SHAKESPEARE IN PRODUCTION

THE TEMPEST

Shakespeare's last play seems unusually elastic, capable of radically different interpretations, which reflect the social, political, scientific or moral concerns of their period. This edition of *The Tempest* is the first dedicated to its long and rich stage history. Drawing on a wide variety of sources, it examines four centuries of mainstream, regional and fringe productions in Britain (including Dryden and Davenant's Restoration adaptation), nineteenth- and twentieth-century American stagings, and recent Australian, Canadian, French, Italian and Japanese productions.

In a substantial, illustrated introduction Dr Dymkowski analyses the cultural significance of changes in the play's theatrical representation: for example, when and why Caliban began to be represented by a black actor, and Ariel became a man's role rather than a woman's. The commentary annotates each line of the play with details about acting, setting, textual alteration and cuts, and contemporary reception.

With extensive quotation from contemporary commentators and detail from unpublished promptbooks, the edition offers both an accessible account of the play's changing meanings and a valuable resource for further research.

SHAKESPEARE IN PRODUCTION

SERIES EDITORS: J. S. BRATTON AND JULIE HANKEY

This series offers students and researchers the fullest possible staging of individual Shakespearean texts. In each volume a substantial introduction presents a conceptual overview of the play, marking out the major stages of its representation and reception. The commentary, presented alongside the New Cambridge edition of the text itself, offers detailed, line-by-line evidence for the overview presented in the introduction, making the volume a flexible tool for further research. The editors have selected interesting and vivid evocations of settings, acting and stage presentation and range widely in time and space.

ALREADY PUBLISHED

A Midsummer Night's Dream, edited by Trevor R. Griffiths
Much Ado About Nothing, edited by John F. Cox
Antony and Cleopatra, edited by Richard Madelaine
Hamlet, edited by Robert Hapgood

FORTHCOMING VOLUMES

Macbeth, edited by John Wilders
Julius Caesar, edited by James Rigney
King Henry V, edited by Emma Smith
Romeo and Juliet, edited by James N. Loehlin
The Taming of the Shrew, edited by Elizabeth Schafer
The Merchant of Venice, edited by Charles Edelman
As You Like It, edited by Cynthia Marshall
Troilus and Cressida, edited by Frances Shirley

.

THE TEMPEST

EDITED BY
CHRISTINE DYMKOWSKI

Reader in Drama and Theatre,

Royal Holloway, University of London

PUBLISHED BY THE PRESS SYNDICATE OF THE UNIVERSITY OF CAMBRIDGE
The Pitt Building, Trumpington Street, Cambridge, United Kingdom

CAMBRIDGE UNIVERSITY PRESS
The Edinburgh Building, Cambridge CB2 2RU, UK   www.cup.cam.ac.uk
40 West 20th Street, New York, NY 10011-4211, USA   www.cup.org
10 Stamford Road, Oakleigh, Melbourne 3166, Australia
Ruiz de Alarcón 13, 28014 Madrid, Spain

© Cambridge University Press 2000

First published 2000

Printed in the United Kingdom at the University Press, Cambridge

Typeface in Monotype Ehrhardt 10/12.5 pt, *System* in QuarkXPress^{TM} [BTS]

A catalogue record for this book is available from the British Library

Library of Congress Cataloging in Publication Data
Shakespeare, William, 1564–1616.
The Tempest / edited by Christine Dymkowski.
p.   cm. – (Shakespeare in production)
Includes bibliographical references (p. 349) and index.
ISBN 0 521 44407 1 (hb)
1. Survival after airplane accidents, shipwrecks, etc – Drama.   2. Shakespeare,
William, 1564-1616 – Stage history.   3. Shakespeare, William, 1564–1616. Tempest.
4. Fathers and daughters – Drama.   5. Castaways – Drama.   6. Magicians – Drama.
I. Dymkowski, Christine, 1950–   II. Title.   III. Series.
PR2833.A2 D9 2000
800.3'3 – dc21   99-053454

ISBN 0521 44407 1 hardback
ISBN 0521 78375 5 paperback

For Pauline

CONTENTS

ILLUSTRATIONS

SERIES EDITORS' PREFACE

It is no longer necessary to stress that the text of a play is only its starting-point, and that only in production is its potential realized and capable of being appreciated fully. Since the coming-of-age of Theatre Studies as an academic discipline, we now understand that even Shakespeare is only one collaborator in the creation and infinite recreation of his play upon the stage. And just as we now agree that no play is complete until it is produced, so we have become interested in the way in which plays often produced – and preeminently the plays of the national Bard, William Shakespeare – acquire a life history of their own, after they leave the hands of their first maker.

Since the eighteenth century Shakespeare has become a cultural construct: sometimes the guarantor of nationhood, heritage and the status quo, sometimes seized and transformed to be its critic and antidote. This latter role has been particularly evident in countries where Shakespeare has to be translated. The irony is that while his status as national icon grows in the English-speaking world, his language is both lost and renewed, so that for good or ill, Shakespeare can be made to seem more urgently 'relevant' than in England or America, and may become the one dissenting voice that the censors mistake as harmless.

'Shakespeare in Production' gives the reader, the student and the scholar a comprehensive dossier of materials – eye-witness accounts, contemporary criticism, promptbook marginalia, stage business, cuts, additions and rewritings – from which to construct an understanding of the many meanings that the plays have carried down the ages and across the world. These materials are organized alongside the New Cambridge Shakespeare text of the play, line by line and scene by scene, while a substantial introduction in each volume offers a guide to their interpretation. One may trace an argument about, for example, the many ways of playing Queen Gertrude, or the political transmutations of the text of *Henry V*; or take a scene, an act or a whole play, and work out how it has succeeded or failed in presentation over four hundred years.

For despite our insistence that the plays are endlessly made and remade by history, Shakespeare is not a blank, scribbled upon by the age. Theatre history charts changes, but also registers something in spite of those changes. Some productions work and others do not. Two interpretations may be entirely different, and yet both will bring the play to life. Why? Without setting out to give absolute answers, the history of a play in the theatre can often show where the energy and shape of it lie, what has made it tick, through many permutations. In this way theatre history can find common ground with literary criticism. Both will find suggestive directions in the introductions to these volumes, while the commentaries provide raw material for readers to recreate the living experience of theatre, and become their own eye-witnesses.

J. S. Bratton
Julie Hankey

This series was originated by Jeremy Treglown and published by Junction Books, and later by Bristol Classical Press, as 'Plays in Performance'. Four titles were published; all are now out of print.

ACKNOWLEDGEMENTS

I would like to thank Royal Holloway, University of London, for one term's sabbatical leave in 1989, 1992, and 1995; the British Academy for a personal research grant that allowed a fortnight's research in Stratford; the Society for Theatre Research for a grant that helped with the acquisition of illustrations; and the copyright holders for permission to reproduce them. I have had enormous help from David Ward of my college library, as well as all the staff at the Shakespeare Centre Library in Stratford (especially Karin Brown and Sylvia Morris) and the Theatre Museum in London (especially Andrew Kirk). I am very grateful to Andrew Gurr for his advice, generous sharing of knowledge and practical help, which included using some of his own research time at the Folger Shakespeare Library to answer my queries; Julie Hankey for patiently working her way through many trees to help me see the wood; Jacky Bratton for combining the good offices of an editor with the kindnesses of a friend; Sarah Stanton for her patience and understanding; David Lindley for his helpful comments and forbearance; Elisabetta Noto for translating the reviews of De Berardinis's production and explaining their references to Italian culture; Joyce Carter for making available her work on Paige's production; Irene Alexander for facilitating my research at the Royal National Theatre; Sarah Morris of the University of Bristol Theatre Collection for locating photographs of Miller's 1988 production; Lynette Goddard and Hannah Rudman for help, respectively, with the bibliography and word-processing; and Audrey Cotterell for her painstaking copy-editing. The many others who gave me access to material on particular productions are credited in footnotes to the relevant sections of the Introduction. My greatest debt is to my parents and to Pauline Gooderson, who has lived with this project as long as I have and who, besides translating French and German reviews, has done so much to help me complete it.

EDITOR'S NOTE

The play-text printed here uses the readings established by David Lindley for the New Cambridge Shakespeare; however, the stage directions as printed in the Folio have been restored, and, in line with the policy of this series, not all additional editorial directions have been adopted. Similarly, the lineation of NCS has, for ease of reference, occasionally been modified.

Shakespeare's play is discussed in the present historical tense, and productions of it in the past tense. Ariel, who has been played by both female and male actors throughout the play's production history, is referred to as 'she' when played by a woman and 'he' when played by a man, in order to keep the actor in the reader's mind; this usage, however, suggests a consistent attitude that did not necessarily exist in the productions themselves. (For example, Ariel, played by Viola Tree in H. B. Tree's 1904 production, is called 'he' in the printed version of the text and 'she' in the hand-written promptbook notes.) The Commentary calls characters by their Shakespearean names even when they have been slightly modified by later adapters (e.g., Alonso's and Antonio's names are sometimes spelled 'Alonzo' and 'Anthonio'); the one exception is Dryden and Davenant's Trincalo, whose difference from Shakespeare's character warrants retention of his new name.

For the reader's convenience, productions are identified by name of adapter/actor-manager/director; for example, 'Tree's Prospero' means the actor in Tree's production, rather than Tree himself. In some cases (for example, 'Kean's Prospero'), the part was in fact played by the actor-manager in his own production. The actors of parts not discussed in the Introduction are identified, where possible and pertinent, when the Commentary first introduces characters in a particular production. In addition, Appendix 2 lists the principal players of productions that feature prominently in the Commentary; in alphabetical order of the person responsible for the production, it allows cross-referencing with the chronological list of productions, which gives fuller production data.

All information about a production, including quotations, is drawn from its promptbook and/or printed text, unless otherwise noted; full details of sources are given in the bibliography. However, because productions evolve and make various changes to the text, stage-business, actors, etc., it should be remembered that no promptbook is definitive; indeed, there are sometimes several versions of a promptbook, reflecting different stages of the same production. Furthermore, the accuracy of promptbooks depends on the thoroughness of their annotators: a feature common to several productions may not have been recorded in each case. Evidence from a promptbook may therefore make a production seem different from others when this is not the case.

Where promptboks have been consulted, all cuts are noted. Half-line cuts are annotated as 'a' or 'b' when the two halves of the line are shared by different speakers or are clearly distinguished by punctuation; the occasional division of a line into three separate speeches or phrases is annotated as 'a', 'b' and 'c'. When division of a line is unclear, the words cut are quoted.

Standard promptbook abbreviations are used and quoted throughout the commentary: e.g., DR or DSR (downstage right); LC (left centre); UL or USL (upstage left); LUE (left upper entrance/exit); R1E (first right entrance/exit); FOH (front of house); FO (facing out); OP (opposite prompt); PS (prompt side). Notations about R and L are always from the on-stage, rather than the audience, perspective. Other abbreviations are given in the list that follows.

Insignificant alterations of the text, such as expansion or use of contractions, changes from singular to plural, and slight differences in word-order, have not been recorded. For reasons of space, quotations do not use ellipsis dots to indicate omission of the beginning or the end of a sentence. Citation of reviews is complete in the Commentary (i.e., author, newspaper, and date); incomplete citation indicates an inadequately identified archival cutting (usually from the Theatre Museum for London and regional productions and from the Shakespeare Centre Library for Stratford and RSC productions). In the Commentary, books and articles are cited only by author and short title; full details may be found in the Bibliography.

ABBREVIATIONS
(Place of publication indicated by context in Commentary)

Ad	*Advertiser*
ANZTR	*Australia & New Zealand Theatre Record*
AP	Associated Press
APJ	*Aberdeen Press & Journal*
AR	*Adelaide Review*
Ath	*Athenaeum*
Aus	*Australian*
BED	*Birmingham Evening Dispatch*
BEM	*Birmingham Evening Mail*
BEN	*Bolton Evening News*
BEP	*Bristol Evening Post*
BG	*Birmingham Gazette*
BgEN	*Birmingham Evening News*
BM	*Birmingham Mail*
BP	*Birmingham Post*
BSM	*Birmingham Sunday Mercury*
Bul	*Bulletin*
BWDP	*Bristol Western Daily Press*
BWP	*Birmingham Weekly Post*
C	*Carlino*
CD	Editor's notes taken during performance
CET	*Coventry Evening Telegraph*
CG	Covent Garden
CiL	*City Limits*
CL	*Country Life*
CM	*Casting Magazine*
CP	*City Pages* (?)
CPi	*Circulating Pines*
CS	*Carlino Spettacoli*
CSM	*Christian Science Monitor*
CT	*Canberra Times*
D	*Dispatch* (St Paul, Minnesota)
DE	*Daily Express*
DET	*Derby Evening Telegraph*

xiv

DG	*Daily Graphic*
DH	*Dudley Herald*
DL	Drury Lane (or down left, depending on context)
DM	*Daily Mail*
DMSR	*Des Moines Sunday Register*
DN	*Daily News*
DS	*Daily Sketch*
DT	*Daily Telegraph*
DW	*Daily Worker*
EJ	*Evesham Journal*
EN	*Evening News*
ES	*Evening Standard*
FR	*Financial Review*
FT	*Financial Times*
G	*Guardian*
GC	*Gloucester Citizen*
GH	*Glasgow Herald*
HC	*Hartford Courant*
HHE	*Hampstead & Highgate Express*
HR	*Hollywood Reporter*
iG	*Il Giorno*
iGe	*Il Giornale*
ILN	*Illustrated London News*
iM	*Il Manifesto*
Ind	*Independent*
IndS	*Independent on Sunday*
ISDN	*Illustrated Sporting and Dramatic News*
ITN	*Italian Tribune News*
JC	*Jewish Chronicle*
L	*Listener*
LAT	*Los Angeles Times*
LC	*Leamington Chronicle*
LDP	*Liverpool Daily Post*
LFMT	*Little Falls Minnesota Tran* (?)
LP	*Liverpool Post*
LS	*London Star*
LSC	*[Royal] Leamington Spa Courier*
LTR	*London Theatre Record*
MA	*Morning Advertiser*
MD	*Minnesota Daily*
MelR	*Melbourne Report*

MG	*Manchester Guardian*
MGa	*Montreal Gazette*
MLD	*Montréal Le Devoir*
MMA	*Minneapolis Metro Area*
MP	*Morning Post*
MR	*Minneapolis Register* (?)
MS	*Morning Star*
MSN	*Minneapolis Skyway News*
MST	*Minneapolis Star Tribune*
MSun	*Mail on Sunday*
MT	*Minneapolis Tribune*
NBB	*New Brighton Bulletin*
NC	*News Chronicle*
NCS	*New Cambridge Shakespeare*
NEC	*Newcastle-upon-Tyne Evening Chronicle*
NEP	*Nottingham Evening Post*
NG	*Nottingham Guardian*
NS	*New Statesman*
NSL	*Newark Star-Ledger*
NTA	*New Theatre Australia*
Nw	*Newsweek*
NYLJ	*New York Law Journal*
NYN	*New York Newsday*
NYO	*New York Observer*
NYP	*New York Post*
NYT	*New York Times*
NYVV	*New York Village Voice*
O	*Observer*
OM	*Oxford Mail*
OT	*Oxford Times*
OTN	*Our Theatre in the Nineties* (G. B. Shaw)
OurT	*Our Town*
P	*Punch*
pb(s)	promptbook(s)
PP	*Plays and Players*
PS	*Paese Sera*
PWI	*Plymouth Western Independent*
R	*Rinascita*
RPB	*Rochester Post-Bulletin*
RS	*La Repubblica Spettacoli*
RSC	Royal Shakespeare Company

RST	Royal Shakespeare Theatre, Stratford
SA	*Sunday Age*
SCG	*Somerset County Gazette*
SCL	Shakespeare Centre Library, Stratford
Sco	*Scotsman*
SCSN	*Sherburne County Star-News*
sd(s)	stage direction(s)
SDR	*San Diego Reader*
SE	*Sunday Express*
SH	*Stratford Herald*
Sk	*Sketch*
SLP	*South London Press*
SMH	*Sydney Morning Herald*
SMT	Shakespeare Memorial Theatre, Stratford
SN	*Soho News*
Sp	*Spectator*
SPD	*St Paul Dispatch*
SPPP	*St Paul Pioneer Press*
SS	*Shakespeare Survey*
St	*Stage*
ST	*Sunday Times*
STel	*Sunday Telegraph*
STT	*Stage & Television Today*
SunH	*Sun Herald*
SundH	*Sunday Herald*
SWCN	*Solihull & Warwick County News*
T	*The Times*
Tab	*Tablet*
Tat	*Tatler*
TCC	*Twin Cities Courier*
TCR	*Twin Cities Reader*
TES	*Times Education Supplement*
TGM	*Toronto Globe & Mail*
TJ	*Theatrical Journal*
TLS	*Times Literary Supplement*
TM	Theatre Museum, London
TN	*Theatre Newsletter*
TO	*Time Out*
TR	*Theatre Record*
Tr	*Tribune*
Tru	*Truth*

TW	*TheaterWeek*
uc	unidentified clipping
V	*Variety*
WA	*Warwick & Warwickshire Advertiser/Warwick Advertiser*
WES	*Wolverhampton Express & Star*
WGH	*Wantage & Grove Herald*
WI	*Western Independent*
WO	*What's On*
WSG	*West Sussex Gazette*
WSJ	*Wall Street Journal*
YP	*Yorkshire Post*
?	Editor's conjecture or unknown information

LIST OF PRODUCTIONS

This list gives basic information about all productions discussed or mentioned in the Introduction and Commentary; asterisks mark those for which cuts have been noted. Venues are in London unless otherwise noted; abbreviations and locations necessary for identification of a theatre are given parenthetically. Design refers to scenery/set *and* costume unless otherwise noted: (s) scenery/set and (c) costume. In order to indicate whether productions played Shakespeare's text or an adaptation of it, the following designations are used: (a) adapter; (a-m) actor-manager; (m) manager; (d) director. Although adapters have consciously altered Shakespeare's text, it should be remembered that each production is to some extent itself an adaptation: actor-managers and directors cut, re-arrange, and interpret the play so that it reflects their own vision of what it means. Consequently, some of the productions of Shakespeare's text noted below include major omissions and interpolations of other material; see the Commentary for further details.

Adapter/ actor-manager/ director	Company	Venue	Design	Music	Date of first performance
	King's Men	Blackfriars? Globe?		Robert Johnson	1610–11?
*William Davenant and John Dryden (a)	Duke's Company	Lincoln's Inn Fields		John Banister, Pelham Humfrey?	7 November 1667
*Thomas Shadwell (a)	Duke's Company	Dorset Garden		Bannister, Humfrey, Matthew Locke, Pietro Reggio, James Hart, Giovanni Battista Draghi	30 April 1674?
James Lacy (m)	Lacy et al.	Drury Lane		Thomas A. Arne	31 January 1746
*David Garrick (a)	Garrick-Lacy	Drury Lane		John Christopher Smith	11 February 1756
*David Garrick (a-m)	Garrick-Lacy	Drury Lane			20 October 1757
Richard Brinsley Sheridan (a?)	Sheridan et al.	Drury Lane	Philip de Loutherbourg	Thomas Linley Jr, Thomas Linley Sr.	January 1777
*John Philip Kemble (a)	Kemble-Sheridan	Drury Lane		Henry Purcell, Arne, Linley Jr.?	13 October 1789
*John Philip Kemble (a)	Kemble & Thomas Harris	Covent Garden	J. H. Grieve (s)	Purcell, Arne, Linley Jr.?	8 December 1806
*William Charles Macready (a-m)	own	Covent Garden	Bradwell & Marshall (s)	Purcell, Arne, Linley Jr.	13 October 1838

*Samuel Phelps (a-m)	own	Sadler's Wells			7 April 1847; also 1849, 1855, 1860
*William Burton (a-m)	own	Burton's, NY			11 April 1854
*Charles Kean (a-m)	own	Princess's	Thomas Grieve, William Telbin, et al. (s)	J. L. Hatton, et al.	1 July 1857
James H. McVicker (a-m)	own	McVicker's, Chicago			1889
*Augustin Daly (a-m)	own	Daly's, NY		Arne, Purcell, K. G. W. Taubert	March 1897
Frank Benson (a-m)	own	touring			1888–1932?
Frank Benson (a-m)	own	Shakespeare Memorial Theatre (SMT), Stratford	Benson (c); W. T. Helmsley (s)	Boggetti, Franz Joseph Haydn, Taubert, Arne, et al.	May 1891; also 1897, 1904, 1908, 1911
William Poel (d)	Elizabethan Stage Society	Mansion House	Jennie Moore (c)	Arnold Dolmetsch, Renaissance music	5 November 1897
Charles Lander (a-m)		Court	H. Potts (s)	Arthur Sullivan	26 October 1903
*Herbert Beerbohm Tree (a-m)	own	His Majesty's	Percy Anderson (c); W. L. Telbin, Helmsley, R. McCleary, R. Douglas (s)	Sullivan, Arne, Raymond Roze, Edward German	14 September 1904
Ben Greet (d)		Royal Victoria Hall (later Old Vic)			1914, 1915, 1916, 1917

Adapter/ actor-manager/ director	Company	Venue	Design	Music	Date of first performance
John Drinkwater (d)		Birmingham Repertory Theatre, Birmingham	Barry Jackson	Clifford Roberts, et al.	17 April 1915; revived 22 April 1916
Ben Greet (d)		SMT, Stratford			August 1916
George Foss (d)		Old Vic			6 November 1918
William Bridges-Adams (d)	Stratford-upon-Avon Festival Company	SMT, Stratford			8 August 1919
Russell Thorndike and Charles Warburton (d)		Old Vic	Wilfred Walter	Sullivan	13 October 1919
Viola Tree and Louis Calvert (d)		Aldwych	Hugo Rumbold, Viola Tree, Percy Anderson (c); R. Rumbold, R. McCleery, et al. (s)	Sullivan, Roze, Arne, Arthur Bliss, et al.	1 February 1921
Robert Atkins (d)		Old Vic	Neil Curtis (c); Wilfrid Walter (s)	Sullivan, Arne	26 February 1921
Robert Atkins (d)		Old Vic	Hubert Hine (Tom Heslewood c?)	Sullivan, Arne	4 February 1924
Beatrice Wilson, Lena Ashwell? (d)	Lena Ashwell Players	Century, and touring		Kate Coates, Johnson, Humfrey, Banister, et al.	2 November 1925

Director	Company	Venue	Designer	Music	Date
Henry Baynton (d)		Savoy	C. and W. May, W. Clarkson (c)		7 January 1926
*William Bridges-Adams (d)	Stratford-upon-Avon Festival Company	SMT, Stratford	Bridges-Adams		5 July 1926; revived 7 July 1930
Andrew Leigh (d)		Old Vic	John Garside		8 November 1926
Harcourt Williams (d)		Old Vic	Owen P. Smith	Coates, et al.	6 October 1930; revived 18 April 1933
Robert Atkins (d)		Open Air (Regent's Park)	Paul Shelving (c)	Purcell, Sullivan, Arne	12 September 1933; also 1934, 1936, 1937, 1938, 1943, 1949, 1960
Tyrone Guthrie (d)		Sadler's Wells/Old Vic	John Armstrong	Herbert Menges, Dennis Arundell	8 January 1934/ 22 January 1934
*William Bridges-Adams (d)	Stratford-upon-Avon Festival Company	SMT, Stratford	Norman Wilkinson, Aubrey Hammond, Bridges-Adams (s); Rex Whistler (c)	Anthony Bernard	16 April 1934; revived 1935 (see below)
	Buskins	Worcester College, Oxford			Summer 1934
*Randle Ayrton (d) (revival of Bridges-Adams's 1934 production)	Stratford-upon-Avon Festival Company	SMT, Stratford	Wilkinson, Hammond, Bridges-Adams (s); Whistler (c)	Bernard	15 April 1935
Ben Iden Payne (d)	Stratford-upon-Avon Festival Company	SMT, Stratford	J. Gower Parks	Bernard	4 May 1938

Adapter/actor-manager/director	Company	Venue	Design	Music	Date of first performance
George Devine and Marius Goring (d)		Old Vic	Oliver Messel	J. S. Bach, W. A. Mozart	29 May 1940
*Ben Iden Payne (d)	Stratford-upon-Avon Festival Company	SMT, Stratford	J. Gower Parks (c); Peggy Neale (s)	Bernard	12 April 1941; revived 4 April 1942
Margaret Webster (d)		Colonial, Boston; Alvin, New York			try-out?; 25 January 1945
*Eric Crozier (d)	Stratford-upon-Avon Festival Company	SMT, Stratford	Paul Shelving	Lennox Berkeley	20 April 1946
*Norman Wright (d)	Shakespeare Memorial Theatre Company	SMT, Stratford	Shelving	Berkeley	9 May 1947
Nevill Coghill (d)	Oxford University Dramatic Society (OUDS)	Worcester College, Oxford	Michael Black (s)?		June 1949
*Michael Benthall (d)	Shakespeare Memorial Theatre Company	SMT, Stratford	Loudon Sainthill	John Wooldridge	26 June 1951; revived 25 March 1952
Julius Gellner (d)	Bernard Miles	Mermaid (St. John's Wood)	Michael Stringer (s); C. Walter Hodges (c)	Elizabethan	17 September 1951
Robert Helpmann (d)		Old Vic	Leslie Hurry	Malcolm Arnold	13 April 1954

Director	Company	Venue	Designer	Music	Date
David William		Open Air (Regent's Park)	Malcolm Pride (c)		1 June 1955
David Scase (d)		Library, Manchester	Scase		13 November 1956
*Peter Brook (d)	Shakespeare Memorial Theatre Company	SMT, Stratford; Drury Lane	Peter Brook	Peter Brook, et al.	13 August 1957; transferred 5 December 1957
Douglas Seale (d) (Dryden/Davenant text)		Old Vic	Finlay James	Purcell, Locke	9 June 1959
John Hale (d)		Theatre Royal, Bristol	Jane Graham	Michael Mellinger, et al.	27 September 1960
Oliver Neville (d)		Old Vic	Leslie Hurry	Michael Tippett	29 May 1962
Gerald Freedman (d)	New York Shakespeare Festival	Delacorte (Central Park), NY			1962
*Clifford Williams with Peter Brook (d)	RSC	RST, Stratford	Abd' Elkader Farrah	Raymond Leppard	2 April 1963
Carey Harrison (d)	Cambridge University Theatre Company	Lauriston Hall, Edinburgh	Carey Harrison and Rod Lack (s); Judith Fulman (c)	David Lord	August 1964
Willard Stoker (d)		Northampton Repertory Theatre, Northampton	Osborne Robinson		11 May 1967
Michael Healey (d)	Meadow Players	Oxford Playhouse, Oxford	Yolanda Sonnabend (s)	Michael Dress	29 April 1968; revived 3 March 1969

Adapter/ actor-manager/ director	Company	Venue	Design	Music	Date of first performance
Peter Brook (work-in-progress)	Peter Brook and Jean-Louis Barrault	Round House	n/a	n/a	July 1968
David Jones (d)		Chichester Festival Theatre, Chichester	Ralph Koltai	Marko Paulos	16 July 1968
Michael Elliott (d)	69 Theatre Company	University Theatre, Manchester	Richard Negri	George Hall	10 September 1969
Jonathan Miller (d)		Mermaid (Puddle Dock)	John Collins (s); Rosemary Vercoe (c)	Carl Davis	15 June 1970
Philip Minor (d)	Minnesota Theatre Company	Guthrie, Minneapolis	John Jensen	John Gessner	20 June 1970
Nagel Jackson (d)	Washington Shakespeare Summer Festival	Sylvan, Washington D.C.	John Peter Halford (c); Robert Troll (s)		Summer 1970
*John Barton (d)	RSC	RST, Stratford	Christopher Morley, with Ann Curtis	cast and Ben Kingsley	15 October 1970
Stuart Burge (d)		Nottingham Playhouse, Nottingham	Robin Archer	John Leach	23 February 1972
Richard Digby Day	New Shakespeare Company	Open Air (Regent's Park)	Kit Surrey (s); Hugh Durrant (c)	Michael Sadler	30 May 1972

*Peter Hall (d)	National Theatre	Old Vic	John Bury	Gryphon	5 March 1974
*Keith Hack (d)	RSC	The Other Place, Stratford	Debbie Sharpe	Stephen Oliver	21 October 1974
John Harrison (d)		Leeds Playhouse, Leeds; Wyndham's	Kitty Burrows (c); Sean Cavanagh (s)	Paul Todd	23 October 1974; transferred 20 February 1975
Giorgio Strehler (d) (translator: Agostino Lombardo)	Piccolo Teatro di Milano	Teatro Lirico, Milan, & touring	Luciano Damiani	Fiorenzo Carpi	1978
*Clifford Williams (d)	RSC	RST, Stratford	Ralph Koltai	Guy Woolfenden	26 April 1978
Pip Simmons (d and a)	Pip Simmons Group	Riverside Studios	Maggie Jones (masks)	Chris Jordan	11 May 1978
David Giles (d)	Edinburgh Festival Productions	Birmingham Repertory Theatre, Birmingham	Kenneth Mellor (s); Pauline Whitehouse (c)		1 August 1978
Michael Bogdanov (d)	Young Vic Theatre Company	Young Vic	Paul Bannister	Stephen Boxer	28 November 1978
Gerald Freedman (d)		American Shakespeare Theatre, Stratford (Connecticut)			Summer 1979
Tina Packer (d)	Shakespeare & Company	The Mount, Lenox (Massachusetts)	Bill Ballou (s); Kiki Smith (c)	Roger Reynolds	30 July 1980
Liviu Ciulei (d)		Guthrie, Minneapolis	Liviu Ciulei (s); Jack Edwards (c)	Theodor Grigoriu	11 June 1981
John Retallack (d)	Actors Touring Company	Treasurer's House, York, and touring; Warehouse	John Neville (s); Jean Turnbull (c)	Paul Sand and Chris Barnes	1 July 1981; revived 24 February 1983

Adapter/actor-manager/director	Company	Venue	Design	Music	Date of first performance
Lee Breuer, with Ruth Maleczech (d)	New York Shakespeare Festival	Delacorte (Central Park), NY	David Mitchell (s); Carol Oditz (c)	Barbara Benary (gamelan); Nana Vasconceles (samba); Disney theme songs	9 July 1981
John Hirsch		Stratford Festival, Ontario	Desmond Heeley	Stanley Silverman	June 1982
*Ron Daniels (d)	RSC	RST, Stratford, and touring; Barbican	Maria Bjornson	Stephen Oliver	5 August 1982; transferred 13 September 1983
Philip Grout (d)		St George's	Lyn Avery (c)	Ian Kellam	28 April 1983
Deborah Warner (d)	Kick Theatre Company	St Cuthbert's Halls, Edinburgh, and touring	Jacqueline Gunn		September? 1983
Glen Walford (d)		Everyman, Liverpool	Sue Mayes	Paddy Cunneen	26 January 1984
Lesley Argent (d)	Trouble & Strife	A.D.C. Theatre, Cambridge	Samantha Hodge		19 February 1985
Nigel Jamieson and Anthony Quayle (d)	Compass	Theatre Royal, Brighton, and touring	Mark Negin	Richard Attree	7 October 1985
Leo De Berardinis (d) (translator: Angelo Dallagiacoma)	Cooperativa Nuova Scena	Teatro Testoni/inter Action, Bologna; Théâtre Gérard Phillippe de Saint-Denis, Paris	Leo De Berardinis	Richard Wagner, Purcell, Anton von Webern, John Coltrane, Indian guitar, et al.	3 April 1986; revived February 1987

Alfredo Arias (d) (translator: Jean–Louis Curtis)	Centre Dramatique d'Aubervilliers and Groupe TSE Festival d'Avignon	?, Avignon			July 1986
Matthew Francis (d)	Chichester Studio Company	The Tent, Chichester; Chichester Festival Theatre	Howard Burden	Mia Soteriou	6 September 1986; transferred 3 October 1986
Ronan Patterson (d)	Northumberland Theatre Company		Frank Thompson		January 1987
Robert Falls (d)		Goodman, Chicago			1987
Alec Bell (d)		New Victoria, North Staffordshire			November? 1987
Michael Goddard (d)		Salford Playhouse, Salford			February/March? 1988
*Peter Hall (d)	National Theatre	Cottesloe, and touring; Olivier	Alison Chitty	Harrison Birtwistle	19 May 1988; transferred 29 September 1988
*Nicholas Hytner (d)	RSC	RST, Stratford; Barbican	David Fielding	Jeremy Sams	7 July 1988; transferred 18 May 1989
Yukio Ninagawa (translator: Yushi Odashima)	Ninagawa Theatre Company	Playhouse, Edinburgh, and touring; Barbican	Toshiaki Suzuki (s); Lily Komine (c)	Ryudo Uzaki	17 August 1988; revived 3 December 1992

Adapter/ actor–manager/ director	Company	Venue	Design	Music	Date of first performance
*Jonathan Miller (d)		Old Vic	Richard Hudson	Carl Davis	6 October 1988
Declan Donnellan (d)	Cheek by Jowl	touring and Donmar Warehouse	Nick Ormerod	Paddy Cunneen	October? 1988; 24 November 1988
John Gaden (d)	State Theatre Company of Southern Australia	Playhouse, Adelaide	Ken Wilby		2 May 1989
Des James (d)	Riverina Trucking Company	Riverina Playhouse, Wagga Wagga (Australia), and touring	Jill Halliday		11 August 1989
Patrick Mitchell (d)		La Boite, Brisbane	Andrew Raymond	Donald Hall	28 February 1990
Gale Edwards (d)	Melbourne Theatre Company	Playhouse, Melbourne	Tony Tripp	Sam Mallet	15 May 1990
Neil Armfield (d)	Company B	Belvoir Street, Sydney	Brian Thomson (s); Jennie Tate (c)	Alan John	30 May 1990; revived 30 May 1995
Braham Murray (d)		Royal Exchange, Manchester	Johanna Bryant	Chris Monks	13 September 1990
Peter Brook (d) (translator: Jean–Claude Carrière)	Centre International de Créations Théâtrales	Les Bouffes du Nord, Paris; Tramway, Glasgow	Chloé Obolensky	Harué Momoyama, et al.	October 1990; 30 October 1990

Mark Rylance (d)	Phoebus Cart	Rollright Stone Circle, Oxfordshire; Globe building site; and touring	Jenny Tiramani and Will Hargreaves	Clare van Kampen	1 June 1991; 19 June 1991
John Retallack (d)	Oxford Stage Company	touring	Julian McGowan	Howard Goodall	19 July 1991
Jennifer Tipton (d)		Guthrie, Minneapolis	John Conklin	Libby Larsen (songs)	13 October 1991
Andrew Hay (d)		Bristol Old Vic, Bristol	Mick Bearwish	John O'Hara	30 September 1992
Robert Lepage (d) (translator: Michel Garneau)	Le Théâtre Repère (Québec) and Théâtre du Manège	Théâtre du Manège, Mauberge (France), and touring	Robert Lepage (s); Nina Reichmann (c)	Guy Laramée	9 October 1992
Michael Bogdanov (d)	English Shakespeare Company	Royalty and touring	Chris Dyer	Robert A. White and Phillip Dupuy	27 November 1992
Sam Mendes (d)	RSC	RST, Stratford; Barbican	Anthony Ward	Shaun Davey	5 August 1993; transferred 7 July 1994
Deborah Paige (d)		Salisbury Playhouse, Salisbury	Isabella Bywater	Peter Salem	16 September 1993
Bill Alexander (d)		Birmingham Repertory Theatre, Birmingham	Ruari Murchison	Jonathan Goldstein	9 September 1994
David Thacker (d)	RSC	Young Vic; Swan, Stratford; and touring	Shelagh Keegan	Adrian Johnston	14 June 1995

Adapter/ actor-manager/ director	Company	Venue	Design	Music	Date of first performance
George C. Wolfe (d)	New York Shakespeare Festival	Delacorte (Central Park), NY; Broadhurst, NY	Riccardo Hernandez (s); Tori-Leslie James (c)	Carlos Valdez and Dan Moses Schreier	11 July 1995; transferred 10 October 1995
Silviu Purcarete (d)	Nottingham Playhouse and Theatre Clwyd	Nottingham Playhouse, Nottingham, and touring	José Manuel Melo	Vasile Sirli	7 September 1995
Nancy Meckler (d)	Shared Experience	Wolsey, Ipswich, and touring	Sophie Jump	Peter Salem	24 October 1996
Adrian Noble (d)	RSC	RST, Stratford; Barbican	Anthony Ward	Stephen Warbeck	25 February 1998; transferred 5 January 1999
Jude Kelly (d)	West Yorkshire Playhouse	Courtyard, West Yorkshire Playhouse, Leeds	Robert Innes Hopkins		2 February 1999

INTRODUCTION

The Tempest is a wonderfully rich play. Although most of Shakespeare's works can take on unexpected and yet convincing shapes in the theatre, his last play seems unusually elastic, its almost miraculous flexibility allowing it to embody radically different interpretations, characterizations and emphases. Prospero and Caliban can not only exchange places as hero and villain, but also vie with each other to occupy both places at once. Ariel can be female or male, a willing or an unwilling servant. Miranda can seem an innocent maiden, a hoydenish tomboy or a rebellious teenager. Antonio can seek forgiveness from his brother or remain sinister until the end. Stephano and Trinculo can present themselves as harmless buffoons or dangerous louts. The island can appear a lush paradise or a barren desert or both at once. The narrative can speak for or against racism or turn into a psychological thriller. The play's final effect can be one of decay and despair or of renewal and hope.

These examples are just a small fraction of the infinite potentialities of Shakespeare's text. Throughout its theatrical life, *The Tempest* has been a mirror powerfully reflecting contemporary concerns, be they social, political, scientific or moral; my intention in this edition is to document its myriad stage interpretations[1] as fully as possible in the Commentary and to offer possible explanations for them in the Introduction. However, with a work like *The Tempest*, whose stage history spans the globe as well as nearly four hundred years, a project such as this can never be definitive: there will always be an interesting production omitted, an important detail unknown, a significant context unavailable. Therefore, although this edition offers its own interpretation of the play's history in performance, it is also intended to serve as a primary resource for

---

1 Because of limitations of space and time, I have excluded radical stage and film adaptations of *The Tempest*, such as Aimé Césaire's *Une Tempête*, Bob Carlton's *Return from the Forbidden Planet*, Fred M. Wilcox's *Forbidden Planet*, Derek Jarman's *The Tempest* and Peter Greenaway's *Prospero's Books*, from the edition; although significant in different ways, all of these versions so thoroughly rework the play that they would demand a disproportionate amount of description and annotation. Because they are readily accessible for viewing and are not particularly noteworthy, I have also excluded straightforward film and video versions of the play, such as John Gorrie's 1980 BBC production.

further research. For this reason, I have not simply amalgamated and paraphrased stage directions and reviewers' opinions, but have quoted them extensively; in this way, readers can make up their own minds about the fairness of my judgements and pursue lines of enquiry different from mine.

An introduction to a volume like this must also choose one of two very different approaches: it can try to offer a microcosmic theatre history, detailing changing conditions and conventions as Shakespeare's play moved from its Jacobean roots into the twentieth century, or it can assume a basic knowledge of such matters. Apart from lightly sketching in essential background for the sake of the novice reader, I have opted for the latter course: there is no point in trying to duplicate – in an inevitably reductive way – the many good specialist studies readily available, particularly when doing so would limit the amount of new material I can offer about the performance history of *The Tempest* itself. So that readers can fill in any gaps that may result, I have cited appropriate studies in my footnotes to the Introduction and, where necessary, glossed specialist theatrical terms.[2]

My introduction is divided into six sections, designed to provide a broad overview of the play in performance as well as a context for further information given in the Commentary. The first section deals with *The Tempest* that Shakespeare wrote, the second with the Restoration adaptations that not only held the stage until the mid-nineteenth century but also influenced subsequent productions of the original text. The next three are devoted, respectively, to changes in the playing of the three main roles: the section on Prospero examines the way the human potential of the part has developed; that on Ariel focuses on the part as a vehicle for the expression of gender ideology; and that on Caliban charts the character's evolution from comic monster to (mostly) sympathetic victim. The final section, looking at different ways of staging the storm-scene and representing the island, outlines thematic approaches taken to the play as a whole. Each section and sub-section follows a chronological order, but the considerable overlaps between them will, I hope, destroy any false sense of linear progression in the play's stage history. Although each section can be read on its own as a separate essay, their sequence is intended to build an increasingly complex picture of the play's performance possibilities and of the cultural forces that create them.

---

2 Simon Trussler's *Cambridge Illustrated History of British Theatre* (Cambridge: Cambridge University Press, 1994) is valuable in reaching beyond traditional canonical accounts of English drama and theatre.

'. . . WHAT'S PAST IS PROLOGUE' (2.1.242):
SHAKESPEARE'S *THE TEMPEST* IN ITS OWN TIME

As many editors of the play point out, *The Tempest* has always attracted considerable attention because of its prominent position as the first play in the first collection of Shakespeare's works ever published, the Folio of 1623.[3] The only extant text of the play, it was carefully prepared for publication: it not only contains very few cruxes but also includes extremely elaborate stage directions. Scholars have made a convincing case that most of the latter are not Shakespeare's own, but embellishments by Ralph Crane, scrivener for the King's Men, the company with which Shakespeare was associated for virtually all of his professional life.[4] As John Jowett has pointed out,[5] the stage directions of *The Tempest* are mostly written from the point of view of an audience member, of someone who has witnessed an effect rather than planned how to achieve it: most notorious is the direction at 3.3.52, which notes that the banquet vanishes 'with a quaint device'. However, even though the Folio stage directions are probably not authorial, they provide the template which all subsequent texts and productions either adhere to or deviate from and are therefore reproduced in the text included in this edition. Editorial stage directions have been added only sparingly – for instance, when Shakespeare's text clearly calls for a particular action or when it fails to note which characters exit; such stage directions are indicated by the square brackets that enclose them.

The Tempest, written about 1610–11, features Shakespeare's most original plot; although the play does borrow from contemporary sources,[6] the

3 My account is indebted to Stephen Orgel's excellent Oxford Shakespeare edition of the play (Oxford: Oxford University Press, 1987) and to Frank Kermode's invaluable Arden edition, 6th edition 1958, reprinted with corrections 1961 and 1962 (London: Methuen, 1964).

4 Peter Thomson's *Shakespeare's Professional Career* (Cambridge: Cambridge Univesity Press, 1992), provides an accessible account not only of the playwright's career but also of Elizabethan and Jacobean theatre.

5 See his influential essay, 'New Created Creatures: Ralph Crane and the Stage Directions in *The Tempest*', *Shakespeare Survey* 36 (1983), pp. 107–20.

6 The editions of Frank Kermode and Stephen Orgel document well the play's borrowings from Golding's 1567 translation of Ovid's *Metamorphoses*, from Florio's 1603 translation of two of Montaigne's essays, 'Of the Cannibals' and 'Of Cruelty', and from contemporary accounts of New World exploration. Orgel, p. 32, notes that the latter subject was 'especially timely in 1611' because of the recent shipwreck of one of the Virginia Company's vessels: 'William Strachey's [1610] account of the adventure is generally considered to have clear echoes in the play. This letter, though not printed until 1625, certainly circulated in manuscript, and Shakespeare was evidently familiar with it. The playwright was associated,

search for one from which the story is taken has proved particularly fruitless. Like the rest of Shakespeare's plays, all of its parts were played by men and boys, as women were not allowed to act in the professional theatre. At the time *The Tempest* was written, Shakespeare's company occupied two different types of playhouse: the large outdoor Globe amphitheatre and the more intimate indoor Blackfriars, which from about 1610 became the winter home of the King's Men. The two kinds of playhouse shared the same basic architectural features: a non-scenic stage with a trap door, a tiring-house facade with a discovery space in the centre and a door on either side, an upper gallery, a music room and a flying device that enabled the descent of thrones and goddesses, among other items. In both playhouses, the audience surrounded the stage on four sides; however, in the Globe those who paid least stood throughout the performance and were closest to the stage, while in the Blackfriars those who paid most sat near or even on it. In both theatres, spectacle was restricted to a sumptuous display of elaborate and colourful costumes; locations were indicated, if at all, by a suggestive prop, such as a throne or a bed.[7]

Despite these physical similarities, there were important differences in performance conditions at the two kinds of theatre. Performances at the outdoor Globe took place in daylight and ran non-stop, while those at the indoor Blackfriars relied on candlelight. The need to tend and trim the candles introduced act-breaks, during which the audience was entertained with music. Andrew Gurr has persuasively demonstrated that '*The Tempest* was the first play Shakespeare unquestionably wrote for the Blackfriars rather than the Globe': the fact that 'Prospero and Ariel leave the stage together at the end of Act 4 and enter together again to open Act 5' provides 'unequivocal evidence that [the play] was conceived with act breaks in mind'.[8] Writing the play for the Blackfriars, whose musicians were

moreover, with a number of members of the Virginia Company . . . [so his] interest in the venture would have been at least partly personal.'

7 For the fullest information on theatre in Shakespeare's time, see Andrew Gurr's *The Shakespearean Stage, 1574–1642*, 3rd edition (Cambridge: Cambridge University Press, 1992) and *Playgoing in Shakespeare's London*, 2nd edition (Cambridge: Cambridge University Press, 1996). *The Revels History of Drama in English*, Volume III, 1576–1613, eds. J. Leeds Barroll et al. (London: Methuen, 1975), includes essays on 'The Companies and Actors' by Alexander Leggatt, pp. 97–117, and 'The Playhouses' by Richard Hosley, pp. 121–235, while *The Cambridge Companion to Shakespeare Studies*, ed. Stanley Wells (Cambridge: Cambridge University Press, 1986), includes essays on 'Playhouses and players in the time of Shakespeare' by Peter Thomson, pp. 67–83, and 'Shakespeare and the theatrical conventions of his time' by Alan C. Dessen, pp. 85–99.

8 '*The Tempest*'s Tempest at Blackfriars', *Shakespeare Survey* 41 (1989), pp. 92–3.

already famous, may also have encouraged Shakespeare to exploit the potential of music for his drama: as Gurr notes, '*The Tempest* is uniquely a musical play among Shakespeare's writings', utilizing 'instrumental music as well as song' to a degree not found in his other plays ('*The Tempest*'s Tempest', pp. 92–3).

Although *The Tempest* was conceived as a Blackfriars play, it would also have played at the Globe: there was no distinction in the repertories of the two theatres nor any need for one, since the indoor theatre did not offer any facilities unavailable at the amphitheatre. Unfortunately, however, there are no surviving contemporary references to the play in performance at either theatre, the only recorded performances in Shakespeare's lifetime having taken place at court.[9] The Revels Accounts show that *The Tempest* was performed for James I at Whitehall, probably in the Banqueting House, on 1 November 1611, and court records of a payment made to the King's Men in May 1613 indicate that it was one of the plays given to celebrate the betrothal and marriage of James's daughter Elizabeth and the Elector Palatine in February of that year.

Knowledge of these court performances, and particularly of the latter one, has sometimes led to a mistaken belief that Shakespeare added the masque of 4.1 as an afterthought; at other times, it has encouraged a misplaced emphasis in the theatre on the play's masque-like elements. However, as Stephen Orgel cautions, 'the masque in *The Tempest* is not a court masque, it is a dramatic allusion to one, and it functions in the structure of the drama not as a separable interlude but as an integral part of the action'.[10] Its presence does not imply the visually spectacular staging associated with the Jacobean court masque, with its perspective scenery and mechanical scene-changes: Shakespeare's play would have been performed with lavish costume but without scenery on a bare stage. This bare stage did not, however, preclude illusion. As Andrew Gurr has admirably demonstrated, the opening scene of *The Tempest*

> is a bravura piece of staging not only in the way it deploys an outdoor effect [the staging of a storm] at an indoor playhouse, but because that effect sets up the ruling conceit for the whole play. A thoroughly realistic

9 Dryden's 1669 Preface to *The Enchanted Island* notes that *The Tempest* 'had formerly been acted with success in the Black-Fryers'. The preface and play are reprinted in Montague Summers, *Shakespeare Adaptations* (London: Jonathan Cape, 1922), pp. 1–103, with the quotation on p. 3.

10 For more information about the court performances and the relevance of the masque, see Orgel, pp. 1–4, 43–50, and Kermode, pp. xxi–xxiv; the quotation is from Orgel, pp. 43–4.

storm, with mariners in soaking work clothes being hampered in their work by courtiers dressed for a wedding, concludes in shipwreck for all. And immediately [with Miranda's entry in 2.1] this realism is proclaimed to be only stage magic, the art of illusion . . . The whole play depends on the initial realism of the shipwreck scene. It is the verification of Prospero's magic and the declaration that it is all only a stage play.[11]

As Gurr's analysis demonstrates, although there are no eyewitness accounts of the play as performed by the King's Men, the explicit and implicit stage directions of the text can offer much evidence about the original performances. The sections of the Introduction that follow, as well as the Commentary, will provide conjectural reconstructions of characterization and action where possible.

ADDING 'MORE AMAZEMENT' (1.2.14): RESTORATION ADAPTATIONS OF *THE TEMPEST*

The version of *The Tempest* most familiar to play-goers throughout much of its performance history has not been Shakespeare's Folio text, but the adaptation by William Davenant and John Dryden, first staged on 7 November 1667 by the Duke's Company at Lincoln's Inn Fields and subsequently published in 1670 by Henry Herringman.[12] This version, which 'includes less than a third of Shakespeare's text',[13] changes the plot of the play and its cast of characters considerably.

The action begins, as in Shakespeare, with a storm at sea, but in this version Stephano is the ship's Master, and Trincalo the Boatswain; they are joined by Mustacho, the Master's Mate, and by Ventoso, a mariner.[14] Their passengers are Alonzo, the Duke of Savoy, who has usurped the dukedom of Mantua rightfully belonging to Hippolito; Antonio, Prospero's brother

---

11 '*The Tempest*'s Tempest', pp. 95–6. Gurr further argues that the scene is 'a supremely adroit and discreet upstaging' of Heywood's complaint in *1 The Fair Maid of the West* that 'Our stage so lamely can express a sea / That we are forc'd by Chorus to discourse / What should have been in action', pp. 96, 91.

12 *The Tempest, or the Enchanted Island. A Comedy. As it is now Acted at His Highness the Duke of York's Theatre.* (London: Henry Herringman at the Blew Anchor in the Lower-walk of the New-Exchange, 1670). The text is reprinted in *Shakespeare Adaptations*, ed. Summers, pp. 1–103; see his Introduction, pp. xli–l, for information about the first performance, publishing history, and Davenant's chief responsibility for the adaptation.

13 Orgel, p. 64.

14 This account gives a general outline of the adaptation; see Commentary for details of the lines retained, which allow for a fuller reconstruction.

and the usurping Duke of Millain; Ferdinand, Alonzo's son; and Gonzalo, a nobleman of Savoy. The opening scene, padded out with nautical directives, is double the length of Shakespeare's (see Appendix 1), but ignores what the original so succinctly establishes: the irrelevance of temporal authority in the face of natural forces, and the differences between the genially optimistic Gonzalo, the rather quiet Alonso and the gratuitously unpleasant Antonio and Sebastian. Instead, Alonzo recognizes that his suffering is caused by his as-yet-unnamed crimes, and, since Sebastian is cut, Gonzalo mouths the curse he speaks at Shakespeare's lines 35–6.

As the victims of the stricken ship exit and Prospero enters with Miranda, his question – 'where's your sister?' – immediately points out another major departure from Shakespeare's text. The rest of Act 1 of the adaptation includes Prospero's considerably shortened account of his past, his interview with Ariel (during which we learn that Caliban has a twin sister called Sycorax), Miranda and Prospero's encounter with Caliban, and a short dialogue between Miranda and her younger sister Dorinda which reveals their total ignorance about sex and the nature of men (see Appendix 1). Following the Restoration, female roles were played not by boys but by women, who were regarded as sexually experienced and available; as a result, as Jocelyn Powell has vividly demonstrated, a double dialogue took place in Miranda and Dorinda's scene, one between the characters on stage and the other between the actors and the audience, 'over the characters' heads'.[15]

Act 2 begins like Shakespeare's, with Gonzalo urging Alonzo to 'be merry', but the rest of their interaction is a radical departure from the Folio text. The bantering conversation of the lords is cut, and in his second speech Alonzo reflects that he and Antonio are being punished for their usurpations of Hippolito and Prospero: in fact, the two are returning from a Portuguese crusade to repulse the Spanish Moors, undertaken in an attempt to expiate their guilt. As they discuss their sins, two off-stage devils sing a duet, 'Where does proud Ambition dwell?', and afterwards enter to produce a show of Pride, Fraud, Rapine, and Murther. As the lords exit to seek some food, Ariel and Ferdinand enter as in Shakespeare's 1.2., with the former singing 'Come unto these yellow sands' and 'Full fathom five'.

The action then shifts to the shipwrecked mariners: because he 'was master at Sea', Stephano declares himself 'Duke on Land' and names Mustacho, his erstwhile Mate, 'Vice-Roy'. Ventoso naturally objects, and the squabbles that ensue, with references to speaking for the people, taking

---

15 Jocelyn Powell, *Restoration Theatre Production* (London: Routledge & Kegan Paul, 1984), pp. 71–2; see also p. 76 for discussion of the same kind of dialogue in relation 'to recent political events in England'.

silence for consent and civil war, satirize the recent Commonwealth years. Although Stephano solves matters by declaring both Mustacho and Ventoso his viceroys, Trincalo's arrival complicates them again: he renounces Stephano's authority and sets himself up as a rival duke. When he meets Caliban, he quickly enlists him as subject and decides to marry Sycorax to 'lay claim to this Island by Alliance'.

In the act's final scenes, Prospero reveals to the audience that, unknown to his daughters, he has also raised Hippolito in a separate part of the island: their ignorance of each other's existence was necessary, since Prospero foresaw that the young man would die if he beheld a woman before a certain time. Because the crucial period is close, Prospero warns Hippolito of 'Those dangerous Enemies of Men call'd women', which Hippolito had 'never heard of . . . before' – an irony as the part was a breeches role (that is, played by a woman). When Hippolito exits, Prospero again warns his daughters of the dangers of men, eliciting some sexual *double entendres* and firing a curiosity that the women promptly gratify once their father leaves. However, because the off-stage Prospero calls Miranda back, only Dorinda speaks to Hippolito: the two are immediately attracted to each other, although they do not understand their feelings.

Act 3 opens with Prospero chastising his daughters for their disobedience and then discussing with Ariel his intentions towards the lords as he does at the beginning of Shakespeare's 5.1. He instructs Ariel to feed them, after which the lords enter: an invisible Ariel sings 'Dry those eyes which are o'reflowing' (*sic*), and eight fat spirits entertain them as a prelude to a genuine feast. The action then shifts to Trincalo's first meeting with the monstrous Sycorax, during which Ariel plays a trick in substituting water for wine, and to another encounter between the two would-be ducal factions. Ferdinand then enters, still led by Ariel's music, and the two sing the Echo Song before Miranda and Ferdinand meet and fall in love as in Shakespeare's 1.2. After imprisoning Ferdinand and chiding Hippolito for his disobedience in speaking to Dorinda, Prospero tells Hippolito to visit and comfort Ferdinand. The act ends with their meeting, during which Hippolito learns there are more women in the world than Dorinda and resolves to have them all. As recent editors of the play explain, Davenant and Dryden's Hippolito is a typical seventeenth-century figure, symbolizing natural man raised in isolation and outside the laws of civilization; his rejection of monogamy illustrates the libertine argument against marriage.[16]

16 Maximillian E. Novak and George Robert Guffey, in their notes to Volume x of *The Works of John Dryden*, gen. ed. H. T. Swedenberg, Jr. (Berkeley: University of California Press, 1970), pp. 319–79, provide a very useful analysis of the play and its changes from Shakespeare's text, setting those changes in their Restoration contexts. The points about Hippolito are made on pp. 330 and 369.

However, the fact that Hippolito was a breeches part implicates both sexes, rather than men alone, in a naturally unrestrained sexuality, a fact already implied by Dorinda's innocent but equally powerful desires, expressed in her first scene with Miranda.

At the beginning of Act 4, Miranda visits Ferdinand with Prospero's permission, but unwittingly arouses her lover's jealousy by asking him to be kind to Hippolito; soon after, Hippolito upsets Dorinda by disclosing his ingenuous desire to have all the women in the world as well as her. Ferdinand then encounters Hippolito and challenges him to a duel; before they fight, however, the action shifts to the two ducal factions, with Stephano appearing to capitulate to Trincalo but in fact using the opportunity to woo Sycorax for himself.[17]

In the duel between the rival lovers, Ferdinand wounds Hippolito, whose refusal to retire results in his apparent death. Prospero berates Ariel for failing to prevent the catastrophe and announces that he will execute Ferdinand for his crime; however, he first reunites Alonzo with his son so that 'the sudden joy of seeing him alive' will lead to 'greater grief to see him dye'. Dorinda, meanwhile, ignorant of what death is, unsuccessfully tries to revive her lover, and then she and Miranda fall out, blaming each other for the turn events have taken. Ariel ends the act with a soliloquy, commenting on the 'Harsh discord reign[ing] throughout . . . [the] Isle' and asking 'Why shou'd a mortal by Enchantments hold / In Chains a Spirit of aetherial mould?'. His reply to himself, 'Accursed Magick we our selves have taught; / And our own Pow'r has our Subjection wrought!', makes his questioning of Prospero's authority seem merely rhetorical.

As Act 5 begins, Miranda pleads unsuccessfully with Prospero for Ferdinand's life, but Ariel intervenes, explaining that after discovering Hippolito's 'Soul was but retir'd, not sally'd out', he had worked through the night to save him. He explains the ministrations still necessary, which Prospero dispatches Miranda to perform; meanwhile, the recovered Hippolito sends Dorinda to Prospero to plead for Ferdinand's life. Consequently, when Dorinda and the freed Ferdinand encounter Miranda with Hippolito, the quartet of lovers quickly dissolves again into mutual misunderstandings, which are then finally cleared. Alonzo and Ferdinand are more happily reunited, the usurped dukedoms willingly rendered back to their rightful holders, and the would-be ducal mariners apprised of the return to the

---

17 Novak and Guffey, *Works*, p. 329, note that the adaptation's three couples (Miranda/Ferdinand, Dorinda/Hippolito, and Sycorax/Trincalo) occupy different places on the scale of love, descending from the platonic to the purely sensual. While the point seems valid in regard to some of the individuals concerned, it is perhaps a bit too schematic to apply to the couples, since, for example, Trincalo finds Sycorax physically repulsive and maintains the alliance only for political advantage.

status quo. Prospero promises Ariel his freedom once he has provided 'calm Seas and happy Gales', and after singing 'Where the bee sucks', Ariel introduces his love Milcha, who has waited for his freedom for fourteen years. The two dance a saraband before Prospero speaks the final lines, dedicating the enchanted isle as 'A place of Refuge [to the afflicted]'.

Davenant and Dryden's adaptation was itself transformed by Thomas Shadwell into an opera, which had its first performance at Dorset Garden, probably on 30 April 1674; retaining John Banister's songs for the 1667 text, it added new music by Matthew Locke, Pietro Reggio and James Hart, dances by Giovanni Battista Draghi, and masques by Pelham Humfrey.[18] The text, which was published by Herringman in 1674, follows that of 1667, apart from the added songs and dances, a slightly different act/scene arrangement, some insignificant scene transpositions and two major changes.[19] The first is the early introduction of Milcha, who joins Ariel at the end of his first scene with Prospero; the second is the masque of Neptune and Amphitrite, an entertainment conjured by Prospero at the end of the play 'to make amends / For the [lords'] rough treatment'.

The extremely popular Restoration adaptations of *The Tempest* held the stage well into the nineteenth century, only finally being ousted with William Macready's reversion to Shakespeare's text in 1838.[20] As a result,

18 Powell, *Restoration Theatre Production*, pp. 62–3; see also Orgel, p. 66. According to J. G. McManaway, Humfrey set 'Where the bee sucks' for the 1667 adaptation; see 'Songs and Masques in *The Tempest* [*c*.1674]', *Theatre Miscellany* (Luttrell Society Reprints No. 14) (Oxford: Basil Blackwell, 1953), p. 79.

19 *The Tempest, or the Enchanted Island*. A Comedy. As it is now Acted at His Highness the Duke of York's Theatre. (London: Henry Herringman, 1674). The text is available in the facsimile edition taken from the copy in the Birmingham Shakespeare Library (London: Cornmarket Press, 1969).

20 Judith Milhous and Robert D. Hume, in their edition of John Downes's 1708 *Roscius Anglicanus* (London: Society for Theatre Research, 1987), p. 74 n. 218, 'judge from fragmentary performance records [that] *The Tempest* was the most popular work on the London stage prior to *The Beggar's Opera* in 1728'. Shakespeare's text received six performances at Drury Lane in 1746, but even these performances retained Shadwell's masque of Neptune and Amphitrite (George Winchester Stone, Jr., 'Shakespeare's *Tempest* at Drury Lane During Garrick's Management', *Shakespeare Quarterly* 7 (1956), p. 1). After assuming management of Drury Lane two years later, Garrick produced in 1756 his own opera adapted from Shadwell's, but its lack of success led Garrick to restore Shakespeare's text the following year; in this version, only 432 lines were cut and 14 added (Stone, Shakespeare's *Tempest*, pp. 5–6). This text remained in the repertory until Garrick retired in 1776, but in 1777, Sheridan, the new manager, 'reintroduced both the masque of Neptune and Amphitrite and the "Grand Dance of Fantastic Spirits" which inaugurates Shadwell's disappearing banquet scene' (Orgel, p. 67). However, even this version of Shakespeare's text was

the play's stage tradition owes much to its earliest revisers rather than to the possibilities inscribed in the Folio text, and it is worth examining the influences the adaptations might have had on performance.[21] For example, the lords in the adaptation have no real dramatic interest: not only is there no sense of tension within the group,[22] but Alonzo and Antonio have already recognized their guilt before the play opens, have attempted to atone for it, and are only too happy to capitulate to Prospero. It is arguable that this untheatrical treatment led to the drastic cutting of the lords' scenes once Shakespeare's text had been restored: their dramatic potential was simply not evident.[23]

A similar point can be made about the tedium of the revised and lengthened storm scene, which may have influenced the long-lasting trend of presenting the scene without any dialogue at all: indeed, apart from partial retention of the dialogue in David Garrick's 1757, William Burton's 1854 and Samuel Phelps's 1855 productions, none of Shakespeare's opening scene was heard on stage until the beginning of the twentieth century.[24] In addition, the emphasis in the Shadwell opera was on spectacle, with 'a thick Cloudy Sky, a very Rocky Coast, and a Tempestuous Sea in perpetual Agitation'; the tempest had 'many dreadful Objects in it, as several Spirits in horrid shapes flying down amongst the Sailers [*sic*], then rising and crossing in the Air', and finally ended with 'a shower of Fire' falling

banished from the stage when John Philip Kemble reverted to the Restoration versions of the play in producing his adaptations of 1789 and 1806.

21 Much has been written about the Restoration adaptations of *The Tempest* which I am unable to rehearse here; see, as already mentioned, Novak and Guffey's edition of the play and Powell's *Restoration Theatre Production*, pp. 62–83, which vividly describes the play in performance and analyses its meaning and effects. Katharine Eisaman Maus, in 'Arcadia Lost: Politics and Revision in the Restoration *Tempest*', *Renaissance Drama* N.S. 13 (1982), pp. 189–209, provides a brilliant political analysis of the differences between Shakespeare's text and that of his Restoration adapters, although I disagree with her evaluation of the final effect made by the Restoration Prospero.

22 Although the group fall out when Ferdinand is under sentence of death, with Gonzalo claiming it as another divine punishment for Alonzo's sins and Antonio describing Gonzalo's upbraiding as unworthy, the discord is both temporary and brief.

23 Although Shakespeare's scene remained available to readers while denied to theatre-goers, theatrical potential is not always evident in words on a page: stage tradition has always played a large part in determining what is seen on stage, as the Commentary makes clear.

24 Although Tree's 1904 pb is the first I have found that restores some of Shakespeare's dialogue, Poel's 1897 platform reading and staging probably retained the scene; see George Bernard Shaw, *Saturday Review* (13 November 1897), reprinted in *Our Theatres in the Nineties*, Volume III (London: Constable, 1932), p. 242.

upon the hapless passengers and crew (opening sd). Jocelyn Powell posits the use of four fly-tracks for the spirits, describing as '[very spectacular t]he interaction of the four figures moving vertically, laterally and diagonally in carefully co-ordinated manoeuvres . . . set against the increasingly anxious movements of the sailors, passing backwards and forwards across the stage with the implements of their work, and accompanied by shouts and screams off stage' (*Restoration Theatre Production*, p. 65). He further describes how, after 'a sudden and considerable drop in [on-stage] light', the audience would have seen a 'gentle golden rain [of St Elmo's fire] at the front of the stage', ushering in a change of scene to the tranquillity of the island (pp. 67–8). It is no wonder that the significance of the opening dialogue, already diluted by Dryden and Davenant's verbal padding and further obscured by such spectacular staging, should have remained hidden until fairly recently.

The adaptations' treatment of Caliban also probably influenced his depiction in Shakespeare's restored text: the Caliban of Dryden–Davenant–Shadwell is essentially a comic creature, a good-natured being who does not plot against Prospero, is happy to serve his new master Trincalo and does not become embroiled in the ducal faction-fighting. The only violence involving him occurs when he is beaten off the stage by his sister Sycorax, expressing her dissatisfaction with the husband he obtained for her. Even the seriousness of Prospero's accusation that Caliban sought 'to violate the honour of [his] Children' is undermined in a comic exchange that characterizes Caliban and his sister as natural innocents rather than sophisticated degenerates: Trincalo confides to Stephano that he found Sycorax 'upon a sweet Bed of Nettles, singing Tory, Rory, and Ranthum, Scantum, with her own natural Brother', but dismisses their incestuousness as 'no matter' (Act 4). Furthermore, the omission of the gaberdine that makes Shakespeare's Trinculo unsure whether the creature beneath it is a man or a fish takes the Restoration Caliban firmly out of the human realm, making him a literal monster whose good nature is all the more appealing.

The Restoration Prospero also bears much responsibility for the enduring failure to see any theatrical excitement in the part. Besides cuts that remove any passion from his expository speeches, this Prospero is mostly seen in a parental role, father as he is to two daughters and father-like guardian to an orphaned prince. In his relations with them he is authoritative, with the unquestioned ability to give and to withhold information, to restrict activity and to order punishment. Although a modern audience may see Prospero himself as undermined by the naivety of his charges, it is more likely that the Restoration audience saw the trio's ineptitude as evidence for the necessity of Prospero's control. Indeed, Davenant and Dryden's decision to transfer to him the 'Abhorrèd slave' speech (1.2.351b–62), which the Folio gives to Miranda, clearly illustrates their own subscription to the patriarchal values acted out by Prospero: as Novak and Guffey point out, one reason for the change was the disobedience that would be implied by Miranda's interruption of her father's dialogue with Caliban.[25]

Although the three young people at times disregard Prospero's strictures, their failure to obey is always followed by a reinstatement of his authority, which allows him to manipulate and direct their behaviour once more. Although Prospero's exercise of power may seem arbitrary, if not tyrannical, to a modern audience, Davenant and Dryden's text inscribes its justice: even Alonzo, having faced Prospero's threat to execute his son, admits that Prospero's 'purpose / Though . . . severe was just. In losing Ferdinand / I should have mourn'd, but could not have complain'd' (Act 5). The Restoration adaptation presents Prospero as an impassive figure of patriarchal authority, an interpretation that has had far-reaching consequences for performances of Shakespeare's own play.

PLAYING PROSPERO 'MORE BETTER' (1.2.19):
CHANGING APPROACHES TO THE ROLE

The passionless approach

As indicated in the previous section, for much of *The Tempest*'s stage history the part of Prospero has not fulfilled its theatrical potential, being regarded simply as a vehicle for the display of rhetorical skills and dignified bearing. Francis Gentleman, for example, who provided the notes to Bell's edition of the 1757 Garrick text, demanded of its actor only 'oratorical ability' and 'venerable appearance'.[26] Even James Boaden, praising Robert Bensley's Prospero in John Philip Kemble's 1789 production for 'a very delicate and nice discrimination . . . when he addressed his daughter, and the spirit Ariel', unwittingly reveals that the nuances the actor dis-

---

25 *Works*, p. 359; the editors add that the adapters would have considered Prospero more likely than Miranda to have taught Caliban to speak and that the speech was in any case too philosophical for a woman to deliver.

26 *The Tempest. A Comedy*, by Shakespeare. As Performed at the Theatre-Royal, Drury-Lane, Regulated from the Prompt-Book, With Permission of the Managers, by Mr Hopkins, Prompter. An Introduction, and Notes Critical and Illustrative, are added by the Authors of the Dramatic Censor [Francis Gentleman]. In Volume III of *Bell's Edition of Shakespeare's Plays*, 1774. (London: Printed for John Bell, near Exeter Exchange in the Strand, and C. Etherington at York, 1773), p. 7.

played in the role were confined within an authoritarian set of relationships:

> They were not two young ladies of the theatre, to whom he announced his pleasure in one common tone of command. He lowered himself parentally to Miranda's innocence and inexperience: it was evidently by his *art* that he raised himself to the control of the spirit Ariel; with whom a kind of personal attachment seemed to mitigate the authority by which that gentlest of his kind was kept in a yet unwilling allegiance.[27]

Similarly, Kemble himself, who played the part in his own 1806 Covent Garden production, displayed 'The majestic presence and dignity of the princely enchanter, conscious of his virtue, his wrongs, and his supernatural power . . . with an undeviating spirit, with that proud composure which seems [his] peculiar property'.[28] George Daniel, commenting in Cumberland's edition, also found Kemble's performance 'impressive', since 'He realized all that can be conceived of the Magi – of one who held in dominion the spirits of the elements. His reproaches of Caliban were in a tone of stern authority, mingled with pity for his debasement – his behests to Ariel were chastened by a tender regard for so graceful and exquisite a being.'[29]

For the most part, such an approach to the role treats Prospero as a quasi-divine character, exempt from human failings and struggles and possessing unshakeable wisdom and serenity. However, William Hazlitt's judgement of Charles Young, who played Prospero in Kemble's 1815 and subsequent revivals, reveals that a spectrum exists even in this kind of treatment: the critic complained that Young was 'grave without solemnity, stately without dignity, pompous without being oppressive, and totally destitute of the wild, mysterious, preternatural character of the original'; rather than the 'potent wizard', he appeared 'an automaton, stupidly prompted by others'.[30]

---

27 *Memoirs of the Life of John Philip Kemble, Esq.*, Volume I (London: Longman, Hurst, Rees et al., 1825), p. 58. Boaden goes on to emphasize that Bensley's Prospero 'was in truth a mighty magician, and the awful accents that he poured out seemed of power to wake sleepers from their graves, and to control those who possessed an absolute mastery over the elements'.

28 Leigh Hunt, *Critical Essays on the Performers of the London Theatres, including General Observations on the Practise and Genius of the Stage* (London: John Hunt, 1807), p. 33.

29 *Cumberland's British Theatre*, Volume VII (London: John Cumberland, n.d.), p. 8.

30 *Examiner*, 23 July 1815, reprinted in *Dramatic Essays*, Volume II, ed. W. Archer & R. W. Lowe (London: Walter Scott, 1895), p. 64.

Even with his return to the Shakespeare text (which Garrick had anticipated in 1757), Macready's performance as Prospero in 1838 was in the same dignified vein as that of Bensley and Kemble. John Forster called it 'very beautiful. His various expression [*sic*] to the inferior creatures around him – to the objects of his affection, the victims of his art, or the ministers of his will – was touched with truth as various. He was indeed a mild Avenger, a dignified Enchanter, a most paternal Sire.'[31] Forster continues that Macready also 'gave us a sort of new thought of Prospero – that kind of habitual melancholy there was, in his most pleased anticipations, so touchingly characteristic of the man who had so long kept company with sad thoughts, and who, also . . . had acquired a little more knowledge than was quite easy to his sense of right'. However, despite Forster's apprehension of something 'new', Macready's variation does not change the basic conception of Prospero as a man wiser and more just than his fellows, of a semi-divine being whose experience of the fallen creatures around him cannot dent his hope that they will rise above their natures. Nineteenth-century Prosperos continued to interpret the character in this way, no doubt bolstered by Thomas Campbell's idea, first mooted in 1838[32] and still found in theatrical journalism today, that *The Tempest* was Shakespeare's conscious farewell to the stage and Prospero an autobiographical character: not only does the play have 'a sort of sacredness as the last work of the mighty workman', but 'Shakespeare, as if conscious that it would be his last, and as if inspired to typify himself, has made its hero a natural, a dignified, and benevolent magician'.[33]

Appraisals of Charles Kean's 1857 Prospero show how limited were the expectations and how fine the discernible subtleties of the part. According to John William Cole, Kean was 'dignified and impressive', but given the writer's opinion that the character has 'neither passion nor variety', requiring only 'sustained solemnity of deportment, with graceful elocution, and here and there an impulse of natural feeling', his judgement of an impressive performance is rather suspect.[34] The *Theatrical Journal*, in two reviews, praised Kean's Prospero in rather vague terms as 'mysterious', 'ethereal' and impressive' (19 August 1857, p. 261), showing 'gentle

31 *Examiner*, 21 October 1838, reprinted in John Forster and George Henry Lewes, *Dramatic Essays*, Volume III, ed. William Archer and Robert Lowe (London: Walter Scott, 1896), p. 70.

32 Orgel, p. 10.

33 Quoted in Horace Howard Furness, *The Tempest*, A New Variorum Edition (Philadelphia, 1892), p. 356, quoted in Orgel, p. 10.

34 *The Life and Theatrical Times of Charles Kean, F.S.A.*, 2nd edition (London: Richard Bentley, 1860), Volume II, p. 223.

patience . . . sublimity of thought, and . . . a refined idea' (26 August 1857, p. 268), but the *Illustrated London News* more concretely commended the actor for 'showing more human emotion than any *Prospero* we have ever seen. His is not a pale and passionless delivery of the text, but a pathetic acting out of the relations to which, however made superior by his art, he is yet bound by nature.'[35] In fact, the range of emotion to which the reviewer alludes seems as narrow as that of Macready's portrayal.

Although this passionless approach to the role has been successfully challenged in the twentieth century, it has not been entirely banished. Max Beerbohm found Acton Bond, who played Prospero in Charles Lander's production of the play at the Court in 1903, 'scholarly and charming', and with 'enough authority' for the part.[36] John Drinkwater's 1915 production for the Birmingham Rep, with sets and costumes by Barry Jackson, pushed to an extreme the presentation of Prospero as a wise and philosophical figure, with Felix Aylmer 'made up to resemble Plato'.[37] A photo in the Theatre Museum, London, shows him in a very flowing white robe resembling an oversized priest's vestment and with a band around his forehead reminiscent of Merlin; he had a bushy beard and carried a long staff patterned with a black-and-white zig-zag design. The *Birmingham Post* reviewer (19/4/15) complained that Aylmer's 'conception [of Prospero] seemed rhetorical and pompous' and his '[utterance] indistinct and unrhythmic', but nevertheless conceded that the performance was 'more than tolerable', showing again how little was expected of actors who undertook the part.[38]

Identification with an ancient Greek philosopher or Celtic seer is not the only conceit possible with an impassive approach to the role. Lena Ashwell regarded Prospero as embodying the 'divine principle in man';[39] programme notes for her production indicate that it was heavily influenced by

35 4 July 1857, p. 11. Hans Christian Andersen, on the other hand, found Kean undistinguished: he 'preached constantly, and ha[d] not at all an agreeable voice' (*Pictures of Travel* (New York: Hurd & Houghton; Cambridge: Riverside Press, 1871), p. 285).

36 *Saturday Review*, 7 November 1903, reprinted in *Around Theatres* (1924; reprint, New York: Simon & Schuster, 1954), p. 297.

37 Claire Cochrane, *Shakespeare and the Birmingham Repertory Theatre 1913–1929* (London: Society for Theatre Research, 1993), p. 58.

38 Michael Billington's comment about Jude Kelly's 1999 production indicates how much this view has changed: 'no Tempest . . . can work if Prospero is played as a resigned recluse, rather than an impassioned figure torn between virtue and vengeance' (*Guardian*, 11/2/99).

39 *Reflections from Shakespeare* (London: Hutchinson [1926]), p. 228.

Colin Still's book, *Shakespeare's Mystery Play*,[40] which argues that *The Tempest* 'dramatis[es] the conflict in the human consciousness of the forces of light and the forces of darkness', with Prospero typifying 'the idea of God'. In yet another vein, Giles Isham, playing the part in Iden Payne's 1938 Stratford production with 'abundant good humour and benevolence beneath the guise of retributive sternness', was 'made up to look like one or several of the idealized portraits of Shakespeare' (respectively, *Stratford Herald*, 6/5/38, and *The Times*, 3/5/38).

Although Prosperos have become more adventurous in their approach to the role as the twentieth century has progressed, many notable actors have subscribed to the benign school of interpretation, among them Alastair Sim in Oliver Neville's 1962 Old Vic production, Paul Scofield in John Harrison's 1974 Leeds Playhouse production and Michael Hordern in Clifford Williams's 1978 RSC production. Hordern, however, managed to incorporate into his kind-hearted portrayal of Prospero a sense of pain and of internal struggle, elements of the character that have become characteristic of modern approaches to the role.

Flawed humanity

Reviewers of Frank Benson's 1891 production were not impressed by his Prospero, Stephen Phillips: he was judged too quiet, grave and sombre, rather than dignified, and also too harsh (see *Stage*, 30/4/1891; *Birmingham Mail*, 25/4/1891; E.C.T., *Stratford Herald*, 1/5/1891). Such descriptions suggest that Phillips did not emphasize Prospero's noble side but his more flawed aspects – aspects that were to become increasingly stressed during the next hundred years, reflecting both the influence of Freud in investigating psychological processes and of Stanislavsky in scrutinizing subtextual nuances. And, of course, since twentieth-century productions have characteristically moved away from substantial textual cuts towards the playing of Shakespeare's full text, there has been more and more subtext for actors playing Prospero to exploit.

An intriguing picture of a complex Prospero comes from *The Times* review of Andrew Leigh's 1926 Old Vic production, where Neil Porter's performance is unfavourably compared with 'the true Prospero' presented five years before by Henry Ainley. Appearing in the Viola Tree and Louis Calvert production at London's Aldwych Theatre, Ainley showed 'a whim-

---

40 *Shakespeare's Mystery Play: A Study of 'The Tempest'* (London: Cecil Palmer, 1921). See pp. 39–40 for a discussion of Ariel's interpretation in the production.

sical, artistic temperament, now fretful and malicious, now tender and sunny, ever forgetful and wandering amid dreams, a forecast of King Louis of Bavaria, and probably a far more intolerable ruler than his wicked but practical brother' (?/11/26). Despite the unflattering comparison to Ainley, the reviewer makes clear that Porter himself freed the part from 'the pompousness of most Prosperos', making him instead into 'a weird, Faust-like creature'. Visually, however, Porter resembled the nineteenth-century conception of the role: a photo from the *Daily Sketch* shows him dressed in an Old Testament-style cloak and long tunic, with a shortish beard and hair swept back from his forehead.

Porter played Prospero again in Bridges-Adams's 1934 Stratford production, and descriptions of his characterization show the continuing constraints of traditional interpretation. Prospero was still in many ways a thankless part, regarded as 'verbose' and 'rather pedantic' (respectively, *Era*, 18/4/34, and *Daily Express*, 19/4/34). Some reviewers, however, saw the greater potential of the part and Porter's attempt to fulfill it: the *Stratford Herald* approved 'a characterisation full of thought, of subtlety, of humility, and of human understanding', but found it 'too delicate a picture for so large a frame' (20/4/34), while *The Times* judged him 'No preaching patriarch . . . but a bold and three-parts successful attempt . . . to set before us the master spirit of the enchanted island' (17/4/34). However, when Ayrton revived the production the following year, the same reviewer was disappointed that Porter 'seemed less like the master spirit of the island and more like the preaching patriarch of bad stage tradition' (*The Times*, 24/4/35).

Although elements of this tradition can still be found in some contemporary productions, its supremacy was effectively shattered by John Gielgud's highly influential interpretations of the part, spanning several decades. The actor tackled the role for the first time at the age of twenty-six, when he played a disillusioned Prospero in Harcourt Williams's 1930 Old Vic production: at a stroke, he freed the character from the double preconceptions of old age and wise omnipotence. Rather than being 'just a bore with a beard', as Ivor Brown had come to expect, Gielgud's Prospero was an 'Italian gentleman . . . rich in . . . melancholy': 'his magic [was] in his mind, as his disenchantment with the world of men [was] in his anguished eye and the dying fall of his declamation'; the *Morning Post* reviewer similarly found Gielgud's 'ascetic, unbearded face, with or without turban . . . a delightful change from the usual conception of Prospero as a dressy old alderman'. Another critic who admired Gielgud's 'dignity and power' was disturbed by the unwonted 'youthfulness which seem[ed] in the early scenes to challenge the pretensions of his daughter's lover'; however, he praised the 'weary cadence of an embittered maturity' in Gielgud's voice and the 'stateliness of a magician impatient of opposition' in his bearing.[41]

Ten years later, Gielgud returned to the Old Vic to play the part in the war-time production by George Devine and Marius Goring;[42] reviews suggest that on this occasion his Prospero combined traces of the traditional approach with his own rethinking of the part. One critic found Gielgud's performance 'a trifle more mature than the [previous] one' and characterized by 'a calm dignity, an almost mystic appreciation of the beauty of the verse and an entire absence of the prosiness often associated with the part' (*Daily Telegraph*, 30/5/40). *The Times* agreed that he was 'never . . . the preaching patriarch, the heaviest of heavy fathers' (30/5/40), while the *Observer* happily remarked that he was 'very far from the usual mixture of Father Christmas, a Colonial Bishop, and the President of the Magicians' Union': rather, he was 'a clear, arresting picture of a virile Renaissance notable (no dotard) who has "a daily beauty in his life" as well as magic powers' (2/6/40). The *Sunday Times* commented that he avoided the 'absurdity' of the part 'not by excess of virtuosity, but through the more subtle method of withdrawal, whereby it seemed that he continually held the centre of an undrawn circle marking him off from even such flesh-and-blood as Miranda owes' (2/6/40?); another reviewer, however, found him tender as well as middle-aged and dignified (*Stage*, 6/6/40). Edwin Smith's photographs show Gielgud with a thin moustache and goatee beard, wearing almost friar-like robes, make-up and costume emblematizing the actor's combination of the new and the old.

It was in fact Gielgud's next Prospero, for Peter Brook's 1957 Stratford production, that broke the nineteenth-century mould most effectively: this Prospero was 'lean, clean-shaven, and grizzled', with a 'harsh and dangerous' look (Harold Hobson, *Sunday Times*, 18/8/57). Several critics saw Gielgud's middle-aged, vigorous, and bitter figure as Timon-like, a resemblance helped by his costume of sandals and knee-length toga, cinched by a sash around the waist. The toga, 'coarsely-woven' and 'mud-coloured',

41 All three reviews, filed in the Theatre Museum, London, are dated 7/10/30. Sources are identified wherever possible, but in some cases names of periodicals and dates are illegible or missing. Unless otherwise noted, for reviews and photographs of Stratford productions I have consulted the relevant clippings and production files at the Shakespeare Centre Library, Stratford-upon-Avon, while for reviews and photographs of other productions I have consulted the production and photograph files of the Theatre Museum, London.

42 He had in the interim also played Prospero in a radio broadcast of 12/11/33 (*The Times*, 13/11/33).

was draped over Gielgud's right shoulder, leaving the left shoulder and arm bare, apart from a cloth band tied around the upper part.[43]

Reviewers unanimously praised Gielgud's portrayal of Prospero, which made prominent the internal struggles of a flawed human being. Anthony Cookman observed that Gielgud seemed to throw light on Prospero's 'own nature', which,

> in spite of its stern schooling, has refractory elements left in it that have not yet found complete release. How if when he comes face to face with [his] enemies . . . he should not be able to forgive them? How if at the last moment he should find it intolerable to bow himself again to human conditions and break his magic rod? . . . It is the actor's triumph to make these questions insistently real.   (*Tatler*, 28/8/57)

T. C. Worsley, recognizing the same features in Gielgud's portrayal, was not so sure of his determination to be forgiving: emphasizing the 'dark side' of the character, Gielgud's Prospero was nearly 'engulfed by his sense of being wronged'; his magic was not just a wonderful but a frightening power, tempting him to give in to his bitterness (*New Statesman*, 24/8/57). Indeed, Roy Walker thought his 'burning . . . resentment of past wrongs . . . threatened to overthrow his reason altogether' ('Unto Caesar', *Shakespeare Survey* 11 (1958), p. 128).

Gielgud's last stage portrayal of Prospero was in Peter Hall's 1974 National Theatre production.[44] This performance, the actor's fourth Prospero and his third on the Old Vic stage, inevitably drew comparisons with his previous appearances; reviews suggest that by this time Gielgud was beginning to seem old-fashioned in his approach, at least to some critics.[45] Irving Wardle found the 1974 interpretation 'in general . . . as I remember it from the 1957 production: aloof, immeasurably elegiac, with the suggestion of internal struggles remote from the surrounding drama' (*The Times*, 6/3/74); however, Michael Billington missed the contrast

---

43 Quotations from, respectively, John Wardle, *Bolton Evening News*, 17/8/57, and Kenneth Tynan, *Observer*, 18/8/57. One critic did not find the costume commanding enough and thought Prospero's magic cloak 'too like a plastic "mack"' (Philip Hope-Wallace, *Manchester Guardian*, 15/8/57; see also *Time & Tide*, 24/8/57).

44 Gielgud also starred in Peter Greenaway's 1991 film adaptation of the play, *Prospero's Books*.

45 In fact, Gielgud was Peter Hall's third choice for Prospero in the 1974 production, after Laurence Olivier and Alec Guinness; see *Peter Hall's Diaries: The Story of a Dramatic Battle* (London: Hamish Hamilton, 1983), pp. 12 and 43. The director thought Gielgud 'perhaps too gentle and too nice' for the part, although he felt he could 'push him into a harsher area of reality' (p. 43).

between 'initial testiness and final benediction' that had been evident in Brook's 1957 production, and John Barber thought Gielgud moved 'more sadly than before from control over mere Nature to control over his own vengeful passions' (respectively, *Guardian* and *Daily Telegraph*, both 6/3/74). Gielgud's acting itself generated quite mixed reactions: one critic complained that he struck 'theatrical poses . . . more appropriate to the Victorian theatre than to the swinging seventies' (Herbert Kretzmer, *Daily Express*, 6/3/74), but Barber judged him 'superb'. Although many reviewers praised his verse-speaking virtuosity, John Elsom thought Gielgud's delivery 'perfunctory' in the sense that 'he never seemed to talk to anyone';[46] other reviewers were similarly disappointed by his 'muted' and 'curiously detached performance' (respectively, Felix Barker, *Evening News*, and Milton Shulman, *Evening Standard*, both 6/3/74). On the other hand, B. A. Young found that Gielgud's Prospero 'dominate[d] the stage constantly; even in scenes where he is not involved, except in so far as he has arranged them by his supernatural powers, he stands regarding his handiwork. He is not a likeable character; actors try sometimes to conceal his cruelty and selfishness, but John Gielgud holds fast to it until almost the end' (*Financial Times*, 6/3/74). For Young, the actor's detachment was not an aspect of Gielgud's performance, but of Prospero's character.

Gielgud's 1974 performance may have muted some of the harsher elements of his earlier interpretations, but other actors soon followed in his iconoclastic footsteps. Ian Richardson, playing Prospero in John Barton's 1970 RSC production, was 'younger and more forthright than usual', showing the 'humanity' of the character, although another critic described him as 'younger and colder than usual'.[47] Benedict Nightingale found him 'a very private man: withdrawn, wry, contemptuous of show, self-mocking. You feel he's pondered much on human inadequacy during his exile, and hasn't shirked from turning a sceptical eye on himself either. His wisdom . . . has [been] won . . . the hard way' (*New Statesman*, 23/10/70). John Barber, noting the same qualities, found them less sympathetic: Richardson's Prospero was 'deeply embittered, soured, by self-pity . . . a cold, weary creature, withdrawn, shambling, hands in sackcloth pockets' (*Daily Telegraph*, 17/10/70). His casual bearing and plain costume seemed to emphasize his ordinary humanity: this Prospero wore 'countryman's trousers' and 'a dun-coloured artist's smock' made of 'holland' for his

---

46 'A Creaking Storm', unidentified clipping, Royal National Theatre archives.
47 Respectively, John Higgins, *The Times*, 17/10/70, and Ronald Bryden, *Observer*, 18/10/70.

magic gown or cloak;[48] Barber felt this 'unclean overall' was of a piece with his 'bedraggled grey beard'.[49]

In the last quarter-century, Prospero's flawed nature has also manifested itself in neurosis, sometimes as part of a thematic approach to interpretation of the play. For instance, in Jonathan Miller's landmark colonialist interpretation of 1970, which opened a few months before Barton's, Graham Crowden's Prospero illustrated Octave Mannoni's point that colonial life attracts those 'who have failed . . . to adapt infantile images to adult reality':[50] he was 'a solemn and touchy neurotic, the victim of a power complex', 'whose need for slaves [was] certainly as great as Caliban's need for a master' (respectively, Barber, *Daily Telegraph*, and Wardle, *The Times*, both 16/6/70). Interestingly, however, this approach did not necessarily make Prospero unattractive: since he was 'unequal to equality . . . the nobility of [his ultimate] surrender [was] all the greater . . . [T]hat his supernaturalism [was] founded in a natural insufficiency [made] Prospero for the first time not only an interesting, but also a sympathetic, even heroic figure' (*Sunday Times*, 21/6/70).

As is evident from this last comment and many others that precede it, focus on the tensions within Prospero's own character gives the play a theatrical momentum that earlier commentators were convinced it lacks. Derek Jacobi, playing Prospero in Ron Daniels's 1982 production for the RSC, emphasized his 'internal struggle between omnipotence and humanity',[51] a struggle encapsulated in costume: Prospero's magic cloak, covered with cabalistic symbols and yoked across the chest by a strip of material, resembled a grand priestly vestment,[52] while his everyday clothes comprised a long dressing-gown-like robe worn over an ordinary shirt and

48 Respectively, *Birmingham Evening Mail*, 16/10/70; Higgins; and Elizabeth Knapp, *TES*, 23/10/70.

49 Reviewers especially praised Richardson for his delivery of the verse: for example, J. C. Trewin felt it was the best speaking of the part since Gielgud (*Birmingham Post*, 24/10/70), and Bryden admired his 'new baritone richness of voice'.

50 Miller's programme reprinted this quotation from Octave Mannoni, *Prospero and Caliban: The Psychology of Colonization* (2nd edn), trans. Pamela Powesland (New York: Praeger, 1964). Mannoni's book, which examined the French colonization of Madagascar, 'was a major force in the transformation of Caliban as the oppressor to Caliban as the oppressed' (Alden T. and Virginia Mason Vaughan, *Shakespeare's Caliban: A Cultural History* (Cambridge: Cambridge University Press, 1991), p. 160).

51 Michael Billington, *Guardian*, 12/8/82.

52 Indeed, one reviewer thought that Jacobi, wearing his magic cloak, looked 'like a rough neck Bishop about to get heavy with his verger' Ariel (City of London Recorder, 29/9/83).

trousers. For Michael Coveney, Jacobi's Prospero was 'interestingly less benevolent than is usual. Throughout the performance there is a sense that this youngish mage resorts to his peculiar art only when realising the shortcomings of his humane instincts' (*Financial Times*, 13/8/82); indeed, to Ned Chaillet, he 'seem[ed] to harbour true vengeance in his heart, and the power to bring it about' (*The Times*, 13/8/82). Robert Cushman found Jacobi's performance 'Technically commanding' and 'psychologically very astute', showing Prospero as 'a man moving from one loneliness to another' (*Observer*, 15/8/82). Other reviewers saw him as a 'hugely human father punctuating fits of rage and irritation with moments of guilty self-awareness' (*Morning Star*, 16/8/82), 'temper[ing] his autocratic strictures with benignity and humour' in a way 'both consistent and believable' (Desmond Pratt, *Yorkshire Post*, 12/8/82).[53] Jacobi's performance was widely and deservedly admired: one reviewer called his Prospero, with its 'tremendous authority', 'one of the finest of our times' (*Scotsman*, 14/8/82), while Billington judged his 'vital and thrilling interpretation . . . the best since Gielgud's'.[54]

Conversely, Michael Bryant's harsh approach to the role in Peter Hall's 1988 National Theatre production sharply divided critical opinion. One reviewer complained that it was 'the most low-key interpretation [she'd] ever seen: A grizzled old sea-dog and small-time alchemist whose choleric mutterings throw away most of the magnificent poetry in his lines' (Maureen Paton, *Daily Express*, 21/5/88). Other reviewers agreed, although some had a more complex response: for example, Jim Hiley described Bryant as a 'bluff, gruff Prospero . . . confined between indignation and fury' but with 'an invigorating earthiness' (*Listener*, 26/5/88), while Michael Billington found the production memorable precisely for Bryant's 'transformation of Prospero from the usual benign schoolmaster into a testy little nut-brown necromancer who is almost a Mediterranean Faust'; reminiscent of Gielgud's 'angry, bare-chested despot' in Brook's 1957 production, he 'pushe[d] the idea much further' (*Guardian*, 21/5/88). Francis King similarly thought Bryant's 'worldly, strong-willed Prospero' the most interesting aspect of Hall's production (*Sunday Telegraph*, 22/5/88).

53 Only Gareth Lloyd Evans demurred, unimaginatively complaining that Jacobi showed Prospero's 'change of mood rather than elements in a thematic or interpretative pattern' (*Stratford Herald*, 20/8/82).

54 Besides admiring Jacobi's interpretation, critics also praised the skill and beauty of his verse-speaking (see, e.g., Coveney, *Financial Times*, 13/8/82). Cushman's review of the London transfer hailed him as 'a superb verse-actor on four counts: tonal colour, lucidity, architecture, and characterisation' (*Observer*, 18/9/83).

Paradoxically, contemporary reviews still insist that it is unusual to portray Prospero as less than benign,[55] even though such interpretations have been dominant in the most influential and prestigious twentieth-century stagings of the play. Such insistence indicates how powerful the traditional passionless approach to the role still is in memory, if not in practice.

Human prosperos and their magic

As my earlier mention of Michael Hordern's 1978 performance has already indicated, aspects of the two divergent approaches to Prospero outlined so far are not mutually exclusive: kind-heartedness can be divorced from Olympian serenity and allied to a depiction of human struggle for fulfil-ment. Even John Gielgud's and Derek Jacobi's performances can be described in this way, with angry drives and vengeful urges eventually over-come by a willed adherence to human virtue.

Prospero's relationship to his magic often plays a crucial role in our per-ceptions of the character's humanity; its importance is neatly highlighted by the different approaches taken by Michael Redgrave, who played Prospero in Michael Benthall's 1951 Stratford production, and by Ralph Richardson, who played the part in Benthall's revival of the production the following year. Although critics were divided on Redgrave's appearance, delivery and bearing,[56] many commented not only on the effort that Pros-pero's magic took, but also on the positive aspects of such an emphasis: his

55 See, for example, Coveney's review of Jacobi's performance and Billington's of Bryant's quoted in the preceding two paragraphs. Even Peter Hall, preparing his 1974 National Theatre production, complained about the traditional interpretation of Prospero as a 'remote old man' and determined to portray him as a 'William Blake-like figure going through the purgatory of the play' (*Peter Hall's Diaries*, pp. 12 and 44).

56 Redgrave wore 'an entirely unnecessary false nose, with dignity, distinction, and even aloofness, and he maintained a certain mellifluous flow, but he was not the equal in depth, tonal quality or bearing' of Robert Harris's 1947 Prospero (*Birmingham Mail*, 27/6/51). The *Stage* felt his heavy clothes made him move uneasily, whereas the *Daily Worker* thought he moved well but 'sometimes mumble[d] through his beard' (29/6/51). The latter critic agreed that he 'looked like one of Blake's prophets' (*Observer*, 1/7/51), while another called him a 'dominant patriarchal figure' (*Berrows Worcester Journal*, 29/6/51). Production photographs confirm the Old Testament impression created by his costume, which had 'twigs growing out of [each] shoulder' (*Daily Express*, 27/6/51). Although his costume and beard clearly evoked the earlier tradition, Redgrave's depiction of Prospero's struggle just as clearly modified their effect, as evidenced by the *Observer*'s reference to Blake's tormented figures.

'mastery must be worked for with increasing toil . . . [E]ach feat of magic was in doubt until it had triumphed and . . . the achievement was paid for by an ensuing exhaustion . . . [I]t was a Prospero easy to believe in' (*The Times*, 27/6/51). Similarly, another reviewer thought that although Prospero as written is 'a bully and a bore', Redgrave, 'with extraordinary skill . . . gives us a nobleman with whose wrongs we sympathise and . . . a practising, an empirical magician, not a mere ringmaster with a wand instead of a whip – whose art we follow with curiosity and admiration. It is a very fine performance' (*Spectator*, 29/6/51). Reviews such as these make clear the still widespread critical belief that Prospero was an unrewarding and unsympathetic role; the *Sunday Times* critic, for one, read the part as that of a 'disagreeable old man' whose supposed omnipotence deprives the play of essential conflict, and he praised Redgrave's display of difficulty in performing magic as a way of obviating such drawbacks: 'His hands tremble and his shoulders heave with effort whenever Prospero goes into action, and he is an exhausted man when he comes out of it. This is excellent' (1/7/51).

Ralph Richardson's notices in Benthall's 1952 revival were generally less enthusiastic than Redgrave's, with many complaints about his delivery of the verse and almost as many about his movements and gestures. For example, Alan Dent in the *News Chronicle* judged that he 'treats the part . . . as rhetoric rather than a[s] poetry, delivers a great deal of it with his right arm extended, and hangs out his great speeches somewhat prosaically' (26/3/52). 'Either he fidgets with the lines', wrote J. C. Trewin, 'splitting them oddly, or else he imposes a new tune of his own. And he has a habit of restless prowling that does not match the noble serenity of the words he utters' (*Sketch*, 9/4/52). Despite these harsh and suspect judgements (predicated as they are on the innate dignity of the role), other reviewers found something to admire in his delivery and/or movement.[57]

Several reviews compared his interpretation to Redgrave's the preceding year; it seems clear from an overview of the criticism that Richardson strongly emphasized Prospero's human side, an approach that many critics found inappropriate. Whereas Redgrave, according to *The Times*, 'was the conscious artist fully aware of his own exceptional gifts', Richardson, on the other hand, was 'the ordinary man conscious of having come through study by extraordinary powers, an enchanter himself half enchanted and marvelling . . . at finding himself the instrument of supernatural purpose';

---

57 See, for example, *Birmingham Evening Despatch*, *Nottingham Guardian* and *Bristol Western Daily Press* (27/3/52) in the SCL cuttings file.

he was, in short, 'a very human Prospero' (26/3/52?). This rather neutral description of the difference between the two interpretations gives way to more partisan response in other accounts. The reviewer for the *Solihull and Warwick County News* found the revival an improvement on the original production because of Richardson's characterization: he

> brings Prospero down to earth. Albeit a magician, here is a human being, a father and a master, and Sir Ralph does not permit him to forget his earthliness even when drawing magic circles and weaving spells. He is less Lear-like in appearance than was Michael Redgrave's Prospero, he resists to a great – but not an entire – degree the temptation to recite his speeches, but there is at times a tendency to over-use those expressive hands.   (29/3/52)

On the other hand, Peter Fleming in the *Spectator* judged Redgrave 'a magician' and Richardson

> an illusionist. Mr Redgrave's attitude to his supernatural agents was commanding, yet at the same time wary, vigilant, rather anxious: very like a huntsman's attitude to hounds. To Sir Ralph the sprites and monsters are little more than the goldfish in his bowl are to a conjuror – stage properties whose punctual appearances and disappearances are managed with a complacent, almost blasé dexterity. His performance is throughout flat and naturalistic . . . his Prospero, though human and likeable, is dangerously deficient both in power and in the quality of wonder.   (27?/3/52)

The question of magic apart, other reviews make clear that the human qualities Richardson brought to the role were those of tenderness and humour rather than the angst and anger that later twentieth-century actors often find in Prospero. According to the *Manchester Guardian*, Richardson was also 'less patriarchal in outward shape' than Redgrave, as well as 'more worldly' (27/3/52); production photographs confirm that Richardson wore simpler, less imposing robes than his predecessor and that he had a trim Van Dyke beard rather than Redgrave's long curled one. Ruth Ellis of the *Stratford Herald* emphasized that his 'alert, energetic, humorous statesman' was 'definitely Miranda's father (*not* grandfather)' (4/4/52).

More recent Prosperos, identifying their magical powers with those of the scientist or the artist, have reflected contemporary concerns about the relationship between the human and the technological, between private and public worlds. For example, in Liviu Ciulei's 1981 production at the Guthrie Theater, Minneapolis, Ken Ruta's Prospero was 'omnipresent' throughout the play.[58] Several reviewers note that he, as well as Miranda and Ariel, were the only characters dressed in contemporary costume; his consisted of a 'shabby old' 'cardigan sweater and baggy [trousers], [making him appear] a reclusive scholar'.[59] His magic staff was 'a mathematician's ruler', but reviewers seem divided about whether his magic garment was 'a painter's stained and ragged smock' or a scientist's 'lab coat'.[60] Frank Rich noted that this Prospero, 'played with worldweary intelligence and great feeling', 'truly seem[ed] capable of miracles', coming across as not only 'a magician, stage manager and poet, but . . . also a modern scientist of genius. Indeed, with his gold-rimmed glasses, ratty cardigan and abstracted demeanor, Mr Ruta could pass for Einstein' (*New York Times*, 4/7/81). The programme's inclusion of photographs of Albert Einstein, J. Robert Oppenheimer, Pablo Picasso, Max Ernst and Albert Schweitzer in fact indicates that the audience were meant to make the artist-scientist connection, while the photograph accompanying Rich's review shows that Ruta, in 'his modern sweater and slacks and his white hair', was in fact made up to look like Einstein (Jack Kroll, *Newsweek*, 29/6/81). As another critic noted, this Prospero's 'books [were] not manuals for necromancy but tools to tackle the mind's frontiers' (T. E. Kalem, *Time*, 27/7/81).

Accordingly, Ruta played Prospero as a 'doubting, struggling artist, constantly and openly making difficult choices, wrestling with his soul just as he is with nature and fate and history . . . [A] steely strength is always mellowed by human doubt' (Steele). Although it was clear that Ruta's Prospero was 'always in charge of his universe', 'he completely resist[ed] the temptation to strike poses and play God. [He was] an in[n]ately kind scholar, even endowed with a sense of humor. His power [was] awesome, yet he [spoke] with a decisiveness tinged with humility, and his love for his daughter [was] quite touching' (Weiser).

Ruta was universally praised for his 'superb performance', in which there was 'very little posturing' (Steele); another critic remarked that the actor's concern 'with the working out of Prospero's private internal conflicts about power and freedom' made the production 'More than in any other . . . Prospero's play' (Jonathan Saville, *San Diego Reader*, 9/81). Purporting to

58 Mike Steele, *Minneapolis Tribune*, 13/6/81. I am grateful to Lara Hughes of the Guthrie Theater for supplying me with copies of reviews and of the programme for each of the Guthrie's three productions of *The Tempest*.

59 Respectively, Lucille Johnsen Stelling, *Minneapolis Skyway News*, 23/6/81, and Steele.

60 Respectively, David Hawley, uc, 14/6/81; David Hawley, *St Paul Dispatch*, 12/6/81; and Mary Weiser, *New Brighton Bulletin*, 2/7/81.

analyse the way Ruta's conception of the role militated against Ciulei's approach to the play, Saville inadvertently shows how well he in fact complemented it: Ruta's

> magisterial inwardness continually compels the rest of the production to revolve around himself, to reflect the struggles of Prospero's heart as he comes to terms with one of life's great problems. What Ruta forces the audience to perceive, not in theory but in palpable experience, is that Prospero's anger toward . . . [Antonio] has made him a prisoner of his own vindictiveness . . . [F]reedom lies not in the power to control but in the power to transcend one's own baser impulses. Ruta's reading of the role changes the meaning of Ciulei's moat of blood [which encircled the stage]: it becomes a symbol of Prospero's own rage, his own internal wars, his own isolation from free human intercourse because he cannot renounce the desire to punish his hateful brother.

There is, of course, no contradiction between the microcosm expressed in Ruta's performance and the macrocosm expressed in Ciulei's set.[61]

Taking a less complex approach, Robert Falls's 1987 production at the Goodman Theatre, Chicago, seems to have presented science as an undoubtedly beneficent force. Dennis Arndt's Prospero was 'a kind, off-beat university professor in khaki [trousers] rolled up to his calves, a loose floursack shirt, and sneakers'; he entered wearing a 'flowing velvet cape [and] carrying an umbrella of silver space-age fabric'.[62] Susan Pellowe adds that although his umbrella-sceptre at first seemed 'a diminution and abomination', its

> subsequent uses . . . [were] typical of the contemporary technologically-oriented magic that this Prospero manipulate[d]: he spread . . . its deflective fabric over sleeping Miranda to protect her [1.2.186sd], he flashe[d] it open as a shield against a weapon [1.2.465sd], he cup[ped] it open in his hand and aim[ed] the handle toward space like a TV dish receiver when he would be in tune with the extraterrestial [1.2.187–8].

More recently, in Silviu Purcarete's 1995 production for Nottingham Playhouse and Theatre Clwyd, Michael Fitzgerald's 'young, slightly effeminate, well-spoken' Prospero was 'more of an artist than a revenging magus' or scientist (Michael Coveney, *Observer*, 17/9/95). Wearing the 'sumptuous robes of an 18th-century monarch', he seemed to one reviewer

---

61 See pp. 88–9 for further discussion of Ciulei's set.
62 Susan Pellowe, 'In Chicago', *Plays International* 3 (August 1987), p. 55.

1 For Silviu Purcarete's 1995 production, Michael Fitzgerald played Prospero as an eighteenth-century aesthete, attended by multiple Ariels who played a variety of musical instruments and whose lines Prospero spoke in voice-over.

like 'one of those princes beloved by Marivaux, performing social experiments on lesser persons' (Jeremy Kingston, *The Times*, 12/9/95); to another, he was 'impressive . . . as an 18th-century rationalist philosopher driven to despair by the darkness of the human heart' (Charles Spencer, *Daily Telegraph*, 18/9/95). Agreeing that Fitzgerald's 'beautifully enunciated and faintly epicene' Prospero 'arrest[ed] the attention throughout', Paul Taylor aptly summed up his characterization as 'a rather mannered aesthete exercised by the competing claims of his seductively solipsistic dreamworld of art and illusion and his responsibilities as father and temporal ruler' (*Independent*, 19/9/95).

Metatheatrical approaches

The viability of treating Prospero's magic power as a metaphorical expression of creative and destructive urges has encouraged some directors to present the play as a meditation on the power of theatre, with Prospero presented as director. In Giorgio Strehler's justly celebrated 1978 production for the Piccolo Teatro di Milano, subsequently seen throughout the world, Tino Carraro's Prospero was 'like a master-illusionist and theatre-director playing God before learning to accept his humanity' (Michael Billington, *Guardian*, 16/11/83). Although his Prospero 'passed through hate to understanding and reconciliation', stressing 'the education of those who wronged him rather than vengeance', the 'contradictions inherent in . . . the role were [not] ignored', but 'were clearly, even though sometimes subtly, suggested'.[63]

The metatheatrical approach, however, can yield less desirable dividends: whereas Strehler's Prospero dominated the stage, Anthony Quayle, in his own co-production with Nigel Jamieson for Compass Theatre in 1985, came across as a stage-manager, 'calling on simple, neatly arranged masque-like visions behind the cloths and taking simple pleasure when his exotic acrobats land[ed] on their feet or negotiate[d] an exit' (Michael Coveney, *Financial Times*, 8/10/85). Consequently, he paid the price of all stage-managers in being 'less interesting than the show he [was] putting on' (Irving Wardle, *The Times*, 9/10/85).

While critics seem to agree that Quayle's approach was unexciting but clear, Timothy Walker's in Declan Donnellan's 1988 Cheek by Jowl production was commanding but impenetrable. Walker played the part 'as a tyrannical young actor-manager . . . who spends much of the time watching the action from a stage-left dressing room. With his lank locks, accosting profile and limping gait', he reminded some critics of Olivier's Richard III: indeed, he was 'positively villainous at times, thanks to hollow red-eyed

---

63 Pia Kleber, 'Theatrical Continuities in Giorgio Strehler's *The Tempest*', in Dennis Kennedy, ed. *Foreign Shakespeare* (Cambridge: Cambridge University Press, 1993), p. 150; she notes, for example, that 'Prospero's role as oppressor of Caliban was expressed in body posture, action, props, and tone of voice'. Strehler's production is discussed more fully below and in the Commentary.

make-up' (respectively, Michael Billington, *Guardian*, 12/10/88, and Martin Hoyle, *Financial Times*, 20/10/88). In fact, Prospero's appearance changed throughout the production, as 'brooding at his reflection' in the mirror, he tried 'to cover his insecurity of purpose by slapping on an increasingly bizarre mask of make-up' (Paul Taylor, *Independent*, 26/11/88). He eventually 'decline[d] into a malignant Dickensian undertaker with pale face, bleeding eyes and the bottoms of his trousers rolled' (Michael Ratcliffe, *Observer*, 13/11/88), although Hoyle thought the latter effect made him appear 'a distant cousin to a Beckett tramp'.

Whereas Donnellan's metatheatrical conception seemed muddled, Yukio Ninagawa's Japanese production was clearly Noh-inspired. When Michael Billington saw it in Edinburgh in 1988, he thought that Haruhiko Joh's Prospero 'emerge[d] as a noble-souled master of ceremonies' rather than the man of 'tortured complexity we have come to expect' (*Guardian*, 19/8/88). Paul Taylor, reviewing the production's 1992 Barbican performances, agreed that in 1988 the 'ravishing ritual . . . [had] upstaged the drama', adding that, 'Now, the tormented complexity of the hero [was] better registered', with Prospero 'Radiating a sense of heart-stricken isolation' (*Independent*, 5/12/92). Prospero, however, was still conceived of as 'a mixture of impresario, director and lead-performer, who, when not dominating the . . . stage, [was] scrupulously following the action or kick-starting each scene with a hand-clap' (Billington, *Guardian*, 5/12/92). Benedict Nightingale thought he 'exude[d] gravity and melancholy power' (*The Times*, 5/12/92), while others found him an 'awe-inspiring' figure, 'a black-garbed, moustachioed autocrat and fixer, with pigtail and hooded eyes' (respectively, Jack Tinker, *Daily Mail*, 4/12/92, and Nicholas de Jongh, *Evening Standard*, 4/12/92).

The metatheatrical approach to Prospero (and indeed to the play as a whole) has other roots besides the one already mentioned. It is, in one respect, a modernization of the nineteenth-century idea that Shakespeare should be identified with his protagonist: the fact that Prospero's literal magic is achieved through theatrical illusion gives the connection a basis in the audience's own experience of the play. The rise of director's theatre during the past century has also led to the development of productions within strong conceptual frameworks, be they metatheatrical, colonialist or something else entirely.

The contemporary Prospero

My concern to identify general trends in the playing of Prospero runs the risk of generating false distinctions between different approaches to the role. In order to demonstrate how one performance can in fact encompass many of the ideas I have discussed, I would like to conclude with a description of the Prospero who, in my experience, most successfully embodied the complex potential of the role: John Wood in Nicholas Hytner's 1988 staging for the RSC.

Wood's Prospero first appeared in a wonderful *coup de théâtre*: as the sails of 1.1. dropped to the floor and were pulled into Prospero's cell, the magician was suddenly revealed behind the central one, leaning on his staff and deep in contemplation. The image presented Prospero – literally – as the power behind the theatrical magic, the lengths of cloth now signifying theatre curtains as well as the ship's sails.[64] His costume, however, was contemporary and informal, an 'open-necked shirt and baggy, unpressed flannels', with 'a long dressing gown' serving as magic cloak (respectively, Francis King, *Sunday Telegraph*, 31/7/88, and Rhoda Koenig, *Punch*, 9/6/89).

Reviewers were violently divided by Wood's performance, which elicited no lukewarm responses: to some he was the production's saving grace, to others its only flaw. Michael Coveney unhesitatingly called him the 'best [he had] seen': 'a demented stage manager on a theatrical island suspended between smouldering rage at his usurpation and unbridled glee at his alternative ethereal power' (*Financial Times*, 28/7/88). Michael Billington found Wood's reading of Prospero as 'a Freudian wreck whose battles are all internal' a 'wholly persuasive' one, 'filled out with myriad detail': 'a man who uses supernatural power to shield himself from human contact', he gave a 'sense of tormented solitude' (*Guardian*, 29/7/88). However, while Jack Tinker praised the way 'Wood's capacity for mercurial mood changes illuminate[d] Prospero's complexities' (*Daily Mail*, 28/7/88), Benedict Nightingale complained that the 'performance lack[ed] coherence, unity and, ultimately, a solid centre . . . [Wood] can switch emotions in the space of a sentence, a phrase, almost a word' and, by doing so, he 'deprive[d] Prospero of dignity, authority, weight' (*Punch*, 12/8/88). While some critics thought that Prospero dominated the stage, others agreed with Nightingale that the character lacked stature.[65]

Most of these complaints derived from dislike of Wood's delivery of the verse: 'indulg[ing] both in extravagant *rubato* and in abrupt alternations

64 My comments are based on notes made at four performances, which include those at Stratford on 3/9/88 and in London on 5/10/89 and 24/10/89.
65 Alex Renton, *Independent* (1/8/88) and D. A. N. Jones, *Sunday Telegraph* (28/5/89) were in the first camp. Christopher Edwards, *Spectator* (3/6/89), Peter Kemp, *Independent* and Martin Hoyle, *Financial Times* (both 26/5/89) were in the second.

between *fortissimo* and *pianissimo*', he 'bark[ed] and whinnie[d] and whisper[ed] the verse until it sometimes sound[ed] unintelligible'.[66] Indeed, Charles Spencer, describing how '[s]ometimes [Wood] accelerate[d] the speed to a frantic gabble [and] at others . . . [ground] to a complete halt in mid-phrase', complained that 'at one point I thought he was cursing cigarettes when in fact he was only referring to . . . Sycorax' (*Daily Telegraph*, 27/5/89). Christopher Edwards found Wood's delivery 'annoyingly patronising – when he comes to a word like "roar", sure enough he roars it out. When wolves howl, they "hoowwl"'; Peter Kemp, choosing the same examples as Edwards, described Prospero's speeches as 'not so much spoken as half sung'. On the other hand, Sheridan Morley thought that 'Not since John Gielgud' had there been 'a Prospero with an entire orchestra in his voice, nor one so willing to use the full range of its music' (*Herald Tribune*, 31/5/89).

Such dichotomized judgements reflect not only individual taste, but also critical preconceptions about Prospero's nature. For the most part, those reviewers dismissive of Wood's performance expected consistency in the characterization, yearning either for an impassive authoritarian mage or for a vigorous duke blazing with rage: they were uncomfortable not so much with Wood's delivery as with his skilful display of Prospero's mercurial personality. Michael Ratcliffe, reviewing the production for the first time upon its London transfer, echoes my own response to Wood's Prospero, finding it 'thrilling':

> I had expected a hysterical eccentric; instead, he is scholar, master, teacher and father, but often harsh and a prey to such brittle rages that even Ariel is shocked . . . [T]he complex tenderness for those in his care, in this age of psychotic, bitter, colonialist Prosperos, amounts to a radical revising of the role which only a classical actor of exceptional gifts, discipline and wit could have accomplished.   (*Observer*, 28/5/89)

In fact, Wood's portrayal was even richer than Ratcliffe suggests: moving easily between Prospero the thoughtless task-master, the gentle guardian, the outraged aristocrat, the socially inept man, the loving father, the blinkered judge of past actions, the lonely child still carried within the adult being, Wood gave a performance that can serve as a summary of the role's possibilities in the late twentieth century.[67] The discussion of other aspects

66 Respectively, King, and Eric Shorter, *Daily Telegraph*, 29/7/88.
67 See, for example, notes to 1.2.16, 25, 38b, 66, 74–7a, 89–92, 179, 252–7; 5.1.109, 130–4a, 288–9, 298–309a.

of the play that follows will, I hope, help explain further how some of these possibilities have been created.

'ARIEL AND ALL HIS QUALITY' (1.2.193):
THEATRICAL REPRESENTATION AND GENDER ISSUES

From the eighteenth century until well into the twentieth, the part of Ariel was a coveted female role; during the past sixty years, however, it became firmly established in England as a part to be played by men, a situation that has only recently and hesitantly begun to be challenged. Some reasons for these shifts in casting can be found in the interplay between the cultural significance of gender and changing attitudes towards the power relationships in the play.

Shakespeare, of course, originally wrote this part, as he did all others, for a male actor. During the play, Ariel uses the male possessive pronoun to refer to himself: he offers 'Ariel and all his quality' as a means 'To answer [Prospero's] best pleasure' (1.2.193 and 190). Ariel's sex would seem by that statement to be firmly established. But Ariel is a spirit, as he later reminds Prospero, without human feeling (5.1.20) – and the variety of disguises the spirit assumes throughout the play suggests a protean being without a fixed human shape. Furthermore, the shapes he subsequently assumes are female: at the end of his first appearance, Prospero commands him to make himself 'like a nymph o' th' sea' (1.2.301); since he is to remain invisible to all but Prospero and the audience, the disguise is not essential to the plot and so must serve some other purpose. Later, Ariel becomes a harpy to punish the 'three men of sin' (3.3.53) and takes the part of the goddess Ceres in the vision Prospero presents to Miranda and Ferdinand (4.1.167).[68] For all we know, Ariel assumed yet other shapes throughout the play that went unremarked in the Folio text.

Keith Sturgess has convincingly argued that the part of Ariel was originally played by a boy-actor,[69] who was used to represent women on the English Renaissance stage. The use of a boy-actor, together with Ariel's myriad guises, suggests that Shakespeare wanted to unfix the spirit's sex: self-defined as male at his first appearance, where he both defies and submits to Prospero's will; siren at the next, luring Ferdinand to the yellow sands with seductive song; then fearsome female monster, snatching away

---

68 When Ariel comments that he 'presented Ceres', the most likely meaning is that he played the part in Prospero's masque; as Orgel notes, 'sheer theatrical economy would argue in favour of Shakespeare using his singer Ariel in the masque of Prospero's spirits' (p. 182, n. 167).

69 *Jacobean Private Theatre* (London: Routledge & Kegan Paul, 1987), p. 77.

the banquet; and subsequently goddess of corn and fertility, blessing the union of Miranda and Ferdinand in Prospero's masque. Shakespeare's treatment of Ariel seems designed to remove the spirit from the human world, to make the character a sexless shape-shifter, an 'it' rather than a 'she' or 'he'.

In contrast, the Restoration versions of the play simplify Ariel's sex, making him firmly male. Among other more drastic changes to Shakespeare's play, the 1667 version by Dryden and Davenant drops Prospero's demand that Ariel appear like a sea-nymph, Ariel's appearance as a harpy and the masque in which Ariel appears as Ceres. Furthermore, at the end of the play, Ariel announces 'I have a gentle Spirit for my Love, / Who twice seven years hath waited for my Freedom, / It shall appear and foot it featly with me', whereupon his consort Milcha appears and the two dance a saraband. Despite Ariel's neutral 'it' in referring to Milcha, the latter was played by a woman. Such sexual symmetry was one of the adaptation's concerns, as is obvious from the addition not only of Milcha, but of Sycorax, Dorinda and Hippolito (see above).[70]

Besides the concern with sex in the main plot, the subplot of the

---

70 My argument is based on the premise that the Restoration Ariel was played by a male actor, even though some scholars assume that Moll Davis played the part: for instance, Elizabeth Howe, in *The First English Actresses: Women and Drama 1660–1700* (Cambridge: Cambridge University Press, 1992), p. 74, presumes that, when Pepys comments 'it is but ill done, by [Mrs] Gosnell in lieu of Mall [*sic*] Davis', the 'it' refers to the role of Ariel. However, I believe the part was more probably played by a man: the character still refers to himself as male when he first greets Prospero and, although the role could have been cross-cast, the Prologue takes great care to announce what appears to be the play's only breeches part, that of Hippolito: 'by our dearth of Youths [we] are forc'd t'employ / One of our Women to present a Boy'. Furthermore, although one might argue that because Ariel is a spirit the issue of sex and therefore of cross-casting does not arise, the adaptation itself sexualizes Ariel by providing him with his consort Milcha. Despite Ariel's use of 'it' to refer to his fellow spirit, the name 'Milcha', by analogy with 'Miranda' and 'Dorinda' and other female names, is probably feminine. While evidence points to Moll Davies and Jane Long both being in the original production, the parts they played are uncertain: Novak and Guffey, *Works*, p. 320, as well as Howe, *The First English Actresses*, pp. 184 and 187, assume that Long played Hippolito and Davis Ariel, while Summers, *Shakespeare Adaptations*, p. xlix, assumes that Davis played Hippolito. However, there is no compelling evidence to place them in any particular part, let alone that of Ariel. Both Orgel, p. 70, and Powell, *Restoration Theatre Production*, p. 71, assume, as I do, that Ariel is male and Milcha female, the former arguing the case that 'Davenant's Ariel is far more male than Shakespeare's' and that 'Dryden's Prologue goes to some pains to point out that in the new theatre . . . men are men and women are women', apart from Hippolito (and perhaps Sycorax, who was cross-dressed in eighteenth-century productions).

Dryden–Davenant adaptation makes it a very political play as well. As already noted (see pp. 7–8), the petty squabbling of the shipwrecked mariners, as they vie for mastery of the island, satirizes the Commonwealth of 1642–60. The satire has a conservative political agenda: a desire to reassert the authority of Charles II, the newly restored king, and to denigrate democratic aspirations. This political purpose finally brings gender into my analysis: given that 'gender is a primary way of signifying relationships of power' and a 'primary field within which or by means of which power is articulated' and constructed,[71] then it is important – even imperative – that Prospero's faithful and willing servant be male. Princely authority is neither demonstrated nor affirmed by female subservience, which simply reflects women's expected obedience to men. Instead, princely authority must be validated by male obedience, by a responsible counterpart to the anarchic mariners.

It can be argued that Shadwell's 1674 opera, itself adapted from Dryden and Davenant's *Tempest*, is even more politically recuperative than its prototype. As already described (see p. 10), Milcha is introduced into the action much earlier, in the play's second scene; the surprise revelation at the end of Shadwell's opera is the appearance of '*a number of Aerial Spirits in the Air*', followed by Ariel's voluntary continuance of service. He promises Prospero that in return 'for the freedom I enjoy in Air, / I will be still your Ariel, and wait / On Aiery accidents that work for Fate. / What ever shall your happiness concern, / From your still faithful Ariel you shall learn.' It is hard to imagine a more telling reinscription of royal authority over the nominally enfranchised.

Although the Dryden–Davenant–Shadwell adaptation long remained a popular play in the repertory, once the topicality of the Restoration had passed, the play lost its overtly political implications. As a result, it was no longer crucial for Ariel to be male and, indeed, as Stephen Orgel notes, 'By the early eighteenth century . . . Ariel . . . had become exclusively a woman's role, usually taken by a singer who was also a dancer . . . In this form, Prospero's servant was the central figure in an increasingly elaborate series of operatic and balletic spectacles' (p. 70). However, the disappearance of a political agenda requiring a male Ariel does not itself explain why the part should have become a female one. While Orgel's mention of the importance of operatic and balletic display might provide a rationale for female assumption of the role, this reasoning begs the question of whether such spectacle followed, rather than necessitated, the introduction of a

71 Joan Wallach Scott, *Gender and the Politics of History* (New York: Columbia University Press, 1988), pp. 42 and 45.

female Ariel. Ariel's change of sex might in fact be a direct legacy of the adaptation's *sexual* politics.

As I have earlier argued (see pp. 12–13), the Restoration version stamped Prospero, in his fatherly dealings with Miranda, Dorinda and Hippolito, as a figure of patriarchal authority, a reading which reaches all the way into twentieth-century stagings and critical interpretations of *The Tempest*. Such a paternalist interpretation of Prospero necessitates a demure Miranda, a beast-like Caliban and an Ariel whose willing servility is seen as natural and inevitable: in other words, a gossamer female fairy. And that is precisely what productions provided for more than a hundred years. Consider not only the gauzy costume with delicate wings worn by Leah Hanman in Benson's 1908 production, her submissive posture and tanta-lizingly revealed thighs (illustration 3), but also the kinds of qualities admired in reviews: Leigh Hunt praised Kemble's 1806 Ariel for 'the air of modesty which this young Lady preserved in a dress necessarily light and thin', while John Forster found Priscilla Horton, Macready's Ariel in 1838, 'perfectly charming' with 'submissive animal spirits'.[72] Charles Kean went one step further and cast the thirteen-year-old Kate Terry as his Ariel in 1857: reflecting women's actual legal status, his casting literally charac-terized female submission as child-like.

Although in Britain Ariel continued to be played by women well into the twentieth century (e.g., in Ben Iden Payne's 1941 and 1942 Stratford revivals), men were reinstated in the part much earlier. The first director to use a male Ariel – albeit partially – was William Poel, in his production for the amateur Elizabethan Stage Society, which received three perfor-mances in November 1897. Poel's programme lists three manifestations of Ariel: 'The Boy', played by Mr H. Herbert; 'The sea-nymph', played by Miss Deane; and 'The Harpy', again played by Mr H. Herbert. Bernard Shaw's review gives us a verbal picture of Ariel as 'armless and winged in his first incarnation', the wings acting as a strait-jacket that prevented the spirit from coming across as a 'tricksy sprite'.[73] A photograph in London's Theatre Museum shows Deane's sea-nymph, in a shimmery dress with a ragged hemline below the knee, elbow-length sleeves, and a mop of curly hair, playing a pipe with one hand and beating a tabor with the other: her mischievous appearance anticipates Shirley Temple's a few decades later. Little information survives about the production and nothing of Poel's intentions, but his treatment of Ariel seems to have been an attempt to

72 Respectively, *Critical Essays*, p. 32, and *Examiner*, 21/10/1838, reprinted in
   Dramatic Essays, Volume II, p. 71.
73 *Saturday Review*, 13/11/1897, reprinted in *Our Theatre in the Nineties*, Volume III,
   p. 244.

2 Leah Hanman, playing Ariel for Frank Benson in 1908, typifies the submissive female fairy, with gauzy wings and revealing costume.

reinforce Ariel's chameleon-like being; however, unlike Shakespeare's treatment, where the single boy-actor playing the part would have embodied a sexual ambiguity, even a sexual amorphousness, Poel's casting simply reflects gender stereotyping, with the appealing nymph played by a woman and the threatening monster by a man. His use of a male actor to play Ariel in some parts of the play proved anomalous: it did not lead to any re-thinking of the role in immediately subsequent productions.

The first production to cast an entirely male Ariel was John Drink-water's for the Birmingham Repertory Theatre, which opened on 17 April 1915. Given Poel's 1897 staging, E. Stuart Vinden was not, as one writer claims, 'the first man to [appear as Ariel] since the seventeenth century',[74] but he does appear to have been the first since the eighteenth century to play the whole part. Little is known about either his performance or his appearance: Cochrane notes only that he was 'grey' (p. 58), but the colour describes his costume, as the *Birmingham Post* reviewer found him 'much like the traditional Puck, except that his face [was] quite wrongly the colour of human flesh instead of the greenish-blue of English fairy lore' (19/4/15).[75] The comparison to Puck suggests a spirit enjoying his supernatural tricks and therefore a willing servant to Prospero; however, the same reviewer's complaint that 'In the beginning . . . Ariel flitted about in a most unfairylike manner' also suggests a move away from the traditional (female) approach.

Despite Drinkwater's reintroduction of a male Ariel, it was another ten years before London saw a man play the part, when Godfrey Kenton appeared as the spirit in the production by the Lena Ashwell Players, which opened on 2 November 1925. It is unclear who had ultimate control of the staging: the programme indicates that the play was produced by Beatrice Wilson, but Ashwell recounts that she herself cast Ariel 'as a man with hair

---

74 Clare Cochrane, *Shakespeare and the Birmingham Repertory Theatre*, p. 55.

75 Besides commenting that the part of Ariel was '*happily* played by a man' (my italics), the same reviewer adds that the production's 'new and interesting interpretations' of Ariel and Caliban 'owe[d] much to the adventures of the Barker–Wilkinson–Clarkson coterie in "The Midsummer Night's Dream" ', referring to those responsible for direction, design and wigs in Granville Barker's groundbreaking Savoy production of 1914. For more information on this production, see my *Harley Granville Barker: A Preface to Modern Shakespeare* (Washington: Folger Shakespeare Library; London and Toronto: Associated University Presses, 1986), pp. 58–77. J. C. Trewin, describing Barry Jackson's costumes for the *Tempest* production in *The Birmingham Repertory Theatre 1913–1963* (London: Barrie and Rockliffe, 1963), p. 34, further notes that 'The island and its people were in every shade of blue, from eggshell to deepest indigo, here and there laced with silver. The strangers wore various reds and browns, and the linking character, Ferdinand, a quiet purple.'

and robes of silver'.[76] Unfortunately, the production seems not to have been reviewed, the only available information about it coming from the programme and a skimpily annotated promptbook.[77] Luckily, the former explains that the play was interpreted 'in accordance with the ideas expressed in Mr Colin Still's book "Shakespeare's Mystery Play"', which argues that the play is a conscious or unconscious allegory dramatizing the conflict between good and evil in human consciousness.[78] In this scheme, Prospero symbolizes God, while Ariel, as his 'chief messenger and minister', stands for conscience (Still, *Shakespeare's Mystery Play*, pp. 208 and 211). As the equivalent of the Old Testament Angel of the Lord, New Testament Spirit and pagan Hermes (p. 208), he is also indubitably male.

While it is impossible to prove whether the Ashwell Players' production influenced subsequent stagings, the correspondence between this silver Ariel and later metallic Ariels played by men suggests a possible link. Also, although it cannot be known whether Godfrey Kenton's performance brought out the Hermes aspect of Still's interpretation of the character, Ashwell's later regret that she had not dressed Ariel 'in orange as a Mercury or Hermes figure' suggests that he might have done (*Reflections from Shakespeare*, p. 227). If so, then it is arguable that the Ashwell production influenced the eventual transformation of Ariel from a delicate female sprite to an unearthly male Mercury-figure, which began in earnest with Leslie French's assumption of the role at the Old Vic in 1930.

This production by Harcourt Williams had an Eastern setting, in which French's Ariel 'was represented as a bronze-skinned, naked youth with golden wings to his head – a sort of Oriental Mercury' (*Morning Post*, 7/10/30). The same reviewer notes the change in Ariel's representation with some misgiving, complaining that it was 'hardly the "delicate Ariel" of Shakespeare's own hinting'. Ivor Brown was more welcoming of this departure from what he called the 'glucose' Ariel: 'instead of the usual insipid songstress wire-dangled', he wrote, 'we have . . . a dancing Ariel of tip-toe poise, athletic, sexless, the very soul of masque' (7/10/30). French was a highly skilled singer and actor who was also trained in ballet; Williams later wrote that, as Ariel, French 'moved . . . differently from the mortals', his 'small, well-shaped, naked body seem[ing] to tread on air'. In addition, 'none of the characters, including Prospero, ever looked at him or touched him, though in his harpy guise he was of course visible to the three

76 *Reflections from Shakespeare*, p. 227.
77 The programme is in the Theatre Museum, London, and the promptbook in the Birmingham Shakespeare Library.
78 See pp. 16–17 above for discussion of the production's treatment of Prospero.

lords'.[79] French became renowned for his depiction of Ariel, playing the part again in the Old Vic revival of 1933 and at the Open Air Theatre in Regent's Park in 1933, 1934, 1936 and 1937.

While French's interpretation undoubtedly influenced many that followed, it would be wrong to attribute the changes in Ariel's depiction simply to an individual performer. For one thing, such a focus isolates the performance from the production as a whole. It should also be remembered that John Gielgud played Prospero in Williams's 1930 production as clean-shaven, youthful, disillusioned and anguished, itself a huge change from the grizzled and wise old patriarch that had become theatrical tradition. What made such a human Prospero possible? The interplay of cultural and political attitudes that eventually reshape theatrical tradition is too complex to allow simple statements of cause-and-effect, but it is worth focusing on two interrelated issues that have profoundly influenced the interpretation and theatrical representation not only of Ariel, but also of Prospero and Caliban: colonialism and evolution.

As other writers have already shown, interest in Darwinism in the late nineteenth century affected theatrical representations of Caliban.[80] He began to be regarded as a missing link, as not simply a beast but a man *manqué*. Beerbohm Tree exemplified this portrayal in his 1904 production, where his Caliban looked like a monster but exhibited human yearnings. The point was especially emphasized in his pro-colonial ending, when the abandoned Caliban stretched out his arms towards the departing ship; Tree later wrote that he intended the tableau to show the possible birth of a civilized – that is, a fully human – Caliban.[81]

In their recent study of *Shakespeare's Caliban*, Alden and Virginia Vaughan write that 'Darwinian conceptions of Caliban continued to dominate the stage until the 1950s', after which his oppressed humanness came to the fore (p. 189). Whether colonialist readings of the play pushed Caliban's portrayal towards the more fully human or whether Caliban's increasing humanity encouraged colonialist interpretations is a moot point; probably the traffic was two-way. What *is* important to this analysis is that just when Caliban became recognizably human on stage, Ariel became firmly established as a male role. Between Lena Ashwell's 1925 production and Peter Brook's 1957 Stratford production, women and men had alternated in the part. In fact, Michael Benthall, who staged the play at

---

79 *Four Years at the Old Vic* (London: Putnam, 1935), pp. 255 and 15.
80 See Trevor R. Griffiths, ' "This Island's Mine": Caliban and Colonialism', *The Yearbook of English Studies* 13 (1983), pp. 159–80, and Alden T. and Virginia Mason Vaughan, *Shakespeare's Caliban*, pp. 109–14, 184–9.
81 See *Thoughts and Afterthoughts* (1913; rpt. London: Cassell, 1915), p. 221.

3

3 and 4 Although nominally his 1951 production, Michael Benthall's change of cast for the 1952 revival significantly affected the play's interpretation: Michael Redgrave's struggling and patriarchal Prospero was replaced by Ralph Richardson's more human figure. Although Alan Badel and Margaret Leighton both played Ariel as a tormented spirit anxious to be free, the change in sex produced very different critical reactions to the interpretation.

4

Stratford in 1951 with Alan Badel as Ariel, revived his production the next year with Margaret Leighton in the role; it appears the actor's sex had little to do with the director's conception of the part. However, an examination of reviews suggests that gender was an important factor in reception of the two performances. Reviews for the 1951 production make clear that Badel stressed Ariel's torment in being denied freedom; those for the revival indicate that Leighton's approach was essentially the same. Interestingly, however, the few reviews that bother to comment on the change of actor for the 1952 revival remark on the strangeness of seeing a woman in the part: this despite more than 200 years of stage history which had only recently – and occasionally – been broken.[82]

The key to this odd response probably lies in the new emphasis on the unfairness of Ariel's bondage. As Caliban became a representative of oppressed humanity, Prospero became less God-like and the parallels between Caliban and Ariel became clearer. Or, to put it another way, as Prospero became less God-like, it was possible to see the oppression of Caliban and Ariel as undeserved. Or, to put it in yet another, once Ariel became male (for whatever reason) within a modern cultural context, it was difficult to be entirely comfortable with Prospero's treatment of him and so his links with Caliban were foregrounded. This nexus of ideas is too tightly interwoven to be easily disentangled, but the symbiotic relationship between its strands is evident: to suggest that the oppression of both Caliban and Ariel is in some way unjust, the one had to become human and the other *male*. Just as a bestial Caliban was seen to deserve Prospero's punishment and restraint, the service of a female Ariel was too culturally normative to be disturbing. To the reviewers who found Leighton's Ariel strange, an unwillingly enslaved female spirit must have appeared a contradiction in terms.

As a result, for more than forty years after Leighton's performance, women Ariels disappeared entirely from the main London and Stratford stages, although they could still occasionally be found in regional productions. For example, Annette Crosbie played the part in 1960 at the Bristol Theatre Royal, and Yolande Bavan in 1968 at the Oxford Playhouse;

82 One reviewer worried that 'in appearance [Leighton's] Ariel is expressive more of a demon than a kindly, helpful, boyish spirit' (Wilfrid Clark, *Warwick Solihull & Warwick County News*, 29/3/52), his comments betraying common expectations of the part when played by a woman: a female Ariel should not only be, but also look, kind, helpful, submissive, unthreatening. When such gender expectations are thwarted, reaction can be damning: Leighton was 'too often . . . shrewish in manner and diction. Her attitude towards Prospero appeared to be malicious rather than whimsical. The result was that Ariel dominated the stage rather than Prospero' (*Coventry Standard*, 4/4/52). Other critics, however, responded positively to the disjunction between the actor's sex and the characterization's gender (see *Evening News*, 26/3/52; *Punch*, 9/4/52; J. C. Trewin, *Lady*). Most were in fact enthusiastic about Leighton's execution of the part, particularly praising its otherworldliness, quicksilver nature and vocal quality, and many stressed her achievement in suggesting materialized thought (see *Stage*; Ruth Ellis, *Stratford Herald*; Trewin, *Illustrated London News*); like Gielgud's Prospero, Richardson's 'was most at ease in his encounters with Ariel' (*Scotsman*, 7/4/52).

however, it is unlikely that such productions reflected a challenging view of Prospero's authority over Ariel. For instance, photographs of Lesley Nunnerley in Willard Stoker's 1967 production for the Northampton Repertory Theatre suggest a conventional approach to the depiction of the female servant/male master relationship: Nunnerley's blonde Ariel wore an off-one-shoulder sequinned garment, gauzes on her arms, and black tights, her appearance both sexualized and submissive.

Despite this overwhelming trend of casting men in the part, the rise of feminist ideas throughout the 1970s and 1980s was likely not only to reinstate some female Ariels on the British stage but also to challenge their traditional representation. The first to do so was Christine Bishop in John Retallack's 1981 production for the Actors Touring Company, revived in 1983: she was 'elegant and graceful as a severe Ariel', 'able to freeze the action by simply beating the tabor strapped to her thigh'.[83] Wearing a 'lovely white and gold' Elizabethan suit, which comprised a 'slashed satin jacket . . . and close-fitting breeches', and with 'gold tipping her ears', she characterized Ariel with 'precise balletic movements . . . frozen stance, and . . . intense manner of speech';[84] she did not, however, 'try to sing Ariel's songs' (B. A. Young, *Financial Times*). Barber, despite having experienced the Ariels of Leslie French, Margaret Leighton, Marius Goring and Wayne Sleep, thought Bishop 'the Ariel of [his] life' and devoted a feature article to her performance; his consistent use of the masculine pronoun in referring to her Ariel attests to the androgynous effect she created:

> His movements were quick and startled, like a wild thing . . . [H]e watched his victims with a gleaming, feasting intensity, frozen still like a fawn but eyes darting, one foot elegantly pointed behind the other . . . [There was] cruelty in the icy sibilants of his voice . . . Under his purity and lightness, the creature shared a dangerous quality with Caliban.

Barber continues that Bishop's Ariel 'was muscular, elegant, wild and dangerous', and 'sexually disturbing, too, being androgynous, alluring while yet neither masculine nor feminine'.

The 1980s and 1990s saw other women Ariels in fringe, regional and touring productions, as well as in major foreign productions, although not on Britain's main national stages. Besides the Kick Theatre and Compass

---

83 Respectively, Milton Shulman, *Evening Standard*, and Michael Billington, *Guardian*. All undated reviews quoted in this paragraph are from *London Theatre Record* 12–25/2/83.

84 Quotations are drawn from John Barber's review in the *Daily Telegraph* (*London Theatre Record* 12–25/2/83) and from his feature article on Bishop (20/6[*sic*]/83; London Theatre Museum clipping).

Ariels, Lesley Argent played the part in her own production for Trouble and Strife in February 1985, while Serena Gordon appeared in Matthew Francis's Chichester Studio Company production, which had five performances in the Tent in September 1986, followed by two in the main house in October. Serena Harrigan played Ariel in Alec Bell's production at the New Victoria Theatre, North Staffordshire, which was set in a 'never-never land' whose mix of costumes ranged from 'Flemish merchants' doublets to Navy-issue life-jackets' (Martin Bell, *Stage*, 19/11/87). Earlier that year, Hilary Ellis intriguingly included the part of Ariel in her Miranda for the six-actor version given by the Northumberland Theatre Company: Miranda was here the 'host body for Ariel's wild spirit', possessed by her when necessary (Elfrieda Ranson, *Stage*, 15/1/87); Ranson adds that this ethereal Ariel made 'seemingly nonchalant, athletic use of the [set's] scaffolding'.

Michael Bogdanov's 1992 touring production for the English Shakespeare Company featured Olwen Fouéré as an androgynous Ariel with short blond hair; she was barefoot and dressed in a suit with rolled-up trousers. She kept very still, making only an occasional hand gesture, and was invisible even to Prospero, who never looked at her.[85] The *Director's Notes* explain that her costume was 'a variation on a lounge-suit, masculine in cut, feminine in colour and fabric and faintly luminous to underline the effect of other worldliness'.[86] Critics viewed her variously as 'an Annie Lennox look-alike with nightclub attitude', an 'androgynous replicant . . . half Rutger Hauer, half Sean Young' and 'a solid, unsmiling lady in a mauve trouser-suit', who looked 'as though she [had] been to one acid-rave party too many, her face blank of any emotion'.[87] However, although Fouéré succeeded in coming across as a 'marvellously agile hermaphrodite',[88] her relationship with Prospero was unproblematic, Bogdanov conceiving of her as the embodiment of Prospero's thought (Neill, *Director's Notes*, pp. 16 and 18).

---

85 My comments are based on notes taken during the matinée performance of 28/11/92.

86 *The Tempest: Director's Notes for Teachers and Students*, compiled by Heather Neill, English Shakespeare Company/*Times Educational Supplement*, 1992, p. 25.

87 Respectively, Michael Arditti, *Evening Standard*, 1/12/92 (see also Ian Shuttleworth, *City Limits*, 3/12/92); Suzi Feay, *Time Out*, 2/12/92; Benedict Nightingale, *The Times*, 30/11/92; and Robert Gore-Langton, *Daily Telegraph*, 3/12/92.

88 Malcolm Rutherford, *Financial Times*, 5/12/92.

On an even more conventional note, Rakie Ayola's Ariel in Bill Alexander's 1994 Birmingham Rep production was a willing and dedicated servant to a Prospero whose authority went unquestioned. Upon entering, she appeared dignified, as well as unaware of Prospero, who chuckled as she unconcernedly hummed a few bars of 'Where the bee sucks'; however, her trembling body and hesitant speech soon made her appear scatter-brained or even feeble-minded.[89] Michael Coveney described her as 'lithe [and] impatient', whereas Michael Billington thought her 'sinuous in watered silk' but certainly not 'yearning for freedom' in the way Simon Russell Beale's Ariel was in Sam Mendes's concurrent RSC production.[90]

When, the following year, the RSC finally cast a woman as Ariel after a forty-three year gap, it was in David Thacker's small-scale touring production of the play, which was also seen at London's Young Vic and Stratford's Swan. Reviewers remarked on the unproblematic nature of the master–servant relationship as played by Paul Jesson and Bonnie Engstrom: Paul Taylor commented that there was 'no tension in [the spirits'] relations with their magician-master', adding that Engstrom's 'primitive, tatterdemalion Ariel [had] none of the suppressed contempt and icy hauteur' that Beale had shown in Mendes's production. Nicholas de Jongh described her as 'airily self-possessed', giving 'no strong sense of hard relations between the ruler and the ruled', while Michael Billington noted that 'Prospero's wishes are carried out by obliging spirits' and that 'the Prospero–Ariel, master–servant tension, highlighted in the . . . Mendes production, [was] conspicuous by its absence.'[91]

As such quotations indicate, Mendes's subversive Ariel epitomized the wrongfully imprisoned male spirit. Beale made him 'an imperious figure', bringing people on 'with an impassive, watchful look of command' (John Peter, *Sunday Times*, 15/8/93). Such disdain was directed at Prospero as well as at the other mortals. Whereas Billington thought Ariel hid 'his rage behind a mask of passivity', other critics found he 'barely conceal[ed] his burning hatred of Prospero', treating him 'with the barely concealed insolence of a head-waiter at a snooty restaurant' (res-

89 My comments are based on notes taken during the matinée performance of 1/10/94.

90 Respectively, *Observer*, 18/9/94, and *Guardian*, 15/9/94. For more information on Beale's Ariel, see below.

91 Respectively, *Independent*, 3/7/95; *Evening Standard*, 3/7/95; and *Guardian*, 1/7/95; the mention of plural spirits alludes to the fact that Ariel was always accompanied by three others.

pectively, *Guardian*, 13/8/93; Rod Dungate, *Tribune*, 20/8/93; Charles Spencer, *Daily Telegraph*, 15/7/94). Ariel's feelings about Prospero were clear 'from the tiny, insubordinate time-lags . . . [he] allow[ed] before he attend[ed] to commands and from the way the Kohl-rimmed eyes slither[ed] with a hint of subversion in that sphinx-like face' (Paul Taylor, *Independent*, 15/7/94). This interpretation seriously altered the balance of the play: as Sheridan Morley put it, 'Not often do you get *The Tempest* starring Ariel rather than Prospero' (*Spectator*, 23/7/94). Beale was 'no limp fairy, darting about to do Prospero's bidding, but a serious rival for authority' (Morley); indeed, to one reviewer, the latter came across 'as a low-status partner to his excessively dignified menial' (Irving Wardle, *Independent on Sunday*, 15/8/93). Ariel's portrayal 'alter[ed] the nature of magic itself [in the play], giving it aggressive potency', and 'also change[d] the balance of power': the 'thuggish Ariel', together with a 'terrifying Caliban' and an 'unusually outspoken daughter', meant that Prospero could not afford to be 'complacent' (Kate Kellaway, *Observer*, 15/8/93).

To sum up, then, the theatrical representation of Ariel, in England at least, has consistently used gender either as a way of legitimizing or of questioning the power of Prospero, be it domestic or political. However, apart from a handful of mostly minor productions, even self-consciously ideological interpretations have simply accepted, rather than challenged, conventional gender hierarchies. Jonathan Miller's stagings of 1970 and 1988, for example, in which black actors played Ariel and Caliban, constituted a critique of colonialism and of its legacies to emergent states. In 1988, Miller toyed with the idea of casting a black woman as Ariel but abandoned it, thus missing a real chance to explore parallels between colonization of blacks by whites and of women by men.[92] Although in staging *The Tempest* the English theatre has often used Ariel's gender as an instrument of ideological struggle, it has rarely used Ariel to contest the dominant cultural view of gender itself.

92 Personal communication from Ella Wilder, who was considered for the part. John Retallack's 1991 treatment of a black woman as Ariel finally brought together the politics of gender and of race on the English stage; however, in keeping with the trend so far outlined, his production was for 'a middle-scale touring company' (programme). Diane Parish's 'wild bird of an Ariel', although 'diminutive' and with 'impish expressions and nimble movements', was 'subversive', bringing to the part 'distinct edge, [and] a suggestion of mocking insubordination' (respectively, Colin Donald, *Scotsman*, 19/9/91; Jill Murawicki, *Somerset County Gazette*; Keren Williams and Gary Shipton, *West Sussex Gazette*, 5/9/91; John Linklater, *Glasgow Herald*, 19/9/91; Linklater).

'A MAN OR A FISH?' (2.2.33): CALIBAN AS
MONSTER OR MINORITY

In the Folio's 'Names of the Actors', Caliban is described as 'a salvage and deformed slave'. As Alden and Virginia Vaughan indicate, 'salvage' describes his cultural inferiority and 'slave' his social status, while 'deformed' suggests some kind of grotesqueness.[93] While Shakespeare's text never makes clear the nature of this deformity, Prospero clearly describes the character as human:

> Then was this island –
> Save for the son that [Sycorax] did litter here,
> A freckled whelp hag-born – not honour'd with
> A human shape.   (1.2.281b–4a)

However, careless reading of the parenthetical description of Caliban's origins, together with Prospero's assertions that Caliban's father was the devil,[94] have often led to the assumption that, rather than being the one human on the island prior to Prospero and Miranda's arrival, Caliban himself does not have a human shape. The misreading can be further compounded by Trinculo's confusion over whether the gaberdine-covered Caliban is 'a man or a fish' (2.2.23) and by Stephano and Trinculo's repeated references to him as a 'monster'. However, Trinculo's doubt, clearly arising from Caliban's smell (see 2.2.23–5), is cleared up when he discovers Caliban's hitherto hidden arms and legs. Similarly, Stephano dubs Caliban a 'monster . . . with four legs' (2.2.57) when the latter is embroiled with Trinculo in the gaberdine; the nickname may then simply stick. As the Vaughans indicate, the term was also generally used in Shakespeare's time to imply physical deformity or 'abnormality, usually . . . manifested in outsized proportions' (*Shakespeare's Caliban*, p. 14 and p. 14, n. 25); Sturgess's suggestion that in the King's Men company the part might have been played by John Lowin, a large-framed actor who 'customarily played the second leads', supports such an understanding of Caliban's grotesqueness (*Jacobean Private Theatre*, p. 77).

Although the text itself seems clear about Caliban's humanness, the possible misapprehensions I have just outlined have led to a wealth of theatrical interpretations of the character: as David Suchet discovered to his 'horror' when researching the role for Clifford Williams's 1978 RSC production, Caliban has been played as '(1) a fish, (2) a dog with one or two heads, (3) a lizard, (4) a monkey, (5) a snake, (6) half-ape, half-man, with

93 See *Shakespeare's Caliban*, pp. 7–15.
94 See 1.2.319–20 and 5.1.271b–2a; Prospero's description may allude to Caliban's character rather than to the literal circumstances of his birth.

fins for arms, (7) a tortoise'.[95] Since the cultural forces informing these varied approaches have been admirably explored in two recent studies already cited, Trevor Griffiths's ' "This Island's Mine": Caliban and Colonialism' and Alden and Virginia Vaughan's *Shakespeare's Caliban: A Cultural History*, my analysis is heavily indebted to these works, although the fuller theatrical history I have been able to uncover allows expansion and refinement of some of their ideas.

As I have already indicated (see p. 12), the Caliban of the Davenant–Dryden–Shadwell adaptations was a comic role. It was also a minor one: 'Caliban's relative insignificance to eighteenth-century productions is understandable. Though audiences enjoyed the seamen's music and antics, Caliban did not fit well with the age's notion of comedy . . . [His] grotesque deformities were not the proper vehicle for good-natured wit; his natural folly was inappropriate to an art form that dealt with manners and artificial follies' (Vaughan, *Shakespeare's Caliban*, p. 178). Even when Kemble restored Shakespeare's lines to Caliban, allowing him 'more room for interpretation', his retention of 'Hippolito, the "natural man" . . . [meant that Caliban] could not signify humanity in a state of nature' (Vaughan, *Shakespeare's Caliban*, pp. 178–9). However, Caliban's potential, even without the distraction provided by Hippolito, was far from evident: Francis Gentleman, writing in Bell's edition of Garrick's 1757 restoration of Shakespeare's text, had directed only that Caliban should speak with a 'rough, malignant costiveness of expression' (p. 17).

John Emery, who played the part in Kemble's 1806 production, was one of the most notable Calibans of the early nineteenth century. William Robson (admittedly pro-Kemble and anti-Macready) considered his Caliban, 'by far, the best that has been seen since that of Charles Bannister'.[96] Leigh Hunt called his performance

> one of the best pieces of acting we have ever seen. He conceived with infinite vigour that union of the man and the beast, which renders the monster so odious and malignant a being; nothing could be more suitable to the character than the occasional growlings which finished the complaints of the savage, and the grinning eagerness of malignity which accompanied his curses on *Prospero*.[97]

95 David Suchet, 'Caliban in *The Tempest*', in *Players of Shakespeare 1*, ed. Philip Brockbank (Cambridge: Cambridge Unviersity Press, 1985), p. 169.
96 *The Old Play-goer* (1846; rpt. Fontwell, Sussex: Centaur Press, 1969), p. 78. As Bannister lived from 1741 to 1804, the praise is perhaps not quite so ringing as it sounds.
97 *Critical Essays*, p. 33.

William Hazlitt, on the other hand, complained that Emery 'had nothing of Caliban but his gaberdine', missing the 'man-monster in contact with the pure and original forms of nature', the 'grossness . . . [without] the smallest vulgarity in it'.[98] James Boaden similarly complained that Emery's Caliban was not only 'a brute' but 'a Yorkshire one', who showed 'no poetry in his conception of the character. It has always been *roared* down the throats of the vulgar; but Caliban is not a vulgar creation.'[99]

Comments such as Hazlitt's and Boaden's reflect the Romantic view of the character, which could not be fully expressed on stage until Macready restored Shakespeare's text in 1838.[100] Besides the wider scope for interpretation offered by the Folio text, Macready's Caliban was played by George Bennett, 'an actor who excelled in tragic as well as comic roles' and who played the part again for Phelps at Sadler's Wells in 1847 (Vaughan, *Shakespeare's Caliban*, pp. 180–1). In Macready's production, his 'first discovery in the hole where [Caliban] is "styed" was singularly picturesque, not less so was his manner of grabbling out of it to fly on Prospero, whose wand in a moment flung the danger of his fury down, and left him merely *dancing mad* with impotent rage'.[101] Forster judged Bennett 'the best Caliban that has been seen since the days of Emery – albeit at times a little too enunciative and syllabical in his delivery, yet redeeming himself the next minute with a genuine humano-brutality and yearning wonderment'. By the time of Kean's production, critical expectation of Caliban's more complex portrayal is apparent in some appraisals. Cole suggests John Ryder's subtlety in the role: 'His execution of this difficult part (difficult, because so easily overdone), was one of [his] best' (*Life and Theatrical Times*, vol. II, p. 223). The *Athenaeum*, however, complained that the actor did not sustain 'the poetic and romantic feeling . . . to the end', while the less demanding *Theatrical Journal* was content with his 'truly savage' performance (respectively, 4 July 1857, p. 859; 19 August 1857, p. 261). Notes in George Ellis's rehearsal workbook call for 'additional foreheads', giving some idea of Ryder's appearance in the role.

Appreciation of the restored role's potential is evidenced in William

---

98 *Examiner*, 23 July 1815, reprinted in *Dramatic Essays*, Volume II, p. 65.

99 *Memoirs of the Life of John Philip Kemble, Esq.*, pp. 224–5, quoted in Vaughan, *Shakespeare's Caliban*, p. 179.

100 Apart from a few tradition-breaking-and-making productions, 'there has been [until quite recently] . . . a thirty-year hiatus between views of Caliban in print and his representation in the theatre' (Vaughan, *Shakespeare's Caliban*, p. 173).

101 John Forster, *Examiner*, 21 October 1838, reprinted in *Dramatic Essays*, vol. III, pp. 70–1.

Burton's decision to play Caliban in his own production in New York in 1854: uncharacteristically, he

> forsook comedy for once and played a threatening Caliban. He was shaggy, misshapen, half-human in appearance, with long talons on his hands and feet, his utterance 'half snarl, half hiss', his manner a kind of 'dull fiendish malice or besotted merriment.' William Keese, who was a boy when he saw this Caliban, tried to forget it: 'It terrified us and made us dream bad dreams.'[102]

Burton's portrayal broke no mould: as the Vaughans indicate, from Emery onwards, performances of Caliban were 'human in their emotional power, animal in appearance and behavior' (*Shakespeare's Caliban*, p. 184). However, as Griffiths further notes, nineteenth-century portrayals of the character 'gradually came to reflect broadly colonial and republican themes' ('"This Island's Mine"', p. 160): one member of Macready's audience, for example, thought Bennett aroused sympathy for 'the rude and uncultivated savage' deprived of 'the advantages of civilisation' (quoted in Griffiths, '"This Island's Mine"', p. 161). Even more explicitly, the republican Caliban in a popular burlesque (William and Robert Broughs's *The Enchanted Isle*) voiced the anti-slavery slogan 'Ain't I a man and a brother?' (quoted in Griffiths, '"This Island's Mine"', p. 161). The slogan, adapted to 'Am I a man and a brother?', was itself later applied to an ape in an 1861 *Punch* cartoon about evolution, thus illustrating 'the close popular inter-linking of ideas about evolution and slavery' (Griffiths, '"This Island's Mine"', pp. 163, 161). Indeed, the spread of Darwinian ideas in the 1860s made Caliban appear a prototype of the 'missing link' and thus assume 'increasingly ape-like characteristics', so that by the late nineteenth-century it became 'particularly difficult to differentiate between Caliban as native, as proletarian, and as missing-link'.[103]

The centrality of Caliban to the expression of such topical ideas meant that, during the late nineteenth and early twentieth centuries, it became the leading role in many productions. Frank Benson, for example, surprised his audience by playing Caliban during the 1891 Stratford Festival, as it was assumed an actor of his stature would play Prospero; however, Caliban was his 'pet part',[104] and he never relinquished it. Inspired by the Darwinian

---

102 Charles H. Shattuck, *Shakespeare on the American Stage* (Washington: Folger Shakespeare Library, 1976), p. 114.

103 Griffiths, '"This Island's Mine"', pp. 161 and 163 respectively. For a fuller discussion of the interlinking of these ideas, see *ibid.*, pp. 160–6.

104 F. R. Benson, *My Memoirs* (London: Ernest Benn, 1930), p. 297.

debate, Benson treated Caliban as 'a sort of missing-link' and emphasized his 'responsive devotion to music' (*My Memoirs*, p. 298). Constance Benson further explains that her husband 'spent many hours watching monkeys and baboons in the zoo, in order to get [their] movements and postures' right, that he wore a 'curious costume, half-monkey, half coco-nut', for the part, and that he 'always insisted on appearing with a real fish in his mouth'.[105] In fact, according to a cast member of his 1929–32 company, Benson 'hung suspended by his feet from a tall palm tree' so naturally that a north of England stagehand asked 'Eh! What 'appens to monkey at t'end of show?'[106]

Benson's innovatory – and comic – approach sharply divided audiences and reviewers. Those who condemned it did so from opposing viewpoints about Shakespeare's Caliban – and Prospero: one correspondent to the *Stratford Herald* remarked that instead of showing the 'terror and sadness' of human vice Benson merely portrayed an amusing animal, while another complained that Benson's conception prevented the audience from rightly sympathizing with the 'ill-used, down-trodden wretch' who is 'wantonly tortured and tormented for not obeying the despot' Prospero.[107] Benson conceded in his *Memoirs* that he 'may have emphasized too much the athletic side in [Caliban's] various antics – weight-carrying, toe-climbing, headlong descents down a rope from the flies' – but defended his conception as interesting and entertaining (p. 298).

J. H. Leigh, starring as Caliban in Charles Lander's 1903 production at the Court Theatre, London, took a different approach from Benson's: Max Beerbohm found him 'duly "savage"', but felt he should have been more '"deformed"'.[108] Leigh stressed Caliban's 'moral, rather than . . . physical, ugliness', presenting him as 'more of a man and less of a four-footed animal than usual'.[109] An unidentified caricature in the Theatre Museum, London, shows him simply with wild hair, moustache and beard.

105 *Mainly Players* (London: Thornton Butterworth, 1926), pp. 97, 179.

106 Olive de Wilton, quoted in J. C. Trewin, *Benson and the Bensonians* (London: Barrie and Rockliff, 1960), p. 259.

107 Respectively Druid and E. C. T., both 1 May 1891. Although Griffiths, '"This Island's Mine"', p. 170, suggests that 'Benson's "missing-link" Caliban was political in the sense that analogies had been drawn between "underdeveloped natives" and the missing link in non-theatrical contexts', the contemporary opinions quoted here suggest that Benson's portrayal in fact interfered with the creation of political meaning.

108 *Saturday Review*, 7 November 1903, reprinted in *Around Theatres*, p. 297.

109 *Era*, 31 October 1903, quoted by Griffiths, '"This Island's Mine"', p. 168.

Most famously, Herbert Beerbohm Tree played Caliban in his own 1904 production at His Majesty's Theatre, London.[110] Dressed in fur and seaweed, he wore a necklace of shells, pearls, amber, coral and 'other precious jewels of the sea' (printed sd); an illustration in the text printed for the fiftieth performance of the production shows him with pointed ears, fang-like teeth, long nails and hair, and a hairy torso. Percy Fitzgerald recounts that Tree 'was determined to make a really original, sensational character of Caliban – a new and striking "monster", that people should wonder at and shrink from in terror'; he therefore made him 'an animal sort of creature . . . with an added tusk, who grovelled and crawled'.[111] Despite his 'physically repulsive' appearance, however, Fitzgerald judged Tree's Caliban as lacking 'the conviction of brutal force and passion' and insufficiently showing the character's '*suffering* side' (*Shakespearean Representation*, p. 75). Contrary to Fitzgerald's appraisal, Tree himself writes that he sought to show, in Caliban's 'love of music and his affinity with the unseen world . . . the germs of a sense of beauty, the dawn of art'.[112] One reviewer in fact noted that Tree's Caliban was 'strangely susceptible to music' (*Illustrated London News*, 24/9/04), while another found that he managed to keep both the pathos and the comedy of the part. His portrayal also 'expanded the political dimensions of . . . Caliban, who was clearly the ignorant native to whom the colonist Prospero had brought an enlightenment which he had spurned before learning its true value'; indeed, 'after Benson's and Tree's performances Caliban was established as a barometer of attitudes to imperialism and democracy'.[113]

Caliban continued to be associated with gorillas, Darwinian missing links and indigenous peoples until well into the twentieth century.[114] The 'first Caliban to have actually blacked up' appears to have been Roger Livesey, whose 'scaly and hairy Caliban [in Tyrone Guthrie's 1934 Vic/Wells production] . . . was generally regarded as bringing out both [his] pathos and his monstrosity' (Griffiths, ' "This Island's Mine" ', p. 175). Griffiths adds that Livesey's innovatory black grease-paint 'excited virtually no critical

110 Details are drawn from Folger Prompt *Tempest* 15, which contains both printed and hand-written stage directions; unless otherwise indicated, information comes from the hand-written sds. The text was also published in London by J. Miles & Co. on 27 October 1904 to mark the occasion of the production's fiftieth performance.

111 *Shakespearean Representation* (London: Elliot Stock, 1908), p. 45.

112 *Thoughts and Afterthoughts*, p. 221.

113 Griffiths, ' "This Island's Mine" ', pp. 170 and 172. Tree's pro-colonialist reading is most evident in the production's final tableau; see note to Epilogue.

114 See *ibid.*, pp. 172–6, and Vaughan, *Shakespeare's Caliban*, pp. 188–9, as well as note to 1.2.320sd for further examples of such Calibans.

comment, except for complaints that the black came off on Trinculo and Stephano'. However, as he indicates, Livesey's portrayal did help some reviewers to develop a political analysis of the play: for example, Ivor Brown defended the interpretation, arguing that 'Caliban should be the oppressed aboriginal as well as the lecherous monster, a case for the radical politician's sympathy as well as for Prospero's punishment.'[115]

More than a decade later, Canada Lee became the first black actor to play the part, appearing in Margaret Webster's 1945 production at the Alvin Theatre, New York. In his study of black Shakespearean actors, *Shakespeare in Sable*, Errol Hill notes that, 'When the establishment theater slowly began to overcome its opposition to interracial casting in Shakespeare, Caliban was one of the first roles offered to black actors. Indeed, as one critic observed of Margaret Webster's production, "Caliban is a perfect role for a Negro".'[116] Hill adds that Webster appreciated the 'racial significance' of the casting, making it clear that although she did not intend ' "to make Caliban a parable of the current state of the American Negro" ' she could see 'a ready parallel. "Prospero has taught Caliban the words of civilization but kept him a slave. Throughout the play . . . Caliban is groping, seeking after freedom. This is in a large part what *The Tempest* is about. Caliban's – and Ariel's – search for freedom".'[117] Despite Webster's views, Lee's performance does not appear to have made critics think of Caliban 'as [a] colonial victim': he was essentially a monster, wearing a 'grotesque mask' and moving 'with an animal-like crouch' (Vaughan, *Shakespeare's Caliban*, pp. 189–90). Lee's widow indicates that the latter

115 *Observer*, 14/1/34. Griffiths, ' "This Island's Mine" ', p. 176, points out that Brown 'was the most consistent propagator of the colonial Caliban' among the critics, 'moving on from his analysis of Livesey's performance to see [Baliol] Holloway as a "dispossessed aboriginal" at Stratford in 1934, Bernard Miles as minimizing "the appeal to sympathy for an oppressed aboriginal" at the Mermaid in 1951, and Michael Hordern as "a most human and even poignant representative of the Backward and Underprivileged Peoples" at Stratford in 1952'. For fuller details of these performances, see note to 1.2.320sd.

116 *Shakespeare in Sable: A History of Black Shakespearean Actors* (Amherst: University of Massachusetts Press, 1984), p. 108. The double-edged nature of the quotation-within-the-quotation is apparent, although Webster herself seems to have been unaware of the potential danger of casting a black actor in the part; she notes that Lee's performance 'was only the second time that a black actor had played in a classic play on Broadway. But at the last minute we almost lost him. Some of his friends had tried to persuade him that it would be derogatory to his race to play the enslaved and brutish Caliban; but the arguments against this type of racism eventually prevailed' (*Don't Put Your Daughter on the Stage* (New York: Knopf, 1972), p. 121).

117 *Theatre Arts*, February 1945, quoted in Hill, *Shakespeare in Sable*, p. 108.

detail was not a feature of the entire performance: because he ' "first appeared onstage in a humpback position akin to Richard III[,] the audience subsequently thought of him only in that curved position, even when he stood tall" '.[118] However, it is clear that his mask and ' "costume of fish scales and long fingernails" ' kept him firmly in the monstrous tradition, with 'the transformation [of Caliban] to an essentially "black" part . . . still in the future' (Vaughan, *Shakespeare's Caliban*, p. 190).[119]

That transformation was shaped partly by the publication of three studies using the Caliban–Prospero relationship as a paradigm of colonialism: Octave Mannoni's *Prospero and Caliban: The Psychology of Colonization* uses the pair to analyse Madagascan–French relationships; Philip Mason's *Prospero's Magic: Some Thoughts on Class and Race* draws analogies between Caliban, Ariel and different types of nationalists in colonized societies; and George Lamming's *The Pleasures of Exile* explores the way language imprisons the colonized Caliban.[120] These analyses, published during the 1960s, helped to make race an explicit issue in subsequent productions of *The Tempest*, often informing both conception and reception of the play.[121]

118 Frances Lee, quoted by Glenda E. Gill, 'The Mercurial Canada Lee', *White Grease Paint on Black Performers* (New York: Peter Lang, 1988), p. 41, quoted in Vaughan, *Shakespeare's Caliban*, pp. 189–90. The quotation following, giving further details of the costume, is also from Lee.

119 It seems that, despite the rise in black consciousness during the sixties in the US, subsequent black Calibans continued in the monstrous tradition: Earle Hyman played the part in 1960 at the American Shakespeare Festival in Connecticut looking 'scarcely human' and 'wearing inflated belly and legs and a grotesque headpiece' (Vaughan, *Shakespeare's Caliban*, p. 190), while, in 1962 in New York's Central Park, James Earl Jones was 'a savage, green-faced lizard darting his red tongue in and out, lunging clumsily at what he wanted and yelping when he was denied it' (Alice Griffin, 'The New York Season, 1961–62,' *Shakespeare Quarterly* 13 (1962), p. 555, quoted in Hill, *Shakespeare in Sable*, p. 173). This mould was broken in 1970 at the Sylvan Theatre in Washington (see below).

120 Mannoni, *La psychologie de la colonisation*, 1950; trans. 1956; 2nd edn, trans. Pamela Powesland (New York: Praeger, 1964); Mason, *Prospero's Magic* (Oxford: Oxford University Press, 1962); Lamming, *The Pleasures of Exile* (London: Michael Joseph, 1960). The studies are discussed by Vaughan, *Shakespeare's Caliban*, pp. 155, 159–61, 166, and by Griffiths, ' "This Island's Mine" ', p. 177.

121 Although these works influenced subsequent stage productions and critical perceptions of them, it is important to note that colonialist readings of the play in production were possible before they were published; see, for example, the discussion of Michael Benthall's 1951 Stratford production and its 1952 revival in the note to 1.2.320sd.

In the 1963 RSC production directed by Clifford Williams in collaboration with Peter Brook, Roy Dotrice played a blacked-up Caliban who
entered 'snarling, slavering and gnawing upon a large bloody bone';[122] this
'lean, dark-skinned practically naked Caliban, with running sores', later
used the 'enormous bone . . . for an effective phallic gesture'[123] that
offended some critics and caused the resignation of one of the front-of-
house staff (Williams, programme note). Caliban's blackness made Alan
Brien, who had read *Prospero's Magic* and thought it a 'stimulating book
on racialism', see anti-colonialist elements in the production, although his
own description of Dotrice's performance does not make him appear
sympathetic to the character: 'This naked, black insurgent, with a bald
dome and tufts of hair in the most distracting places, sweats an evil energy
and an aboriginal lust which would frighten Genet' (*Sunday Telegraph*,
7/4/63). Indeed, J. W. Lambert thought the portrayal actually fostered
racism: this 'naked, beetling, grossly priapic Caliban has a skin too dark to
make it possible to avoid [the] implication' that 'the coloured races . . . [are]
mere brutes to be driven down' (*Sunday Times*, 7/4/63). Reviewers unconscious of their racism described 'a buffoon in burnt cork' and a 'hideously
negroid' savage who was 'a little too much like a black mamba'.[124] A photograph in the *Stratford Herald* (5/4/63) shows Caliban with a bulbous
brow, making his skull look primitive.

No critics besides Brien and Lambert discussed the racial implications
of Dotrice's performance, but reactions to the character ranged from
deserved 'sympathy' for a 'suffering creature', to 'pity . . . stirred . . . [by]
ignorance destroying itself', to the loss of 'any sympathy' whatsoever.[125]
Richard Findlater, who liked Dotrice's 'near-naked black-devil', thought
the actor had played the part 'for terror and symbol, not for pathos', but
remains silent about the symbol's nature and implications (*Observer*,
7/4/63). Another reviewer, complaining that 1.2 had never been 'so
tedious' as it was here, added that 'The production came alive . . . only with
the appearance of Caliban'; Dotrice's interpretation 'was interesting and at
times valuable . . . though . . . unsupported by the text' (*Coventry Evening
Telegraph*, 3/4/63).

A more conscious use of race was evidenced in two 1970 productions,

---

122 Conrad Wilson, *Scotsman*, 4/4/63.
123 R. B. Marriott, *Stage & Television Today*, 4/4/63.
124 Respectively, Denis Blewett, *Daily Sketch*, 3/4/63; Bernard Levin, *Daily Mail*,
     3/4/63; and *Bolton Evening News*, 3/4/63.
125 Respectively, *New Daily*, 8/4/63; *Leamington Spa Courier*, 5/4/63; and *Worcester
     Evening News*, 3/4/63.

one in the US and the other in Britain.[126] Nagel Jackson's production of the play at Washington's Sylvan Theatre featured black actors as both Caliban and Ariel, with Henry Baker's Caliban

> savage enough, but neither deformed nor servile. He was, indeed, rather darkly beautiful in his glistening fish scales and his great natural dignity . . . [V]iolent and arrogant . . . he was powerful and intractable from beginning to end. He never actually obeyed the command of his new master Stephano to kiss his foot. And even when he spoke of his fear of pinching, he did not cower. Most significantly of all, he never uttered the final resolve . . . that he would be wise hereafter and go seek grace. He admitted his folly in worshipping a drunkard, but, after rejecting the 'dull fool', strode angrily off stage, an enigma reverberating in the memory.[127]

Paraphrasing Roberts, Errol Hill remarks that, 'Seeing this role played by Baker with his black skin, flawed diction, and minstrel-type mouth painted on a greenish face, and combining that impression with the use of the word "slave" in the play, the Washington audience could not fail to identify him with a black American' (*Shakespeare in Sable*, p. 158). Roberts herself teases out the implications of such an identification, commenting that the casting of black actors as both Caliban and Ariel 'suggested on a symbolic level that the black man could be both a threat and an instrument of salvation to the white society' ('The Washington Shakespeare Summer Festival', p. 481). However, as she also recognizes, both casting and characterization might simply have confirmed prejudices and stereotypes: Darryl Croxton's Ariel was 'such a light shade of black as to reinforce the vulgar prejudice that lighter is better', while the 'angry and recalcitrant' Caliban and the 'witty, amenable, and even compassionate' Ariel could tempt one 'to conclude facetiously that [the former] was a black militant and [the latter] an Uncle Tom' (pp. 481–2).

   During the same summer, at the Mermaid Theatre, London, Jonathan Miller directed a production of *The Tempest* that 'was certainly the most overtly colonial since Tree's'.[128] Influenced by Mannoni, as well as by

---

126 It is unclear which production opened first, as the primary source on the American production, quoted below, does not give the date of the opening performance, noting only that it comprised the 1970 Washington Shakespeare Summer Festival. Jonathan Miller's production opened on 15 June.

127 Jeanne Addison Roberts, 'The Washington Shakespeare Summer Festival, 1970', *Shakespeare Quarterly* 21 (1970), p. 481.

128 Griffiths, ' "This Island's Mine" ', p. 177; he postulates that 'the new willingness to present the colonial dimension arose from a sense that it was now feasible to approach the colonial elements more dispassionately than had been possible during the retreat from Empire'.

'accounts of the Elizabethan voyages of exploration and a production of Lowell's *The Old Glory*, with its . . . Puritan sailors making Indians drunk', Miller also cast black actors both as Ariel and as Caliban, using them as 'examples of two opposing ways in which native black populations responded to the Europeans' (Griffiths, ' "This Island's Mine" ', p. 177). Ariel represented 'the accomplished servant who learnt European ways' (*ibid.*, p. 177), while Caliban, played by Rudolph Walker (who repeated the part for the same director in 1988), was 'the ex-African degraded into the New World slave, used solely for Prospero's profit', 'the incurable dependent who is anxious only to exchange one bondage for another' (respectively, *Punch*, 24/6/70, and Irving Wardle, *The Times*, 16/6/70). Other reviewers described him as a 'great giggling Caliban', 'a grinning mooncalf angrily swatting at flies', and a 'grumbling creature . . . [with] the endearing [*sic*] quality of a rasping, grovelling, ingratiating Uncle Tom'.[129] Miller's well-received colonial interpretation, which 'embraced all the characters', made one reviewer feel that it would be 'hard . . . ever again to see *The Tempest* as the fairytale to which we are accustomed – or indeed to see it in any other terms than as Shakespeare's account . . . of the impact of the Old World on the New'.[130]

The distorting perspective of the Old World on the New was very evident in Peter Hall's 1974 production for the National Theatre. Denis Quilley's 'Cheyenne-like' Caliban was 'recognisably human . . . deformed not in body but in spirit', although a third critic mentioned his 'dragging [a] bandaged leg' and the wig plot shows he had a bald head with a deformed lump on it; yet another critic found him 'scrofulous, but rather charming'.[131] Surprisingly, these reviewers make no mention of what Irving Wardle thought 'the most original performance in the production. [Quilley's] makeup [was] bisected: on one half the ugly scrofulous monster whom Prospero sees, on the other an image of the noble savage'.[132]

129 Respectively, Peter Lewis, *Daily Mail*; John Barber, *Daily Telegraph*; and Milton Shulman, *Evening Standard*, all 16/6/70; Shulman adds that he wore a 'soiled, army greatcoat'. Interestingly, while Jeanne Roberts implies that the Washington Ariel came perilously close to an Uncle Tom caricature, the strong political context of Miller's production avoided simple replication of a stereotype: Prospero's treatment of his servants helped to explain the genesis of 'Uncle Tom'-ish behaviour in Caliban.

130 Respectively, Griffiths, ' "This Island's Mine" ', p. 178, and Hilary Spurling, *Spectator*, 27 June 1970, quoted in *ibid.*, p. 178.

131 Respectively, Michael Billington, *Guardian*, 6/3/74; B. A. Young, *Financial Times*, 6/3/74; John Elsom, 'Creaking Storm'; and John Barber, *Daily Telegraph*, 6/3/74.

132 *The Times*, 6/3/74; given this description, Wardle contradictorily adds that, 'as Mr Quilley plays him, he is striving to break from the first stage into the second'.

5 and 6 In 1988, Declan Donnellan treated the masque as a classical extravanga and anarchic dance in which Miranda and Ferdinand (Cecilia Noble and Lloyd Owen) joined, while Jonathan Miller highlighted cultural imperialism by his use of black goddesses (Melanie E. Marshall, La Verne Williams, Dorothy Ross), dressed in African beads and straw farthingale skirts, singing in baroque style; Ariel (Cyril Nri) can be seen in the background.

David L. Hirst writes that the director 'employed this [bisected] device . . . to subtle effect, often counterpointing Caliban's appearance with his words and with the action on stage', but at least one reviewer did not find the character 'credible'.[133]

In the same year, Keith Hack's RSC production at The Other Place cast black actor Jeffery Kissoon in the part. Many critics had difficulty with this Caliban, 'whose superb physique [made] him an unlikely target for phrases like "misshapen knave"'; he was 'a slave simply because of his colour'.[134] Although agreeing that Kissoon was 'much too beautiful' to be a monster, another critic thought he 'suggest[ed] the pent-up savagery of Caliban very well', while yet another admired the way he 'twist[ed] his agile frame into fantastic poses to convey the acrimony of his feelings'.[135] However, other reviewers thought the racial politics of casting a black actor in the part had not been considered carefully enough. Sheila Bannock argued that the temptation 'to see connotations of racial oppression in Caliban's role' could be 'very misleading': in her view, his 'innate instinct to destroy' demands a character who is believably 'monstrous', and to present him otherwise alters our understanding of the play (*Stratford Herald*, 25/10/74). Another reviewer complained that Hack's attempt 'to illustrate the white man's mental and physical cruelty to the black races . . . succeed[ed] only in being offensive to them' (*Coventry Evening Telegraph*, 23/10/74); the critic was perhaps referring to what Charles Lewsen called Stephano's 'uncompromising . . . humiliation of Caliban'.

While the conception of Caliban in Giorgio Strehler's 1978 production of *La Tempesta* for his Piccolo Teatro di Milano was similar to Hack's, the use of a blacked-up white actor seemed to obviate the unease Kissoon's Caliban had evoked in critics. There are two possible reasons for these different reactions: either unconscious racism prevented acceptance of the dignity of a Caliban who was actually black, or white racial guilt caused so much discomfort that only a blacked-up white actor could function as a symbol of black oppression, since the presence of a black actor could recreate both racial oppression and stereotyping as a reality during the performance. For example, just as the Coventry reviewer quoted above found Hack's treatment of his black Caliban offensive, Errol Hill criticizes Gerald

---

133 Respectively, Hirst, *The Tempest: Text and Performance* (London: Macmillan, 1984), p. 48, and Milton Shulman, *Evening Standard*, 6/3/74.

134 Such critics include John Peter, *Sunday Times*, 3/11/74, from whom the first quotation is taken, and Eric Shorter, *Daily Telegraph*, 23/10/74. The second quotation is from Charles Lewsen, *The Times*, 24/10/74.

135 Respectively, Don Chapman, *Oxford Mail*, 23/10/74, and *Evesham Journal*, 31/10/74.

Freedman's 1979 production at Stratford, Connecticut, in which Joe Morton, 'the only black actor in the cast . . . played Caliban as a bowlegged, barbaric creature with bared fangs. Only [his] considerable energy and fine speaking voice saved his characterization from being a banal caricature worthy of the minstrel stage' (*Shakespeare in Sable*, p. 198, n. 9). Indeed, Freedman exploited another racist stereotype in conceiving of Caliban 'as an aspect of Prospero's character – the libido that cannot be controlled'; he also 'had him sing his freedom catch to jazz tunes' (Vaughan, *Shakespeare's Caliban*, p. 194). Although the Vaughans argue that 'this Caliban still symbolized a repressed minority' (pp. 194–5), it seems likely, given Hill's analysis, that he more accurately reflected a prejudiced rather than a realistic view of his race.[136]

At least three actors played Caliban during the life of Strehler's production: Michele Placido, Piero Sammataro and, on video, Massimo Foschi; however, descriptions of the different performances indicate that conception and execution of the part remained the same. This Caliban was 'a black, naked, physically beautiful noble savage with no hint of deformity', who embodied the pathos of the exploited.[137] However, his first appearance was 'sinister with two hands creepily emerging from his underground cave': 'very slowly, one black arm after the other emerged from the [trap], holding onto the frame of the opening and heaving up the rest of Caliban's body'.[138] Because, at first, his bowed head was out of sight and his hands were lying flat on the stage on either side of the trap, with his arms forming an inverted V with the elbow at the apex, it appeared as if a giant black spider were emerging from the hole: the entrance cleverly

136 My remarks apply to productions during the 1970s, when there was less white sensitivity to racial stereotyping and oppression than there is now. Reviewers of Neil Armfield's 1995 revival of his 1990 production at Belvoir Street Theatre, Sydney, for example, were powerfully struck by the new 'casting [of] Aboriginal actor Kevin Smith in the part' (James Waites, *Sydney Morning Herald*, 1/6/95). Armfield 'deliberately loaded the work with the politics of Australian colonialism' by the portrayal's evocation of the 'famous Aborigine . . . Bennelong': 'to watch Smith [in loin cloth and tattered redcoat jacket] swagger around the stage like Jacky-Jacky, beaten, berated and plied with alcohol; to feel the power of his impotent anger at his dispossession; and to listen to him explain the music of his island to the drunken imperial clowns he has taken up with, is profoundly affecting' (respectively, Stewart Hawkins, *Telegraph Mirror*, 2/6/95; John Trigger, *Capital Weekly*, 16/6/95; and John McCallum, *Australian*, 2/6/95). I am grateful to Susan Pfisterer for supplying reviews of the production.

137 The quotation is from Roger Warren, *Times Literary Supplement*, 9/3/84, and the point about pathos from Michael Billington, *Guardian*, 16/11/83.

138 Respectively, Michael Billington and Pia Kleber, 'Theatrical Continuities', p. 148.

suggested some kind of monstrous animal which Caliban's actual appearance then belied.[139] Kleber notes that 'Most of the time, [Caliban] stayed
close to the earth, often sitting, lying down, or crouching when he walked',
his 'postures and facial expressions disclos[ing his] . . . hatred for and fear
of the man who had taken the island away from him and reduced him to
slavery'; she adds that his body, 'painted coal-black, stood in sharp contrast
to . . . [Prospero's and Miranda's] white clothes' ('Theatrical Continuities',
p. 148). Caliban himself wore only the skimpiest of loin-cloths (video).

A similar treatment of Caliban was evident in Clifford Williams's 1978
RSC production. David Suchet, who played the part, conceived the
character 'as a mixture of different types of native . . . whose land has been
taken away'.[140] Not wanting 'to be instantly recognizable as . . . an African
native or an Indian or an Eskimo or an Aborigine', Suchet wore 'two layers
of dark brown makeup all over [his] body and then sprayed it pewter-
coloured. Under the stage lighting the effect was that sometimes [he] would
look black, sometimes pewter, and sometimes . . . even . . . greenish . . .'
('Caliban in *The Tempest*', p. 179). In addition, he had 'an African nose' and
'two rubber prosthetics which covered [his] eyebrows and gave [him] a pre-
historic-looking forehead'; the top of his head was made to 'appear bald
and lumpy by placing dollops of porridge on it and covering the whole top
of [the] head with latex'. His 'physical movements were very slightly ape-
like without *being* an ape. For example, [he] would be slightly crouched and
bent forward with [his] movement, and . . . would squat rather than sit'.
His voice was 'slightly stilted . . . to make it clear that [he] had been taught
to speak' (p. 179). Because Suchet felt that Caliban is 'totally instinctive' in
thought, action and speech, he played him as 'at times dangerous and at
times childish, but at all times totally spontaneous' (pp. 177–8). Caliban's
only clothing was a pair of Prospero's cast-off breeches: coming to below
the knee, they had 'slits in them' and 'were a dirty fawn colour' (p. 179).

Reviews tended to reflect Suchet's conception of the character; Jack
Tinker, for example, called him 'a proud, black Caliban whose nobility
has clearly been betrayed by birth and fate' (*Daily Mail*, 4/5/78),
while Michael Billington praised 'a stunning performance with both the
anger and the pathos of the unreasonably exploited' (*Guardian*, 15/5/78).
However, two critics were puzzled by the 'open and glaring contradiction
at the centre' of the production: as Irving Wardle wrote, 'Of all the characters Mr Suchet's Caliban approaches closest to the simple kindness of

139 Details from my notes, taken while watching the VideoRai production of
Strehler's *La Tempesta*, made by Carlo Battistoni.
140 Suchet, 'Caliban in *The Tempest*', p. 173.

Prospero: he is also the only one whom Prospero treats with implacable unforgiving hatred' (*The Times*, 3/5/78). Robert Cushman reversed Wardle's equation but saw a similar problem: Caliban's 'grudge against Prospero is difficult to understand as they are both such thoroughly nice people . . . [Prospero] shows no bitterness towards Caliban which, read it how you will, robs the play of a dimension' (*Observer*, 7/5/78). Reviews also mention that Caliban carried 'a manikin-type model of Prospero which he view[ed] with suitable hatred', 'a voodoo doll to help him curse his enemy' (respectively, Billington and Bernard Levin, *Sunday Times*, 7/5/78). A production photograph reprinted in Suchet, 'Caliban in *The Tempest*', p. 168, shows him clutching the long slender doll in his right hand as he spoke the curse at 1.2.339–40.

By the early 1980s, stage Calibans were used to represent not only blacks, but 'any group that felt itself oppressed'; for instance, 'In New York, he appeared as a punk-rocker, complete with cropped hair, sunglasses, and cockney accent'.[141] In Robert Falls's 1987 Chicago production, Bruce A. Young's Caliban won the audience's 'sympathy as a maltreated, powerless underdog': although the 'analogy [was] not pressed . . . [this Caliban was] the trained underemployed, bored with his status, ripe for thoughtless rebellion and potentially dangerous' (Pellowe, 'In Chicago', p. 55). In Michael Goddard's 1988 Salford Playhouse production, Paul Walker's Caliban was a menacing, loud-mouthed Millwall fan, dressed in leather jacket and chains.[142] And in Braham Murray's 1990 production at the Manchester Royal Exchange, Dan Hildebrand, a white actor, played the part in 'rags, Rasta-style locks and gaudy tattoos . . . a cross between some alienated North London squatter and the Cowardly Lion in the *Wizard of Oz*'; his 'buttocks thrust through shreds of evening dress', and he had 'crudely tattooed spiders on his torso'.[143] An 'exploited victim', he was kept 'Tearful and afflicted . . . in a kennel made of rock and chained by one leg'.[144] Benedict Nightingale added that it was 'possible to see both why Caliban looks for a leader when planning violence, and why Prospero keeps him chained', as there was 'something both feeble and feral about [Hildebrand's] hooliganism'.

141 Vaughan, *Shakespeare's Caliban*, p. 194; their example fits Lee Breuer's Caliban, Barry Miller, who played him as 'a snarling Cockney punk rocker' (John Beaufort, *Christian Science Monitor*, 20/7/81).
142 Martin Hoyle, *Financial Times*, 2/3/88.
143 Respectively, Benedict Nightingale, *The Times*, 15/9/90; Jeffrey Wainwright, *Independent*, 15/9/90; and Michael Schmidt, *Daily Telegraph*, 17/9/90.
144 R. V. Holdsworth, *Times Literary Supplement*, 21–7/9/90.

Caliban has even been played by women in two French-speaking versions of *La Tempête*, although, surprisingly, reviews do not comment on such a radical departure from tradition. Marilu Marini played the part in Alfredo Arias's 1986 Avignon production as a 'horrible human animal with a raucous voice', wearing a sack-cloth like Prospero's,[145] while Anne-Marie Cadieux appeared as Caliban in Robert Lepage's 1992 production for Le Théâtre Repère. Cadieux played the part as an 'utterly uninhibited Caliban, who recite[d] his/her speeches to rock 'n' roll rhythm while dancing maniacally', producing the 'most convincingly anarchic Caliban' one reviewer had ever seen.[146] Another, mentioning the 'optimum opportunity for overacting' that the part provides, described her 'frenetic Caliban' as 'a punk-rocker on speed', while a third deplored her shameless barnstorming and directionless performance.[147] It is possible to see both Marini's and Cadieux's performances either as expressions of feminist rebellion or as reactions to the perceived threat of feminism, but not enough is known about the productions to substantiate either claim.

Obviously, the now firmly established trend of presenting Caliban as a member of an oppressed minority can sometimes produce complex analyses and sometimes send culturally confusing signals. An example of the first is arguably found in the 1980 production of *The Tempest* at The Mount in Lenox, Massachusetts, in which black actor Joe Morton again played Caliban. Although one reviewer thought the casting 'raised the troubling questions of bondage and servitude with which the play abounds', he felt the casting of another black actor, Gregory Uel Cole, as Stephano 'added yet another layer of meaning: "The servant who comes upon a captive monster and, in the name of freedom, makes the monster his own slave, is not just a fool but a representative of the unending chain of power society provides."'[148] In other words, the issue of exploitation was not reduced to

---

145 Anthony Curtis, *Financial Times*, 18/7/86.
146 Ray Conlogue, *Toronto Globe & Mail*. I am grateful to Michael Morris and
     Rachel Feuchtwang at the production company Cultural Industry, London, for
     making available to me press clippings about and photographs of the production.
147 Respectively, Pat Donnelly, *Montreal Gazette*, 7/6/93, and Robert Lévesque,
     Montréal Le Devoir.
148 Terry Curtis Fox, *The Village Voice*, 10 September 1980, quoted in Hill,
     Shakespeare in Sable, p. 184. The Vaughans, drawing on Peter Erickson's account,
     'A *Tempest* at the Mount', *Shakespeare Quarterly* 32 (1981), pp. 188–90, describe
     this production as reflecting a trend in which 'the actor's blackness was
     insignificant' and 'Caliban's monstrosity . . . reemphasized', *Shakespeare's
     Caliban*, p. 195. While Caliban's large hands and circled eyes may have put him
     into the monstrous camp, I do not think that they necessarily served to remove
     him from the black one, given the race-consciousness of 1980s America.

a simple racial equation but grounded in a wider understanding of power and class.[149]

An example of a confused interpretation might be found in Ron Daniels's 1982 RSC production, in which Bob Peck made one reviewer rethink his first impression of Miranda's wildness: 'Like Miranda's his hair is braided but it is a filthy mass and, along with his beard, knotted and studded with beads; in fact there is more than a touch of the Rastafarian about him.'[150] Caliban's Rastafarian dreadlocks were noted by several reviewers, but only one commented that they gave the character 'a slightly worrying racial slant', adding that this was not reflected in the white actor's 'witty playing'.[151] Peck wore a loin-cloth, had a humped back covered 'in festering sores', and walked with knees bent in a crouched position, which Michael Coveney rightly described as 'awkward'.[152]

Despite Ned Chaillet's comment on the wit of Peck's playing, there was no critical consensus about either the effects or the effectiveness of his performance. In one view he was 'predominantly savage', in another 'strangely human and sympathetic'.[153] Chaillet himself, describing Peck's 'virility' as Caliban, thought he could be 'a rapist or a revolutionary', but to another critic he was 'a comic creation of half-man, half-beast loping around the stage and swinging from the set's rigging like an orangoutang'.[154] Similarly, one reviewer thought him 'rather striking', but others found him 'disappointingly average' and 'more remarkable in appearance than in performance'.[155] Peck's voice also produced sharply divided reactions: 'too

149 As my previous note implies, the production could also be accused of stereotyping its black Caliban as bestial: Peter Erickson's review notes that Caliban wore 'leather gloves which, blended in with his blackened skin, gave the illusion of enormous hands'; that he was 'typically [positioned] on or near the ground', walking 'bent over at the waist, torso swaying up and down or shaking vigorously in an animal-like posture'; and that 'An assortment of convincing groans and growls served as background' to his speech ('A *Tempest*', p. 189, quoted in Vaughan, *Shakespeare's Caliban*, p. 195). On the other hand, since Caliban was not the only black actor in the cast, it is also arguable that the audience would not have perceived these characteristics as racial ones.

150 Christopher Edwards, *New Statesman*, 20/8/82.

151 Ned Chaillet, *The Times*, 13/8/82.

152 The description is drawn from Chaillet, my viewing of the archive video and Coveney, *Financial Times*, 13/8/82.

153 Respectively, *Oxford Times*, 20/8/82 (see also *Wantage & Grove Herald*, 19/8/82), and Brian Jarman, *South Wales Argus*, 12/8/82 (see also Desmond Pratt, *Yorkshire Post*, 12/8/82).

154 *Kidderminster Shuttle*, 20/8/82.

155 Respectively, James Fenton, *Sunday Times*, 15/8/82; Robert Cushman, *Observer*, 15/8/82; and *Sunday Telegraph*, 15/8/82.

external, a bit mechanical even', it 'didn't match the animality of his appearance', according to Edwards. J. C. Trewin thought it was 'rather too glib', while, on the other hand, Judith Cook admired the way Peck made Caliban 'unusually articulate and intelligent'.[156]

Interestingly, recent years have also seen white Calibans imprisoned by black Prosperos; while such a staging could express white male backlash to perceived threats from militant minorities, neither production under consideration fits into such a mould. The first is Peter Brook's 1990 production of *La Tempête* for his Centre International de Créations Théâtrales, in which Caliban was played by David Bennent, well known for having acted the boy in the film version of Günter Grass's *The Tin Drum* (dir. Volker Schlöndorff, 1979). He was dressed in a large burlap sack with an opening for his head and holes in each corner from which his limbs protruded (programme photograph). Michael Billington found him 'a thuggish, boyish Caliban who wield[ed] a clump of wood like an axe and who [had] wild, staring eyes that pierce[d] through people like laser-beams . . . [He was a] steely, dangerous menace' (*Guardian*, 19/10/90). Paul Taylor agreed that he was 'No brutish hulk' but 'a furious, stunted-looked urchin, much given, in the first half, to bashing turnips to death with a wooden log. [He was a] rolling bundle of frustration' (*Independent*, 2/11/90). Michael Coveney called him 'a capering, dwarfish white boy . . . who live[d] in a rotting cardboard box and . . . [was] transformed only from a priapic scavenger into a guzzling wine cask on withered legs'; consequently, he acted as 'a symbol of sensual deformity in dignified primitivist surroundings' (*Observer*, 4/11/90). Martin Hoyle also thought him 'small, tough and frightening' but was disappointed that Brook mistakenly 'undercut' his tragic potential (*Financial Times*, 2/11/90). Irving Wardle was alone in thinking that Bennent 'convey[ed] the idea of an angry innocent rather than a mutinous beast' (*Independent on Sunday*, 4/11/90). As Coveney suggests, given the quiet dignity of Sotigui Kouyate's saintly Prospero (see note to 1.2.0sd), the only possible symbolic reading, if one was intended, was the contrast

---

156 Respectively, *Birmingham Post*, 12/8/82, and *Scotsman*, 14/8/82. Reviews of the London transfer suggest that Peck's characterization of Caliban changed somewhat during the run. Francis King called his performance 'outstanding', showing Caliban as 'at once repellent and pathetic', though Stephen Brook thought he 'misse[d] the pathos in his grovelling' to Stephano as well as a sense of real menace towards Prospero and Miranda. Giles Gordon thought he was 'more mischievous than at Stratford', while Robert Cushman complained that he gave to the part 'too little of anything' but comedy. See King, *Sunday Telegraph*, Brook, *New Statesman*, Gordon, *Spectator* and Cushman, *Observer*, all reproduced in *London Theatre Record* 10–23/9/83.

between an imagined Third World simplicity and purity and First World destructiveness and ugliness.

The other production, Bill Alexander's in 1994 for the Birmingham Repertory theatre, featured Richard McCabe, one of the most moving Calibans I have seen, as the only white actor among the play's quartet of main characters.[157] Michael Coveney described him, not altogether aptly in view of his clear human status, as a 'simian Caliban [who] swagger[ed] like a Mongolian warrior, gaping and staring wildly, and snatching at phrases and examples like a greedy toad'; he nevertheless rightly judged this 'self-conscious performance . . . a very fine one' (*Observer*, 18/9/94). Michael Billington was nearer the mark in seeing McCabe's 'extraordinary Caliban . . . [as] a natural man of the kind the captain of the Beagle brought back from Tierra del Fuego for purposes of social experiment'; he added that, 'with his distempered face and crouching lope, [Caliban was] particularly touching in his puzzled curiosity about these new creatures who have landed on his former island', being 'especially tickled by the boatswain's bald pate' (*Guardian*, 15/9/94). Billington hints at what I found the strongest element of the portrayal: that this Caliban was a simple-minded innocent, capable of great affection and great hurt. Since in this production a black Prospero also controlled a black Ariel, it was clear that race alone was not an element in the trio's power relationships; indeed, since Ariel herself sometimes appeared feeble-minded, Prospero's relationship to both her and Caliban could be seen as paternal.[158]

Since the late 1980s, the monstrous tradition has re-emerged to coexist with the oppressed victim, sometimes even within the same performance. For example, in Peter Hall's 1988 production for the National Theatre, Tony Haygarth's Caliban was naked apart from a rectangular box restraining his penis; it was fastened by two belts and padlocked onto his body, much of which oozed blood. His diabolical inheritance was clearly signposted by short horns on his forehead, as well as fangs and talons.[159] The costume plot also notes that he wore white contact lenses, which increased his alien appearance.

Haygarth's performance was a critical triumph, one reviewer justifiably calling it 'a *tour de force*'.[160] The actor gave no suggestion of Caliban as 'a

---

157 That is, Prospero, Ariel, Caliban and Miranda.

158 Prospero slapped Caliban at 1.2.349 ('O ho, O ho! would't had been done!', but showed him physical affection at 5.1.275b ('I shall be pinch'd to death'); see note to 5.1.274b–5a.

159 Details are drawn from my notes of the performance of 19 May 1988.

160 David Evans, *What's On*, 12/10/88.

poor, bullied colonial subject', playing him instead as 'a comic unpolitical' monster who 'cowers and fawns and snarls like a chained dog'.[161] However, this filth-caked 'monster of mutilated and self-mutilating brutishness' spoke the verse with a beauty that was both 'unexpected' and 'heart-touching'; 'slavish and strangely moving', he was 'True to Hall's discomfiting reading of the play'.[162] The performance was 'outstanding: fierce, sensual and ecstatic', 'as touching as it [was] uncompromising'.[163]

Similarly, in Nicholas Hytner's 1988 RSC production, John Kane's Caliban had blue markings all over his body, almost like abstract tattoos, which perhaps represented his being 'freckled' (1.2.283) in a monstrous way. The same gold speckly substance that glittered in his hair could also be seen in places on his hands and legs.[164] Kate Kellaway described Caliban as having 'gold lichen growing on his chest, looking as though a wicked doodler has scribbled over him', while Benedict Nightingale saw him as 'a pristine skinhead tattooed with blotches of mud' and Michael Billington as 'a surly, mud-caked menace'.[165] A 'gravel-covered monster with a voice to match', he communicated 'in raw, guttural croaks'.[166] Clive Hirschhorn thought he was 'a victim more to be pitied than scorned', a sentiment shared by Rhoda Koenig, who found him 'a piteous monster in his homeless-man's tattered blanket'.

In an altogether different vein, Yukio Ninagawa's Caliban, Yutaka Matsushige in Edinburgh in 1988 and Hiroki Okawa in London in 1992, was a somersaulting, fish-tailed creature on clogs; comic and unthreaten-

161 The first two quotations are from Martin Hoyle, *Financial Times*, 1/10/88, and the third from Ros Asquith, *City Limits*, 26/5/88.

162 Respectively, Peter Kemp, *Independent*, 21/5/88; Francis King, *Sunday Telegraph*, 22/5/88; David Nathan, *Jewish Chronicle*, 27/5/88; Christopher Edwards, *Spectator*, 28/5/88; and Kemp.

163 Respectively, Michael Ratcliffe, *Observer*, 22/5/88, and Jim Hiley, *Listener*, 26/5/88.

164 Details are drawn from my notes of the performance of 3 September 1988. Apart from this aspect of Caliban's appearance, Hytner's costuming and staging stressed the similarities between Prospero's two servants: they were both bare-chested, with Caliban dressed in ragged shorts that had the same soft appearance as Ariel's fringed trousers, and both had blonde hair, with Caliban's a glittery gold colour and the spirit's a colourless white. Caliban's literal confinement in the rock (see note to 1.2.320sd) mirrored Ariel's in the pine and gave force to Prospero's pretended threat to the spirit to rend an oak and peg him within it (see note to 1.2. 294–6).

165 Respectively, *Observer*, 31/7/88; *Punch*, 12/8/88; and *Guardian*, 29/7/88.

166 Respectively, Clive Hirschhorn, *Sunday Express*, 28/5/89, and Alex Renton, *Independent*, 1/8/88; see also Rhoda Koenig, *Punch*, 9/6/89, and Jack Tinker, *Daily Mail*, 26/5/89.

ing, he appeared to have a paralysed hand.[167] Other critics described him as 'half-punk, half-mermaid', his 'wild spiky hair and . . . long fish's tail . . . creating the impression of a punk sturgeon'; he also had a 'flamboyantly warpainted face'.[168]

The approach taken by Ninagawa is an anomaly, a throwback to earlier times: most contemporary productions emphasize Caliban's status as victim and portray him as essentially human, albeit grotesque or deformed in some way, rather than as an out-and-out monster. Although still often played by black actors, the role of Caliban has increasingly reverted to white performers in recent years, as the note to 1.2.320sd further illustrates. However, whatever the race of the actor playing the part, its overall interpretation continues to serve as an accurate index of which groups in society are presently alienated, disadvantaged and vulnerable, and, for that reason, threatening to and threatened by those with more power.

LOOKING AT THE 'FABRIC OF THIS VISION' (4.1.151): SPECTACLE, DESIGN AND MEANING

Although throughout its performance history *The Tempest* has proved to be perhaps the most visually spectacular of Shakespeare's plays, it was written to be performed on a virtually bare stage. Whether it played at the outdoor Globe or at the indoor Blackfriars, there was no scenic decoration apart from a few representative properties. The stage itself represented the ship of Act 1, Scene 1, with the lords emerging from a trap as if from below deck and with mariners positioned not only on the 'main deck' of the stage but also on the 'mast' of the upper gallery (see notes to 1.1 for further details). Elsewhere, characters entered through the tiring-house doors, and Prospero probably gestured to the discovery space to indicate his cell.

Shakespeare's original staging, like his text, prevailed only for the first three decades of *The Tempest*'s life. While the Restoration returned the monarchy and the Stuarts to Britain, it did not restore the native theatrical tradition that had been so successfully disrupted by the closing of the theatres during the inter-regnum years (1642–60); rather, it introduced a continental style of theatrical presentation to England. Not only did women begin to play women's parts and playhouses move firmly indoors, but perspective scenery, with its attendant visual spectacle, became the

---

167 The description is drawn from my notes of the performance of 3 December 1992.

168 Respectively, Paul Taylor, *Independent*, 5/12/92; Benedict Nightingale, *The Times*, 5/12/92; and Nicholas de Jongh, *Evening Standard*, 4/12/92.

norm. Stage directions in the printed text of Shadwell's 1674 adaptation, for example, explain that the painted scene at the beginning of 1.1 represented a cloudy sky, rocky coast and agitated sea (see pp. 11–12); in the middle of the shipwreck's 'shower of fire' the lights dimmed, during which the 'cloudy sky, rocks, and sea' vanished, to be replaced by 'that beautiful part of the island' that is Prospero's home. The scene now showed 'three walks of cypress-trees', with the walks on either side each leading to a cave (which belonged respectively to Prospero's daughters and to Hippolito) and the middle walk, 'of a great depth', leading to 'an open part of the island'. The mechanics of scene-changing, with wings and shutters sliding along grooves in full view of the audience, were as much an attraction as the scenes themselves: Baron von Schwerin, who attended a performance of Shadwell's version on 14 June 1674, commented that 'because of the changing of the scenes [it] was well worth seeing'.[169]

Such emphasis on visual spectacle continued for at least the next two and a half centuries, leading to an increasing concern with realism, often at the expense of the text. William Macready's 1838 production, for example, opened with a 'grand panoramic spectacle' that showed a 'tranquil sea' and a view of 'the Neapolitan fleet in the distance'. Suddenly, however, a storm with thunder and lightning dispersed the fleet, with dark clouds descending and hiding the painted vessels, while 'demons appear[ed] above, waving intermitting lights'. Then, on the right, a workable ship appeared: already shattered, it proceeded to lose its mast and then foundered, whereupon Ariel flew 'over the stage, waving an[other] intermitting light'. This kind of elaborate staging was made possible by the omission of all of Shakespeare's dialogue, a practice established well before 1838 and continuing long afterwards.[170] Whether it compensated for the sacrifice of the playwright's lines is a moot point: John Forster found Macready's staging impressive, commenting that 'the hugest vessel that we ever beheld on the stage laboured in a genuine and most tremendous gulf of waters',[171] while the reviewer for *John Bull* complained that the 'mimic

169 Quoted in *London Stage 1660–1800, Part 1: 1660–1700*, ed. William Van Lennep (Carbondale: Southern Illinois University Press, 1965), p. 216. For more information on perspective scenery, see Sybil Rosenfeld's *A Short History of Scene Design in Great Britain* (Oxford: Basil Blackwell, 1973) and Arnold Aronson's entry on 'Theatre Design' in *The Cambridge Guide to Theatre*, ed. Martin Banham (Cambridge: Cambridge University Press, 1995), pp. 1090–3.

170 Quotations are from Pattie's 1839 edition of *The Tempest*, which Charles Shattuck notes was printed from Macready's promptbook (*The Shakespeare Promptbooks: A Descriptive Catalogue* (London and Urbana: University of Illinois Press, 1965). For further examples of productions that omitted the dialogue of the first scene, see note to 1.1.

171 *Examiner*, 21 October 1838, reprinted in *Dramatic Essays*, Volume III, p. 68.

7 Thomas Grieve's set for Act 2, scene 1 of Charles Kean's 1857 production shows the literalism of nineteenth-century scenic design, with a forbidding landscape for the 'men of sin'; it also incidentally shows a female Ariel in the fairy mould.

vessel . . . outrageously bumped and tossed about on waves that we can liken to nothing save tiny cocks of hay, painted green and afflicted with a spasm'.[172]

Charles Kean's 1857 production similarly omitted the first-scene dialogue. The play began with a workable ship in a storm; it carried about thirty boys, who played the crew and in this scene doubled for the courtiers, Master and Boatswain, their small size making the stage ship appear larger. During the storm, the lights were 'quite down', and the effects included 'Rolling and shaking Thunder, Chains, Braces, Wind, Rain, Lightning, Wood crashes, Windlass, [and] Crash Box', which continued until the vessel sank.[173] Herman Charles Merivale, who saw the production, explains how some effects were achieved: 'Over a floor above the stage was spread a sheet of iron, and in the corner, revolving on a pivot, a mighty box all full of

172 Quoted in J. C. Trewin, *Mr Macready* (London: Harrap, 1955), p. 150.

173 The promptbook from which these details are drawn, hereafter referred to as Edmonds pb, is now in the Folger Shakespeare Library (Prompt *Tempest* 10); Shattuck, who lists it as *Tempest* number 19 in his *Shakespeare Promptbooks*, describes it as a final or souvenir promptbook made in 1859 by Kean's prompter, T.W. Edmonds.

cannon-balls. You had but to tip the box and the storm came on. It burst in a sudden crash with all the cannon-balls, then growled itself out in declining fury as they ran about the floor.'[174] Notes in another promptbook prepared by George Ellis[175] make clear that there were also a large and a small rain box and two wind machines.

Ellis's notes further reveal much of the mariners' detailed and realistic business during the storm. The Captain (*sic*) and Boatswain were on the quarter deck, whence certain members of the crew carried out their orders. One of the sailors fell overboard and was hauled back on ship by a rope; one mast, blown over by the wind, dragged its tackling with it. A group of sailors, massed together like a 'swarm of bees', went to cut away the foremast with hatchets, while another group of sailors threw out the anchor, which was lost when its rope snapped. Finally, the ship itself sank.[176]

Hans Christian Andersen, who attended the first night of Kean's production as a guest of Charles Dickens, vividly describes the storm scene from the audience's perspective:

> During the overture, a storm was heard muttering, the thunder rolled, cries and screams were heard from behind the stage; the entire prelude was thus given while the curtain was still down; and when it rolled up, great waves seemed to be rolling toward the footlights, the whole stage was on a furious sea, a great ship was tossed back and forth . . . seamen and passengers tumbled about, there was a death shriek, the masts fell, and then the ship was swallowed up by the sea.[177]

While the reviewer for the *Illustrated London News* also found the staging of the storm scene 'entirely new and appalling in the extreme', the *Athenaeum*'s critic remarked that 'striking and startling' though it was, 'it lasted too long; [because] it survived the moment of surprise . . . the spectator was . . . enabled to discover the contrivance'.[178] Dickens in fact

---

174 *Bar, Stage and Platform* (London: Chatto & Windus, 1902), p. 139.

175 This promptbook, hereafter referred to as Ellis pb, is now in the Folger Shakespeare Library (Prompt *Tempest* 11); Shattuck, who lists it as *Tempest* number 21, describes it as the rehearsal workbook of Ellis, who was Kean's stage manager.

176 Edmonds notes that at this point the green curtain descended, and after a pause the overture was played, allowing time for the stage to be cleared; according to the *Theatrical Journal*, twenty minutes were needed (19 August 1857, p. 261).

177 *Pictures of Travel*, p. 283. It is unclear whether the overture Andersen mentions was a feature changed after the first night or whether his memory was faulty; both Ellis and Edmonds note that the overture was played between the storm scene and the rest of the play, and contemporary reviews confirm this arrangement.

178 Both 4 July 1857, respectively p. 11 and p. 859.

explained the contrivance to Andersen: 'it turned out . . . that the whole ship was made of air-tight linen, which had been puffed out, and from which they now all at once let out the air; the great hulk shrunk together into a piece of cloth, and was hidden by the waves which rose to half the height of the stage' (Andersen, *Pictures of Travel*, p. 283).

Such nineteenth-century literalism in the handling of the storm scene extended well into the latter part of the twentieth century, as the Commentary to 1.1 shows. However, during the past seventy years, many productions have featured stylized presentations of the shipwreck, ranging from the simply non-illusionistic to the totally abstract. The reasons for this shift are many, ranging from a desire for originality, to a need for economy, to a belief in fidelity to the spirit of Shakespeare's original staging, to an acknowledgement that theatrical resources for the creation of illusion cannot compete with cinematic ones.

Robert Atkins's successive stagings of the play at the Open Air Theatre, Regent's Park, encapsulate several possible strategies for representing the shipwreck, his handling of the scene appearing constant in some respects, subject to change in others. The 1933 production saw 'more of tempestuous music than speech in the opening scene', while 1934 saw it 'ambitiously staged'.[179] In Ivor Brown's description, 'the tempestuous start [involved] a large number of young ladies [becoming] impermanent waves and undulat[ing] with conviction'; however, the way 'the barque went down by the boughs . . . rather suggested a crashed aeroplane than a foundering galleon' (*Observer*, 10/6/34). In 1938 Atkins again used 'a dance of sea nymphs to suggest the wild waters' as the ship 'founder[ed] among the wind-ruffled bushes', but in 1949 the vessel became 'a tiny rocking-horse ship, beside which as it was drawn in, the lords and mariners walked gravely, while the surrounding waves were mimed by dancers'.[180] Michael Benthall, similarly eschewing a realistic depiction of the storm in his 1951 Stratford production, seems to have followed Atkins's lead, with one reviewer complaining of his 'hotch-potch of symbolism, surrealism, mime, and pseudo-balletic movement' (*Birmingham Gazette*, 27/6/51).

179 Respectively, *The Times*, 13/9/33, and unidentified clipping, 6/6/34, Theatre Museum, London.
180 Respectively, *The Times*, 29/6/38, and Arthur Colby Sprague, 'Robert Atkins as a Shakespearian Director', in Robert Atkins, *An Unfinished Autobiography*, ed. George Rowell (London: Society for Theatre Research, 1994), p. 136. More recently, Adrian Noble showed a 'model sailing boat bob[bing] along on a turbulent sea of billowing silk, before . . . [moving] in for a cinematic close-up of the battling mariners and the frightened, garrulous nobility' (Charles Spencer, *Daily Telegraph*, 2/3/98).

8 Ralph Cleaver's sketches of Herbert Beerbohm Tree's 1904 production illustrate the continuing literalism of scenic design, with a realistic shipwreck and sets drawn from textual description; costume design shows a conventional approach to character, with a patriarchal Prospero, sprite-like Ariel, and missing-link Caliban (*The Sketch*, 21 September 1904, p. 347).

Nevertheless, another critic admired the

> most masterly opening when [the] transparency curtain . . . dissolves into
> the stranded ship with the long-drawn hiss of waves not yet roused to
> fury. There is a touch of real magic when one sees that these waves are
> the shrouded arms of swimming sea-maidens, though the mystery has
> been lost by the time the unmistakeably human wave-nymphs have been
> stirred to the tempest pitch.[181]

In the same year, Julius Gellner took an entirely different approach in
the inaugural production at Bernard Miles's Mermaid Theatre, a 'private
venture' located in his garden at St John's Wood, London.[182] Designed by
Michael Stringer and C. Walter Hodges and built at Nettlefield Film
Studios, the Mermaid was not a reproduction of a particular Elizabethan
theatre but a representation 'in style and general arrangement . . . of the
"gorgeous playing places" in which Shakespeare's plays were first performed' (programme). Reviews make clear that it had 'the ordinary appur-
tenances of the Elizabethan playhouse': apron stage with proscenium doors
at either side, inner stage (*sic*), and upper gallery with two windows, 'all
richly coloured and gilded like an elaborate inlaid cabinet'[183] or, in another
view, 'as gaily painted as an Eastern pagoda'.[184] Reviewers, like that of *The
Times*, were pleasantly surprised – not to say astounded – by 'the variety
and ingenuity of the stage effects' such architecture made possible:

> The play opens with a clap of thunder, and down from the roof come
> ropes and rigging, while a trap-door opens to represent the hold and the
> balustraded gallery becomes the poop. The scene ends, the crowd scatters,
> the rigging drops from the roof and vanishes through the trap-door,
> which closes, and in a twinkling the stage has become the island.

A. C. Sprague further noted that 'a ship's lantern swung back and forth'
in each of the two gallery windows and that 'Sailors, shouting orders, clung
for support to the pillars, or swarmed up the tackling'.[185] W. A. Darlington found the 'storm scene . . . so exciting' that he forgot critical custom

181 *Manchester Guardian*. Production photographs show the nymphs in 'sea-green
   draperies' (*Solihull & Warwick County News*, 30/6/51), from which protruded
   only their heads, covered in scarves.
182 *Observer*, 23/9/51; this first Mermaid should not be confused with the
   permanent one built for Miles in 1959 at Puddle Dock, Blackfriars.
183 *The Times*, 18/9/51; the notion of an inner stage has since been discredited by
   scholars of Elizabethan theatre and replaced by that of a discovery space.
184 *Sunday Times*, 23/9/51; see also *Theatre Newsletter*, 29/9/51, and *Observer*,
   23/9/51.
185 *Shakespearian Players and Performances* (1954), p. 157, quoted in Sturgess,
   Jacobean Private Theatre, p. 81.

and nearly applauded (*Daily Telegraph*, 18/9/51), while the *Sunday Times* mused on 'the unusual and unusually successsful notion of showing a ship-wreck by missing out the ship'. The *Theatre Newsletter* thought it 'no less lovely [a spectacle] than anything at Stratford' although, unlike Benthall's production, 'here the spectacle did not compete with the poetry'.[186]

Using a somewhat similar staging some years later at Stratford, Peter Brook gave his audience 'a magical storm of alternating fury and silence'; the wreck was 'swiftly suggested, silhouetted against an indeterminately violet-green storm-sky' (respectively, John Courtenay, *Truth*, 23/8/57, and J. C. Trewin, *Illustrated London News*, 24/8/57). Production photographs show that the whole stage was set as the deck of the ship, with railings running the width of the stage at front and back, ropes and rigging rising from the stage floor into the flies, and a '20ft. [high] top-mast lantern' near the front railing (*Evesham Journal*, 23/8/57). The play began in 'total dark-ness, except for a swaying ship's lantern, and then, with startling abrupt-ness, [there was] all the terror and the turmoil' of a shipwreck:

> Sailors . . . clambering with frantic haste over the perilously shaking rigging, officers dash[ing] from one group to another, shouting last-minute orders, fireballs flam[ing] intermittently from stem to stern and, amidst the growing confusion, the royal passengers . . . at prayer. Oarsmen start upon a last frenzied effort to keep the ship afloat and just before it sinks the cry 'All lost' rings out with agonising intensity.
>
> (Geoffrey Tarran, *Morning Advertiser*, 24/8/57)

As the ship foundered, the lantern swung 'slowly through half the compass, striking a note of vertigo . . . and we stare[d] at the stage, amazed that its rigid horizontal [could] seem to pitch and climb'.[187] Harold Hobson con-firmed the effectiveness of Brook's lantern, finding the 'half-dozen actors writhing and reeling . . . the customary dreary stuff' but the 'lighted lamp' a 'new and curiously exciting' addition to what had become hackneyed staging.[188]

186 Reviewers remarked that there was 'nothing of austerity about the costumes and properties' (*Observer*) and that the settings and costumes 'constantly made [the eye] happy' (*Evening Standard*, 21/9/51).
187 *Punch*, 21/8/57. In fact, several reviewers compared the wreck to the excitement of watching *Moby Dick* in CinemaScope.
188 *Sunday Times*, 18/8/57. Hobson in fact makes clear that Brook used two lanterns: 'the front lamp is of extraordinary height. When the play begins, it is lying flat on the stage, and then it rises to describe a huge semi-circle, and fall extinguished on the other side. As soon as it has drawn its great arc, another lamp, much smaller, at the back of the stage, behind the sinking mariners, gives a faint reflection of its tremendous span.'

9 John Barton's 1970 production, designed by Christopher Morley with Ann Curtis, handled the shipwreck simply and suggestively, using trap, lights and rigging to create location and effects.

While Brook's magical storm of 1957 still contained realistic action, Leo De Berardinis, in his 1986 production for the Bologna-based Cooperativa Nuova Scena company, only 'gravely hinted' at the tempest: 'a group of men-mummies . . . emerge[d] bit by bit from the dark background'[189] as the prelude to Wagner's *Parsifal* played.[190] White-haired 'zombies who slowly advance[d]', they were 'made heavy by unnatural costumes'; with their faces covered by masks that allowed only a glimpse of their dark eyes, they looked like 'exhausted human larvae'.[191] Speaking quietly in De Berardinis's characteristic 'musical-oratorial style',[192] they used their voices to imply the storm they had suffered, employing (in Grande's description) tones of 'fright, anguish, expectation, panic, bewilderment';

189 Maurizio Grande, *Rinascita*, 19/4/86. I am grateful to Roberta Gandolfi for supplying me with copies of reviews and to Elisabetta Noto for translating them and explaining their references to Italian popular culture.
190 Giovanna Zucconi, *Paese Sera*, 5/4/86, and others.
191 Zucconi supplies the information about masks, while quotations are from, respectively, Sergio Colomba, *Carlino Spettacoli*, 5/4/86; Gianni Manzella, *Il Manifesto*, 1/4/86; and Ugo Ronfani, *Il Giorno*, 6/4/86.
192 Ugo Volli, *La Repubblica Spettacoli*, 5/4/86.

the effect created was of the characters reliving the storm as they spoke.[193] Similarly, Nicholas Hytner's handling of the scene in his 1988 RSC production was notable for its eerie and effective stillness. Although the production opened with music and the sounds of sea, wind and thunder, my chief memory is of the Master swaying slightly in a crow's nest suspended from the flies, a line of mariners ranged horizontally across the stage moving in the same rhythm, and dialogue quietly spoken in the hush of real and impending disaster.[194] At the same time, the effect was very unreal, reminiscent of slow motion without being played in slow motion: one critic described the actors as 'sleepwalking, as if hypnotised' (D. A. N. Jones, *Sunday Telegraph*, 28/5/89).

Contemporary avoidance of realism in the presentation of the storm scene is also due to the current emphasis on finding conceptual frameworks for the play. For example, Glen Walford's 1984 production at the Everyman Theatre, Liverpool, presented the island 'as a circus ring peopled by clowns and acrobats' (Martin Hoyle, *Financial Times*, 31/1/84). As Hoyle explains, the action began with ring-master Prospero standing on 'the central podium . . . crack[ing] his whip like something out of *Lulu*. The company [then] enter[ed] as a parade of clowns', with 'the grey-skinned Ariel [trundling on] in a giant hamster's wheel[,] the young lovers . . . suspended in a skeletal crescent moon high above the action[, and other] Actors awaiting their cue sit[ting] round the ring adding to the isle's noises by humming or playing instruments'. Another reviewer makes clear that these 'fantastic' clowns 'spout[ed] the speeches of the drowning bosun, mariners, and courtiers,' their screams 'gleefully orchestrate[d by a star-bangled Ariel and sneering Prospero]'.[195]

In a similar vein, Declan Donnellan's 1988 Cheek by Jowl production treated the play as metatheatre,[196] interpreting Prospero as an actor-

---

193 Anna Adriani, *La Repubblica*, 3/4/86.

194 My notes add that the chaos of flickering lights in which we could see the still figures eventually gave way to an eerie peacefulness and a quiet wind. Christopher Edwards gives a similar impression: 'At first the storm rages furiously. A fluttering blue silken topsail descends, the Master appears suspended on his bridge high above, and his crew brace themselves against the torrent on the tilting deck below. Then all is weirdly silent' (*Spectator*, 3/6/89). Edwards adds that not only did this staging allow the dialogue to be heard, but it also created a sense of the storm's magic.

195 Irene McManus, *Guardian*, 27/1/84. Hoyle adds that the production's textual cuts could 'be condoned, given the Everyman's predominantly young audience'.

196 The most widely admired metatheatrical production of *The Tempest*, that of Giorgio Strehler, is discussed above and in the Commentary, as is that of Yukio Ninagawa.

manager: the stage was presented as a rehearsal/dressing room, with the set consisting simply of piano, costume rail, two baskets, and dressing table with lighted mirror. Consequently, the storm was presented as an acting improvisation, with the thunder hammered out in piano chords:[197] 'The actor who is to play Prospero, wearing dark glasses and slicked back hair, rushes manically around the auditorium controlling the proceedings while the other characters, in jeans, T-shirts and tracksuits, mime the shipwreck like first-year students at drama school.'[198] Robert Lepage took the same approach in his 1992 production of *La Tempête*, setting the play in a 'rehearsal room equipped with a balance bar, a wall of mirrors, some gym lockers, and a couple of green-topped conference tables', which were 'pushed together so that the cast [could] sit around them with scripts in hands'.[199] A photograph by Emmanuel Valette shows a small square stage, with tiled walls on two conjoining sides: the mirror with practice bar in front covers the SR wall, and four slender gym lockers occupy the centre of the SL wall, on which a clock also hangs; most of the chequer-board floorspace is taken up by the tables, which form a square in the centre of the stage. Simple wooden chairs surround the tables, above which hangs a neon strip-light. Pat Donnelly explains that, as the play began, 'A director . . . [went] over the script with his cast', while 'To one side a musician twirl[ed] an instrument that [made] harp-like sounds'; Ray Conlogue adds that an 'interpolated opening speech, where the director/Prospero compare[d] *The Tempest* to the writing of Jorge Borges', made clear that the audience was watching 'a rehearsal of the play'. Donnelly notes that the storm scene 'arrived' when 'Suddenly the tables beg[a]n to undulate while a tiny toy sailing ship move[d] across them', but that the movement from 'rehearsal' to full-scale 'production' was very gradual: 'Actors reading dutifully from scripts blossom[ed], step-by-step[,] into full-blown Shake-spearean characters. Only in Act V [did] they graduate into full make-up and costume.' Other reviewers make clear that little by little the actors used a prop, a costume, a small gesture to effect a very gradual transition to full realization of the play.[200]

---

197 Details are drawn from my notes of the performance at the Donmar Warehouse, London, on 23/11/88.
198 Charles Spencer, *Daily Telegraph*, 28/11/88. Martin Hoyle, who reviewed the production while it was on tour, more generously describes them as 'miming and humming up a storm on the bare stage' (*Financial Times*, 20/10/88).
199 Respectively, Pat Donnelly, *Montreal Gazette*, 7/6/93, and Ray Conlogue, *Toronto Globe and Mail*.
200 Marion Thébaud, *Le Figaro*; Robert Lévesque, *Montréal Le Devoir*; Urs Jenny, *Der Spiegel* 46 (1992), p. 262.

As my discussion has already implied, twentieth-century preoccupation with thematic approaches to *The Tempest* has affected not only the spectacle of the storm scene but also the design of Prospero's island. While the Restoration adapters and their eighteenth-, nineteenth- and even early twentieth-century successrs were content to depict luxuriant foliage, golden sands, gleaming seas and any other natural feature mentioned in the text, modern directors and designers often use the set to signal their approach to the meaning of the play: the set becomes metaphor rather than illustration. Although this development is fairly recent, the potential for it was created early in the twentieth century with the arrival of permanent sets: that is, a single (although often modifiable) setting in place of myriad scenes to depict each new location Shakespeare creates.

Permanent sets were introduced as a means of achieving the speed and continuity that had been possible on the bare Elizabethan stage;[201] they acted as functional statements of a production's style, but did not contribute to an overall interpretation of the play's meaning. J. Gower Park's design for Ben Iden Payne's 1938 Stratford production, for example, was inspired by Cubism, as one reviewer explained: 'Prospero's island is represented not by palm trees and wooded vistas, but by an arrangement of wooden bricks . . . [which] carve out a seashore of red rock mounting up to a promontory which serves Prospero as a pulpit'; however, despite the design's abstraction, it conveyed a suggestion, 'deepened by the painted seascape', that 'the magic island lay just off the shores of Devon' (*The Times*, 3/5/38). Black-and-white production photographs do not so much suggest bricks as huge machine cogwheels stacked concentrically on each other, the largest at the bottom and the smallest on top, in the middle of the stage; two flat, multi-sided 'bricks' are set DSL and DSR, while a false proscenium, painted with undulent tree-trunks at the sides and unrealistic foliage at the top, is set behind the actual proscenium arch. The backcloth is painted with a view of placid water, identified in several reviews as a blue

201 Scenic productions of Shakespeare had almost as much (if not more) time devoted to scene-changes as to playing of the text: for example, the first performance of Kean's *Tempest* lasted five and a half hours, even though the individual timings for each act in Edmonds's promptbook amount only to two hours and nine minutes. By 7 July, an hour had been shaved off the time needed by the 140 stage-hands for scene-changes (see *Illustrated London News*, 11 July 1857, p. 35), while Edmonds's pb notes an even better final playing-time of three hours and twenty minutes. For discussion of changing modes of Shakespeare production, see, for example, J. L. Styan, *The Shakespeare Revolution* (Cambridge: Cambridge University Press, 1977) and my *Harley Granville Barker: A Preface to Modern Shakespeare*.

lagoon, while in front of it, below but parallel to the horizon, is a line of 'bricks', here arranged like the teeth of a saw.

Critical reaction to Park's set varied, but discussion centred on its aesthetic effect rather than on any possible meaning it might have conveyed. The reviewer for the *Birmingham Gazette* was eventually won over by it:

> Prospero is seen silhouetted on a [C]ubist conglomeration of rock which looked like nothing so much as the end of a promenade in course of construction at one of our more popular seaside resorts. Presently, as the storm subsides, the lights go up and we see that . . . [it] was really a boy's box of bricks strewn about the stage . . . which was all angles and flat surfaces. The curious thing is that this conjunction of Shakespeare with Cubism is effective . . . [T]hese rocks . . . really did suggest a wild and rugged coast.   (3/5/38)

On the other hand, the *Observer* reviewer remained unconvinced: he found that the

> rectangular and triangular slabs of old red sandstone . . . painfully resembles the yard of a brick and tile works or a dump for red Cheshire cheeses. This hot and raddled country is harsh to the eye and destructive of that fancy in which the play abounds. The view is happier after sunset when the lagoon begins to resemble a most desirable bathing-pool.
>   (8/5/38)

Ultimately, Park's set elicited no more than a revelation of personal taste from the reviewers. The only significant comment comes from *The Times* critic, who praised the set for its 'two great virtues of speed and simplicity' and for the freedom it allowed the actors – but who made no mention of any meaning it may have contributed. Nevertheless, the uncomfortableness of the *Observer* critic with what he saw as Park's 'harsh' and 'destructive' stage-setting points to the potential of design in creating atmosphere – atmosphere that can then contribute powerfully to an audience's reception of the play. For example, Loudon Sainthill's set design for Michael Benthall's 1951 Stratford production arguably complemented Michael Redgrave's portrayal of Prospero as a man struggling with the weight of his magical powers. Sainthill's design generated much critical comment, both positive and negative, and although none of the reviewers explicitly remark on its meaning, the strong impressions the set created clearly helped to shape their experience of the play.

Many reviewers shared the impression of the *Daily Telegraph* critic that Sainthill's grey-green island was somehow submerged, its surface consisting 'of submarine plants, sea shells and sharp pinnacles of rock'. The *Daily Express* critic liked 'the floating mystery of a cave under the sea [where w]eird stalagmites melt into aquarium-like transformation scenes [and r]ocks turn into elves', while the *Daily Worker* more graphically described the 'great sea shells that become "shapes" and do [Prospero's] bidding'. *The Times* commented, admiringly, that 'all things seemed to aspire to the shape of cactus', while the *Scotsman* praised the 'dominant low pinnacles of grey rock rising abrubtly from a level mist-swept plain'. However, the reviewer for *Truth* found the island grotesque: 'On either side of the foreground were rocky heights of macabre contours; and high-water mark was decked with giant whelk shells and smooth boulders from beneath which crawled sinister, gargoyle-faced goblins.' While this critic passed no judgement on the effects of the island's appearance, the *Daily Worker* found that despite the 'fashionably pointed Gothic mountains . . . it is like the island of a nightmare. It should be like the island of a dream.'[202] Both these comments, but especially the last, are particularly telling of the way Sainthill's design, as well as Redgrave's performance, helped to wrest the play away from the cosy interpretation many reviewers still expected.

By the time the play was next seen at Stratford, in Peter Brook's 1957 production, at least one reviewer was able to make an explicit connection between design and the director's overall approach to the play: Roy Walker commented that although the play's 'scenery [had never been] more obtrusively scenic', Brook's interpretation of Prospero as 'a man whose wrongs haunted him through the winding caverns and overgrown jungles of the mind . . . largely justified the strangely subterranean settings and tangled hothouse vegetation' that Brook had himself designed.[203] Production photographs show that 1.2 was set in Prospero's cave, a 'plain, non-distracting, action-inviting, cavernous court', which took up the whole of the stage and

202 All reviews are dated 27/6/51, except for the *Daily Worker* (29/6/51), *Truth* (6/7/51) and *Scotsman* (?/51). In addition to the reviews quoted above, the *Spectator* thought the island's 'seaward prospect suggest[ed] . . . [it was] part of an archipelago of ant-hills' (29/6/51), while Ivor Brown in a 1952 *Observer* review condemned the 'stony space with stalactites growing the wrong way up' for being 'as monotonous as shiversome'. While Brown further commented that the set was 'both gloomy in its grey monochrome and nonsensical in relation to the coral tints and gold-glitter of the poet's rocks and beaches', the *Scotsman* found it a 'compelling study in grisaille' (7/4/52). The *Nottingham Guardian* noted in 1951 that 'Most of the scenic pieces and islandic tropical properties [were] located on the fore-stage, and through them the actors ma[d]e their entrances and exits.'

203 'Unto Caesar: A Review of Recent Productions', *Shakespeare Survey* 11 (1958), p. 135. It should be noted that Brook also designed the costumes and helped to compose the music.

apron; both sides of the proscenium were covered by huge rocks with cavernous openings, which in one view made 'somewhat tiresome exits'.[204] Photographs also show swirling rock formations at the back of Prospero's vast cell, which reflected 'shimmering light from the [unseen] water' outside it (*Oxford Mail*, 14/8/57); there were three rock-seats downstage, one at right, one a few feet to its left and another at left. Several reviews also mention that Brook's sets seamlessly transformed themselves from one scene to the next: 'Long, wide vistas open and close between the towering rocks: at one moment it is luxuriant with growth, at the next [it shows] bare sea-swept caves.'[205]

While Brook's set simply suggested a link between the island's appearance and Prospero's state of mind, other designs more explicitly determine audiences' understanding of the play. For example, the programme note for Michael Bogdanov's 1978 Young Vic production, which was designed by Paul Bannister, states that, for Prospero, 'all action has become a form of mental chess. Trapped inside his head [he] sits in exile and dreams of revenge on the brother who deposed him.' Consequently, the play began with 'A portly, bearded exile looking a bit like Henrik Ibsen sit[ting] at a white table in the centre of the octagonal stage. A bottle of vin rouge and some cheese [were] in front of him, [and] chansons [could] be heard in the background'; he continued to sit there 'until Act 5 while the action rage[d] about him'.[206]

Although very different from Bannister's, Tony Tripp's set for Gale Edwards's 1990 Melbourne Theatre Company production also helped to locate Prospero's mind as the source of the play's action. Tripp's set comprised a 'silken, sandy disc' with 'a huge revolving sculpture' at centre: one side of it was 'chiselled into a stone-like representation of Prospero's head', while the 'cave-shaped' back, 'in effect Prospero's brain', was 'left open'

---

204 The first quotation is from the *Evesham Journal*, 23/8/57, and the second from Ellen Foxon, *Birmingham Weekly Post*, 16/8/57.

205 T. C. Worsley, *New Statesman*, 24/8/57. Although Brook's sets changed from one scene to the next, the basic set was permanent: production photographs suggest that changes were effected, for example, by opening or closing the doors of the cave, by suspending streamers from the flies, and by changing the backcloth.

206 Respectively, Michael Billington, *Guardian*, and B. A. Young, *Financial Times*, both 29/11/78. Billington thought 'Bill Wallis's Prospero carrie[d] admirably the burden of having not only to act but also to react to the strange fantasies that inhabit[ed] his head', while Young felt that his fantasies should have been more elaborately represented on stage: the idea of a 'purely mental *Tempest*', though good, was inappropriate to such a Spartan production. Billington notes that the storm itself was 'represented by a cluster of figures in military uniform who for once allow[ed] us to hear Shakespeare's words'.

10 and 11 Photographs of Act 5, Scene 1, *c.* lines 266–75 of Peter Brook's 1957 production, designed by the director, and of Nicholas Hytner's 1988 production, designed by David Fielding, exemplify both changes and continuities in late twentieth-century theatrical treatment of the play. Although John Wood's anguished Prospero had its roots in the fallible–human tradition established by John Gielgud, John Kane's recognizably human Caliban looked very different from Alec Clunes's simian monster (Brian Bedford's Ariel can incidentally be seen behind the latter). While Fielding provided an abstract set and more or less contemporary costuming, Brook's use of period costume and scenery suggestive of Prospero's state of mind still finds contemporary adherents: although his scenic representation is now outmoded, his provision of a conceptual framework for design is standard.

(Rosemary Neill, *The Australian*, 17/5/90). Other reviewers give further details of the sculpture's appearance, describing it variously as 'the eroded head of Prospero', 'a huge, shattered head half-buried in the sand', and 'the massive head of a classical statue, fractured and tilted into the sand'.[207] Not only was Prospero accordingly played by John Gaden as 'a man of near irreconcilable extremes', 'complex, confused and erratic',[208] but Frank Gallacher's Caliban made a spectacular entrance 'when his webbed hand grotesquely protrude[d], spider-like, from inside the sculpture's mouth', thereby 'suggesting his source is indeed Prospero'.[209]

Building a much more complex framework for the play, Romanian director Liviu Ciulei's 1981 production for the Guthrie Theater, Minneapolis, was 'deliberately eclectic', reflecting his concept of Prospero's magic as 'a metaphor for the power of art', of Prospero himself as 'the magician–artist–scientist', and of his island as at once 'a theatrical space' and 'a studio or laboratory' for exploring the human 'mind, soul and morality' (director's programme notes). After re-designing the Guthrie stage to make it 'wider and much deeper', Ciulei, who designed the set himself, 'placed a large rectangular platform stage over the familiar . . . thrust, bringing things even closer to the audience'.[210] He then surrounded the stage with

> a moat of blood (a less aggressive image than it sounds) filled with cultural artifacts from handless clocks to a suit of armor, the Mona Lisa and, on shore, familiar sculptures, a head of a Venetian horse from San Marco sitting next to a stuffed chicken pulled from a Rauschenberg collage. A broken rowboat, obviously Prospero's entree [*sic*] to his island, [lay] in ruin at the front of the stage. Scientific equipment from Galileo's period [sat] over a battered and legless grand piano propped up, as [was] the stage itself, by books.[211]

207 Respectively, Chris Boyd, *Melbourne Times*, 16/5/90; Helen Thomson, *Sunday Herald*, 20/5/90; and Paula Carr, *Melbourne Report*, 6/90.

208 Respectively, Boyd, and Rosemary Neill. Neill continues that 'upon acknowledging his darker side, [Prospero made] peace with his enemies and himself'. Another critic, however, offered quite a different view of Gaden's performance, seeing him as 'a gentle, dignified figure, less authoritarian than is sometimes the case and one for whom forgiveness comes just as easily as anger. He exudes warmth towards his daughter, and towards the audience, drawing them into his confidence' (Leonard Radic, *The Age*, 18/5/90).

209 Respectively, Carr and Thomson.

210 Respectively, David Hawley, uc, 14/6/81, and Mike Steele, *Minneapolis Tribune*, 13/6/81.

211 Steele. The piano was workable: characters 'hammer[ed] out everything from sprightly tunes to symphonies' (Steele), with Miranda at one point playing Mozart's Sonata K. 545 (Jonathan Saville, *San Diego Reader*, 9/81).

In addition to the objects noted by this reviewer, there were also 'a Greek marble Venus, a modern rifle', 'a smashed typewriter', 'a vintage cash register', and 'chairs';[212] T. E. Kalem, assuming the armour contained 'an unseen corpse' floating 'face down in the moat', found that prop 'most disquieting'. Critical reaction makes clear that the set helped the audience to think through the metaphysical implications of the play without predetermining what they would be for each viewer. For Jack Kroll, the setting 'transmit[ted] the feeling of a great force that has stopped history in its tracks with thunderbolt power'. For Frank Rich, it signified that human 'attempts to create a beautiful and humane civilization have always, finally, been drowned in the blood of wars', but that Prospero's success might bring, 'at long last, an end to history's self-destructive cycle'. Kalem's similar analysis implies a more modest optimism, seeing as perpetual the struggle between artistic order and existential chaos.

Leo De Berardinis's set for his own 1986 production appears to have worked on similar lines to Ciulei's. The director, who intended to present the play as a journey 'towards knowledge and awareness', set it in an 'empty scenic space' with a 'contrivance of mirrors [and] panels' that went up and down; 'white [was] the predominant note' for both set and costumes.[213] The panels converged towards a bi-level background, and the mirrors not only doubled, multiplied and distanced the images reflected in them, but in so doing blurred the line between illusion and reality.[214] There were also two curtains on stage, an 'extremely traditional one, vertical, in red velvet, which open[ed], as convention requires, at the beginnings of the two parts in which the show [was] divided', and another, 'white and horizontal', which changed the shape of the playing-space[215] and 'allow[ed] illusionist games of mysterious displacements'.[216] Various objects were dotted around the stage: Maurizio Grande notes 'a little tree in a small vase at the centre of the scene' and 'a globe on the left reflected in another on the right'; Ugo Ronfani 'fossils and geometric forms'; Gastone Geron 'shells, corals, branches of peach-tree and almond-tree'; and Giovanna Zucconi drums and a xylophone. The last-mentioned critic called the set 'a Magrittian island, floating amongst the clouds' and, indeed, Ronfani identified it

---

212 Respectively, Jack Kroll, *Newsweek*, 29/6/81; Frank Rich, *New York Times*, 7/4/81; T. E. Kalem, *Times*, 27/7/81; and David Hawley, *St Paul Dispatch*, 12/6/81.

213 Respectively, Anna Adriani, *La Repubblica*, 3/4/86; Claudio Cumani, *Carlino*, 25/3/86; Sergio Columba, *Carlino Spettacoli*, 5/4/86; and Adriani.

214 My description is drawn from Giovanna Zucconi, *Paese Sera*, 5/4/86; Maurizio Grande, *Rinascita*, 19/4/86; and Ugo Ronfani, *Il Giorno*, 6/4/86.

215 Ugo Volli, *La Repubblica Spettacoli*, 5/4/86.

216 Gastone Geron, *Il Giornale*, 6/4/86.

as the 'stony island shown in the backdrop . . . of Magritte's "Chateau des Pyrenees"'. Reviewers' comments suggest that the set helped to convey the mystical impression De Berardinis had intended: Zucconi regarded the production as 'a Zen exercise'; Ugo Volli felt it 'allude[d] with extreme modesty to a cosmic mystery'; and Geron thought it restored the play's 'elevating magic element, without repeating [Strehler's] exquisitely meta-theatrical projection'.

Although Ciulei's and De Berardinis's sets seem to have successfully provided rich cultural frameworks for the play, designers' concepts can sometimes lead to a confusing ambiguity, with the audience unsure whether to read the image on stage as literal, metaphorical or both. For example, Maria Bjornson's set for Ron Daniels's 1982 RSC production was 'A great ship . . . foundered on a hostile shore, her timbers gaping, her back broken', with 'her massive spars', 'strained planking', 'elaborately-carved rails' and 'storm-rent canvas' all clearly visible;[217] another reviewer called it 'a decaying hulk' reminiscent of 'the Ancient Mariner's doomed vessel finally at rest'.[218] While most reviews admired the 'astonishing scene change from ship to island where the ground literally swallows up the vessel' of scene 1 'to reveal Prospero standing on his own wreck, his staff raised to make the storm',[219] critical understanding of Bjornson's conception covered a wide spectrum. One reviewer commented on its useful ambivalence: 'The shredded rigging in the background suggested the luxurious growth which some of the castaways see on the isle, while in the for[e]ground the rippled sand[,] which half buries the old ship, invokes the barren land the others find' (*South Wales Argus*, 12/8/82). However, others objected that the 'vast static object absolutely confine[d] the action to one place' and that it rather undermined Prospero's version of events: the ship 'look[ed] more impressive than you might guess from the paranoid tale he tells his daughter'.[220] Yet another critic viewed the set emblematically: 'Prospero's island is . . . revealed as a broken ship of state, with a severely crushed foredeck, leaning

217 *Evesham Journal & Four Shires Advertiser*, 19/8/82.
218 *Morning Star*, 16/8/82. Production photos show the prow, reduced to its beams, facing SR and tilting DS; all that remains of the rest of the ship are masts and rigging. A tall mast with huge crow's nest is C, US of the prow and tilted towards SR; one mast US of the prow leans SL and appears to rest on the crow's nest, while another mast running from SR to SL appears to hang suspended above the stage. Looped and tattered sails are draped between the crow's nest and the SL side of the suspended mast.
219 Respectively, *Shropshire Star*, 12/8/82, and Ned Chaillet, *The Times*, 13/8/82.
220 Respectively, Gareth Lloyd Evans, *Stratford Herald*, 20/8/82, and Robert Cushman, *Observer*, 15/8/82.

12 For Ron Daniels's 1982 Stratford production, Derek Jacobi was a youthful and vigorous Prospero, Alice Krige a credibly young Miranda and Mark Rylance an other-worldly Ariel; Maria Bjornson's permanent set, first seen in Act 1, Scene 2, produced both literal and symbolic readings.

mast with crow's nest, and tattered sails' (Michael Coveney, *Financial Times*, 13/8/82).

Similar dissent about its significance greeted Richard Hudson's set for Jonathan Miller's second colonialist interpretation of the play, staged at the Old Vic in 1988. The steeply raked stage extended over the orchestra pit and the first three rows of the stalls,[221] and its permanent set, covered for the storm scene by a heaving silk sail that gave the impression of waves, consisted of two hollow white cubes, ten feet tall: one emerged from the blue cyclorama at the back of the stage, while the other was set at an angle midstage among sandy-yellow rocks.[222] The cube at centre contained a telescope derided by one critic as 'a piece of intellectual luggage' not 'earn[ing] its keep as a stage prop', since Prospero never looked through it; however, another read it as signalling his status 'as a scientific magus'.[223]

221 Roy Farndon's interview with Richard Hudson, *Independent*, 12/10/88.
222 Details are drawn from my notes of the performance of 20/10/88 and from Nigel Andrews, 'Critics' Forum' (BBC Radio 3), 15/10/88.
223 Respectively, John Peter, *Sunday Times*, 16/10/88, and Michael Billington, *Guardian*, 12/10/88.

Yet another, seeing Prospero rather as 'a magus suspended between the acquired magical practices of Caliban's mother, Sycorax, and the late Renaissance breakthroughs in science and astronomy', found 'These tensions . . . reflected in [the] extraordinary tilted geometric setting . . . Here is a strange and dangerous limbo between Old and New Worlds, Prospero's square walled cell, decorated merely with a white Copernican telescope, nestling awkwardly against the cream boulders of a surreal landscape' (Michael Coveney, *Financial Times*, 12/10/88). As these quotations suggest, the traffic between design and meaning is two-way: sets do not simply determine a reading of the play, but are themselves read in the light of prior understanding of what the play means – or in the light of programme notes, which themselves increasingly set the parameters of interpretation for a particular production.[224]

The design possibilities discussed so far do not, of course, exhaust the manifold potentialities of *The Tempest*. As Margaret Webster rather conservatively noted, 'You can make it mystical, political, psychiatric; Prospero can be anything from God to Lyndon B. Johnson in a huff; Ariel and Caliban have been interpreted in staggeringly different ways according to the personal whims of designers and directors and the social background of their time.'[225] Indeed, Michael Bogdanov recently directed *The Tempest in Butetown*, 'a production for BBC Wales . . . which sets the play in Cardiff's notorious docklands and draws its cast and much of its crew from the area's famous "rainbow society"'.[226] Filmed on location and reflecting 'the residents' perspective [that] the past 40 years have seen their homes, their way of life, indeed the very name of their area [Tiger Bay] sacrificed to the redevelopers', the adaptation turns 'the usurping Duke of Milan and his cronies . . . [into] property developers' and makes 'Prospero and his sprites . . . the guardians of the true Butetown . . . the film cuts between Shakespeare's take on dispossession and the men and women on the street having their say'. As fact and fiction mirror each other in this *Tempest*, reality becomes a design concept used to critique commercial values.

224 Indeed, the programme for Miller's 1988 production contains an article on 'The Emergence of Science' by Martin Cinnamond and extracts from the work of Frances Yates about Renaissance occult philosophy, as well as an article on New World 'Discoveries' by Gordon McMullan and extracts from Mannoni's *Prospero and Caliban*. The printed text is complemented by a wealth of visual material depicting Renaissance astronomers and occultists, as well as astronomical diagrams and instruments and occult books.
225 *Don't Put Your Daughter on the Stage*, p. 120.
226 Brian Logan, *Guardian*, 12/7/96, section 2, p. 6. The programme was broadcast on BBC2 Wales on Sunday, 9 March 1997, at 9:30 p.m.

EPILOGUE

It is appropriate to a play like *The Tempest* to end not with a conclusion but with an 'additional word'. The play itself ends without any sense of closure: uniquely in Shakespeare, the character Prospero, not the actor playing the part, speaks the Epilogue, inviting the audience to release him from the island and to return him to Milan 'With the help of [their] good hands' (10). This opening-out of the action to a potential rather than a certain future invites speculation, just as Antonio's silence at the end of the play does: witness, as one example, W. H. Auden's imaginative response to *The Tempest*'s openness in his poem *The Sea and the Mirror* (1944), in which the story continues as Prospero packs and the courts of Milan and Naples set sail for home. This openness can also create moments in the theatre where the play refuses to end: as Prospero asks 'Let your indulgence set me free' (20) and then stands immobile, waiting for the requested release, the audience very often sits silent, expecting something else to happen, some signal that the play is over, not realizing that it is up to them to declare it done.

But, of course, as I hope this introduction has demonstrated, there is no way in which *The Tempest* is ever over and done with: it is a play whose 'charms crack not' (5.1.2), its protean nature finding ever new ways to voice contemporary social, political and cultural concerns and to voice them powerfully. Although I have tried to show a broad range of the play's possibilities in this Introduction, the following Commentary shows that my selection in fact captures only a narrow spectrum of the play's rich theatrical life during the past three hundred and ninety years.

LIST OF CHARACTERS

ALONSO, *King of Naples*
SEBASTIAN, *his brother*
PROSPERO, *the right Duke of Milan*
ANTONIO *his brother, the usurping Duke of Milan*
FERDINAND, *son to the King of Naples*
GONZALO, *an honest old councillor*
ADRIAN and FRANCISCO, *lords*
CALIBAN, *a savage and deformed slave*
TRINCULO, *a jester*
STEPHANO, *a drunken butler*
MASTER *of a ship*
BOATSWAIN
MARINERS
MIRANDA, *daughter to Prospero*
ARIEL, *an airy spirit*
IRIS
CERES
JUNO ⎬ *spirits*
NYMPHS
REAPERS

The scene an uninhabited island

THE TEMPEST

✛ ✛
✛

ACT 1   SCENE 1

A tempestuous noise of thunder and lightning heard.

Enter a SHIPMASTER *and a* BOATSWAIN

MASTER Boatswain!

BOATSWAIN Here, master. What cheer?

MASTER Good; speak to th' mariners. Fall to 't yarely, or we run ourselves
  aground. Bestir, bestir!   *Exit* [MASTER.] *Enter* MARINERS

BOATSWAIN Heigh, my hearts! Cheerly, cheerly, my hearts! Yare,   5
  yare! Take in the topsail. Tend to th'master's whistle. Blow till
  thou burst thy wind, if room enough!

1.1 For the way in which the architecture of Shakespeare's stage represented the ship, and for
Restoration stagings, see the Introduction. Shadwell's painted scene was revealed during the
overture, played by twenty-four violins, harpsichords and theorbos and accompanied by
voices; the orchestra, playing in the pit rather than in the gallery, was twice the usual size
(Edward J. Dent, quoted in Vickers, *Shakespeare: The Critical Heritage*, vol. 1, p. 8).

   Eighteenth- and nineteenth-century productions usually relegated 1.1 to the second scene
of the play and/or cut its dialogue. Garrick's 1756 opera opened with Ariel coming on stage to
sing 'Arise, arise, ye subterranean winds' and to speak 1.2.196–206a (with a change to the
future tense); she exited to 'repeated flashes of lightning, and claps of thunder'. Both Kemble
versions began with Shakespeare's 1.2, taking it up to 374 and adding new material; the shipwreck became 2.1, but none of Shakespeare's dialogue was spoken. The scenery showed a
storm-driven ship at sea; Ariel and other spirits assisted the tempest, the chorus singing
'Arise! ye spirits of the storm!': they all disappeared after the ship sank. Macready restored
the shipwreck to the play's opening but omitted Shakespeare's dialogue, as did Phelps. The
latter presented the spectacle by means of panoramic scenery, which first showed the
Neapolitan fleet sailing over a calm sea (this concealed a 'double row of trick waters to
change to rough sea'). The soft humming music that accompanied its passage was soon
replaced by storm sounds, while a gauze 'storm Horizon of Clouds [appeared] at c' containing 'spirits of every imaginable and fanciful form'; they disappeared to reveal a 'Dark Storm
Horizon' and 'two additional rows of storm waters'. A ship was trucked on from L2E to C of
the working water pieces, which were formed of whalebone flaps and aprons and so able to
yield to the ship as it veered about the stage and finally foundered on a rock; thereupon, a

dark cloud cloth descended, the ground cloth (with ground row) was pulled up, and the whole enclosed (Phelps/Creswick pb).

Some of Shakespeare's dialogue began to be restored early in the twentieth century, although there had been three notable earlier exceptions: Garrick (1757), who retained about two-thirds of the original 1.1 dialogue; Burton, whose fidelity in restoring some of Shakespeare's text was all the more remarkable considering a Kemble/Dryden version of the play had been revived in New York's Bowery a year before; and Phelps, staging the play for a third time in 1855. Poel's influence on Atkins led to his playing a relatively full text in his Old Vic productions, a fact 'repeatedly mentioned at the time' (Sprague, 'Atkins', p. 134), but his 1933 and 1934 outdoor stagings incorporated elements adapted from Shadwell's and Garrick's operas: for instance, in 1933, a Singing Devil performed Purcell's 'Arise, Ye Subterranean Winds' at the start of the play (programme). Lena Ashwell was most unusual in cutting only a half-line from 1.1; Ariel was on stage during the storm but the pb notes no business for him.

Although many twentieth-century productions have used elaborate shipboard sets for 1.1, as the notes to osd show, directors have increasingly played the opening scene on the permanent set for Prospero's island; consequently, it is useful to note here, rather than in the commentary for 1.2, the salient features of some recent settings. Farrah's basic set for the Williams/Brook production was a cyclorama, 'The bottom half of [which] . . . [was] made of perspex, the top half of cinema-screen plastic lit by four projectors on trolleys . . . giv[ing] the idea of a magic wall, a mirror which splinters whenever and wherever you want it to' (Farrah, programme). Some critics criticized its 'painted or projected abstract decorations of varying patterns' as a meaningless hodge-podge, while others appreciated the set's flexible simplicity (*EJ* 5/4/63); in addition to the cyclorama, there was 'A kind of conveyor belt, flush with the stage', which carried actors, props and scenery on and off (*WA* 6/4/63). Koltai's set for Jones had some similar features: it comprised 'a huge white saucer dominated by a white disc and globe, like a dead moon and sun. Across these move[d] projections of the play's imagery – storm-clouds, water, brain-coral, dense green leaves' (Ronald Bryden, *O* 21/7/68). Similarly, Bury's set for Hall (1974) consisted of 'a raised disc with an upstage promontory' that 'descend[ed] to floor level for the entrance to the cell'; 'artificiality [was] underlined with wafer-thin trees smothered in leaves like sequins and an orange sun suspended on two visible cords' (Irving Wardle, *T* 6/3/74). In addition, 'tall sliding flats [were used] for scene-changes, sometimes with a magical effect, as when two flats, crossing at the back of the stage, leave there when they pass a blossom-hung tree that was not there before' (B. A. Young, *FT* 6/3/74). A less admiring view called the 'jagged, mobile, mirrored sets . . . the essence of primitive chic' (Michael Billington, *G* 6/3/74).

The 1970s also marked a trend towards stark sets. Healey's was 'Bosch-like', with a 'vast, glittering silver funnel for elemental action' (Wardle, *T* 8/5/68). Miller's was 'austere' and the costumes 'bleak', the staging simple 'on a rather ugly ramp' (respectively, R. B. Marriott, *St* 18/6/70; Marriott; Wardle, *T* 16/6/70). Barton's was 'stark', its 'plain blue walls sloping inwards to meet a vast wedge-shaped shutter suspended overhead. The effect [was] like looking down a dark corridor, with at the end a square black door'; the 'latticed white roof [of this wind-tunnel] heave[d] and bellie[d] ingeniously into sail, ceiling or clothes-line', while 'Naked-looking spirits vaguely undulate[d] behind the transparent blue walls' (respectively, Elizabeth Knapp, *TES*, 23/10/70; John Barber, *DT* 17/10/70; Bryden, *O* 18/10/70; Benedict Nightingale, *NS* 23/10/70; see note to 1.2.239–46). Burge's 'austerely plain stage' showed 'a large circular [severe grey] island surrounded by smaller hexagons stained with a triangular green motif' (respectively, Eric Shorter, *DT*; Charles Lewsen, *T*, both 28/2/72). Hack 'Visually . . . stripped the play down to essentials': 'Prospero's island [was] an irregularly shaped raked wooden platform from which [rose] a single scaffolding tree, and sea and sky [were] represented by a silvery-grey-blue curtain running across the back' (Sheila Bannock, *SH* 25/10/74). Despite its simplicity, the set evoked different perceptions: 'more or less bare boards with just a spiral of wooden steps' became in another view 'an elaborate arrange- ment of platforms on barrels', with a 'grubby curtain', that most often 'suggest[ed] a Fellini circus tent' (respectively, Shorter, *DT* 23/10/74; Lewsen, *T* 24/10/74). Similarly, a general consensus that Williams's 1978 set was sparse, stylized and/or surreal belies very different emphases in description: one critic thought it 'an anonymous waste land', while another found it 'distinctly Dr Who-ish, with curved, highly-coloured plastic' (respectively, Robert Cushman, *O* 7/5/78; Gareth Lloyd Evans, *SH* 5/5/78).

Conklin's set for Tipton provides a more recent example of such an approach: it was a 'broken expanse of wooden planking . . . [that] might [have been] the deck of a ship or an island or just a stage' (Shyer, 'Disenchanted', p. 28). Its 'most prominent feature . . . [was] a large, ragged hole in the middle . . . as if a howitzer had lobbed a shell into it. A couple of rusty oil barrels st[oo]d, like abandoned derelicts, at one side . . . Overhead, a bent steel girder dangle[d] at a sharp angle; and just as the performance [was] about to begin, a light attached to this girder [fell] several feet before being caught by a safety cord' (Roy M. Close, *SPPP* 15/10/91). In addition, the 'rugged, wooden stage . . . [was] dotted with huge rocks, plexiglass configurations' and chairs, while to one side sat an 'enormous lens' (respectively, Mike Steele, *MST* 15/10/91; Tad Simons, *TCR* 23–9/10/91). There was also a 'tangled construc- tion of wood and rigging . . . entwined with a fibre-optic lightning bolt'; this tangle stretched twenty-five feet from the ceiling to the floor, where it plunged into the 'dark abyss . . . which Prospero treat[ed] as a cauldron' (respectively, Shyer, 'Disenchanted', p. 29; Mary Anne Welch, *CP* 23/10/91). This hole looked as if it had been caused by burning or rotting, and the 'sagging . . . gridwork' overhead seemed 'about to break away from the ceiling' (Shyer, 'Dis- enchanted', p. 26). In one view, the set's elements represented 'the intersecting worlds' of the play, with the rocks standing for nature, the 'transparent cubes and disks' for art and magic, and the 'chairs and oil drums' for humankind (*ibid.*, p. 29).

Elegant simplicity has also been a hallmark of many later twentieth-century sets. Strehler used a 'wooden rectangular platform' with 'Two wooden runways connect[ing] it to the wings'; it was 'bisected diagonally on both sides', allowing each US corner to be raised to represent different locations (Kleber, 'Theatrical Continuities', p. 144, and video). The platform had three traps, a square one DSC that served as Caliban's home and a long narrow rectangular one at SR and SL that served as prop and costume stores; in the middle of the platform was a circle of sand, a 'zodiac design' outlining it, and behind the platform a 'vast cyclorama' (video; quotations from, respectively, Kleber, 'Theatrical Continuities', pp. 144–5, and Roger Warren, *TLS*, 9/3/84). Hytner's set was a white oval or disc, steeply raked and tilted to one side, with concentric floorboard markings; at C was a romanesque arch-shaped trap that later descended to indicate Prospero's cell. To the cell's R was a rectangular trap; to its L, on roughly the same horizontal plane, stood a large rock, covered by a cloth during 1.1. The DSL quadrant of the disc held a second rectangular trap, and a grey cyclorama stood US, with a curtain behind its scrim; a curved walkway ran DS of the disc (CD). The set received mixed notices, at once praised for its 'spectacular elegance and simplicity' and derided for the 'single rock which look[ed] disconcertingly like a jacket potato' (respectively, Michael Ratcliffe, *O* 28/5/89; Kate Kellaway, *O* 31/7/88).

Sand has proved a prominent feature of many sets since Strehler's. Hall's (1988) comprised 'a pale wooden floor, with a circle in the centre, a wall at the back and a golden astrological disc above' (Ratcliffe, *O* 22/5/88). The circle was filled with sand, while a blue-and-white projection on the back wall, which had seven classical pillars, gave an impression of cloud, sky, rain and hills; there were traps in the wooden floor at DSR and DSL (CD; the set was also used for Hall's *Cymbeline* and *Winter's Tale* with minor modifications). Gaden's set, 'plain [and] uninspiring', was 'A giant sloping slab covered in painted marbling and surrounded by a ring of sand'; 'flanked by unadorned wing flats and backed by a black cyclorama', it had Caliban's 'perfectly-square hole-cave' cut into it (respectively, Tim Lloyd, *Ad* 3/5/89; Lloyd; Leigh Sutton, *NTA* 8/89; Peter Ward, *Aus* 4/5/89, all in *ANZTR* 5/89). Brook (1990) used 'a tennis court-shaped stretch of sand set amidst red shale borders and the exposed brickwork of the Tramway [Theatre]' in Glasgow (Paul Taylor, *Ind* 2/11/90). A single rock stood USL, while part of the Tramway wall held dangling ropes and a high perch for Ariel (CD). Despite 'this stark framework . . . the island's lushness' was conveyed in the course of the play by 'green clad attendants, who . . . [held] palm fronds or invisibly wav[ed] butterflies on the ends of stalks before the bewildered eyes of the shipwrecked interlopers' (Martin Hoyle, *T* 2/11/90). Alexander had 'a large black polystyrene cave with a circular sandpit', the latter 'echoed by an upstage vertical disc full of scudding clouds and beating waves'; gigantic black books lined the sandpit's circumference (respectively, Michael Coveney, *O* 18/9/94; Billington, *G* 15/9/94; CD). Wolfe used a 'simple, sand-covered circle with no scenery', although, like Brook, 'When foliage [was] needed, actors appear[ed], carrying leafy bits of greenery that evoke[d] an almost supernatural jungle' (Michael Kuchwara, AP 11/7/95); Prospero's 'meager cell' was also visible, 'jutting out on a promontory over the [Central Park] lake' (Jeremy Gerard, *V* 17–23/7/95).

Trunks have also proved popular in recent RSC productions. At the start, Mendes's stage was set only with a large wicker trunk on the apron, which was formed of vertical wooden slats, and with a semi-circular blue-black gauze US, which was virtually filled by a huge red sun; 'precarious ziggurats of weighty tomes' were visible behind the gauze, as well as a ladder (CD; Taylor, *Ind* 13/8/93). Although Thacker's 'music and Jacobean costumes [gave] the sense of some eastern isle', the in-the-round stage was quite bare, set with only three trunks, one of them C; the other two were near the circumference of the stage, as was Prospero's rough three-legged chair and desk fashioned from a crate (respectively, Nicholas de Jongh, *ES* 3/7/95; CD).

A production's permanent set often reveals its conceptual framework. Ciulei regarded the stage as Prospero's 'island-studio' (programme note), and reviews make clear that his set suggested 'an Old World study', 'a scholarly sea-captain's cabin' or 'an old warehouse converted into an artist's studio' (respectively, Frank Rich, *NYT* 7/4/81; T. E. Kalem, *Time* 27/7/81; Robert H. Collins, KSJN Public Radio typescript; see also Introduction). 'Double sets of stairs [rose] to what look[ed] like the captain's bridge ripped from an ancient ship, wooden railings circling it. The back wall [was] covered with an enormous, industrial window from some faceless factory, yet when lights change[d], a window and door emerge[d] in the gloom framing bright, Magritte-like seascapes leading outdoors' (Steele, *MT* 13/6/81). Ninagawa, who subtitled the play 'a rehearsal of a Noh play on the island of Sado', had his set dominated by a traditional thatched Noh stage and its raised bridgeway (CD). Murray's psychologically oriented production showed Prospero's cell as a 'large pink sea-shell', the mouth of which looked like a 'vulval conch', while Caliban inhabited 'a geometrical slate outcrop'; in addition, the theatre's gallery was 'walled with mirrors, at intervals asymmetrical pieces of reflecting glass drop[ped] from the roof, and the floor itself [was a] gilt mirror' (respectively, Michael Schmidt, *DT* 17/9/90; Jeffrey Wainwright, *Ind* 15/9/90; Schmidt; Wainwright). Rylance's outdoor performances were given at sites 'at which ley-lines cross', since the director wanted 'to harness [their] psychic energies . . . and to present Prospero as a Rosicrucian Adept': 'In each quadrant of the stone circle [stood] a pavilion: black and rocky for Earth; a blue bath aquabed and shower for Water; a red tent topped with fruit for Fire; and for Air a fanciful assemblage of yellow furniture, fully open to the rain-bearing wind' (respectively, Taylor, *Ind* 11/6/91; Taylor; Jeremy Kingston, *T* 10/6/91). Hay set the action against 'a giant cabalistic symbol', a 'monochrome . . . open tilted pentangle . . . with matching floor-plan' (respectively, Kirsty Milne, *STel* 11/10/92; Andrew St George, *FT* 5/10/92).

Purcarete took as his starting point Caliban's description of the island at 3.2.122b–3: the 'focus [was] on sound, where everything is connected to sound and music – time, rhythm, and so on' (Purcarete, quoted by Lynne St Claire, *NEP* 1/9/95). Consequently, there was 'scarcely a moment of silence: we hear[d] the wind humming . . . the sounds of the sea, tantalising fragments of elusive melody and song' (Charles Spencer, *DT* 18/9/95). The setting was a simple 'diamond-shape wooden platform, point-on to the audience . . . set with mother-of-pearl' (Timothy Ramsden, *TES*, 8/9/95), a 'basic. . . . black box' with 'a revolving centre' (St Claire, 11/9/95). A 'shimmering blue drape [was] the only device used to demarcate different spaces on stage, and once or twice [it] breeze[d] across the entire stage acting as a "wipe" behind which performers [could] exit invisibly' (Ian Shuttleworth, *FT* 16/9/95).

However, this 'minimalist triumph' of 'a bare, reflective square' also powerfully reflected the production's emphasis on sound, making 'much use . . . of a movable set of wires, like the strings of an instrument, stretched across the performance area' (respectively Robin Thornber, *G* 12/9/95; Thornber; St Claire); this 'bank of steel wires . . . evoke[d] both a cluster of musical staves and the strings of the thousand twangling instruments Caliban speaks of' (Taylor, *Ind* 19/9/95). Stretching across the entire width of the stage, they did not remain fixed, but at various points moved up and down or took on a diagonal slant (CD).

Of course, music was itself important for Purcarete's focus on sound: Sirli composed an original score, but Mozart themes were also used, 'reworked, mixed and repeated' (Purcarete, quoted by St Claire); some of the music was played live by on-stage musicians (see note to 1.2.188sd), and some recorded by the REEA string quartet. However, even in productions with a different conceptual framework, the music so prevalent in Shakespeare's play can be used to good effect. For example, in one view, Neville's ironical production used Tippett's 'sophisticated music [as] a superior laugh at the expense of Caliban's naive talk of "sweet airs that give delight" ' (Alan Roberts, *Tat* 20/6/62; see note to 1.2). Burge, harnessing 'the mystery, magic and supernatural powers which Renaissance Europeans believed to be the province of the Eastern World', used music 'strongly Turkish in feeling', returning 'to the more comfortable rhythms of Western Renaissance culture' when Prospero renounced his magic (respectively, Burge, programme; Lewsen, *T* 28/2/72; Burge).

Lighting can be used to similar effect. Duane Schuler's for Ciulei became 'a kind of visual music', 'used almost as another instrument, constantly changing from bright to dim, underscoring mood changes, sometimes even changing on key words' (respectively, Jack Kroll, *Nw* 29/6/81; Steele, *MT* 13/6/81). Indeed, 'each scene [was] filled] with dozens of major shifts in illumination . . . sometimes screechingly bright, or filled with mistlike haze' (David Hawley, *D* 12/6/81). The lighting plot contained 'such intricate subtleties that every mood of the play seem[ed] to have its own special color tone' and the lights themselves had 'as much a part in the play as any actor' (respectively, Marilyn Stasio, *SN* 15/9/81; Mary Weiser, *NBB* 2/7/81). Likewise, changes in De Berardinis's lighting led to 'chromatic explosions', and 'constantly created and re-created [the scene] . . . in deep reds and liquid blues', while the 'gloomy shadow' allowed the actors to appear and disappear rather than simply to enter and exit (respectively, Ugo Ronfani, *iG* 6/4/86; Giovanna Zucconi, *PS* 5/4/86; Maurizio Grande, *R* 19/4/86).

Although the conceptual frameworks noted above were deliberate, contemporary events can project unintended meaning onto a production. Edwin Smith's photographs of the Devine/Goring collaboration, for example, show a surrealistic landscape full of mouth-like cavernous openings (TM); reviews make clear that Messel's designs were restricted by the need for war-time economy. However, *The Times* was disappointed that the setting 'fail[ed] to capture' the play's 'harmony' and thus its perceived relevance to the war-time situation (30/5/40). Another reviewer made much the same point in remarking that the opening scene 'sounds a keynote for these stormy days when the stout-hearted mariners cry "Cheerly,

cheerly, my hearts! Yare! Yare!" ' (*St* 6/6/40). Indeed, the programme, in advising the audience to continue watching the performance in case of air raid rather than leave for the nearest shelter, itself embodies the way Shakespeare can be used both to assert British tradition and to construct communal identity in the face of mortal danger to nation and individual. (Interestingly, Foss's 1918 programme notes similarly stress the play's relevance to the post-war situation, 'for undoubtedly the moral of it is: Forgive your enemies! – after you have reduced them to impotence, publicly exposed their secret crimes, and compelled them to make whatever restitution is possible.')

Finally, it is worth noting that five years after his collaboration with Williams, Brook again experimented with the play at the Round House, London, in 'a series of actors' exercises aimed at generating emotions required for [*The Tempest*] and gestures to express them' (Bryden, *O* 21/7/68). Although Brook's experiment, just over an hour long, was not a production, it informed his subsequent interaction with the play and therefore its salient features are of interest. The storm was created by a crouching 'Japanese actor . . . vocalising wind and terror while the rest huddled together whimpering and trembling' (Bryden); it was 'a terrifying suggestion of shipwreck and thunderous storm' (J. C. Trewin, *ILN* 27/7/68). Brook also showed 'How Prospero and Miranda came to the island . . . Halfway through Prospero's usually tedious speech his lines [were] taken over by his usurping brother, and father and daughter [were] seen being pushed out to sea in their boat. Cast ashore on the other side of the arena they [found] huge Sycorax and her son, and in the following telling passage where Prospero teaches Caliban to speak, *you* and *me* leads ruthlessly on to *slave* and *master*. The usurped is shown becoming the usurper' (Kingston, *P* 31/7/68). Brook's experiment also showed an internationalism: 'The Japanese Noh was an important source . . . [as was] the idea of ritual followed by Bacchanalia' (Frank Marcus, *STel* 21/7/68); Ariel wore a 'kimono' and Prospero 'a crumpled coolie suit' (Harold Hobson, *ST* 21/7/68). The actors and the audience occupied the same space, and the use of scaffolding allowed for some neat juxtaposition: 'Sebastian and Antonio from upper parts . . . plot[ted] to kill the King of Naples while down below them Caliban and his confederates [were] stealthily advancing upon the sleeping Prospero' (Kingston). Ten years later, and less attractively for many critics, Pip Simmons's ninety-minute version was an 'act of textual disruption' that involved 'redistributing speeches, telescoping characters, [and] introducing action in violent contrast to expected meanings' (Wardle, *T* 10/5/78); it was Shakespeare 'illustrated by Fuseli or even Bosch' (Anne Morley-Robinson, *St* 18/5/78).

osd Shakespeare's play opens with the sound effects of a storm. The noise of thunder was created by a ' "roul'd bullet" (a metal ball trundled down a metal trough) and "tempestuous drumme" '; the lightning was probably implied, at least at Blackfriars, since, although amphitheatres used fireworks or rosin for lightning flashes, indoor theatres avoided their offensive smell (Gurr, '*The Tempest*'s Tempest', p. 95). The original staging may also have used sea and wind machines, respectively 'small pebbles revolved in a drum' and 'a loose length of canvas turned on a wheel' (Sturgess, *Jacobean Private Theatre*, p. 81).

Dryden and Davenant in 1667, followed by Shadwell in 1674, considerably expanded the shipwreck scene to include more accurate nautical actions and orders (see Appendix 1). Even in this century, Harcourt Williams took great care to establish the precise action implied by the Boatswain's orders; for his 1930 production, he consulted John Masefield about the exact meaning of nautical terms, sequence of whistles, et al. (see his *Four Years*, pp. 85–7). Similarly, Neville inserted extra dialogue, most of it for sailors responding to the Boatswain's instructions.

The very literal handling of the storm and shipwreck, exemplified by Macready and Kean (see Introduction), extended well into the twentieth century. The most talked-about feature of Bridges-Adams's 1934 production, for example, was the elaborately realistic shipwreck, designed by the director himself: after a 'slow, impressive [overture] . . . the curtain rose . . . [on] a real galleon' that was 'high above the level of the stage' (respectively, *BG* and *DM*, both 17/4/34); it 'rocked, staggered and heaved and finally plunged beneath the waves at the correct angle demanded by marine experts' (*BG*). While the production 'only lack[ed] . . . real water', even this was 'simulated' on a back cloth by a film projector 'to give an effect more realistic in heaving seas than the cinema has ever obtained' (*BG*). As the action began, the Boatswain hacked with an axe at a broken mast and two sailors threw wreckage overboard.

One recurring difficulty with realistic treatment of the storm is lack of audibility, a complaint levelled against Bridges-Adams and many other directors, including Minor, Williams (1978), Miller (1988) and Armfield – even though Williams minimized movement, with the 'shipwreck victims, absolutely stock-still . . . dimly-perceived' behind the front screen (Warren, 'A Year of Comedies', p. 202). Hall (1988) overcame the difficulty by careful orchestration of sound and speech: 'The storm is allowed only to punctuate the declamations of the sailors with the odd crash. There is a stillness at the heart of it which helps make Prospero's magic . . . all the more eerie' (Christopher Edwards, *Sp* 28/5/88).

The last century has, of course, also seen simplified, suggestive treatments of the storm and shipwreck. Shaw preferred Poel's simple staging to elaborate attempts at realism: he 'says frankly, "See that singers' gallery up there! Well, lets [*sic*] pretend that it's the ship." We agree; and the thing is done' (*OTN*, vol. III, p. 242). Devine/Goring's opening scene, a 'masterpiece of chiaroscuro', was 'based on a medieval picture: the figures larger than the ship', which 'pitched enough to make the characters all seasick' (respectively, *St* 6/6/40; Williams, *Old Vic Saga*, p. 165; Williams). Reviewing Bridges-Adams's 1926 production, one critic much preferred the staging some thirty years earlier at Birmingham's Theatre Royal: 'The stage was set to imitate the deck of an old-time sailing vessel, littered with casks, broken spars, and torn remnants of sails. Lights were lowered, crew and passengers rushed hither and thither, imitation rain fell, thunder and lightning played their part, and, though the ship never moved, the general effect was achieved.' Bridges-Adams, in contrast, seems to have unsuccessfully combined a variety of realistic storm effects with symbolic staging: 'the curtains parted a few feet and revealed the Boatswain . . . in seamanlike attire, perched upon a soapbox, near a very steady "binnacle lamp," bawling in stentorian tones. His coadjutors on board assisted in the prodigious noise, and rushed past the curtain gap frequently. Other raucous voices seemed to come from the wings.' When the soap-box remained 'immovable and permanently level upon a fast-wrecking ship', the audience dissolved into laughter (*SH* 20/8/26).

Indeed, the balance between suggestion and embodiment is hard to achieve: Iden Payne's 1941 storm, for instance, was 'not much more than a dirty night on the Norfolk Broads': 'It would be far better to sink that absurdly rocking mast and, by lighting effects and better speech, allow Shakespeare to convey his own dirty weather. Semi-realism is never convincing' (respectively, *SH* 2/5/41; John Bourne, [*SH*?] 17/4/42). David William's solution relegated the storm 'entirely off-stage', relying simply on 'a realistic storm upon the loudspeakers', a tactic Arias also employed to 'ear-splitting' effect' (respectively, *MG* and *T*, both 3/6/55; Anthony Curtis, *FT* 18/7/86). Similarly, Breuer began with Prospero 'sweeping the spotless floor', while the tempest itself was 'phoned in, over the loudspeakers, in the form of static' (respectively, Douglas Watt, *DN*, and Rich, *NYT*, both 10/7/81). The storm's casualty was a toy helicopter, whose propellers Prospero twirled and which he eventually disposed of with Ariel's help (John Beaufort, *CSM*, and Kalem, *Time*, both 20/7/81).

More satisfying solutions have been found, often with reference to non-Western theatrical styles. Brook's 1990 Ariel entered 'ceremoniously [balancing on his head] a [long African] wooden tube which emit[ted] a watery hiss when he [held] it upright'; 'others in the company form[ed] a diagram of the ship with bamboo sticks' (Wardle, *IndS*, with additional interpolated detail from Coveney, *O*, both 4/11/90). As Ariel 'move[d] across the stage tilting the magic staff this way and that to raise wind and sea . . . the black-clad mariners slowly transform[ed the] bare poles into the straining masts and sails of the storm-tossed ship' (Hoyle, *T* 2/11/90). Ninagawa suddenly 'and spectacularly evoked' the storm when 'A couple of spread sheets violently flutter[ed] into turbulent waves. Chunks of carved wood, swung into place by the performers, lock[ed] together to form the prow of a galleon. With lurching precision, the actors mime[d] the impact of the sea's buffetings', the stylized water shaken by a visible stage hand (respectively, Taylor, *Ind* 5/12/92; Peter Kemp, *Ind* 19/8/88; CD). Similarly, Wolfe's storm was 'enacted with two long segments of blue fabric undulating on poles, as in Chinese theatre'; they were waved 'by stiltwalkers in African tribal costume' (respectively, Edward Karam, *T* 14/7/95; Michael Feingold, *NYVV* 18/7/95). Although in one account the 'configuration of actors [represented] the physical body of the ship', in others 'a toy ship' was 'tossed in [the] sea of floating blue fabric' (respectively, Ben Brantley, *NYT* 12/7/95; Kuchwara, AP 11/7/95; Marjorie Gunner, *ITN* 27/7/95).

Sheer theatricality has, of course, also offered some splendid stagings, relatively simple in means while magical in effect. Daniels used fairly continuous storm noises, punctuated by thunder, rumblings, creaks, sea-claps, etc.; the very dark and smoky stage was taken up by a huge ship whose 'prow push[ed] out towards the audience', its 'large black sail billow[ing] in the wind' and 'lit by lightning flashes' (respectively, Coveney, *FT* 13/8/82; Coveney; Billington, *G* 12/8/82). This sturdy-seeming vessel was actually made of cloth and held rigid by unseen poles; between lightning flashes, the audience could see the ship 'break up' and sink, disappearing without trace (archive video). Strehler 'start[ed], rivettingly, with an ear-splitting crack of thunder; a vision of a galleon projected onto a billowing sail; blue sheets rippling, in imitation of waves, on top [of] the four ground-rows at the front of the stage; a mast splintering in two; a topsail descending on the heads of the mariners. [It was] both very exciting and highly theatrical' (Billington, *G* 16/11/83). Alexander's storm, like Hytner's (see Introduction), was very quiet, with some of the mariners suspended on a large, swaying horizontal platform; the actors all faced out, looking past the audience as if at something threatening. The sound of thunder and wave crashes then travelled from the back of the auditorium across the audience to the stage, where lightning flashed: the effect for the audience was of being engulfed by a terrifying wave (CD). Billington thought it 'the best storm since Strehler's' (*G* 15/9/94).

Directors have sometimes added to the opening action not in the interest of nautical accuracy but as part of an interpretative strategy or attempt at originality. John Harrison began with a 'sing-song on deck in which even the King's party join[ed] in the shanties' (Young, *FT* 21/2/75): the songs eventually gave way 'to the catch "flout 'em and scout 'em" with its significant refrain "thought is free" ', with the latter line repeated several times; this emphasis resurfaced in 'the play proper . . . [as] all passages concerning freedom [were] reverentially delivered, the word itself isolated as if hung about with invisible quotation marks' (*O* 23/2/75). Ninagawa showed the actors all getting ready on stage, 'Some of them flail[ing] away at drums . . . their faces hidden by devil's masks': 'Then Haruhiko Joh, who play[ed] a weird shifting palimpsest of roles – the contemporary director, Shakespeare's exiled duke and (implicitly) the Prospero-like figure of Zeami – gather[ed] the cast around him and smack[ed] the play alive with a summary clap of his hands' (respectively, Nightingale, *T*, and Taylor, *Ind*, both 5/12/92). Meckler added 'a pre-storm dumb show [in which] a nubile Miranda frolic[ked] with Caliban. Innocent games turn[ed] to sexual awareness, leapfrog to lust' (Lyn Gardner, *G* 1/2/97).

Tipton began her production '10 minutes before curtain time. Slowly at first, then mounting to a crescendo, the sound of waves crashing . . . [was] heard' (Joan Bunke, *DMSR* 20/10/91). One light then suddenly dropped from the grid (see note to 1.1), 'spilling light in a gradually dwindling arc as it [swung] back and forth over the stage' and revealing Ariel 'toying with the tempest, controlling its fierce howl' (respectively, Shyer, 'Disenchanted', p. 31; Bunke). The 'rush of sea and wind [grew] deafening as the house lights dim[med] and members of the company, dressed in what could be street clothes, file[d] in and [took] their places' in the semicircle of 'black, straight-backed chairs' arranged on stage (respectively, Shyer, 'Disenchanted', p. 31; Close, *SPPP* 15/10/91). The already-costumed actors who were to play 'the inhabitants of the island' stood 'in the darkness' behind those who were seated; as the latter began to read the storm scene from the scripts in their hands, 'an unseen Ariel move[d] among [them] with two rocks which she clap[ped] together, turning the sound of the tempest on and off like a radio' (Shyer, 'Disenchanted', p. 31) so their lines could be heard

(Close). Eventually, Ariel 'approache[d] the actor playing the boatswain, snatche[d] his pages and tosse[d] them in the air. It [was] as though the tempest had blown the script out of his hands, sweeping him and everyone else into the play' (Shyer, 'Disenchanted', p. 31).

Purcarete's production actually began in the foyer, with Alonso 'in his wheelchair and the rest of the party of nobles process[ing] through the theatre's bars and lobbies', 'exploring [the] strange land in stately silence' (respectively, Shuttleworth, *FT* 16/9/95; Marion Gleave, *DET* 12/9/95); my own impression was that they were on shipboard. They eventually assembled at the doors to the auditorium, behind which the tempest could be heard raging; the doors were then flung open to reveal a smoking inferno that sucked in the lords and swiftly closed again. When the audience thereafter filed into the theatre, they saw a virtually empty stage over which played waves created by lighting. At USC stood a bewigged figure dressed in white who was sometimes bathed in light, sometimes in shadow; he was eventually joined by another figure who climbed onto his back, and the two (whom the production would eventually reveal to be Prospero and Miranda) slowly revolved 180 degrees. All the while, the lines of 1.1 were whispered by a single voice in a barely distinguishable voice-over; when it reached 'we split' (54), Prospero and Miranda left the stage. As the scene played, members of the audience continued to file in and take their seats, both the scene and the seating finishing at the same time (CD).

Some productions suggest or reveal Prospero's control over the storm from the outset, a staging that can weaken the play's own dramatic strategy while sometimes creating a different one of its own. Benson's 1891 Prospero and Miranda were on-stage throughout the wordless storm scene. The Williams/Brook production began 'with Prospero shaking his staff', his back to the audience (respectively, Don Chapman, *OM* 3/4/63; Trewin, *BP* 3/4/63); there were then 'two resounding crashes like glass and chains falling from a height, and into the sphere which is the island the characters beg[a]n to break, leaving behind them jagged-edged places in the setting' (Marriott, *STT* 4/4/63). The ship's crew and passengers were in fact 'drawn in on a conveyor belt under [Prospero's] piercing gaze' (*T* 3/4/63); the belt must also have taken them off-stage, as subsequently the 'passengers and crew reappeared in the well of the forestage' where they 'lurch[ed] together to denote a storm' and were finally engulfed 'by stupid little plastic waves' (respectively, Trewin; John Coe, *BEP* 6/4/63; Edmund Gardner, *SH* 5/4/63). Hack had his company enter and surround the stage area, while Prospero, Ariel, Miranda and Caliban stood on the stage itself; Prospero beat the ground with his staff and spoke the opening words, 'Bestir, bestir', in his one really energetic gesture of the production (Coveney, *FT* 4/11/74; see Appendix 1). Ciulei's 'Prospero [was] everywhere present, even holding center stage' during 1.1: 'As the play began, [he] sat staring acutely at the replica of a ship which he held across the palms of his hands. At his conjuring, a tempestuous noise of thunder and lightning was heard, and a crew of men suddenly came bursting on stage' (respectively, Steele, *MT* 13/6/81; Sallie Stephenson, *TCC* 25/6/81); as the storm raged, Prospero continued to 'quietly hold . . . [the] ship's model and contemplate . . . the havoc he ha[d] wrought' (Hawley, 14/6/81). Armfield's storm was 'wrought in the shallows of half a 50-litre drum which Prospero whip[ped] into a whirlpool with his staff', an 'inversion of macrocosm and microcosm' that proved 'a disturbing image' (Bob Evans, *SMH* 31/5/90). Murray also began with Prospero, 'standing in a velvet smoking jacket behind an elegant desk, unleash[ing] the storm' and thereby confusing anyone unfamiliar with the play: there was 'no visual impression of a ship in a storm and the dialogue [was] virtually inaudible' (John Peter, *ST* 23/9/90). Instead, as Prospero cast his spells C, 'his spirits dart[ed] about among the mariners' (R. V. Holdsworth, *TLS*, 21–7/9/90). Another critic, however, found this a 'spectacular opening', 'The tempest ris[ing] from the stillness of Prospero's cupped hands yet its roaring rack[ing] him as much as those aboard ship' (Wainwright, *Ind* 15/9/90). Kelly had Prospero enter and add 'another chalk mark to the wall, as though counting off the days of his exile' (Taylor, *Ind* 11/2/99); then he 'conjure[d] the fateful storm by dropping a toy boat in a tin bath, lighting the flames in a circle of stones and blessing his magic cloak, his plastic robe, with a chaste kiss' (Coveney, *DM* 12/2/99). The storm scene itself took place 'upstage, behind a large grey plastic sheet, with the characters visible only as shadows', while Prospero remained DS, '[lying] calmly on his back' (respectively, Peter, *ST* 14/2/99, and Alastair Macaulay, *FT* 12/2/99).

As some of the preceding examples show, Prospero's agency is sometimes displayed by the presence of Ariel and other spirits, with or without that of the controlling magician. Benthall had a variety of creatures on-stage at the opening: two 'monsters', two 'barnacles', two 'hedgehogs', and nine nymphs; waves, thunder, wind, bird-cries and the creaking of the ship sounded besides the music, with Ariel entering after the second bird-cry. Minor imaginatively evoked the storm through 'lights and a few props', comprising two 'pieces of railing[,] a trapdoor', and a 'billowing sail' on which Prospero's face was shimmeringly projected (respectively, Nick Baldwin, *MR*; Dave Duff, *MMA* 24/6/70; Duff). The huge sail, which also had a 'heraldic design', was 'pulled . . . into furious motion [by black-clad sprites]', while the 'sounds of wind and thunder' and 'flashes of light' were accompanied by human 'waves' wearing 'black leotards and silvery masks, crouching along the outer side of a ship's railing, and rhythmically miming the rise and fall of stormy water'; Ariel, dressed in 'black and glittery silver', also 'dance[d] about', performing Prospero's commands (Anne Merrick, *LFMT* 17/7/70). Miller (1988) showed Ariel visibly stage-managing the waves (CD), while Mendes's production 'jerk[ed] into life when . . . Ariel [sprang], jack-in-the-box-like, from [the wicker] basket and clap[ped] his hands. A storm lantern descend[ed] to the summons whereupon the tricksy spirit initiate[d] the tempest and *The Tempest* by setting the lamp swinging, his kohl-rimmed eyes following the wide arcs it [made] with the unnerving dispassion of a cat watching the twitches of a butterfly' (Taylor, *Ind* 13/8/93). His action was accompanied by 'a crackle of thunder and a flash of lightning; and, quite suddenly . . . frantic figures [were] lurching this way and that,' as 'to a cry of "bosun" the play [began]' (Nightingale, *T*, respectively 15/7/94 and 13/8/93). Prospero stood US, 'Dimly [visible] through the translucent backcloth of clouds and red sunset', 'on a high step-ladder watching over the pandemonium' (de Jongh, *ES* 14/7/94). Thacker had his spotlit Prospero gesture with his staff, whereupon a mast

was lit, revealing Ariel atop it (CD); his 'opening offer[ed] the combined spectacle of the conjuring Prospero, the voyagers playing chess on a swaying ship's table, and Ariel (who [spoke]
the show's first words) releasing the tempest from above' (Wardle, *IndS* 2/7/95). Paige's Ariel
remained onstage throughout the play (Carter, *'The Tempest* at Salibury Playhouse', p. 21).

1 Donnellan's Prospero spoke 'Boatswain!' as he pulled an actor to C to start the improviza-
tion: it was a command to a member of the company to play a part rather than an address to
a character (CD).

1–2 The Master's shout and the Boatswain's reply indicate that in the original staging the two
would have entered by separate doors, or, alternatively, the Master may have appeared on
the balcony (Gurr, *'The Tempest*'s Tempest', p. 96).

1–4 Thacker dispensed with the Master; Ariel spoke his lines as if they were part of the spell being
worked (CD).

4sd Although the Master exits and does not re-appear, his whistle is heard regularly throughout
the rest of the scene (e.g., at 6 and 12). Tree had four boys dressed as mariners pretend to
speak the lines that were in fact delivered by off-stage actors: 'gauged in relation to the size
of its mariners, the vessel appear[ed] to be full-scale' (Nilan, ' "The Tempest" ', p. 120). Iden
Payne (1942) cut the mariners' entrance: they were either on-stage from the beginning or
unseen presences off-stage. Hall (1974) cut the Master's exit and had the mariners enter at
the start. Mendes used no mariners, apart from the Master and Boatswain; three traps provided entrances and exits (CD).

5–7 Miller (1988) cut 'Heigh . . . yare!' and 'Blow . . . enough!'; thunder sounded at 'whistle'.
Garrick (1757) cut one 'cheerly'.

Thacker's storm snapped into life as the Boatswain delivered 5–7. However, at some point
during the ensuing lines, Ariel approached the lords, making them freeze; the physical calm
surrounding her interaction with them again suggested the casting of the storm-spell for this
group of characters (see note to 1–4). When the storm again raged, Ariel in fact 'flamed
amazement' as she shot fire from her hands into the air, an effect achieved by placing flash
paper and black powder in a cigar tube together with a striker (CD).

6 As Gurr points out, it is unclear whether there would have been ropes on-stage at the Blackfriars theatre: the Boatswain's order to 'Take in the topsail' may be directed to mariners on-
or off-stage (Gurr thinks the latter more likely, *'The Tempest*'s Tempest', p. 97).

Burton and Bridges-Adams (1934) cut 'Take in the topsail'. Between the Boatswain's
'topsail' and 'Tend', Neville had four sailors speak the following lines: 'Topsail yards fast',
'– Yards fast', '– Fast', '– Aye aye Sir'. Sometime later, the Master shouted 'Strike your
topmast to the cap', to which the same four sailors replied 'Topmast away', 'Lay hold, lay
hold', 'Away' and 'Away'; the Master then told them to 'Make it sure'.

Hytner's mariners moved slightly US to hold the three sails of billowing blue silk that
dropped from the US flies and were suspended above the stage; they were visible after a
lightning 'flash' travelled down the proscenium arch from one bulb to another (Stratford
pb and CD).

Enter ALONSO, SEBASTIAN, ANTONIO, FERDINAND,
GONZALO *and others*

ALONSO Good boatswain, have care. Where's the master? Play the
men.

BOATSWAIN I pray now, keep below.   10

ANTONIO Where is the master, boatswain?

BOATSWAIN Do you not hear him? You mar our labour – keep your
cabins. You do assist the storm.

GONZALO Nay, good, be patient.

BOATSWAIN When the sea is. Hence! What cares these roarers for   15
the name of king? To cabin. Silence! Trouble us not.

GONZALO Good, yet remember whom thou hast aboard.

7sd Cut by Williams (1978), who had all the characters on-stage from the start of the play; he
seems to have ignored the scene's subsequent exits and entrances. Garrick (1757) cut '*and
others*', while Hall (1974) substituted 'Adrian' for them: during the storm, 'All [was] dark-
coloured, until from the open hold emerge[d] the useless figures of Alonso's courtiers in
their bright costumes' (Young, *FT* 6/3/74). Daniels's courtiers were already on deck when the
Master entered.

8–9 Cut by Miller (1988). Just before Alonso's first line, Brook (1957 DL) had the Boatswain
announce 'the king', which was then repeated by the other mariners.

11–13 Miller (1988) cut 'Where . . . him?' and 'you do assist the storm'. Rather than blowing his
whistle, Iden Payne's Master called 'yare, yare' from off-stage.

14 Cyril Luckham's Gonzalo for Brook (1957) impressed J. C. Trewin: 'His first words . . .
disarmed me, with his cheerful assumption that the Boatswain "hath no drowning mark
upon him" ' (*BP* 21/8/57). Brook was 'the only director . . . to have got two legitimate
laughs in the usually blurred storm scene' (Trewin, *BP* 14/8/57); this may have been one of
them.

15–16 Miller (1988) cut 'When . . . king?' After 'Hence', Brook's 1957 Gonzalo reproached the
Boatswain with a reminder that he was speaking to 'the king', thus prompting the next sentence. At 15, Hytner's mariners fell over when a huge (invisible) wave hit the deck (Stratford
pb).

16–60 Tree cut all dialogue following 'king?'; the question was followed by a great crash of thunder,
and Ariel was seen steering the ship, which caught fire and began to sink as the curtain fell.
Grove elaborated on this printed sd, noting that, following lightning and a thundercrash, the
mast broke and the ship's bow swung as far DS as possible. After another crash of thunder,
'steam and flames with red light' were turned on in the ship. The curtain lowered on a picture
of the vessel 'still rocking and starting to sink' and another crash of thunder and lightning.

BOATSWAIN None that I more love than myself. You are a councillor;
    if you can command these elements to silence, and work a peace
    of the present, we will not hand a rope more – use your authority.   20
    If you cannot, give thanks you have lived so long, and make your-
    self ready in your cabin for the mischance of the hour, if it so hap.
    Cheerly, good hearts. Out of our way, I say.   *Exit* [BOATSWAIN]
GONZALO I have great comfort from this fellow. Methinks he hath no
    drowning mark upon him, his complexion is perfect gallows.   25
    Stand fast, good Fate, to his hanging; make the rope of his

The gauze was taken up before the house lights were raised. One unidentified reviewer found this staging 'most realistic', with the ship 'disappear[ing] into the darkness'.

18–23 Burton cut 'You are . . . say'; Barton 'give thanks . . . hearts!' (21–3); Miller (1988) 'You are . . . hearts!'.

At 'Councillor', Hytner's mariners began to sway, facing US, in time with the Master's basket overhead (Stratford pb); at the end of 23, the Boatswain moved US to the other mariners and stood C between them, also facing US and swaying.

Hall (1974) had lightning flash at 'if it so hap' (22) and then a big lurch DS in a counter-clockwise direction: it threw the lords forward, Ferdinand DSC, and Adrian onto the deck. One of the mariners crossed below the hatch to DSC on a rope, two others fell and crawled L of the hatch on a rope, and the rest tumbled about, trying to control the ropes. At 'Out of our way' (23), there was another big lurch back (US in a clockwise direction): the lords were thrown back, while Alonso reached DS and pulled Ferdinand into the hatch. The two fallen mariners staggered USR, steadying the rope, while the first got behind the hatch and stayed there; another mariner took over his rope. Lightning flashed again at 'I say'.

23–3sd The Boatswain implies that the courtiers hamper the mariners' movements. As Gurr points out, the exits of the mariners and the courtiers are not clearly marked: he suggests that the Boatswain and mariners exit at 23, while the courtiers do so at 28 ('*The Tempest*'s Tempest', p. 98). Benthall's Boatswain pushed past Antonio, prompting Sebastian to respond with insults: 'Blackguard, insolent cur'. Neither Hall's (1974) nor Miller's (1988) Boatswain exited.

24–8 Hall's 1974 storm was comparatively calm; the mariner who had taken over the rope (see note to 18–23) took on another one or two and looked down the hatch at the lords, while the rest of the mariners worked on the ropes. In contrast, in 1988, Hall had all the characters freeze as Gonzalo spoke.

24–33 Burton cut from 24 to some ill-defined point around 'Yet again!'.

25–7 Wright cut from 'Stand fast', Barton from 'make the rope' and Miller (1988) from 'his complexion' to 'advantage'.

destiny our cable, for our own doth little advantage. If he be not
born to be hanged, our case is miserable.

Exit [ALONSO, SEBASTIAN,
ANTONIO, FERDINAND, *and* GONZALO]

Enter BOATSWAIN

BOATSWAIN Down with the topmast! Yare, lower, lower! Bring her
to try with main-course.   30

A cry within

A plague upon this howling! They are louder than the weather,
or our office.

Enter SEBASTIAN, ANTONIO *and* GONZALO

Yet again? What do you here? Shall we give o'er and drown?
Have you a mind to sink?

28sd Cut by Williams (1978), whose characters remained on stage throughout the scene; Hall's
1974 Boatswain also remained on stage. In 1988, Hall punctuated the end of Gonzalo's
speech with a lightning flash and thunder crack and started the wind and storm voices again;
Gonzalo and the other lords exited in the Cottesloe but remained on-stage in the Olivier.
    As Neville's Gonzalo exited, the four sailors spoke 'Topsail to leeward', 'Leeward', 'Bear
away', 'Bear away', after which the Boatswain entered, looked and shouted his next line.

29   After 'topmast', Neville's four sailors spoke 'Aye aye, Sir', 'Aye aye', 'Away she goes', 'Away
she goes' as they executed the order, the Boatswain directing them further with 'yare! lower,
lower!'; he then paused before continuing. Hall (1974) had the yard-arm slowly lowered, the
sail ropes unclipped, and the sail wound round the yard-arm, while the ship continued to
lurch and fall; Hytner's mariners and Boatswain knelt (London pb).

29–32 Bridges-Adams (1934) had this speech spoken in the ship's stern during 24–8; the ship
lurched throughout.

30sd The Folio runs together 30sd and 32sd after 'plague', but 31–2 suggest the courtiers are
responsible for the 'cry within'. Benthall had them cry 'Look to the king', etc., while Barton's
howled and Hytner's screamed from the traps. Crozier, in contrast, had the mariners shout
'Ware rocks!'. Garrick (1757) transposed 'A plague upon this howling!' (31) and *A cry within*,
so that 30sd was immediately followed by 32sd; it is unclear whether the re-arrangement
was made for the typesetter's convenience or whether it reflected the Boatswain's reaction
to the howling of the storm rather than of his passengers.

31–4 Garrick (1757) cut 'they are louder . . . sink?'; Wright 'they . . . office' (31–2); Brook (1957)
'A plague . . . office' (31–2).

31–53 Miller (1988) cut 'A plague . . . Mercy on us!'

SEBASTIAN A pox o'your throat, you bawling, blasphemous,   35
incharitable dog.

BOATSWAIN Work you then.

ANTONIO Hang, cur, hang, you whoreson, insolent noisemaker, we
are less afraid to be drowned than thou art.

GONZALO I'll warrant him from drowning, though the ship were no   40
stronger than a nutshell, and as leaky as an unstanched wench.

BOATSWAIN Lay her a–hold, a–hold; set her two courses. Off to sea
again; lay her off!

Enter MARINERS, *wet*

35 Burton cut 'pox'.

37 Iden Payne's Boatswain drank before speaking. Hytner had another wave hit the ship,
causing everyone to duck and the mariners to kneel (Stratford pb).

38 Burton cut 'whoreson'; Hall's 1988 Antonio grabbed the Boatswain.

40–1 Cut by Burton; Ashwell, Bridges-Adams (1926/30), and Wright cut 'as leaky as an unstanched
wench'. Hall (1988) had everyone but Gonzalo freeze and the storm sounds subside as at
22–3; at 'wench', there was a lightning flash and low roar of thunder, and the wind and
metalmouth sounds restarted.

42–3 The Folio punctuates the line as 'set her two courses off to sea again', and in most produc-
tions the line has been delivered in that way; Daniels, however, used the reading given here.
After the second 'ahold!', Neville's four sailors spoke 'Away, away', 'Yare, yare', 'Fast, fast',
'– Away'.

'Lay her off' often marks the ship's final foundering. For example, Bridges-Adams (1934)
had the ship crash and the first mast fall, while Crozier had a 'big lurch DS' that threw Sebastian, Antonio and Gonzalo to their knees. Daniels had the characters fall, with two mariners
rolling into the lords and the Boatswain falling off the prow. Hall's 1974 mariners repeated
'off to sea again' and then froze for four beats; at 'lay her off', the ship struck the rocks with a
big lurch. The Boatswain left the bridge, slipped onto the deck and sprawled out, while a
mariner fell, screaming 'To prayer', and crawled USL where he waited fearfully. Another fell
DSC, got up, and crossed USR to pray. A third shouted 'To prayers' and fell CR, while the rest
were thrown to the deck around the yard-arm, where they muttered prayers. In the quiet that
followed, only prayers could be heard from the mariners US and from the courtiers below
the hatch. In contrast, the prayers of Hytner's mariners were counterpointed by the cursing
of the lords (CD).

43sd As Gurr argues, because the storm is eventually revealed to be magical in origin, it needs 'the
emphatic though momentary illusion of reality' provided by the mariners' entry in wet
clothes ('*The Tempest*'s Tempest', p. 101). The contrast between the wet mariners and the
courtiers in their splendid wedding clothes marks 'the beginning of the end', 'a token that

MARINERS All lost! To prayers, to prayers, all lost!

BOATSWAIN What, must our mouths be cold?   45

GONZALO The king and prince at prayers! Let's assist them,

     For our case is as theirs.

SEBASTIAN   I'm out of patience.

ANTONIO We're merely cheated of our lives by drunkards.

     This wide-chopped rascal – would thou mightst lie drowning

     The washing of ten tides!   50

GONZALO   He'll be hanged yet,

disaster is looming for the well-dressed passengers' (p. 98). Indeed, Burton's topsail blew away as a crashing noise sounded, while Wright's mariners entered L and exited R, saying things like 'we sink', 'we split', 'all lost', etc.; at the same time, a microphone picked up the sound of a crack and of water pouring through it.

    Benthall sounded a bird-noise that all on board registered; Ariel appeared at the UR end of the ship, directing the sea-nymphs to increase the violence of the storm, and exited in a literal flash above the R arch, as the ship crashed, wind roared and music played. One 1951 reviewer described the 'hissing water-nymphs' and another the 'ship being tossed on a green, eerie sea of living water as nymphs waved their arms in unison to distant music' (respectively, *EJ* and *WA*, 29/6/51).

    Brook (1957 DL) transposed 43sd–4 to the end of the scene (see note to 60sd).

45 Cut by Wright and Hytner (London pb). Bridges-Adams's Boatswain (1934) drank from a bottle slung around his neck and Benthall's swigged brandy, giving some credibility to 48. In contrast, since Crozier's rudder only worked from side to side from this point, loss of control seems to have prompted the line.

45–60 (end of scene) Cut by Garrick (1757), whose characters exited after 44. Burton and Ayrton cut 45–52.

46 Hytner's mariners moved slowly back, crawling and staying low near the deck, to form a group on the C trap; they took with them the guide ropes from their respective sails (Stratford pb).

46–7a Cut by Brook (1957). At Stratford, the Master called for 'Oars, Oars', whereupon four oarsmen got into place.

47 Bridges-Adams's Boatswain (1934) started to fight with the mariners in the bow, seeming to validate the courtiers' view of him. Similarly, Daniels's Boatswain sat on the deck and drank from his flask, somewhat justifying Antonio's complaint (48).

50a Bridges-Adams's 1934 bow started to sink, with the vessel then sinking steadily for the rest of the scene.

50b-2 Bridges-Adams (1926/30, 1934) and Brook (1957) cut 51–2. After 51, Benthall's 1952 Ariel entered and stirred up the waves, making all those on board fall; she then exited. After 52,

Though every drop of water swear against it,
And gape at wid'st to glut him.

A confused noise within

'Mercy on us!' –

the 1951 Ariel appeared with a 'sheet flame and flash', went DS and off L, only to come on again behind the ship. Hall (1988) had all the characters but Gonzalo freeze and the storm sounds abate as at 22–3 and 39.

52sd As Gurr and others argue, although the Folio arrangement seems to give 53–5 to Gonzalo, it is more likely that they comprise the 'confused noise' heard within; the Boatswain and mariners probably make their final exit at this point (*'The Tempest*'s Tempest', pp. 98, 99). Cut by Wright and Barton.

Many productions show or suggest that the ship is beginning to sink or to break up. Shadwell darkened the theatre, and 'a shower of Fire' fell upon the vessel, accompanied by lightning and 'several Claps of Thunder, to the end of the Storm' (opening sd; see Appendix 1). The anonymous poem *The Country Club* (1679) suggests that Restoration productions used realistic effects for the shipwreck: 'Such noise, such stink, such smoke there was, you'd swear / The *Tempest* surely had been acted there' (quoted in Vickers, *Shakespeare: The Critical Heritage*, vol. I, p. 9).

Williams (1978) used sound effects to suggest the ship's splitting, while Hall (1974, 1988) used business with ropes and rigging. Tipton used synecdochic spectacle: 'as the ship threaten[ed] to break apart . . . Ferdinand leap[t] out of his chair', which burst 'into flame and plunge[d] into the hole at the center of the stage. In the tumult, the other actors overturn[ed] their chairs, which remain[ed] on stage for the rest of the play, becoming – along with a few scattered pages of the script – the debris that has washed up on the island' (Shyer, 'Disenchanted', p. 31). An accompanying photograph shows the still-seated actors holding their scripts and calmly looking at the flaming chair in their midst (p. 29).

As another wave hit Hytner's ship, the C trap started to open and the mariners to sink into it. The SL trap in which Antonio had appeared at 31 slammed shut and he exited US; Sebastian came out of the SR trap in which he had appeared at the same point and also exited US; and the Master flew out in the basket. Gonzalo, still in the SR trap, was left alone in darkness, apart from a light shining on him. Prospero, unseen by the audience, entered in the black-out and positioned himself behind the central sail, the bottom of which had previously been fully lowered to the stage (Stratford pb; CD).

53–5 Cut by Barton and by Wright, whose mariners uttered similar words on their last entrance and exit (see 43sd).

The lines have been divided and handled in myriad ways. Crozier split them between the Master and mariners, while Brook (1957 DL) retained only 'We split', interpolating the rest at the end of the scene (see 60sd). Hall (1974) distributed them among the mariners, with 'we split' repeated by all of them three times. Williams (1978) included the lords: someone cried

'We split, we split!' – 'Farewell, my wife and children!' –
'Farewell, brother!' – 'We split, we split, we split!'   55
ANTONIO Let's all sink wi' th' king.
SEBASTIAN Let's take leave of him.

　　　　　　　　　　　　　　　[*Exeunt* SEBASTIAN *and* ANTONIO]

GONZALO Now would I give a thousand furlongs of sea for an acre
　　of barren ground – long heath, brown furze, anything. The wills
　　above be done, but I would fain die a dry death.   60

　　　　　　　　　　　　　　　　　　　　Exit [GONZALO]

'Mercy on us!', Gonzalo (?) 'We split, we split', the Master 'Farewell, wife and children',
Alonso 'Farewell, brother' and Gonzalo 'Farewell, life! farewell, living!' Neville elaborated the
lines: after 51, two sailors screamed 'We split, we split', followed by another two sailors
simply screaming. Sebastian said 'Get below' and Antonio 'Away, away', while Alonso asked
for 'Mercy on us'; Adrian and Francisco then screamed, which made two sailors laugh. The
Master's 'There she goes' was followed by another sailor's 'We split, we split'. Francisco
asked for 'Mercy on us', with Adrian replying (to him?) 'Farewell, brother.' Another sailor
spoke 'Farewell, my wife and children', followed by three sailors, and perhaps the Master,
screaming. Some recent Prosperos have joined in the action: Donnellan's, a 'directorial
figure in dark glasses', 'arrange[d the actors] in place [throughout the storm scene], and to
reiterated cries of "We split!" flail[ed] the air with his staff' (Hoyle, *FT* 20/10/88). As Murray's
'join[ed] in the desperate cries from below . . . his scholar's desk [was] riven and his gentleman's clothes pulled from either arm' (Wainwright, *Ind* 15/9/90).

55 Burton accompanied 'We split' with the sound of a loud crash, whereupon an imp swung
　　aboard the ship with a flashbox and drove the crew and passengers below, apart from Fer-
　　dinand and two sailors who leapt into the sea; at the same time a thunderbolt struck the ship
　　and it fell to pieces, with red fire coming up the hatchway. The imp flew up to hover over the
　　vessel, while the stern was pulled off and the mast fell, followed by the bulwarks. The sea
　　cloth was pulled over them, and the first grooves closed in.
　　　　McVicker had an invisible chorus sing 'Arise ye terrors' after 'We split' (Becks's pb).

56–7 Wright reversed the speech-headings.

56–60 (end of scene) Cut by Burton, Bridges-Adams (1934), Ayrton and Iden Payne.

57 Benthall (1951) had a lull in the nymphs' activity.

58–60 Cut by Crozier. Wright cut 'but . . . death' (60); his Gonzalo longed for 'ling, heath, broom,
　　firs' (59). Miller (1988) changed 'brown' to 'broom' (59).
　　　　Brook's 1957 storm scene played with sudden shifts between sound and silence: 'Just
　　before the ship split, Gonzalo staggered to the bulwark and, crouching across it, uttered [his
　　final speech] into a sudden silence' (Trewin, *BP* 21/8/57).

60sd The ship's sinking can be signalled in various ways, from the literal to the metaphoric.
　　Reviewers vividly described the final moments of Bridges-Adams's 1934 wreck: 'as a green

flood surges over her, the lights from the vessel's poop disappear and she sinks from our sight, with a wail of terror from the doomed sailors' (W. A. Darlington, *DT* 17/4/34); 'the despairing faces of the sailors are seen, caught in a noose of light among the green and swirling waters. Then blackness, silence, and a moment later we are looking at Duke Prospero' (*BP* 17/4/34). Ayrton's 1935 pb reveals the mechanics of the staging: when the lift on which the ship was perched reached stage level, there was a black-out behind it during which film was projected onto the scrim (?), the lift sank to its 'bottom limit', and the cave was rolled into position. Brook (1957 DL) simply had the mariners enter wet and speak 44, followed by the 'confused noise' and cries (see 53–5), while Strehler had a tall mast crack in half once the stage was empty of actors (CD). Other directors add to the scene: for example, Wright's mariners re-entered for a tableau, a pb sketch suggesting vigorous movement suddenly frozen; when the tabs closed on the tableau, Ariel performed a mime on the forestage. Benthall (1951) showed Ariel on the ship's prow in a sheet of flame; Ferdinand pushed past him and dived into the waves. In 1952, Ariel was suspended above the boat, and Ferdinand, as he leapt, spoke the words reported at 1.2. 214–15: 'Hell is empty / And all the devils are here.' A 1951 reviewer remarked that the 'stationary figures of sea deities come to life as the storm moves to a climax, and wildfire plays over the vessel. The waves disclose themselves as sea nymphs to receive the prince and bring him safely to land' (*Sco*). Brook's 1990 staging was one of the simplest and most effective I have witnessed: two spirits held each end of the pole that Ariel had carried on at the beginning of the scene, gradually raising it horizontally in front of Gonzalo as otherwise alone on stage he spoke his final speech. Eventually, as he said his last words, it was raised over his head, and he 'drowned' (CD).

Like Bridges-Adams, many directors provide a seamless transition to 1.2. Hall's 1974 ship split 'with a great crack; in the dimness, flats slide in their grooves, and the lights go up on Prospero's island' (Young, *FT* 6/3/74). In 1988, his Gonzalo exited, taking the tarpaulin which covered Miranda; she then stepped forward into the light to begin 1.2. Hytner released the sails which then disappeared down the C trap, revealing Prospero alone on stage, as the sounds of the raging storm and splitting ship cross-faded into that of a distant sea (Stratford pb), while 'At the height of the [storm] excitement [Donnellan had] an actress leap . . . on to the skip [clothes basket?] with the words "My dear father" – and we [were] on the island' (Hoyle, *FT* 20/10/88).

None of Thacker's actors exited during the production: they simply lay down around the circumference of the stage as if they were charmed into oblivion when not needed (CD). As a result, the stage 'often look[ed] like some congested dossers' hostel' (Taylor, *Ind* 3/7/95), the small 'cluttered' stage having 'a distracting rush-hour look' (Nightingale, *T* 1/7/95).

ACT 1   SCENE 2

Enter PROSPERO *and* MIRANDA

MIRANDA If by your art, my dearest father, you have
Put the wild waters in this roar, allay them.
The sky it seems would pour down stinking pitch,
But that the sea, mounting to th'welkin's cheek,
Dashes the fire out. O I have suffered   5

1.2 Ernest Law posits that the 1611 Whitehall performance may have used rock, cloud, sea shore and cave properties built for *Oberon* and other recent court masques (see Sturgess, *Jacobean Private Theatre*, p. 78), but the play at the Blackfriars and Globe would have had no scenic decoration apart from a few representative properties. Although the text frequently mentions Prospero's cell, no action is set within it apart from Miranda and Ferdinand's chess-game in 5.1: it is therefore likely that the discovery-space served as the cell.

Kemble opened both versions with 1.2, setting it on 'a rocky part of the island' in 1789 and in Prospero's cell in 1806. Macready also set it in a 'Rocky part' near the entrance to Prospero's cell, with most of the scenery recycled from the unsuccessful Easter pantomime, *Sinbad the Sailor* (*Sp*, cited in Downer, *The Eminent Tragedian*, pp. 178–9); Marshall's imaginative scene painting allowed the viewer to conjure 'odd fantastic shapes . . . out of the various rocky trees or rocky passes – as though the sylphs that dwelt there had gambolled and twisted them into sylph-like meanings' (Forster, 'Macready's Production', p. 69). Other nineteenth-century settings were similar, with Phelps also using a three-dimensional bank and a large sloat for Ariel's descent (the latter was a kind of batten that 'rose and fell' in a [vertical] channel'; see Leacroft, *The Development of the English Playhouse*, pp. 212–13). Burton used two trick trees, a 'foreign' one from which Ariel emerged and a large one that lowered on cue from a vertical to a horizontal position. Kean compensated for his shallow stage by setting the scenery 'slantwise, to give depth through perspective' (Merivale, *Bar, Stage and Platform*, p. 137).

Twentieth-century design has tended to create mood or meaning rather than to re-create place. Jackson's design for Drinkwater was 'a symphony in purple' and blue, the landscape reflected in the costuming with a 'grey Ariel and blue Caliban'; the intrusive court wore a contrasting red (respectively, *BP* 19/4/15; Cochrane, *Shakespeare and the Birmingham Repertory Theatre*, pp. 57–8). Hurry's 'hideous' set reflected Neville's emphasis that 'irony underlies all the romance of the story. The island does not in fact belong to Prospero, but to the man monster Caliban, both by inheritance and by right': the set was consequently 'ironical, a mockery of the enchanted isle idea' (respectively, Roberts, *Tat* 20/6/62; programme notes; Roberts). Tripp's design for Edwards allowed the visions conjured by

Prospero to appear in his cell and all action to take place front stage: 'entrances and exits occur[red] from behind the central rock, not the wings, suggesting the action spinning like a top at the command of Prospero' (Helen Thomson, *SundH* 20/5/90, with additional information from Alison Croggan, *Bul* 29/5/90).

Meaning created through design can sometimes interfere with critical perception of the play's own meaning. Harcourt Williams's 'Persian-cum-Japanese decor' made the set 'a kind of "Willow Pattern", with a little Chinese bridge above [Prospero's] cell' (Williams, *Old Vic Saga*, p. 95). Not only did it create 'stage pictures of a rare beauty' as Prospero stood, 'long crimson mantle sweeping over dark green robe, on a high bridge of lacquer red', but the 'definitely Eastern background . . . set a gulf between the forces of culture and the forces of anarchy', so disguising the way in which all the characters are 'of a piece' (respectively, *MP* 7/10/30; *DT*; uc 7/10/30; uc 7/10/30). Some design, although attractive, awkwardly restricts the play. Jensen's set for Minor consisted of 'free-form metal constructions', made from 'wrought iron' or 'harsh metals and meshes welded together' (respectively, John H. Harvey, *SPD* 22/6/70; Duff, *MMA* 24/6/70; Laurance Tucker, *RPB* 22/6/70). Although these 'tree-like sculptured pieces' looked imaginative and, with 'casters to move about on', seemed 'functional', they 'were bunched together, nearly invisible in the gloom and shadows but nevertheless restricting the stage area . . . and hampering' free movement (*MD* 26/6/70). For other sets, see Introduction and note to 1.1.

Prospero's cell has itself been depicted as anything from forbidding to homely. Burton's 1st groove 'Storm Cave flats' showing the 'dark and dismal mouth of a large cave' presumably represented Prospero's home, while Tree showed a cosy setting 'fitted out with books', couch, rock-seat and table; Drinkwater had a grander cell 'carved out of the rock like a bluestone classical temple' (respectively, pb; Nilan, ' "The Tempest" ', p. 120, and pb; Cochrane, *Shakespeare and the Birmingham Repertory Theatre*, pp. 57–8). Williams's 1978 Prospero had only 'a severely unadorned shield from the elements' (Warren, 'A Year of Comedies', p. 202), while Hall's (1988) occupied a bookish hermit's cell, 'a Faustian study' with 'salt-bleached doors', desk and chair (Ratcliffe, *O* 22/5/88; prop setting list). In Mendes's production, there was something 'touching and convincing about Prospero's makeshift study, desert flowers on a desk, untidy books piled up against a blue sky' (Kellaway, *O* 15/8/93).

The transition from 1.1 to 1.2 has often been not only seamless but magical or unexpected: Bridges-Adams's 1934 shipwreck, for example, wondrously merged into a view of the island: 'pantomime has never given us a better transformation scene' (*BG* 27/4/35). Ciulei's storm 'Abruptly . . . disappear[ed], replaced by doors to [Prospero's] studio that [swung] open to reveal a glorious seascape' (Hawley, 14/6/81). Donnellan's director-figure 'whip[ped] into the costume rail and pull[ed] on Prospero's clothes. During his exposition [he pulled] various actors forward as if casting them', to 'urgent and thrilling' effect (respectively, Hoyle, *FT* 20/10/88; Ratcliffe, *O* 13/11/88). See notes to 1.1.60sd and 1.2.0sd for further examples.

osd   Sturgess posits that Richard Burbage would have played Prospero and Richard Robinson, 'the principal company juvenile at the time', either Miranda or Ariel; Prospero's magic garment was probably 'a robe covered in cabalistic signs' (*Jacobean Private Theatre*, pp. 75, 77, 79). Although the characters had to enter on Shakespeare's stage, subsequent productions have sometimes discovered them: Tree, for instance, raised the curtain on Prospero sitting and reading, while Thacker's genial Prospero was already on stage, seated at his desk, as he had been throughout 1.1. Modern entrances can sometimes be surprising: Gaden's Prospero, for example, 'descend[ed] on a trapeze' (Murray Bramwell, *AR* 6/89).

Many Prosperos, like Kean's, are first seen 'superintending the effect of his art' (Cole, *Life and Theatrical Times*, vol. II, p. 221), though some make a much more spectacular first appearance than Kean's discovery on a high rock. Daniels, for example, achieved 'an astonishing transformation when in the space of a blackout and a peal of thunder the tempest-tossed ship [of 1.1.] disappear[ed] to reveal [in its place] Prospero the magician conjuring the storm' (*BSM* 15/8/82); the audience's 'first glimpse of him between lightning flashes [was] of a swirling cloak' (Edwards, *NS* 20/8/82). This first sight of the spell-working Prospero can help to define his magic power and his relationship to it: while Jacobi 'trembl[ed]', 'convulsed in a magical orgasm', Gielgud (for Brook 1957) wielded his staff 'as if it [were] truly an instrument of power' (respectively, Stephen Brook, *NS* 9/83; Wardle, *T* 14/9/83; Trewin, *ILN* 24/8/57). In contrast, Ralph Richardson (for Benthall 1952) used it as if it were a cooking utensil (Trewin): as he raised it, thunder sounded; then he put it down, turned a page of his book, and picked up a crystal, causing the wind to blow. Observing the book again, Prospero made another gesture, cueing thunder; he then looked at his book, lifted his hour-glass, looked at the book again and used his dividers.

Prospero's costuming ranges from the Jacobean to the contemporary, taking in the exotic and the downright eccentric along the way. In 1974, Hall's wore a cream lace ruff, a floor-length long-sleeved brown gown cinched by a leather belt, a heavy brown magic cloak covered with large cabalistic symbols and a black skullcap; he also sported the 'long grey beard of a Jacobean necromancer' (photos and costume lists; quotation from Felix Barker, *EN* 6/3/74). In contrast, Quayle's Prospero was a 'dabbling artist in gumboots and rustic smock', and James's was 'rigged out in a dry-as-a-bone coat and akubra hat' (respectively, Coveney, *FT* 8/10/83; Ann Nugent, *CT* 23/8/89). In keeping with the director's Eastern focus, Burge's Prospero wore a 'tunic, patchwork cloak, Turkish trousers, anklets and boots' (Foulkes, review, p. 7). De Berardinis's Prospero, who went through a 'purgatorial journey' to reach 'a superior level of consciousness', wore a 'solemn tunic' of white and a 'vaguely Indian' mask of silver (respectively, De Berardinis interviewed by Claudio Cumani, *C* 25/3/86; De Berardinis; Ugo Volli, *RS* 5/4/86; Gastone Geron, *iGe* 6/4/86). Atkins's 1933 Prospero looked decidedly eccentric, with his cap, knee-length baggy trousers, embroidered short-sleeve shirt and strapped sandals that reached above the ankle (1933 photo, *DS*).

Costuming for other characters encompasses the same options as for Prospero: Burge's Miranda, for instance, wore 'muslin pantaloons' under her 'English pastoral dress', while Hall's 1974 costumes were 'sumptuous' and 'extravagantly courtly, with plumed head-dresses and helmets' (respectively, Lewsen, *T* 28/2/72; Barber, *DT* 6/3/74; Wardle, *T* 6/3/74).

Recently there has been a marked tendency towards eclecticism: Tipton's costumes ranged in style, connecting 'the Renaissance with a "Star Trek" future' (Steele, *MST* 15/10/91), while Purcarete's were a mixture of eighteenth-century and modern. Murray's mainly consisted 'of evening dress for the people and tattered silver-gilt tails for the spirits', while Hay dressed the court in 'Period costume' and the spirits in 'outlandish designer gear' (respectively, Schmidt, *DT* 17/9/90; Robert Gore-Langton, [*DT*?] 10/10/92). Similarly, Wolfe's islanders wore 'raggedy but colorful' costumes and the courtiers 'traditional Renaissance dress' (respectively, Michael Bourne, W8GO 11/7/95 (broadcast typescript), and Michael Sommers, *NSL* 12/7/95).

The general approaches to Prospero outlined in the Introduction have had other exponents than those discussed there. Youthful figures include those for Atkins (1933, 1934), Iden Payne (1938) and Rylance, with Iden Payne's also 'made up to look like one or several of the idealized portraits of Shakespeare' (uc); Crozier's, also influenced by the Shakespeare connection, played the part as 'a sad, serene farewell' (*EJ* 27/4/46). More recently, Brook's 1990 Prospero was 'a dignified African mage with no discernible character beyond his spiritual superiority to the surrounding company' (Wardle, *IndS* 4/11/90); dressed in his long, white, voluminous robe, he resembled both 'a tall, black El Greco saint' and a 'gentle, unblinking village elder' (respectively, CD; Taylor, *Ind* 2/11/90; Coveney, *O* 4/11/90). Lepage's was 'a kind of theatre director', 'serene and beautifully-spoken', while Warner's had the 'slightly dingy, slightly demented air of authority of a Victorian showman' (respectively, Ray Conlogue, *TGM*; Conlogue; Colin Affleck, *Sco* in *LTR* Edinburgh Festival Supplement 1983).

Less pleasant Prosperos also abound. That of the Williams/Brook collaboration was 'fierce and angry', a stern figure who 'could settle anyone with one of his small, hard, calculating glances' (respectively, *APJ* 5/4/63; Conrad Wilson, *Sco* 4/4/63). Hirsch's was 'in ungovernable temper' throughout the play, while Wolfe's 'moody, tense' Prospero was 'very angry' (as indeed were most of the characters in this production; respectively, Young, *FT* 30/6/82; Margo Jefferson, *NYT* 16/7/95; Brantley, *NYT* 12/7/95). Armfield's, who found it 'difficult to experience real human contact', showed 'a sort of detached ferocity', while Murray's was 'a likeable, essentially unassuming person, tragically driven to fits of rage and vindictiveness by his past mistreatment, and further dehumanized by [his] magic' (respectively, director's programme note, quoted by Ken Healey, *SunH* 3/6/90; Evans, *SMH* 31/5/90; Holdsworth, *TLS*, 21–7/9/90). Tipton's Prospero was 'troubled, slightly askew and not totally sympathetic', an 'impure and calculated . . . [and] joyless manipulator of people' (respectively, Terry Wigand, 24/19/91; Steele, *MST* 15/10/91). Kelly's was 'a moody, embittered man in late middle age: a tired magician, crabby and a little self-righteous' (Peter, *ST* 14/2/99).

There are, of course, exceptions to the major approaches to the role discussed in the Introduction. In 1981, Retallack made Prospero the deposed Queen of Milan, with the necessary textual adjustments to 'lady', 'mother' and 'mistress' (Nightingale, *NS* 2/83). Reviewers seemed to have little difficulty with the change in Prospero's sex, and many were intrigued by its effects on the character and on character relationships. Wardle thought that Valerie

Braddell split the character 'in two: half tenderly maternal (even shedding tears over Caliban) and half the witch from *Snow White*', complaining that this split, together with her 'prolonged pauses and spiritless delivery of the verse', robbed 'Prospero of authority and emotional clarity' (*T* 25/2/83). Barber, however, implied that emotional clarity does not necessarily make Prospero interesting: Braddell made 'a noble impression in the role', revealing 'a stern figure of justice but also a disturbed woman, capable of enfolding the monster Caliban in her arms, and with a mother's warm concern for her girl's well-being and chastity' (*DT* 2/83). Other critics also emphasized her motherliness and unusual protectiveness and the effects these qualities had, particularly on her attitude to Caliban (see Young, *FT* 2/83; Billington, *G* 2/83; Nightingale). Some recent productions, like Brook's (1990) and Alexander's, have also reversed another theatrical convention by casting black actors as Prospero and/or Miranda and a white actor as Caliban: for Walford, Ricco Ross was 'a super cool young black Prospero' who, although 'vigorous', gave a 'sombre interpretation' of the part (respectively, Irene McManus, *G* 27/1/84; Hoyle, *FT* 31/1/84; Hoyle).

John Phillips, 'faced with the task of reconciling Shakespeare's Prospero with the avuncular figure in the Restoration text' of Seale's Dryden/Davenant revival, 'adopted an impassioned gravity that failed to extract the best from either' (*T* 10/6/59); despite his 'efforts, [Prospero] seem[ed] more than ever a bossy old conjuror' (*O* 14/6/59). In contrast, Simmons's Prospero was sinister and manipulative, in keeping with the director's interest in showing 'images of power, sadomasochism and sexual confusion'; very few of his main speeches were left intact (Coveney, *FT* 10/5/78, with additional information from *Vogue*, 5/78).

Critical opinion concerning Miranda seems to reflect conflicting tastes about the attractions of young womanhood rather than any theatrical reality. Early reviews imply that, besides grace, charm and tenderness, not much was demanded of actors taking the role. In 1933, Atkins's was variously praised for 'delicate sincerity and sense of wonder' and the 'dreamlike quality' of her charm, as well as disliked for sometimes being 'too self-confident' and 'a shade too sophisticated' (respectively, *DT* 13?/9/33?; *T* 13/9/33?; Ivor Brown, *O* 17/9/33; George W. Bishop, *ST* 17/9/33). In 1951, Benthall's was on one hand praised as 'full of girlish charm' and on another damned for being 'docile' and 'unassertive' (respectively, *MG*; *SWCN* 30/6/51). Brook's 1957 Miranda was more interesting, 'allowing herself a much greater range of passion than the part is traditionally supposed to bear: when did a Miranda make her first entrance in so violent a storm of tears?' (*LSC* 16/8/57). However, apart from this substantiated judgement, critics offer a range of disparate and seemingly subjective responses to a Miranda variously seen as 'fresh and unsophisticated' (Ellen Foxon, *BWP* 16/8/57); too 'subservient' to Prospero (*LDP* 14/8/57); 'sweet on a too contemporary note' (*CET* 14/8/57); 'a character of interest' (*BM* 14/8/57); and too realistic (*T* 14/8/57).

With the advent of explicitly ideological interpretations and of feminism, the role has offered actors more opportunities. In 1970, Miller's conception of Prospero affected the presentation of Miranda: a 'stooped, sad, dreary girl' who was 'distressingly submissive', she came across as 'a little Charlotte Brontë of a Miranda, a frail country girl with a shut-in imaginative life of her own' (respectively, Milton Shulman, *ES* 16/6/70; *ST* 21/6/70; Barber, *DT* 16/6/70). Angela Pleasence's portrayal was 'revolutionary', eschewing the two traditional interpretations of 'radiant innocent and gauche innocent' for a more sensible 'bemusement'; she was 'slow-speaking, intent, intense and weird, brilliantly managing the difficult art of listening' (*P* 24/6/70). Hack's showed 'rare quality and originality' in making Miranda 'credible and convincing' (*CET* 23/10/74); for instance, even though 'her gurgling speech [was] genteel, [her] animal crouches well suggest[ed] a girl brought up in the wilds' (Lewsen, *T* 24/10/74). Daniels's Miranda, Alice Krige, seemed 'At first sight . . . a wild thing – bare shouldered, her hair in long braids', her 'boyish gaucheness . . . wholly believable' (respectively, Edwards, *NS* 20/8/82; Paul Vallely, *MSun* 18/9/83). Rescuing Miranda 'from the insipidity which often bedevils her', she still 'display[ed] the careful tutelage of her father's care, innocent and yet emotionally wise' (respectively, *WGH* 19/8/82; Ned Chaillet, *T* 13/8/82). She was in fact 'the best' Miranda the *Morning Star* had seen, 'full of . . . precocious certainty and passionate teenage concern' (16/8/82); indeed, other reviewers commented that Krige actually managed to seem fifteen (Barber, *DT* 9/83; Young, *FT* 14/9/83).

   Other recent Mirandas have emphasized the character's tomboyishness: Wolfe's acclaimed Miranda, for example, was 'a fiery, impetuous hoyden' 'androgynously dressed in her father's hand-me-downs' (Brantley, *NYT*, 12/7/95); wearing 'dirty breeches and [waistcoat]', she looked 'like a tousle-haired boy' (Alexis Greene, *TW* 31/7-6/8/95). However, productions often manage to undercut such an image or to recuperate it entirely. Ciulei's Miranda, a 'fresh and pure product of nature, tomboyish and curious and innocent', started off in 'jeans and man's shirt, knotted at the waist', but ended 'in a lovely long gown with a high waistline' (respectively, Steele, *MT* 13/6/81; Lucille Johnsen Stelling, *MSN* 24/6/81; Grace Gibas, *CPi* 6/8/81). Miller's 1988 Miranda was dressed like Prospero or even in his clothes, but she was played as 'quiveringly neurasthenic', a 'nervy' and 'hysterical clinger' (respectively, Coveney, *FT* 12/10/88; Gardner, *MSun* 16/10/88; Ratcliffe, *O* 16/10/88). Hytner's, clad in a 'white nightshirt', was, in one view, 'a sunburned wild-child of nature with instinctive warmth and passion' and, in another, 'yet another pretty, golden-haired . . . pastoral heroin[e], tripping about the stage like a cross between a sit-com bimbette and a children's tv presenter' (respectively, Kellaway, *O* 31/7/88; Maureen Paton, *DE* 26/5/89; Dominic Gray, *WO* 31/5/89). Although one critic complained she 'caw[ed] her lines breathlessly and hop[ped] about like a boy-crazy co-ed', another saw her delivery as part of Hytner's use of 'distinct and surprising tonal qualities' for 'each of his main players': 'Miranda, frantically emotional in Thaw's convincing performance, is a shrieker' (respectively, Rhoda Koenig, *P* 9/6/89; Alex Renton, *Ind* 1/8/88). Mendes's was 'unusually outspoken' and 'combative' but 'delightfully emphasize[d] the tendency to overreact to everything: weeping at the storm, crying (for joy)' (Kellaway, *O* 15/8/93); she was also 'unusually randy' (Billington, *G* 13/8/93).

   As is obvious from some of the preceding examples, productions often sexualize Miranda. Baynton's resembled a flapper, with bobbed hair, long beads and loose sheath dress with scooped neck, while Guthrie's wore a long diaphanous evening dress (photos, TM). More blatantly, Barton's wore 'the tattered remnants of a baby doll nightdress', while Hall's 1988 'exotic South Seas maiden covered in fake tan' was dressed 'in a sarong-like garment' (respectively, Knapp, *TES* 23/10/70; Paton, *DE*, and Kemp, *Ind*, both 21/5/88). Simmons's was 'discovered naked, except for a very unbecoming mob-cap, in a tin bath-tub' and remained 'regularly naked' throughout the rest of the performance; losing most of her dialogue, she was 'compensated . . . by being allowed to steal all the scenes in which she was not listening to her father or playing the flute, by having mock intercourse with any characters not otherwise engaged' (respectively, Germaine Greer, *Sp* 20/5/78; Coveney, *FT* 10/5/78; Greer). Quayle/Jamieson's took 'the romantic initiative and [swept] Ferdinand off his feet', though a less charitable view saw her as 'a distinctly unvirginal Miranda', who, 'in an unflattering nightshirt, [leapt] at . . . Ferdinand as though she knew exactly what to do with him' (respectively, Wardle, *T* 9/10/85; Coveney, *FT* 8/10/83). Walford's, though 'plumed like an exotic bird' (McManus, *G* 27/1/84), luckily had a 'forthright strength' that her 'feathered tutu' could not disguise (Hoyle, *FT* 31/1/84). Armfield's, with her 'fleshy, sensual' handling of the role, made her scenes with Prospero 'rich with a mix of filial affection and simmering sexuality' (Paul McGillick, *FR* 1/6/90).

As the last point indicates, Miranda's relationship with her father has also been variously portrayed. Neville's Prospero was 'very much his daughter's father', unlike other Prosperos who take no 'notice of the girl' (Trewin, *ILN* 16/6/62). Similarly, Daniels's Prospero showed 'the strongest yet gentlest affection for Miranda. For once you believe they've lived in close harmony for nearly twenty years [*sic*]' (Nightingale, *P* 12/8/88). In contrast, Hall's 1988 Prospero interacted brusquely with his daughter: 'untender as a Guards sergeant-major, even when he is reminding Miranda of her misfortunes', he was 'tetchy and hectoring' to her, showing far 'more tenderness' to Ariel (respectively, Hoyle, *FT* 1/10/88; Kemp, *Ind* 21/5/88; Francis King, *STel* 22/5/88). For Wolfe, Prospero's relationship with his daughter was 'clearly conflicted', 'seesaw[ing] carefully between rage and heroic restraint', but their first scene had 'genuine intimacy', Miranda standing 'arms akimbo while listening to Prospero, or else nose to nose in defiance' (respectively, Brantley, *NYT* 16/7/95; Brantley; Howard Kissel, *DN* 12/7/95; Karam, *T* 14/7/95).

1 Dryden/Davenant interpolated new material before 1.2.1, which Shadwell retained:
PROSPERO Miranda! where's your sister?
MIRANDA I left her looking from the pointed rock, at the walk's end, on the huge beat of waters.
PROSPERO It is a dreadful object.
MIRANDA If by your art, my dearest father, you have put them in this roar, allay 'em quickly.

Both Kemble versions opened with Prospero's lame question. The 1789 text followed Dryden/Davenant for the next three lines, apart from cutting 'at . . . end' and giving Prospero's second line to Miranda. The 1806 Miranda answered Prospero differently, retaining some of 6b–7: 'Sir, I saw her / Climbing tow'rds yon high point, whence I am come / From gazing on the ocean: – A brave creature, / Who has, no doubt, some other creatures in her, / Toss'd on the waste of waters –'.

With those that I saw suffer! A brave vessel,
Who had no doubt some noble creature in her,
Dashed all to pieces. O the cry did knock
Against my very heart! Poor souls, they perished.
Had I been any god of power, I would   10
Have sunk the sea within the earth, or ere
It should the good ship so have swallowed, and
The fraughting souls within her.
PROSPERO   Be collected;

From the beginning of 1.2, Miller (1988) had Ariel present on-stage, watching and listening to Prospero and Miranda; his bluey-grey body was clothed in a loin-cloth, and there was a black badger stripe down the centre of his gold hair (CD). His appearance was based on John White's drawing of a Roanoke medicine man in Virginia in 1585 (H. R. Woudhuysen, *TLS* 21/10/88).

1–13a Dryden/Davenant cut 3–9, 13a; Shadwell 3–15 (adding 'I have so order'd, that not one crea-ture in the ship is lost' before 16); Garrick (1756) 3–5a, 6b–9 (with Miranda's air, 'Hark how the winds rush from their caves', inserted after 13a); Kemble (1789) 1–13a, (1806) 1–6a (with changes of tense and words since the shipwreck had not yet occurred; Miranda also had some of Dorinda's ignorance with 'vessel' (6) changed to 'creature'); Macready and Kean 3–5a, 10–13a; Phelps 3–5a, 8b–9a, 10–13a; Daly 3–5a, 6b–8a, 9b–13a; Tree 3–5a.

Miller's 1970 Miranda 'enter[ed] from above and deliver[ed] her plea for the storm victims straight out to the audience, as if in a dream, while Prospero [sat] below in his cell'; in such ways the production 'adopt[ed] the tone of a masque without the spectacular trimmings' (Wardle, *T* 16/6/70). Strehler's blue silk 'waves' calmed and receded, while the cyclorama was 'suffused with glowing light', suggestive of a hazy sun (Warren, *TLS* 9/3/84; CD); in the course of the play the 'sun slowly descend[ed] behind the cyclorama suggesting . . . the events of a single day' (Billington, *G* 16/11/83).

Daniels's Prospero continued to work his spell throughout Miranda's speech, delivered with 'force[ful] . . . grief', only stopping when he spoke his first line (pb; Shorter, *DT* 13/8/82). Alexander's was still bleary from his exercise of magic (CD). Paige's 'Prospero would several times have reassured [Miranda] if he could have got a word in'; when he finally raised his voice at 'No harm', he 'got her attention' (Carter, '*The Tempest* at Salisbury Play-house', p. 11).

1–37 Purcarete's Prospero was lying asleep and Miranda addressed her words to a mannikin, dressed in Prospero's cloak and wig; Prospero's replies were given in voice-over. At 'ope thine ear' (37), Prospero woke up and spoke (CD).

13b–15 Shakespeare's 15, divided into three between two speakers, suggests urgency as well as Pros-

No more amazement. Tell your piteous heart
There's no harm done.
MIRANDA   O, woe the day.
PROSPERO   No harm.   15
I have done nothing but in care of thee –
Of thee my dear one, thee my daughter – who
Art ignorant of what thou art, nought knowing
Of whence I am, nor that I am more better
Than Prospero, master of a full poor cell,   20
And thy no greater father.
MIRANDA   More to know
Did never meddle with my thoughts.

pero and Miranda's quick responsiveness to each other; Dryden/Davenant's change of 15c to 'There is no harm' deadens the effect. They cut 14a; Garrick (1756) 13b–14a, 15b–c; Kemble 14–15; Daly 14a, 15b, with 15c given to Miranda.

    Benthall's 1952 Prospero busily wrote in his book as he spoke 13b; Daniels's was slow 'to shake off the effect of such a mighty act of magic' (Chaillet, *T* 13/8/82). Hytner's Miranda squatted on 15b (pbs); such 'contemplative crouching on the ground with arms bound . . . in "a sad knot" ' was 'An attitude repeated so often by different characters that it [became] a hallmark' of the production (Kellaway, *O* 31/7/88). As Thacker's Prospero assured Miranda 'No harm' was done, Ariel and three other spirits watched them (CD).

16 Hytner's father–daughter relationship was 'touching: when Prospero claims that all he has done is motivated by care for Miranda it [was] convincing' (Kellaway, *O* 31/7/88).

16–65 Compressed by Garrick (1756) into eight lines, seven of them spoken by Prospero: 'Tell your piteous heart, there's no harm done; / I have done nothing but in care of thee, / My child, who art ignorant of what thou art; / But I will now inform thee – pray attend: / ' Tis twelve years since thy father was the duke / Of Milan – be not amaz'd, my daughter; / Thou art a princess of no less issue'; Miranda responded 'O the heav'ns, what foul play had we!'

17 Rewritten by Dryden/Davenant, Shadwell and Kemble to include Dorinda.

18–21a Dryden/Davenant and Shadwell corrected Shakespeare's grammar, changing 'nought' to 'not' (18) and cutting 'Of' and 'better' (19); they also made Prospero 'unhappy' (21a) and his cell 'narrow' (20).

21b–2 Dryden/Davenant and Shadwell changed 21b–2a to 'I ne're endeavour'd to know more than you were pleas'd to tell me' and cut 22b.

PROSPERO   'Tis time
I should inform thee farther. Lend thy hand
And pluck my magic garment from me – so –
[PROSPERO'S *cloak is laid aside*]

23a   As Burton's Miranda started to undo his clasps, Prospero (enjoined in the pb never to
produce any magical effect without his wand and magic cloak) waved his wand, causing a
large practicable tree trunk, about fifteen feet long, to fall gently onto C stage from its position on the R front wing and form an armchair-like seat amongst its branches; Prospero lay
his mantle on a branch or rock and his wand near it. Hall's 1974 storm subsided, allowing
Prospero to relax; Daniels's Prospero relinquished his wand and book but was still very agitated (pb; archive video).

23b–33a   Dryden/Davenant cut 23b–5a, 29b–33a (the latter replaced by 'that not one creature in the
ship is lost'); Shadwell 23b–33a; Kemble (1789) 23b–7, 29b, 32, (1806) 25b–7, 29b, 32a (with
an added phrase before 28 in both); Kean 23b–5a (Edmonds pb only). Dryden/Davenant
changed 'provision . . . So' to 'a pity', while Kean changed 'provision' to 'prevision' (28).

24   Daly's Prospero waved his wand and 'a young tree [sprang] up . . . upon which he [hung] his
robe and rest[ed] his wand'.

At mention of the 'magic garment', Donnellan's Prospero took a black shawl or cloak from
the clothes rail and handed it to Miranda (CD). Murray's Prospero switched 'from a strained,
incantatory tone when Miranda [took] off his robe' (Holdsworth, *TLS* 21–7/9/90); likewise,
Alexander's Prospero was visibly relieved when his black cloak was removed (CD).

24sd   Prospero's 24b–5a indicates his magic garment is removed and laid down. The garment can
vary enormously: for Poel, it was a robe based on the 1584 'The Discoverie of Witchcraft'
(Mansion House programme); for Brook (1957), a cloak of silver; for Williams (1978), 'a black
schoolmaster's gown' (Young, *FT* 3/5/78); for Daniels, a 'cloak covered in cabalistic symbols'
(Edwards, *NS* 20/8/82); for Gaden, 'an electric blue mantle' (Lloyd, *Ad* 3/5/89); for Mendes,
a dressing-gown embroidered with gold flowers (CD); for Thacker, a sleeveless floor-length
cloak of rough cloth (CD).

Since Barton's Prospero 'was dressed in plain beige, his magic cloak offering no contrast
and suggesting no formality', 'there was no apparent need [for him] to ask Miranda to help
"pluck" it off . . . The effect was to . . . [present] Prospero as a man feeling his way through a
crisis, not as a strange, powerful magician' (Brown, 'Free Shakespeare', p. 129). Strehler's
Prospero wore a large off-white rectangle of cheese-cloth across his shoulders and upper
arms; he and Miranda here folded it in the way two people fold a large sheet. However, the
action had a ritualistic air, achieved not only by Prospero and Miranda's gravity and slowness, but also by Carpi's haunting music, sung as a high-pitched lyrical chant; it occurred at
all the magic moments in the production, including Ariel's appearances. When the mantle
was folded, Prospero lifted the SR trapdoor, which was shaped like a long plank, and
Miranda placed it inside (CD).

Lie there my art. Wipe thou thine eyes; have comfort.   25
The direful spectacle of the wrack which touched
The very virtue of compassion in thee,
I have with such provision in mine art
So safely ordered, that there is no soul,
No, not so much perdition as an hair   30
Betid to any creature in the vessel
Which thou heard'st cry, which thou saw'st sink. Sit down,
For thou must now know farther.
MIRANDA   You have often
Begun to tell me what I am, but stopped
And left me to a bootless inquisition,   35
Concluding, 'Stay: not yet.'
PROSPERO   The hour's now come;
The very minute bids thee ope thine ear,
Obey, and be attentive. Canst thou remember

---

25 Hytner's Prospero either dried Miranda's eyes with her hair or 'Absent-mindedly . . . wipe[d] away . . . [her] tears . . . with the cuff of his collarless shirt' (respectively, Stratford pb; Renton, *Ind* 1/8/88).

26 Strehler's Prospero produced his magic 'book' from his pocket, as if to assure Miranda that his art were indeed responsible for the storm; it was a folded sheaf of large parchment papers (CD).

32 Garrick (1757) substituted 'attend' for 'sit down', suggesting that the actors stood. Wright's Prospero physically sat Miranda down on the cell steps, while Williams's (1978) embraced her. Hytner's Prospero directed 'which thou *saw'st* sink' as much to the audience as to Miranda (CD). Before telling Miranda his story, Alexander's Prospero touched the tip of his staff and turned US, making the storm clear and the cyclorama-disc turn blue (CD).

35–7 Dryden/Davenant and Shadwell cut 35–6a, 37; Daly 35–6a.

36–47 Phelps seems originally to have made some cuts, but the Phelps/Creswick pb restores them.

38a Hall's 1974 Prospero was 'no more than coolly paternal as he relate[d] to Miranda . . . the story of their exile' (Young, *FT* 6/3/74), while Daniels's Miranda clasped Prospero's leg at 'Obey' and Prospero put his hand on his daughter's head at 'be attentive' (archive video; pb).

38b McVicker's production began here and generally followed Shakespeare's dialogue to 175a (Becks's pb); see note to 175b–307 for further description of his first and second acts.
    Hytner's Prospero made 'the word ['*before*'] eclipse the present and then passionately relate[d] their history, repeatedly holding his hand to the side of his face as if to pillow memory' (Kellaway, *O* 31/7/88).

A time before we came unto this cell?
I do not think thou canst, for then thou wast not   40
Out three years old.
MIRANDA   Certainly, sir, I can.
PROSPERO By what? By any other house, or person?
Of any thing the image, tell me, that
Hath kept with thy remembrance.
MIRANDA   'Tis far off;
And rather like a dream, than an assurance   45
That my remembrance warrants. Had I not
Four or five women once, that tended me?
PROSPERO Thou hadst, and more, Miranda. But how is't
That this lives in thy mind? What seest thou else
In the dark backward and abysm of time?   50
If thou rememb'rest aught ere thou cam'st here,
How thou cam'st here thou mayst.
MIRANDA   But that I do not.
PROSPERO Twelve year since, Miranda, twelve year since,
Thy father was the Duke of Milan and
A prince of power –

39 His scene-setting made Kemble change 'cell' to 'isle' (1789); similarly, Kean changed 'cell' to 'island' (Edmonds pb) and 'house' to 'place' (42; Ellis pb).

42–4a Dryden/Davenant and Shadwell cut 42 and rearranged the rest to 'Tell me the image then of anything which thou dost keep in thy remembrance still'; Tree cut 43–4a. Brook's 1990 Prospero used a stone to charm Miranda into her remembrance (CD).

44b–52 Dryden/Davenant and Shadwell cut 44b–6a, 48b–9a, and changed 'abysm' to 'abyss' (50). Kemble, Phelps, Burton, Kean and Tree cut 48b–52, with Tree also cutting 46a. Crozier, Wright, Barton and Hytner followed 52b with a pause, signalling Prospero's hesitation or uncertainty or a psychologically significant moment.

53 Dryden/Davenant, Shadwell and Kemble put Prospero and his family on the island for fifteen rather than twelve years, so that Miranda was nearly eighteen rather than nearly fifteen; the additional years gave greater propriety to the romances that ensue. Macready, Burton and Kean added yet another year to their banishment, while Tree cut 53.
   Mendes's Prospero took out his ducal crown and blew off the dust (CD); Purcarete's raised his magic staff, in this production a conductor's baton (CD).

54–5a Tree emphasized Prospero's announcement by having it spoken without musical backing. Indeed, the *Blackwood* critic commented disparagingly about the nearly continuous music, provided by a full-sized orchestra 'hidden beneath a mass of vegetables': 'As the cast always

MIRANDA   Sir, are not you my father?   55
PROSPERO Thy mother was a piece of virtue, and
                    She said thou wast my daughter; and thy father
                    Was Duke of Milan; and his only heir,
                    And princess, no worse issued.
MIRANDA   O the heavens!
                    What foul play had we, that we came from thence?   60
                    Or blessèd was't we did?
PROSPERO   Both, both, my girl.
                    By foul play, as thou say'st, were we heaved thence,
                    But blessedly holp hither.
MIRANDA   O my heart bleeds
                    To think o'th'teen that I have turned you to,
                    Which is from my remembrance. Please you, farther.   65

        speaks to musical accompaniment, generally slow, it is surprising that they make a single
        speech intelligible' (quoted in Nilan, ' "The Tempest" ', p. 123).
55b–9 Dryden/Davenant and Shadwell changed 'a piece of' (56) to 'all' and cut 57b–9a, adding 'and
        thy sister too' to the end of 57a. Many later producers, such as Kemble (1806), Kean, Tree
        and Ayrton, cut the lines entirely, presumably unhappy with the impropriety of Miranda's
        questioning her paternity. Macready retained them, enigmatically punctuating 57 as 'She
        said – thou wast . . .' Uncertainty about the lines stretched well into this century – Phelps,
        Iden Payne (1942) and Hack all originally cut and then restored them; Bridges-Adams
        (1926/30, 1934) funked the issue by cutting only 56–9, so that Miranda did not wait for an
        answer. Some recent handlings of the exchange, such as Hall's (1988), have suggested Pros-
        pero's suspicion of women; Hytner's Prospero spoke 'Thy mother' (56) with some distaste,
        but then changed his tone to continue (CD). In contrast, Alexander's Prospero clearly regis-
        tered Miranda's question as an expression of her inability to think of him as a duke, with his
        reply a gentle and humorous way of affirming the truth (CD); the laugh of Williams's 1978
        Prospero at 57a may have conveyed the same meaning. Daniels's Prospero spoke the lines
        very gently (archive video).
    57 Wright's Prospero rose and crossed C, a movement that marked the beginning of a pattern
        throughout the scene in which Prospero's moves were shadowed a few lines later by
        Miranda, and vice versa, suggesting the closeness between father and daughter.
    58 Donnellan's Prospero 'tosse[d] Miranda's rich dress to the actress' playing her (Hoyle, *FT*
        20/10/88).
  61–5 Dryden/Davenant and Shadwell cut 62–3a; Kean 61–5; Daly 65a. In accommodating
        Dorinda's existence, Dryden/Davenant lost the sense of peril shared by Prospero and
        Miranda: 'How my heart bleeds to think what you have suffer'd' replaced 63b–5a.

PROSPERO My brother and thy uncle, called Antonio –
I pray thee mark me, that a brother should
Be so perfidious – he, whom next thyself
Of all the world I loved, and to him put
The manage of my state, as at that time   70
Through all the signories it was the first,
And Prospero the prime duke, being so reputed
In dignity, and for the liberal arts

Drinkwater's Miranda 'declared with cheerful emphasis that "her heart bleeds" . . . but she smiled as gaily as if he had made a joke she did not quite understand' (*BP* 24/4/16, quoted in Cochrane, *Shakespeare and the Birmingham Repertory Theatre*, p. 51).

66 Prospero's exposition, beginning here and continuing until 186, has often been condensed: passionless Prosperos found it difficult to sustain audience interest, and yet the cutting undertaken to solve the problem only compounded it by draining the account of any emotional content. The more psychologically complex Prosperos of this century have more successfully animated the tale. Gielgud's performance for Devine/Goring, for example, made 'one really listen . . . and realise . . . that Prospero is not just a verbose conjuror on a never-never island, but an Italian noble who has preferred theory to practice in life and has studied the arts instead of ruling men' (*O* 2/6/40). Barton's Prospero relived the experience, his 'eyes never light[ing] on Miranda but mov[ing] away to some distant spot' (John Higgins, *T* 17/10/70). Hall's 1988 Prospero became very excited when he spoke Antonio's name, looking out C and seeming to see him in his mind's eye (CD); since 'this Prospero has spent 12 years simmering with rage', the exposition became 'a passage of recollected fury: he goes almost purple at the very thought of his brother' (Billington, *G* 21/5/88). Wood's handling of the exposition was one of the highlights of Hytner's production: 'The painful and difficult exposition of exile has rarely been so clear'; speaking 'as though the memory of [past events] were still so raw that he can only succumb now to grief and now to rage as he relives them', Prospero 'vacillate[d] between tearful, frustrated anger at the memory and a touching need for emotional reassurance from his daughter' (respectively, Ratcliffe, *O* 28/5/89; King, *STel* 31/7/88; Helen Rose, *TO* 3/8/88). Prospero had clearly been 'seething throughout his exile': 'adversity has not taught him stoicism. . . . he weeps, shouts and shakes with rage, which certainly for once keeps us and Miranda awake' (Hoyle, *FT* 26/5/89). Similarly, Prospero's account in Wolfe's production became 'more a definition of a divided soul than the usual leaden piece of exposition': he 'isolate[d] the phrase "my brother" and dispense[d] it in an angry roar, anger being the production's motivating force' (respectively, Brantley, *NYT* 12/7/95; Gerard, *V* 17–23/7/95). However, not all modern Prosperos are angry: Burge's evinced 'childlike astonishment' at his betrayal, while Miller's (1988) showed

'passive suffering, rather than splenetic outrage' (respectively, Lewsen, *T* 28/2/72; Taylor, *Ind* 13/10/88).

   Some recent productions have semi-dramatized Prospero's account. As Donnellan's Prospero told Miranda his history, he plucked the actor who was to play Antonio from the circle of actors seated on the floor around them (CD): 'The simulated improvisation work[ed] wonders for [this] long scene of exposition . . .' (Ratcliffe, *O* 13/11/88). The way Prospero 'chucked his ridiculously chin-strap-fitted crown onto the floor in the direction of Antonio, as though it were a bone in some game of "Fetch" ', highlighted 'a real ambiguity about the extent to which the magician's bookishness tempted his brother to vicious usurpation' (Taylor, *Ind* 26/11/88). The practice of identifying not only Antonio but also Alonso and Gonzalo during Prospero's long exposition has since become something of a commonplace, serving both to dilute potential monotony and to avoid later audience confusion: Brook's 1990 Antonio, Alonso and Gonzalo came on-stage when mentioned, as did Mendes's lords (CD). Thacker's Antonio had simply to rise from where he lay on-stage, while Purcarete's were lit behind the scrim (CD). Bogdanov's 1992 Prospero took a photograph out of his wallet and handed it to Miranda at mention of his brother (CD).

66–88a Cut by Garrick (1756), with 75 interpolated later. Garrick (1757) cut 79–88a; Kemble (1789) 70b–6a, 79–88a, (1806) 68b–9a, 70b–5, 80b–3a; Macready 72b–4, 78–83a; Kean 78–84; Phelps 80b–3a; Daly 72–4, 78b–87; Tree 70b–7a, 79–83a, 85b–7a; Bridges-Adams (1926/30) 70b–6a, 81b–3a, (1934) 81b–3a; Ayrton 70b–88a; Iden Payne 70b–4 (apart from 'the liberal arts being all my study'), 80–4a. Since Moore's pb marks Macready's cuts in red and Burton's in pencil, they are not easily distinguishable on microfilm: Burton appears to have restored 72b–4a but may have cut 74b–6a; he also cut 78–83a. (Because of the difficulty of differentiating the two sets of cuts, a question mark identifies doubtful Burton ones.)

66–186 Greatly compressed by Dryden/Davenant, who reduced Prospero's narration to sixty-one mostly prose lines. The result is a rational account of the usurpation, without any sense of Prospero's self-absorption and mental reliving of events the reality of which he can still scarcely believe; thus, his reversions to the present tense in 148 are carefully corrected, and his admonitions to Miranda appear the habit of a dull school-teacher to an unappreciative student. The following lines were cut: 67–9a, 70b–6, 81b–5a, 88b, 91–2a, 93b–102a, 103b, 105, 109b–11a, 114–20 (Miranda's 116b is changed to 'False man!'), 123–8a, 132b–8a, 139b–40a, 141b–3, 154–7a, 162a, 169b–70, 172b–80a. These cuts reinforce Antonio's past villainy, not only by making him the executor as well as the agent of Prospero's banishment, but also by omitting Prospero's unwitting emphasis on his abdication of rightful duties to pursue secret studies. The cuts include reference to Antonio's paternity, probably less for reasons of propriety than of length (the earlier question about Miranda's paternity is left intact) and to Prospero's tearful sea-journey. Exact geographical details are added to his account: he was hurried from Milan 'to Savoy, and thence aboard a bark at Nissa's port' (144). The language Prospero uses about his magic is also changed: his 'prescience' is replaced by 'skill', 'zenith' by 'mid-heaven' and 'auspicious' by 'most happy' (180b–2a),

Without a parallel; those being all my study,
The government I cast upon my brother,   75
And to my state grew stranger, being transported
And rapt in secret studies. Thy false uncle –
Dost thou attend me? –
MIRANDA   Sir, most heedfully.
PROSPERO Being once pèrfected how to grant suits,
How to deny them; who t'advance, and who   80
To trash for over-topping; new created
The creatures that were mine, I say, or changed 'em,
Or else new formed 'em; having both the key
Of officer, and office, set all hearts i' th' state
To what tune pleased his ear, that now he was   85
The ivy which had hid my princely trunk,
And sucked my verdure out on't – thou attend'st not!

defining him more precisely as an astrologer. (Dryden's belief in astrology is documented; see Thomas, *Religion and the Decline of Magic*, p. 346). Shadwell adopted the Dryden/Davenant version and also cut 78, 107–8a, 112a, 148b–51a.

74–7a Prospero's attitude to his responsibilities can be made an issue. Neville's Prospero spoke 'ruefully but with confidence that his course [had been] the right one', while Hytner's tossed 75 away, emphasizing his brother's betrayal without seeing his own role in laying the ground for it (respectively, J. W. Lambert, *ST* 3/6/62, and CD; see note to 89–92).

78 Prospero's question is not necessarily prompted by Miranda's inattentiveness. Williams's 1978 Miranda was 'curious about the family history her father thinks must bore her', whereas Paige's provoked the reminder simply by 'looking away to digest all the information he was giving her' (respectively, Young, *FT* 3/5/78; Carter, 'The Tempest at Salisbury Playhouse', p. 11). Benthall's 1951 Prospero had inadvertently made a sign at 77a, causing Miranda to grow sleepy and sink onto her haunches; she 'jerk[ed] up' on 78b (see notes to 86, 92b and 105b–6).

For Brook (1957), Gielgud's '"Dost thou attend me?" to Miranda (an experienced captive audience) [was] a waspish challenge to any Father's-off-again attitude that might spoil self-pity's satisfaction' (*P* 21/8/57); 'his sharp asides . . . to make sure she is heeding him [were] thrown off in a manner which suggest[ed] it doesn't really matter if she isn't' (Peter Rodford, *BWDP* 15/8/57). Daniels's Prospero was 'a very bad-tempered father', though he was 'gentle with his constant reminders to [Miranda] to pay attention' (Young, *FT* 14/9/83). Hall's 1988 Prospero did not focus on Miranda during much of his speech, instead directing his attention to Ariel's off-stage presence; Miranda stood and moved at 77b, prompting Prospero's question (CD).

86 Benthall's 1951 Prospero made another sign, presumably again causing Miranda to grow sleepy.

MIRANDA O good sir, I do.

PROSPERO   I pray thee mark me:
I, thus neglecting worldly ends, all dedicated
To closeness, and the bettering of my mind   90
With that which, but by being so retired,
O'er-prized all popular rate, in my false brother
Awaked an evil nature; and my trust,
Like a good parent, did beget of him
A falsehood, in its contrary as great   95
As my trust was – which had indeed no limit,
A confidence sans bound. He, being thus lorded
Not only with what my revènue yielded,
But what my power might else exact – like one
Who having into truth by telling of it,   100
Made such a sinner of his memory

88b–108a Garrick (1757) cut 89–97a; Kemble (1789, 1806) 89–97a, 99b–108a (with 88b cut in 1806 and 98–9a in 1789); Daly 93b–9a ('my trust . . . exact'); Tree 91–108a; Bridges-Adams (1926/30) 93b–7a, 99b–108a (retaining 102–3's 'believe / He was indeed the duke'), (1934) 93b–7a; Ayrton 88b–97a, 99b–102a; Iden Payne 91–2a; Benthall (1952) 88b–106; Wright 89–106; Brook (1957) and Williams (1978) 91–2a, 99b–102a; Barton 98–100; Daniels 91a, 92a, 100–2a.
          Macready and Kean, having transposed 88a and 88b, cut 89b–92a, 93b–105a and 106–8a, thereby reducing the passage to 'I, thus neglecting worldly ends, in my false brother awak'd an evil nature. Hence, his ambition growing, he needs will be absolute Milan.' Phelps originally cut as Macready but restored 91–6 and 101–8; Burton cut 88b–97a and 99b–108a, perhaps retaining 105b. Hack cut 89–92 so that they read 'all dedicated to the bettering of my mind, in my false brother'.

88b–186   Compressed by Garrick (1756) into thirty-five lines, with word order changed and simplified: 88b–90, 75, 102b–5, 111b, 112b, 121b–2a, 124–32a, 144–7a, 149b–50a, 171–5a, 177b–84a, 185–6. Prospero sang the air, 'In pity, Neptune smooths the liquid way', to describe their idyllic journey to the island, and Miranda sang 'Come, o sleep, my eyelids close' before giving way to the 'good dullness'.

89–92   Hytner's Prospero spoke in a tone that justified his pursuit of secret studies and his neglect of official duties (CD). Perhaps because of this self-justification, Billington commented that, 'although the experience still scorches, this Prospero knows that he lost power through scholarly negligence and that his moral claim to his island retreat is shaky' (G 29/5/89).

92b   Benthall's 1951 Prospero again made a sign, causing Miranda to nod off with her head on his knees and so miss the rest of his speech.

100–1   Changed by Benthall (1951) to read 'Who having minted truth, by telling of it, / Made such a finer of his memory'.

To credit his own lie – he did believe
He was indeed the duke, out o'th'substitution
And executing th' outward face of royalty
With all prerogative. Hence his ambition growing –   105
Dost thou hear?

MIRANDA   Your tale, sir, would cure deafness.

PROSPERO To have no screen between this part he played,
And him he played it for, he needs will be
Absolute Milan. Me, poor man, my library
Was dukedom large enough. Of temporal royalties   110
He thinks me now incapable; confederates –
So dry he was for sway – wi' th' King of Naples
To give him annual tribute, do him homage,
Subject his coronet to his crown, and bend
The dukedom yet unbowed – alas, poor Milan –   115
To most ignoble stooping.

MIRANDA   O the heavens!

103b–5a Cut by Bridges-Adams (1934), Ayrton, Iden Payne, Benthall (1951), Barton, Hack, Williams (1978) and Daniels.

105b–6 On 'growing', Benthall's 1951 Prospero realized the power in his hand, lowered it and raised Miranda's head, waking her on 'Dost thou hear?' A long pause followed 106b, after which Prospero repeated 105b. Although the business may seem curious, it apparently helped to overcome the boredom reviewers often complained of in this scene: Redgrave's 'skilful management of the lengthy, and too often wearisome, monologue in which Miranda, and the audience, are lectured . . . makes fully credible Miranda's "Your tale, sir, would cure deafness" ' (*BEN* 28/6/51).

105–30 Hytner's Stratford pb marks pauses after 'growing' (105), 'Milan' (109), 'enough' (110), 'brother' (127), 'levied' (128) and 'Milan' (130). 'Recounting the indignity of exile from his dukedom, [Prospero shook] his eyes [*sic*] with a trembling hand and [went] to pieces at the memory' (Koenig, *P* 9/6/89).

110–11 'Real rage erupt[ed in Hall's 1988 Prospero] even in speeches about what happened 12 years earlier: "Of temporal royalties / He thinks me now incapable", he fume[d], red-faced with fury, of his perfidious brother' (Kemp, *Ind* 21/5/88).

112–13 For clarity, Barton added 'Alonso called' to the end of 112 and, in order to keep the scansion, cut 'do him homage' from 113. Mendes's Alonso emerged from behind the screen, while Thacker's got up from where he lay on the stage (CD). Tree cut 112a.

114–27b Cut by Kemble (1789); Kemble (1806), Daly, and (?) Burton cut 116b–27b (each retained 127c, 'whereon').

115 At 'unbow'd', Thacker's Antonio knelt to Alonso (CD).

PROSPERO Mark his condition, and th' event, then tell me
     If this might be a brother.
MIRANDA   I should sin
     To think but nobly of my grandmother –
     Good wombs have borne bad sons.
PROSPERO   Now the condition.   120
     This King of Naples, being an enemy
     To me inveterate, hearkens my brother's suit,
     Which was, that he, in lieu o' th' premises
     Of homage, and I know not how much tribute,
     Should presently extirpate me and mine   125
     Out of the dukedom, and confer fair Milan,
     With all the honours, on my brother. Whereon,
     A treacherous army levied, one midnight
     Fated to th' purpose did Antonio open
     The gates of Milan, and i' th' dead of darkness   130

117–20 This second questioning of paternity, like 55b–9, is often cut, though not simply for reasons of propriety: Macready retained the former lines but cut these, his omissions creating a less excitable Prospero, one who seems to be retelling rather than reliving the past. Kean, Ayrton, and Iden Payne also cut 117–20; Tree and Hack 117–20a; Phelps and Bridges-Adams (1926/30, 1934) 118b–20a; Garrick (1757) 120a. Burton cut either 116b–27a or 117–20 (see note to 114–27b).
     Bogdanov's 1992 Prospero took the photograph of Antonio back from Miranda and replaced it in his wallet (CD).
121 Changed by Barton to 'Alonso, King of Naples, enemy'.
     Donnellan's Prospero pulled in the actor who was to play not the King but the Queen of Naples (CD). Anne White portrayed her as 'a handbag-clutching Margaret Thatcher doppel-ganger in navy and pearls', wearing 'one of those clipped little hats of circumspection that match the sour, tight mouth of royal displeasure' (respectively, Annalena McAfee, *ES* 28/11/88; Ratcliffe, *O* 13/11/88). Other critics noted the similarity to Thatcher, but, in one view, 'presenting her as a hard Leaderene-lookalike obscure[d] the fact that of all the shipwrecked malefactors, Alonso experiences the greatest inner change, when the supposed death of his son reduces him to a morally enlarging despair' (Taylor, *Ind* 26/11/88).
123–31 Tree cut 123b–4, 129a, 131 ('The . . . purpose').
127–32a When Hall's 1988 Prospero 'describe[d] how he and Miranda were "heaved" out of Milan the humiliation still burn[ed]' (Billington, *G* 21/5/88).

> The ministers for th' purpose hurried thence
> Me, and thy crying self.
> MIRANDA   Alack, for pity!
> I, not remembering how I cried out then,
> Will cry it o'er again; it is a hint
> That wrings mine eyes to't.
> PROSPERO   Hear a little further,   135
> And then I'll bring thee to the present business
> Which now's upon's; without the which, this story
> Were most impertinent.
> MIRANDA   Wherefore did they not
> That hour destroy us?
> PROSPERO   Well demanded, wench;
> My tale provokes that question. Dear, they durst not,   140
> So dear the love my people bore me; nor set
> A mark so bloody on the business; but
> With colours fairer painted their foul ends.
> In few, they hurried us aboard a barque,

132 Kemble's Prosperos made due reference to Dorinda. Mendes's Antonio and Alonso exited (CD).

132b–8a Cut by Macready, Phelps, Kean and Tree. Kemble (1789) cut 133–8a; Kemble (1806) and Iden Payne 133–5a; Bridges-Adams (1926/30, 1934), Ayrton and Barton 134b–8a; Ashwell 135b–8a; Daly, Iden Payne and Hack 137b–8a.

139b Miranda's question delighted Daniels's Prospero (archive video); Hytner's Prospero made clear that he had never before wondered why they had not been murdered (CD).

139b–40a Cut by Kemble (1806), Macready, Kean and Daly.

140b–1a Perhaps because of 'dear' in 141a, Kemble changed 'Dear' in 140b to 'Girl', Kean to 'My child', and Daly to 'Child'.

    Brook's 1957 Prospero put 'Much pride and profound emotion . . . into his answer to Miranda's question' (*MA* 24/8/57). In contrast, the claim of Hack's Prospero 'sound[ed] like an empty boast; indeed, one suspect[ed] from his nervy paranoia, as well as from the overt tyrannizing of Ariel and Caliban, that this Prospero was banished from Milan because he was a dictator' (Lewsen, *T* 24/10/74).

141b–3 Cut by Daly and Tree.

144–52a Alexander's Prospero was very agitated during his exposition and lost in the story he told; it was clear when he talked about the ship and its rats that he was there in the past, only realizing it was the present when Miranda rushed up to and embraced him (CD). Similarly, as Donnellan's Prospero described the voyage, the cast made sea and wind noises, thus re-

Bore us some leagues to sea, where they prepared   145
A rotten carcass of a butt, not rigged,
Nor tackle, sail, nor mast – the very rats
Instinctively have quit it. There they hoist us
To cry to th' sea, that roared to us; to sigh
To th'winds, whose pity sighing back again   150
Did us but loving wrong.

MIRANDA   Alack, what trouble
Was I then to you!

PROSPERO   O, a cherubin
Thou wast, that did preserve me. Thou didst smile,
Infusèd with a fortitude from heaven,
When I have decked the sea with drops full salt,   155
Under my burden groaned; which raised in me
An undergoing stomach, to bear up
Against what should ensue.

MIRANDA   How came we ashore?

PROSPERO By providence divine.
Some food we had, and some fresh water, that   160

creating it (CD). In contrast, Garrick (1757), Kemble, Burton and Kean changed 'have' (148) to
the past tense, thus missing Prospero's reliving of the horrible moment.

The voice of Hytner's Prospero 'soar[ed] into incredulity at the way the two of them were
thrust into "a rotten carcass of a butt" ' (Billington, *G* 29/5/89). Daniels cut 147a; Miranda
hugged Prospero's knees at 151b.

152 Many Prosperos embrace Miranda, including Macready's, Burton's, Benthall's (1952) and
Purcarete's; Daniels's Prospero and Miranda held hands (archive video). Kemble's
Prosperos duly referred to 'two cherubin'.

153 Benthall's 1951 Prospero kissed Miranda.

153b–8a Many productions omit Prospero's account of his tears and his images suggestive of preg-
nancy. Kemble (1806), Burton and Kean cut 155–6a; Hack 155–8a; Tree 156–8a; Daly, Ayrton
and Iden Payne 156b–8a. Phelps originally cut 153b–6a, but Creswick marks them 'In'; Kean
changed 'An undergoing stomach' (157) to 'A courage'. Benthall's 1951 Miranda nuzzled
against Prospero's chest at 158a.

159 Thacker's spirits lifted their hands, making Gonzalo rise so that Miranda could see him; they
then lowered their hands, allowing him to lie down and go back to sleep (CD).

160–1 Purcarete's Prospero started to rise from his bed, putting on one shoe at 'Some food' (160a)
and the other at 'Gonzalo' (161b).

A noble Neapolitan, Gonzalo,
Out of his charity – who being then appointed
Master of this design – did give us, with
Rich garments, linens, stuffs, and necessaries
Which since have steaded much. So, of his gentleness,   165
Knowing I loved my books, he furnished me
From mine own library, with volumes that
I prize above my dukedom.

MIRANDA   Would I might
But ever see that man.

PROSPERO   Now I arise,

---

161   Brook's 1957 Gonzalo, Cyril Luckham, was 'wise and endearing', thus making understand-
able 'Prospero's affectionate smile as he remembered the noble Neapolitan's charity'
(Trewin, *ILN* 24/8/57). For Hall (1988), Prospero's 'wry chuckle at the mention of . . .
Gonzalo hint[ed] that his humanity is not quite dead' (Billington, *G* 21/5/88). Mendes's
Gonzalo came out from behind the screen (CD).

162b–3a   Tree cut the reference to Gonzalo's being 'appointed / Master of [the] design' to set Prospero
and Miranda adrift.

166b   Purcarete's Prospero left his bed but, bent over as he walked towards the mannikin, had to
be helped by Miranda (CD).

168a   Hytner's Prospero spoke 'prize above my' enthusiastically, but then paused before speaking
'dukedom' quietly and doubtfully (CD).

169a   Mendes's Gonzalo exited (CD).

169b   Prospero's half-line is an implicit sd, which some directors have changed. Garrick (1757) substituted 'attend' for 'I rise', strengthening the suggestion that the actors remained standing
during the scene (see notes to 32 and 170). Macready and Burton gave 169b to Miranda, who
was then told by Prospero to 'Sit still'; Wright's Miranda began to rise but was stayed by a
gesture from her father. Kemble (1806), Phelps, Daly, Tree and Hack cut 169b; the latter's
Prospero had risen *c*. 159.

Purcarete's Prospero, helped by Miranda, reached the mannikin, hugging it as he spoke
169b; at 171a he put on the cloak it had worn, and at 174b its wig. The staging implied that the
exercise of his magic had drained him to the point where it was difficult to walk; assuming
the magic garb restored some of his strength (CD).

Daniels's Prospero stood and Miranda slid forward (pb); there was a sudden sense of
urgency in Prospero's manner, and he appeared distracted during the following lines
(archive video). One critic praised the actor's 'wonderful and dramatic avoidance of the
deadly traps of that long first speech to Miranda' (Evans, *SH* 20/8/82), while another
remarked that he passed 'with ease' the test of holding the audience's attention, thanks to his

Sit still, and hear the last of our sea-sorrow.   170
Here in this island we arrived, and here
Have I, thy schoolmaster, made thee more profit
Than other princes can, that have more time
For vainer hours, and tutors not so careful.
MIRANDA Heavens thank you for't. And now I pray you, sir –   175
For still 'tis beating in my mind – your reason
For raising this sea-storm?
PROSPERO   Know thus far forth:
By accident most strange, bountiful Fortune,
Now my dear lady, hath mine enemies

'beauty of diction and authority of presence' (*STel* 15/8/82). Implying its unusualness, one
reviewer commented that 'wide-eyed Miranda really [had] listen[ed] to her father's story'
(Chapman, *OM* 12/8/82).

170 Cut by Tree; Garrick (1757) cut 'Sit still', while Kemble changed it to 'Attend' (1789) and 'Mark
me' (1806).

171–4 Barton's 'Prospero to begin with [was] very much the Victorian parent, proud of having
done the right thing by his daughter under trying circumstances. His self-esteem
stem[med] not from his magical powers but from his learning and the fact that he ha[d]
transmitted a little of this to Miranda even though Caliban remain[ed] untouched' (Higgins,
T 17/10/70).

173 The meaning has long exercised actor-managers as well as editors: Garrick (1757) and
Kemble (both versions) used 'princes', and Macready 'princess'; other variants are
'princesses' and 'princess's'. Prospero either means he has taught Miranda more than the
tutors of other princesses have done or that Miranda has learned more than other
princesses.

175b–307 McVicker opened his production with 1.2.38b–175, running it straight into 308–74 to consti-
tute scene 1. His second scene was the storm that opens Shakespeare's play, while the third
ran 1.2.1–17 straight into 175b–307. The act ended with scene 4, the 'Yellow Sands' sequence
(Becks's pb).

177a Changed by Kemble (1789) to 'For this purpos'd storm'.

178b–9a Cut by Daly.

179 'More maternal than fatherly', Hytner's Prospero picked Miranda up in his arms; 'when he
carries her . . . it seems he is carrying their past: she could again be the child he first brought
to the island' (Kellaway, *O* 31/7/88). Miranda remained in his arms through the rest of his
speech (CD).

Brought to this shore; and by my prescience   180
I find my zenith doth depend upon
A most auspicious star, whose influence
If now I court not, but omit, my fortunes
Will ever after droop. Here cease more questions.
Thou art inclined to sleep. 'Tis a good dullness,   185
And give it way; I know thou canst not choose.

[MIRANDA *sleeps*]

180a Kemble (1789) changed 'to this shore' to 'on these seas'. Tree's Miranda moved as if to speak, whereupon Prospero made a 'hypnotic movement, causing Miranda to feel sleepy'.

180b–4a Cut by Daly and Tree. The Williams/Brook production may have connected the 'most auspicious star' (182a) to 'the flame-coloured disc that glares balefully at us like a huge cyclopean eye at the beginning, goes into eclipse during the tempest, moves on an orbit across the backcloth, briefly becomes a planet, and burns itself out like the setting sun at the end' (*OM* 3/4/63).

184b–6 After 184a, Kemble (1806) added the sd 'Takes up his wand, and charms Miranda to sleep'; she fell asleep after 186, at which point Prospero put on his mantle, thereby suggesting that to command Ariel requires greater magical powers than the staff alone can give. Tree's Prospero led Miranda slowly to the couch at 184b, whereas Brook's (1957) held his arm out to her, making her sink to rest against a rock (DL pb); Thacker's waved his staff in front of her eyes (CD). At 185, Burge's Prospero made 'hypnotic hand movements' to make Miranda sleep (Foulkes, review, p. 8), while Hack's caressed her. Alexander's used an obvious spell that involved touching his staff: Miranda went into a trance and walked slowly to DSC where she slept (CD). Brook's 1990 Prospero charmed Miranda to sleep with a stone; see note to 42–4a. Paige's Prospero fixed his eyes on Miranda at 185a, who looked at him 'protestingly' at 185b–6a; at 186b, he 'held out his hand, palms down, fingers extended towards her', causing her to 'drop like a stone' from the standing position she had assumed at 177a (Carter, '*The Tempest* at Salisbury Playhouse', p. 14). Other Prosperos, such as Hall's (1974) and Ninagawa's, put on their magic garment and took up their wand. Garrick (1757) and Kemble (1789) made 186b an aside.

186sd Miranda is asleep by this point, as Prospero's 187 indicates that he is 'ready now' for Ariel. Miranda's being asleep when Ariel first appears leaves open the question of her knowledge of the spirit.

Come away, servant, come; I'm ready now.
Approach, my Ariel. Come!

Enter ARIEL

ARIEL All hail, great master, grave sir, hail! I come
To answer thy best pleasure; be't to fly,   190

187 Cut by Garrick (1756), whose Prospero simply ordered 'Approach, my Ariel' (188); Daly cut
187b. Dryden/Davenant and Shadwell changed 'servant, come' to 'my spirit'.
   Kean showed a thunderbolt descending behind a bush (Edmonds pb): a perpendicular
stream of light shone from above, while the bush opened and the lights were gradually
raised, lime light and Kerr's light being used at the same time (Ellis pb); the latter allowed the
'strongly-illuminated head of a person [to be] projected upon a semi-transparent screen . . .
by means of a silvered glass or metallic reflector and a case cointaining two achromatic
lenses' (quoted in Rees and Wilmore, *British Theatrical Patents*, p. 13). Benthall's Prospero
gestured, whereupon the hedgehogs and barnacle ran on to clear things. Barton's Prospero
put on his cloak and '[hummed t]o summon spirits' (pb; Barber, *DT* 17/10/70). Purcarete's
Prospero was almost sick as he spoke (CD).
188 Benthall's 1952 Prospero summoned Ariel 'without raising his voice, as though Ariel was a
very well-trained sheepdog' (Peter Fleming, *Sp*). In contrast, Williams's 1978 Prospero was
'most unsure of his own powers: clenching his eyes in dreadful uncertainty when he
summon[ed] . . . Ariel, and mastering the mutinous spirit only at great cost to himself'
(Wardle, *T* 3/5/78). Hytner's Prospero made clear that he did not know where Ariel was (CD).
188sd Based on Inigo Jones's sketch of an 'Aery Spirit' and Ben Jonson's description of Jophiel, a
spirit in his 1626 masque *Fortunate Isles*, Ernest Law posits that the original Ariel would have
worn a 'close fitting tunic of silk in rainbow colours, wings tinctured in harmony with it, a
scarf over his shoulders, buskins or blue silk stockings, and on his head a chaplet of flowers'
('Shakespeare's "Tempest" ', p. 20). Sturgess persuasively argues that Ariel would have been
played by a boy, since Prospero treats the spirit 'like a child' and 'as someone small of
stature', using words like ' "delicate", "dainty" and "chick" ' (*Jacobean Private Theatre*, p. 77);
in addition, Ariel spends much of the play in female costume, the preserve of the boy-actor.
Richard Robinson, the principal boy-actor in the King's Men at the time, would probably have
played either Ariel or Miranda (Sturgess, *Jacobean Private Theatre*, p. 77); the other part
may have been played by John Rice (see Saenger, 'Costumes', p. 334, for Rice's part in a sea-
pageant acted by two of the King's Men).
   Variants exist in the two main approaches to Ariel outlined in the Introduction – either
submissive or resistant to Prospero – and indeed, the two may sometimes be combined.
Harcourt Williams's Ariel managed to convey, despite his obedience, 'the melancholy of his

exile and his passionate foreknowledge of liberty' (*T* 19/4/33). Wright's 'gave feeling to a character who is usually shown with all too little', her 'spirit of independence and pride [shining] through the subservience' (respectively, *WES* 10/5/47; *BM* 10/5/47). Ciulei's was 'very down-to-earth', 'delightfully offhand', 'exceptionally funny and dashing', 'yet with a snappingly brittle edge' (respectively, Weiser, *NBB* 2/7/81; Dan Sullivan, *LAT* typescript fax, 20/8/81; Rich, *NYT* 4/7/81; Carla Waldemar, *TCR* 18/6/81). Daniels's, sometimes 'anxious to please' and sometimes sulking, 'emphasise[d] Ariel's impatience to return to the elements' (Edwards, *NS* 20/8/82). De Berardinis's felt the 'servitude of love' that cannot 'completely renounce freedom', expressing the contradiction by slow movement and vocal quality (Grande, *R* 19/4/86). Often, the relationship between Prospero and Ariel is not simply complex but difficult to read: in one view, Hack's Ariel was 'sombre' and 'bristling with over-sharp resentment', while in another his relationship with Prospero was 'most imaginatively established' as 'bitter-sweet' (respectively, Peter, *ST* 3/11/74; Chapman, *OM* 23/10/74). Similarly, the relationship between Daniels's pair produced conflicting opinions: some reviewers sensed a struggle in Ariel's need to 'choose freedom' over love, while others felt that Prospero's friendship was 'unreciprocated' by the 'exploited' spirit (respectively, James Fenton, *ST* 15/8/82; Coveney, *FT* 13/8/82; Billington, *G* 14/9/83).

Other Ariels impatient or anxious for liberty include that of Devine/Goring, 'a quivering, mercurial' spirit 'passionately eager for freedom' (respectively, *DT* 30/5/40; *T* 30/5/40). Atkins's 1949 Ariel 'admirably disclose[d] . . . [her] passion to be free again' (*T* 19/7/49), speaking 'crisply' and doing 'her best to overcome a rather unhappy get-up vaguely reminiscent of a teashop waitress' (*DT* 19/7/49). The 'readiness [of Armfield's Ariel] to enact her master's commands [had] a testy impatience to it' (Evans, *SMH* 31/5/90; however, see note to 5.1.314b–16a for a very different final image of the spirit). Tipton's was 'a dour fairy . . . a dutiful, slightly angry tomboy who [found] neither humor nor any particular joy in her magic' (Steele, *MST* 15/10/91). Meckler's Ariel played the part 'rather brilliantly . . . as a recalcitrant and otherworldly teenager bowed by parental expectation'; her relationship with Prospero '[made explicit w]hat is implicit in the relationship between father and daughter' (Gardner, *G* 1/2/97). Such impatient or angry Ariels can sometimes prove frightening: Benthall's (1951) was 'a rather terrifying unearthly sprite, reminiscent of Mercury', while that of Williams/Brook showed a 'poised eeriness . . . faintly underlined by a sense of danger'; similarly, Murray's, with his 'air of wildness and menace', was 'a far cry from the Peter Pan tradition' (respectively, *WA* 9/6/51; Richard Findlater, *O* 7/4/63; Holdsworth, *TLS* 21–7/9/90).

Some Ariels, like Bridges-Adams's (1934), emphasize 'the spirit's remoteness from all human emotion' (*DT* 17/4/34). Iden Payne's (1938), making a welcome departure from 'the pretty-pretty singing fairy of tradition', showed 'sublime detachment from the human world in which [he] was confined' (respectively, *SH* 6/5/38; *BP* 3/5/38). Hall's (1988) seemed 'eerily dispassionate – staring at the mortals' unruly behaviour with the cold fascination of a child who has a quick intelligence but no empathy with adult emotions' (Kemp, *Ind* 21/5/88). In addition, Bridges-Adams's Ariel also stressed her acrobatic agility, from one moment to the next 'riding a cloud . . . leap[ing] from the heart of a crag or glid[ing] down the sheer face of a steep rock' (*BM* 17/4/34). Lepage's was not only 'acrobatic [and] puckish', using the neon-strip 'light fixture as both a trapeze and a perch', but also 'a sort of stage manager' to Prospero's 'theatre director' (respectively, Pat Donnelly, *MGa* 7/6/93; Donnelly; Conlogue, *TGM*; Conlogue). Similarly, Hall's 1974 androgynous Ariel emphasized his protean nature: besides having seven costume changes, Ariel sang 'sweetly on occasions as both counter-tenor and tenor' (John Elsom, 'Creaking Storm'). In such ways, some approaches overlap with others.

Not all modern productions problematize the master–servant relationship. Brook's 1990 Ariel 'enjoy[ed] executing Prospero's will' and, indeed, proved 'A bit bashful throughout about bringing up the subject of his manumission'; Edwards's Ariel even gave 'a hint of eroticism between [her and Prospero]' (respectively, Billington, *G* 19/10/90; Taylor, *Ind* 2/11/90; John Larkin, *SA* 20/5/90). Similarly, even though Wolfe cast African-American actors as both Ariel and Caliban 'to reflect the experience of African slaves' and Aunjanue Ellis played Ariel as 'a sassy black woman, often full of attitude', most critics agreed that her relationship with Prospero had too much of a sexual edge (respectively, Brantley, *NYT* 14/7/95; Kissel, *DN* 12/7/95). She was 'costumed like a modern cabaret star', wearing a 'gold bodice and a belly-dancer's see-through skirt' suggestive of the 'harem'; her hair was 'brilliant red' and 'her face dusted with gold' (respectively, John Heilpern, *NYO* 31/7/95; Malcolm Johnson, *HC* 16/7/95; Cindy Nemser, *OurT* 20/7/95; Martin Gottfried, *NYLJ* 14/7/95; Karam, *T* 14/7/95).

Other conceptual approaches, however, can prove more successful. In keeping with his idea of the play as a 'colonial parable', Miller (1970, 1988) cast black actors as both Ariel and Caliban but 'allot[ted] to each a separate rank in the colonial order': his 1970 Ariel was 'the lordly African colonized by the European Prospero, impatient for independence' (respectively, Wardle, *T* 16/6/70; Wardle; *P* 24/6/70; however, another reviewer, while recognizing his difference from Caliban, saw him an 'a sulky house-boy, elegant in black breeches' (Barber, *DT* 16/6/70)). Similarly, his 1988 Ariel 'obey[ed] Prospero with an element of privately-enjoyed irony, almost within secret inverted commas. His riveting eyes slither[ed] from side to side with lazy, sly humour . . . [He was] the ambivalent smart-ass co-operating for his own ends', 'sly and indolent yet apparently the perfect servant' (respectively, Taylor, *Ind* 13/10/88; Paul Anderson, *Tr* 21/10/88).

As some of the preceding examples indicate, Ariel's costumes vary as greatly as interpretation of the part. The gauzy fairies and classical figures described in the Introduction can sometimes be combined: Benson's 1897 Ariel, for example, wore a short Greek tunic with medium-sized dragon-like wings and an indeterminate decoration sprouting from the top of her head (*DG* 21/4/1897). Similarly, the classical approach can be allied to an emphasis on physicality: both Harcourt Williams and Benthall (1951) dressed Ariel in a loin-cloth; the former also wore a winged helmet, while the latter's hair had the curls of a Greek statue and his body an unearthly sheen (production photos). Despite its focus on the human body, near-nakedness itself is sometimes used to signify otherworldliness, as with the Ariels of Neville and Barton. The latter was 'an androgynous figure, uncovered except for a G-string and a pony-tail of blond hair falling over the shoulders. The movements [were] graceful, the [face and] body powder white and . . . the voice . . . a childish, sexless chant' (Higgins, *T* 17/10/70).

Barton's use of body powder and stress on androgyny are echoed by many other Ariels, though not always in conjunction. Hytner's 'stone-grey' or 'icy-tinted' Ariel, for example, was 'a figure of unearthly, sleek-haired pathos', managing to be both 'manly and ethereal' (respectively, Kellaway, *O* 31/7/88; Kemp, *Ind* 26/5/89; Billington, *G* 29/7/88; Clive Hirschhorn, *SE* 28/5/89). Other androgynous or hermaphroditic Ariels include those of Daniels, Hall (1974, 1988), Jamieson/Quayle, Mitchell and Edwards, while tinted ones include Wright's 'ash-blue' Ariel, Williams/Brook's 'slight pale-bluish spirit', Jones's 'scaly silver being', and Noble's 'blanched' and 'spectral' spirit (respectively, *NC* 16/5/47; Marriott, *STT* 4/4/63; Bryden, *O* 21/7/68; de Jongh, *ES* 26/2/98; Nightingale, *T* 27/2/98).

Other Ariel costumes turn the body inside-out: at Stratford, Daniels's was 'sexually ambiguous', 'a silver sprite with a tangle of red and blue veins leading up his body to blue hair mottled with pink', brushed straight up from his crown in punk style (respectively, Billington, *G* 12/8/82; Chaillet, *T* 13/8/82); in London, however, he wore an 'ugly loincloth' instead of the veiny costume and his own hair slicked back in place of the punkish wig (respectively, Giles Gordon, *Sp* 9/83; *O* photo, 18/9/83). David William's Ariel was a 'blanched' skeletal version of Prospero, 'made up from head to foot in chalky white, [with] . . . the lines of his muscles . . . drawn in all over in black. He looked exactly like a diagram from an old medical text-book' (respectively, *T* 3/6/55; *G* 3/6/55).

Ariel's costume can also directly refer to theatrical tradition. Strehler's, a white-faced pierrot in a white skull-cap, wore a loosely billowing body-suit over her tight-fitting body stocking; her 'costume [was one] traditionally associated with . . . Deburau', a 'version of Pierrot [that] allowed Strehler to communicate the superiority of Ariel as a character of dignity, if still a servant' (Kleber, 'Theatrical Continuities', p. 152). For her first entrance, Ariel descended over Prospero's head and continued to fly during much of their ensuing conversation. As she cavorted in the air, the diaphanous material of her costume made her sometimes seem an ectoplasmic shape-shifter; at other times, she seemed a weightless pet-spirit, as she 'sat' on Prospero's arm, 'stood' on his shoulder, or straddled his chest, wrapping her legs around his back (CD). Although seemingly free in her movements, 'the flying-wire attached to [her] back' symbolized her 'enslavement': she '[spun], cycle[d] and plummet[ed] through the air . . . yet at the same time, you sense[d] the passionate hunger for true liberty' (Billington, *G* 16/11/83). Hers was the 'key' performance of the production, since she was 'the practical executant of Prospero's theatrical shows' (Warren, *TLS* 9/3/84).

Other Ariels dress more ordinarily: Bogdanov's (1978) was 'an impassive figure in cricket-flannels', while Ciulei's wore 'sneakers', 'black trousers and a white open-necked shirt' and Falls's a white vest, track bottoms and trainers (respectively, Billington, *G* 29/11/78; Larry Larson, *SCSN* 30/7/81; Jonathan Saville, *SDR* 9/81; Pellowe (photo), 'In Chicago', p. 55). Murray's wore a 'silvered parody of formal dress', whereas Tipton's 'dresse[d] like a street-wise punk' (respectively, Wainwright, *Ind* 15/9/90; Brad Canham, uc). Mendes's, looking a bit like Boy George with kohl-rimmed eyes and white face, wore a silk Mao suit that was 'sometimes white, sometimes lilac, sometimes midnight blue' (Kellaway, *O* 15/8/93). In quite a different vein, Thacker's Ariel wore ragged Jacobean clothes, her appearance reminiscent of early prints of American natives, with a painted face and Indian-style hair decorated with a single feather; the three spirits who accompanied her were similarly costumed (CD).

Some Ariels have been played by several actors in one production (see Introduction for Poel's). Thorndike/Warburton divided the part into three: 'an airy Spirit' (Kitty Carlton), 'a Nymph' (Ogna Hicks) and 'a Harpy' (Winifred Oughton) (programme). James's was played by three actors, with Stephen Boyle, who also played Ferdinand, predominant (Nugent, *CT* 23/8/89); the others were Elizabeth Newman, who doubled as Miranda, and Paul Taylor, who doubled as Adrian. Although Arias's Ariel was played by Clotilde Mollet in formal page-boy livery, she had 'two lookalikes who bob[bed] up alternatingly from the opposite direction' after her exits (Curtis, *FT* 18/7/86). Breuer's Ariel was played simultaneously by eleven actors, ranging in age, sex and race, although there was a chief one 'garbed as a sumo wrestler with matching gestures and grunts' (Kalem, *Time* 20/7/81). The voice of Purcarete's Ariel, recorded by Michael Fitzgerald, who played Prospero, was heard only as a voice-over, with Ariel himself represented by seven actors, five of them musicians, supplemented by three mannikins; they were dressed in eighteenth-century costume and wore powdered wigs like Prospero (programme; CD). Fitzgerald's Ariel-voice, spoken 'in an unchangingly neutral tone', 'possibly . . . suggest[ed] an Ariel so disembodied that he [had to] borrow Prospero's voice'; similarly, the spirit's 'visible manifestations . . . fit his master's 18th-century notion of what servants should look like' (Kingston, *T* 12/9/95).

Like Purcarete, other directors have found theatrical means to embody a particular conception of the spirit. Warner emphasized Ariel's 'immateriality' by the 'flashing mirror' Prospero had to use to communicate with her (respectively, Affleck, *Sco*, in *LTR* Edinburgh Festival Supplement 1983; Randall Stevenson, *TLS* 16/9/83). Because Tipton's Ariel was ' "the rightful possessor of the island . . . whenever Ariel appear[ed] something strange . . . happen[ed] in sound" ': 'When she touche[d] the edge of a large transparent disk it resonate[d]; at times her laughter [could] be heard moving around the perimeter of the theatre; when she drop[ped] a rock into the hole in the middle of the floor there [was] a long silence – as though the space below the stage were a thousand feet deep – and then a distant explosion' (respectively, sound environment designer Hans Peter Kuhn, quoted in Shyer, 'Disenchanted', p. 30; Shyer, 'Disenchanted', p. 30). Bogdanov's 1992 Ariel 'cross[ed] the stage on a tightrope when she [was] casting a spell', but unfortunately Fouéré concentrated 'so hard on not falling off that enchantment [was] the last thing she project[ed]' (Nightingale, *T* 30/11/92).

Although the text demands 'shapes' for the banquet and masque, other spirits often accompany Ariel throughout the play: Williams/Brook had Ariel attended by 'four zombie-like mock Ariels' (*LP* 3/4/63), while Barton and Daniels both provided a 'train' of spirits 'in [Ariel's] likeness' (Knapp, *TES* 23/10/70, and archive video; see note to 239–46). Hall's 1988 Ariel was accompanied throughout by 'alternately masked and faceless' spirits, 'sinister bald elves who turn[ed] into monstrous, black-winged birds or red-eyed hounds' (respectively, Jim Hiley, *L* 26/5/88; Billington, *G* 21/5/88).

Nineteenth-century Ariels made spectacular first entrances. Macready's 'crosse[d] the stage from R to L in the form of a ball of fire' and disappeared into the L trap (189–93a were spoken from 'without'). Phelps copied and eventually varied the business: after the fireball appeared, 301–4 were interpolated, and Ariel rose 'from the sea in a Marine shell' or was 'drawn in a slote [sloat] from R' in the guise of a sea-nymph (Creswick pb); in another version Ariel descended the OP2E sloat (Williams pb). Kean's Ariel came up on a small trap L, presumably through the opened bush (see note to 187): 'when Prospero summons [Ariel], a shooting-star falls from heaven and touches the grass; it burns with blue and green flames, and then one suddenly sees Ariel's beautiful angelic form . . . clad in white, with wings from his shoulder reaching to the ground; he appeared to have come with the shooting-star' (Andersen, *Pictures of Travel*, pp. 283–4). Every appearance of Ariel was different and beautiful: she would 'appear suddenly, hanging by the hand, in a garland of vine leaves' or float over the stage (p. 284); she also rose 'gently from a tuft of flowers', sailed on a dolphin's back, glided over sands as a noiseless water-nymph, perched on a rock or a bat's back, and split the air 'with the velocity of lightning' (Cole, *Life and Theatrical Times*, vol. II, p. 220).

Twentieth-century entrances range from the elaborate to the simple. Hall's 1974 and 1988 Ariels respectively 'descend[ed] from the flies on a bow-like trapeze' and 'a whalebone' (Wardle, *T* 6/3/74; Coveney, *FT* 20/5/88), whereas Falls's made an 'earthbound' first entrance, 'all the better to delight by contrast later: black-clad stagehands roll[ed] in a hydraulic stage lift prominently marked with the brand name *Genie* and they lower[ed] the high platform so that Ariel . . . [could] remove the safety chain and step off. But thereafter he dance[d], he [leapt], he [flew] out over the audience . . . He appear[ed] from nowhere to mystify the already befuddled. He haunt[ed] the shipwrecked sailors by playing the violin . . . Wearing the likeness of a NASA space suit and suspended between two slender harness lines, he perform[ed] a weightless, breathtaking ballet' (Pellowe, 'In Chicago', p. 55). More simply, Brook's 1990 Ariel entered 'bearing on his head a miniature ship which he then remove[d] to show how he "flamed amazement" . . . amongst the masts and decks', knocking and tossing it in demonstration (Billington, *G* 19/10/90; CD).

189 The Williams/Brook Ariel was first heard as 'a haunting, disembodied voice' (Chapman, *OM* 3/4/63). Similarly, Hytner's Ariel was invisible and his voice unplaced as he spoke 189, making Prospero search for him with his eyes up, down and around the stage; at 'I come', he appeared at the top of the SL proscenium arch and glided down it, supported by a pole (CD; Stratford pb). Donnellan split Ariel's opening lines among the cast, including Miranda, with Prospero pointing a stick to direct them to speak (CD); then 'the eventual player of the part advance[d], almost trance-like, as if taken over by the role' (Hoyle, *FT* 20/10/88).

Miller's 1988 Ariel spoke with an African accent (CD). The 'hostile sarcasm' with which Wolfe's Ariel (and Caliban) 'intone[d] the word "master" [was] perhaps overdone' (Brantley, *NYT* 12/7/95).

To swim, to dive into the fire, to ride
On the curled clouds. To thy strong bidding task
Ariel, and all his quality.

PROSPERO   Hast thou, spirit,
Performed to point the tempest that I bade thee?

ARIEL To every article.   195
I boarded the king's ship. Now on the beak,
Now in the waist, the deck, in every cabin,
I flamed amazement. Sometime I'd divide
And burn in many places; on the topmast,
The yards and bowsprit, would I flame distinctly,   200
Then meet and join. Jove's lightning, the precursors
O' th' dreadful thunder-claps, more momentary
And sight-outrunning were not; the fire and cracks
Of sulphurous roaring the most mighty Neptune
Seem to besiege, and make his bold waves tremble,   205
Yea, his dread trident shake.

PROSPERO   My brave spirit!
Who was so firm, so constant, that this coil
Would not infect his reason?

192–3a Hytner's Ariel appeared distracted, as if he had something (his freedom?) on his mind (CD).

193a Dryden/Davenant, Shadwell and Garrick changed 'quality' to the plural so that Ariel no
longer meant fellow spirits but her/his own characteristics. When Daniels's Ariel said
'quality', five other 'Ariels' ran forward (archive video); Coveney found the 'attendant spirits
. . . well used throughout as goddesses, swains, scene shifters and vocal background'
(*FT* 13/8/82). Some critics thought them less effective, and, when the production transferred
to London, Chaillet was relieved that the 'hordes of fairies' were 'gone now, present only for
the massive acts of magic' (*WSJ* 9/83).
     Garrick's Ariel followed 193a with the air 'In the bright moonshine, while winds whistle
loud'. Macready interpolated 301–4 after 193a, whereupon Ariel emerged from the trap
wearing green weeds and a coral wreath (Downer, *The Eminent Tragedian*, p. 251).

193b–239 Condensed by Garrick (1756) to five lines: 'Spirit, thou hast perform'd to point / The tempest
that I bade thee, and dispos'd / The ship and princes exactly to thy charge / But there's more
work: what is the time o'th'day?'; Ariel responded 'Past the mid-season', whereupon
Prospero sang the air 'We must work, we must haste'. Kemble changed 'Perform'd' to
'Prepar'd' to accommodate his change of scene order and cut 196–238.

198b–208a Dryden/Davenant and Shadwell cut 198b, 200a, 201–6a, the latter adding 'Nay once I rain'd
a shower of fire upon 'em' to remind the audience of the scenic effects of Scene 1. Macready

ARIEL   Not a soul
     But felt a fever of the mad, and played
     Some tricks of desperation. All but mariners   210
     Plunged in the foaming brine and quit the vessel,
     Then all a-fire with me; the king's son Ferdinand,
     With hair up-staring – then like reeds, not hair –
     Was the first man that leaped; cried 'Hell is empty,
     And all the devils are here'.
PROSPERO   Why that's my spirit.   215
     But was not this nigh shore?
ARIEL   Close by, my master.
PROSPERO But are they, Ariel, safe?
ARIEL   Not a hair perished;
     On their sustaining garments not a blemish,
     But fresher than before. And as thou bad'st me,
     In troops I have dispersed them 'bout the isle.   220
     The king's son have I landed by himself,
     Whom I left cooling of the air with sighs
     In an odd angle of the isle, and sitting,
     His arms in this sad knot.
PROSPERO   Of the king's ship,

and Kean cut 198b–203a, 206b–8a; Burton 198b–201a, 203b–8a; Daly 201b–8a; Hack
      201b–2a. Brook's 1990 Ariel was very pleased with Prospero's praise, doing a backwards
      somersault and dancing (CD).
209   Garrick (1757) changed 'mad' to 'mind'.
212a Cut by Dryden/Davenant and Shadwell.
215b–16 Cut by Daly and Hack, but Daniels's Prospero showed 'generous joy' in expressing his delight
      with Ariel (*OT* 20/8/82).
217a Daniels's Prospero asked his question in a very worried tone (archive video).
218–19 Cut by Dryden/Davenant, Shadwell and Hack.
221   Macready's Ariel made Ferdinand sound like a prize fish: 'The king's son have I landed by
      myself' (my italics). Daniels's Prospero glanced at Miranda.
222–37a Cut by Burton. Macready cut 229b–32a; Kean 227c–9 ('where . . . there'), 231; Daly 228b–9a
      ('to . . . Bermoothes'); Barton 231, 233; Hack 224b–6a (replacing them with 'And the king's
      ship?'), 227b–9, 232b–7a. Dryden/Davenant and Shadwell had Ferdinand *warming* the air
      with sighs' (222; my italics).
224   Ariel's words demand an illustrative action; most fold their arms.

The mariners, say how thou hast disposed,   225
And all the rest o'th'fleet?
ARIEL   Safely in harbour
Is the king's ship, in the deep nook, where once
Thou call'dst me up at midnight to fetch dew
From the still-vexed Bermudas, there she's hid;
The mariners all under hatches stowed,   230
Who, with a charm joined to their suffered labour,
I've left asleep. And for the rest o' th' fleet –
Which I dispersed – they all have met again,
And are upon the Mediterranean float
Bound sadly home for Naples,   235
Supposing that they saw the king's ship wracked,
And his great person perish.
PROSPERO   Ariel, thy charge
Exactly is performed; but there's more work.
What is the time o'th'day?
ARIEL   Past the mid season.
PROSPERO At least two glasses. The time 'twixt six and now   240
Must by us both be spent most preciously.

226 Paige's Ariel 'drew a map in the sand with his finger' to show where he had left the ship
     (Carter, '*The Tempest* at Salisbury Playhouse', p. 15).

228 Mendes's Ariel had a 'brilliant momentary pause when he remind[d] Prospero "thou
     called'st me up at midnight" as if he's spent his life in sleepless servitude' (Billington,
     G 15/7/94). In contrast, Thacker's Ariel showed no sense of anger but rather an eagerness to
     please, a sense of pleasure in herself and what she has done in Prospero's service (CD).

229a After 'Bermoothes' (the Folio's word for 'Bermudas'), Daniels's Ariel cleared his throat,
     eliciting audience laughter (archive video).

237b-8 At 238b, Benthall's 1951 Prospero used his power to stop Ariel (from exiting? protesting?).
     Miller's 1988 Ariel intended to exit at 237b-8a, but 238b stopped him. The music that
     Purcarete's Ariels were playing suddenly trailed off at 'more work' (CD).

239-41 Cut by Kean. Kemble (1789) cut 240a, while Macready ran it into Ariel's preceding line. Tree
     cut 239-40, retaining only 'The time' (240).

239-46 Barton's spirit-voices could be heard, offering 'resistance to Prospero'. Many reviewers
     allude to the figures, mentioning, for example, 'sculptural spirit-shapes dimly discernible
     behind the blue-green scrim' (Bryden, *O* 18/10/70; see note to 1.1).

240-318sd Reduced by Garrick (1756) to thirty lines, with those spoken to and by Caliban omitted:
     243, 245-6, 250b, 258a, 285b-6a (the former changed to 'the dam of Caliban'),

ARIEL Is there more toil? Since thou dost give me pains,
          Let me remember thee what thou hast promised,
          Which is not yet performed me.
PROSPERO   How now? Moody?
          What is't thou canst demand?
ARIEL   My liberty.   245
PROSPERO Before the time be out? No more.
ARIEL   I prithee,
          Remember I have done thee worthy service,
          Told thee no lies, made no mistakings, served

251b–6, 286b–7a, 291b–3a, 277b–8a, 294–6, 301–2a, 318. Ariel exited after 318, and Miranda and Prospero after 307a.

242 Phelps's Ariel turned 'moodily away', and Burton's was sulky. Other Ariels, like those of Strehler and Williams (1978) reacted angrily; Daniels's shouted 242a, and Thacker's stamped her foot several times (archive video; CD).

242–99 Up to 242, the relationship between Paige's master and servant had been one of 'warm complicity'; now, 'Prospero's voice hardened'. During the ensuing scene, Ariel argued his case reasonably until Prospero mentioned freeing him from the pine; at that point 'he stood up and turned away, not quite sulkily, but as one who has heard and resented all this before, and yet must bear it again'. Since Prospero also stood up at the mention of Sycorax (263b), he and Ariel 'were almost nose to nose' for the rest of their argument; then 'the tension at once fell away, and Ariel's voice became warm and enthusiastic again' (Carter, 'The Tempest at Salisbury Playhouse', p. 15).

244b The tone of Daniels's Prospero was indulgent (archive video); his description of Ariel as 'moody' had 'never been more a case of the pot and the kettle' (*MS* 16/8/82). Purcarete's Ariels closed around Prospero in a circle at 'moody?' (CD).

245b Ariel's self-confidence is variable. Williams's (1978) had a long pause before speaking; in one view, his 'relationship with his master [was] compounded of wary respect and sullen impatience', while, in another, he showed 'a frightening malevolence' when he demanded his freedom (respectively, Evans, *SH*; *DH*, both 5/5/78). Burton's Ariel spoke 'with slight trepidation' and gradually became bolder, while that of Williams/Brook was subject to 'frenzied trembling' (Higgins, *FT* 3/4/63). Strehler's Ariel tugged at her flying-rope, making it clear that it constituted an imprisonment (video), so that, as Jan Kott put it, the theatrical 'prop suddenly [became] a metaphor' (quoted in Kleber, 'Theatrical Continuities', p. 145).

246a Daniels's Prospero shouted.

246b–50a Phelps's Ariel spoke 'entreatingly', while Wright's Ariel knelt. Strehler's Ariel 'tried to hide in embarrassment like a scolded child behind Prospero's stick, which had been stuck in the sand' (Kleber, 'Theatrical Continuities', p. 145), whereas Brook's (1990) climbed onto a perch

Without or grudge or grumblings. Thou did promise
To bate me a full year.

PROSPERO   Dost thou forget   250
From what a torment I did free thee?

ARIEL   No.

PROSPERO Thou dost! And think'st it much to tread the ooze
Of the salt deep,
To run upon the sharp wind of the north,
To do me business in the veins o' th' earth   255
When it is baked with frost.

ARIEL   I do not, sir.

PROSPERO Thou liest, malignant thing. Hast thou forgot
The foul witch Sycorax, who with age and envy
Was grown into a hoop? Hast thou forgot her?

on the SR wall to put some distance between himself and his master (CD). Purcarete's Ariels lay down at 'no more!' (CD); one reviewer commented that Prospero's 'increasing grief at liberating his spirit [was] intensified because he [was] bidding farewell to a part of himself' (Shuttleworth, *FT* 16/9/95).

246b–50 Williams's 1978 Prospero had a long pause before 250b; Daniels's Prospero read his book during 246b–50a, only shutting it to speak (archive video).

251b Burton's Ariel trembled with horror, and Iden Payne's fell on her knees; Williams's (1978) had a long pause before answering.

252–7 Garrick (1757) cut 252–6; Daly 252b–7a. Burton's Ariel spoke 256b apologetically (pb), whereas Thacker's was defiant (CD). Hytner's Prospero was visibly wrapped up in his own scheme, unaware of any imposition on Ariel; to him, it was clearly no burden for the spirit to do his bidding, compared to his possible fate of perpetual imprisonment: in fact, he implied it must be fun (CD).

257b–98b Kemble (1789), Macready and Kean cut 263b–8, the latter also cutting 'with child' (269), 'And here was left' (270) and 287b–91a. Daly cut 258b–9a, 260b–3a ('Where . . . forget'st'), 265–9 (retaining 269's 'was hither brought'), 270a, 275–6, 280b–1a, 286b–91a; Tree 264–74 (retaining 274's 'did confine thee'), 286b–91a; Iden Payne 276; Hack 260b–1a, 263b–8, 288b–9a; Miller (1988) 266b–70a (?). Benthall changed 'blue' to 'blear' (269); Barton changed 270–1 to 'and here was left. Thou, slave, was then her servant' and cut 274a, 275–6.

At 260a, Phelps's Ariel shuddered, Burton's spoke submissively and Tree's turned away in fear. In contrast, Hytner's Ariel really had forgotten Sycorax, so that Prospero made him relive a forgotten experience (CD). Likewise, Alexander's Ariel genuinely could not remember Sycorax, and the attempt at recall made her frustrated and distraught: by 298b, she had

ARIEL No, sir.
PROSPERO   Thou hast. Where was she born? Speak. Tell me.   260
ARIEL Sir, in Algiers.
PROSPERO   O, was she so? I must
              Once in a month recount what thou hast been,
              Which thou forget'st. This damned witch Sycorax,
              For mischiefs manifold, and sorceries terrible
              To enter human hearing, from Algiers   265
              Thou know'st was banished. For one thing she did
              They would not take her life. Is not this true?
ARIEL Ay, sir.
PROSPERO This blue-eyed hag was hither brought with child,
              And here was left by th' sailors. Thou, my slave,   270
              As thou report'st thyself, was then her servant;
              And for thou wast a spirit too delicate
              To act her earthy and abhorred commands,
              Refusing her grand hests, she did confine thee,
              By help of her more potent ministers,   275
              And in her most unmitigable rage,
              Into a cloven pine, within which rift
              Imprisoned thou didst painfully remain
              A dozen years; within which space she died,

completely covered her head with a cloth and was beating it with her fist (CD). Thacker's Ariel grew increasingly uncomfortable, and Donnellan had Sycorax embodied in front of Ariel as Prospero recounted her history (CD).

Prospero's attitude to Ariel can vary greatly: Brook's (1957) spoke with 'sadistic relish' (*P* 21/8/57), while Williams's (1978) was 'schoolmasterly in manner, impatiently tapping his foot as he made Ariel repeat the origin of Sycorax' (Warren, 'A Year of Comedies', p. 203). Hall's 1974 Prospero spoke 269 loudly, while Ariel writhed on the rostrum with 'cramps' that continued until 293. Miller's 1988 Prospero cuffed Ariel on the head at 'Dull thing' (285), making Ariel hold his head in pain until 293b (pb; CD).

Prospero's description of Ariel's imprisonment (277) often marks a crisis: Benthall's 1951 Prospero raised his staff, while Ariel 'attitudinise[d] freeze' (*sic*), seemingly re-imprisoned in an imaginary pine. Barton's uneasy spirit voices, which had started again at 269, reached a crescendo. Hytner's Ariel suddenly remembered his imprisonment, the horrid cruelty of which Prospero emphasized, and screamed: the sound was a 'thin shriek . . . like hearing a tree scream'; he then accompanied Prospero's description of his past groans (281a) with present ones (CD; quotation from Koenig, *P* 9/6/89). Mendes's Prospero took out what

And left thee there; where thou didst vent thy groans   280
As fast as mill-wheels strike. Then was this island –
Save for the son that she did litter here,
A freckled whelp, hag-born – not honoured with
A human shape.

ARIEL   Yes, Caliban her son.

PROSPERO Dull thing, I say so: he, that Caliban   285
Whom now I keep in service. Thou best know'st
What torment I did find thee in. Thy groans
Did make wolves howl, and penetrate the breasts
Of ever-angry bears. It was a torment
To lay upon the damned, which Sycorax   290
Could not again undo. It was mine art,
When I arrived and heard thee, that made gape
The pine, and let thee out.

ARIEL   I thank thee, master.

PROSPERO If thou more murmur'st, I will rend an oak
And peg thee in his knotty entrails till   295
Thou hast howled away twelve winters.

appeared to be a pine cone or some other 'relic of the cloven pine', causing Ariel to back
away two steps (CD; quotation from Billington, *G* 13/8/93); the latter transmitted 'blinking,
outraged pride . . . when reminded that he needed to be freed by Prospero from the magic
of Sycorax' (Taylor, *Ind* 13/8/93). In contrast, the pleasure Strehler's Prospero took in recall-
ing the power of his art to free Ariel was evident in his face: his eyes showed he was reliving
the moment in his mind, as he smiled with satisfied but unselfconscious delight (video). The
crisis's turning-point often comes at 291b–3: at 293a, Benthall's 1951 Prospero made a tree-
splitting motion, thus releasing Ariel from the imaginary pine; Barton's Ariel relaxed and the
spirit voices stopped, while Hall's 1974 Ariel stopped writhing. Phelps's Ariel was prostrate at
293b, while Burton's spoke gratefully and Crozier's bowed.

282–5 Dryden/Davenant and Shadwell made the lines accommodate the existence of Caliban's twin
sister, Sycorax. Daniels substituted 'Safe' for 'Save' (282), at a stroke changing both syntax
and meaning: in this reading, rather than being excepted from the description, Caliban
became a creature 'not honour'd with/A human shape'. In contrast, Donnellan had the
'actor' presenting Caliban get up from the gorilla stance he had assumed and look irritated
(CD). Burton's Ariel spoke 284b as a respectful correction of Prospero.

294–6 Whether or not Prospero's threat is genuine is open to interpretation. Daniels's Prospero
stressed 'oak', eliciting audience laughter, but Billington thought 294–5 'a realistic, whis-

ARIEL   Pardon, master.
          I will be correspondent to command
          And do my spriting gently.
PROSPERO   Do so; and after two days
          I will discharge thee.
ARIEL   That's my noble master!
          What shall I do? Say what? What shall I do?   300

pered threat' (archive video; *G* 12/8/82). Hall's 1988 Prospero stood over Ariel, making the
other spirits recoil, while Miller's 1988 Prospero twisted Ariel's ear so violently that he afterwards nursed it (CD). Wolfe gave the lines a 'disquieting impact': as Prospero 'threaten[ed] to
return Ariel to the imprisonment of a tree trunk . . . an ensemble of actors in black
advance[d] menacingly with tall bamboo poles that encage[d] the hauntingly terrified sprite'
(Brantley, *NYT* 12/7/95). In contrast, Hytner's Prospero made clear that he was merely acting
the threat to Ariel (CD).

  Ariel's response can also vary: Phelps's spoke 296b despondingly, while Williams's (1978)
came 'close!' to Prospero, the pb's punctuation suggesting some threat even though his
words were apologetic. Brook's 1990 Ariel put his head on Prospero's knee, and the latter
stroked it (CD).

299 Phelps's Ariel exclaimed 299b 'with great animation', and Burton's spoke it 'joyfully, not
    boisterously'. Barton's Ariel made a circle, going through Prospero's legs, while Hack's
    Prospero slapped Ariel's face after forgiving him (Coveney, *FT* 4/11/74).

  At 299b, Shadwell interpolated new material in order to introduce Milcha:

ARIEL Thanks, my great master. But I have yet one request.
PROSPERO What's that, my spirit?
ARIEL I know that this day's business is important, requiring too much toil for one alone. I
have a gentle spirit for my love, who twice seven years has waited for my freedom: let it appear,
it will assist me much, and we with mutual joy shall entertain each other. This I beseech you
grant me.
PROSPERO You shall have your desire.
ARIEL That's my noble master. Milcha!
Milcha flies down to his assistance
MILCHA I am here, my love.
ARIEL Thou art free! welcome, my dear! what shall we do? Say, say, what shall we do?

300 Because 301–4 had been interpolated earlier, Macready's Ariel sang 'O, bid thy faithful Ariel
    fly' after 300 and exited. Barton's spirit voices sounded 'light' and 'happy'; Strehler's Ariel
    again flew up to sit on Prospero's chest, straddling it with her legs (video).

PROSPERO Go make thyself like to a nymph o' th' sea.
            Be subject to no sight but thine and mine, invisible
            To every eye-ball else. Go take this shape
            And hither come in't. Go! Hence with diligence.

                                                    Exit [ARIEL]

301–4 Dryden/Davenant and Shadwell cut 301 and 303b–4a, with the former adding 'My daughter
        wakes. Anon thou shalt know more' before Ariel's exit; Shadwell adopted only the second
        sentence and had his spirits *'both fly up and cross in the air'* to exit.
            Both Kemble versions interpolate new material. The 1789 Prospero instructed 'Go; and
        with Grineldo, spirit of earth, / And others under thy command, let loose the tempest; / And
        then disperse the stranded wanderers / Through the isle', while the 1806 Prospero directed
        Ariel to 'Go, with the spirits under thy command, / Let loose the Tempest, as I bade thee;
        then, / Disperse the stranded crew about the isle, / And bring the king's son Ferdinand to my
        cell', followed by 302–3a. The spirit agreed to her master's commands and then sang 'Oh, bid
        thy faithful Ariel fly.'
            Phelps cut 301–4 but seems to have interpolated the lines earlier in some productions (see
        note to 188sd). In their place Ariel sang 'Oh bid thy faithful Ariel fly', then exited and pre-
        pared for flight; after the song, Prospero spoke 317, went to L2E to speak 318a and whispered
        to Ariel, who replied with 318b. Ariel, who had had time to get into harness, then flew off
        RUE, and the scene resumed with 305.
            Many subsequent productions have omitted Prospero's instruction that Ariel appear as a
        sea-nymph, presumably for economy of time or budget. McVicker cut 301, using Kemble's
        1806 lines instead, and included 'O bid thy faithful Ariel fly.' Hack cut 301 and 304, interpolat-
        ing 317–18a in place of the latter. Other productions make a feature of the lines: Benthall's
        1951 Ariel immediately began to act like a sea-nymph, but the pb gives no further detail; the
        1952 Ariel made sea-noises. Strehler's Prospero opened the SL trap and handed Ariel the
        sea-nymph costume (video), while Miller's 1988 Prospero 'consult[ed] a learned tome to
        instruct Ariel to "go take this shape" pointing to the appropriate illustration'; at such
        moments he suggested 'simultaneously a John Dee-type magician and someone who
        rejoices in his power over the enslaved' (Billington, *G* 12/10/88). Daniels's Ariel hesitated
        during the lines, seeming loath to depart, until Prospero ordered him 'hence with diligence!'
        (archive video).
304sd Before Ariel's exit, Daly interpolated 'O bid thy faithful Ariel fly', while Tree's answered
        'Master it shall be done' (handwritten pb interpolation). A black-out and a roll of thunder fol-
        lowed the latter's exit, and the curtain and gauze lowered for Tree's Scene 3 (The Yellow
        Sands, painted by Telbin). In the darkness an off-stage chorus of sea-nymphs faintly sang
        375–84 to Sullivan's music; as the curtain was raised, the 'lights gradually c[a]me up to

PROSPERO Awake, dear heart, awake; thou hast slept well,   305
    Awake.
MIRANDA   The strangeness of your story put
    Heaviness in me.
PROSPERO   Shake it off. Come on,
    We'll visit Caliban, my slave, who never
    Yields us kind answer.
MIRANDA   'Tis a villain, sir,
    I do not love to look on.
PROSPERO   But as 'tis   310
    We cannot miss him. He does make our fire,
    Fetch in our wood, and serves in offices

purple disclosing nymphs playing on the water and on the sands': the former effect was achieved by four nymphs suspended on wires behind the first water row (handwritten pb notes). Eventually Prospero entered to wake Miranda (305).

At 303a, Hall's 1974 Prospero turned US and opened his cloak to mask Ariel's unseen, walking exit. Thacker's Ariel, like the rest of the characters, did not exit, but went behind a trunk and made a shape with her legs reminiscent of a mermaid (CD).

305–6 Dryden/Davenant and Shadwell cut 305a and 306a so that Miranda's sleep and waking appeared natural rather than the result of magic; 'strangeness' became 'sadness' (306b).

Macready's Ariel re-appeared at the back of the stage after 305, and 317–18 were interpolated. Ariel seems then to have spoken 306a, suggesting that Prospero had difficulty in waking Miranda and therefore whispered an instruction for Ariel to do so; she flew off afterwards. Burton may have interpolated 317–18 after 306a, but this may just be Moore's notation of Macready's staging (see note to 309–13).

Neville's Prospero used 'unlooked-for intonations', such as 'Thou *hast* slept well!' (Trewin, *ILN* 16/6/62). Hytner's Prospero was visibly upset as he woke Miranda; Ninagawa's used a charm to do so (CD). Daly's Miranda spoke 306b–7a as she was waking on Prospero's final command, whereas Tree's entered from the cave on 306a.

307 Daniels's Prospero pulled Miranda to her feet at 'Shake it off.'

308 Kemble's Prospero (1789) proposed a solo visit to Caliban: 'I'll visit . . .'

309–13 Dryden/Davenant and Shadwell changed 'villain' to 'creature' (309b). Miranda is often apprehensive at the thought of meeting Caliban: Benthall's 1951 Miranda spoke 309b–10a hesitantly, while Williams's 1978 Miranda broke to the L proscenium as Prospero approached Caliban's hole. At 310a, Daniels's Miranda hugged Prospero, who held her shoulders, pushing her back; Miller's 1988 Prospero and Miranda hugged each other during 309–12. Garrick (1757), Kemble (1789), Macready and Daly had her exit at 313a. Prospero sometimes shares Miranda's wariness: Brook's 1957 Prospero picked up a whip at 310b

That profit us. What ho! Slave! Caliban!
Thou earth, thou! Speak!
CALIBAN *Within*   There's wood enough within.
PROSPERO Come forth, I say; there's other business for thee.   315
Come, thou tortoise, when?

Enter ARIEL *like a water-nymph*

(Stratford pb), while Paige's Prospero and Miranda both 'looked very apprehensive at the prospect of facing Caliban'; when they approached his cell, Miranda was 'stopped dead as if by an invisible forcefield' caused by a magic gesture from her father (Carter, 'The Tempest at Salisbury Playhouse', p. 16). In contrast, Hytner's Prospero was 'suitably shame-faced about the fact that Caliban "serves in offices that profit us"' (Billington, G 29/5/89).

Moore's notation of Burton's staging is not exact: Prospero and Miranda exited after 313a, and the set changed to a 'bright view' with 'yellow sands' in the 5th groove and the cave at R2E. The Caliban scene began with soft music playing while a fountain rose C.

316sd Sturgess infers that 'Ariel's costume confers invisibility by making him look like a sea-nymph'; however, Prospero's instruction at 302 does not necessarily suggest that Ariel's invisibility is linked to this particular manifestation. Sturgess's point is worth noting, nevertheless, because of his consequent speculation that the tiring-house facade might have been 'hung with curtains representing a seascape' into which the sea-nymph costume might have 'merged', creating the illusion of invisibility; as he recognizes, however, the inclusion in the Admiral's Men inventory of a 'robe for to go invisible' indicates a theatrical convention not dependent on realistic illusion (*Jacobean Private Theatre*, p. 87). Saenger has more recently argued that Ariel's sea-nymph costume was that previously worn by the nymph Corinea in a sea-pageant scripted by Anthony Munday to celebrate the investiture of Henry as Prince of Wales in May 1610 ('Costumes', p. 334); the costume, which comprised a 'watrie habit yet riche and costly, with a Coronet of Pearles and Cockle shelles', was given to the King's Men as part payment for their actors' participation in the event (Saenger, 'Costumes', p. 335; Munday, quoted in Egan, 'Ariel's Costume', p. 63).

Subsequent sea-nymph costumes have varied greatly: Burge's wore 'green trousers apparently [made] of layers of leaves', and Hall's (1974) was dressed in a chiffon costume of 'sea-blue wisps', complemented by 'flowing hair' (respectively, Foulkes, review, p. 9; costume list; Young, *FT*, and Wardle, *T*, both 6/3/74). Hall's 1988 Ariel had 'long blonde locks and bulging mammaries' that were clearly made of plastic; he also wore a half-mask (to which the wig was attached) and a pleated silk muslin dress (CD; costume plot; quotation from Billington, G 21/5/88). More simply, Hytner's Ariel sported a new blonde cone-shaped wig, blue at the tip, which some reviewers likened to a paintbrush (CD). Donnellan's wore a black cape and a white half-mask, while Brook's (1990) wore a blue veil and carried a shell in

> Fine apparition! My quaint Ariel,
> Hark in thine ear.

ARIEL   My lord, it shall be done. *Exit* [ARIEL]
PROSPERO Thou poisonous slave, got by the devil himself
> Upon thy wicked dam, come forth.   320

Enter CALIBAN

his hand and on a stick; similarly, Ninagawa's Ariel wore a mask and a different veil as the sea-nymph (CD).

Some Ariels, like those of Dryden/Davenant and Shadwell, did not dress as a water-nymph, whereas others, like those of Kemble, Daly, Tree, Strehler and Alexander, did not reenter at all. Since Macready had earlier interpolated 301–4 and 316sd–18, 316 was immediately followed by Caliban's appearance at the mouth of the cave, Prospero's lines to him (319–20) and Caliban's entrance (320sd). Similarly, since Phelps had interpolated 317–18 earlier, Prospero's 316 ran straight into 319–20. However, Kean's Ariel came up the C trap riding on a dolphin's back, with Kerr's light again used; she floated off still riding the dolphin at 318b. Burton's water-nymph Ariel entered through the fountain.

317–18 Cut by Kemble, Daly and Tree, and interpolated earlier by Macready, (?) Burton, Phelps, Hack and (?) Miller (1988).

317–18 Daniels's Prospero whispered to Ariel after 318a, whereas Hytner's Ariel was some distance from Prospero; the latter was able to talk to him intimately without his physical proximity (CD). Ciulei's Prospero, throughout the play, sent Ariel 'out to spread his spells . . . by touching fingers, an image straight from Michelangelo's ceiling' (Steele, *MT* 13/6/81). Wright transposed Caliban's 330b after 318a; it was spoken off-stage.

319a Brook's 1957 Prospero put down his wand and picked up a whip (DL pb).

319–74 Cut by Garrick (1756).

319b–20a Cut by Daly and Tree.

320b Strehler's Prospero took off his belt, ready for use as a weapon, before summoning Caliban (video).

320sd Sturgess suggests that, as the King's Men Ariel exited through one stage door in his sea-nymph costume, Caliban entered through the other, thus visually reinforcing Shakespeare's opposition of the airy spirit and the earthy slave (*Jacobean Private Theatre*, p. 84); William, however, wonders if a trap-door served for Caliban's rock ('*The Tempest* on the Stage', p. 149). Saenger's argument that Caliban's costume was that of the triton, a ' "deformed sea-shape" ' in Munday's sea-pageant, is based on the dubious premise that Caliban should indeed look like a fish ('Costumes', pp. 335–6).

Trends outlined in the Introduction have remained current throughout twentieth-century productions: Caliban may be monstrous animal, primitive human, exploited minority or a combination thereof. Drinkwater's was 'a hybrid of ape and aborigine' (*BP* 19/4/15), while Baynton's had 'a fish-like body, with green scales and a most dejected green face' (St John Ervine, uc 8?/11/26). In 1919 Bridges-Adams's was 'a monster half-seal, half-man' (*St* 8?/19), but in 1934 he was 'a kind of grotesque green gorilla with a pair of terrifying tusks' (*DT* 17/4/34). Harcourt Williams's 'Mongolian monster', with 'his hair in long strings and tonsured head and a face like a Mongolian devil-mask', looked like 'ogre in a Japanese fairy-tale' (respectively, Williams, *Old Vic Saga*, p. 95; *MP* 7/10/30; Ivor Brown, 7/10/30). More recently, Minor's Caliban was 'the creature from the Black Lagoon, slimy, crawling, scaly and rather than being natural man [was] the essence of unnatural creature' (Steele, *MT* 22/6/70). Hideous appearance, however, is not always a clue to interpretation: Bridges-Adams's 1934 Caliban, for example, was 'rather comically docile' (*St* 19/4/34). Similarly, although Edwards's Caliban was visually a 'lumbering humped-back' 'semi-amphibious creature, part-fish, part-frog' (respectively Paula Carr, *MeIR* 6/90; Thomson, *SundH* 20/5/90), his portrayal was 'essentially compassionate', communicating both 'baseness and savagery' and 'touching innocence' (Croggan, *Bul* 29/5/90).

As the last quotation suggests, not even the most bestial manifestation of Caliban can now entirely occlude his more sympathetic – and human – aspects. Although Leigh's Caliban was physically presented 'as a mixture of hog and gorilla', the actor 'properly denied' his make-up and showed 'a creature aspiring to be a man' (Ervine). Similarly, Atkins, who had played the part for Greet at Stratford in 1916 and in his own productions at the Old Vic during the 1920s and Open Air Theatre during the 1930s and 1940s, 'redeemed by imaginative power a Caliban rather ridiculously ape-like in appearance' (*T* 13/9/33): George W. Bishop regarded him as 'one of the best Calibans [he had] ever seen . . . vigorous and brutal, but . . . excit[ing] pity . . . for the poor enslaved wretch' (6/6/34), while Ivor Brown thought that he 'achieved pathos, passion, and a poignant abundance of frustration' (10/6/34). Brook's 1957 'shaggy [and] red-eyed' Caliban wore a gorilla suit that several reviewers labelled obscene, presumably because of its pronounced breasts; however, although his 'gait and behaviour' matched his gorilla form, his 'seedy intellectual[ism]' did not (respectively, *DM* 14/8/57; Derek Granger, *FT*; 'Prompter' [Wendy Trewin], *WI* 18/8/57). More recently, Walford's Caliban, 'finny and primitive like a grey lizard with a bald head', came across as 'the archetypal victim, the exploited savage' (McManus, *G* 27/1/84).

As these quotations make evident, most sympathy for Caliban derives either from his aspiration to full humanity or from his exploitation by Prospero, and twentieth-century productions have continued to portray him as either missing link or degraded slave or a combination of the two. Greet's 1917 programme note described him as 'savage – a member of an almost prehistoric race with witches as ancestors'. Russell Thorndike, playing the part in his own 1919 co-production with Warburton, was 'hideous enough to have been studied from the new gorilla at the Zoo, [but he] managed to combine the grossness with flashes of almost profound intelligence, just in the way that one feels Shakespeare meant his inspired aboriginal to do' (*Era* 15/10/19, quoted by Griffiths, ' "This Island's Mine" ', p. 173). Baliol

Holloway, despite his costume, played Caliban for Atkins (1936) 'not [as] an aspirant beast, but the human intellect fallen, and haunted all the time by memories at once dreadful and ancestral of a paradise lost yet capable of being regained' (*T* 8/7/36). More recently, John Harrison's semi-human Caliban had a 'blue complexion' and was bald and earless, with some other organ (gills?) where his ears should have been (Young, *FT* 21/2/75; Zoë Dominic's photos, TM); in contrast, Giles's human Caliban, inhabiting a set that suggested an eastern Mediterranean island with Greek-like ruins, was costumed as a ragged Turk (Young, *FT* 23/8/78).

As the Introduction notes, colonialist readings of Caliban were available before Miller's 1970 landmark production, although sporadic: in some cases, reviewers responded to their own conception of the character and, in others, to elements of the performance itself. Although one critic saw Iden Payne's 1938 Caliban as 'speak[ing] up for the oppressed aboriginal with appropriate venom' (*Sk* 11/5/38), most agreed that his appearance was clearly sub-human: a 'Missing Link' 'reaching up to the human' (respectively, *SH* 6/5/38; *BM* 3/5/38). Later, another critic complained that Gellner's Caliban 'minimise[d] the appeal to sympathy for an oppressed aboriginal', instead playing the part as 'a scaly, hirsute monster with a marvellous range of bronchial rumblings and gastric grunts' (*O* 23/9/51). Benthall's 1951 Caliban, described by one critic as 'a fretful porcupine with barnacles on its chest', disappointed another in 'suggest[ing] only a man who has been degraded to a beast' instead of 'the pathos and the pretensions of a beast promoted to human status' (respectively, *ES* 25/6/51; *Sp* 29/6/51). Interestingly, however, no critics mention one aspect of his appearance: with blackened face, enlarged nostrils and whitened bottom lip, this African caricature did not engender any colonialist readings. Only the *Daily Worker*, remarking that the portrayal of 'the savage slave' was not as sympathetic as Shakespeare had intended it to be, even intimated that such servitude might be an issue in the play (29/6/51). In the revival the following year, however, Michael Hordern imbued Caliban with an emotionally human character despite his physical appearance, helping to support colonialist readings of the play: 'What is [Caliban] if not the symbol of men surrounded by a gracious world, but unable to realise it, unable to enjoy it because they are allowed only such knowledge as will enable them to be slaves' (Hugh Phillips, *DW* 29/3/52); he was 'a most human and even poignant representative of the Backward and Underprivileged Peoples: he makes one feel that Prospero did sometimes mingle the sadist with the scholar in his colonial policy' (Brown, *O* ?/3/52). In a similar yet differently costumed vein, Ciulei's Caliban, Czechoslovakian actor Jan Triska, was 'Dressed in drooping grey flannel huggers . . . the most outlandish bushy vest [waistcoat] . . . and a cap' (Stephenson, *TCC* 25/6/81). Playing him as 'part buffoon, part motley peasant with a vaguely prehistoric look . . . a very lumpen prole not far from the primal ooze', Triska made him 'a creature of wonderful irony, charm, humor and pathos' (Steele, *MT* 13/6/81). 'From his pulling of a switchblade to his lyric rhapsody over music, Triska's Caliban embodie[d] the outsiders – whether slaves, savages, Third Worlders – who have haunted the conscience of the West' (Kroll, *Nw* 29/6/81).

Many recent Calibans have been simply human in appearance: for example, Bogdanov's (1978) was a 'human figure wearing only a loincloth and a coating of dirt', Retallack's (1981) 'only an ugly, bandy-legged human', who seemed 'a gormless idiot', and Gaden's 'a restlessly malicious, ugly, raggedy man' (respectively, Young, *FT* 29/11/78; Young, *FT*, and Shulman, *ES*, both in *LTR* 12–25/2/83; Ward, *Aus* 4/5/89). Rylance's 'splendidly gormless', 'Smike-like' Caliban was 'bedecked in the heads of Barbie dolls', while Tipton's, with his 'Wild hair and wire-rimmed glasses', was 'less a savage than an [honest] anarchist' (respectively, McAfee, *ES* 1/7/91; Kingston, *T* 10/6/91; St George, *FT* 21/6/91; Wigand, 24/10/91; Close, *SPPP* 15/10/91). Donnellan, reversing the modern convention of a white Miranda and a black Caliban, made the latter 'a dim, white, gentle buffoon', 'a mutinous lout more funny than threatening . . . kept in check by magically-induced torments rather than the innate superiority of his master' (respectively, Ratcliffe, *O* 13/11/88; Hoyle, *FT* 20/10/88); he surprisingly changed his top in honour of the visit from Miranda and Prospero, and looked and acted like a rather tatty waiter, spitting in a cup to clean it (CD). Bogdanov's 1992 Caliban, wearing only 'mud-like make-up and a modified G string', was 'a filthy, half-naked primitive with a phallic effigy of the god Setebos rammed down his loin-cloth'; the Russian actor who played him 'cleverly utilise[d] his own foreign accent to suggest alienation from language' (respectively, Neill, *Director's Notes*, p. 25; Taylor, *Ind* 30/11/92; Michael Arditti, *ES* 1/12/92). Mendes's Caliban, 'built like a wrestler with an alarming white body, a bald, talcumed head and a mouth full of black teeth', portrayed 'a man spiritually deformed by subjugation' (respectively, Kellaway, *O* 15/8/93; Billington, *G* 13/8/93). Thacker's fully human Caliban was swathed in ragged strips of cloth, almost mummy-like, and could not use his legs: although he could occasionally get himself into a standing position, he moved by dragging himself across the floor with his hands and arms (CD).

Human Calibans can, of course, embody directorial concepts. Armfield's 1990 Caliban, dressed 'in a tattered red military coat, lashed on by ropes that end[ed] in a hangman's knot', (Evans, *SMH* 31/5/90), evoked both Australia's origins as a British penal colony and colonization of its original inhabitants. Wolfe's Caliban, monstrous 'only [in] his near nakedness and a red-capped skull', was played, like Ariel, by an African-American; he was 'meant to reflect the experience of African slaves', speaking the word 'master' with 'hostile sarcasm' (Brantley, *NYT* 12/7/95) and 'sneer[ing] while promising subservience' (Greene, *TW* 31/7–6/8/95). Purcarete, describing Caliban as 'the artist's dark side' (Ramsden, *TES* 8/9/95), envisaged him not as a 'savage' but as 'the weak mind . . . the mind of the child before society', evincing 'non-comprehension', 'fear leading to violence' and 'extreme sensitivity' (programme); accordingly, he was 'a hulking infant in a nappy-like dhoti, given to curling up in moments of stress into the foetal position' (Shuttleworth, *FT* 16/9/95).

As with Miller's 1970 and 1988 productions, directors sometimes make links between Caliban and Ariel, often to comment on Prospero. Most recently, Kelly dressed both characters in 'outfits identical to Prospero's own', either to suggest 'they are reflections of his own personality' or to provide a 'serious reminder that this is a play about colonial oppression'

CALIBAN As wicked dew as e'er my mother brushed
    With raven's feather from unwholesome fen
    Drop on you both! A south-west blow on ye,
    And blister you all o'er!
PROSPERO For this, be sure, tonight thou shalt have cramps, 325
    Side-stitches that shall pen thy breath up; urchins
    Shall, for that vast of night that they may work,
    All exercise on thee; thou shalt be pinched

(respectively, Georgina Brown, *MSun* 14/2/99; Spencer, *DT* 11/2/99; Billington, *G* 11/2/99). Similarly, Noble made the pair 'positive and negative photographic images of each other'; with Caliban 'covered in black slime' and Ariel in 'white body-paint' and 'both dressed in unflattering loin cloths', they suggested 'different aspects of Prospero's psyche, the super ego and the id perhaps' (Spencer, *DT* 2/3/98).

  Caliban often makes a striking or even spectacular first entrance. Phelps's staging was similar to Macready's: Caliban entered 'crawling out on all fours, like a beast', and then rose, threatening Prospero, who raised his wand to check him; Caliban then 'recoil[ed] as if spell struck' (Phelps/Creswick pb). In Tree's production, a rock opened and Caliban crawled out, carrying a fish in his mouth, while Coghill's Caliban 'made his first entry *out of* the lake. This effect was achieved by sinking a small, empty cast-iron water tank into the lake, against the bank, thus producing a more or less dry space where Caliban could crouch unseen . . . until his entrance' (Moore, 'Footing it Featly', p. 15); at the end of the play, he 'sank back into his submerged tank' (Hodgson, 'Rough Magic', p. 16). Hytner's Caliban had a magnificent first entrance from behind the rock in which he was apparently immured, appearing to burst out from within it, arm first, accompanied by the sound of stone cracking and dropping, which stopped when he emerged (CD; pbs); similarly, Noble's Prospero prised Caliban from a 'huge horned shell' (Macaulay, *FT* 28/2/98). Lepage's Caliban 'entered' when the tables were up-ended to reveal her in the spot where Ariel had disappeared. Caliban's entrance can make Miranda exit, as did Kemble's (1806), or retreat to the mouth of the cave, as did Tree's. However, rather than being afraid of Caliban, John Harrison's Miranda 'treat[ed] him rather as an English girl would treat a horse' (Young, *FT* 21/2/75).

321–4 Daly cut 321–3a. Kean's Caliban rushed at Prospero, and Daly's threatened him; both Prosperos used their wands to control him. Hack's Prospero tapped his staff on the ground in response to Caliban's curses. Donnellan's Caliban, in 'scruffy waiter's garb', threw the contents of his tea-cup in Prospero's face; from this point on, the 'actors' wore costumes instead of their rehearsal gear, with Miranda here putting on a dress (CD; quotation from Hoyle, *FT* 20/10/88).

325–30a Dryden/Davenant and Shadwell changed 327–8a to 'Urchins shall prick thee till thou bleed'st.' Daly cut 326b–30a, and Macready 328b–30a; Phelps cut as Macready but then restored the lines.

As thick as honeycomb, each pinch more stinging
Than bees that made 'em.

CALIBAN   I must eat my dinner.   330
This island's mine by Sycorax my mother,
Which thou tak'st from me. When thou cam'st first
Thou strok'st me and made much of me; wouldst give me
Water with berries in't, and teach me how
To name the bigger light, and how the less,   335
That burn by day and night. And then I loved thee
And showed thee all the qualities o' th' isle,
The fresh springs, brine-pits, barren place and fertile –
Cursèd be I that did so! All the charms
Of Sycorax – toads, beetles, bats – light on you!   340

Benson's Caliban, reacting to Prospero's threats, 'screamed and chattered, grimaced and crouched, and showed [his] teeth . . . making all kinds of inarticulate noises (not indicated by the text)' (letter from 'The Druid', *SH* 1/5/1891). Tree's simply groaned at 'cramps' and interpolated 330b after 328a: ignoring Prospero, he came DR with his fish and sat cross-legged, throwing the fish away at the end of Prospero's speech. Benthall's 1952 Caliban, backing DR, picked up a stone, presumably to threaten Prospero, but then dropped it. Hytner's Prospero made clear that his threats to Caliban (unlike those to Ariel) were genuine, while Miller's 1988 Miranda hopped 'up and down in delight' at hearing the torments her father proposed for Caliban (CD; H. R. F. Keating, *Tab* 22/10/88).

330b Tree interpolated 330b after 328a, and Hack cut it. In 1951 Benthall's Caliban, eating his fish, rushed to C, while in 1952 he edged towards it. Brook's 1957 Caliban sat on a rock, chomping on 'a blade-bone' (Trewin, *BP* 14/8/57), while Purcarete's Caliban extracted clothes-pegs from his loin-cloth (CD).

Many Calibans begin to exit, but are stopped by Prospero: Barton's Prospero trapped Caliban's chain by shutting the trapdoor on it; Daniels's Prospero slammed the trap shut, preventing Caliban's exit through it; Hall's 1988 Prospero stopped him with his staff.

331–44a Kemble (1789) cut 341–2a (Caliban's claim that Prospero is a usurper), and Daly 333b–6a, 338 and 339b–42a.

Caliban's speech is usually forceful in performance: Macready's roared 339b–40; Phelps's was 'Stamping, and gabbling with fury' at 338; Burton's roared and yelled 339a with rage; Tree's, having half-risen at 331, made a 'cat sound' at 339a. Miller's 1988 Caliban interpolated 'No!' before 331(pb), which he 'crie[d] . . . with the pathos of the territorially-deprived' (Billington, *G* 12/10/88); Murray's Caliban similarly gave 331 'heroic weight' (Holdsworth, *TLS* 21–7/9/90). Paige's Caliban manoeuvred himself past Prospero to claim ownership of the island from the C sandcastle and rope, the sand having a totemic significance that Caliban

For I am all the subjects that you have,
Which first was mine own king; and here you sty me
In this hard rock, whiles you do keep from me
The rest o' th' island.

PROSPERO   Thou most lying slave,
Whom stripes may move, not kindness! I have used thee,   345
Filth as thou art, with humane care, and lodged thee
In mine own cell, till thou didst seek to violate
The honour of my child.

conveyed by touching, gathering and carrying it about with him (Carter, '*The Tempest* at Salisbury Playhouse', pp. 16–17). In contrast, Mendes's Caliban, who only left the basket after 331, was clearly afraid of Prospero's wand (CD); Spencer's comment that there were 'moments of real cruelty in Prospero's treatment of Caliban' suggests why (*DT* 16/8/93).

Some recent productions have suggested a bond between Caliban and Miranda: Thacker's Caliban looked at Miranda at 336b, causing her to look away in reverie, perhaps somewhat uneasy with her recollections (CD). Purcarete's Caliban sat DSC, FO, for his speech, all the while sticking clothes-pegs on his midriff and ears; at 338 Miranda began to approach him from behind, appearing to be compulsively drawn (CD).

344b–51a Dryden/Davenant and Shadwell changed 'child' to 'children' (348). Kemble cut the references to Caliban's attempted rape of Miranda; in 1789, 344b was immediately followed by 352, whereas, in 1806, 344b–51a were cut, with 345b–6a interpolated after 353a. Macready and Kean changed 'violate / The honour of my child' (347–8) to 'abuse my gentle child' and cut 349–53a. Phelps cut 344b–51a; a copy of the pb probably made by Sarah Flower restored 344b–8 but cut 349–53a (SCL 50.31/1870.3047 (f.98)). Burton and Daly cut 345–53a, the latter retaining 345a.

The exchange between Prospero and Caliban has been theatrically realized in both expected and unexpected ways. Barton's Caliban grabbed at Miranda at 351a, causing her to retreat US and Prospero to strike him. Daniels's Caliban sat with his hands over his head at 346, and at 348 gave a long groan redolent of sexual desire and mischief (archive video). Mendes's Caliban 'ogle[d] Miranda with an affecting mixture of animal lust and human awe' (Andrew Billen, *O* 17/7/94), whereas Miller's (1988) moved towards Miranda and appeared to point to his crotch on 'Thou didst prevent me', raising the question of castration (CD). However, Retallack's 1981 (female) Prospero 'maternally wrapp[ed] Caliban under her cloak' at 345b–6a (Billington, *G* 2/83), and Falls's 'Miranda would [have] like[d] to like Caliban, caressing his head in her lap as Prospero recounts his story' (Pellowe, 'In Chicago', p. 55); the comment must refer to 345b–8a, unless Prospero took Miranda's 'Abhorrèd slave' speech (351b–62). Purcarete's Caliban threw Miranda a clothes-peg at 349, which she was eager to have: the sight of the pegs had seemingly drawn her towards him. Caliban delivered 349–51a

CALIBAN O ho, O ho! Would't had been done.
                 Thou didst prevent me – I had peopled else   350
                 This isle with Calibans.
      MIRANDA   Abhorrèd slave,
                 Which any print of goodness wilt not take,
                 Being capable of all ill! I pitied thee,
                 Took pains to make thee speak, taught thee each hour
                 One thing or other. When thou didst not, savage,   355
                 Know thine own meaning, but wouldst gabble like
                 A thing most brutish, I endowed thy purposes
                 With words that made them known. But thy vile race –
                 Though thou didst learn – had that in't which good
                       natures
                 Could not abide to be with; therefore wast thou   360
                 Deservedly confined into this rock,
                 Who hadst deserved more than a prison.

in a giggly rather than vicious way, taking the clothes-peg away from Miranda as he finished
speaking (CD).

351b–62 Dryden/Davenant and Shadwell gave this speech to Prospero, regarding it as too indecorous
for Miranda to speak; both cut 362 and changed 'vile' to 'wild' (358). Until recently, most subsequent adaptors and directors have followed suit in assigning the speech to Prospero; those
who have done so include Garrick (1757), Kemble (1789, 1806), Macready, Phelps, Kean,
Burton, Daly, Tree, Bridges-Adams, Benthall, Brook (1957, 1990), Neville, Daniels and
Purcarete. Of all the pbs I have examined, Ashwell's is the first to restore the speech to
Miranda, cutting 358b–62. Iden Payne's 1942 pb has the speech-heading 'Miranda' written
in but crossed out; it is unclear whether she was given the speech in 1938 or 1941.
      Garrick (1757) and Kemble (1789) cut 358b–62, the latter strengthening Prospero's con-
demnation of Caliban by changing 'capable' to 'guilty' (353); in 1806, Kemble interpolated
345b–6a after 353a and restored 358b–62. Macready's cut of Caliban's preceding speech
extended into this one (349–53a); he also cut 358b–62, as did Phelps, Kean, (?) Burton, Daly
and Tree. The latter also cut 352–3a; as Prospero spoke 353b–8a, Caliban found an oyster,
which he opened and ate.
      The interaction of the three characters can vary enormously. Benthall's 1952 Caliban grov-
elled at Prospero's feet at 358a. Hall (1974) had Miranda and Caliban move frequently, indicating the shifting dynamic between them: at various times, he approached her, she
approached him, she turned to him, he turned away from but then crossed to her. Strehler's
Caliban looked 'desperately sad, shy, almost a timid boy' (Jan Kott, quoted in Kleber, 'Theatrical Continuities', p. 149), whereas Barton's spat a mouthful of fish at Miranda when she

CALIBAN You taught me language, and my profit on't
      Is, I know how to curse. The red plague rid you
      For learning me your language!
PROSPERO   Hag-seed, hence!   365
      Fetch us in fuel; and be quick, thou'rt best,
      To answer other business. Shrug'st thou, malice?
      If thou neglect'st, or dost unwillingly
      What I command, I'll rack thee with old cramps,

called him a savage (355); Prospero held and comforted her at 362. Murray's Miranda 'retain[ed] tenderness . . . for a Caliban . . . present[ed] as closely human' (Wainwright, *Ind*, 15/9/90), but Mendes's rushed at Caliban as she began speaking, causing him to fall back and sit on the floor, 'cower[ing] timorously'; she then sat next to him, speaking gently and prompting some response, but becoming angry again at 358b (CD; quotation from Billington, *G* 13/8/93). Paige's Miranda and Prospero showed great care for each other, Prospero ready to defend his daughter and Miranda ready to lend her father moral support; thus, when Caliban so stunned Prospero with 349b–51a that he was lost for words, Miranda came to the rescue. As she spoke, Caliban appeared hurt; they looked into each other's faces, both making it clear that the lessons she had given him were 'a happy memory . . . gone sour'. At 358b, Miranda sank to her knees, almost in tears, while Caliban 'crouched in sympathetic body language' (Carter, '*The Tempest* at Salisbury Playhouse', p. 17). Purcarete's Prospero stood behind Caliban, removing the clothes-pegs from his head. The actual meaning of the pegs was by no means clear: they could as easily have represented a childish game as a harmless sexual fetish. However, while their meaning was elusive, their significance was plain, signalling some sort of bond between Miranda and Caliban that Prospero was concerned to stop (CD).

363–5a Dryden/Davenant and Shadwell changed 'Plague' to 'botch' (364). Williams's 1978 Caliban directed 364b–5a to Prospero, Miranda having exited after 364a; Daniels's Caliban came right up to Prospero for 364b–5a, backing away before 365b (archive video). Miller's 1988 pb directs Caliban to curse after 364a, which suggests his next line was delivered as a formal imprecation. Similarly, Thacker's Caliban delivered 364b as 'The – red – plague – rid –', after which he lunged at Miranda, unsuccessfully because of his crippled legs (CD).

    Tree's Caliban, having half-risen to speak, rushed at Prospero at 365a, trying to strike him with both hands; Prospero held up his wand, using his magic to force Caliban to sink slowly to the ground, where he crouched. In contrast, Iden Payne and Crozier had Caliban move towards Miranda before being stopped by Prospero. Strehler's Caliban adopted a 'crouching position . . . loaded with tension, as if he wished to attack Prospero. But Prospero quickly reversed the situation by a body movement which physically threatened Caliban, who instantly changed into a frightened position' (Kleber, 'Theatrical Continuities', pp. 148–9). In

Fill all thy bones with aches, make thee roar,   370
That beasts shall tremble at thy din.
CALIBAN   No, pray thee.
[*Aside*] I must obey; his art is of such power,
It would control my dam's god Setebos,
And make a vassal of him.
PROSPERO   So, slave, hence.

Exit [CALIBAN]

Enter FERDINAND, *and* ARIEL *invisible, playing and singing*

SONG

ARIEL Come unto these yellow sands,   375

contrast, Paige's Caliban had moved towards Miranda at 362, in what appeared to be
genuine concern, but Prospero made a warning gesture; in response, Caliban opened his
hand to show him a piece of orange he had been holding. Prospero therefore let him continue, but the former's 'mistrust [gave] rise to [Caliban's] next gesture of hostility': as he held
out the fruit to Miranda, who reached for it, he spoke very gently until, at 'curse' (364a), 'he
squirted the orange right in her face. She recoiled, [as] hurt and rejected' as he was (Carter,
'*The Tempest* at Salisbury Playhouse', p. 17).

365b–71a Kemble's attention to proper verse-speaking led to a bisyllabic pronunciation of 'aches'
(370); his perseverance in the pronunciation despite the disapproval of the pit caused such
an uproar that the line had to be cut. Phelps and Kean solved the metrical problem by adding
'and' after 'aches'. Dryden/Davenant and Shadwell cut 'thou'rt best' (366), and Daly 'Hag-
seed' (365b), replacing it with another 'hence!', and 368–71.
    While Prospero's 367b suggests only that Caliban shrugs, some have protested more vig-
orously: for example, Burton's growled and Tree's made an angry gesture. More recently,
they have defied Prospero with cool insolence: Thacker's nonchalantly ate a banana, and
Purcarete's blew a raspberry (CD). Both Daniels's and Miller's Prosperos reinforced their
threats with some show of magic: Miller's (1988) used his cloak (pb; CD), and Daniels's 'literally threaten[ed] to throw the magic book at him' (Billington, *G* 12/8/82).

371b Macready's Caliban knelt; Phelps's crouched; Purcarete's seemed in genuine rather than
anticipated pain (CD).

373–4a Cut by Daly, who added another 'I must obey' for Caliban. Brook's 1957 Caliban touched the
floor with his R hand at mention of Setebos (Stratford pb).

374sd Dryden/Davenant and Shadwell had Prospero and Caliban exit, followed by the first
Miranda/Dorinda scene, during which the audience might have seriously questioned Prospero's care as a tutor if they had not been entertained by the sexual innuendo resulting from

his pupils' ignorance: not only do Miranda and Dorinda show little knowledge of the facts of life, but the latter does not even know what a ship is. Between that scene, which closes their Act 1, and Ferdinand and Ariel's entrance, Dryden/Davenant also interpolated some of Shakespeare's 2.1 and new material to open their own Act 2; Shakespeare's 1–3a, 8b–9, 100–1a, 106b–14a (with Francisco's speech given to Antonio), 115b–16 are more or less retained, but only Alonso, Antonio and Gonzalo figure in the scene apart from unnamed attendants. (See Introduction for further details.) Shadwell located the corresponding scene even later in Act 2 (after one between Stephano, Mustacho, Ventoso and Caliban, composed of new material and Shakespeare's 2.2, and another invented scene involving Prospero, Hippolito, Miranda and Dorinda), but mainly followed the Dryden/Davenant structure, cutting additional lines (109b–15a) and adding more song and spectacle: besides three devils singing 'Where does the black fiend Ambition reside?', another devil sang 'Arise, arise! ye subterranean winds', at the end of which there was a dance of '*winds*'. When it ended, '*Three winds s[a]nk, [and] the rest dr[o]ve Alonzo, Antonio, Gonzalo off*', marking the end of Act 2; Ferdinand's entrance with the invisible Ariel and Milcha began Act 3. Kemble kept the Restoration Miranda/Dorinda scene, the last of Act 1, in both versions, making only minor changes; Ariel and Ferdinand entered only after the playing of interpolated scenes, two in 1789 and four in 1806, so that the 'Yellow Sands' segment became, respectively, scene 4 and scene 6 of Act 2.

Many nineteenth-century and some twentieth-century producers, such as Macready, Phelps, Burton, Daly, Tree and Daniels, had Prospero and (if she were still present) Miranda exit before Ariel and Ferdinand's entrance; some Prosperos, such as Benthall's (1951), Hall's (1974), Alexander's and Thacker's, charmed Miranda, either directly or through spirits, into closing her eyes. McVicker ended the scene at 374 with a general exeunt; the tempest scene (1.1) followed, and then 1.2.1–17, 175b–307, with 307 reading 'Come shake it off' (Becks's pb). Tree introduced elaborate action, with Caliban, alone on stage, moving threateningly towards Prospero and Miranda's cave until suddenly arrested by music: he tried to dance to it, at the same time 'making inarticulate sounds as if attempting to sing' (printed sd). As he exited, Ariel entered and commanded her nymphs (in mime) to bring her a comb, a shell, a necklace, a head-dress and a bullrush (or a cloak), with which they then dressed her. Forming a circle, they danced around her until they were interrupted by the opening bars of 'Come unto these yellow sands', sung off-stage, whereupon they gradually vanished. Ariel disappeared as she began singing and then 're-enter[ed] immediately, waving on Ferdinand' (Grove's pb notes). Strehler's Caliban, who had grovelled throughout his scene, stood upright when dismissed and made a slow, dignified exit, pausing to look back solemnly at his tormentor: 'His beautiful, majestic black body defied' Prospero's description of him as a slave (video; Kleber, 'Theatrical Continuities', p. 149). Alexander's Caliban mocked Prospero by mimicking his gestures; his later enthusiastic imitations of Stephano suggested that his copying of Prospero had originated in admiration (CD).

The King's Men Ariel might have accompanied himself on the lute for both songs; he also 'had a chorus of off-stage spirits' to sing the burthen and 'music from above . . . so that

Ferdinand cannot place its origin' (Sturgess, *Jacobean Private Theatre*, pp. 89, 83). Although Sturgess, *Jacobean Private Theatre*, p. 83, posits that 'a broken consort of strings and wood-wind . . . was probably augmented by an organ to produce the sonorous and unearthly music the play requires' in later scenes, Gurr does not include organs in his index listing of playhouse instruments (*Shakespearean Stage*, p. 277). Some Ariels do not sing: Garrick (1756) cut 'playing and singing' from Ariel's sd; Kean had the songs performed by 'Miss Poole and choristers behind the scenes' (*Ath* 4/7/1857, p. 859); Crozier's Ariel pre-recorded the songs, which were relayed over the loud-speaker system; Ninagawa's Ariel was on top of the Noh stage during the song but did not sing it himself (CD).

Daly's Ariel entered, floating in the air, playing an unspecified instrument, and singing 'Full fathom five', with Ferdinand following. Benson's 1891 Ferdinand was 'dragg[ed] on . . . by two rather large-sized, rosy Cupids', whose antics distracted the audience from any 'interest in the shipwrecked and unhappy prince' (E.C.T., *SH* 1/5/91). Bridges-Adams (1934) had him led on by four elves, who followed a pipe-playing Ariel, while Crozier's was brought on by a sea-nymph. Brook's 1957 production provided a moment of 'complete enchantment . . . when Ariel and the blindfolded Ferdinand [were] seen in a strange grey light far away, but beyond the mouth of the darkened cave, floating . . . dreamlike in space' (*LSC* 16/8/57). Much less ethereally, Strehler's Ariel, wearing a curly sea-nymph wig, appeared in the ground-row waves below stage level, sometimes disappearing beneath them, and pulled on a fishing-line; once she had clambered onto the stage, she reeled it in, eventually drawing Ferdinand, to whose wrist it was attached, in her wake (video). Falls's Ferdinand made an even more 'startling entrance': 'Naked and as if playing beach games, he roll[ed] on in a hoop looking like DaVinci's familiar drawing of a man whose arms and legs extend to the perimeter of a circle' (Pellowe, 'In Chicago', p. 55). In contrast, Thacker's Ferdinand, like the other performers, simply got up from the floor to make his entrance as a very dignified and attractive prince, earnest but not 'wet'; in choosing a black actor to play Ferdinand and a white one to play Caliban, Thacker reversed one recent casting cliché (CD).

Reviews suggest that the demands and possibilities of Ferdinand's role are more complicated than one might expect. Curiously, although Kean made it a breeches part, played by Miss Bufton, the casting attracted no comment from Andersen and *ILN* and praise from Cole and the *Theatrical Journal*; only the *Athenaeum* doubted the 'propriety of representing [Ferdinand] by a female' (4/7/1857, p. 859). At Stratford, Greet's 1916 Ferdinand, Ion Swinley, took an original approach, 'show[ing] the weaker side of that caitiff's character to a nicety' (*St* 10/8/16), but more recently, Mendes's Ferdinand, Mark Lewis Jones, attracted generally negative reviews for playing him as 'a plodding, if amiable dolt' (Malcolm Rutherford, *FT* 13/8/93). In between, Ferdinand has been played by Alec Guinness as 'flawlessly romantic' for Devine/Goring (*T* 30/5/40); with 'taking frankness' by John Harrison for Crozier (*BP* 10/5/47); as 'awestruck and lovestruck' by Richard Burton for Benthall in 1951 (*St*); as 'fiery' by Richard Johnson for Brook in 1957 (*P* 21/8/57); with 'a sly touch of self-mockery' by Alan Rickman for Williams in 1978 (Bernard Levin, *ST* 7/5/78); as a 'hangdog personality' by

Christopher Ashley for Bogdanov in 1978 (Young, *FT* 29/1/78); 'like a rough and randy high school jock' by David Marshall Grant for Breuer (Kalem, *Time* 20/7/81); and as 'unappealingly graceless and hostile' by James Clyde for Murray, making Prospero's treatment of him 'forgivable' and Miranda's 'adoration . . . weak-headed' (Holdsworth, *TLS*, 21–7/9/90).

Recent reviews make clear that Ferdinand is now regarded as a rather unrewarding part, requiring originality and a playing-against-(what is seen as)-the-grain: for example, in one view, Peter Woodward managed to make 'something vigorous and sympathetic of the mimsy Ferdinand' for Hall (1988), but, in another, he was 'a cartoon Italian prince, romantic but little else' (respectively, Coveney, *FT* 20/5/88; Hoyle, *FT* 1/10/88). Aden Gillett, for Miller (1988), was praised for being not only 'sympathetic and well-spoken', but also the least 'wet Ferdinand any Miranda could [wish] for' (respectively, Charles Osborne, *DT* 13/10/88; Jack Tinker, *DM* 12/10/88). Hay's Ferdinand, John Lloyd Fillingham, was 'refreshingly cheeky' (Milne, *STel* 11/10/92), and Bogdanov's (1992), Charles Simpson, 'a spoilt young man growing up by finding a wiser father than his own' (Douglas Slater, *DM* 3/12/92). The presentation of Donnellan's Ferdinand, Lloyd Owen, 'as a bewigged, powdered Restoration fop', together with the queen's Thatcherite similarities, led 'to some uncertainty as to whether we [were] meant to grieve with the bereaved parent' (Hoyle, *FT* 20/10/88); however, in another view, the 'artifice of [Ferdinand's] world [was] highlighted by his curling wig, greasepaint, foppish clothes and elaborate language, all of which [were] lost as the play progresse[d]' and the character matured (Hilary Hutcheon, *Tr* 9/12/88).

375–85 The original setting has not survived. Macready arranged the choruses so that they 'fill[ed] the air', coming from 'above, beneath, on either side, or from the depths of Prospero's cell' (Forster, 'Macready's Production', pp. 68–9). Kean assigned the whole song to an invisible chorus of spirits in the flies. Cole found this execution of the music 'One of [Kean's] most strikingly original conceptions': the 'invisible choir, led by Miss Poole, whose mellow voice sounded with the rich, full clearness of a bell in the midst of, and above, the accompanying melody', prevented Ariel from seeming 'too material and terrestial' (*Life and Theatrical Times*, vol. ii, p. 220); the *Athenaeum* disagreed, judging that it '[took] away from Ariel a great charm' (4/7/1857, p. 859). Benson and Hack cut the song, while Daly interpolated it at the end of the scene (see note to 500–500sd); his Ariel entered singing 'Full fathom five', whereupon Ferdinand spoke 386–94 and Prospero and Miranda re-entered from the cave. See following notes for line cuts.

Ariel's songs have received a variety of musical treatments, some more effective than others. Brook's 1957 settings disappointed reviewers, with one complaining that 'A vague wash of sound will not do . . . but it is all [Ariel] gets for accompaniment, and against it he merely intones the words, like a vicar at matins, occasionally even breaking into speech' (*LSC*; see note to 5.1.88–94). Murray's composer, Chris Monks, made his 'music run . . . so at odds with the lyrics that it sound[ed] like deliberate subversion' (Schmidt, *DT* 17/9/90). Although Birtwistle's settings for Hall (1988) were 'tautly ethereal . . . Ariel's miming of them to a recorded voice' was loathsome (Coveney, *FT* 20/5/88). Some directors dispense

And then take hands.
Curtsied when you have, and kissed,
The wild waves whist.
Foot it featly here and there,
And sweet sprites the burden bear.   380

with music: Thacker's song was almost spoken, and Purcarete's was spoken in voice-over (CD).

Some of the most successful recent settings have been ethereal in nature. For Williams (1978), Charleson's Ariel 'deal[t] beautifully with the most haunting songs Guy Woolfenden has ever composed': 'full of unearthly strange harmonies', the 'drugged lullabies and ethereal dances memorably transmit[ted] the island's poetry' (respectively, Cushman, *O* 7/5/78; Desmond Pratt, *YP* 4/5/79; Wardle, *T* 3/5/78). There has also been a trend towards singing Ariel's songs as a counter-tenor: in Barton's production, Kingsley's 'haunting falsetto [was] perfectly suited to [his own] arrangements of the songs' (Knapp, *TES* 23/10/70). Stephen Oliver's music, one of the highlights of Daniels's production, provided 'a diversity of sounds that [was] sometimes . . . perfect, especially just the pipes, and sometimes . . . strained and anachronistic . . . [T]he songs . . . veer[ed] from the light fantastic to the heavy operatic' (Shorter, *DT* 13/8/82); their 'twangling sonorities' and 'ingenious settings' made Rylance sound 'almost like a counter-tenor' (respectively, Wardle, *T* 14/9/83; Coveney, *FT* 13/8/82; Coveney). Similarly, Mendes's Ariel sang the 'Sondheimian tunes' in a '[sweet] counter-tenor' voice, 'his singing . . . one of the joys in a production which [took] at face value the sounds of "a thousand twangling instruments" '; only when he sang 'in a beautiful tenor voice [did] he seem to understand anything about human feeling' (respectively, James Christopher, *TO* 18/8/93; Carole Woddis, *WO* 18/8/93; Tinker, *DM* 12/8/93; Taylor, *Ind* 13/8/93). In contrast, Burton's song was sung 'gaily', and Jonathan Goldstein's music for Alexander was 'a fascinating mix of Asian and Afro-Caribbean rhythms' (Billington, *G* 15/9/94).

Hall's 1974 Ariel played with Ferdinand throughout the song: for example, on 375, he stretched his hands out to him, without touching him; on 376, he quickly drew Ferdinand to C; on 377, he curtsied to Ferdinand, who curtsied back; on 379, he got up and raised his arms, and Ferdinand followed him; on 380, he somehow 'escaped', and Ferdinand felt the air. Although the pb is not clear on the point, it would appear that Ariel was visible to Ferdinand. As Daniels's Ariel began to sing, six other 'Ariels' entered and swirled about the stage (archive video) or, less charitably, 'prance[d] about in plastic capes', giving 'just a hint of louche Las Vegas cabaret' (respectively, Shorter, *DT* 13/8/82; Billington, *G* 12/8/82). Miller's 1988 Prospero tried to cut the song off (CD). Brook's 1990 spirits, carrying ferns and two butterflies on sticks, 'tease[d] the newly arrived Ferdinand . . . by shifting around comically broken bits of greenery, some of it sprouting between their toes' (CD; Taylor, *Ind* 2/11/90).

376 Kemble (1806) had three dancing sea-nymphs enter.

377–8 Cut by Kemble (1806) and Kean; Hytner had 378 sung twice.

380 Altered by Phelps to 'And let the rest the burden bear.'

Burthen dispersedly Hark, hark

Bow-wow

The watch-dogs bark

Bow-wow

ARIEL   Hark, hark! I hear

The strain of strutting Chanticleer,

Cry cock-a-diddle-dow.   385

FERDINAND Where should this music be? I'th 'air, or th'earth?

It sounds no more; and sure it waits upon

Some god o'th'island. Sitting on a bank,

381–2 Shadwell and Williams (1978) had Ariel sing the burthen; Garrick (1756) cut it. Many producers, such as Kemble, Kean, Daly, Williams (1978) and Hytner (London), cut the 'Bow-wow's';
others, such as Macready, Burton and Miller (1988), treated the phrase as the dispersed
burthen, with Ariel singing the rest of the song (but not 385 for Miller). At 381sd, Phelps's
Ariel waved her wand, 'as if directing the Chorus, which [was] first sung at back of stage, then
in the flies'. Daly's Ariel sang 381a and 382a, which other voices then echoed.

383–5 Cut by Garrick (1756) and given by Kemble to the chorus. Kemble (1806) and Kean cut 'strutting', while Daly's voices twice echoed 'chanticleer' (384); Williams (1978) had 385 sung
twice, but Kemble (1789), Phelps, Kean, Daly and Hytner cut it, the latter ending the song
with 375 sung twice, accompanied by a fading chorus of sea-sounds (Stratford pb). After 380,
Daniels's Ariel sang 'Bow wow wow wow' three times and then 'Hark, the watchdogs bark!
Hark I hear / The strain of strutting Chanticleer', followed by 'Cock-a-diddle-dow' twice, with
the chorus taking up the cockcrows. Barton transposed 385 and 386; Miller (1988) made 385
part of the burthen, while Purcarete had Prospero speak it.

   Garrick (1757) followed 385 with 'A Dance of Spirits'; Tree and Benthall had Ariel exit.
Strehler's Ariel took off her sea-nymph wig and then crowed loudly to wake the sleeping
Ferdinand; she also made various animal and bird sounds, meowing and chirruping, teasing
Ferdinand with her unseen but locatable presence. As she sang an air (a reprise of 'Yellow
sands'?) and Ferdinand sat, Ariel put her head in the triangular space between Ferdinand's
arm, his torso and the ground, again teasing him with her heard but unseen presence
(video).

386 Kemble (1806) and Daniels had Ferdinand enter. His question unintentionally provoked
much audience laughter during the first night of the Williams/Brook production, since the
songs were 'rasped and hissed' 'by sprites dressed like skin divers with hair nets' (respectively, *BEN* 3/4/63; *EN* 3/4/63).

388 Dryden/Davenant changed the punctuation, so that Ferdinand supposed the 'god o' th'
island' was sitting and weeping for Alonso's loss. Shadwell's punctuation was confused: 'god
i' th' island; sitting . . . against the duke; my father's wrack'd'.

Weeping again the king my father's wrack,
This music crept by me upon the waters,   390
Allaying both their fury and my passion
With its sweet air. Thence I have followed it –
Or it hath drawn me rather; but 'tis gone.
No, it begins again.

SONG

ARIEL Full fathom five thy father lies,   395
    Of his bones are coral made;

389   Miller's 1988 Ariel mimicked Ferdinand's posture and continued to mimic 'how [he] looks
    about' (409); it was unclear to one reviewer whether he was impressed by or mocking the
    mortal (Claire Armitstead, *PP* 12/88). Wardle saw him simply as Prospero's 'friendly ally . . .
    playing a mirror game [with mischievous enjoyment]' (*T* 12/10/88), but Billington thought he
    'mimic[ked] human gestures as if he had mortal longings in him' (*G* 12/10/88). See note to
    Epilogue 20sd.
390–2 Dryden/Davenant and Shadwell changed 'crept' to 'hover'd' and 'sweet' to 'charming';
    Garrick (1756) adopted 'hover'd', but changed 'sweet' to 'chearing'.
393   Shakespeare's text clearly calls for music between Ferdinand's 'But 'tis gone' and 'No, it
    begins again', and all productions provide it. Benthall's Ariel re-entered.
394   Cut by Kemble.
395–403 The lutenist Robert Johnson, the king's musician, composed a setting, either for a court
    revival or for the original production; his music, which survives, is 'surprisingly cheerful,
    almost gay' (Sturgess, *Jacrobean Private Theatre*, pp. 83, 89). Both Kermode, p. 157, and
    Orgel, pp. 223–4, reprint it.
      Shadwell, Garrick (1756), Kemble, Williams (1978) and Miller (1988) cut 402. Garrick
    (1757), Macready and Kean transposed 402 and 403; Benthall cut 403. Williams's 1978 Ariel
    sang 'Ding-dong, bell' (403) three times; Daniels treated 401–3 as a three-part burthen, while
    Ninagawa's on-stage audience provided the burthen of 'ding-dong-dong' (CD). Atkins (1937)
    left 'too little to the imagination. When sea nymphs are mentioned, swarms of whinnying
    chits answer the cue with prentice eurythmics, and Ariel's ding-dong-bell has its amplified
    deputy in the orchestral brake' (*O* 29/8/37).
      Phelps had 402 sung in the flies, with Ariel slowly ascending the OP sloat between 401–3,
    'lying and waving wand, as if directing chorus'; Ashwell's Ariel sang from the pit. Strehler's
    sang from the ground-row waves below the stage and approached Ferdinand when she
    finished, clashing finger-cymbals at him; as he reached out towards the sound, Miranda saw
    him for the first time, but he did not yet see her (video). Ariel, however, does not always sing
    the song: Shadwell used Milcha instead. Kemble (1789) had a spirit sing 395–400 and the

Those are pearls that were his eyes;
Nothing of him that doth fade,
But doth suffer a sea-change
Into something rich and strange.   400
Sea-nymphs hourly ring his knell.
                              Burthen: Ding-dong
ARIEL   Hark, now I hear them, 'ding dong bell'.
FERDINAND The ditty does remember my drowned father.
This is no mortal business, nor no sound   405
That the earth owes. I hear it now above me.

chorus 401 and 403, but in 1806 Ariel sang the song, arranged as in 1789. Walford had Prospero sing (Hoyle, *FT* 31/1/84), while Hall's 1988 Ariel mimed the song to recorded voices.

Williams/Brook 'modernised [Ariel's songs] so that "Full fathom five" . . . beg[an] "Full fathom" (long pause) "five-thy-father-lies" ' (Wilson, *Sco* 4/4/63). The voice of Retallack's 1981 female Ariel evinced 'inhumanity . . . as he callously informed Ferdinand of Alonso's death' (Barber, *DT* 20/6[*sic*]/83). Similarly, Wolfe's 'strident musical arrangements [made] Ariel's sweet songs turn harsh and unappealing', with 'Full fathom five' sung 'to a Latin rhythm' (respectively, David Sterritt, *CSM* 13/7/95; Karam, *T* 14/7/95). In contrast, during the song in Edwards's production, 'partly stylised gesture and movement . . . suggested the world beneath the sea . . . or the state of dreaming itself' (Thomson, *SundH* 20/5/90); the 'lyrical music . . . add[ed] to the emotional mood of the play, in the flute playing of the spirits and in Ariel's wistful singing' (Carr, *MelR* 6/90). Likewise, Hytner had 'distant voices accompanying Ariel', and Sams's 'elusive music' did 'indeed create an isle full of noises, sounds and sweet airs' (Hoyle, *FT* 26/5/89). Purcarete had the song spoken rather than sung (CD).

During the song, Donnellan's Prospero, who had already pushed his trousers up over his knees and donned one shoe and one boot, grayed his face and blacked his teeth (CD). Rylance's 'Ferdinand [was] subjected to a vision of the fully-clothed Alonso having a waterless scrub-down in a dilapidated shower stall' (Taylor, *Ind* 11/6/91). At the end of the song, Tree, Benthall and Brook (1957 SMT) had Ariel exit. Williams's 1978 Prospero and Miranda entered, with Prospero waving his hand over Miranda's face to disenchant her, presumably at 407. Miller's 1988 Prospero beckoned Miranda from the cell and hugged her.

404–6 Ferdinand's remark that he now hears the music above him (406b) indicates either that the music of 'Full fathom five' continues throughout 404–6 or that music is re-introduced following 406a. Garrick (1757), Kemble and Tree reintroduced it at 406a, while Burton had his chorus resume at 403a. Garrick (1756) cut 404; Kean 406b; Daly 404–6.

After 406, Dryden/Davenant and Shadwell added 'However I will on and follow it', after which Ferdinand and Ariel exited. Both texts changed 'owes' to 'owns' (as did Garrick 1756, 1757 and Kemble 1789) and 'above' to 'before', the latter indicating that Ariel (and Milcha)

PROSPERO The fringèd curtains of thine eye advance,
              And say what thou seest yond.
MIRANDA   What is't? A spirit?
              Lord, how it looks about! Believe me, sir,
              It carries a brave form. But 'tis a spirit.   410

did not fly at this point. Garrick (1757) and Kemble (both versions) also had Ferdinand exit, the latter thereby ending his second act.

Following Ferdinand's exit in Dryden/Davenant, Stephano, Mustacho and Ventoso entered, drinking and eventually discussing the need for government on the island. After manoeuvring, argument and a near duel, Stephano emerged as duke with the other two as viceroys; further complications ensued with the arrival of Trincalo and then of Caliban. The scene was followed by one involving Prospero, Hippolito, Dorinda and Miranda. Shadwell used the same material but changed its order (see note to 374sd). Garrick's 1756 opera imported a shortened version of the 1667 and 1674 echo scene, with its duet between Ariel and Ferdinand, after 406; it was followed by scenes between Stephano, Ventoso, Mustacho and Trincalo, after which Shakespeare's scene was resumed.

407 Miranda is sometimes charmed from seeing Ferdinand until now, and sometimes simply physically prevented. Macready's Prospero and Miranda only emerged from the cell at 406a, while Daniels's Prospero kept one hand in front of Miranda's eyes. Purcarete's Miranda was wrapped up and unable to see (CD). Hall's 1974 Miranda, having been uncharmed by Prospero's passing his hand over her head, opened her eyes.

407–500sd (end of scene) Cut by Dryden/Davenant and Shadwell, with 407–24a, 427b–35 and 439b–99 interpolated elsewhere. Garrick (1757) changed the scene to another part of the island, whereupon Ariel and Ferdinand entered on one side, and Prospero and Miranda on the other. Kemble made this section Act 3, Scene 1 of both versions. The 1789 Prospero and Miranda entered as they did for Garrick, Prospero beginning the scene with 'Look, Miranda: say, what thou seest yond.' The more elaborate 1806 version began the scene with Ariel and other spirits singing the final lines of 'Full fathom five' (401, 403) off-stage, during which Prospero and Miranda entered and began the dialogue at 407; Ferdinand, Ariel and attendant spirits remained off-stage until line 415.

408 Barton's Prospero opened his cloak at 408a, presumably thus allowing Miranda to see Ferdinand; it is unclear whether he had literally covered her in it or simply used its magic powers.

Constance Benson was praised for her playing of Miranda's first encounter with Ferdinand: 'there was something very captivating in the sweetness of her manner, the grace of her movements, and the musical quality of her tones. Her points were made with remarkable ease and naturalness' (*St* 30/4/1891). Daniels's Miranda, Alice Krige, was 'poised on tenterhooks of admiration all the time – for father, lover and men in general' (Barber, *DT* 9/83).

409–10 Garrick (1756) cut 409a, perhaps because the action it implies would have harmed Ferdinand's dignity. According to Edmonds, Kean cut 409–10, but Ellis marks business against the

PROSPERO No, wench, it eats, and sleeps, and hath such senses
As we have, such. This gallant which thou seest
Was in the wrack; and but he's something stained
With grief – that's beauty's canker – thou might'st call him
A goodly person. He hath lost his fellows,   415
And strays about to find 'em.

MIRANDA   I might call him
A thing divine, for nothing natural
I ever saw so noble.

PROSPERO [*Aside*]   It goes on, I see,
As my soul prompts it. Spirit, fine spirit, I'll free thee
Within two days for this.

FERDINAND   Most sure the goddess   420
On whom these airs attend. Vouchsafe my prayer
May know if you remain upon this island,

lines. Garrick (1757) and Kemble (1789) made Miranda less adamant about Ferdinand's
nature, having her ask, respectively, 'But is't / is it a spirit?'. Brook (1957 DL) had Ariel exit at
410.

411–20a Cut by Kemble (1789). Garrick (1756) cut 412b–13a, 415b–16a, 418b–20a; Kemble (1806),
Burton, Kean and Daly 415b–16a; Macready 416a; Tree 418b–20a. The often cut 416a may
have presented the same problem as 409a. Garrick (1756) followed 418a with Ferdinand's air
'What sudden blaze of majesty'.
    Williams's 1978 Prospero 'found much humour in lines like the over-explanatory "It eats,
and sleeps" . . .' (411; Warren, 'A Year of Comedies', p. 203). Miller's 1988 Ariel mirrored
Ferdinand's gestures, so that they were in identical postures at 'nothing natural / I ever saw
so noble' (417b–18a), Miranda unwittingly commenting on Prospero's exploitation of Ariel
(pb; CD). At 418a, Benthall's Ferdinand saw Miranda as a result of Prospero's magic, whereas
Hytner's Miranda very slowly moved to Ferdinand and put her hand on his shoulder. Mendes
changed the lighting state for Prospero's aside to Ariel (418b–20a); when it was over, Ferdinand saw Miranda (CD). Armfield's Prospero and Miranda had 'not the intimacy . . . one
would have expected . . . but a more formal association which found Prospero delightfully
capable of surprise when Miranda and Ferdinand fall so movingly in love' (Jeremy Eccles, *Bul*
12/6/90).

420b–6a Ferdinand discovers Miranda's presence on (or just before) 420b. Brook's 1990 Ariel used a
magic stick to point him in her direction, then whipped it and slapped his back to make him
come forward to speak; Purcarete's Ferdinand was put under a spell, waking from it to speak
and to find himself sitting entwined with Miranda (CD). Garrick (1756) cut 421b–6a.

> And that you will some good instruction give
> How I may bear me here. My prime request,
> Which I do last pronounce, is – O you wonder –   425
> If you be maid, or no?
> MIRANDA   No wonder, sir,
> But certainly a maid.
> FERDINAND   My language? Heavens!

Iden Payne's 1938 Ferdinand had 'the right air of baffled, spellbound ecstasy' (*O* 8/5/38), while Brook's 1957 Miranda, meeting Ferdinand, finally '[caught] fire after being merely sincere and competent' (*St* 15/8/57). Miller (1970) 'imbued [their meeting] with a powerful feeling of love': they 'pick[ed] their way with intense care through the lines, and examin[ed] one anothers' [*sic*] hands as though they had never seen such things before' (respectively, *P* 24/6/70; Wardle, *T* 16/6/70). Similarly, Miller's 1988 courtship of Miranda and Ferdinand was, 'for once, really touching rather than merely soppy' (Gardner, *MSun* 16/10/88), with Miranda 'an eager, sexually-impassioned girl tugging at [Ferdinand's] shirt and ears with something more than scientific curiosity' (Billington, *G* 12/20/88).

   When Retallack's 1981 Ferdinand met Miranda, 'he sensibly addresse[d] her as if she were unlikely to understand English' (Young, *FT* 2/83); Hytner's Ferdinand spoke in the same way, while Mendes's used sign language to help him communicate (CD). Daniels's Ferdinand knelt and spoke his first lines in the tone of a fervent prayer (archive video and pb). Mendes's Miranda laughed at being called a 'goddess' (CD), while the boyish and ragged appearance of Wolfe's Miranda made Ferdinand's appellation 'sound . . . momentarily odd' (Greene, *TW* 31/7–6/8/95).

426b–7a Cut by Garrick (1756). Nerves made Constance Benson once deliver the line as 'No maid, sir, and certainly no wonder!'; she writes that Prospero and Ferdinand 'could hardly finish the scene' as a result (*Mainly Players*, p. 96). Barton's Miranda 'really convinced you that she was meeting a young man for the first time in her life' (*GC* 18/10/70).

427b Daniels's Ferdinand addressed 'My language!' to the audience, eliciting a laugh (archive video). Mendes's Ferdinand also got a laugh, as the actor appeared to send up the character (CD).

427b–48a Garrick (1756) cut 429b–46a (i.e., Prospero's interventions were cut and other speeches shortened, with minimal new material added where necessary); Prospero's air 'In tender sighs he silence breaks' followed 448a. In 1757 he improved Prospero's grammar ('more brave' in 438), cut 440b–1a where Prospero speaks to Ariel, and had Prospero address 439b–40a to Ariel instead. In 1789 Kemble cut 427b–47a, and in 1806 436b–9a (see note to 442). Kean, Bridges-Adams (1926/30, 1934) and Ayrton cut 436b–9a; Kean also cut 441b–6a and changed 'a virgin' to 'unmarried' (446b). Burton, Tree, Iden Payne and Brook (1957) cut

I am the best of them that speak this speech,
Were I but where 'tis spoken.

PROSPERO   How the best?
What wert thou if the king of Naples heard thee?   430

FERDINAND A single thing, as I am now, that wonders
To hear thee speak of Naples. He does hear me,
And that he does, I weep. Myself am Naples,
Who, with mine eyes, ne'er since at ebb, beheld
The king my father wracked.

MIRANDA   Alack, for mercy!   435

FERDINAND Yes, faith, and all his lords, the Duke of Milan
And his brave son being twain.

PROSPERO [*Aside*]   The Duke of Milan
And his more braver daughter, could control thee
If now 'twere fit to do't. At the first sight
They have changed eyes. Delicate Ariel,   440
I'll set thee free for this! [*To Ferdinand*] A word, good sir;
I fear you have done yourself some wrong; a word.

437b–9a; Barton 436–9a; Hack 429b–33a, 437b–48a (with 443–7a later interpolated in place of 456–8). See following notes for stagings.

429a Miller's 1988 Prospero shed his magic cloak, perhaps suggesting that he had controlled Miranda's and Ferdinand's first responses to each other.

437b–51 Brook (1990) had Prospero freeze Miranda and Ferdinand during his asides (CD). Mendes also had the couple freeze, as Ariel 'drop[ped] his prayerful, hands-raised, spirit-summoning pose and wait[ed], with an inscrutable hint of insolent impatience, while Prospero offload[ed] a thought or two on such subjects as the spirit's promised freedom' (Taylor, *Ind* 13/8/93). Alexander's Prospero kept breaking through the lovers at 'one word' (CD).

439b In Brook's 1957 production, Miranda's love for Ferdinand made Prospero's 'manner soften' (Pratt, *YP* 14/8/57).

440a Bogdanov's 1992 Ferdinand kissed Miranda's hand erotically (CD).

441b Prospero apparently demands that Ferdinand approach him; the two then talk in the background while Miranda speaks her following lines to the audience. However, how far Ferdinand obeys Prospero is a matter for the individual director. Mendes's Prospero had clearly not planned to enslave Ferdinand, only now hatching the plot because the lovers were too enamoured of each other (CD).

442 Kemble (1806) substituted an order to Ariel ('Attend') for 'a word' addressed to Ferdinand, adding a sd that Prospero should talk apart to Ariel; he thus provided a naturalistic opportunity for the lovers' ensuing conversation. Daniels's Prospero made it clear that he was only acting angry at Ferdinand (archive video).

MIRANDA Why speaks my father so ungently? This
          Is the third man that e'er I saw; the first
          That e'er I sighed for. Pity move my father   445
          To be inclined my way.
FERDINAND   O, if a virgin,
          And your affection not gone forth, I'll make you
          The Queen of Naples.
PROSPERO   Soft, sir, one word more.
          [*Aside*] They are both in either's powers; but this swift
              business
          I must uneasy make, lest too light winning   450
          Make the prize light. [*To Ferdinand*] One word more. I
              charge thee
          That thou attend me! Thou dost here usurp

443   Hall's 1974 Miranda addressed her question to the audience, as did Daniels's (respectively,
      pb and archive video). Purcarete's Ferdinand was lying on his back with Miranda's head on
      his chest; Prospero was lying prone (CD).

446b Hytner's Ferdinand dragged both himself and Prospero out of the cell to kneel next to
      Miranda (CD).

448b–55a Garrick (1756) cut 449b–53a, replacing them with 'Young sir, a word.' Phelps, Barton and
      Hack cut 448b; Kean changed it to 'One word' (Ellis) and later substituted 441b for it
      (Edmonds). Bridges-Adams (1926/30, 1934) and Ayrton cut 448b, 449–51a. Kemble (1806)
      cut 453, while Kean and Daly changed its 'ow'st' to 'own'st'.
          During 448b–51, Tree's Miranda found a shell and gave it to Ferdinand, who put it in his
      tunic. Daniels's Prospero addressed the audience at 449 (archive video). Burton's Ferdinand
      was so lost in admiration of Miranda that on Prospero's 451b he unconsciously waved his
      hand to silence him. At Stratford, Brook's 1957 Prospero came between Miranda and Ferdi-
      nand at 452; the 'fine, manly Ferdinand [bore] with fortitude his harsh treatment' by Pros-
      pero (*WA* 15/8/57). Williams's 1978 Prospero banged his staff at 451c, causing the lovers to
      break apart.
          At 451, Hytner's Prospero stamped his foot to get Ferdinand's attention, his 'fit of petty
      anger' bringing both lovers to their feet (CD; Hoyle, *FT* 26/5/89). It was clear that Prospero
      was genuinely pleased at their developing relationship and merely acting his anger (CD):
      Wood 'extract[ed] an unusual amount of laughter from the incongruities of a Prospero who
      organises his daughter's love-match, must appear to resist it, gets worried by its growing
      intensity, yet still wishes it to progress' (Nightingale, *P* 12/8/88). In contrast, Wolfe's Pros-
      pero, genuinely jealous 'at losing Miranda', did not counterbalance the emotion with 'the
      loving resignation of a father who, after all, has set the whole process in motion' (Gerard,
      V 17–23/7/95).

> The name thou ow'st not, and hast put thyself
> Upon this island as a spy, to win it
> From me, the lord on't.

FERDINAND   No, as I am a man.   455

MIRANDA There's nothing ill can dwell in such a temple.
> If the ill spirit have so fair a house,
> Good things will strive to dwell with't.

PROSPERO   Follow me.
> Speak not you for him: he's a traitor. Come!
> I'll manacle thy neck and feet together;   460
> Sea water shalt thou drink; thy food shall be
> The fresh-brook mussels, withered roots, and husks
> Wherein the acorn cradled. Follow.

FERDINAND   No!
> I will resist such entertainment, till
> Mine enemy has more power.
>   *He draws, and is charmed from moving*

MIRANDA   O dear father,   465

455b Changed by Kean to 'as I am alive'; since Ferdinand was played by a woman, the change suggests that audiences would not have entirely accepted the convention.

456 Miranda's protest made Daniels's Prospero turn around and look at her with clear amazement (archive video).

456–8 Garrick (1756) and Kean cut 457–8; Hack cut 456–8a, interpolating 443–7a in their place, and changed 458b to 'Come'.

Phelps's Miranda interceded for Ferdinand at 458b, provoking Prospero's 459; Burton's Prospero spoke 458b threateningly, prompting Miranda's 'gesture of intercession'. Hytner's Miranda followed and grabbed Prospero at 458 (London pb), whereas Miller's 1988 Prospero pulled Ferdinand US, at the same time pulling Miranda, who was apparently holding onto her lover.

459–63a Hack cut 461b–3a. During 459–63a, Strehler's Ariel got a sword out of the SL trap and put it DS of the sand circle, ready for Ferdinand's use at 465sd (video). After 'cradled' (463a), Crozier's Miranda interpolated 'Father'.

463b Crozier's Ferdinand drew his sword but found it charmed. Benthall's 1951 Ferdinand had to make a great effort to draw his sword, whereas Daniels's, having drawn his, looked to see whether Miranda were suitably impressed (archive video).

465sd Ferdinand is clearly charmed from using his sword at some point during the ensuing lines, but the director has some leeway as to when the spell takes effect: it can be here or at 472 or even at 482; at these points Prospero is either threatening Ferdinand or taunting him for his inability to act as he wishes. The charm's effect has also been handled in myriad ways:

Make not too rash a trial of him, for
He's gentle, and not fearful.
PROSPERO   What, I say,
My foot my tutor? Put thy sword up, traitor,
Who mak'st a show, but dar'st not strike, thy conscience
Is so possessed with guilt. Come from thy ward,   470
For I can here disarm thee with this stick,
And make thy weapon drop.
MIRANDA   Beseech you, father!

Bridges-Adams's 1934 Ariel caught the dropped sword so that Ferdinand 'marvel[led] to see it float before him' (*SH* 20/4/34). Brook (1990) showed a real physical struggle as Ariel bent back Ferdinand's sword, whereas Ninagawa's Prospero threw white streamers at Ferdinand, who was thereafter imprisoned in a circle of light (CD). Alexander's Ferdinand had his sword pinned to one spot on the ground, making him go round and round, trying to lift it, to no avail; Thacker's, accompanied by eerie music, desperately and unsuccessfully struggled to lift his inexorably descending sword (CD). Hall's 1988 Prospero simply waved his staff, making Ferdinand fall to his knees. See following notes for other stagings.

465b–72a Kemble (1806) cut 465b–8a; Hack 469–70. At 465b, Tree's Miranda rushed to Ferdinand, took down his sword and dragged him away from Prospero, while Hall's 1974 Miranda got between her father and Ferdinand and protected the prince. Alexander's Miranda also showed a spirited response to her father's behaviour; Prospero himself seemed to be responding to the situation as it developed, not having planned this treatment of Ferdinand from the start (CD). Benthall's 1952 Miranda knelt to Prospero on 465b; he raised her at 468a as Ferdinand raised his sword and then turned to him at 472a, making him lower it.

467–84 Garrick (1756) followed 467a with the air 'Sweetness, truth, and ev'ry grace' and cut 467b–84, with 473 interpolated later.

468b Strehler's Ariel sat near the tip of Ferdinand's sword and placed her finger on it, very gradually bending it down into the ground. Once it lay on the floor, she patted it into the sand as if magically fixing it; Ferdinand struggled hard but unsuccessfully to lift it (video).

471 Phelps's Prospero waved his wand and touched Ferdinand's arm, which dropped paralysed.

472a Kemble (1806) and Macready had Ferdinand drop the point of his sword to the ground, while Hall (1988) and Hytner had him drop the sword entirely. As Ferdinand was about to advance, Burton's Prospero raised his wand and made the sword fall to the ground; Ferdinand, however, remained transfixed in an attitude of attack. Tree's Ferdinand tried to strike Prospero but the latter raised his wand and moved it downwards, forcing the prince to lower his sword until it fell from his hand. Mendes's Prospero tapped Ferdinand's sword with his stick, making the prince himself fall to the floor (CD).

472b–82a Kemble (1789) cut 475b–82a; in 1806, he cut 477–82a, the restored lines substituting the now

PROSPERO Hence! Hang not on my garments.

MIRANDA   Sir, have pity;
I'll be his surety.

PROSPERO   Silence! One word more
Shall make me chide thee, if not hate thee. What,   475
An advocate for an impostor? Hush!
Thou think'st there is no more such shapes as he,
Having seen but him and Caliban. Foolish wench,
To th'most of men this is a Caliban,
And they to him are angels.

MIRANDA   My affections   480
Are then most humble. I have no ambition
To see a goodlier man.

PROSPERO   Come on, obey.

---

omitted 468a for 476a (see note to 465b–72a). Macready cut 477–82a; Kean 472b–82a;
Burton 473b–82a. Phelps originally cut 473b–82a, but Creswick marks the lines 'In'; copies
presumably made from this pb show the cuts in slightly different versions.

   The interaction between Prospero and Miranda varies greatly. Crozier's Miranda was
about to speak after 476a, but Prospero responded 'Hush, foolish wench!' (i.e., 478b was
transposed here); Miranda nevertheless again tried to address him, saying 'Father'. Hytner's
Prospero momentarily touched the side of Miranda's face at 476b, but at 481a she stood
between him and Ferdinand (Stratford pb). Tree's Prospero turned his face away from
Miranda to conceal a smile at 479. Williams's 1978 Prospero was praised for his 'confident
delivery [which] moved from mock indignation ("An advocate for an imposter") via anger
("Hush!") to ironic humour ("Thou think'st there is no more such shapes as he, / Having seen
but him and Caliban!") in one short speech' (Warren, 'A Year of Comedies', p. 203).

   Ferdinand's behaviour also varies. Hall's 1974 Ferdinand slowly collapsed at 476, whereas
Williams's (1978) retrieved his sword at 478b. Williams/Brook had him 'fall flat at Miranda's
feet – almost as if he were Trinculo' at 481b–2a (Trewin, *BP* 3/4/63); Ian McCulloch made him
'a modern beatnik whose poetry fell as flat as he did . . . at [this] awful moment' (*DW*
4/4/63).

482b Cut by Kean and Burton. Tree's Prospero presumably directed 'obey' at Miranda, taking her
by the hand and swinging her to the R. Crozier's Miranda picked up Ferdinand's sword.
Whereas Benthall's 1952 Prospero gestured to make Ferdinand come out of his trance,
Brook's 1957 Ferdinand put his hands into chains that had just descended, while Miranda lay
on the floor (SMT pb). Hall (1974) had both music and magic stop as Ferdinand collapsed
onto the floor, while Purcarete's Ferdinand stood up under the bed, which remained
strapped to his back, and was blindfolded (CD). Strehler's Ariel cued magical chant-music

    Thy nerves are in their infancy again
    And have no vigour in them.
FERDINAND   So they are.
    My spirits, as in a dream, are all bound up.   485
    My father's loss, the weakness which I feel,
    The wrack of all my friends, or this man's threats,
    To whom I am subdued, are but light to me,
    Might I but through my prison once a day
    Behold this maid. All corners else o' th' earth   490
    Let liberty make use of; space enough
    Have I in such a prison.
PROSPERO [*Aside*]   It works. [*To Ferdinand*] Come on!

and took up a position like Ferdinand's; moving her body, she 'made' him mirror her movements, culminating in his sinking to the ground (video).

483 Thacker's Ferdinand fell to the ground and dropped his sword (CD).

484a Following a pause after 484a, Burton's Prospero waved his wand to release Ferdinand from the spell. Barton's Prospero took Ferdinand's sword, while the latter crouched on the floor.
      Kean's Prospero retired US, and Ariel appeared at the top of a high rock; she had made only a brief appearance earlier when leading Ferdinand to the yellow sands (Edmonds pb). Kerr's light was again used (Ellis pb).

484b Phelps's Ferdinand spoke in a bewildered tone. Brook's 1957 Ferdinand backed away, holding his arms up; Ariel chained him at 488 (DL pb).

487–8 Garrick (1757) improved Ferdinand's grammar, changing the Folio 'nor' to 'and' and 'are' to the subjunctive 'were' (this *NCS* reading changes 'nor' to 'or').

489 Tree's Ferdinand held out his arms and Miranda slowly crossed to him, whereupon he embraced her.

490 Miller's 1988 Miranda slowly went to Ferdinand, and they held hands.

490b–2a Cut by Daly. Kean's Ariel appeared again at 492a, this time on the sloat (see note to 484a).

492b–500 During these lines Miranda speaks to Ferdinand, and Prospero to Ariel, Ferdinand and Miranda. Prospero clearly directs 493a, 494a and 497b–9a to Ariel and 500b to Miranda, while 492c seems an appropriate command to Ferdinand (cf. 482b); 493b and 500a can be directed either to Ferdinand alone or to Miranda alone or to both. Prospero's comment on the mutual love between Ferdinand and Miranda ('It works') can be spoken either as an aside or as a comment to Ariel or even (as Hytner's did) to the audience (CD).
      Garrick (1756) cut 492b–9, interpolating 473 after 492a and transposing the two halves of 500; the scene ended with a new line ('This door shews you to your lodgings'). Kemble (1806) cut 496b–7a, with 'ne'er, till this day, / Saw I him touch'd with anger so distemper'd'

Thou hast done well, fine Ariel. Follow me.

[*To Ariel*] Hark what thou else shalt do me.

MIRANDA [*To Ferdinand*]   Be of comfort;

My father's of a better nature, sir,   495

Than he appears by speech. This is unwonted

Which now came from him.

PROSPERO   Thou shalt be as free

As mountain winds; but then exactly do

All points of my command.

ARIEL   To th'syllable.

PROSPERO Come follow. Speak not for him.   500

Exeunt

(4.1.144b–5) substituted instead; Kean 492b–c; Tree 492c; Kean, Tree and Williams (1978) 493b; Daly 497b–9. See following notes for stagings.

493 Macready's Prospero spoke 'Follow me' to Ferdinand and Miranda. Tree's Prospero waved his wand at 'fine Ariel!', whereupon the spirit quickly entered. Brook's 1990 Prospero and Ariel turned round to the lovers, but, realizing that Miranda had not yet finished speaking to Ferdinand, they turned back again to give them more time (CD).

494 Prospero's 494a suggests that he gives Ariel further instructions, unheard by the audience, during Miranda's speech to Ferdinand (494b–7a). Both Kemble versions add the sd that Prospero should talk apart to Ariel, thereby allowing the lovers naturalistic space for Miranda's comforting words. Burton's Miranda crossed hastily to Ferdinand as her father spoke to Ariel; Benthall's Ariel entered.

495–7a It was hard to believe Hirsch's Miranda, since 'she took all [Prospero's] fury, beginning with his first lines, for granted' (Young, *FT* 30/6/82).

497a Miller's 1988 Miranda and Ferdinand kissed.

497b–9a Ayrton's Prospero spoke in response to Ariel's gestured appeal.

499 Kemble's 1789 Ariel exited. In 1806, she stayed behind with Ferdinand and the attendant spirits after Prospero and Miranda's exit at 500, singing 'Kind fortune smiles, and she / Hath yet in store for thee / Some strange felicity: / Follow me, follow me, / And thou shalt see.' The Chorus of Spirits repeated the last two lines, after which all exited to close the scene. Inchbald adds that Miranda continued her supplication as she exited with her father.

Tree's Ariel quickly ran between Miranda and Ferdinand and exited. Caliban then appeared, coming over the rocks, carrying faggots and a log; seeing Ferdinand, he dropped the faggots, quickly climbed down the rocks and raised the log, ready to strike him. Prospero, however, had seen Caliban's approach and used his wand to make him retire.

Thacker's Ariel promised, somewhat testily, to obey Prospero 'To the sylla*bull*' (CD).

500–500sd Phelps's Miranda was about to speak after 'follow', provoking Prospero's next words; she and her father then exited into the cave. Ariel waved Ferdinand off into (another?) cave as the chorus sang eight bars of 'Sea nymphs hourly' in the flies, the act drop descending slowly upon the picture. Kean and Burton also reprised 'Sea nymphs hourly'; the latter's Miranda followed her father but looked back all the while at Ferdinand. McVicker ended the act with Ariel's song 'Kind fortune smiles', but it is unclear whether the actor or an invisible chorus in the flies sang it. Like Phelps, many directors add a gesture or remark by Miranda to prompt 500b; Iden Payne's gestured, while Crozier's interpolated 'Sir, have pity.' Brook's 1990 Ariel carried Ferdinand off (CD).

Some directors have interpolated more elaborate business to end the first act. After 500, Daly had other spirits enter and dance around Ferdinand 'as if to distract him from Miranda', who exited into the cave; Ariel then sang 'Come unto these yellow sands' (see note to 375–85). This 'climactic tableau, featuring song and dance', was repeated in the other three act-endings (Nilan, ' "The Tempest" ', p. 116). Tree had Prospero and Miranda exit slowly, with Ferdinand following; at the same time, Caliban picked up his faggots and crawled into his cell. In the distance the chorus sang 'Come unto these yellow sands', its volume gradually swelling as the enraptured Ferdinand, the last to leave the stage, exited and the curtain fell on the first act. Strehler had Ariel remain on stage, picking up props and replacing them in the trap before exiting; at one point, she picked up a large sea-shell and held it to her ear, 'an allusion to the music which permeates the island' (video; Kleber, 'Theatrical Continuities', p. 147).

Modern productions, from Iden Payne's onwards, usually run the scene straight into 2.1. After Benthall's Prospero had spoken 500, the audience could hear voices off-stage: Alonso calling 'Ferdinand, my son' and Gonzalo and Francisco 'My good Lord Ferdinand'. The 1951 pb notes further business regarding the shapes, 'Small, quizzical, prickly monsters [that] dwel[t] in the interstices of [the] foreshore' and 'seem[ed] to derive from the painting of Bosch and Breughel' (respectively, *Sp* 29/6/51; *NC* 27/6/51). Apparently already on-stage, they stopped what they were doing when they heard the lords' voices and ran to the mouth of the hole; when the lords laughed, they stopped again, looked around and scuttled down it. After Hall's 1974 Prospero exited, followed by Ariel and a stumbling Ferdinand, the DS wings wiped, nearly catching the latter; by the time Miranda, having watched him go, exited, the back wing flats had gone off, leaving the trees in position for the next scene. At 'Come', Hytner's Ferdinand crossed to Prospero, who directed him into the cell; Miranda went to follow, but Prospero stopped her and exited into it himself. As the lords came into view for 2.1, Miranda and Ariel exited (Stratford pb). Mendes's Ariel remained on stage during the transition to 2.1, overseeing spirits who carried on giant flowers and the screen (CD).

ACT 2   SCENE 1

Enter A L O N S O, S E B A S T I A N, A N T O N I O, G O N Z A L O,
A D R I A N, F R A N C I S C O *and others*

GONZALO Beseech you, sir, be merry. You have cause –
So have we all – of joy; for our escape
Is much beyond our loss. Our hint of woe
Is common; every day some sailor's wife,

2.1 Shadwell set the scene on 'a wild island', starting a trend for scenic display in many productions that followed. Phelps, for example, showed 'A large lake, surrounded by a luxuriant
landscape', Burton 'Gorgeous foliage', and Daly 'a dense ravine' with 'cavernous entrance'.
osd Seventeenth- and eighteenth-century productions often cut the full complement of courtiers,
with a consequent loss of dialogue, presumably because their theatrical potential was not
realized; Francis Gentleman, for instance, thought that 'If this half-drowned King, and his
sea-soused attendants, are decent figures and decent speakers, they walk through well
enough' (Bell's edition, p. 24). Dryden/Davenant and Shadwell had only Alonso, Antonio
and Gonzalo enter (with attendants in 1667). Most of Shakespeare's lines were cut, the only
ones retained in some form being 1–3a, 8b–9, 100–1a, 106b–14a, 115b–16 (Shadwell also cut
109b–15a); Francisco's lines were given to Antonio, making him a more sympathetic character (see note to 1.2.374sd). Garrick's 1756 opera likewise limited the number of courtiers to
three, but his 1757 reversion to Shakespeare's text cut only Adrian and the unnamed 'others'.
Kemble again omitted Sebastian and the lesser lords and placed the scene much later in the
play, making it Act 3, Scene 4; it was preceded by Shakespeare's 3.2 and 3.1, both amended.
Macready restored the full complement of courtiers, as have most of the nineteenth- and
early twentieth-century directors who followed him; Kean even added two unnamed lords.
In the interests of economy, however, more recent productions have often cut Adrian and/or
Francisco or amalgamated them (e.g., Burge, Bogdanov (1978), Warner, Walford, Donnellan,
Murray, Brook (1990), Rylance, Lepage, Paige, Alexander, Thacker, Wolfe and Purcarete).
Modern directors have also sometimes turned financial constraint to interpretative advan-
tage by doubling the courtiers with other characters. In Retallack's first production, Jack Ellis
doubled Gonzalo and Caliban, Chris Barnes Antonio and Trinculo, and Raymond Sawyer
Sebastian and Stephano; Warner similarly doubled the parts of Sebastian and Stephano and
of Antonio and Trinculo.

Many directors have enlivened the scene with invented business. Tree discovered Ariel in
a bower of trees 'from which wild honey-suckle [hung] in profusion' (printed sd). Singing
'Where the bee sucks', she was accompanied by an off-stage fairy chorus of children and
Arne's traditional music. On the appropriate words, Ariel 'flutter[ed] and rustle[d] the

pendent leaves and tendrils, as though actually riding the bat'; this was done 'in a pleasing and fanciful way' but her earlier peeping out of the bush was 'grotesque and artificial . . . as if the property garlands, leaves, etc., were placed there on purpose' (Fitzgerald, *Shakespearean Representation*, p. 45). On the second 'After summer merrily', Ariel was lowered to the stage, where she sang the refrain, danced, repeated the last line of the refrain and exited. Then the courtiers entered, with Gonzalo pantomimically trying to cheer Alonso; he began his lines as Sebastian and Antonio came on.

Crozier invented business involving the lords themselves: Alonso was discovered lying on his cloak, while voices off called in search of Ferdinand. First, all the voices called 'Prince Ferdinand. Halloo', followed by three voices, now nearer, calling 'Prince. Halloo'. Two voices then urgently shouted 'Prince Ferdinand. Halloo', followed by all calling 'Prince Ferdinand' and then two voices again halloo-ing. At this point, Antonio and Sebastian entered, and Alonso raised himself; they nodded and sat down away from him. In the meantime, two voices again halloo-ed, followed by two calling 'Prince Ferdinand' and (another?) two repeating his name. At some point Gonzalo entered, making Alonso sit up expectantly and sink back disappointed again. Gonzalo then approached Alonso, followed by Adrian; Francisco did not enter until much later in the scene. The care apparent in Crozier's handling of the scene elicited praise for the courtiers: they were 'well cast players whose acting (coupled with the firm line taken by the producer) avoids the tedium often created' (*EJ* 27/4/46).

Bridges-Adams (1934) seems simply to have exploited visual interest in his handling of the lords: dressed in 'rich Elizabethan finery', his courtiers 'tried in speech and movement for all the stateliness possible within an acting convention that remained naturalistic' (respectively, *BM* and *T*, both 17/4/34). Antonio (Kenneth Wicksteed) reminded two reviewers of 'a kind of Guy Fawkes in black steeple hat and enormous black ostrich feather' (*MP* 17/4/34), making his conspiracy seem 'burlesque melodrama' in one view but 'nothing comical' in the other (*BP* 17/4/34; since he 'flapped his black coat most suggestively – the compleat villain', the former judgement might be more sound (*LC* 20/3/34)).

Individualizing the courtiers has often proved a stumbling-block to actors and directors. Harcourt Williams (1933) relied on a very strong cast that included George Devine as Alonso, Alaistair Sim as Antonio and Marius Goring as Adrian; because of Sim's ability to find the natural humour of a line, the 'Elizabethan cross-talk achieved the elegance and thrusting strokes of a fencing bout' (Williams, *Four Years*, pp. 225–6). Similarly, although usually 'such anonymous bores', the lords in the Devine/Goring production were 'given individuality, life, and humour as never before', providing 'unexpected comic gleams'; Lewis Casson's Gonzalo, for example, was 'made up to look like Sir Thomas Beecham' (respectively, *O* 2/6/40; *O*; *T* 30/5/40; Philip Page, *DM* 30/5/40). Benthall created interest in the lords visually, as well as through characterization. His courtiers were 'decked as in tinsel: their inspiration the old penny-coloured figures of the toy theatre', and they were 'handled . . . so cleverly that delicious differences of character appeared in these dull dogs' (respectively, *DW* 29/6/51; *T* 27/6/51). William Squire (Sebastian) and William Fox (Antonio) were an 'excellent pair of villains . . . who turn[ed] the "sleepy language" of the King and courtier scenes into sparkling comedy' (Ruth Ellis, *SH* 29/6/51). However, in the 1952 revival, Benthall 'so clutter[ed] his players with ornament and overload[ed] them with stylised gesture that they [were] constantly struggling, as it were, between pose and poetry' (*BG* ?/3/52).

Brook's 1957 handling of this scene received much praise from J. C. Trewin in various reviews: it was timed with an 'almost Chekhovian [care]. Its pattern, its flow, became curiously exciting' (*BP* 21/8/57); Trewin could not remember a production of the scene that had 'so enlivened it without obvious fussing' (*ILN* 24/8/57). The critic thought Brook reasonable to 'run Adrian and Francisco into a single character' (Adrian, played by Toby Robertson) and found that Antonio (Mark Dignam) and Sebastian (Robin Lloyd) had 'a menacing quality these petty villains usually lack' (*BP*). In contrast, the set for the Williams/Brook collaboration appears to have been less static than the actors, who were described as 'deep-frozen puppets' (*BM* 3/4/63). The scene was 'an exercise in perpetual motion', as bits of scenery moved along the travelator from the beginning of 2.1. until Antonio and Sebastian's conspiracy (Gardner, *SH* 5/4/63). In a more spectacular vein, Breuer's lords arrived 'simulatedly, in a real helicopter' (Clive Barnes, *NYP* 10/7/81); 'all in white suits and panamas, and packing pistols, [they] resemble[d] leftovers from an old Fellini movie, with a jive-talking guard, and a silk-shirted Antonio who sport[ed] long sideburns, a shoulder holster and a comic Italian gangster accent' (Watt, *DN* 10/7/81). In fact, each of the lords spoke 'in a different B-movie accent' (Rich, *NYT* 10/7/81).

As the last example suggests, directors have found different ways to comment on the courtiers, some using costume, set and lighting emblematically. Jackson's costumes for Drinkwater's shipwrecked court emphasized the way they intruded 'Into [the] secluded, shadowy land' of the same designer's set: they were 'all attired in patterned robes of rich, warm red – an Italianate livery. The contrast [was] as admirable as it [was] simple; as effective as it [was] bold' (*BP* 19/4/15). De Berardinis's lords wore 'milk-white costumes' that made 'any weight or consistency of character evaporate'; not only their clothing but also their gestures denoted the 'fraudulent and blunt power . . . of a baroque courtier's art' (Grande, *R* 19/4/86): they were 'mere shapes', 'dressed in white and gold, with sticks and wigs' (Zucconi, *PS* 5/4/86). While Hytner had the 'scenes with Ariel glimmer with an unearthly blueish tinge', when 'the guilty nobles appear[ed], rainy-grey drifts of gauze obscure[d] the light or, bunched up into shapes like storm clouds, just [hung] menacingly in the sky' (Kemp, *Ind* 26/5/89).

Simmons compressed the courtiers into three characters: Gonzo, the usurping King of Milan, who combined elements of Alonso and Gonzalo; Antonio, an 'ambitious duke' like Sebastian; and Ferdinand, played by a woman 'in pert drag' (Coveney, *FT* 10/5/78). They made 'a splendid mock-majestic entrance in red cloaks and blowing trombones' (Coveney), for which the audience had to stand before being pelted with 'pseudo-wholemeal buns' (Greer, *Sp* 20/5/78). The arrival of the 'bedraggled regalia [was] accompanied on the keyboard by a pith-helmeted Prospero and Caliban bashing away on drums' (Wardle, *T* 10/5/78).

Flexible handling of the lords also lends itself to overtly ideological interpretation. As already noted, Donnellan turned Alonso into the Queen of Naples (Anne White), presenting her as a Margaret Thatcher-figure, complete with handbag, hat and walk (CD); her lords, dressed in morning suits and with swords in their walking-sticks, were 'a toadying Cabinet of courtiers' (CD and Taylor, *Ind* 26/11/88). Flexibility can also allow more parts for women in a production: Thacker turned Adrian into Lady Adriana. Such cross-casting had not been seen since the First World War, when a shortage of male actors made Greet (1917) cut Francisco and cast Betty Potter and Winifred Oughton as Sebastian and Antonio respectively; Foss's production similarly featured Oughton as Gonzalo and Katharine Herbert as Antonio, with Molly Veness and Catherine Willard playing Adrian and Francisco respectively. Most recently, Kelly's use of the same ensemble company to perform *The Tempest, The Seagull* and *Present Laughter* necessitated cross-casting of Alonso, Sebastian and Antonio (the only lords featured in the production); most critics agreed that it was unsuccessful.

Brook's 1990 scene began with the entrance of Gonzalo and two island-spirits carrying ferns, water and a green scarf (CD): the 'green-clad spirits who simply [brought] nature on with them. . . . simulate[d] birdsong, carr[ied] palms and leaves against which people's faces brush[ed] and even brandish[ed] rods on the end of which [were] beautiful butterflies' (Billington, *G* 19/10/90). In contrast, Bogdanov's 1992 court, who appeared 'to hail from the Napoleonic era', was 'smokily farted onto the island through the opening of [the] huge concrete [sewer] pipe' (Taylor, *Ind* 30/11/92). They 'pour[ed]' onstage in a procession of ambassadors, bandsmen, cinema commissionaires, Gilbertian admirals, Salvation Army generals, and clones of Edward VII' (Nightingale, *T* 30/11/92); Bogdanov 'wanted the colours . . . heightened as in a dream' (Neill, *Director's Notes*, p. 24). Mendes's Ariel oversaw the scene change from 1.2 to 2.1, during which the other spirits brought on ten giant flowers and dotted them about the stage. The lords came on slowly, only beginning the scene after Ariel clapped his hands for a change of lighting state; Ariel remained on stage during it, standing behind and above the screen (CD). Just before Purcarete's lords entered, Caliban could be briefly glimpsed at USR, where he howled like a wolf or coyote; Stephano also made a brief appearance before exiting from the front of the stage. Alonso came on in his wheelchair, wearing his crown, together with Gonzalo, Antonio, Sebastian and Adrian/Francisco; they were all dressed in underwear, braces, black socks held up by garters, and shoes, with Gonzalo and Adrian/Francisco also carrying umbrellas. Prospero watched the lords during the ensuing scene (CD).

1 In Falls's production, Edgarr Meyer's Gonzalo was a 'particular joy': 'Recognizing that he may appear old-fashioned, nonetheless he remains idealistic, devoted, and sincere. His braces dangle awkwardly, a symbol of his preoccupation with more important matters. He has an irresistible innocent humanity about him' (Pellowe, 'In Chicago', p. 55).

3a Hall's 1974 Alonso met Antonio's stare on 'loss'.

3–9a Cut by Garrick (1756). Kemble (1789) cut 3–8a, but restored 3a in 1806; Macready, Daly, Tree and Brook (1957) followed Kemble's final cut. Kean and Burton cut 3b–6a, the latter perhaps

        The masters of some merchant, and the merchant   5
        Have just our theme of woe. But for the miracle –
        I mean our preservation – few in millions
        Can speak like us. Then wisely, good sir, weigh
        Our sorrow with our comfort.
ALONSO   Prithee, peace.
SEBASTIAN He receives comfort like cold porridge.   10
ANTONIO The visitor will not give him o'er so.
SEBASTIAN Look, he's winding up the watch of his wit,
        By and by it will strike.

       also cutting 6b–8a. (Because this scene has been so heavily and variously cut, the notes fol-
       lowing do not always amalgamate cuts under single line-headings, since such presentation
       can obscure both general trends and individual approaches; cf., for example, the three notes
       immediately following, which could be headed 9b–107a.)
9b–54 Macready and Daly cut 10–43; Phelps 10–46, with 25–6 retained; Burton 10–54. Kean cut
       10–24, 'But yet' from 25, 26–33, 35–6, 38–40, 42–3, 45–54, running the remaining lines
       together as one speech: 'Though this island seem to be desert, uninhabitable, and almost
       inaccessible, it must needs be of subtle, tender and delicate temperance. The air breathes
       upon us here most sweetly.' Brook's 1957 pbs cut 9b–43, but cues written against 9b–41 and
       then crossed out in the SMT pb suggest that these lines were retained at Stratford and only
       cut for the London transfer; in that case, only 42–3 were cut at SMT and 9b–43 at DL.
10–63 Garrick (1757) and Kemble (1789) cut 10–63. Kemble restored 55–6 and 58–9 in 1806; the
       latter line was joined to 64 ('That our garments . . . are notwithstanding as fresh as . . .') and
       was addressed to Alonso, 'your' being substituted for 'the king's'.
10–107a All but 103a cut by Garrick (1756).
   11 'Never was there a Sebastian more proud, handsome and worthless than Bryan Coleman, or
       an Antonio more suitably like Basil Rathbone than Ferdy Mayne', who both appeared in
       Gellner's production: 'The way in which these two exploited their rather distracting side-chat
       about what Gonzalo and the others are saying vindicated the lines as a real asset and not, as
       they often seem, a rather tiresome liability'. The reviewer compared the production
       favourably to Benthall's, which 'cut the "Widow Dido" altogether' (*TN* 9/9/51).
       Hytner's 'wickedly debonair' Antonio threw a pebble at Gonzalo (Koenig, *P* 9/6/89, and
       pb).
       Miller's 1988 courtiers 'began to gabble on top of each other's lines in the "Citizen Kane"
       manner' (Osborne, *DT* 13/10/88). Probably referring to this aspect of the staging, Jane
       Edwardes complained that 'The court scenes had unwonted humour foisted upon them (thus
       losing the dignity of Alonso's grieving for Ferdinand)' (*Sp* 22/10/88). Billington, on the other
       hand, found the humour intentional: 'the courtiers are an amusing lot with strong hints that
       Alonso is fed [*sic*] to the back teeth with hearing about the loss of his son' (*G* 12/10/88).

GONZALO Sir, –

SEBASTIAN One: tell.   15

GONZALO When every grief is entertained that's offered,
        Comes to the entertainer –

SEBASTIAN A dollar.

GONZALO Dolour comes to him indeed; you have spoken truer than
    you purposed.   20

SEBASTIAN You have taken it wiselier than I meant you should.

GONZALO Therefore, my lord –

ANTONIO Fie, what a spendthrift is he of his tongue.

ALONSO I prithee, spare.

GONZALO Well, I have done. But yet –   25

SEBASTIAN He will be talking.

ANTONIO Which, of he or Adrian, for a good wager, first begins to
    crow?

SEBASTIAN The old cock.

ANTONIO The cockerel.   30

SEBASTIAN Done. The wager?

ANTONIO A laughter.

SEBASTIAN A match!

ADRIAN Though this island seem to be desert –

ANTONIO Ha, ha, ha!   35

SEBASTIAN So: you're paid.

14–26 Cut by Benthall.

19 Tree's Gonzalo turned to Sebastian, suggesting that until now he ignored his and Antonio's sarcasm; he turned back to Alonso at 22.

22–43 Cut by Hack. Wright cut 23 and 'But yet' (25).

25 Crozier's Gonzalo wandered sadly down to the proscenium rock and indicated to Adrian that he should try to talk to Alonso.

27–33 Cut by Tree; Ashwell cut 31b–3. Barton added 'young' before Adrian's name (27). As Benthall's Antonio and Sebastian shook hands at 33, Gonzalo and Adrian both drew breath, preparing to speak at the same time. The business was repeated, after which Gonzalo gestured to Adrian to speak.

34 Tree assigned this line, together with 37 and 41, to Gonzalo rather than to Adrian. Williams's 1978 Adrian spoke it, as well as 37, to Francisco.

35–6 The Folio gives 35 to Sebastian and 36 to Antonio, but the latter has actually won the bet; either the speech headings have been reversed or 'you're' is a misprint for 'you've' (see

ADRIAN Uninhabitable, and almost inaccessible –
SEBASTIAN Yet –
ADRIAN Yet –
ANTONIO He could not miss't.   40
ADRIAN It must needs be of subtle, tender, and delicate temperance.
ANTONIO Temperance was a delicate wench.
SEBASTIAN Ay, and a subtle, as he most learnedly delivered.
ADRIAN The air breathes upon us here most sweetly.
SEBASTIAN As if it had lungs, and rotten ones.   45
ANTONIO Or as 'twere perfumed by a fen.
GONZALO Here is everything advantageous to life.
ANTONIO True, save means to live.
SEBASTIAN Of that there's none, or little.
GONZALO How lush and lusty the grass looks! How green!   50

Kermode). Many directors have followed the Folio reading, but Ashwell assigned both lines
to Sebastian and Miller (1988) both lines to Antonio. Like the *NCS* reading, Williams (1978)
and Hytner reversed the Folio's speakers, so that Antonio laughed and Sebastian replied
(respectively, pb, CD). Benthall kept Sebastian's laugh, after which Adrian made a puzzled
sound: 'Huh?' (1951) or 'Ha?' (1952). Tree cut 36, while Barton interpolated the Folio 35–6 into
the middle of 34, after 'island'.

42 Hytner's Antonio threw another pebble at Gonzalo here (London pb); however, either the
   actor's aim was bad or the target changed, as I saw him throw it at Adrian (CD).

42–3 Cut by Tree and Benthall. Bridges-Adams (1926/30, 1934) cut 43.
   Benthall's Adrian breathed in the air to emphasize his point; Antonio imitated him, both of
   them breathing out at the same time.

44 Barton gave Adrian's line to Francisco, thus adding another voice to Gonzalo's and Adrian's
   praise of the island; the birdsong that played during the following exchange also substantiated this positive view and undercut Antonio's and Sebastian's. Hack, having cut Adrian and
   Francisco from the play, gave the line to Gonzalo.

45–54 Cut by Macready and Daly. Tree cut 45–6; Bridges-Adams (1926/30, 1934) 45–6, 49, 53–4;
   Phelps and Williams (1978) 50–4; Barton 52–3; Iden Payne 53–4.
   Brook's 1990 spirits, who had produced a green scarf near Gonzalo, produced a red one
   near Antonio and Sebastian at 45–6, causing a bad smell and hence their different reaction
   to the island (CD).

47 As Miller's 1988 Gonzalo praised the island's advantages, Alonso smacked a mosquito biting
   his face, not for the first time (CD).

50 Benthall's 'somewhat sombre caverns . . . and the ever-recurring pinnacles, reminiscent of
   greenish icebergs, make Gonzalo's line . . . ring false' (*NG* 1952).

ANTONIO The ground indeed is tawny.

SEBASTIAN With an eye of green in't.

ANTONIO He misses not much.

SEBASTIAN No, he doth but mistake the truth totally.

GONZALO But the rarity of it is, which is indeed almost beyond   55
    credit –

SEBASTIAN As many vouched rarities are.

GONZALO That our garments being, as they were, drenched in the
    sea, hold notwithstanding their freshness and glosses, being
    rather new-dyed than stained with salt water.   60

ANTONIO If but one of his pockets could speak, would it not say he
    lies?

SEBASTIAN Ay, or very falsely pocket up his report.

GONZALO Methinks our garments are now as fresh as when we put
    them on first in Afric, at the marriage of the king's fair daughter   65
    Claribel to the King of Tunis.

SEBASTIAN 'Twas a sweet marriage, and we prosper well in our
    return.

50–1 Strehler's Gonzalo seemed to focus on the flowers on the tree in front of him, while Antonio broke off a barren twig and snapped it in two (video).

52 Benthall's Sebastians picked a blade of grass from the ground.

54 Benthall interpolated some business after Sebastian's line: Gonzalo interjected 'Huh?'; Antonio imitated him and looked at Sebastian, at which point they both shook their heads at Gonzalo and said 'huh-huh!'.

57–64 Burton cut 'As many. . . . Methinks'. Kean cut 57, 61–4 ('If but . . . garments'). Phelps cut 57, 59–64 ('their freshness and glosses' to 'Methinks our garments'), so that the line read 'That our garments, being, as they were, drenched in the the the sea, notwithstanding are now as fresh', etc. Williams (1978) cut 57; Macready, Daly, Tree, Bridges-Adams (1926/30, 1934), Iden Payne and Benthall 61–3.

During 59–64, the wires of Purcarete's set were set at a diagonal and, when Gonzalo mentioned their freshened garments, a suit whizzed down the wires on a hanger as if it were coming from a dry cleaner (CD).

64–6 Versified by Kemble (1789), and given by Barton to Francisco. Kean had a general movement of surprise from all on stage, as each lord examined his garments (Ellis's pb). Mendes's Gonzalo took out photos of the wedding, prompting 'ahs' from other lords (CD).

67–99 Cut by Garrick (1757) and Kemble (both versions).

68 Crozier's still-offstage Francisco again called 'Prince Ferdinand', and Adrian and Gonzalo changed places; the former paused before speaking 69.

ADRIAN Tunis was never graced before with such a paragon to their
    queen.   70
GONZALO Not since widow Dido's time.
ANTONIO Widow? A pox o'that! How came that widow in? Widow
    Dido!
SEBASTIAN What if he had said 'widower Aeneas' too? Good Lord,
    how you take it!   75
ADRIAN Widow Dido, said you? You make me study of that. She
    was of Carthage, not of Tunis.
GONZALO This Tunis, sir, was Carthage.
ADRIAN Carthage?
GONZALO I assure you, Carthage.   80
ANTONIO His word is more than the miraculous harp.
SEBASTIAN He hath raised the wall, and houses too.
ANTONIO What impossible matter will he make easy next?
SEBASTIAN I think he will carry this island home in his pocket, and
    give it his son for an apple.   85
ANTONIO And sowing the kernels of it in the sea, bring forth more
    islands.
GONZALO Ay.
ANTONIO Why in good time.
GONZALO Sir, we were talking, that our garments seem now as fresh   90
    as when we were at Tunis at the marriage of your daughter, who
    is now queen.
ANTONIO And the rarest that e'er came there.

69–89 Cut by Macready, Phelps, Kean, Burton, Daly, Benthall and Hack.
69–101a Cut by Tree.
  72–5 Cut by Iden Payne and Wright; Williams (1978) cut 74–5, and Crozier and Barton 'Good Lord
    . . . it!' (74–5). Bogdanov's 1992 Antonio echoed Gonzalo at 72 with 'widow diddly Dido' (CD).
    76 Bridges-Adams (1926/30, 1934) cut 'you make me study of that'.
    80 Barton's Adrian accepted Gonzalo's correction with an 'Oh'.
  81–9 Cut by Bridges-Adams (1926/30, 1934), Ayrton, Wright and Williams (1978). Iden Payne cut
    83–9; Barton 81–2, 84–7; Ashwell 88–9. Crozier's off-stage Francisco called 'Prince
    Ferdinand' at 89.
90–2 Cut by Burton and Hack.
93–9 Cut by Macready, Phelps, Daly and Bridges-Adams (1926/30, 1934). Kean cut 93–5, 97–9 ('I
    mean . . . wore it') and changed 96 to 'Are not, sir, my garments . . . them?'; his changes
    present Gonzalo as garrulous in an insensitive way rather than as someone trying, in spurts,

SEBASTIAN Bate, I beseech you, widow Dido.

ANTONIO O widow Dido? Ay, widow Dido.   95

GONZALO Is not, sir, my doublet as fresh as the first day I wore it –
    I mean, in a sort –

ANTONIO That sort was well fished for.

GONZALO – when I wore it at your daughter's marriage?

ALONSO You cram these words into mine ears, against   100
    The stomach of my sense: would I had never
    Married my daughter there. For coming thence
    My son is lost, and, in my rate, she too,
    Who is so far from Italy removed
    I ne'er again shall see her. O thou mine heir   105
    Of Naples and of Milan, what strange fish
    Hath made his meal on thee?

FRANCISCO   Sir, he may live.
    I saw him beat the surges under him,
    And ride upon their backs; he trod the water
    Whose enmity he flung aside, and breasted   110

to raise the king's spirits. Burton cut 93–5, 97–9; Benthall 93–5; Barton 94–5; Hack 93–5, (?) 99.

    Benthall's Gonzalo desperately tried to engage the despondent Alonso with his talk of garments at 96; he looked despairing at Alonso's response. In 1952, Raymond Westwell received widespread praise for his playing of the part, which he made 'thoroughly charming': his 'endearing' Gonzalo was 'the best kind of maiden aunt, humorous' (Ellis, *SH* ?/3/52). Hall's 1974 Sebastian sniggered at 98.

101   Brook (1957) had a pause between 101a and b (DL pb).

102b–5a   Cut by Hack.

103b–7a   Cut by Garrick (1757), Kemble (both versions), Phelps and Tree. Macready and Kean cut 103b–5a and 106b–7a. Burton, Daly and Ashwell cut 103b–5a; Iden Payne 105b–7a.

105a   Just as Purcarete's Alonso spoke, Ferdinand crossed the stage with his burden of wood, so that he was present to the audience as his father wondered about his fate. Alonso got up slightly from his wheelchair at the same time (CD).

107b–16a   Following Dryden/Davenant and Shadwell, Garrick's 1756 opera transferred these lines to Antonio and cut 109b–15a; both Kemble versions followed suit. Garrick's 1757 reversion to Shakespeare's text, which restored the lines to Francisco, cut 109b–11 and 114b–15a. Kean and Bridges-Adams (1926/30, 1934) cut 109b–15a. Phelps gave the lines to Gonzalo, as did Burton, Daly, Benthall and Hack; Burton and Daly cut 109b–11a, and Hack either 109b–15a or 112b–15a. Benthall's 1952 Adrian encouraged Gonzalo to continue following 107b; in 1951 'Adrian and Francisco join[ed] in' presumably the same sort of encouragement.

The surge most swol'n that met him. His bold head
'Bove the contentious waves he kept, and oared
Himself with his good arms in lusty stroke
To th' shore, that o'er his wave-worn basis bowed,
As stooping to relieve him. I not doubt   115
He came alive to land.
ALONSO   No, no, he's gone.
SEBASTIAN Sir, you may thank yourself for this great loss,
That would not bless our Europe with your daughter,
But rather lose her to an African,

Barton gave 107b to Gonzalo; the rest of the speech to 115a remained Francisco's. Adrian spoke 115b–16a, so that Gonzalo, Francisco and Adrian were all involved in the attempt to console Alonso. Miller's 1988 Francisco feebly repeated 107b, trying to break into Alonso's grief (CD).

117–29 Benthall's Sebastian really rubbed in Alonso's responsibility, as the latter's actions showed: he rose, broke away, etc.

117–316 (end of scene) Cut by Garrick (1756), who followed 116b with a short dialogue between Alonso and Antonio in which the former pointed out their guilt; it was similar to the 1667 and 1674 versions (see note to 1.2.374sd). At this point, however, Garrick conflated the action with the later banquet scene: a banquet rose and Ariel sang 'Dry those eyes, which are o'erflowing' from '*behind the scenes*'. As the courtiers discussed whether it were safe to eat, the banquet vanished, Ariel appeared with 'strange shapes' and sang 'Around, around, we pace', after which the spirits danced and drove the three off. Prospero entered to speak 'My charms work; mine enemies, knit in their / Destruction, are now within my pow'r' (taken from 3.3.88b–90) and to sing the air 'Upon their broken peace of mind', which ended the scene.

Both Kemble versions followed Garrick's lead, cutting the rest of the scene, incorporating Alonso's recognition of retribution being visited upon him and interpolating material from 3.3. The 1789 version had 'Two spirits rise with a Table spread', disappearing after making the delivery; the table vanished with a 'strange noise' as the courtiers approached to eat; the latter were then surrounded by Furies, two of whom sang the duet 'Where does the black fiend ambition reside?' before being answered by the chorus ('In hell, in hell in flames they shall reign, / And for ever, for ever shall suffer the pain'). The 1806 adaptation had Ariel enter to sing 'Dry those eyes' while other spirits carried on the banquet and incorporated more of Shakespeare's 3.3 before the Furies' entrance (see notes to 3.3 for more detail).

119 Cut by Burton and Daly, thus omitting reference to Claribel's marriage to an African. Hytner's Francisco, played by a black actor (Patrick Miller), visibly reacted to Sebastian's slighting reference to Claribel's African husband, as did Donnellan's Adrian, also played by a black actor (Paterson Joseph; respectively, pbs and CD).

> Where she, at least, is banished from your eye,   120
> Who hath cause to wet the grief on't.

ALONSO   Prithee, peace.

SEBASTIAN You were kneeled to and importùned otherwise
> By all of us; and the fair soul herself
> Weighed between loathness and obedience, at
> Which end o' th' beam should bow. We have lost your son,   125
> I fear for ever. Milan and Naples have
> More widows in them of this business' making
> Than we bring men to comfort them. The fault's
> Your own.

ALONSO   So is the dearest of the loss.

GONZALO My lord Sebastian,   130
> The truth you speak doth lack some gentleness,
> And time to speak it in; you rub the sore,
> When you should bring the plaster.

SEBASTIAN   Very well.

ANTONIO And most chirurgeonly.

120–8 Cut by Macready, Phelps, Tree, Burton and Daly. Kean cut 120–5a and 126b–8, thereby retaining 'We have lost your son, / I fear, for ever.' Ashwell cut only 120–1a, 122–5a; Hack 120–1; Bridges-Adams (1926/30, 1934) 124–5a; Iden Payne 126b–8. Barton cut 120–1a; his Antonio interrupted Sebastian at the end of 122 and spoke the rest of the speech himself, with 'at . . . bow' (124b–5) and 'Milan . . . them' (126b–8) cut.

126a In London, Hytner's Francisco pulled at Sebastian, presumably now reacting to his cruelty rather than to his racism; Sebastian shook him off.

129 Tree's courtiers moved at 129a, presumably in surprise at Sebastian's plain speaking; Alonso's reply was cut.

Donnellan's queen wept as she spoke, to the surprise of her lords (CD). In this way, too, she was reminiscent of Margaret Thatcher, who, 'When her son, Mark, disappeared during a trans-Sahara motor rally in January 1982 . . . spent six days in a state of extreme anxiety, frequently weeping, sometimes in public' (Young, *One of Us*, p. 308).

133a After 'plaster', Garrick's 1757 Alonso replied: 'Still let me hope. Good Francisco, look / Out again, scout round the rocks, and bring my / Heart some comfort with my son', whereupon Francisco exited. Phelps and Kean had Ariel enter with a lyre and music for 174sd, since intervening lines were cut.

133b–6 Cut by Garrick (1757) and Tree; Daly cut 133b–4; Bridges-Adams (1926/30, 1934) 134–6; Hack 134. Bogdanov (1992) changed 'chirurgeonly' to 'surgically' (CD).

133b–74 Cut by Macready, Phelps and Kean.

GONZALO It is foul weather in us all, good sir,   135
    When you are cloudy.
SEBASTIAN   Foul weather?
ANTONIO   Very foul.
GONZALO Had I plantation of this isle, my lord –
ANTONIO He'd sow't with nettle-seed.
SEBASTIAN   Or docks, or mallows.
GONZALO – And were the king on't, what would I do?
SEBASTIAN 'Scape being drunk, for want of wine.   140
GONZALO I' th' commonwealth I would by contraries

135 Gonzalo's comment made everyone, including Donnellan's crying queen, burst out laughing (CD).
136 Hall's 1988 Sebastian and Antonio spoke 136b and c as asides to each other. Daly's punctuation gives some idea of delivery: '*Foul weather!*' Williams's 1978 Sebastian asked 'Fowl weather?', clarifying his meaning by clucking; Mendes repeated the business (CD).
137 Bogdanov's 1992 Adrian and Francisco sang 'All our thoughts are holiday' to Alonso just before Gonzalo spoke this line (CD).
138 Cut by Garrick (1757), Burton, Daly, Bridges-Adams (1926/30 and 1934) and Crozier.
140 Tree's Gonzalo looked at Sebastian when the latter scoffed ''Scape being drunk', which made him pause before finishing; when he did, Francisco and the others laughed. Hack's Alonso asked Gonzalo 'What would you do?' after 140, implying a reprimand to Sebastian's rudeness.
140–59 Cut by Garrick (1757), who retained of the commonwealth speech only Gonzalo's dream that 'I would with such perfection govern, sir, / To excel the golden age' (160–1a).
141–57 The handling of Gonzalo's speech often reflects current ideologies: it is not surprising that in nineteenth-century England Macready, Phelps and Kean cut it entirely, while in the US Burton retained it. To a reviewer of Bridges-Adams's 1919 production, it smacked of 'arrant Bolshevism' (*St* 28[?]/8/19), while a critic of Benthall's 1951 staging 'liked particularly [Gonzalo's] day-dream of a welfare state "without sweat or endeavour"' (*LSC* 29/6/51): the construction of Gonzalo's commonwealth as a 'welfare state' reflects the aims and achievements of Britain's post-war Labour government, while the idea of attaining it so easily suggests wishful fantasy. Donnellan's court – particularly the Thatcher-like queen – had difficulty in suppressing its laughter at Gonzalo's communal values, though his desire for 'No sovereignty' (150a) brought a rebuke from the queen, who just before could not contain her mirth (CD). Brook's 1990 Gonzalo appeared to see the sand-castles the spirits had made during the scene, knocking them down during his speech: he seemed either to mock his own pipe-dream or to implicitly acknowledge the distance between dream and reality.

Exècute all things. For no kind of traffic
Would I admit; no name of magistrate;
Letters should not be known; riches, poverty,
And use of service, none; contract, succession,   145
Bourn, bound of land, tilth, vineyard, none;
No use of metal, corn, or wine, or oil;
No occupation, all men idle, all;
And women too, but innocent and pure;
No sovereignty –
SEBASTIAN   Yet he would be king on't.   150
ANTONIO The latter end of his commonwealth forgets the beginning.
GONZALO All things in common nature should produce
Without sweat or endeavour. Treason, felony,
Sword, pike, knife, gun, or need of any engine
Would I not have; but nature should bring forth   155
Of it own kind, all foison, all abundance
To feed my innocent people.
SEBASTIAN No marrying 'mong his subjects?
ANTONIO None, man, all idle; whores and knaves.
GONZALO I would with such perfection govern, sir,   160
T'excel the Golden Age.
SEBASTIAN   'Save his majesty!
ANTONIO Long live Gonzalo!
GONZALO   And – do you mark me, sir?

Burge cut the whole speech (Foulkes, review, p. 12), while Wright cut only 143b–4a ('no name . . . known'), thereby making Gonzalo's commonwealth seem more attractive, for in the excised line he rules out law, literature and learning ('magistrate' and 'letters'). Wright also cut 151, and Daly 151, 153–5.

Tree interpolated 'And women too?' after 148 as a sneering question from Sebastian, with Gonzalo then repeating the words as statement; Benthall's 1952 Adrian showed the line's possible implication by gasping after 149a and then laughing after 149b.

159b Daly cut 'whores and knaves'; Tree retained only 'None, man'.

160–1a Brook's 1957 Gonzalo, Cyril Luckham, spoke these lines so that they 'rang in the mind as if new'; his Gonzalo was an 'honest lord' and 'honourable man' rather than a 'straw-stuffed, beard-wagging ancient' (Trewin, *BP* 21/8/57).

161b–2a Cut by Garrick (1757).

162 Cut by Daly. Iden Payne's Ariel entered after 'do you mark me, sir?'.

162b–74 Cut by Tree and Hack.

ALONSO Prithee, no more; thou dost talk nothing to me.

GONZALO I do well believe your highness, and did it to minister
occasion to these gentlemen, who are of such sensible and   165
nimble lungs, that they always use to laugh at nothing.

ANTONIO 'Twas you we laughed at.

GONZALO Who, in this kind of merry fooling, am nothing to you;
so you may continue, and laugh at nothing still.

ANTONIO What a blow was there given!   170

SEBASTIAN And it had not fall'n flat-long.

GONZALO You are gentlemen of brave mettle; you would lift the
moon out of her sphere, if she would continue in it five weeks
without changing.

Enter ARIEL [*invisible*] *playing solemn music*

163–82a Garrick's 1757 Alonso continued with added lines after 163: 'Let us sit down upon / This bank,
and rest our sorrows'; Gonzalo replied 'I will, my Lord; for I am very heavy', and they lay
down on the bank. Ariel did not appear in the early part of the scene, and 164–82a were cut.

170 Benthall's Gonzalo turned and, tripping on the shell, fell. In 1951 he had to be picked up,
whereas in 1952 Adrian and Francisco caught him.

170–4 Cut by Daly. Barton cut 'if she would . . . changing' (173–4).

173 Hall's 1974 Ariel was flown in at 'sphere', dressed as a sentinel in white felt tunic and green
fibreglass helmet.

174sd Ariel, according to the direction given by Prospero at 1.2.302–3a, is invisible to everyone else;
s/he has variously played a lyre (Phelps), a harp made of a large conch shell (Burton) and a
tambourine (Alexander). The solemn music apparently acts as a charm on all the lords but
Antonio and Sebastian: if Ariel simply plays the music, these two seem to be impervious to
the spell rather than specifically exempted from it. However, Ariel often directs the charm at
particular lords, so that the exclusion of Antonio and Sebastian seems to be part of a plan to
tempt them to more villainy. For example, Burton's Ariel touched the lords with her harp at
pauses in the music, making each drowsy, while Paige's Ariel charmed them asleep by
advancing 'arm extended . . . singing, on only two notes, the name of each in turn, on a
gently swelling then fading electronic chord' (Carter, '*The Tempest* at Salisbury Playhouse',
p. 21). Some Ariels dispense with music; for example, Strehler's Ariel threw sand at the lords
individually to charm them to sleep (video), while Miller's 1988 Ariel '[shot s]leep from a
blow-pipe at all the courtiers but Antonio and Sebastian', thus making it 'plain that Prospero
is actively arranging the conditions in which his brother can re-demonstrate his evil nature'
(Taylor, *Ind* 13/10/88). Mendes's Ariel, who had been on stage throughout the scene, moved
among the nobles during Gonzalo's speech, passing his hand in front of their eyes to charm
them asleep. One of Thacker's spirits itself acted sleepy to enact the spell (CD).

SEBASTIAN We would so, and then go a-batfowling.   175
ANTONIO Nay, good my lord, be not angry.
GONZALO No, I warrant you, I will not adventure my discretion so
    weakly. Will you laugh me asleep, for I am very heavy?
ANTONIO Go sleep, and hear us.
    [*All sleep except* ALONSO, SEBASTIAN *and* ANTONIO]
ALONSO What, all so soon asleep? I wish mine eyes   180
    Would with themselves shut up my thoughts; I find
    They are inclined to do so.
SEBASTIAN   Please you, sir,
    Do not omit the heavy offer of it.
    It seldom visits sorrow; when it doth,
    It is a comforter.
ANTONIO   We two, my lord,   185
    Will guard your person while you take your rest,
    And watch your safety.
ALONSO   Thank you. Wondrous heavy.
    [ALONSO *sleeps. Exit* ARIEL]

175 Cut by Macready, Phelps, Kean, Daly, Tree, Iden Payne, Benthall, Hack and Barton.

179 Hack cut 'and hear us'.

179sd Alonso's 180 makes clear that Gonzalo, Adrian, Francisco and the other lords must fall asleep by this point, but the manner of their doing so gives the director some scope: it can be instantaneous or gradual, simultaneous or staggered.

    Brook's 1990 Ariel rubbed Gonzalo's head and eyes to make him sleepy, while he waved his hand in front of Alonso to charm him to sleep; it was clear that Alonso felt his presence (CD). During the run, Paige's Sebastian 'took to falling, in imitation, immediately after Gonzalo', almost fooling Antonio; 'then they both laughed' (Carter, '*The Tempest* at Salisbury Playhouse', p. 21).

180 Hack cut 'all', as only Gonzalo was asleep, Francisco's and Adrian's parts having been cut.

182b–7 Cut by Hack, with only 'Wondrous heavy' (187c) retained.

185 Hytner's Antonio crossed to Alonso and started to drape a cloak gently over him; when the king fell asleep before he had finished, he tossed it carelessly down (CD).

187–187sd Alonso's 'Wondrous heavy' makes clear that he too succumbs to Ariel's magic at this point. Although the Folio does not mark it, Ariel presumably exits now, since the charm (from which Sebastian and Antonio are exempt either intentionally or unintentionally) is complete. It is clear that Ariel is not meant to remain on stage during the ensuing scene, as the spirit re-enters at 285sd, prompted by Prospero; however, many directors have Ariel present throughout (e.g., Strehler and Hall 1988). Garrick's 1757 Ariel did not appear in this part of

SEBASTIAN What a strange drowsiness possesses them?

ANTONIO It is the quality o'th'climate.

SEBASTIAN Why

Doth it not then our eyelids sink? I find 190

Not myself disposed to sleep.

ANTONIO Nor I; my spirits are nimble.

They fell together all, as by consent

They dropped, as by a thunder-stroke. What might,

the scene; all the courtiers but Sebastian and Antonio fell asleep at 'heavy', while soft music played.

When Strehler's Alonso fell asleep, the crown fell from his head; Sebastian picked it up, holding it either ruefully or covetously for the merest fraction of a second, before placing it near his brother's head (video). Brook's 1990 Alonso 'manage[d] to mutter "Merci" as Ariel lower[ed] him to the floor' (Taylor, *Ind* 2/11/90). Purcarete's Antonio and Sebastian tipped Alonso's wheelchair into a 'sleeping' position, the king remaining in it, and immediately lit up cigarettes once he was asleep. As they smoked, Prospero set up a music stand at SL and another at SR; when they were in position, Sebastian and Antonio each took up a place at one (CD; see note to 193b–263).

188 Ninagawa's Antonio tapped Gonzalo with a branch; he shooed it away in his sleep (CD).

190 Miller's 1988 scene between Antonio and Sebastian was 'excellently played. Peter Wear's saturnine, effete Antonio trie[d] to nudge Sebastian's thoughts to crime with the quietly exasperated, ironic patience of a don coaching one of nature's Lower Seconds. In a pointedly witty touch, Peter Guinness's slit-eyed Sebastian fiddle[d] throughout with an obviously marked and rigged pack of cards, beautifully distinguishing his mundane small-time crookedness with Antonio's sweeping, incorrigible evil' (Taylor, *Ind* 13/10/88).

191a Iden Payne's Ariel exited.

191b Cut by Tree. Williams's 1978 Ariel exited. Hytner's Antonio tapped Gonzalo with his foot (Stratford pb).

192 Hack changed 'all' to 'both'.

193 Hytner's Antonio half-unsheathed his sword at 'thunderstroke', replacing it at the second 'what might?' (194; Stratford pb). He stood on Caliban's rock as he broached his plot, during which the actors emphasized Antonio's cleverness and Sebastian's slow wit (CD).

193b–263 Strehler's Antonio played the political conspiracy almost as a physical seduction, at various points standing very close behind Sebastian, holding him, laying his head on Sebastian's when the latter fell on the ground in distress, etc. (video).

Purcarete's Sebastian and Antonio stood at the music stands on either side of the stage, watched by Prospero and the Ariels at C; Sebastian seemed to be reading his lines from the

Worthy Sebastian, O, what might? – No more.
And yet, methinks I see it in thy face,   195
What thou shouldst be. Th' occasion speaks thee, and
My strong imagination sees a crown
Dropping upon thy head.

SEBASTIAN   What? Art thou waking?

ANTONIO Do you not hear me speak?

SEBASTIAN   I do, and surely
It is a sleepy language, and thou speak'st   200
Out of thy sleep. What is it thou didst say?
This is a strange repose, to be asleep
With eyes wide open; standing, speaking, moving,
And yet so fast asleep.

ANTONIO   Noble Sebastian,
Thou let'st thy fortune sleep – die rather; wink'st   205
Whiles thou art waking.

SEBASTIAN   Thou dost snore distinctly;
There's meaning in thy snores.

ANTONIO I am more serious than my custom. You
Must be so too, if heed me; which to do,
Trebles thee o'er.

SEBASTIAN   Well: I am standing water.   210

ANTONIO I'll teach you how to flow.

SEBASTIAN   Do so – to ebb
Hereditary sloth instructs me.

ANTONIO   O!
If you but knew how you the purpose cherish
Whiles thus you mock it; how in stripping it

stand as he responded to Antonio's proposals (CD). Taylor, however, felt the words of both
were scripted: 'Prospero has rigged the experiment, not just throwing temptation in their
path by keeping the pair awake but placing their respective scripts on music-stands . . . As
they proceed unwittingly through this inset play, it's a fine touch that Fitzgerald's Prospero
keeps his eyes on his wicked sibling' (*Ind* 19/9/95)

196b–217a This section has suffered major cuts in production. Kean cut 'the occasion . . . sloth'
(196b–217a), and Tree 'What, art thou waking? . . . sloth' (198b–217a). Garrick (1757) cut
199–207a, apart from 204b–5a ('Noble Sebastian, / Thou let'st thy fortune sleep'), while
Macready, Phelps, Burton and Daly cut 'and surely . . . to sloth' (199b–217a). Benthall cut
209b–17a, Ashwell 210b–17a, Iden Payne and Brook (1957) 212b–17a, Barton 214b–15a and
Bridges-Adams (1926/30 and 1934) 214b–17a.

You more invest it. Ebbing men, indeed,   215
Most often do so near the bottom run
By their own fear, or sloth.

SEBASTIAN   Prithee say on.
The setting of thine eye and cheek proclaim
A matter from thee; and a birth, indeed,
Which throes thee much to yield.

ANTONIO   Thus, sir: 220
Although this lord of weak remembrance, this,
Who shall be of as little memory
When he is earthed, hath here almost persuaded –
For he's a spirit of persuasion, only
Professes to persuade – the king his son's alive,   225
'Tis as impossible that he's undrowned
As he that sleeps here, swims.

SEBASTIAN   I have no hope
That he's undrowned.

ANTONIO   O, out of that 'no hope'
What great hope have you! No hope that way is
Another way so high a hope that even   230
Ambition cannot pierce a wink beyond,
But doubt discovery there. Will you grant with me
That Ferdinand is drowned?

218–32a This section has also suffered frequent abbreviation, Tree doing away with the lines entirely,
Garrick (1757) cutting 221–32a, and Phelps, Bridges-Adams (1926/30 and 1934) and Iden
Payne cutting 218–20a. Burton cut 221–5a ('this . . . persuade'), retaining 223b, so that the
lines read 'Although this lord of weak remembrance hath here almost persuaded the king his
son's alive'; Daly followed suit. Kean cut 'of weak . . . earth'd' and 'here' (221–3) and
224–25a, so that the lines read 'Although this lord hath almost persuaded the king his son's
alive'. (The lord to which Antonio refers has sometimes changed: Williams's 1978 Antonio
pointed to Francisco, Wright's indicated Gonzalo and Benthall's nonsensically referred to
Alonso.) Phelps cut 224, and Macready, Wright, Benthall, Brook (1957) and Barton 224–5a;
Ashwell and Hack cut 'only / Professes to persuade' (224b–5a). Kean cut 227b–33b ('I have
no hope . . . He's gone'), and Ashwell, Bridges-Adams (1926/30 and 1934), Iden Payne,
Benthall, Brook (1957), Barton and Hack 229b–32a.

220a Miller's 1988 Sebastian threw his cards (down?) and lay down.

233c–55a This section has also been severely truncated. Garrick (1757) cut 234b–49a, substituting
'What mean you?' for 'Claribel' as Sebastian's answer to Antonio's question in 234a. Kean cut

SEBASTIAN   He's gone.

ANTONIO   Then tell me,
    Who's the next heir of Naples?

SEBASTIAN   Claribel.

ANTONIO She that is Queen of Tunis; she that dwells   235
          Ten leagues beyond man's life; she that from Naples
          Can have no note, unless the sun were post –
          The man i' th' moon's too slow – till new-born chins
          Be rough and razorable; she that from whom
          We all were sea-swallowed, though some cast again –   240
          And by that destiny, to perform an act
          Whereof what's past is prologue; what to come
          In yours and my discharge.

SEBASTIAN   What stuff is this? How say you?
          'Tis true my brother's daughter's Queen of Tunis,
          So is she heir of Naples, 'twixt which regions   245
          There is some space.

ANTONIO   A space, whose ev'ry cubit
          Seems to cry out, 'How shall that Claribel
          Measure us back to Naples? Keep in Tunis,
          And let Sebastian wake.' Say this were death
          That now hath seized them, why, they were no worse   250
          Than now they are. There be that can rule Naples
          As well as he that sleeps; lords that can prate
          As amply and unnecessarily
          As this Gonzalo; I myself could make
          A chough of as deep chat. O, that you bore   255
          The mind that I do! What a sleep were this
          For your advancement! Do you understand me?

234b–55a, and Tree 233c–55a. Brook (1957) cut 235b–43a, Wright 236b–9a, Benthall
236b–43 (apart from 'What stuff is this!' in 243), Macready and Ashwell 236b–46a, Burton
and Daly 236b–49a, Barton and Hack 238b–9a, and Phelps 239b–43a. Garrick (1757),
Macready, Phelps, Daly and Ashwell cut 252b–5a, and Benthall and Barton 254b–5a.

235 As he spoke about Claribel, Mendes's Antonio screwed up the wedding photo he still had in
      his hand; he later tossed it off-stage (CD).

249a Hytner's Sebastian moved worriedly away from Antonio, impatient because he did not
      understand his innuendoes (CD).

257a Tree's Sebastian touched his dagger on 'Methinks I do.'

SEBASTIAN Methinks I do.

ANTONIO   And how does your content
    Tender your own good fortune?

SEBASTIAN   I remember
    You did supplant your brother Prospero.

ANTONIO   True;   260
    And look how well my garments sit upon me,
    Much feater than before. My brother's servants
    Were then my fellows, now they are my men.

SEBASTIAN But for your conscience?

ANTONIO Ay, sir: where lies that? If 'twere a kybe   265
    'Twould put me to my slipper; but I feel not
    This deity in my bosom. Twenty consciences
    That stand 'twixt me and Milan, candied be they,
    And melt ere they molest. Here lies your brother,
    No better than the earth he lies upon,   270
    If he were that which now he's like – that's dead;
    Whom I with this obedient steel, three inches of it,
    Can lay to bed for ever: whiles you doing thus,
    To the perpetual wink for aye might put
    This ancient morsel, this Sir Prudence, who   275
    Should not upbraid our course. For all the rest,
    They'll take suggestion as a cat laps milk;
    They'll tell the clock to any business that
    We say befits the hour.

258–9a Cut by Burton and Daly. Kean's Ariel floated across the stage at 258a, accompanied by music.

260a Some directors have underlined the mention of Prospero: in London Brook's 1957 Prospero entered above at PS (pb), while Mendes had a gong sound (CD).

264 In response to Sebastian's question, Purcarete's Antonio set fire to the 'music' on his stand (CD).

265b–9a Garrick (1757) was the first of many producers to cut the puzzling reference to a 'kybe' from the dialogue of the restored text; he, Phelps, Iden Payne and Hack cut 265b–7a. Macready, Tree, Benthall, Brook (1957) and Barton cut 265b–6a, Kean 262b–9a, Burton and Daly 265b–9a, Tree and Bridges-Adams (1926/30 and 1934) 267b–9a.

267b Garrick (1757) modified Antonio's ruthlessness: he defied only ten consciences, rather than Shakespeare's twenty.

271b Macready and Kean cut 'that's dead'.

276b–9a Cut by Macready, Phelps, Burton, Kean and Daly. Garrick (1757) cut 277.

SEBASTIAN   Thy case, dear friend,
              Shall be my precedent. As thou got'st Milan,   280
              I'll come by Naples. Draw thy sword; one stroke
              Shall free thee from the tribute which thou payest,
              And I the king shall love thee.
ANTONIO   Draw together:
              And when I rear my hand, do you the like
              To fall it on Gonzalo.
SEBASTIAN   O, but one word. [*They talk apart*]   285

279b–80a Cut by Barton.

279–85 During this scene, one of Brook's 1990 spirits had put Sebastian's hand on his heart and
        pushed him to look at Alonso as Antonio hatched his plot; the spirits now put sword-sticks
        into the conspirators' hands (CD).

  281a Brook's 1957 Prospero exited (DL pb). Purcarete's Sebastian emulated Antonio, setting fire to
        the 'music' on his own stand (CD).

  283a Macready nonsensically transposed the first two words. Daniels's Sebastian held his hand
        out to Antonio, who kissed it; as Sebastian tried to withdraw his hand, Antonio held on to it,
        only releasing it after 'Draw together' (283b).

  283b Antonio and Sebastian clearly draw out their swords either here or at 295a, since on waking
        Alonso questions them about being drawn (297). If they draw here, the director has a further
        choice: Sebastian can immediately stay Antonio with 'O, but one word' (285b) or the two
        may be about to strike their victims when Sebastian has a sudden thought.
            In keeping with their costumes, Paige's conspirators had no swords: 'Sebastian had a
        dagger in an inner pocket . . . and Antonio used [Gonzalo's] sword-stick', which had 'fall[en]
        beside him in the sand'. Sebastian 'appeared reluctant' to assault his own brother, 'but quite
        content for Antonio to do so' (Carter, '*The Tempest* at Salisbury Playhouse', pp. 21–2).
        Purcarete's music stands were transformed into weapons, as the conspirators lifted the tops
        out of the bases and pointed the tips at their intended victims (CD).

284–5a Cut by Tree.

   285 As noted at 283b, Sebastian's 285b can be part of a continuous conversation or an interrupt-
        ing afterthought – e.g., Burton's Antonio had drawn his sword and was nearing Gonzalo
        when Sebastian called him back at 285b; they then conversed apart.
            Some Ariels charm Antonio and Sebastian. Barton's Ariel made some sort of signal on
        'Gonzalo' (285a), causing them to freeze. At 'word', Hall's 1974 Ariel, who had presumably
        hovered high above the stage throughout the scene, quickly dropped to twelve feet above
        the rostrum and charmed Sebastian and Antonio, who were poised to strike. Paige's con-
        spirators were also ready to use their weapons 'when another note from Ariel . . . caused
        Sebastian to draw Antonio aside' (Carter, '*The Tempest* at Salisbury Playhouse', p. 22).

285b–95a Many directors have cut or re-arranged some of these lines, thereby compacting the action.

Enter ARIEL [*invisible*] *with music and song*

ARIEL My master through his art foresees the danger
      That you, his friend, are in, and sends me forth –
      For else his project dies – to keep them living.
          Sings in Gonzalo's ear
      While you here do snoring lie,
      Open-eyed conspiracy   290
        His time doth take.
      If of life you keep a care,
      Shake off slumber and beware.
        Awake, awake.
ANTONIO Then let us both be sudden.

Burton cut 286–8, as did Tree's printed text (Grove, however, re-inserted them). Benthall and Brook (1957) cut 285b. Bridges-Adams (1926/30, 1934) cut 285b–8 and 295a, so that Antonio's instruction that Sebastian kill Gonzalo at the same time Antonio kills Alonso was immediately followed by Ariel's song (accompanied by music) and Gonzalo's waking line; Ayrton and Benthall (1952) cut 295a. Donnellan cut 285b and Antonio and Sebastian's talking apart; instead, Ariel woke the court while the conspirators' swords were drawn and pointed at their would-be victims' heads and necks (CD). Hack cut 285b–91 and had Ariel jump on Gonzalo's stomach to wake him, presumably while delivering 292–4. Hytner transposed 294–5a, so that Ariel's 'Awake, awake!' followed Antonio's 'Then let us both be sudden.' Thacker cut Sebastian's 285b, putting Antonio's 295a in its place; at 'sudden', both conspirators drew back and froze, their swords pointed at their victims' throats, as Ariel delivered 286–94 (CD).

285sd Some Ariels re-enter several lines earlier. Strehler's conspirators froze as they stood over their intended victims, swords poised in both hands which were lifted above their heads, ready to stab down; Ariel, however, ran over to the sleepers with a tambourine, waking them by singing and tapping on the instrument (video).

288sd Benthall's 1951 Ariel cast another spell, making Gonzalo snore in response. After speaking 286–8, Hall's 1974 Ariel left his stirrup and crossed to Gonzalo, where he crouched, tapping his drum and holding his spear across Gonzalo and Alonso to protect them. Hay's sleepers heard the warning sounds through 'a vast alpine horn' (Gore-Langton, 10/10/92).

289–94 Wright cut all of Ariel's song, except for one 'awake', which was presumably spoken. Hall (1974) and Miller (1988) had Ariel repeat 'awake' (294) three times; Hall's Sebastian and Antonio were uncharmed at the end of the song (see note to 285).

295 Although the courtiers clearly wake after this line, the director has some latitude: Gonzalo may wake to speak 295b–6a, or he may call out during his Ariel-inspired sleep. His words rouse the others.

GONZALO   Now, good angels   295
          Preserve the king.
ALONSO Why, how now? ho! Awake? Why are you drawn?
          Wherefore this ghastly looking?
GONZALO   What's the matter?
SEBASTIAN Whiles we stood here securing your repose,
          Even now, we heard a hollow burst of bellowing,   300
          Like bulls, or rather lions; did't not wake you?
          It struck mine ear most terribly.
ALONSO   I heard nothing.
ANTONIO O, 'twas a din to fright a monster's ear,
          To make an earthquake. Sure it was the roar
          Of a whole herd of lions.
ALONSO   Heard you this, Gonzalo?   305

     Tree's Ariel spoke a third (interpolated) 'awake' after 295a, as Antonio and Sebastian suddenly rushed at their intended victims; as Antonio stood above Alonso with his sword drawn, and Sebastian above Gonzalo with a dagger, the music swelled loudly and then stopped dead, as the lights also came up. Hack cut 295b.

296 Phelps's music stopped at 'Preserve the king', and the sleepers woke up.

297a Phelps and Tree cut Alonso's first words on waking ('Why . . . awake?'). Benthall's Alonso directed 297a to Gonzalo; in 1951, Gonzalo interpolated 'Good sir, awake' before Alonso's line. Williams (1978) gave 'Why . . . awake?' to Gonzalo. Hytner's Alonso woke up as he began his line (Stratford pb); Antonio's sword was already sheathed by the time the king asked 'Why are you drawn?' (CD).

297b Purcarete's conspirators threw away their music-stand weapons in response to Alonso's question (CD).

297–8 Daly gave Alonso's 297–8a to Gonzalo, and Gonzalo's 298b to Alonso, which he spoke as he awoke. Benthall (1952) cut 298b.

300 Tree's Antonio interjected 'bellowing', presumably to help a faltering Sebastian; the courtiers 'f[e]ll back terrified'.

301a Following Sebastian's 'Like bulls', Bridges-Adams's 1934 Antonio either murmured or cleared his throat, his implied criticism prompting Sebastian's 'or rather lions'. Bogdanov's 1992 Antonio similarly cleared his throat after 'bulls'.

303–5a Cut by Macready, Phelps and Kean. Tree's Sebastian said 'lions' (305a), either now helping Antonio or nervously interrupting him (see note to 300).

305b Garrick (1757) cut 'Gonzalo', perhaps making the enquiry more general. Kean's Ariel reappeared about here.

GONZALO Upon mine honour, sir, I heard a humming,
  And that a strange one too, which did awake me.
  I shaked you, sir, and cried. As mine eyes opened,
  I saw their weapons drawn. There was a noise,
  That's verily. 'Tis best we stand upon our guard,   310
  Or that we quit this place. Let's draw our weapons.
ALONSO Lead off this ground, and let's make further search
  For my poor son.
GONZALO   Heavens keep him from these beasts:
  For he is sure i' th' island.
ALONSO   Lead away.
ARIEL Prospero my lord shall know what I have done.   315
  So, king, go safely on to seek thy son.

Exeunt

308a Cut by Kean; Phelps and Tree cut 308a, and Hack changed 'shaked' to 'saw'.
309b–10a Given by Barton to Francisco.
310 Garrick changed 'verily' to 'verity', as did Macready, Kean and Daly.
310b–11 Barton gave 310b–11a to Adrian and 311b to Francisco; Hack cut 311b.
313b–16 (end of scene) Cut by Hack, who retained only 'Lead away' (314b).
314b Cut by Barton. Phelps's courtiers exited L1E, with Sebastian and Antonio in the rear making threatening actions towards Alonso. Burton had Ariel appear USL on a flower, which changed to a bat and ascended with her to close the scene.
315–16 Cut by Garrick (1757). Phelps's Ariel ascended up the sloat as she spoke, accompanied by music which continued until Scene 2 began. Kean's Ariel went behind the LC rock setpiece after speaking; there was a peal of thunder and then her double flew across LC to R, with the action moving straight into 2.2. When Tree's courtiers were all off, Ariel spoke from the honeysuckle bower and then broke into eight bars of 'Merrily, merrily'; as she sang, the curtain descended for a ninety-second scene-change. Mendes's Alonso remained on stage while Ariel spoke (CD).
316sd Crozier led this scene straight into the next; when the courtiers had exited, their calls of 'Prince Ferdinand. Halloo. Halloo' could be heard off-stage. Benthall's Alonso interpolated 'Ferdinand, my son' after Ariel's final line.
  Barton's Ariel hummed and sang a reprise of 'Come unto these yellow sands.' Strehler's piled up the lords' discarded clothes as they exited, placing on top of them the sea-shell to which she had earlier enjoyed listening, and carried them off (video).

ACT 2   SCENE 2

Enter CALIBAN, *with a burden of wood. A noise of thunder heard*

CALIBAN All the infections that the sun sucks up
        From bogs, fens, flats, on Prosper fall, and make him
        By inch–meal a disease. His spirits hear me,

2.2 The scene order in post-Restoration adaptations is different from Shakespeare's. In the Dryden/Davenant and Shadwell versions, Caliban entered after the political machinations of Stephano, Ventoso and Mustacho and the arrival of Trincalo (who was given the songs sung by Stephano in the original text). His entry followed the exit of the first three and was visible to Trincalo: 'Hah! Who have we here?'. Garrick's opera transposed part of 3.1 before Caliban's entrance, but the 1757 version followed Shakespeare's text. Still 2.2 in Kemble's 1789 version, the scene became 2.5 in 1806; the first adaptation set it in 'A Barren Heath', the second in 'A naked Part of the Island'.

    While some productions, like those of McVicker, Daly and Brook (1957), ran the previous scene straight into this one, others marked the scene-change. Garrick (1757) and Macready, for example, set the scene in 'Another part of the island', the latter set magically transforming itself from the more inviting area around Prospero's cave: 'the fantastic and varying tints of enchantment vanish, and on a bare and rocky strand, amongst strange volcanic vestiges, we can see "not a twig", no, not one, to [shelter] Trinculo' (Forster, 'Macready's Production', p. 69). Tree similarly opened the scene on a 'barren waste' painted by R. Douglas, while Strehler lowered the raised USR corner of the platform, had the tree descend into the ground-row, and raised the USL corner (video).

osd The amount of wood Caliban carries can indicate the scale of his oppression; comparisons with Ferdinand's log in 3.1 are also instructive. Daniels's Caliban carried a sizeable load of wooden planks on his shoulders (pb and archive video), while Strehler's dragged in a large tree trunk. Bogdanov's 1992 Caliban carried in a great cruciform beam, as did Ferdinand in 3.1, 'Christ imagery' that one reviewer found 'cheap' (CD and Arditti, *ES* 1/12/92). Purcarete's Caliban carried not a burden of wood but a huge skeleton (CD), which some reviewers took to be that of Sycorax; Taylor thought it set up 'awkward *Psycho*-echoes' (*Ind* 19/9/95). Donnellan's Caliban, on the other hand, simply entered with a black bow tie around his neck and with one arm in his shirt sleeve, the other hanging loose (CD).

    Dryden/Davenant and Shadwell cut Shakespeare's thunder, while Kemble (1806) added wind and rain to the thunder-effects.

1 Dotrice's performance as Caliban in the Williams/Brook production was particularly good in this scene. Although elsewhere the actor's voice was 'much too "normal" and polite' and there was 'not enough anger and resentment in him when he turns on [Prospero]', 'when

And yet I needs must curse. But they'll nor pinch,
Fright me with urchin-shows, pitch me i' th' mire,   5
Nor lead me like a firebrand in the dark
Out of my way, unless he bid 'em; but

Caliban is muttering to himself, slouching about doing his wood-gathering labours, celebrating what he believes to be his release into freedom, and at last returning to the protection of Prospero [in 5.1], he is excellent' (Marriott, *STT* 4/4/63).

1–3a Many Calibans treat the first 2½ lines as a formal curse or an attempt to cast a spell. As Strehler's Caliban dropped his burden, thunder sounded and frightened him into hiding behind the raised corner of the stage. When he re-emerged, he held an ornate stick and wore what looked like a hooded jacket, but on closer inspection turned out to be a long strip of some kind of animal-skin, complete with paws. After shaking his stick at the sky, Caliban hesitated before jumping into the C of the sand-circle, where he used his stick to describe a magic circle and then intoned his opening curse. As he did so, tribal beats sounded, and Caliban bounced on his haunches to their rhythm, at the same time patting his face with sand, which eventually decorated it like war-paint: his forehead and cheeks were white with the sand, leaving black stripes under his eyes. Although clearly feeling defiant, he collapsed quivering when thunder again sounded; crying, he threw away his magic stick and picked up a handful of sand, only to throw it down dismissively (video).

Miller's 1988 Caliban used a short stick to cast his spell, abandoning it when thunder sounded after 'disease' (CD and pb). Brook's 1990 Caliban tried to spell-bind Prospero by sticking a feather in a sweet potato and putting it on a stump; he then hit it with a log, making it disintegrate (CD). Bogdanov's 1992 Caliban simply directed the lines to his idol (CD). Alexander's Caliban made a magic circle and broke twigs into pieces to curse Prospero; between 2a and 2b, he looked up to see if the heavens were responding (CD).

3 Caliban's comment that Prospero's spirits 'hear' him demands some sort of stimulus after 3a. In Crozier's production, it was Trinculo calling 'Hallo' off-stage; in Hall's (1974), it was an 'island noise' that made Caliban cringe. Hytner's Ariel, who at Stratford had remained on stage since the preceding scene, slammed the trap shut, causing Caliban to turn and run USC. Thacker's Caliban managed to stand for a moment at 'disease' but then fell, presumably blaming the spirits for his crippling (CD).

3b–14a Emery, Kemble's 1806 Caliban, 'approache[d] to terrific tragedy, when he describe[d] the various tortures inflicted on him by the magician and the surrounding snakes that "stare and hiss him into madness"'. He embodied 'all the loathing and violence of desperate wretchedness: the monster hugs and shrinks into himself, grows louder and more shuddering as he proceeds; and when he pictures the torment that almost turns his brain, glares with his eyes and gnashes his teeth with an impatient impotence of revenge' (Hunt, *Critical Essays*, p. 111).

4a Crozier's courtiers could be heard off-stage calling 'Hallo', presumably answering Trinculo's

> For every trifle are they set upon me,
> Sometime like apes, that mow and chatter at me
> And after bite me; then like hedgehogs, which   10
> Lie tumbling in my barefoot way and mount
> Their pricks at my footfall; sometime am I
> All wound with adders, who with cloven tongues
> Do hiss me into madness.

Enter TRINCULO

Lo, now lo!

call at 3a; Caliban moved DL. Hytner's Ariel exited, and Caliban moved back to DSC (Stratford pb).

4b–17 Cut by Garrick (1756); his Trinculo entered after Caliban's first speech.

10b–12a Cut by Daly. Burton and Kean changed 'pricks' to 'prickles'.

12 Hytner's Trinculo (Desmond Barrit) started to climb the rear ramp, walking around it from SL to SR. Barrit's performance as Trinculo was one of the undoubted high points of the production: a pink and green Pierrot with a very fat stomach, dressed in a satin or silk shift with dangling gloves clipped to his sleeves, he extracted more comedy than one would have thought possible from his passive, depressed, wimpish and effeminate portrayal (CD). With 'lacquered black hair and a tiny rouged mouth', he was 'a camp and nervous jelly, get[ting] his laughs through his poised falsetto as much as anything else' (respectively, Nightingale, *P* 12/8/88, and Renton, *Ind* 1/8/88). '[S]porting a kiss-curl', 'smudged lipstick' and 'rouge smudged with tears', this 'corpulent and dainty' Trinculo was 'as much a triumph of costume as of performance' (respectively, Edwardes, *TO* 31/5/89; Rose, *TO* 3/8/88; Kellaway, *O* 31/7/88; Tinker, *DM* 28/7/88; Kellaway). He spoke lines 'with a slow plaintive dryness which [made] them sound wittier than they are' and was 'brilliantly inventive – his routines [were] freshly minted and [took] this part well beyond the usual clowning buffoonery', his 'hilariously querulous Trinculo' finding instead a 'wealth of original lugubrious comedy' (respectively, Hoyle, *FT* 26/5/89; Edwards, *Sp* 3/6/89; Kemp, *Ind* 26/5/89; Kemp).

14a Many Trinculos, such as Burton's, Kean's and Tree's, are heard off-stage to explain Caliban's 'Lo, now lo!'; Kemble's 1806 called 'O,O,O-' and Phelps's 'Hillio! ho! ho!' Crozier's Trinculo, nearer but still off-stage, again called 'Hullo' (*sic*) after 'madness' (see note to 3); after 'Lo, now lo!', the court responded with its own 'Hullo', followed by another from Trinculo, causing Caliban to '[move?] back quickly'.

Daniels's Trinculo (Alun Armstrong, Stratford; Ian Talbot, London) entered from USR and crawled into the wreck. Reviewers variously describe Armstrong's Trinculo as 'surly, working class', 'rather sour' and 'innocent, much-offended', but agree that he was 'splendid' and 'infinitely watchable' (respectively, Billington, *G* 12/8/82; *OT* 20/8/82; Pratt, *YP* 12/8/82; Evans, *SH* 20/8/82; and *NEC* 2/3/83).

14b Cut by Dryden/Davenant and Shadwell, who changed 15 to 'Hah! Yonder stands one of his spirits sent to torment me.' The Williams/Brook pb notes 'stand by balloons', probably referring to the thundercloud that received wide mention in reviews: 'a silly little cardboard black cloud with a pawnbroker's appendage which pops off fireworks at the hint of a thunderbolt' (Gardner, *SH* 5/4/63). The 'three huge globes' suspended from the cloud reminded innumerable reviewers of pawnbrokers' balls, though two were more struck by their resemblance to beetroots (*EJ* 5/4/63; *BSM* 7/4/63).

14sd On Shakespeare's platform stage, Trinculo had to enter sometime before his speech beginning at 18; Caliban's 14b–17 covered his long walk DS. The naturalism of the proscenium theatre precludes such an arrangement, since Trinculo would be supposed to have seen Caliban; consequently, many Trinculos enter later – Kemble's, for example, came on at the end of Caliban's speech. The part was probably originally played 'by the King's Men's regular comedian, Robert Armin', wearing 'the Fool's outfit of suit of motley and coxcomb' and perhaps carrying a 'bauble' (Sturgess, *Jacobean Private Theatre*, pp. 77, 80).

   In Retallack's ATC production, Chris Barnes played both Trinculo and Antonio, and Raymond Sawyer both Stephano and Sebastian. The doubling 'device . . . ha[d] strong and developing dramatic point, reinforcing the unitary quality of the plot, and projecting the regal Stephano into a grotesque reflection of the usurping Duke' (Wardle, *T* 25/2/83); the doubling was also 'an effective comment on the farcical aspects of political warfare' (*CL* 17/3/83). Warner used the same doubling.

   Barrit's wan Trinculo (described in note to 12) belongs to one strand of interpretation of the part. Gellner's Trinculo, Toke Townley, was admired for his 'quiet style', 'with just the right touch of pathos behind the humour' (respectively, *DT* 18/9/51; *TN* 29/9/51). Neville's Trinculo, Robert Eddison, was 'pale and piping', 'a timorous, wrinkled reed of a fellow', who seemed 'a mad maiden aunt out of Gilbert and Sullivan' (respectively, Peter Lewis, uc; Trewin, *ILN* 16/6/62; Hope-Wallace, *G* 30/5/62). David Warner, for Williams/Brook, played 'a skinny lamp[-p]ost of a Trinculo given to swooning', who was delivered on stage by conveyor-belt (respectively, 'Prompter' [Wendy Trewin], *PWI* 7/4/63; Chapman, *OM* 3/4/63).

   In Brook's 1957 production, Clive Revill was 'a very melancholy jester, a delectably timorous zany with something of Chico Marx's truculent incredulity and something of Stan Laurel's pallid dejection', who managed to get 'the right laughs with the slightest movement or simple glance' (respectively, *OT* 16/8/57, and *EJ* 23/8/57). A kind of 'Goon show character' who wore 'a sou'-wester . . . sideways', 'yellow, quilted jacket, running shorts and Turkish slippers', he appeared a 'comic Aladdin' to one reviewer and a 'fisherman . . . [wearing] his hat over his night gear' to another (respectively, Philip Hope-Wallace, *MG* 15/8/57; *P* 21/8/57; *P*; *OM* 14/8/57; Rodford, *BWDP* 15/8/57). Reviewers repeatedly refer to him and to Patrick Wymark's Stephano as a music hall double act, a kind of Laurel and Hardy, whose comic scenes were immensely successful.

Although the Folio describes Trinculo as a jester, many directors turn to other, more relevant or familiar, clown traditions for interpretation of the part. Strehler's, wearing clown-like white clothes, a red cloak, a tall brimless white hat and a black eye-mask, was 'drawn directly from *commedia dell'arte*', as were Ariel and Stephano; however, where Ariel was based on Deburau's early nineteenth-century pierrot, the comic characters came from an older tradition (Kleber, *Theatrical Continuities* pp. 151–2, and video). They did not wear 'the highly individualistic character masks of later *commedia*, but a more generic-form of the half-mask. Nevertheless . . . Trinculo had many similarities with the Pulcinella figure', wearing 'the distinctive tall hat unique' to him and 'speak[ing] in a southern Italian dialect' (p. 154). Ciulei's Trinculo, Adam Redfield, entered 'singing the barber's song from "The Barber of Seville" as he shave[d]'; he and Stephano, Richard Hilger, were dressed as 'period burlesque clowns' and showed 'some of the divine madness of the Marx Brothers' (respectively, Steele, *MT* 13/6/81, and Sullivan, *LAT* typescript fax, 20/8/81). De Berardinis dressed his Trinculo, Ivano Morescotti, in 'a black-and-red circus outfit' of 'red bowler hat and tails' (respectively, Ronfani, *iG* 6/4/86; Zucconi, *PS* 5/4/86); Zucconi found him incoherent and jerky, like 'a Buster Keaton or a Charlot [Chaplin's tramp]', while another reviewer thought he came across as a 'stand-up comedian' (Sergio Colomba, *CS* 5/4/86). He was a ' "cretin" ', speaking the 'Romagna dialect of Ferrini' (Gianni Manzella, *iM* 12/4/86), an obtuse Bolognese character from a popular television show who would have been readily recognizable to the audience.

As De Berardinis partly did, directors sometimes turn to different show-business characters and traditions to portray Trinculo. Breuer's was played by Lola Pashalinski as a 'blowsy demimondaine' speaking like Mae West (respectively, Kalem, *Time* 20/7/81; Rich, *NYT* 10/7/81, et al.). Miller's 1988 Trinculo, the comedian Alexei Sayle, was very much himself: a 'bald, thuggish, Magwitch-like Trinculo', 'whose bemusement hardens into Scouse resentment (and a lovely un-Shakespearian cry of "bastards")' (respectively, Billington, *G* 12/10/88; Coveney, *FT* 12/10/88). He 'rant[ed] and judder[ed] in familiar fashion', his style 'more Sayle than Shakespeare with his head-butting swagger and asides to the audience' (respectively, Hiley, *L* 20/10/88; Rose, *TO* 19/10/88). Karl James, in Retallack's 1991 production, was 'a jester in loud check [suit] and battered straw hat reminiscent of Tommy Trinder' (Jill Murawicki, *SCG*; *TES* photo, 13/9/91). A 'reincarnation of Max Miller, "the cheeky chappie" ', he 'deliver[ed] a line, click[ed] his two-tone shoes, doff[ed] his straw hat, and [threw] open his arms to receive laughs as Shakespeare may not quite have conceived them' (John Linklater, *GH* 19/9/91). David Bradley, for Mendes, was 'a hilariously jittery ventriloquist with dyed carroty hair, woebegone Northern vowels, Little Titch shoes and a dummy who [was] his double', with the same red hair and checked trousers (Taylor, *Ind* 13/8/93; CD); they shared Trinculo's speeches between them (CD). Wolfe's Trinculo, Bill Irwin, was 'a cross between Bert Lahr and Daffy Duck', 'teetering on his heels and speaking with heavily salivated sibilants' (respectively, Donald Lyons, *WSJ*, and Karam, *T*, both 14/7/95).

Purcarete's Trinculo, Sean McKenzie, was first seen as he slid down the set of wires, which

Here comes a spirit of his, and to torment me   15
For bringing wood in slowly. I'll fall flat,
Perchance he will not mind me.
TRINCULO Here's neither bush nor shrub to bear off any weather at
all, and another storm brewing – I hear it sing i'th'wind. Yond same
black cloud, yond huge one, looks like a foul bombard that would shed   20
his liquor. If it should thunder as it did before, I know not where to

were positionally diagonally. He then entered properly, dressed as a chef in a big hat and
white clothes (CD).

16–17 Caliban lies down and, in an attempt to disguise his presence, covers himself with his
gaberdine. Cut by Dryden/Davenant and Shadwell.
        Strehler's Caliban hid himself DS not by 'fall[ing] flat', but by kneeling with the top of his
head resting on the floor; his narrow animal-skin lay along the top of his back leaving him
clearly visible at the sides (video). Daniels's Caliban fell flat on his stomach at C, with his
head facing DSL (pb); his head was covered by the gaberdine, which was 'scaled . . . like a
fish', but his hands and feet and part of his legs protruded from it (archive video; quotation
from Young, *FT* 14/9/83). Mendes's Caliban fell flat with his bottom up, making him look
rather like a rock (CD).

17 As Crozier's Caliban fell on his face, the still off-stage Trinculo yelled 'Hi' and was similarly
answered by the off-stage courtiers. Trinculo then called 'Hi hi' and was again answered by
the court's 'Hi hi'. After Trinculo's final 'Hallo', thunder sounded and Trinculo entered.
        Williams's 1978 'white pierrot' Trinculo, Richard Griffiths, entered after Caliban's speech;
his first word was "Loo!', followed by a pause (Warren, 'A Year of Comedies', p. 203). Griffiths's 'endearingly funny teddy-bear Trinculo' was generally admired: he had 'the unhurried
dignity of the weighty and a Jack Benny-like ability to deliver crushing judgments in a flat,
low key style' (respectively, Levin, *ST* 7/5/78; Billington, *G* 15/5/78).

18–23 Brook's 1990 Caliban moved under the gaberdine to make Trinculo notice him; eventually he
uncovered his legs and arms so that Trinculo could not miss him (CD).

18–35 Condensed by Dryden/Davenant and Shadwell to seven lines; references to the storm were
cut (and therefore the business with the gaberdine), as well as the barbed comment on the
lack of English charity. Garrick's 1756 opera similarly cut the speech to eight lines, but added
some clarification ('A man, or fish? for it resembles both: / 'Tis some amphibious monster of
the isle'); the lack of alms was not mentioned but the satirical 'In England any monster
makes a man' was included. Kemble's 1806 adaptation cut the lines about the 'black cloud'
(19–21) and the reference to England (25–9).

19–21 Burton cut 'yond huge one . . . liquor' (20–1); Daly 'yond same . . . liquor' (19–21). Hytner's
Trinculo spoke in a small voice at first; his resentful pointing to 'yond same black cloud, yond
huge one' could make one believe the foul bombard were persecuting him personally (CD).

hide my head. Yond same cloud cannot choose but fall by pailfuls. What have we here – a man, or a fish? Dead or alive? A fish, he smells like a fish; a very ancient and fishlike smell; a kind of, not-of-the-newest poor-John. A strange fish. Were I in England now – as once I   25

22 Macready's Trinculo discovered Caliban at 'pailfuls'. So did Phelps's: 'going backwards looking off R. as if fearing the storm, he stumble[d] against Caliban'. Similarly, Tree's Trinculo, who had been looking off L, fell over Caliban at 'pailfuls' as thunder sounded. Many subsequent directors have continued the tradition.

23 Harley, Macready's Trinculo, was 'quaint and astonished as becomes Harleyism in contact with a "monster" ' (Forster, 'Macready's Production', p. 71).

Phelps's Trinculo held his nose at 'A fish', 'as if offended with the smell'; Rylance's 'gulp[ed] down fresh air before inspecting [Caliban's] noisome limbs' (Kingston, *T* 10/6/91); Thacker's emitted an 'ugh!' when he smelled him (CD). In contrast, after spotting Caliban, whose feet and arms protruded from the tarpaulin, Purcarete's Trinculo sniffed around him a good deal, before producing salt, fork and knife, which he proceeded to sharpen. Just as he was about to dig in, Caliban's feet shot up (CD).

After asking 'What have we here?', Strehler's Trinculo lifted the end of the animal-skin covering Caliban and, pointing to the latter's bottom, announced 'a man'; he then kicked Caliban's bottom, making him fall flat. After this, Trinculo played toreador with his red cloak, trying to rouse the still immobile Caliban to no avail. He then started to get a whiff of Caliban's smell, making him decide he was in fact a fish (video). Paige's Trinculo, on the other hand, danced and shuffled around the tarpaulin before finally 'pluck[ing] up courage to feel under it at both ends' at 30 (Carter, '*The Tempest* at Salisbury Playhouse', p. 23).

Bridges-Adams (1926/30) transposed 'dead or alive?' and 'a man or a fish?'.

24–5 Tree, Bridges-Adams (1926/30) and Hack cut 'a kind . . . poor-John', and Brook (1957) 'poor-John'. Alexander's Trinculo talked instead about 'dried hake' (CD).

Ashwell's Trinculo sneezed after 'poor-John', while Daniels's Trinculo let out a telling 'orgh!' (archive video); Coveney found the latter 'hilariously sensitive to foul smells' (*FT* 13/8/82). At some point, Williams's 1978 Trinculo addressed 'Hello fish face' to the hiding Caliban.

At 'poor-John', Hytner's Trinculo started feeling Caliban through the cloak, happening instantly on his genitals; once he had made them out through touch, he announced 'strange fish!' to general audience merriment (CD).

25–9 Macready cut from 'A strange fish!' to 'dead Indian'; Kean and Daly from 'Were I in England' to 'dead Indian'.

Trinculo's comment on the English lack of charity is sometimes emphasized: Hytner's delivered 29 harshly (CD) and Miller's (1988) added 'Bastards' after 'Indian'. At 'Indian' in

was – and had but this fish painted, not a holiday-fool there but would
give a piece of silver. There would this monster make a man; any
strange beast there makes a man. When they will not give a doit to
relieve a lame beggar, they will lay out ten to see a dead Indian. Legged like a man – and his fins like arms. Warm, o'my troth! I do now let 30
loose my opinion, hold it no longer: this is no fish, but an islander, that
hath lately suffered by a thunderbolt. [*Thunder*] Alas, the storm is
come again. My best way is to creep under his gaberdine; there is
no other shelter hereabout. Misery acquaints a man with strange
bedfellows. I will here shroud till the dregs of the storm be past. 35

    Enter STEPHANO [*carrying a bottle and*] *singing*

STEPHANO I shall no more to sea, to sea,
        Here shall I die ashore.

Mendes's production, Trinculo's dummy suddenly yelled 'whowho', making Caliban shout
and fall flat. When Trinculo explained 'No, I said dead Indian', the dummy responded 'I
thought you said red Indian' (CD).
30 Trinculo's words make clear that he now touches Caliban to ascertain what he is. The 'o' my
troth' of Purcarete's Trinculo seemed to be prompted by feeling Caliban's genitals (CD). Just
before announcing Caliban was 'Legged like a man!', Strehler's Trinculo lifted Caliban's leg
and counted its toes, before counting his own to confirm the number was right; only when he
hit Caliban's foot did it come down again (video). Miller's 1988 Trinculo cut 'o' my troth' and
knelt by Caliban, who put his legs in the air.
32sd Trinculo's next sentence indicates that the storm manifests itself again, probably by a
thunder sound-effect. When Strehler's thunder sounded, Trinculo unwittingly covered his
face with his cloak and thought it had gone completely dark before discovering his mistake
(video).
33–5 Sometime during these lines, Trinculo creeps under Caliban's gaberdine, allowing business
rich in varied comic effect. Phelps's and Burton's found it difficult to cope with Caliban's
stench, the former having to make several attempts to get under the covering. Benson's 1891
Caliban carried Trinculo 'on his back about the stage', 'pantomimic business' which the *Stage*
enjoyed (30/4/1891), but which the *Stratford Herald* found 'exaggerated and prolonged'
(24/4/1891). Benthall's (1952) crept under the gaberdine during 33 and spoke 34 ('Misery . . .
bed-fellows') peeping out from under it. Mendes's Trinculo put his nose down between
Caliban's legs and inhaled in disgust (CD).
    Daniels's comic business was more elaborate. At 'gaberdine', Caliban lifted his head
briefly, giving the audience a startled and comic look at this new turn of events (archive

video). At 'hereabout', Trinculo lifted the gaberdine, reeled back SR, put his hanky over his nose and then wrung it out (presumably it was wet with sea-water). After a pause, he crawled underneath Caliban crossways, with his head DSR, first lying on his back and then on his side, facing US; he then pulled the gaberdine over him and philosophized about misery and its strange bed-fellows. A pb sketch shows the two in an X formation, Caliban's head DSL and feet USL and Trinculo's head DSR and feet USR. The archive video shows that at his first approach Trinculo actually crept in under the gaberdine and then came out again, voicing another 'orgh!' at the smell.

Hytner's Trinculo paused after announcing he would 'creep under [Caliban's] gaberdine' and looked at the audience in a way that appeared either slightly defensive, guilty or ratio-nalizing; he waited for a laugh and then fixed an audience member with his eye as he shouted harshly (and in a lower register than he had previously used) 'there is no other shelter hereabout'. However, there was no further development of this apparently gay subtext, apart from Trinculo's later jealousy of Caliban's devotion to Stephano (CD). After a pause, Trinculo moved back up to C, pulled the DS edge of the cloak out flat and flipped the DSL edge of it back as if it were a bedsheet. He then slid under the cloak on the DSL side, his legs facing SR, and sitting half-way under it, spoke the rest of his speech to the audience; at the end he pulled the cloak over his head, and Stephano was then heard singing from behind the ramp at USC (Stratford pb). Trinculo's actions were very fastidious and resigned: he clearly felt put upon by the situation (CD).

To get under the gaberdine, Paige's Trinculo lay on his back, his head between Caliban's legs; he 'then pulled the tarpaulin down to cover his own [legs], thereby *un*covering Caliban's head and arms'. Once Stephano had entered, Caliban sat up 'and looked in amaze-ment at Trinculo's feet behaving totally independently. He pulled the tarpaulin and Trinculo pulled it back', whereupon they 'decided to investigate underneath it' (Carter, '*The Tempest* at Salisbury Playhouse', p. 23).

Purcarete's Caliban lay under the gaberdine in a posture that mimicked Alonso's in the previous scene: his head and back lay flat on the ground, but his legs and feet were raised in an inverted L. Trinculo crawled under the gaberdine with his torso parallel to the ground and his knees in a kneeling position: his head, pointing SR like Caliban's, passed between Caliban's thighs and rested on the monster's chest (CD).

34–5 Barton transposed 'misery acquaints . . . strange bed-fellows' and 'I will here shroud . . . be past'.

35sd Cut by Hack. The original Stephano 'would have been costumed as Butler to the King to make his assumption of regal power the more ridiculous' (Sturgess, *Jacobean Private Theatre*, p. 80). Poel had him dressed in sober black and wearing a chain of office (photograph, TM), but more recent productions have costumed him in varied ways: Goddard's wore a 'Carmen Miranda hat bearing squeezy plastic lemons to alleviate thirst' (Hoyle, *FT* 2/3/88), while Donnellan's entered in mask, snorkel and flippers (CD). Ninagawa's carried a Greek wine-skin and was dressed only in a chef's hat, apron and black knee bands: a 'bald, bare-bummed', and 'great, shiny hulk' (respectively, CD; Billington, *G* 5/12/92; Nightingale, *T* 5/12/92). Some Stephanos, like those of Kemble (1806) and Burton, carried a keg rather than a bottle.

Kean had elaborate storm effects here: thunder crash, rolling and shaking thunder, wood crash, wind, rain.

Jay Laurier played Stephano in all three of Iden Payne's Stratford revivals 'as a music hall "drunk"' and was widely acclaimed for his portrayal: 'from his first entrance . . . carefully climbing down rocks which offered only a few inches of danger, and as nonchalantly leaping o'er fearsome precipices', Laurier's performance was 'tremendous fun' (respectively, *BED*; *BM*; *BM*, both 3/5/38); all 'his antics, gestures, darting glances and quaint explosive utterances' embodied 'grand professional fooling, cordial, comforting, and perfectly timed' (respectively, *SH* 6/5/38; *O* 8/5/38).

Brook's 1957 Stephano, Patrick Wymark, came on 'with the narrow-brimmed bowler and stick of the music-hall comedian' (*EJ* 23/15/57). He reminded most reviewers of George Robey and several of Tweedledum, since besides the bowler he wore a 'tight-fitting garment' with 'barrel-like yellow and black stripes' reminiscent of a turn-of-the-century bathing-suit (respectively, Rodford, *BWDP* 15/8/57; Foxon, *BWP* 16/8/57). 'Fat, red-faced and pompous, something like the late Oliver Hardy, he contrast[ed] excellently' with Revill's Stan Laurel-like Trinculo, making Stephano 'just drunk enough, just comic enough, always a living character and not a caricature' (*St* 15/8/57); he also 'adroitly suggest[ed Stephano's] bonhomie' (*OT* 16/8/57). With its 'Chaplinesque' comic timing, Wymark and Revill's 'manic-depressive lunacy . . . [was] funny and at the same time pitiful' (respectively, *OM* 14/8/57; *Sp* 13/12/57). In a somewhat different vein, Arthur Lowe, for Hall in 1974, was a 'Robeyish' but 'very male, dry little Stephano', who 'excel[led] in his tincture of authority with absurdity' (respectively, Barber, *DT*; Jane Gaskell, *DM*; Young, *FT*, all 6/3/74); he made Stephano 'a dangerous buffoon with powerful [*sic*] sense of his own dignity' and the 'enslavement of Caliban . . . genuinely disturbing' (Wardle, *T* 6/3/74).

Many Stephanos emphasize the character's sinister side even more than Lowe. In keeping with Miller's overall concept, Mike Pratt (as well as Ron Pember's Trinculo) 'exhibit[ed] colonialism in a brutally primitive form' (Wardle, *T* 16/6/70), while the 'drunken cupidity' of Williams's 1978 Stephano, Paul Moriarty, highlighted his menace: he was 'enflamed less with drink than with the ambition of repeating Antonio's coup and taking over the island' (respectively, Evans, *SH* 5/5/78; Wardle, *T* 3/5/78). Barton's Stephano, Patrick Stewart, was 'a moustached pocket-führer from the Midlands', 'more batman than butler, but . . . aggressive enough to keep his Trinculo and Caliban . . . in order' (respectively, D. A. N. Jones, *L* 22/10/70; Higgins, *T* 17/10/70). Alexander's 'inebriate Celtic Stephano', Andy Hockley, made visible the process of Stephano's corruption through power: on his first entrance, he held his liquor well and clearly had no thought of exploiting Caliban until Caliban himself gave him the idea (CD; quotation from Billington, *G* 15/9/94).

As with their treatment of Trinculo, Italian directors have exploited the *commedia* tradition in portraying Stephano. Strehler's appeared in the ground-rows with a chianti-type bottle, dressed in white, with a cloak, a black eye-mask and a feathered two-cornered hat, worn pirate-fashion across his head (video). He was drawn from the Arlecchino and Brighella figures of the older *commedia* tradition, wearing the sailor-type hat reminiscent of the former and speaking in a northern Italian accent that reflected the origins of both; like Brighella, Stephano was 'more crafty' than Pulcinella/Trinculo, as well as 'dishonest, unscrupulous, opportunistic, and vengeful' (Kleber, 'Theatrical Continuities', p. 154). De Berardinis, playing Stephano in his own production, gave him 'the body, the voice, the gestures of Toto', the comic Neapolitan actor with a foolish character similar to Pulcinella's, who was popular from the 1940s through the 1970s and is now an iconic figure of tragi-comic genius (quotation from Manzella, *iM* 12/4/86). He wore Toto's trademark 'black cloak', 'bowler hat and tailcoat', spoke his 'philosophical Neapolitan', and embodied his 'pseudo-noble malice' (respectively, Manzella; Ronfani, *iG* 6/4/86; Ronfani; Zucconi, *PS* 5/4/86).

Retallack's 1991 Stephano, Patch Connolly, 'enriched [the lowlife scenes] by a humorous cocktail of Shakespearean quotations': he had 'a tendency to improvise lines from other Shakespearean plays' and 'thoroughly exploited' Stephano's 'absurd airs of superiority' (respectively, Ramsden, *TES* 13/9/91; Linklater, *GH* 19/9/91; Keren Williams and Gary Shipton, *WSG* 5/9/91; Williams and Shipton). Other recent Stephanos have also emphasized the character's desire for upward class mobility. Daniels's, Christopher Benjamin, had a 'comic dignity' and spoke with 'pseudo upper-class vowels', having 'just the right measure of affected, genteel solemnity' (respectively, Shulman, *ES* 9/83; Barber, *DT* 9/83; Edwards, *NS* 20/8/82). Mendes's, Mark Lockyer, played the part with a pot-belly, buck teeth and Hooray Henry accent (CD), with one reviewer thinking that his 'clubland voice betray[ed] a lifetime of resentful servility to the aristocracy' and another that he sounded like the Queen (respectively, David Nathan, *JC* 20/8/93; Kellaway, *O* 15/8/93). A 'loathsome cross of Oliver Reed and Terry-Thomas', he seemed 'like a mad parody of Prospero himself' (respectively, Billen, *O* 17/7/94; Billington, *G* 15/7/94).

While most Stephanos simply come on, some have had more idiosyncratic entrances. Williams/Brook's entered via the conveyor-belt, 'off which [he was] frightened by a white rat' (Chapman, *OM* 3/4/63). Mendes's Ariel brought in the basket which contained Stephano, while Purcarete's got on stage as if he were swimming onto it from the orchestra pit; he eventually leaned against the set of wires, which were strung horizontally across the bottom half of the stage, and got entangled in them (CD).

35sd–49sd   Assigned by Dryden/Davenant and Shadwell to Trincalo, who entered 'with a great bottle, half drunk', prior to Caliban's entrance.

36–7 Hytner's Stephano (Campbell Morrison) sang these lines twice while still off-stage; as he repeated 37, he climbed onto it. Most critics fastened on his Hibernian incarnation, simply describing him as a 'roaring Glaswegian' 'lager lout' who provided a 'robust counterpoint' to Barrit's Trinculo (respectively, Koenig, *P* 9/6/89; Tinker, *DM* 26/5/89; Tinker). He had a large build similar to that of Caliban and Trinculo, with Caliban's ironically the least 'monstrous' (CD).

This is a very scurvy tune to sing at a man's funeral. Well, here's
my comfort. *Drinks*

   Sings The master, the swabber, the boatswain and I,   40
            The gunner and his mate,
        Loved Mall, Meg, and Marian, and Margery,
            But none of us cared for Kate.
            For she had a tongue with a tang,
            Would cry to a sailor, 'Go hang!'   45
        She loved not the savour of tar nor of pitch,
        Yet a tailor might scratch her where'er she did itch.
            Then to sea, boys, and let her go hang!
  This is a scurvy tune too; but here's my comfort. *Drinks*
CALIBAN Do not torment me! O!   50

Alexander's Stephano vomited at some point; he wiped his mouth and then flicked his finger, the discarded matter hitting Caliban in the eye. Caliban then appeared to wipe it away and taste it. As the scene proceeded, Caliban began to copy Stephano's gestures, imitating him and occasionally echoing him: he did here in admiration what he had earlier done in angry, disillusioned response to Prospero (CD).

36–9 Cut by Tree and Hack.

36–49sd Garrick (1756) cut all but the first two lines, which were spoken rather than sung; the second 'to sea' (36) was also omitted.

39 Falls's Stephano 'brandishe[d] his bottle and call[ed] "He-e-e-re's my comfort" in a parody of Ed McMahon's nightly introduction for TV personality Johnny Carson' (Pellowe, 'In Chicago', p. 55).

40–8 Macready cut 42–8; Phelps and Kean 45–7; Kemble (both versions), Burton and Daly 46–7; Tree 46–8. Bridges-Adams (1926/30 and 1934) and Ayrton had 48 sung twice.

    Mendes's Stephano urinated during his song; he intended to do so into the basket, but aiming too high, he missed, 'his copious arcs [of urine] landing everywhere but'. When he finished, he burped (CD; quotation from Taylor, *Ind*, 15/7/94)).

50–5 Tree cut 50 and 'For it hath . . . nostrils' (53–5); Hack 'What's the matter?' from 51; Daly 'Do you put . . . Ha?' (51–2).

    The singing of Donnellan's Stephano prompted Caliban's plea, during which he clung to Stephano's foot (CD).

    The four legs that protrude from Caliban's gaberdine generate rich and varied comic business. Phelps simply had the pair shake their legs in the air, presumably in fear of Stephano, who then became somewhat frightened himself; Tree, Bridges-Adams, Ayrton and Benthall used similar business, though the latter's 1952 Stephano found it amusing the second time it happened. Other directors have devised more elaborate business. Strehler's Trinculo and

STEPHANO What's the matter? Have we devils here? Do you put tricks
upon's with savages and men of Ind? Ha? I have not scaped drowning to be afeared now of your four legs. For it hath been said, 'As proper a man as ever went on four legs, cannot make him give ground';
and it shall be said so again, while Stephano breathes at' nostrils.   55
CALIBAN The spirit torments me! O!
STEPHANO This is some monster of the isle, with four legs, who hath
got, as I take it, an ague. Where the devil should he learn our language? I will give him some relief if it be but for that. If I can
recover him, and keep him tame, and get to Naples with him, he's   60
a present for any emperor that ever trod on neat's leather.

Caliban were both on their hands and knees, with Trinculo's head under Caliban's stomach
and Caliban's head on Trinculo's back. In reaction to Stephano's voice, Trinculo backed SL,
taking Caliban with him; they soon moved SR again and eventually rocked up and down, as
each in turn raised his bottom (video). Daniels invented 'a brilliant piece of pantomime . . .
which had both adults and children in fits' (Edwards, *NS* 20/8/82); it involved Trinculo and
Caliban getting into various 'spider' positions. The first, at 50, had Trinculo, lying on his
stomach, put his head under Caliban's crotch and then kneel, a manoeuvre that forced
Caliban's head onto Trinculo's bottom (pb); Caliban uttered a Trinculo-like 'orgh!' as his nose
came to rest there (archive video). Trinculo then lay down, he and Caliban forming a 'flat
spider'. Stephano turned to look at them and, surprised by what he saw, spilled his liquor
down his front; between 51 and 64, he walked all around the 'spider'. Lepage's Caliban wore
'a green plastic garbage bag [to avoid the rain]'; once Trinculo also climbed inside it, there
was 'a remarkable series of physical manoeuvres based on the exact breaking point of the
bag's strength', with Caliban 'at her grotesque best tearing her way out of' it (Conlogue,
TGM; Conlogue; Donnelly, *MGa* 7/6/93).

50–61 Cut by Dryden/Davenant and Shadwell.
51–98 Garrick (1756) condensed these lines to three spoken by Trinculo: 'A sensible monster, and
speaks my language. / Dear Tortoise, if thou hast the sense of taste, / Open thy mouth, and
know me for thy friend'; after this, Trinculo poured wine down Caliban's throat.
56 Interpolated by Tree and Barton after 'ague' in 58.
57–8 On 'four legs' (57), Benthall's 1951 Stephano prodded Caliban and Trinculo all over, making
them shake in fear. On 'ague' (58), Benthall's 1952 Stephano kicked Trinculo's bottom, which
made the pair move back to their original position and lie down again, shaking and making
noise. In both productions, Caliban repeated 56 after 'ague'.
59–61 Hall's 1974 Stephano delivered 'If I can recover him . . .' to the audience.
At 61, Daniels's Trinculo knelt facing US, his head still on the floor. His action made
Caliban's head come up, facing DS and still resting on Trinculo's bottom ('cheeks spider').

CALIBAN Do not torment me prithee! I'll bring my wood home faster.

STEPHANO He's in his fit now, and does not talk after the wisest. He shall taste of my bottle. If he have never drunk wine afore, it will go near to remove his fit. If I can recover him, and keep him tame, I will not take too much for him; he shall pay for him that hath him, and that soundly. 65

CALIBAN Thou dost me yet but little hurt; thou wilt anon, I know it by thy trembling. Now Prosper works upon thee. 70

STEPHANO Come on your ways. Open your mouth; here is that which

Trinculo then began shuffling around, making the 'swivelling spider'. Sometime before 71, Stephano went US of the 'spider' and then DSL, while the 'spider' jerked twice and then trembled before becoming still (pb notes and sketch).

63 Kemble (1806) added '0,0,0!' after 'faster'.

64–8 Dryden/Davenant and Shadwell, whose Trincalo spoke a version of these lines, cut the references to Caliban's fit and to the plan to exploit him. Daly cut 'and . . . wisest' (64); Tree 'If I can . . . soundly' (66–8); Barton 'If he have . . . fit' and 'I will not . . . for him' (65–7).

At 64, Benthall's 1952 Stephano stroked Caliban's head; at 66, his 1951 Stephano tried to let Caliban drink, but Caliban bit him and shouted, making Stephano jump back – Stephano then stroked him. Bogdanov's 1992 Caliban and Trinculo, partially standing up under the gaberdine, looked like a rather tall tortoise (CD).

69–72 Dryden/Davenant and Shadwell cut 69–70; Daly 'now . . . thee' (70); Tree 'Thou dost . . . cat' (69–72).

71–4 Stephano gives Caliban his first taste of liquor during these lines, but both the degree of Stephano's coerciveness and the extent of Caliban's initial enthusiasm are open to directorial discretion. Strehler's Caliban 'seem[ed] born for subjugation, a point that [was] graphically made by the way Trinculo [Stephano?] shove[d] the neck of his bottle between his lips in a gesture of phallic domination' (Billington, *G* 16/11/83), while Bogdanov's 1992 Caliban showed his idol to Stephano and muttered 'psht' in an attempt to prevent the intrusion; he proceeded to spit out his first mouthful, swallow the second and enjoy the third (CD). Bridges-Adams's Stephano (1926/30, 1934) held the bottle to Caliban's mouth at 73, only to have his finger bitten; Ayrton repeated the business, with Caliban also grabbing at the bottle. Mendes's Stephano sang 'Come on your ways. Open your mouth' in a falsetto (CD).

Dryden/Davenant and Shadwell, whose Trincalo spoke a version of 71–4, cut the references to Caliban's shaking and need for 'language'; at the end of his speech, Trincalo poured wine down Caliban's throat. When Daniels's Stephano poured drink into Caliban's mouth, the latter spat it out; after a pause, Trinculo's hand appeared, feeling his damp bottom. Trinculo then crawled SL, with him and Caliban in the 'cheeks spider' position (see note to 59–61).

will give language to you, cat. Open your mouth; this will shake
your shaking, I can tell you, and that soundly. You cannot tell who's
your friend: open your chops again.

TRINCULO I should know that voice. It should be – but he is   75
drowned, and these are devils. O defend me!

STEPHANO Four legs and two voices; a most delicate monster! His
forward voice now is to speak well of his friend; his backward
voice is to utter foul speeches, and to detract. If all the wine in
my bottle will recover him, I will help his ague. Come. Amen.   80
I will pour some in thy other mouth.

TRINCULO Stephano.

STEPHANO Doth thy other mouth call me? Mercy, mercy! This is a
devil, and no monster. I will leave him; I have no long spoon.

72 Bridges-Adams's 1934 Stephano looked at Caliban's face before addressing him as 'cat'; considering Holloway's appearance as a 'Green-skinned, gorilla-faced, tusked and web-
fingered' creature (*DM* 17/4/34), the appellation may well have raised a laugh.

75–98 Cut by Dryden/Davenant and Shadwell.

76 Daniels's 'spider' got into the 'dog' position: Trinculo put his head and feet (knees unbent) on
the floor, thereby raising his bottom in the air, Caliban's head still resting on it (pb notes and
sketch).

77–9 Barton interpolated 'a most delicate monster' (77) after 'detract' (79). Garrick (1757) changed
'utter' to 'spatter' (79).

80 'Come. Amen' suggests that Stephano again offers Caliban the bottle but that the latter
drinks too greedily for his liking; thus he decides to offer some of the liquor to Caliban's
'other mouth'. When Kean's Caliban finished drinking, Stephano took the bottle and said
'Amen' in surprise at how much Caliban had consumed. Barton's Caliban burped after
'Come', presumably motivating Stephano's 'Amen', while Daly cut 'Amen'.

81 Shakespeare's line suggests that the actor must change position here. Hytner's Stephano
went to put the bottle under the tarpaulin into Trinculo's bottom (Stratford pb); Purcarete
went a step further, Stephano goosing Trinculo with the neck of the bottle and then finding it
difficult to pull out (CD).

82 Hytner's Trinculo repeated Stephano's name three or four times at Stratford and twice in
London, shocking him.

83–4 Kemble (1806) cut 'This is a devil . . . spoon', and Daly 'Doth thy other mouth call me?' (suggesting that Trinculo's head was not at Caliban's feet) and 'I . . . spoon'. Hack changed 'This
is . . . monster' to 'This is but a devil.'
    At 83, Daniels's Stephano ran DSL when he heard his name called; by the end of his ques-
tion he was crossing to SR. Meantime, Trinculo and Caliban changed from the 'dog' (see note
to 76) to the 'cheeks spider' position (see note to 59–61).

TRINCULO Stephano! If thou beest Stephano, touch me, and speak to   85
me; for I am Trinculo – be not afeared – thy good friend Trinculo.

STEPHANO If thou beest Trinculo, come forth! I'll pull thee by the
lesser legs. If any be Trinculo's legs, these are they. Thou art
very Trinculo indeed! How cam'st thou to be the siege of this
moon-calf? Can he vent Trinculos?   90

TRINCULO I took him to be killed with a thunder-stroke. But art
thou not drowned, Stephano? I hope now thou art not drowned.
Is the storm over-blown? I hid me under the dead moon-calf's
gaberdine for fear of the storm. And art thou living, Stephano?
O Stephano, two Neapolitans 'scaped!   95

86 Daniels's Stephano crossed to US of the 'spider', which collapsed into the 'flat spider' position. Bogdanov's 1992 Trinculo finally saw Caliban, who tried to ward him off with his idol
and another 'psht'. At some point, Trinculo hit his nose on Stephano's bottom (CD).

88 The text explicitly describes the action required: Stephano pulls Trinculo out by the legs,
revealing him at 89. The action is often embellished: after being pulled out, Kean's Trinculo
caught his first sight of Caliban's face and looked alarmed; Strehler repeated the business.
Tree's Stephano took Trinculo by both legs, turned him on his back, and dragged him out.
Seeing Stephano, Trinculo gave 'a laugh of recognition, and turn[ed] onto his hands and
knees to rise'; since Caliban did so at the same time, Trinculo came face to face with him as
he turned and his laughing stopped dead. After a pause, Caliban tried to claw Trinculo's face,
and the latter shrank back to Stephano, who helped him to his feet. In quite a different vein,
the smell of Trinculo's feet made Williams's 1978 Stephano momentarily abandon the task.
Kemble (1806) cut 'if any . . . they'.

89 Hack changed 'siege' to 'turd'; Williams (1978) changed it to 'sewage'.

90 Kean, Daly, Tree, Ashwell, Bridges-Adams (1926/30, 1934) and Ayrton cut 'Can . . . ?'

91–4 Garrick (1757) and Kemble (both versions) cut 'But art . . . fear of the storm'. Daly cut 'Is the
storm . . . fear of the storm' (93–4), and Miller (1988) 'But art . . . art not drowned' (91–2).
Macready changed 'gaberdine' to 'laberdine' (94). Hall's 1974 Trinculo kept touching
Stephano, presumably to assure himself that Stephano was not a ghost.

95–6 Shakespeare's text clearly indicates the required action: in his joy at their escape from
drowning, Trinculo embraces Stephano and whirls him about. When Ciulei's Trinculo and
Stephano were reunited, they 'embrace[d] and [broke] into "O Sole Mio" ' (Steele, *MT*
3/6/81); it also 'occasion[ed] a lusty Neapolitan duet' in Retallack's first production (Wardle, *T*
5/2/83). Miller's 1988 Trinculo and Stephano turned about, hugging each other, with
Stephano nearly vomiting, while Caliban imitated them (CD and pb). In particular, Caliban
'desperately copy-cat[ted Stephano's] and Trinculo's pugilistic gestures in an effort to be
accepted' and 'seize[d] on [Trinculo's] two-fingered gesture', mimicking it 'with uncompre-

STEPHANO Prithee do not turn me about, my stomach is not constant.

CALIBAN [*Aside*] These be fine things, and if they be not sprites. That's a brave god, and bears celestial liquor. I will kneel to him.   100

STEPHANO How did'st thou 'scape? How cam'st thou hither? Swear by this bottle how thou cam'st hither. I escaped upon a butt of sack which the sailors heaved o'erboard, by this bottle – which I made of the bark of a tree, with mine own hands, since I was cast ashore.

hending glee' (respectively, Taylor, *Ind* 13/10/88; Hiley, *L* 20/10/88; Hiley). Donnellan's Stephano *did* vomit – into Trinculo's trousers (CD).

98–100 Hall's 1988 Caliban stood CR, admiring Stephano and Trinculo at C, where Ferdinand had been when Miranda (US) first saw him; the blocking of the admired figures highlighted the similarity of Miranda's and Caliban's responses (CD).

99–100 Kemble (1806) cut 'I . . . him'; Miller's 1988 Caliban spoke the words but did not kneel to Stephano. Daniels's Caliban fell onto his back, having become drunk with his first swig of liquor.

99–114 Garrick (1756) cut from 'I'. After 'liquor', Trinculo asked Caliban if, like him, he would 'live soberly, and become my subject?' Caliban swore to serve him, sang 'No more dams' (155–60), and was given another drink by Trincalo with 'Here, kiss the book'. Caliban swore by 'Settibos' that the 'liquor's not earthly' (106) and then Shakespeare's dialogue was resumed.

101 Brook's 1957 Trinculo tried to answer Stephano's question: the pb interpolates 'I swum . . .' for Trinculo after 'How camest thou hither?', but Stephano carried on talking (DL pb).

Strehler's Trinculo went US and drank liberally from Stephano's bottle, which had been left there; Stephano was still DS, asking Trinculo questions. When Stephano realized what Trinculo was up to, he hit him on the head and took back the bottle. During the ensuing lines, a small tambourine was thrown to Trinculo from off-stage, and he and Stephano cavorted about before Trinculo finally tossed the tambourine back off-stage; he and Stephano then collapsed flat on their backs (video).

101–2 Stephano's 'Swear by this bottle' precipitates a good deal of business with the bottle that carries on throughout the following lines. Stephano appears to retain the bottle at this point, but offers it to Trinculo at 107 ('Here. Swear then') and 110 ('Here, kiss the book'); he also offers it to Caliban at 120.

101–4 Cut by Dryden/Davenant and Shadwell and replaced by a speech in which Trincalo asks Caliban to be his subject.

103–6 Kemble (1789) cut 103–4 ('by this bottle . . . cast ashore'); in 1806 he cut 103–6 ('by this . . . earthly'). Macready, Kean and Daly cut from 'which I made' to 'not earthly'; Tree, Bridges-Adams (1926/30, 1934), Ayrton, Iden Payne and Hack from 'which I made' to 'cast ashore' (103–4). This popular cut presumably reflected the difficulty of providing a bottle that looked

CALIBAN I'll swear upon that bottle to be thy true subject, for the   105
    liquor is not earthly.
STEPHANO Here. Swear then how thou escap'dst.
TRINCULO Swum ashore, man, like a duck. I can swim like a duck,
    I'll be sworn.
STEPHANO Here, kiss the book. Though thou canst swim like a   110
    duck, thou art made like a goose.
TRINCULO O Stephano, hast any more of this?
STEPHANO The whole butt, man. My cellar is in a rock by the sea-side,
    where my wine is hid. How now, moon-calf, how does thine ague?
CALIBAN Hast thou not dropped from heaven?   115

hand-carved from bark: Devine/Goring's Stephano drank out of one 'shaped like a golf-bag'
(*O* 2/6/40). Wright cut only Caliban's lines (105–6).
    Daniels's Caliban finally succeeded in kneeling at 'o'erboard' (103; see note to 99–100).
Hall's 1988 Trinculo acquired his own 'home-made' bottle in the course of the play (props
list).

105–25 Purcarete's Stephano and Trinculo, respectively SR and SL, bounced about on the wires and
sent the bottle back and forth along them; Caliban was C in front of the wires (CD). One
reviewer enjoyed the comic scenes for the 'pure European-tradition clowning' they
employed (Thornber, *G* 12/9/95).

106 Daniels's Caliban fell over.

107–14 Cut by Dryden/Davenant and Shadwell. Kemble (1806) cut 107 (adding the question 'How
escaped'st thou?' for Trinculo to answer) and 'I can swim . . . goose' (108–11). Macready cut
'I'll be sworn . . . like a duck' (109–11), giving the rest of 111 to Trinculo. Barton gave 110–11 to
Trinculo, making it self-referential: 'Though I canst swim like a duck, I be made like a goose.'
Miller (1988) cut 109.

110 Stephano's 'kiss the book' is an invitation to drink from his bottle, and most productions
incorporate the action although it is not always noted in pbs.

113 Brook's 1957 Stephano drank 'flamboyantly' and spoke ' "The whole butt, man" with a smile
so seraphic that he [stood] for a moment in the company of the great topers' (*CET* 14/8/57).
Strehler's Caliban, who had been lying on his back DSC, got up and did a somersault, visibly
drunk (video). Williams (1978) interpolated 'Horah!' (*sic*) after 'man', presumably for Trinculo, who went to grab the bottle but was pushed away by Stephano.

115 Emery, for Kemble (1806), 'inimitably display[ed]' both Caliban's 'roughness of manners and
his infinite awe at the divinity of the sailor who had made him drunk . . . particularly in the
vehement manner and high voice with which he curse[d] Prospero, and that thoughtful
lowness of tone, softened from its usual hoarse brutality, with which he worship[ped] his
new deity' (Hunt, *Critical Essays*, pp. 110–11). Wright's Trinculo sniggered at Caliban's
question.

STEPHANO Out o' th' moon I do assure thee. I was the man
     i'th'moon, when time was.

CALIBAN I have seen thee in her; and I do adore thee. My mistress
     showed me thee, and thy dog, and thy bush.

STEPHANO Come, swear to that! Kiss the book – I will furnish it   120
     anon with new contents. Swear.

TRINCULO By this good light, this is a very shallow monster. I afeared
     of him? A very weak monster. The man i' th' moon? A most poor,
     credulous monster. Well drawn, monster, in good sooth.

CALIBAN I'll show thee every fertile inch o' th' island. And I will   125
     kiss thy foot – I prithee be my god.

TRINCULO By this light, a most perfidious and drunken monster –
     when's god's asleep he'll rob his bottle.

116–17 Given by Dryden/Davenant and Shadwell to Trincalo. Williams's 1978 Stephano admitted he
     was 'De man in de moon'.

   118 Iden Payne's Stephano and Trinculo both laughed at Caliban's professed adoration.

118–24 Dryden/Davenant and Shadwell cut 118–21 and all but the first sentence from 122–4, with the
     final sentence interpolated below (see note to 127–35). Garrick (1756) changed 'mistress' to
     'mother' and cut 120–4 in 1756, 122–4 in 1757. Kemble cut 122–4 in 1789 and gave 124 ('Well
     drawn . . . sooth') to Stephano in 1806. Kean cut 'My . . . bush (118–19), while Hack added
     (Trinculo's?) 'woof woof' to its end; Burton's Trinculo laughed at Caliban's ignorance. Tree
     cut 'I will furnish . . . contents' (120–1), while Donnellan's Stephano urinated into the bottle
     as he spoke the line (CD). Barton cut 'A very weak monster' (123).

125–62 Mostly cut by Garrick (1756), who retained only some of 125–6 (transposed), 136, 144, 147:
     'Pray be my god, and let me drink again. *Drinks again.* / I'll shew thee ev'ry fertile inch i' th'
     isle, / Where berries, nuts, and cluster'd filberds grow.' The rest of the scene comprises new
     material, including an air for Caliban and a trio for Trinculo and two of the mariners who now
     entered.

   126 Dryden/Davenant and Shadwell added 'and let me drink' to the end of the sentence.
     Benson's Caliban 'slavishly lick[ed] the dust from the footsteps of the drunken butler as he
     implore[d] him to be his god'; he also 'positively lap[ped] the drops of spilt wine from the
     ground . . . as a thirsty dog would water from a stream' (respectively, A. H. Wall, *ISDN*,
     2/5/1891; E.C.T., *SH* 1/5/1891). At Caliban's offer, Purcarete's Stephano stuck his foot out and
     Caliban kissed it; Trinculo did the same, but Caliban only spat at it (CD).

   127 Hytner's Trinculo got between Caliban and Stephano, appearing to be jealous (pbs and CD).

127–35 Cut by Dryden/Davenant and Shadwell with Trincalo's 'Well drawn, monster, in good faith'
     (124) interpolated here.

CALIBAN I'll kiss thy foot; I'll swear myself thy subject.

STEPHANO Come on then: down and swear.   130

TRINCULO I shall laugh myself to death at this puppy-headed mon-
    ster. A most scurvy monster. I could find in my heart to beat him –

STEPHANO Come, kiss.

TRINCULO – but that the poor monster's in drink. An abominable
    monster.   135

CALIBAN I'll show thee the best springs; I'll pluck thee berries;
    I'll fish for thee, and get thee wood enough.

    A plague upon the tyrant that I serve!

    I'll bear him no more sticks, but follow thee,

    Thou wondrous man.   140

TRINCULO A most ridiculous monster, to make a wonder of a poor
    drunkard.

129 Hall's 1988 Caliban wore fangs that 'affect[ed] his enunciation: 'I will kish thy foot . . . show
    thee the besht shprings' (Edwards, *Sp* 28/5/88). Miller's 1988 pb notes 'no[t?] true' at 'kiss
    thy foot': presumably, Caliban did not perform the action, just as he did not kneel to
    Stephano earlier (see note to 99–100).

129–35 Cut by Garrick (1757) and by Kemble (both versions).

130 Tree's Caliban kissed Stephano's foot, business that Fitzgerald found ill judged: 'How nobly
    grovelling, with yet a sort of canine attachment, [should be] the kissing of the traveller's
    boots, where here was made a bit of comic or funny "business" ' (*Shakespearean Represen-*
    tation, pp. 45–6).

132 Trinculo's unfinished line has been variously interpreted. Burton's Trinculo was 'Half inclined
    to beat [Caliban] there and then but [was] deterred by his formidable appearance'; Kean's by
    Caliban's savage glance. Bridges-Adams's 1934 Caliban snarled at being called a 'scurvy
    monster' and again when Trinculo considered 'beat[ing] him'; Ayrton's Trinculo backed away
    when Caliban snarled. Tree's Caliban stroked Stephano's legs, presumably ignoring Trinculo.

132–3 Brook (1957) interpolated Stephano's 133 ('Come, kiss') into Trinculo's 132, between 'puppy-
    headed monster' and 'A most scurvy monster!'. When Ninagawa's Caliban kissed Stephano's
    foot, the latter screamed several times, apparently because it tickled (CD).

134 It took Tree's Trinculo three attempts to say 'abominable'.

136–40 Purcarete's Caliban rocked Stephano in his arms as he spoke 136b; his delivery of the whole
    speech was gentle, apart from his imprecation against Prospero at 138 (CD).

137 Tree's Caliban rose to take the bottle hanging from Stephano's shoulder; as Stephano slowly
    turned to prevent him, Caliban followed him around, trying to grab it: forming a complete
    circle, he ended up in his original position.

140–2 Cut by Dryden/Davenant and Shadwell; Trincalo's response was 'The poor monster is loving
    in his drink.' Kemble's 1806 Trinculo added 'Ah me!' after 'drunkard' (142). Daly cut 141–2.

CALIBAN I prithee let me bring thee where crabs grow;
And I with my long nails will dig thee pig-nuts,
Show thee a jay's nest, and instruct thee how   145
To snare the nimble marmoset. I'll bring thee
To clust'ring filberts, and sometimes I'll get thee
Young scamels from the rock. Wilt thou go with me?
STEPHANO I prithee, now lead the way without any more talking.
Trinculo, the king and all our company else being drowned, we   150
will inherit here. Here; bear my bottle. Fellow Trinculo, we'll
fill him by and by again.

144   Tree's Caliban scratched Trinculo's eye.

146–7   Daly cut 'I'll bring thee . . . sometimes'.

147b–8a   Dryden/Davenant and Shadwell cut the puzzling reference to scamels. Garrick (1757)
retained the lines, changing 'scamels' to 'shamois', which Kemble adopted in 1789 and which
he replaced in 1806 with 'sea-mells'. Macready and Kean adopted 'sea-mells' and, following
Garrick (1757), also changed 'filberts' to 'filberds' (147a).

    Tree's Caliban apparently had no trouble with the idea of a 'scamel': on 148a, he mimed
snatching one, which made Trinculo stagger forward curiously, asking 'Eh?' Caliban then
suddenly opened his hand under Trinculo's nose, which made the latter stagger back to R.
Alexander handled the crux inventively: when Caliban offered to get 'scamels', Stephano
looked at Trinculo and mouthed the word with a puzzled shrug; Caliban then gave him a
shellfish, which clarified the matter. Caliban's enunciation of his speeches was deliberate,
lingering on 'd' and 't' at the ends of words, making it clear that he was not a native speaker
(CD).

149–53sd   Cut by Dryden/Davenant and Shadwell; new material was interpolated after 148 and after
Caliban's song in which Trincalo learned of Sycorax's existence and planned to marry her in
order to claim the island 'by alliance'.

151   Stephano's 'Bear my bottle' may be addressed either to Caliban or to Trinculo, and its handling often generates comic business. Kemble's 1806 Stephano spoke the words to Caliban,
who then drank the keg empty; Stephano added 'and lead the way, monster' before consol-
ing Trinculo with the promise of a refill. Tree's Stephano gave the bottle to Caliban, who took
it US and was about to drink when Trinculo snatched it from him, wiped its mouth with his
sleeve, and took it DR; in pantomime Caliban appealed to Stephano, who took the bottle
away from Trinculo and gave it again to Caliban. Bridges-Adams's 1934 Caliban tried to take
the bottle but Stephano gave it to Trinculo instead, whereas Iden Payne's Stephano only gave
Caliban the bottle because it was empty.

152   Benthall's Stephano pointed to Caliban's gaberdine, which Trinculo put on Stephano as a
kingly cloak, handing him the bottle as a sceptre.

CALIBAN *Sings drunkenly* Farewell, master; farewell, farewell.

TRINCULO A howling monster; a drunken monster.

CALIBAN No more dams I'll make for fish,   155
    Nor fetch in firing
    At requiring,
    Nor scrape trenchering, nor wash dish,
    Ban, ban, Ca-caliban
    Has a new master – get a new man.   160

153–62   Kemble cut 155–61 in 1789 and 153–4, 161–2 in 1806. Inchbald notes that Stephano, Trinculo and Caliban all sang the last two lines of Caliban's song. Despite his enthusiasm for Emery's performance, Hunt complained about his acting here: 'after he had drunk so much of a liquor to which he was unaccustomed, and indeed after he had acknowledged it's [*sic*] power by reeling on the stage, he should not have displayed so sober a voice in his song: we think that Shakespeare intended this song to be given in the style of a drunkard, by the breaks which he has marked in the line – – ban – ban – Ca – Caliban – which could hardly have been a chorus' (*Critical Essays*, p. 33). Ryder, Kean's Caliban, sang with 'some rough heartiness . . . but the preternatural and the monstrous were not equally impressive' (*Ath* 4/7/1857, p. 859); 161 was cut. In contrast, Harcourt Williams's 1933 Caliban performed the song with a 'terrifying animalism' (Williams, *Four Years*, p. 226).

    David Suchet, Clifford Williams's 1978 Caliban, saw the final song 'as a dance and song of freedom . . . I beat my feet on the floor rather like a tribal dance – threw away my effigy of Prospero with "Farewell master; farewell, farewell". And then sang very loudly the song "No more dams I'll make for fish", etc., and when I got to "Freedom, high-day, high-day freedom, freedom high-day, freedom", I stopped singing but let those words come out of my body as though released from the depths of my soul; sometimes the words would literally lift me off the floor. And in this state of wild exuberance the scene closed' (Suchet, 'Caliban in *The Tempest*', p. 176).

159   Williams's 1978 Caliban sang the line twice and then repeated 158–60, again delivering 159 twice. Daniels's Caliban made four 'splod jumps' on the line, on the first, second, fourth and sixth syllables.

160   At 'get a new man', Tree's trio joined hands and danced around in a circle three or four times, the dance getting wilder and wilder. Then they broke the circle and took each other by the arm, Caliban C, Stephano DS and Trinculo US. As they danced towards the L, Caliban suddenly broke away from them, turned to the R and drank; Trinculo and Stephano grabbed his arms and dragged him off L, 'dancing more wildly than ever' and singing the (unspecified) refrain.

160–1   Hall's 1974 Caliban directed 'Has a new master' to Stephano and 'get a new man' to his logs; his 'delivery of the word "freedom" even in the catch (which the three plotters sing in charac-

Freedom, high-day, high-day freedom, freedom high-day, freedom.
STEPHANO O brave monster, lead the way!

Exeunt

ter) echoe[d] with more passion and meaning than anything else' in the production (Wardle,
T 6/3/74). Alexander's Caliban was exceptionally moving towards the end of this scene, the
pathos engendered by his search for someone to admire (CD).

161–2 Dryden/Davenant and Shadwell gave Caliban's excitement limited expression ('Heigh-day,
freedom, freedom!') and cut Stephano's line. Trincalo led Caliban away to his butt, at which
point Prospero entered alone and explained why he had kept Hippolito and his daughters
apart: his astrological skill predicted that Hippolito would die if he saw any woman's face
before a certain time. An extended scene followed involving Prospero, Hippolito, Miranda
and Dorinda.

Tree's Caliban shouted 'Freedom, hey-day! hey-day, freedom!' as the three revellers made
their singing and dancing exit; the rest of 161 and 162 were cut. The curtain then fell for a one-
minute scene-change. Brook (1957) transposed 161 and 162 (DL pb). Daly, Bridges-Adams
(1934) and Iden Payne cut 162; Bridges-Adams instead had Stephano and Trinculo repeat the
unspecified chorus, as they circled round Caliban or the stage.

At 161, Donnellan's Trinculo and Stephano went into a double singing and dancing act;
they began it three times, each time unsuccessfully trying to include Caliban, who instead
kept coarsely hitting the ground with a flipper and yelling a simple phrase. Eventually, the
twosome's refrain echoed Thatcher's pronouncement that 'There's no such thing as society'
(CD). Hoyle thought the pair resembled 'a cross between panto slapstick and the Crazy
Gang', while Taylor complained that their refrain 'suggest[ed] the glimmerings of an (albeit
half-baked) capacity for political abstraction when, by rights, this couple can be seen as not
just more vulgar than Caliban . . . but a good deal less intelligent' (respectively, *FT* 20/10/88;
Ind 26/11/88). Billington found them 'a couple of second-rate, front-cloth vaudeville enter-
tainers who use[d] Shakespeare's words largely as a cue for song . . . Caliban's cry of
"Freedom, high-day" here [became] an excuse for another number', thus losing sight of the
way the two 'nourish Caliban's desire for liberty' and later 'pose a positive threat to Prospero' (*G* 12/10/88).

162sd Modern directors often place the single interval here. Neville followed the scene with 3.3.

ACT 3   SCENE 1

Enter FERDINAND, *bearing a log*

FERDINAND There be some sports are painful, and their labour
Delight in them sets off. Some kinds of baseness
Are nobly undergone; and most poor matters
Point to rich ends. This my mean task
Would be as heavy to me as odious, but   5
The mistress which I serve quickens what's dead,

3.1 Almost the entire log-bearing scene was cut by Dryden/Davenant and Shadwell; only 68 and
73b–4a were retained with some of the sense of 61b–3a. Act 3 began with a new scene
between Prospero and Miranda, and Prospero and Dorinda. Then the following lines, with
some adjustments, deletions and additions, were interpolated: 5.1.1–2; 4.1.33–7a; 5.1.3b–5a
(with 'sixth hour' changed to 'fourth'), 6b–8, 10–28; 4.1.42b–9a (Shadwell cut 44–9a);
3.3.1b–10 (Shadwell cut 2–4a, 9b–10), 12–13a (which became a heartening remark to Alonso
that Shadwell cut), 18, 20a; 1.2.408–25a, 428b–36, 440b–500. Garrick (1756) cut the scene
completely; Neville had 3.3 precede it.
     Kean showed a rocky terrain with bare trees and a dark sky, representing another part of
the island (sketch, Edmonds pb); however, the lights were all up for the scene (Ellis pb).
     Brook (1957) festooned the stage with tangled streamers running from flies to floor and
suspended mid-way between them. There were three rock-like seats and an abstract ten-
drilled plant with 'outsize tropical fruit hang[ing] from branches as thick as drain-pipes' (production photo; quotation from 'Prompter' [Wendy Trewin], *PWI* 18/8/57).
     As the audience returned at the end of Donnellan's interval, the 'actors' were doing some
kind of warm-up with steps; the play proper began again with Prospero, now looking rather
like Martin Luther, menacingly banging a stick on the ground (CD).
osd The size and weight of Ferdinand's log(s), as well as his manner of working, provide instructive comparisons with Caliban in 2.1 and can shape our responses to both characters.
Phelps's Ferdinand was 'discovered, seated on pile of logs', and Daniels's was 'a bit idle',
while Burton's entered with a large and heavy log (pbs and Young, *FT* 14/9/83). Hall's 1988
Ferdinand picked up the large log left by Caliban, while Bogdanov's 1992 Ferdinand, his neck
chained to his ankles, entered with the same cruciform beam Caliban had carried in the previous scene; Hytner's Ferdinand began to work towards the end of the interval, carrying in
armfuls of logs, sweating as he did so and running energetically to get his next load (CD).
     Strehler's Ferdinand entered from the C trap in an echo of Caliban's first entrance, naked
except for his breeches. He walked SL to a pile of wood, picked up a piece and carried it back
to the trap; about to drop it in, he was so exhausted he had to put it down (video). Not only

And makes my labours pleasures. O, she is
Ten times more gentle than her father's crabbed –
And he's composed of harshness. I must remove
Some thousands of these logs, and pile them up,   10
Upon a sore injunction. My sweet mistress

did Ferdinand's appearance mirror Caliban's, but 'both characters convey[ed] a real sense of sweating, back-breaking servitude', the parallel 'strongly imply[ing] that Prospero [was] using the theatrical devices which represent[ed] his magic art to put all those in his power on trial' (Warren, *TLS* 9/3/84). Brook's 1990 Ferdinand also worked hard, accompanied by frenetic music; however, as he circled the stage piling up logs, Ariel and another spirit unpiled them (CD). These 'unseen spirits who tease[d] and torment[ed], scattering poor Ferdinand's neatly collected logs . . . [made] the sport really "penible" rather than the mere laboursome of the English' (Hoyle, *T* 2/11/90). Hirsch's Prospero, on the other hand, had quietly touched Ferdinand with magic, so that he could 'twirl on his little finger great logs' that Caliban found difficult to move (Young, *FT* 30/6/82, implying that the audience was unlikely to note the magical interference and would therefore be confused by the staging).

Donnellan ingeniously let Ariel act as Ferdinand's logs: once put down, he returned to his original place to be carried again. Thacker repeated the business, with the accompanying spirits as well as Ariel turning into logs and Ferdinand seeming always to think he had carried the final one: then another miraculously appeared as he was dealing with the current one. He carried them in different ways, struggling with each to comic effect (CD).

Some Prosperos, like those of Alexander, Thacker and Purcarete, were present on stage from the scene's beginning. The latter's placed a goblet of wine on the revolve at about the same time Ferdinand entered from SR, blindfolded and carrying what appeared to be a giant cello frame; Miranda also entered from SR, but further DS, and headed straight for the wine, which she gave to Ferdinand (CD). The moment 'show[ed] Prospero poised between remaining in a rather creepily watchful control of the proceedings and preparing to bow out of them' (Taylor, *Ind* 19/9/95).

1   Miller's 1988 Ferdinand carried in a log and made two journeys off-stage for more before speaking; he began his lines as he exited again and then continued to fetch logs from off-stage regularly during the scene (CD and pb).

2b–4a   Cut by Macready, Kean, (?) Burton and Daly.

3   Miller's 1988 Ferdinand re-entered with another log.

6   Benthall (1951) changed 'serve' to 'love'. Miller's 1988 Ferdinand re-entered with another log.

7b–15a   Cut by Kean.

9   Garrick (1757) changed 'remove' to 'move', wording which perhaps indicates the stage-business.

11   Miller's 1988 Miranda entered as Ferdinand re-entered with another log and then took a break.

Weeps when she sees me work, and says such baseness
Had never like executor. I forget.
But these sweet thoughts do even refresh my labours,
Most busy, least when I do it.

Enter MIRANDA, *and* PROSPERO [*following at a distance*]

MIRANDA   Alas, now pray you   15
Work not so hard. I would the lightning had
Burnt up those logs that you are enjoined to pile.

13 Ferdinand indicates that he has forgotten to perform his task while talking about Miranda: he now begins to deal with the logs again.

13b–15a Cut by Macready (and probably) Burton.

15a The Folio reads 'Most busy lest, when I do it.' Directors have dealt with the crux in different ways: Garrick (1757) changed 'busy lest' to 'busyless'; Bridges-Adams (1926/30, 1934) and Iden Payne used 'busiest'; Benthall and Williams (1978) adopted 'Most busiest when idlest'; Brook (1957), Hack and Miller (1988) cut it.

15sd Garrick (1757), Macready and Phelps had Miranda enter without Prospero; some Prosperos, like Macready's, Phelps's, Tree's and Brook's (1957), entered later, while others, like Kean's and Atkins's (1938), did not appear at all. Burton's Miranda entered slowly, watching off-stage (presumably for Prospero); when she saw Ferdinand, she ran to him and laid her hand on his shoulder. Prospero then entered and remained at the back watching.

Strehler's Ferdinand went down into the trap, at which point Miranda ran on from SR; she was standing behind the trap when he re-emerged, but he was so intent on his work he did not see her. He walked to the pile of logs at SL, picked one up, and, with head bent, turned and went back to the trap, still without seeing her. As he stopped near the trap, she grabbed hold of his log and pushed it in. Prospero was DSC, facing US to watch them; he turned DS to speak his asides to the audience (video).

Brook's 1990 Ariel and two other spirits brought Miranda on between six poles; Prospero also appeared between two long sticks (CD). The 'bamboo poles . . . held upright by spirits, suggest[ed] a protective grove' where the lovers talked (Taylor, *Ind* 2/11/90).

15b–16a Atkins's 1936 Miranda 'deserve[d] a more vigorous Ferdinand': 'Her "Alas, now, pray you work not so hard!" is unnecessary advice' (uc, 10/7/36). Retallack's 1991 Miranda and Ferdinand 'appear[ed] to be in love in a sexual rather than a vague Renaissance way' (Colin Donald, *Sco* 19/9/91); Ray Fearon played his part 'with great sincerity and not a little passion', he and Miranda making 'an unusual and spirited pair' (Murawicki, *SCG*).

15b–59a Purcarete's Ferdinand stood L, still bearing on his back the oversized cello frame, while Miranda crouched R; at some point during their exchanges, Prospero circled behind Miranda and got between the lovers, leaning his face close to his daughter's to look intently at her. The impression created was one of awe at the emotions she was experiencing (CD).

Pray set it down, and rest you. When this burns
'Twill weep for having wearied you. My father
Is hard at study; pray now, rest yourself –   20
He's safe for these three hours.

FERDINAND   O most dear mistress,
The sun will set before I shall discharge
What I must strive to do.

MIRANDA   If you'll sit down
I'll bear your logs the while. Pray give me that;
I'll carry it to the pile.

FERDINAND   No, precious creature,   25
I'd rather crack my sinews, break my back,
Than you should such dishonour undergo,
While I sit lazy by.

MIRANDA   It would become me
As well as it does you; and I should do it

18–21 Kean cut 'Pray . . . O most'.

19b Benthall's 1951 Miranda pointed to the cave, while Prospero entered LC through the arch. Brook's 1957 Prospero entered and remained at OP with his wand (DL pb).

20a When Williams's 1978 Miranda mentioned her father's being 'hard at study', Prospero 'clock[ed] audience' – that is, he registered a look at them, presumably wry.

21a Hytner's Prospero was coming on as he heard Miranda tell Ferdinand her father would not be seen for 'these three hours'; with a sigh he began obligingly to exit, but was arrested by Ferdinand's reply to Miranda. Standing USC on the ramp (i.e., below stage level), he then leaned on the stage to watch the lovers, 'rest[ing] his chin on his hand and lean[ing] on his elbow, beaming vacantly and indulgently' as he watched Miranda and Ferdinand 'fall in love' (CD; quotation from Koenig, *P* 9/6/89).

21b Benthall (1951) changed 'O most dear' to 'O no dearest'.

23a Miller's 1988 Ferdinand went to fetch another log.

24–5 Miranda often tries to take Ferdinand's log during this exchange, as in the productions by Crozier, Benthall, Brook (1957), Hall (1974, 1988), Williams (1978) and Hytner (pbs); Alexander's lovers really fought over it (CD). Bogdanov's 1992 lovers struggled for the beam, with Miranda finally letting go just before 32a, making Ferdinand fall with it across his legs, while Ninagawa's lovers moved the logs together, as if they were playing a game (CD). Mendes's Miranda easily took from Ferdinand logs he had found heavy and made them appear light (CD), whereas Miller's 1988 Ferdinand deposited his log and returned for another before beginning his reply; he and Miranda fought over the new one at 29. Benthall (1951) cut 25b.

25b–32a Cut by Macready, Phelps, Kean, (?) Burton and Daly. Garrick (1757) and Tree cut only Prospero's aside (31b–2a).

With much more ease, for my good will is to it, 30
And yours it is against.
PROSPERO   Poor worm, thou art infected;
This visitation shows it.
MIRANDA   You look wearily.
FERDINAND   No, noble mistress, 'tis fresh morning with me
When you are by at night. I do beseech you
Chiefly, that I might set it in my prayers, 35
What is your name?
MIRANDA   Miranda. – O my father,
I have broke your hest to say so.
FERDINAND   Admired Miranda,
Indeed the top of admiration, worth
What's dearest to the world. Full many a lady
I have eyed with best regard, and many a time 40
Th' harmony of their tongues hath into bondage
Brought my too diligent ear. For several virtues
Have I liked several women, never any
With so full soul but some defect in her
Did quarrel with the noblest grace she owed, 45
And put it to the foil. But you, O you,

32b Miller's 1988 Ferdinand lay prostrate on his back while Miranda sat at his head, waving a frond to cool him (CD and pb).

34 The Ferdinands of Macready, Burton and Phelps were conscientious workers, carrying their logs out before returning to continue the conversation with Miranda. In contrast, Bridges-Adams's 1934 Ferdinand drew Miranda onto a rock and then sat with her.

36a Purcarete's Ferdinand asked Miranda's name in response to her 32b; 33–5 were cut (CD).

37a Macready's Prospero appeared at the cell-entrance. Hytner's waved his hand in a gesture that indicated Miranda's disobedience was of no consequence, much to the amusement of the audience (CD).

37b–9a Cut by Kean.

37b–48a Donnellan's Ferdinand used very mannered eighteenth-century gestures (CD).

40b–6a Cut by Macready, Kean, (?) Burton and Daly. Phelps cut 42b–6a, the retained lines making clear Ferdinand's previous 'bondage' to other women. Benthall's 1951 Miranda caught her breath at Ferdinand's admission.

46b Acting was so 'smothered' by spectacle in Tree's production that 'even so perfect a Ferdinand as . . . Gill, with his graceful poses and fervent tones, backed by so pretty, though so arch, a Miranda as . . . Kerin, [could] not win the love-scenes their due' (*ILN* 24/9/04).

So perfect and so peerless, are created
Of every creature's best.

MIRANDA   I do not know
One of my sex; no woman's face remember,
Save from my glass, mine own. Nor have I seen   50
More that I may call men than you, good friend,
And my dear father. How features are abroad
I am skilless of; but by my modesty,
The jewel in my dower, I would not wish
Any companion in the world but you;   55
Nor can imagination form a shape
Besides yourself, to like of. But I prattle
Something too wildly, and my father's precepts
I therein do forget.

FERDINAND   I am in my condition
A prince, Miranda; I do think a king –   60
I would not so – and would no more endure
This wooden slavery than to suffer
The flesh-fly blow my mouth. Hear my soul speak.
The very instant that I saw you, did
My heart fly to your service, there resides   65
To make me slave to it, and for your sake
Am I this patient log-man.

MIRANDA   Do you love me?

FERDINAND O heaven, O earth, bear witness to this sound,

48b–54a Cut by Macready, Kean and (?) Burton; Daly cut only 54a and Barton 50b–2a.
54b Macready's Miranda, Helena Faucit, 'seemed to second the gentlemanly love of Mr Anderson
[Ferdinand] with just such tones of trusting impulse as peculiarly fitted her' for the part
(Forster, 'Macready's Production', p. 71).
57 Phelps's Prospero entered.
57b–9a Cut by Garrick (1757). Tree's Prospero entered at 59a.
59b–63a Cut by Tree, Burton and Daly; Macready cut 61b–3a, and Kean 61–3. Purcarete's Prospero
removed the wine goblet from Miranda's hand at 60a, she being too preoccupied with
Ferdinand to notice (CD).
65b–7a Kean cut 65b–6a and Daly 66b–7a.
67b Donnellan's Miranda's 'transfiguring cry, "Do you love me?", had a startling intensity'
(McAfee, *ES* 28/11/88), her ardour far outweighing Ferdinand's (see note to 73a).
68 Purcarete's Ferdinand made 'his "O heavens!" [*sic*] a delightful Shakespearean equivalent of
"O gosh!" ' (Kingston, *T* 12/9/95).

And crown what I profess with kind event
If I speak true; if hollowly, invert   70
What best is boded me to mischief. I,
Beyond all limit of what else i' th' world,
Do love, prize, honour you.

MIRANDA   I am a fool
To weep at what I'm glad of.

PROSPERO   Fair encounter
Of two most rare affections. Heavens rain grace   75
On that which breeds between 'em.

FERDINAND   Wherefore weep you?

MIRANDA At mine unworthiness, that dare not offer
What I desire to give, and much less take
What I shall die to want. But this is trifling,
And all the more it seeks to hide itself   80
The bigger bulk it shows. Hence, bashful cunning,
And prompt me, plain and holy innocence.
I am your wife, if you will marry me;

69–71 Cut by Kean; Macready cut 70–1 and Daly 70b–1.

73a Donnellan's Ferdinand could not at first bring himself to say 'love': Miranda had to mouth the word at him four times or so before he could utter it (CD).

73b–6a Garrick (1757), Burton, Kean, Daly and Barton cut 74b–6a; Bridges-Adams (1926/30, 1934) cut 75b–6a, while Wright interpolated 74b–6a before 73b–4a. At some point, Ciulei's 'brave new lovers . . . gaze[d] into the red moat, seeing only their own faces. [Miranda] stir[red] the water, not seeing it as blood' (Sullivan, *LAT* typescript fax, 20/8/81). Hytner's Prospero was genuinely moved and pleased by Miranda's and Ferdinand's declarations of love (CD). At 76a, Benthall's 1952 Prospero exited; Purcarete's handed the wine goblet back to Miranda, again without her noticing (CD).

77b–83 Kean cut 77b–9a; Burton 78b–81a; Daly, Bridges-Adams (1926/30, 1934) and Ayrton 79b–81a; Hack 80–2.
     Miranda's boldness at 81b seems to have alarmed Tree's Ferdinand: he took a step back. Daniels's Miranda kissed Ferdinand on the cheek after 'innocence' and spoke 'I am your wife' in a pleased tone; then she paused and continued the next clause uncertainly (archive video). Really suggesting a fifteen-year-old, 'when [Krige] tells Ferdinand "I am your wife", she is only acting out what she has read in a book' (Young, *FT* 14/9/83); however, when Miranda kissed Ferdinand, 'Prospero . . . is so agonised that he hides his face from the couple, like Adam from God. His child has become woman' (Gordon, *Sp* 9/83). When Hytner's Miranda offered herself as wife, Prospero made a worried gesture (CD).

> If not, I'll die your maid. To be your fellow
> You may deny me, but I'll be your servant   85
> Whether you will or no.
> FERDINAND   My mistress, dearest,
> And I thus humble ever.
> MIRANDA   My husband then?
> FERDINAND Aye, with a heart as willing
> As bondage e'er of freedom. Here's my hand.
> MIRANDA And mine, with my heart in't; and now farewell   90
> Till half an hour hence.
> FERDINAND   A thousand thousand.
> *Exeunt* [FERDINAND *and* MIRANDA *separately*]

84b–6a Cut by Hack.

86b–7a Ferdinand's 'thus humble' suggests an appropriate posture, with most directors having him kneel. Kean's Ferdinand had apparently kept working sporadically throughout the scene and now laid his logs down and knelt to Miranda. While Cole felt that Carlotta Leclerq and Miss Bufton 'were delightfully coupled as *Miranda* and *Ferdinand*' (*Life and Theatrical Times*, vol. II, p. 223), the *Athenaeum* was 'not so well pleased with the love-scenes . . . The propriety of representing [Ferdinand] by a female . . . is doubtful; – the real contrast of the sexes in this instance is decidedly wanting'; however, the reviewer conceded that 'The lady-lover . . . was graceful in her attitudes, and though deficient in force, was not unpleasing' (4/7/1857, p. 859). Tree's Miranda knelt first, at 85, Ferdinand mirroring her at 'humble ever' and Miranda raising him on 87b. Hytner's Ferdinand kissed Miranda on the lips at 'dearest', as Prospero smiled, genuinely rejoicing in their happiness (CD).

87b–9a Cut by Kean. Strehler's Miranda and Ferdinand chastely embraced each other, but Prospero, from his DS position, threw a stone which landed near them, causing them to break their embrace (video).

89a   Hall's 1974 Miranda broke to Ferdinand and knelt; then Ferdinand offered her his hand. Williams's 1978 Ferdinand held out his hand and, presumably noticing grime, brushed it off before again offering his hand to Miranda, who laughed.

Because Hytner's Ferdinand had worked so hard during this scene, his link with Ariel and Caliban was very clear as he spoke the words. Similarly, Donnellan's Ferdinand pointed to Ariel as he spoke, presumably indicating his own desire to be rid of the bondage of log-carrying (see note to 3.1.0sd); however, the gesture had an added resonance for the audience, who saw the enslaved spirit where Ferdinand saw only enslaving logs (CD).

90a   At 'in't', Daniels's Miranda kissed Ferdinand twice, first briefly and then at greater length; Prospero crossed to SL of the mast. Miller's 1988 lovers held a long silence during which they remained kneeling and holding hands.

90b–1   Cut by Tree. Hack cut 91b.

PROSPERO So glad of this as they I cannot be,
          Who are surprised with all; but my rejoicing
          At nothing can be more. I'll to my book,
          For yet ere supper-time must I perform   95
          Much business appertaining.   *Exit*

91sd Kean's Ferdinand, still kneeling, kissed Miranda's hand and exited, gazing after Miranda as
      he did so. As Prospero did not appear in this scene, his final speech was cut, and the action
      moved straight into 3.2.
          According to Daly's printed pb, after Ferdinand and Miranda exited, Prospero summoned
      Ariel and the scene then went straight into Shakespeare's 4.1., starting at 165b; however, as
      Shattuck notes, pencilled additions by Miss Hoswell, who played Iris, show further revisions
      to the text. Here, she writes 'song' and 'curtain' before Prospero calls Ariel, indicating that the
      lovers' exit marked the end of Daly's Act 2; the interval followed. The New York Public Library
      pb elucidates that Ariel performed 'Where the bee sucks' and that there was another dance
      of attendant spirits (Nilan, ' "The Tempest" ', p. 116).
          Daniels's Ferdinand paused after 'A thousand'; once he had spoken the second 'thou-
      sand', he and Miranda stood. Then Miranda piled the logs into his arms, kissed him over
      them and exited USR, while Ferdinand exited through the L proscenium. In one view,
      Miranda was 'a little innocent learning fast, and there's a nice touch when she suddenly
      realizes that Ferdinand . . . will be her slave and makes him carry the firewood' (Norah
      Lewis, *BEM* 12/8/82). In another, 'the young lover pair [made] the centrepiece of the play
      with the wonderment of sudden self-revelation and maturity in . . . Krige's lovely virginal girl
      and . . . Maloney's handsome, honest Ferdinand' (Pratt, *YP* 12/8/82).
  92 Benthall's 1951 Prospero came out from the niche he had entered at 31b; in 1952, he appeared
      at the cell door.
          Daniels's Prospero broke DS for his speech. In one view he showed 'a quite moving kindly
      contentment in his acceptance of the love of Ferdinand for his daughter', while in another he
      was able 'to overcome his possessiveness' (respectively, Pratt, *YP* 12/8/82; *SLP* 30/9/83).
92–6 (end of scene) Cut by Garrick (1757), Kean, Daly and Ashwell. Tree cut 95–6, his Prospero exiting
      on 'I'll to my book' (94).
 96sd According to the printed pb, Daly's Prospero did not exit here, as the text was so rearranged
      that the latter part of Act 4, interpolated into 3.2, followed straight on from Miranda and
      Ferdinand's exit at 91sd; however, see note to 91sd for revisions made during rehearsal and
      note to 4.1.165b–93sd for a further description of the printed text.
          Following Prospero's exit at 94, Tree's 'lovers kiss[ed] for the first time. They walk[ed]
      slowly up[stage] and look[ed] out to sea. A silence [fell]; the light [began] to fade. Miranda's
      head [fell] on Ferdinand's shoulder, sweet music [was] heard, and the scene fade[d] out'

(printed sd). The music, probably Sullivan's, covered the scene change into Tree's Act 2, scene 4, which was not Shakespeare's 3.2 but 3.3.

Since Benthall transposed 3.2 and 3.3, as this scene ended cries of 'Ferdinand', 'My son', 'My lord', etc. could be heard off-stage.

Purcarete's Miranda did not exit but was wrapped up by Prospero, as she had been at 1.2.407 before seeing Ferdinand for the first time (CD).

Brook (1957) and Hall (1974) placed the interval here.

ACT 3   SCENE 2

Enter CALIBAN, STEPHANO *and* TRINCULO

STEPHANO Tell not me. When the butt is out we will drink water,
not a drop before; therefore bear up, and board 'em. Servant
monster, drink to me.

TRINCULO Servant monster? The folly of this island! They say
there's but five upon this isle; we are three of them – if th' other   5
two be brained like us, the state totters.

3.2   Cut by Dryden/Davenant, Shadwell and Garrick (1756); some elements of the scene remain
in 1667 and 1674 in Caliban's desire to lick Stephano's shoe and in Ariel's tricking of the
sailors, substituting water for their wine.

    Kemble set the scene on 'An open part of the Island', Phelps on 'a rough sea shore' in the
second groove, and Tree at 'The Cliffs', painted by W. T. Helmsley.

    In Daly's printed text, this scene, with interpolations from Act 4 (see note to
4.1.165b–93sd), ended Act 2. However, Hoswell's pencilled-in changes indicate that in fact
Act 2 ended with the previous scene between Miranda and Ferdinand (3.1), rounded off with
a song. Act 3, in both the printed text and Hoswell's rehearsal copy, began with Shakespeare's 3.3 (the banquet scene); in the printed text, this was immediately followed by the
masque scene (the first part of 4.1), while in the revised version, the frippery scene (3.2 with
4.1 interpolations), intervened between the banquet and the masque. Both Tree and Benthall
transposed 3.2 and 3.3; Shakespeare's 3.2 became Tree's Act 3, Scene 1, and Benthall's first
scene after the interval.

osd   The characters are sometimes discovered. Tree's Caliban sat 'on the shore listening to sweet
music in the air, and weaving a wreath of flowers wherewith to crown his his new-found
master' (printed sd); he then put the wreath on his own head and looked at his reflection in
the pool. Stephano and Trinculo were heard off-stage singing 'Flout 'em and scout 'em'
before entering. Bridges-Adams's 1934 trio were sprawled out on the ground before Caliban
woke, sat up, crawled over to a bowl of water and drank from it; Stephano then got up onto
his knees, pulled Caliban away from the bowl and spoke his first line. Benthall's 1951
Stephano and Caliban were asleep, sitting against the butt of wine, as Trinculo rose hiccup-
ping and giggling; when Trinculo went to steal some wine, Stephano woke, snoring.

    Donnellan's trio appeared in front of a red curtain, with Caliban now a part of Trinculo and
Stephano's stand-up comedy/clown act: he wore the same sparkly hat, bow-tie and vest with
patches as they. Caliban was very excited at his inclusion, coming up to members of the
audience and pointing to his name on the program (CD). Their costumes comprised

STEPHANO Drink, servant monster, when I bid thee; thy eyes are
almost set in thy head.
TRINCULO Where should they be set else? He were a brave monster
indeed if they were set in his tail.   10
STEPHANO My man-monster hath drowned his tongue in sack. For
my part, the sea cannot drown me – I swam, ere I could recover
the shore, five and thirty leagues off and on. By this light, thou
shalt be my lieutenant, monster, or my standard.

'sequinned bowlers and bow-ties, gaudily patched trousers and baseball boots' (Hutcheon,
Tr 9/12/88). Mendes's trio re-entered in the basket, Caliban now wearing a sign saying
'monster' around his neck and an open shirt; he also had a moustache and eyebrows painted
on his face and wore a steward's jacket like Stephano's (CD and programme photo).
Alexander's Stephano sat on a 'throne' formed from three crates full of bottles; Caliban was
catatonic until spoken to at 7 (CD). Purcarete's Stephano sported clothes-pegs; Caliban, who
came on atop Trinculo's shoulders, imitated Stephano's gestures (e.g., swimming motions).
They were accompanied by three Ariels (CD). Ciulei's Caliban, presumably reflecting his new
Neapolitan influence, 'down[ed] a bowl of spaghetti' at some point (Stelling, *MSN* 23/6/81).

1   Burge's Caliban carried a barrel of wine similar in size to his log in 2.2 (Foulkes, review,
     p. 16).
         Hytner's Stephano led Trinculo out of the SL trap by means of the latter's gloves, which
     were attached to his sleeves by long strings (Stratford pb). Stephano's hair was no longer
     tied in a pony-tail and his shirt was off, while Trinculo's mascara and lipstick were smudged
     and he no longer wore shoes (CD).

1–36 Cut by Daly, who interpolated much of 4.1.165b–93sd in its place (see note to 4.1.165b–93sd).

3   Tree's Caliban crowned Stephano with the wreath.

4–7 Kemble (1806) cut 'Servant-monster? . . . bid thee'.

6   Bogdanov's 1992 Trinculo hit his head on a tray at 'brained'.

8   Tree's Caliban 'pick[ed] up flowers' (Grove's pb notes).

9   Crozier's Caliban tried to speak, but finding no sound coming from his mouth, he sat.

10   Hytner's Stephano, who had been helping Caliban sit up, let him go (Stratford pb).

11–20 Kemble (1789) cut 16–18; Kemble (1806) 'For my part . . . light' (11–13); Tree 11–20; Barton
       17–18; Hack 'but . . . neither' (17–18). Benthall seems to have cut 'For my part . . . nothing
       neither' (11–18); however, the 1951 pb has a lot of pushing, falling and slapstick business
       pencilled in against the lines, including the note that Trinculo is 'hysterical'.

13   Kemble (1789), Macready and Kean made 'By this light' the end of the preceding sentence;
     Miller (1988) punctuated the sentence as 'on, by this light; thou'.
         Stephano's boast is often highlighted as absurd. Burton's Trinculo looked 'incredulous',
     while Iden Payne's interpolated 'What?', presumably sceptical rather than admiring. After

TRINCULO Your lieutenant if you list; he's no standard.   15
STEPHANO We'll not run, monsieur monster.
TRINCULO Nor go neither; but you'll lie like dogs, and yet say
    nothing neither.
STEPHANO Moon-calf, speak once in thy life, if thou beest a good
    moon-calf.   20
CALIBAN How does thy honour? Let me lick thy shoe. I'll not serve
    him, he is not valiant.
TRINCULO Thou liest, most ignorant monster; I am in case to jostle

    boasting about his feat, Bridges-Adams's 1926/30 Stephano paused and then modified his claim ('off and on'); his qualification was prompted by Trinculo's 'eh' in 1934 and 1935. Many subsequent directors have repeated the business. Thacker's Trinculo spoke 'five-and-thirty leagues' in unison with Stephano, as if he had heard the account many times; Stephano added 'off and on' in an off-hand, sheepish manner (CD).

14–15 Caliban often falls, provoking Trinculo's pun on 'standard'. Some, like Macready's, dropped without being touched, while others, like Burton's and Kean's, fell when clapped on the shoulder by Stephano.

17–18 Strehler's Trinculo 'kicked back sand in a manner resembling a dog covering its urine', showing Pulcinella's ' "kind of stupid wit or witty stupidity essentially gross and vulgar" ' (Kleber, 'Theatrical Continuities', p. 154, quoting Allardyce Nicoll).

19–36 Phelps's Caliban generally spoke his speeches 'either kneeling, sitting, or on all fours like a beast' (Phelps/Williams pb).

    21 Bridges-Adams's 1934 Caliban tried to lick Stephano's shoe while Trinculo vainly held out his own foot for attention; Ayrton's Trinculo offered his foot to Caliban, who growled, causing him to back away. Hytner's Stephano, who had helped Caliban sit up at 19, dropped him again and with difficulty started to remove his own shoe (Stratford pb); he finally removed it at 28. Donnellan's Caliban started to lick Stephano's shoe, which surprised and perturbed the latter; then, as Caliban and Trinculo started to have a genuine fight that ruined the 'act', the 'performers' went 'backstage'.

21–9 Benthall (1952) used a lot of slapstick business (rising, falling, running) between Caliban and Trinculo during these lines. At 'shoe' (21), Stephano leaned back, while Caliban kissed his foot over the barrel and Trinculo giggled. At 'constable' (24), Trinculo tried to get up, but fell backward; he then rose, picked up the bottle and crossed towards Caliban. At 'Lo' (27), Caliban picked up the barrel as if he were going to throw it at Trinculo and chased him DL. At 'Wilt' (27), Caliban fell below the UL arch, and Trinculo ran across the front of the stage to R of shell and sat. At 'Lo, lo' (29), Caliban tried to get up but fell, and Stephano went over to him.

23–4 Kemble (both versions) cut 'I am . . . constable'. Crozier's Caliban tried to rise when Trinculo called him a 'deboshed fish' (24); he finally managed to do so in time to deliver 27ff.

> a constable. Why, thou deboshed fish thou, was there ever man
> a coward, that hath drunk so much sack as I today? Wilt thou   25
> tell a monstrous lie, being but half a fish, and half a monster?

CALIBAN Lo, how he mocks me. Wilt thou let him, my lord?

TRINCULO 'Lord', quoth he? That a monster should be such a natural!

CALIBAN Lo, lo again! Bite him to death, I prithee.

STEPHANO Trinculo, keep a good tongue in your head. If you prove   30
  a mutineer, the next tree. The poor monster's my subject, and
  he shall not suffer indignity.

CALIBAN I thank my noble lord. Wilt thou be pleased to hearken
  once again to the suit I made to thee?

STEPHANO Marry will I. Kneel, and repeat it. I will stand, and so   35
  shall Trinculo.

Enter ARIEL *invisible*

---

25 Tree's Trinculo inadvertently kicked Stephano as he stepped over him. Caliban grabbed
Trinculo by the neck and pushed him away, then returned to Stephano, brushing the place
Trinculo had kicked and placing two flowers on him.

28 Tree's Trinculo picked up a flower and placed it on Stephano's foot, presumably mocking
Caliban's gesture at 25.

30 Stephano's approach to Trinculo was menacing in Macready's and Burton's productions;
however, Tree's Stephano simply rose onto his elbow to deliver the warning. Bogdanov's
1992 Stephano, who during the previous lines had struck Trinculo and tried to hit him with a
brick and a pole, hit him again (CD).

31–2 Macready's Stephano caressed Caliban on 'subject'. Thacker's very assertive Trinculo was
flabbergasted by Stephano's threat to hang him (CD).
   Directors often highlight the irony of Stephano's comment on Caliban. Williams's (1978)
spoke them as he 'pinn[ed Caliban] down by the back of the neck' (Warren, 'A Year of Comedies', p. 203), while Mendes's pushed the kneeling Caliban flat on the floor. Hytner's Caliban
kissed the sole of Stephano's shoe, which the latter happened to hold in front of his face.
Although Miller's 1988 Stephano made Caliban kiss his hand, Caliban then reciprocated, to
Stephano's disgust (CD).

35 Many Stephanos, like those of Kean, Bridges-Adams (1934), Ayrton and Iden Payne, needed
Trinculo's support to stand. Purcarete's Stephano and Trinculo both promptly collapsed,
whereas Miller's 1988 Trinculo made the V-sign, presumably at Stephano's order to stand
(CD).

36sd Kean's Ariel came up on a sloat through the trap behind a tree LC, where Trinculo was standing; the Kerr's light was again used.

CALIBAN As I told thee before, I am subject to a tyrant, a sorcerer,
    that by his cunning hath cheated me of the island.
ARIEL Thou liest.
CALIBAN   Thou liest, thou jesting monkey thou.
    I would my valiant master would destroy thee.   40
    I do not lie.
STEPHANO Trinculo, if you trouble him any more in's tale, by this
    hand, I will supplant some of your teeth.
TRINCULO Why, I said nothing.
STEPHANO Mum then, and no more. Proceed.   45
CALIBAN I say by sorcery he got this isle;
    From me he got it. If thy greatness will
    Revenge it on him – for I know thou dar'st,
    But this thing dare not –

    Hall's Ariel entered in a white parody of Trinculo's costume, which included a green and
white jester's hat (staging plans 6/12/73; costume list).

39 Many Ariels, like Phelps's, quickly run between Stephano and Trinculo to make it sound as if
Trinculo has spoken. Most Calibans become furious, but Tree's simply hit Trinculo lightly on
the head. Trinculo's puzzlement over the voice also leads to comic business: Burge's Trinculo
thought his 'familiar' was responsible for Ariel's interjections (Foulkes, review, p. 17). Similarly, Mendes's Trinculo held out his dummy but when Ariel provided its voice, he looked at it
in surprise in a 'wonderful perplexed moment' (CD and Taylor, *Ind* 13/8/93). Miller's 1988
Trinculo looked down his shirt, presumably feeling the voice had come from there, while
Paige's Ariel was 'an excellent mimic' who 'sounded *very* like Trinculo' (Carter, '*The Tempest*
at Salisbury Playhouse', p. 25). Strehler's Ariel, who like Trinculo and Stephano was partly a
commedia figure, entered into the clowns' routines with abandon (Warren, *TLS* 9/3/84),
while Alexander's Ariel was not playing a trick on Trinculo and Stephano at all: she vigorously
shouted 'Thou liest' at Caliban, intent on defending Prospero against a false accusation and
so unwittingly getting Trinculo into trouble (CD).

41 Thacker's Caliban spoke earnestly, not angrily (CD).

42–50 At 42, Macready's and Burton's Stephanos again approached Trinculo menacingly. During
42–5, Benthall's 1952 Ariel and Trinculo both rose, and Trinculo made a threatening gesture
behind Stephano's back; then Ariel and Trinculo sat down again. Williams's 1978 Stephano
slapped Trinculo at 45, while Purcarete's Stephano tried hard to be dignified during 42–50
(CD). Phelps's Caliban was on all fours at 47–9, 'occasionally getting to a sitting position'.
Bridges-Adams's 1934 Trinculo laughed at Caliban's high opinion of Stephano's courage (48).

49–54a Kemble (both versions) cut 'But this thing . . . my lord'. At 49, Kean's Trinculo turned contemptuously away from Caliban; at 53, Tree's Caliban caught some flies from Stephano's
head, which he killed and trampled.

STEPHANO That's most certain.   50

CALIBAN Thou shalt be lord of it, and I'll serve thee.

STEPHANO How now shall this be compassed? Canst thou bring me
   to the party?

CALIBAN Yea, yea, my lord, I'll yield him thee asleep,
   Where thou mayest knock a nail into his head.   55

ARIEL Thou liest, thou canst not.

CALIBAN What a pied ninny's this? Thou scurvy patch!
   I do beseech thy greatness give him blows,
   And take his bottle from him. When that's gone,
   He shall drink nought but brine, for I'll not show him   60
   Where the quick freshes are.

STEPHANO Trinculo, run into no further danger. Interrupt the
   monster one word further, and by this hand, I'll turn my mercy
   out o' doors, and make a stockfish of thee.

54b Phelps's Caliban 'chuckle[d] at the idea'. Kean had a lay figure of Ariel appear in the bush L,
   near which Trinculo was standing; it disappeared after Ariel's line (56).

55 Williams's 1978 Caliban, presumably demonstrating his plan, hit his head with Stephano's
  help.

56 Brook's 1990 Trinculo wanted to sit but was pulled to his feet by Ariel, who proceeded to
  speak and to point Trinculo's finger as if the latter were talking. At some point he made Trinculo hit Stephano, whereupon Trinculo pretended to be hitting a bee. Mendes's Trinculo was
  drinking when his dummy suddenly spoke, making Trinculo spit out his drink in amazement.
  Thacker's Ariel shook Trinculo's jester's stick; Trinculo was shocked, looking at it as if it had
  spoken (CD).

57 Daly cut 57a. Tree's Caliban advanced on Trinculo, threatened him with his hand, and turned
  back to Stephano, whereupon Ariel beat him with a lily; thinking Trinculo was to blame,
  Caliban then beat him. Miller's 1988 Caliban floored Trinculo when the two fought.

59a Daly interpolated 4.1.194–5 and 219–33 (to 'Be you quiet, monster' inclusive) after 59a;
  Trinculo probably spoke 233, since in the next line spoken (62) Stephano warns Trinculo not
  to interrupt Caliban again. Tree's Trinculo hugged his bottle, while Ninagawa's tried to empty
  it (CD).

59–61 Cut by Kemble (1806). Daly cut 59b–61. At 61, Barton's Stephano stepped on Trinculo's foot,
  while Williams's 1978 Stephano 'interrupt[ed]' Trinculo from hitting Caliban with a cup.

62 Tree's Ariel tickled Caliban's nose with the lily; assuming it was a fly, he tried to catch it. Iden
  Payne cut 'run into no further danger'.

64 Kean had another figure of Ariel work on from behind at R2E, which disappeared after Ariel
  spoke 67 from behind a transparent rock RC at back. Thacker's Stephano hit Trinculo's
  jester's stick; there were no real fisticuffs between them, as Trinculo got away (CD).

TRINCULO Why, what did I? I did nothing. I'll go farther off.   65
STEPHANO Didst thou not say he lied?
ARIEL Thou liest.
STEPHANO Do I so? Take thou that! As you like this, give me the
    lie another time.
TRINCULO I did not give the lie. Out o' your wits, and hearing too?   70
    A pox o' your bottle! This can sack and drinking do. A murrain
    on your monster, and the devil take your fingers!
CALIBAN Ha, ha, ha!
STEPHANO Now forward with your tale. Prithee stand further off.

65 Strehler's Trinculo was about to hit Stephano on the head with a bottle when Stephano yelled
    at him, making Trinculo change his mind and 'go farther off' (video).

68 Shakespeare's 'take thou that' indicates that Stephano does something abusive to Trinculo,
    but its nature must be determined by actors and directors. Garrick (1757) and Kemble (1789)
    had him beat Trinculo; Kemble (1806) had him strike him. Hall's 1974 Stephano thumped
    Trinculo in the stomach, causing him to double over, whereupon Stephano thumped him on
    the back. Williams's 1978 Stephano gave the bottle to Trinculo and then pulled his hair,
    whereas Hall's 1988 Stephano kneed him in the groin, making him fall to the ground.
    Daniels's Stephano kicked Trinculo's bottom twice, while Hytner's punched him in the eye
    (Stratford pb). Brook's 1990 Stephano threatened him with the stump of a tree, and Pur-
    carete's broke his bottle over Trinculo's head (CD). Donnellan's Stephano showed real
    menace, pulling a knife on Trinculo and generating a genuine sense of danger (CD).

68–72 Daly cut 70–2. Kemble (1806) and Burton had Trinculo preface 70 with 'You lie', thus giving
    Stephano the lie again; they and Kean also changed 'pox' to 'plague' (71). Tree interpolated
    'and that' after 'that!' (68) and cut 'As you like this . . . fingers!' (68–72).

70 In defending himself, Mendes's Trinculo threatened to use his dummy's removable head as a
    club (CD).

71 Daniels's Stephano took Trinculo's bottle away and kicked him again, whereas Miller's 1988
    Trinculo hit Stephano.

72 Hall's 1974 Stephano kicked Trinculo, whereas Williams's 1978 Trinculo bent Stephano's
    fingers, who retaliated by stamping on his foot; when Trinculo bent forward in pain, Ariel
    pinched his bottom. Daniels's Trinculo swung at Stephano, ineffectually hitting his head, and
    Stephano swung at Trinculo, ineffectually slapping him, before kicking him again (pb and
    archive video). When Hytner's Stephano turned for a moment to look at Caliban, Trinculo
    took the opportunity to slap him on the arm (Stratford pb).

73 Thacker's Caliban, who was dressed in strips of rags tied about his body, laughed at Trinculo
    while shaking his penis at him; it was clothed in its own ragged sheath (CD).

74 Tree's Stephano turned to Caliban, who rather curiously, given his enthusiasm for Trinculo's
    beating, shrank from him; Stephano then suddenly turned on Trinculo, who had followed

CALIBAN Beat him enough; after a little time   75
　　　　　I'll beat him too.
STEPHANO　　　　　　　　Stand farther. Come, proceed.
CALIBAN Why, as I told thee, 'tis a custom with him
　　　　　I' th' afternoon to sleep. There thou mayst brain him,
　　　　　Having first seized his books; or with a log
　　　　　Batter his skull, or paunch him with a stake,   80
　　　　　Or cut his wezand with thy knife. Remember
　　　　　First to possess his books; for without them
　　　　　He's but a sot, as I am, nor hath not
　　　　　One spirit to command - they all do hate him
　　　　　As rootedly as I. Burn but his books;   85
　　　　　He has brave ùtensils – for so he calls them –
　　　　　Which when he has a house, he'll deck withal.
　　　　　And that most deeply to consider, is

---

him C, making him stagger away fearfully. Williams's Ariel met Stephano and pulled his ear, making him look around in surprise.

75–6 Kemble (1806) cut 'Beat him . . . Stand farther.' Tree interpolated 75–6a after 73, which itself followed 68; Caliban spoke through Stephano's lines as the latter beat Trinculo, who howled with pain (Grove's pb notes). He also cut 'Stand farther. Come' from 76b, with Caliban again shrinking away from Stephano. Hack interpolated 75–6a after 72.

81–95 Kemble (1789) cut 'Remember . . . brave brood'; in 1806 the cut began at 85b, thus retaining references to Prospero's book-inspired power and to his spirits' hatred of him. Both versions omitted the plan for Miranda to 'become [Stephano's] bed'. Macready, Phelps, Kean, (?) Burton and Daly cut 84b–95, thus omitting reference to the spirits' hate. Tree cut 84b–5a, 86–7, and only 'become . . . warrant / And' from 94–5, retaining the comment on Miranda's ability to produce a 'brave brood' for Stephano. Barton cut 86–7 and Crozier 94–5. After speaking 94–5, Strehler's Caliban went to the USR corner of the platform and, facing US, retched three times (video).

84b–5a The face of Thacker's Ariel was impossible to read as Caliban averred that Prospero's spirits hate him: she appeared interested in the comment but gave nothing away. As the plot was hatched during the next lines, Prospero was asleep at his desk, the staging suggesting that his loss of consciousness allowed the conspiracy to happen (CD).

86–93a Alexander's Stephano was not really interested in usurping Prospero at this point, so Caliban began to search for ways to tempt him, his pauses indicating his grasping for possible incentives, such as Prospero's utensils and Miranda's beauty (CD).

88–95 Hytner's Caliban seemed to want to hold his crotch while talking about Miranda (CD).

The beauty of his daughter. He himself
Calls her a nonpareil. I never saw a woman   90
But only Sycorax my dam, and she;
But she as far surpasseth Sycorax
As great'st does least.
STEPHANO   Is it so brave a lass?
CALIBAN Ay, lord, she will become thy bed, I warrant,
And bring thee forth brave brood.   95
STEPHANO Monster, I will kill this man. His daughter and I will be
king and queen – save our graces! – and Trinculo and thyself
shall be viceroys. Dost thou like the plot, Trinculo?
TRINCULO Excellent.
STEPHANO Give me thy hand. I am sorry I beat thee. But while thou   100
liv'st, keep a good tongue in thy head.

89a Purcarete's Trinculo, still floored from Stephano's blow, sat up looking interested at the
mention of Miranda but promptly fell back again (CD).

93a Tree's Caliban indicated Stephano on 'great'st' and himself on 'least', whereupon he made a
low bow.

96–8 Cut by Kemble (both versions); Phelps cut 'his daughter . . . queen' (96–7).
Alexander's sozzled Stephano looked forward to being 'quing' and 'keen' with Miranda
(97): he realized it sounded odd, but could not think how to correct it (CD). Bridges-Adams's
Stephano kicked Trinculo before asking his question (98); Ayrton's Stephano kicked him
afterwards.

99 Kemble's 1789 Trinculo continued with his own proposition: 'Thou shalt be king and I will be
viceroy over thee.' His 1806 Trinculo cut the seeming agreement of 'Excellent' and substituted a version of the speech that Dryden/Davenant had assigned to Mustacho: 'Stephano,
hear me: I will speak for the people, because there are none on the island to speak for themselves. – Know then, we are all content that Stephano shall be king, on condition I may be
viceroy over him. Speak, good people, are you agreed? What, no man answer? Then, we may
take their silence for consent.'

100 The line clearly calls for a hand-shake, although some modern directors ignore the text to
make Stephano more of a bully. Williams's 1978 Stephano, for example, took Trinculo's hand
and then squeezed his fingers, the pain forcing Trinculo to stand. Hytner's Trinculo took
Stephano's hand, proffered with a pleasant tone of voice, but Stephano wrenched or
squeezed Trinculo's hand, causing him to bend over in pain (Stratford pb and CD). In contrast, Tree's Stephano and Trinculo not only shook hands but wept, and Alexander's
Stephano sincerely tried to make up with Trinculo. Brook's 1990 Ariel put Stephano's hand
out to shake Trinculo's, while Mendes's Trinculo did not take Stephano's proffered hand.

CALIBAN Within this half hour will he be asleep,
Wilt thou destroy him then?
STEPHANO   Ay, on mine honour.
ARIEL This will I tell my master.
CALIBAN Thou mak'st me merry. I am full of pleasure,   105
Let us be jocund. Will you troll the catch
You taught me but whilere?
STEPHANO At thy request monster, I will do reason, any reason.
Come on, Trinculo, let us sing.
Sings Flout 'em, and scout 'em, and scout 'em, and flout 'em.   110
Thought is free.

Purcarete's Trinculo shook his head 'no' at Stephano's 'Give me thy hand', whereupon
Stephano offered his apology, and the two hugged each other (CD).
100–4 Cut by Daly.
101 Miller's 1988 Stephano had Trinculo in a half-nelson hold.
102 Tree's Caliban joined in the weeping.
103b–5a Thacker's Caliban made a backward somersault, while Trinculo tap-danced (CD).
104 Kemble (both versions), Phelps, Ashwell, Brook (1957) and Daniels had Ariel exit; Hack,
changing the line to 'I must tell my master', had Ariel exit and immediately re-enter.
105 Purcarete's Caliban, who was holding a mallet and a large nail, banged his foot on the stage
five times (CD).
108 After Stephano's 'any reason', Tree interpolated the following lines:

TRINCULO Flout 'em and scout 'em?
STEPHANO Scout 'em and flout 'em.
TRINCULO No, no, flout 'em and scout 'em. Thought is free.
STEPHANO Come sing Trinculo.

Although left in the printed text, 109 was presumably cut.
109 After 'inviting' Trinculo to sing, Bridges-Adams's 1934 Stephano seized him by the scruff of
the neck. Donnellan's Stephano delivered these words as a command to Trinculo, who was
still upset (CD).
109sd Despite the singular sd, Trinculo and Stephano usually sing together, as 109 implies, with
Caliban often joining in.
110–11 Kemble (1789) cut 111. Williams (1978) repeated 111 three times, so that each of the trio could
sing it: Trinculo danced as Stephano sang first; then Caliban sang, followed by Trinculo,
whom Caliban stopped. Crozier's Stephano and Trinculo sat back to back, legs apart, beating
the time before beginning the song. Hall (1974) treated it as a round, with Stephano beginning alone; Stephano and Trinculo ended after three rounds, Caliban finishing alone, shouting. Daniels also treated the song as a round, with Stephano losing the tune after the first

CALIBAN That's not the tune.
> *Ariel plays the tune on a tabor and pipe*

STEPHANO What is this same?

TRINCULO This is the tune of our catch, played by the picture of
Nobody.   115

STEPHANO If thou beest a man, show thyself in thy likeness: if thou
beest a devil, take't as thou list.

'Flout 'em' and beginning again; after the third round Trinculo went 'operatic', whereupon
Caliban grabbed him, making him cower, but then simply said 'That's not the tune' (112) in a
patronizingly gentle tone (archive video). Hytner's version ran 'Flout 'em and scout 'em /
And scout 'em and flout 'em / Flout 'em and scout 'em / Thought is free', which Stephano and
Trinculo sang three times, Trinculo in harmony the final time. Lepage's trio sang 'a drunken
rap song on top of the lockers' (Donnelly, *MGa* 7/6/93).

Donnellan's trio came back onto the 'stage' for a reprise of 'Thought is free / Flout 'em and
scout 'em / No such thing as society / Freedom – available now in the foyer' (CD). Critics
were generally dismissive of these comments on contemporary political attitudes, complaining of 'low music-hall *shtick* with sequin patches, Stanley Holloway routines, and derisive
anti-Thatcher refrains', with the 'punchline . . . too obvious and insufficiently witty to justify
the departure from the text' (respectively, Ratcliffe, *O* 13/11/88; McAfee, *ES* 28/11/88).

112 Phelps had the music of tabor and pipe come from R, provoking Caliban's comment. Burton
and Daly cut it, while Tree's Caliban said it twice 'in deep pain' (printed sd). Hall's 1974
Caliban spoke as Ariel played the tune on a penny-whistle, while Hytner's was responding to
Trinculo's singing in harmony (CD). Hack changed the line to 'Listen' and then Ariel sang, as
elsewhere in the production, 'with oddly moving harshness' (pb and Lewsen, *T* 24/10/74).

112sd Cut by Phelps. In between playing, Burton's Ariel laughed, enjoying Stephano's and
Trinculo's embarrassment. Kean's pbs suggest Ariel was not present on stage as the tune was
played. Daly's Ariel played while 'a number of other spirits enter[ed] and torment[ed] the
men'. Hoswell's revised rehearsal copy has the scene ending as the three were driven off-
stage; the action continued with the beginning of 4.1. The printed text retained more of this
scene, as outlined in the notes below.

Not all Ariels play the tabor and pipe. Tree cued in a tabor and had Ariel whistling the time
at the back, whereas Strehler's Ariel gently sang and played a tambourine (video). One of
Purcarete's Ariels played a mouthbow (CD), Falls's played a violin (Pellowe, 'In Chicago',
p. 55) and Hytner's, wearing a throat microphone that gave an echoing effect, whistled the
tune, accompanied by 'woman's chords' (pbs and CD). Ninagawa's Ariel, hovering in the air,
beat real drumsticks on an imaginary drum; when it stopped, Caliban whistled to the air,
hoping it would begin again (CD). Whereas Ninagawa's effect was magical, Bridges-Adams's
(1919) was disconcerting: 'When Ariel enters . . . she bore a long golden trumpet. This Leah

TRINCULO O forgive me my sins!

STEPHANO He that dies pays all debts! I defy thee! Mercy upon us!

CALIBAN Art thou afeared?   120

STEPHANO No, monster, not I.

CALIBAN Be not afeared, the isle is full of noises,
         Sounds, and sweet airs, that give delight and hurt not.
         Sometimes a thousand twangling instruments
         Will hum about mine ears; and sometime voices,   125
         That if I then had waked after long sleep,
         Will make me sleep again; and then in dreaming,
         The clouds methought would open, and show riches

Hanman manipulated with skill; it really looked as if she were playing. Reed music, however, does not come from a brass instrument as a rule' (*SH* 15/8/19).

113–15   Cut by Daly.

118   Many Trinculos fall on their knees, while some run about in fear.

118–19   Strehler's Ariel, who had been gently singing, banged her tambourine loudly a few times, so frightening Trinculo and Stephano; afterwards, she again sang gently, causing Caliban to stretch out on the ground to luxuriate in the sound (video).

119   Many Stephanos fall to their knees after initial bravado. Burton's, for example, spoke 'I defy thee' (119) 'boastingly', at which the pipe and tabor sounded again and he fell to his knees in terror. Kean answered Stephano's defiance with a blast of wind instruments under-stage. Tree's Stephano struck at Ariel with his staff, whereupon Ariel touched his face with the lily, provoking 'Mercy upon us!' Benthall's 1952 Ariel motioned towards Stephano's knees just before he fell to them. Daly cut 'He that dies pays all debts'.

122–30   Kemble (1789) and Daly cut 124–30; Hack interpolated 123–30 at the end of the scene, after Ariel, Stephano and Trinculo had exited.

Baliol Holloway, playing Caliban for the first time in Leigh's production, 'spoke, not as one uttering a purple patch, but as one who looks up from his slime and sees the stars . . . [Caliban's] pleased mystification . . . at this point was beautifully done' (Ervine, uc 8?/11/26).

Strehler's Caliban lay USR for his speech (video). While he 'sensuously stretche[d] himself full length on the floor to enjoy the "sounds and sweet airs" of the island, Ariel delicately accompanie[d] them on a tabor, and the clowns [sat] slumped in a maudlin alcoholic stupor . . . a strange harmony [took] over the stage, from which the clowns [were] not excluded' (Warren, *TLS* 9/3/84). In contrast, Donnellan's ' "thousand twangling instruments" [were] so thunderous that the delicacy of [Caliban's] famous speech [became] a joke' (Keith Brown, *TLS* 2/12/88). The speech appeared to raise hidden fears in Stephano (CD).

Hay used 'black light effects [to] produce magically detached hands holding musical instruments' (Gore-Langton, 10/10/92).

> Ready to drop upon me, that when I waked
> I cried to dream again.   130

STEPHANO This will prove a brave kingdom to me, where I shall
have my music for nothing.

CALIBAN When Prospero is destroyed.

STEPHANO That shall be by and by: I remember the story.

TRINCULO The sound is going away; let's follow it, and after do our   135
work.

STEPHANO Lead, monster, we'll follow. I would I could see this
taborer, he lays it on.

TRINCULO Wilt come? I'll follow Stephano.

Exeunt

135–9 Cut by Daly, except for 'Lead, monster, we'll follow' (137).

138 Tree's Ariel led the three about the stage 'like a will-o'-the-wisp' and then flew above them still playing the tune; Caliban tried to dance and sing while Trinculo and Stephano watched him 'curiously' (printed sd). Hack changed 'taborer' to 'singer'.

139 Cut by Tree and Iden Payne. Kemble (1806), Burton, Kean and Miller (1988) gave Trinculo's 'Wilt come?' to Stephano; Burton's Trinculo answered timidly. Macready's Trinculo had screwed up his courage (presumably asking 'Wilt come?' with some bravado), but the music suddenly became louder, causing him to lose heart and sneak off after the others (Moore's notes in Burton pb).

139sd McVicker's Caliban sang 'The owl is abroad' after Trinculo and Stephano followed the music off-stage.

Daly's printed text repeats the music and resumes the dance of the spirits, who 'sing and annoy the drunkards and drive them out', marking the end of his Act 2.

Tree ended the scene with the characters still on stage; there followed a minute-and-a-half scene-change before Tree's 3.2, which was Shakespeare's 4.1. Similarly, because Benthall had transposed 3.3 and 3.2, the next scene to be played was 4.1.

After Hack's Ariel, Stephano and Trinculo exited, Caliban spoke 123–30, beginning his speech 'This isle is full of noises'; then he too exited.

Tipton's 'moments of spectacle' were 'touched by an element of menace. When the clowns attempt[ed] to follow Caliban across the raked platform at the back of the stage, it suddenly veer[ed] up, becoming a towering vertical wall that block[ed] their way – the single chair placed on its surface now pitched at a terrifying angle' (Shyer, 'Disenchanted', p. 64; Shyer does not clarify whether this moment occurred at the end of this scene or of 2.2, but it seems more probable here).

As Mendes's Caliban dragged out the wicker basket, he sensed Ariel; reaching out, however, he felt only air (CD).

ACT 3   SCENE 3

Enter ALONSO, SEBASTIAN, ANTONIO, GONZALO,
ADRIAN, FRANCISCO *and others*

GONZALO By'r lakin, I can go no further, sir,
    My old bones aches. Here's a maze trod indeed
    Through forth-rights and meanders. By your patience,
    I needs must rest me.
ALONSO   Old lord, I cannot blame thee,
    Who am myself attached with weariness   5
    To th' dulling of my spirits. Sit down, and rest.
    Even here I will put off my hope, and keep it
    No longer for my flatterer. He is drowned
    Whom thus we stray to find, and the sea mocks
    Our frustrate search on land. Well, let him go.   10
ANTONIO [*Drawing Sebastian aside*] I am right glad that he's so
    out of hope.
    Do not for one repulse forgo the purpose
    That you resolved t'effect.

3.3 Cut by Dryden/Davenant and Shadwell, with the following lines interpolated elsewhere:
  1b–10 (2–4a, 9b–10 cut in 1674), 12–13a (spoken hearteningly to Alonso), 18, 20a. Garrick
  (1756) cut the scene, but incorporated the vanishing banquet earlier in the opera (see note to
  2.1.117–316). Kemble treated the scene similarly to Garrick (1756) but retained many of
  Shakespeare's lines, particularly in the 1806 version. The scene marked the beginning of
  Daly's Act 3; Tree and Benthall transposed 3.2 and 3.3. Neville had the scene follow 2.2.
    Phelps's set was a foreign landscape with 'wings to match', containing at C a trick rock that
  changed into the banquet and then back into a rock; there was also a high box trap at C with
  rock masking (Phelps/Creswick pb). Burton similarly used a large trick tree, hinged about
  three feet from the ground so that the upper part fell on cue to form a table for the banquet.
osd Garrick (1757) cut Adrian. Strehler's nobles entered looking bedraggled (video). Purcarete
  had a cello-carrying Ariel lead in Alonso's empty wheelchair, which the lords crawled after;
  once they were ranged across the width of the stage, they sat down, DS FO (CD).
1–17 Cut by Kemble in 1789, with 7a and 8b–10a restored in 1806. Hack, opening the scene with
  13b–17, had Alonso and Gonzalo enter at 17, whereupon 1–13a were spoken and Sebastian
  repeated 'I say tonight'. Burton and Daly cut 2–3, Kean 2b–3a, 14b–17 and Macready 9–10;
  Barton re-assigned 2b–3a to Adrian.
4a Phelps's Gonzalo sank into Adrian's arms.

SEBASTIAN [*To Antonio*]   The next advantage
          Will we take throughly.
ANTONIO   Let it be tonight;
          For now they are oppressed with travail, they   15
          Will not, nor cannot use such vigilance
          As when they're fresh.
SEBASTIAN   I say tonight: no more.

Solemn and strange music, and [enter] PROSPERO *on the top, invisible*

ALONSO What harmony is this? my good friends, hark!
GONZALO Marvellous sweet music.

17sd and 19sd Although the Folio runs these sds together after 17a, 18–19 make clear that the music
          sounds before any of the shapes appear; the two halves of 20 seem to mark, respectively,
          their arrival and disappearance. Where Prospero stood is a matter of conjecture: although
          some scholars posit a music gallery above the upper stage gallery (see Orgel, p. 164, n. 17.1,
          and Sturgess, *Jacobean Private Theatre*, p. 91), none of the plays written for the Blackfriars
          refer to a third level above the stage and the upper gallery. Gurr suggests that the music-
          room was itself in the upper gallery and that *'on the top'*, which seems 'to refer to [a place]
          above the upper playing area . . . may have been the topmost spectators' galleries, or a
          place adjacent to the heavens or the huts – possibly even the trumpeter's place' (*Shake-
          spearean Stage*, pp. 147–8). Alternatively, since Prospero would not have been visible to
          many spectators from the latter positions, he may have stood in the music gallery or
          appeared looking down out of the roof-trap (private conversation with Gurr, 19/12/97). His
          entrance has often been cut (e.g., by Garrick (1757), Ayrton, Iden Payne) or delayed until the
          end of the scene (e.g., by Burton, Wright and Hack).
              The 'banquet' was originally a trick table, probably 'covered with a thick fringed cloth'
          (Adams, 'The Staging of *The Tempest*', p. 405), and has generated some spectacular stagings.
          Macready had 'several tabular columns[,] crowned with foliage and fruit, rise from beneath
          the stage'. Kean gradually transformed the scene from barrenness to luxuriant vegetation:
          the courtiers spoke 18–20a while trees shot up, flowered and bore fruit; waterfalls gushed
          from rocks; and springs bubbled beside them (see Cole, *Life and Theatrical Times*, vol. II,
          p. 221; Andersen, *Pictures of Travel*, p. 284; *TJ* 26/8/1857, p. 268). Brook (1957) had 'phantom
          feasts [drop] from the heavens' 'in glorious colours' (respectively, *P* 21/8/57; *NG* ?/12/57),
          while Mendes had spirits place dishes of food, bowls, beakers, pitchers and plates on an out-
          stretched cloth, which 'magically' supported them when an unseen table rose up underneath
          (CD). Recent directors have often opted for the greater simplicity of individual banquets for
          the lords: Hytner, for example, had shapes carry on six globes, each containing fruit and
          seafood (CD). Still others, like Brook (1990) and Thacker, have simply had the lords mime
          eating.

The shapes have themselves received spectacular treatment. Kean provided twelve naiads, twenty-four dryads, twelve satyrs (six of them dancing) and three or four boy satyrs to harmonize with the mythological harpy. Iden Payne's, with full-head masks, resembled some kind of amphibious creatures (pb and production photos), while Burge's, orange- and flame-coloured, had insect heads but no mouths or eyes (Foulkes, review, p. 18). Jamieson/Quayle's, 'whirl[ing] on like a group of windblown flowers', were 'writhing, somersaulting spirits who resemble[d] a bed of sea anaemones (respectively, Wardle, *T* 9/10/85; Coveney, *FT* 8/10/85). Most spectacular of all were Hall's 1974 '[Hieronymous Bosch-like] grotesques', 'an awesome retinue of spirits sprouting multiple heads, limbs, and genitalia' (respectively, Shulman, *ES*; Wardle, *T*, both 6/3/74). Besides the double-headed animal with 'crawling heads', 'Fat double-breasted lady', green lizard, 'half-man body' and two shapes with upside-down torsos and green shoes with toes attached, there were three shapes even more grotesque: one had extra arms sprouting from the shoulders and extra legs behind; another had the top half of a baby protruding from the chest and the bottom half from the back; the final one had twins sprouting from the chest (costume list). Noble's, less elaborately, were 'encased in sewn-up rectangles of purplish cloth', resembling an 'avant-garde advertisement for teabags' rather than spirits (Taylor, *Ind* 27/2/98).

Other directors have emphasized the shapes' otherness without making them grotesque. Although there are no details of Burton's costuming, his staging estranged the shapes, who responded to four chords: on the first they said 'you', on the second 'of this', on the third 'eat' and on the fourth 'we are your slaves'. Gestures accompanied the chords: during the first three the shapes held dishes up with both hands over their heads, and on the fourth they put them on a table, which had been formed by the falling tree. Although Hytner's wore grey balaclavas at Stratford and had blue face-masks and hands in London, he highlighted their similarity to Prospero, dressing them in the same contemporary brown baggy trousers, white shirts and wide belts; they made friendly but awkward gestures to the court, their social unease anticipating Prospero's in the play's final scene (CD).

Treatment of the shapes in recent productions has also emphasized cultural otherness. Alexander used four masked Indian dancers, an innovation that called attention to Birmingham's juxtaposition of different cultures (CD), while Wolfe had 'Bunraku puppets serve the banquet', the 'bamboo-wielding puppeteers imparting a semivoodoo, semibunraku tone to the island's spirits' (respectively, Karam, *T*; Lyons, *WSJ*, both 14/7/95). Thacker's native American-like Ariel and spirits approached the courtiers 'in the style of trusting islanders receiving a party of future colonists: a process that massively recharge[d] their subsequent descent into snarling, vindictive frenzy' (Wardle, *IndS* 2/7/95).

The banquet has sometimes been cut altogether, as by Bogdanov (1978; see Young, *FT*, and Billington, *G*, both 29/11/78). With only eight actors in the cast, Retallack (1981) was unable to stage it, but substituted for it a moment that took one critic's 'breath away': 'Ferdinand and Miranda [came on] in the likeness of two drowned ghosts to torment Alonso' (Wardle, *T* 25/2/83).

Enter several strange shapes, bringing in a banquet, and dance
about it with gentle actions of salutations, and inviting the King,
etc. to eat, they depart

ALONSO Give us kind keepers, heavens! What were these?   20
SEBASTIAN A living drollery! Now I will believe
   That there are unicorns; that in Arabia
   There is one tree, the phoenix' throne, one phoenix
   At this hour reigning there.
 ANTONIO   I'll believe both;
   And what does else want credit, come to me   25
   And I'll be sworn 'tis true. Travellers ne'er did lie,
   Though fools at home condemn 'em.
 GONZALO   If in Naples
   I should report this now, would they believe me?
   If I should say I saw such islanders –
   For certes, these are people of the island –   30
   Who though they are of monstrous shape, yet note
   Their manners are more gentle, kind, than of

18 McVicker added an invisible chorus of 'Dry thine eyes, which are o'erflowing', during which Ariel danced, waving a wand, while the banquet table appeared: the song's final line explained that 'Ceres' blessing – So is on you.'

19 Cut by Kemble in 1789 and restored in 1806, after which Ariel entered with three other spirits, sang 'Dry those eyes, which are o'erflowing', and made the banquet appear from the C trap by waving her wand.

20a Cut by Ashwell.

21–39 Cut by Kemble (both versions), Macready, Phelps and Kean; Macready and Kean interpolated 27b–8 elsewhere (see note to 42b–9a). Burton cut 21b–6a, (?) 29 and 34b–9. Bridges-Adams (1926/30 and 1934) cut 21b–7a, 29–39, and Tree 22b–7a, 30–9. Daly cut 21b–6a, transferring 26b–7a to Sebastian, and 27b–39. Garrick (1757), Ayrton, Iden Payne and Wright cut 34b–6a and 39b. Barton re-assigned 26b–7 to Francisco and cut 34b–9; Hack cut 29–39 and, since his shapes were portrayed by slide projections rather than by actors, changed 'living' (21) to 'strange'.

28 Daniels's shapes wheeled the banquet orb DS to C; reminding some reviewers of an astrolabe, the orb contained a Star of David surrounded by six candles, each candle set between the star's points (pb and archive video; see Coveney, *FT* 13/8/82, and Billington, *G* 12/8/82). The design's implications were clear from the programme's references to cabala, alchemy and astrology: there were quotations from Frances Yates and Elizabeth M. Butler, as well as reproductions of a John Dee portrait and an engraving of a 'Cabalist Alchemist'.

Our human generation you shall find
Many, nay almost any.
PROSPERO [*Aside*]   Honest lord,
Thou hast said well – for some of you there present   35
Are worse than devils.
ALONSO   I cannot too much muse,
Such shapes, such gesture, and such sound, expressing –
Although they want the use of tongue – a kind
Of excellent dumb discourse.
PROSPERO [*Aside*]   Praise in departing.
FRANCISCO They vanished strangely.
SEBASTIAN   No matter, since they   40
Have left their viands behind; for we have stomachs.
Wilt please you taste of what is here?
ALONSO   Not I.
GONZALO Faith, sir, you need not fear. When we were boys,
Who would believe that there were mountaineers,
Dewlapped like bulls, whose throats had hanging at 'em   45
Wallets of flesh? Or that there were such men
Whose heads stood in their breasts? Which now we find
Each putter-out of five for one will bring us
Good warrant of.
ALONSO   I will stand to, and feed

34a Burton's Gonzalo looked suspiciously at Antonio and Sebastian.

36a Purcarete had two Ariels carry in a large birthday cake with candles and set it on a round table at C, which four other Ariels had carried on (CD).

40a–2 After 40a, Garrick (1757) had thunder sound and two devils rise out of the stage, together with a decorated table. Both Kemble versions gave Francisco's words to Antonio and Sebastian's to Gonzalo; 41a was cut in 1789. Ashwell gave 40a to Adrian, her pb suggesting that Francisco's part was amalgamated with Adrian's during rehearsal. Barton gave 42a to Adrian; Hack cut 40–1.

42b–9a Cut by Macready, Burton, Kean, Daly, Tree, Bridges-Adams (1926/30, 1934), Iden Payne and Barton; Macready and Kean interpolated 27b–8 between 42a and 49b. Garrick (1757) and Phelps cut 43b–9a, and Kemble 43–9a (both versions), the latter making this substitution: 'Well, Sir, I will: / I am hungry. The devil may fright me, / But he shall not starve me.' Benthall cut 48–9a and assigned the rest of the speech to Antonio.

43 Purcarete's Gonzalo and Adrian/Francisco each took a piece of cake and began eating, while Antonio and Sebastian looked at it hungrily (CD).

Although my last; no matter, since I feel   50
The best is past. Brother, my lord the duke,
Stand to and do as we.

Thunder and lightning. Enter ARIEL, *like a harpy, claps his wings*
upon the table, and with a quaint device the banquet vanishes

ARIEL You are three men of sin, whom Destiny –
That hath to instrument this lower world,
And what is in't – the never-surfeited sea   55
Hath caused to belch up you. And on this island,
Where man doth not inhabit – you 'mongst men
Being most unfit to live – I have made you mad;

50b–2 Kemble (both versions) and Hack cut 51b–2; Barton cut 50b–1a.

52sd Ariel's original entrance was presumably a descent from the heavens. The wings of the
costume, which may have included 'a bird mask and claws', would have been, if 'reasonably
proportioned . . . some four feet long and two feet wide' (respectively, Sturgess, *Jacobean
Private Theatre*, p. 91, and Adams, 'The Staging of *The Tempest*', p. 409). The 'quaint device'
which made the banquet vanish will never be known for certain: Adams reasonably posits a
stage-hand hidden in the table who, when Ariel clapped his wings over it, removed a 'false
top' holding the food (p. 408).

   The Ariel-harpy has descended from the flies, ascended through a trap and, more prosaically, simply run on. Kean had 'most strange noises' fill the stage and 'a volcano [erupt] in
the distance' as the courtiers approached the banquet (respectively, *TJ* 26/8/1857, p. 268;
Ath 4/7/1857, p. 859); Ariel came up a trap through the C of the banquet flowers. Tree's
entered in black-out and, once on the table, switched on lights in her head-dress. At Stratford, a 'telescopic mushroom' ushered in Brook's 1957 Ariel, reminding J. C. Trewin, 'with
irrelevance, of Alice growing and shrinking' (respectively, *Lady* 29/8/57, and *ILN* 24/8/57);
Brook dispensed with it at DL. Mendes's Ariel burst up through the middle of the table in a
spectacular *coup de théâtre*, the white Mao suit he wore in place of his blue one covered with
blood and his fingers transformed into talons (CD); he reminded some reviewers of Banquo
(see Billen, *O* 17/7/94, and Tom Morris, *TO* 20/7/94). Noble's Ariel was 'thrillingly surreal',
hanging 'suspended . . . on huge red wings', 'like some dangerous angel breathing fire and
brimstone' (respectively, de Jongh, *ES* 26/2/98; John Gross, *STel* 1/3/98; de Jongh).

   As Mendes's costuming shows, some harpy costumes are more stylized than others:
Benthall (1952), for example, had Ariel wear a half-mask, from the top of which protruded
two long plumes, and insert her arms into extremely long feathery wings; the latter were
stylized, no wider at the top than at the bottom and with their edges snipped into starkly cut
plumes (photograph). In contrast, Hall's 1974 Ariel had 'powerful pinions', 'gnarled claws'

and prop faeces (props list; quotations from, respectively, Young, *FT*, and Wardle, *T*, both 6/3/74). Williams (1978) enclosed the Ariel-harpy 'within a circle, arms and legs out-stretched, after Leonardo's famous illustration of Vitruvius's "Proportions of the Human Figure"; but the historical link did not inhibit him from vividly ferocious cawing' (Warren, 'A Year of Comedies', pp. 202–3). Hytner's harpy, with 'huge, feathery, Icarus-like' wings, was a colourless white or grey, the only exception the slash of blood on his mouth; when he flew in, making the lords freeze, Prospero could be seen behind him, arms outstretched in a posture reminiscent of his first appearance, when he was revealed as conjuror of the storm (CD and Stratford pb; quotation from Koenig, *P* 9/6/89). Wolfe's harpy was 'pterodactyl-like', 'with scarlet-streaked wings and malevolent claws'; although the 'glowing' wings had an astonish-ing 'thirty-foot' span, the sight of her ascending a stepladder was 'disconcerting' (respec-tively, Sommers, *NSL* 12/7/95; Sterritt, *CSM* 13/7/95; Aileen Jacobson, *NYN* 12/7/95; Marc Raphael, *CM* 18–28/7/95; Johnson, *HC* 16/7/95).

Ariel does not always dress as a harpy or even appear at all: Kemble (both versions) cut the sd, making the table vanish with 'a strange noise' in 1789 and to 'sounds of discordant Instruments' in 1806; although the revision had three harpy-spirits descend on the table and vanish with it, 'amidst flames and groans' (Inchbald), Ariel was not one of them. Macready had Prospero enter instead, surrounded by red fire, while Williams/Brook's table 'overturn[ed] to reveal a giant spider': Ariel in the guise of 'a giant Queen Tarantula' (respec-tively, Wilson, *Sco* 4/4/63, and Higgins, *FT* 3/4/63; a programme photograph suggests that the spider was in fact a separate creature). Miller's 1970 staging was 'a true invocation to the-atrical magic': 'Instead of the apparition of the harpy and parade of spectral waiters in cornu-copian headgear . . . Ariel descend[ed] on a bare stage, slow-moving and dignified as ever in his black costume, while the courtiers stare[d] in amazement at a vision above the audience, stretch[ed] out their hands and [froze]' (Wardle, *T* 16/6/70). As they 'stare[d] transfixed at nothing we [could] see . . . simultaneously the right hands of all six dr[e]w white kerchiefs from their doublets to serve for napkins. This simultaneity [was] a moment of producer's magic infinitely more effective than the gaudiest spread of plaster peacock pies bright-lit the other side of gauze' (*P* 24/6/70).

If, unlike Miller, the director has provided an actual banquet, it can disappear in a number of ways. Hall's 1974 table had a solid rim and a middle cut into three sections; when Ariel flew in and landed on the table, he defecated on the food, making the middle tip it and the crock-ery into a box underneath the lid (staging plans 6/12/73). The bottoms of Hytner's individual banquet-globes were opaque and the tops see-through glass: as the lords tried to get at the food, the fruit inside suddenly flipped over, revealing in its place a little pile of sand (CD). Ninagawa simply had the lords freeze in a red light, whereupon the stage crew removed the food. Since Paige's lords only mimed eating, the banquet 'vanished' when each courtier 'was overturned' by the spirit behind him (Carter, *The Tempest* at Salisbury Playhouse', p. 26).

Courtiers have occasionally been able to taste and even to eat some of the banquet. Donnellan's Queen made Sebastian and Antonio eat first, Gonzalo having already tasted her food of his own accord; Ariel interrupted them after they had taken their first bite, but Adrian hungrily ate all three left-overs during the harpy speech (CD). Purcarete had a figure in a red leotard and a mask suddenly pop up through the cake, from which Gonzalo and Adrian/Francisco had already taken a piece; all through the ensuing accusations (53–82), the two stood DSR, enjoying their treat, unaware of what was going on behind them (CD).

53–82 Macready, Phelps and Daly assigned Ariel's speech to Prospero; Hack's Prospero spoke 77–82.

Garrick (1757) cut 54–5a. Kemble (1806) cut 58b–82 and condensed 53–8a, which were spoken by 'A Voice from below': 'You men of sin, whom destiny hath caus'd / The never-surfeited sea to cast up, / And on this isle, where man doth not inhabit, – / You amongst men being most unfit to live, – '; he capped them with the admonition to 'Remember Prospero', punctuated with thunder and lightning (pb and Inchbald). Macready cut 58b–60a, 61b–8a, 69a, 73–6, 77b–8a, altering 60b–1a to 'Behold the ministers of Fate.' Phelps cut 58b–60a, 61b–9 (except the final two words) and 73–8a. Kean cut 54–5a, 58b–60a, 61b–68a, 73–6, 77b–8a and 80–1a. Daly cut 58b–66a (except for 'You fools!' in 60), 69 ('For . . . that'), 73–6, 77b–8a and 79b–81a. Ashwell cut 71; Ayrton 58b–68a and 75b–82; Hack 60b–1a ('I . . . Fate') and 65b–6a; Bridges-Adams (1926/30, 1934) and Iden Payne 61b–6a; Barton and (?) Daniels 65b–6a; Wright 66b–8a.

Because Ariel addresses only Alonso, Antonio and Sebastian, the other lords are some-times removed from the action. Hack's Gonzalo exited as Ariel entered, as did Williams's (1978) Gonzalo, Adrian and Francisco. Alexander's Gonzalo and Adrian were unconscious.

53–109 (end of scene) Cut by Kemble (1789), who added the following material:

ALONSO   It is as I suspected – see, 'tis vanish'd! –
         Shall we always be haunted with these fiends? -
ANTONIO This isle's enchanted ground; for I have heard
         Swift voices flying by my ear, and groans
         Of ghosts lamenting.
ALONSO   Good Heav'n deliver me from this dire place,
         And all the after actions of my life
         Shall mark my penitence! Lead from this spot.

Before the courtiers could move, Furies entered and surrounded them; two of them sang the duet 'Where does the black fiend ambition reside?' and, after the chorus sang the final two lines, a general exit ended the scene (see note to 2.1.117–316).

Burton cut 53–69 (apart from a few words of 60–1 and 69), 73–6 and 79b–end, condens-ing the harpy's speech to 'You fools! Behold ministers of fate. You three', followed by 70–2 and 77–9a. Then the lights went down, and Prospero appeared above in coloured fire, accompanied by thunder, crashes, music and 'Discordant Noises of any and every kind'. The banquet sank, while demons entered up traps and from the sides with flash boxes, accompa-nied by fiery serpents. Flaps changed the set pieces and flats to a 'withered and blasted land-scape' which was 'still identified with the previous scene'; red fire lit all. The scene ended

And even with suchlike valour men hang and drown
Their proper selves.
　　　　　　[*The lords draw their swords*]
　　　　　　　　　　You fools! I and my fellows　　　　　　60
Are ministers of Fate. The elements
Of whom your swords are tempered may as well
Wound the loud winds, or with bemocked-at stabs
Kill the still-closing waters, as diminish
One dowl that's in my plume. My fellow ministers　　65
Are like invulnerable. If you could hurt,
Your swords are now too massy for your strengths,
And will not be uplifted. But remember –
For that's my business to you – that you three
From Milan did supplant good Prospero;　　　　　70
Exposed unto the sea – which hath requit it –
Him, and his innocent child; for which foul deed,
The powers, delaying, not forgetting, have
Incensed the seas and shores, yea, all the creatures
Against your peace. Thee of thy son, Alonso,　　75
They have bereft; and do pronounce by me

with a tableau of the mortals looking horror-stricken, with Ariel flying above waving the now-familiar intermittent light.

　　Tree cut 58b–60a, 65b–8a, 73d–6a ('have/Incensed . . . bereft; and do') and 78–109 (end of scene); he followed 77, his last line of the scene, with a crash of thunder and a black-out, during which Ariel exited and the table was lowered. When the lights came up again slowly, the courtiers were 'standing in amazement, gazing at vacancy' (printed sd), and the curtain lowered on Act 2.

60sd Ariel's subsequent lines indicate that some or all of the courtiers draw, or attempt to draw, their swords and perhaps try to stab him or his 'fellows'; however, they are charmed from doing so. Benthall's 1951 Antonio, Alonso and Sebastian, for example, rushed forward to strike Ariel at 65, but at 66a were unable to lift their swords and at 67 sank to the ground with the swords' weight. Thacker's lords were unable to hold up their swords; they themselves collapsed at 68a (CD).

60b Mendes had red streamers suddenly burst from Ariel's talons (CD).

63a Hytner's Antonio and Sebastian stopped their attacks at 'winds' and put their swords across their faces (Stratford pb).

70 Prospero's name has been punctuated by thunder (Bridges-Adams 1934) and by guilty reactions: Ayrton's Antonio dropped to his knees, and Hall's three lords (1974) cried out in anguish.

Ling'ring perdition – worse than any death
Can be at once – shall step by step attend
You, and your ways; whose wraths to guard you from –
Which here, in this most desolate isle, else falls   80
Upon your heads – is nothing but heart's sorrow,
And a clear life ensuing.

He vanishes in thunder; then, to soft music, enter the shapes
again, and dance, with mocks and mows, and [then depart]
carrying out the table

PROSPERO Bravely the figure of this harpy hast thou
Performed, my Ariel; a grace it had devouring.
Of my instruction hast thou nothing bated   85
In what thou hadst to say. So, with good life
And observation strange, my meaner ministers
Their several kinds have done. My high charms work,
And these, mine enemies, are all knit up
In their distractions. They now are in my power;   90

82sd The original Ariel probably flew out, winched up into the heavens from which he had
descended. Some directors focus on the mechanics of Ariel's exit: according to the
Phelps/Creswick pb, a fan with a demon painted on it was raised in front of the table so that
Ariel could get away, presumably down the trap, whereupon a double of Ariel ascended into
the flies and the fan disappeared. Others, like Hytner, emphasize the reactions and treatment of the guilty lords: in Stratford, as Alonso crawled towards a globe, Antonio rolled backwards and Sebastian moved towards the trap, shapes grabbed the latter two. In London,
however, three shapes held Sebastian, Alonso and Antonio as another three shapes stabbed
each in the chest with a red dart (pb and CD).
    After McVicker's Ariel vanished, a Demon Chorus sang 'Where does the black fiend ambi-
tion reside?', ending the act with a tableau.

83–93 Cut by Garrick (1757), Kemble (1806), Macready, Kean, Daly, Ayrton and Iden Payne;
however, Macready interpolated 83–91a later (see note to 4.1.257–61). Phelps cut 83–8a
(Williams pb; Creswick cuts more but is unclear). Bridges-Adams (1926/30, 1934) cut 83–8a,
91–3 and transposed 88b–90 and 94–102a, the only other lines retained from the rest of the
scene. Hack cut 86b–8a, 91–3. Benthall, Strehler, Williams (1978) and Purcarete transposed
Prospero's speech to the end of the scene; see notes to 109a and 109sd.
    Hall's three lords (1974) were frozen during Prospero's speech. Thacker's Prospero
walked among the courtiers, becoming excited as he looked at them; he left them at 93, thus
breaking the spell and allowing them to get up off the floor where they had collapsed at 68a.
The spirits, however, worked a subsequent charm on them (CD).

And in these fits I leave them, while I visit
Young Ferdinand, whom they suppose is drowned,
And his and mine loved darling.   [*Exit*]
GONZALO I' th' name of something holy, sir, why stand you
In this strange stare?
ALONSO   O, it is monstrous: monstrous!   95
Methought the billows spoke and told me of it,
The winds did sing it to me, and the thunder,
That deep and dreadful organ-pipe, pronounced
The name of Prosper. It did bass my trespass;
Therefore my son i' th' ooze is bedded; and   100
I'll seek him deeper than e'er plummet sounded,
And with him there lie mudded.   *Exit*
SEBASTIAN   But one fiend at a time,

93sd Although the Folio marks no exit for Prospero, he announces his intention to leave at 91. As
       Hytner's Prospero exited, Alonso, Antonio and Sebastian screamed and, in London, pulled
       the darts from their chests.
94–5a Cut by Kemble (1806), Kean and Benthall. Hack cut 94a and had Gonzalo re-enter. Williams
       (1978) also had Gonzalo, Adrian and Francisco re-enter.
94–109 Strehler placed this section immediately after Ariel's exit.
95b Benthall's Antonio and Sebastian stabbed at invisible shapes as Alonso spoke.
98a Kemble (1806) cut 'That . . . pipe'.
99 Directors often underline the mention of 'Prosper'. Bridges-Adams (1934) had thunder,
     Barton's Sebastian and Antonio let out a cry, and Hytner's Adrian and Francisco looked at
     Gonzalo (Stratford pb).
99b–109 (end of scene) Kemble (1806) cut the rest of the scene and again included the 1789 interpola-
       tions (see note to 53–109). The courtiers exited to thunder and lightning, pursued by the
       demons.
101 Bridges-Adams's Alonso (1934) rushed down the C steps into the orchestra pit, provoking
      cries of 'My lord, my lord' from everyone on stage.
102a Ayrton's Alonso collapsed on the ground.
102sd Daly's spirits re-entered to torment the courtiers.
102b–9 (end of scene) Cut by Bridges-Adams (1926/30, 1934). He seems to have retained 103a in 1934;
       either after that or after Alonso had rushed into the orchestra pit, the courtiers all turned and
       saw Prospero, at which they knelt in awe. Prospero spoke 88b–90, and the curtain fell for the
       interval.
       After 103b, Ayrton had shapes enter and seize the courtiers; he and Iden Payne cut the rest
       of the scene. Kean cut 104–6a; Macready and Daly 106b–9 (end of scene), with Daly retaining

I'll fight their legions o'er.

ANTONIO   I'll be thy second.

Exeunt [SEBASTIAN *and* ANTONIO]

GONZALO All three of them are desperate. Their great guilt,

Like poison given to work a great time after,   105

Now 'gins to bite the spirits. I do beseech you,

That are of suppler joints, follow them swiftly,

And hinder them from what this ecstasy

May now provoke them to.

ADRIAN   Follow, I pray you.

Exeunt omnes

109b. After 106a, Macready had spirits enter 'with torches blazing intermittingly, which they
wave[d] over the heads of Gonzalo, Alonzo, and the rest'; Ariel also 'passe[d] over the stage,
waving an intermitting light'. Hack cut 106b–7, since he omitted Adrian and Francisco.

109a In 1951, Benthall's Ariel appeared and made a bird-cry; Prospero then came out of the cave
to deliver 83–93, the other characters having exited. In 1952, Francisco exited and Adrian
stopped to speak to Gonzalo. There was a bird-cry; Gonzalo stopped talking in order to listen
to it and then exited, presumably with Adrian. Prospero came out of his cell to begin his
speech to Ariel; as he spoke Ariel's name (84a), the spirit appeared.

109b Cut by Garrick (1757) and Hack, who cut Adrian from the play.

109sd The Folio direction applies to Gonzalo, Adrian, Francisco and the unnamed 'others'.

After the courtiers' exit, Kean's shapes re-entered in wild confusion and then danced to
end the act. Daly's printed text has the action moving straight into 4.1; however, in Hoswell's
revised version, the frippery scene (3.2 with later parts of 4.1 interpolated) was interposed
between 3.3 and 4.1. See notes to 3.2 and to 4.1.165b–93.

Strehler, Williams (1978) and Purcarete interpolated 83–93 here. After Strehler's lords had
exited, Ariel walked on carrying her harpy costume; as Prospero congratulated her ('bravo'),
the two shook hands, the moment 'underlin[ing] the combination of pretence and theatrical
craft' (video and Billington, *G* 16/11/83). Similarly, Ninagawa's Prospero gave notes to his
'actors' at the end of the scene (CD).

ACT 4   SCENE 1

Enter PROSPERO, FERDINAND *and* MIRANDA

PROSPERO If I have too austerely punished you
　　　　　Your compensation makes amends, for I
　　　　　Have given you here a third of mine own life,
　　　　　Or that for which I live; who once again
　　　　　I tender to thy hand. All thy vexations　　　　　5
　　　　　Were but my trials of thy love, and thou

4.1 Cut by Dryden/Davenant and Shadwell, with 33–7a and 42b–9a (44–9a cut in 1674) interpolated elsewhere. Daly's printed text has this scene immediately follow the exit of the courtiers at the end of 3.3. Changes made during rehearsal put the frippery scene (3.2 with later parts of 4.1 interpolated) before it; Prospero's entrance with Miranda and Ferdinand followed the driving-off of Caliban, Stephano and Trinculo by spirits at 3.2.112sd. Benthall's transposition of 3.2 and 3.3 meant this scene followed 3.2.

　　Most illusionistic productions set the scene in or before Prospero's cell, study or cave. Many sets, such as Benson's (1891), were designed to accommodate the masque: his foreground showed 'precipitous rocks, painted on gauze', which disappeared when lit to reveal the vision (*SH* 24/4/1891).

osd The Folio text does not make clear how the three characters enter: is Miranda arm-in-arm with Ferdinand or with her father? Prospero indicates that he has already 'given' Miranda to Ferdinand (3); however, he gives her to him again at 5 and yet again at 14. Many productions incorporate the father's solemn handing-over of daughter to future husband at some point during the opening lines, while others take advantage of Prospero's repetition to suggest his hesitation and conflict at losing her. Some directors, like Barton, run the preceding scene straight into this one, with Prospero remaining on stage at the end of 3.3 and Miranda and Ferdinand entering to him. Kemble (both versions) cut Ferdinand and Miranda, beginning the scene at 139.

　　Strehler's Prospero led on Miranda and Ferdinand in a kind of ritual: they walked side by side and he in front of them, carrying a sheaf of wheat and lighted torch and making a complete circle of the stage. Paige's Miranda entered alone, 'sighed to herself, and began writing [Ferdinand's name] in the sand'; she looked very guilty and quickly wiped it out when Prospero and Ferdinand entered (Carter, '*The Tempest* at Salisbury Playhouse', p. 28). Bogdanov's 1992 Prospero gave Miranda the key to unlock the still chained Ferdinand; Thacker's Ferdinand was still busily shifting the spirit 'logs' (CD). Purcarete's Miranda entered in a wedding dress, while Ferdinand was still blindfolded and miming a heavy load (CD). Hytner's Ferdinand somersaulted out of the C trap and sat FO, while Prospero led

Hast strangely stood the test. Here, afore heaven,
I ratify this my rich gift. O Ferdinand,
Do not smile at me, that I boast her of,
For thou shalt find she will outstrip all praise   10
And make it halt behind her.
FERDINAND   I do believe it
Against an oracle.
PROSPERO Then, as my gift, and thine own acquisition
Worthily purchased, take my daughter. But

Miranda out by the hand; Donnellan's Ferdinand appeared henceforward in a morning-coat rather than his previous period costume (CD).

1–11a Bogdanov's 1992 Prospero twice held up his magic rod so that the lovers could not get to each other (CD).

1–14 Strehler's Prospero gave Miranda the wheat and the torch and, standing behind her, gently moved her to walk towards Ferdinand; when they met, she gave him the wheat. Later (*c.* 15–32), Prospero took the torch from Miranda and, stubbing its top on the floor, extinguished its flame; afterwards, he took half the wheat from Ferdinand and gave it to Miranda. The lovers then sat opposite one another on either side of the sand-circle (video).

Alexander's Prospero was reluctant to let Miranda go: he kept 'giving' her to Ferdinand and holding her back (CD). Lepage's Miranda 'silently exercise[d at the dancer's *barre* in front of the mirror], unaware that in a magical reality on the other side of the mirror, Prospero and Ferdinand calmly discuss[ed] giving her away in marriage' (Conlogue, *TGM*).

1–138sd Cut by Kemble (both versions).

3 Garrick, following Theobald in both versions, changed 'third' to 'thread', as did Macready, Burton, Kean and Daly.

4a Hytner's Prospero really emphasized 'that for which I live' (CD).

4b–8a Cut by Garrick (1756). Macready, Kean, Brook (1957) and Barton cut 4b–5a, in which Prospero 'again' tenders Miranda to Ferdinand.

7a When Retallack's female Prospero remarked on Ferdinand's 'having "strangely stood the test" of her persecution, it sound[ed] a bit like a citation at a school prizegiving' (Nightingale, *NS* 2/83).

8a Donnellan's Miranda appeared in a wedding gown; 'Prospero's dividedness over the love of Miranda and Ferdinand . . . [was] ludicrously overstressed in a strange ceremony, when, Dracula-pale and wearing a Victorian funeral director's outfit, he [gave her] away' (Taylor, *Ind* 26/11/88).

11a–12 Garrick (1756) cut 11a and interpolated Ferdinand's air 'Have you seen but a bright lilly [*sic*] grow' after 12.

13–14 Brook's 1957 Prospero blessed the pair with 'a most moving quality of tempered wisdom and controlled resignation' (*St* 15/8/57). Barton's Ferdinand drank from a bowl on 'daughter',

If thou dost break her virgin-knot before   15
All sanctimonious ceremonies may
With full and holy rite be ministered,
No sweet aspersion shall the heavens let fall
To make this contract grow; but barren hate,
Sour-eyed disdain and discord shall bestrew   20
The union of your bed with weeds so loathly
That you shall hate it both. Therefore take heed,
As Hymen's lamps shall light you.

FERDINAND   As I hope
For quiet days, fair issue, and long life,
With such love as 'tis now, the murkiest den,   25

presumably in some sort of ritual fashion. Mendes's lovers were about to kiss when
Prospero's 'but' (14b) stopped them (CD).

13–23a Unlike later revisers, Garrick (1756) retained Prospero's admonitions about chastity,
although he, Macready, Phelps and (?) Burton cut 19b–22a, his threats. In contrast, Kean,
McVicker and Tree cut 15–23a; Daly 15–17, 19–22. Ashwell and Bridges-Adams (1926/30,
1934) cut 13–23a, which included reference to Ferdinand's purchased 'acquisition' of
Miranda. Iden Payne's 1942 pb retains the 'virgin-knot' reference, although his previous productions appear to have cut it. Hack cut 23a.

   Some Prosperos direct their words to Ferdinand, and others to the couple. Since Daniels's
Miranda and Ferdinand were both 'so keen to make it in the sand that Prospero's restraining
paternal hand ha[d] some point', he changed the punctuation to 'hate it. Both, therefore,
take heed' (pb and Billington, *G* 12/8/82). Hytner's Prospero, not looking at the lovers, was
stern, even 'awe-inspiring', seeming 'to grow a foot and lose 20 years in age' (CD and
Renton, *Ind* 1/8/88). Paige's, in contrast, 'took Ferdinand to one side' so that Miranda was
'out of earshot', smiling 'sweetly' at her lover; Ferdinand gave 'a little smile' as he replied
(Carter, '*The Tempest* at Salisbury Playhouse', p. 28). Wolfe's Miranda, on the other hand,
was greatly embarrassed: with an ' "oh-Dad-stop-it" wincing', she held 'her face, her hands
and all but shouted . . . out "Daddy, don't!" ' (respectively, Lyons, *WSJ* 14/7/95; Barnes, *NYP*
12/7/95). In quite a different vein, Pip Simmons's Miranda was 'raped . . . by Antonio while
her father [was] holding forth on prenuptial restraint to Ferdinand (played by a girl)'
(Wardle, *T* 10/5/78).

23b–31a Garrick (1756) cut 23b–7a and 30–1a, substituting 'Nothing' as subject of the sentence.
Macready, Phelps and (?) Burton cut 25b–6a and 28b–31a. Kean and Tree cut 23b–31;
McVicker 23b–32a; Daly 25b–6a, 28, 30–1a. Benthall (1951) cut 25a, and Brook (1957)
25b–6a, 30–1a.

   Alexander's Ferdinand was annoyed by Prospero's injunction (CD); Barton's handed the
bowl back to Prospero at 31a.

The most oppòrtune place, the strong'st suggestion
Our worser genius can, shall never melt
Mine honour into lust, to take away
The edge of that day's celebration,
When I shall think or Phoebus' steeds are foundered,   30
Or night kept chained below.

PROSPERO   Fairly spoke.
Sit then, and talk with her, she is thine own.
What, Ariel! My industrious servant Ariel!

Enter ARIEL

ARIEL   What would my potent master? Here I am.
PROSPERO   Thou and thy meaner fellows your last service   35
Did worthily perform; and I must use you
In such another trick. Go bring the rabble –
O'er whom I give thee power – here, to this place.
Incite them to quick motion, for I must
Bestow upon the eyes of this young couple   40
Some vanity of mine art. It is my promise,
And they expect it from me.

31b   Hytner's Prospero regained his good humour (CD).

32a   Garrick (1756) cut 32a, but some Prosperos, like Williams's (1978), found 'much humour' in it after his admonitions: Hordern stressed 'talk', showing 'a world of Puritanism . . . in that emphasis' (respectively, Warren, 'A Year of Comedies', p. 203; Young, *FT* 3/5/78); Mendes followed suit (CD). Purcarete's Ferdinand was about to kiss Miranda when Prospero issued his instruction (CD).

33sd   Burton's female Ariel entered 'as boy fairy'.

34   Thacker's Ariel spoke 'potent master' somewhat sarcastically (CD).

35–9a   In general, Neville's Prospero treated Ariel 'as though the creature were his own quicksilver essence, that he [knew] must in the end escape back into the void' (Lambert, *ST* 3/6/62).

35–50sd   Mostly cut by Garrick (1756), who interpolated 5.1.7–8, 11b–12, 14, 15b–17a, 18–19a, 21–2, 24, 28b–30a in its place. Prospero concluded: 'Go, bring them, Ariel, hither; and let thy / Meaner fellows fetch the rabble [i.e., the mariners rather than the other spirits], o'er whom / I gave them pow'r to do it presently.' Ariel answered with the air 'Before you can say, come and go' (44–8 with an added verse).

37b–9a   Cut by Hack.

41a   Mendes's Prospero showed Ariel the pop-up toy theatre book he wanted enlarged for the masque (CD).

ARIEL   Presently?

PROSPERO Ay: with a twink.

ARIEL Before you can say 'come' and 'go',
                And breathe twice, and cry 'so, so',   45
                Each one tripping on his toe,
                Will be here with mop and mow.
                Do you love me master? No?

PROSPERO Dearly, my delicate Ariel. Do not approach
                Till thou dost hear me call.

ARIEL   Well; I conceive.   *Exit*   50

42b Thacker's Ariel, grouchy and rebellious, spoke as if Prospero were demanding much of her (CD).

44–8 McVicker's handling is unclear: Becks notes that he retained 44–8, but adds the following reading, cobbled together from 39b–41a and 57b, without indicating where they were placed: 'Come my Ariel; bring a corollary / I must bestow upon the eyes of / This young couple some vanity of mine art.' The masque of 'Ceres, Iris, Juno, Nymphs, & Foresters' followed. Daly cut 48, and Hack 46–7.

     Directors have treated these lines in varied ways: Garrick's 1757 Ariel sang them; Phelps's spoke them 'archly'; Daniels's, carried away, said 44–7 with great vehemence, pausing before 48 (archive video). Indeed, the final line has often received special emphasis, although of different types. For example, Macready's Ariel was exiting at 47 when she suddenly turned to Prospero and asked 48 with a 'pretty, winning contradiction of [her] own doubt' (Forster, 'Macready's Production', p. 71). Williams's (1978) paused after 'master?' and then answered his own question: '[W]ithout the second note of interrogation . . . the "No" becomes a grief-stricken realisation' (Levin, *ST* 7/5/78). Barton had music play during 44–7, which stopped as Ariel turned to deliver 48 (see note to 49–50). In Hytner's production, the silence following 48 further emphasized the poignancy of Ariel's delivery of it (CD); the relationship between servant and master was 'complex and increasingly interesting: when Ariel asks . . . "Do you love me, master?", Prospero is for once perplexed, his duties in the happiness of his creations has [*sic*] not occurred to him' (Renton, *Ind* 1/8/88). Mendes's Ariel demanded 'Do you love *me*' and then paused before adding 'master?', finally asking 'no?' in a small voice, while Purcarete's Ariels all went limp as they asked 'no?' (CD). Wolfe's sensual Ariel laid her head on Prospero's shoulder 'for a moment' as she asked 'Do you love me?' (Jefferson, *NYT* 16/7/95), whereas Noble's Prospero reached for Ariel and 'violently recoil[ed] when they ma[d]e contact' (Edwardes, *TO* 4/3/98).

49–50 Garrick (1757) cut 50b; Daly 49–50; Tree 49b–50a, substituting 58b in its place; Bridges-Adams (1926/30, 1934) 49b–50. Many Ariels, like Macready's, Kean's and Burton's, spoke 50b from off-stage; Burton's Prospero did not raise his voice even though Ariel was distant, so 'convey[ing] the idea that the latter is conscious of his thoughts rather than his words'.

PROSPERO Look thou be true! Do not give dalliance
    Too much the rein. The strongest oaths are straw
    To th' fire i' th' blood. Be more abstemious,
    Or else good night your vow.
FERDINAND   I warrant you, sir,
    The white cold virgin snow upon my heart   55
    Abates the ardour of my liver.

Barton, in only cutting Prospero's instruction to Ariel at 49b–50a, made the exchange focus entirely on their relationship. Indeed, some reviewers found it the production's 'key-moment' or 'crux', but were troubled by what they saw as the homoerotic implications of such an 'ambiguous and unclarified attachment', especially given Ariel's long pony-tail, high-pitched singing and nakedness, as well as the use of male spirits to play the goddesses (respectively, Hobson, *ST* 18/10/70; Knapp, *TES* 23/10/70; Knapp). For Higgins (*T* 17/10/70), however, the exchange encapsulated the 'humanity' of Richardson's Prospero: 'The potential prig and bully is a man who can feel loss and most particularly the loss of Ariel. "Do you love me, Master? No? Dearly, my delicate Ariel." For the first time the voice hesitates and breaks. A few moments later Prospero stretches out to take his spirit's hand and finds only air.'

The responses of other Prosperos have varied greatly: Garrick's (1757), changing 'Dearly' to 'Why', seemed noncommittal; Williams's (1978) made it 'almost a brush-off' (Young, *FT* 3/5/78); Daniels's showed deep feeling (Shrimpton, 'Shakespeare Performances', p. 154); Mendes's was surprised (CD).

51–4a Cut by Kean, Tree, Iden Payne and Bridges-Adams (1926/30, 1934). Macready and Phelps cut 52b–3, Burton and Daly 52b–4a. When Retallack's Ferdinand was caught 'necking with Miranda', Prospero spoke 'Milton's "sage and serious doctrine of virginity" speech from Comus . . . as a homily . . . to the lubricious' pair (respectively, Nightingale, *NS* 2/83; Billington, *G* 2/83).

As with Retallack, Prospero's speech is sometimes prompted by Miranda and Ferdinand's behaviour: Benthall's couple laughed (1951), Bogdanov's kissed (1992), Paige's held hands (Carter, '*The Tempest* at Salisbury Playhouse', pp. 28–9). Hack's Ferdinand more provocatively showed 'a youthful impatience with the old man's strictures and a healthy desire for the flesh and the fleshpots' (*CET* 23/10/74), while Ciulei's Miranda and Ferdinand were likewise 'uncontainably erotic young lovers' (Rich, *NYT* 4/7/81).

54b–8 Kean, Tree (interpolating 58b earlier), Iden Payne and Bridges-Adams (1926/30, 1934) cut 54b–8. Burton and Daly cut 54b–6a; Macready 55–6a; Phelps and Brook (1957) 55–6; Garrick (1757) and Hack 57–8; and Daly 57b–8a.

Hytner's Prospero greeted Ferdinand's protestations 'with a deeply cynical "Well" as if he has heard that one before' (Billington, *G* 29/7/88); his delivery was extremely funny (CD).

56a–261 (end of scene) Garrick (1756) followed 56a with Miranda's air 'Hope waits upon the flow'ry prime' and cut the rest of Shakespeare's scene.

PROSPERO   Well.
  Now come, my Ariel – bring a corollary,
  Rather than want a spirit; appear, and pertly.
                    Soft music
  No tongue! All eyes! Be silent!

                    Enter IRIS

59 Garrick (1757) 'judiciously made [the masque] half as short again as the original' (Francis
    Gentleman, Bell's edition, p. 47), changing it considerably. Juno entered first and sang a
    recitative:

      Hither, Hymen, speed your way,
      Celebrate this happy day,
      Hither, Ceres, haste away,
      Celebrate this happy day:
      With blithsome look, and jocund mien,
      Come, and tread the short grass green,
      Leave behind your grief and care,
      Come, and bless this happy pair.

    Hymen and Ceres then entered, Hymen singing 106–9 (changing 'Juno' to 'Hymen' in 109),
    Ceres 110–13, and both 106–9 again. A duet followed, with Ceres singing 'Scarcity and want
    shall shun ye [116] / Ceres sings her blessings on ye' and Hymen 'Hourly joys be still upon ye,
    / Hymen sings his blessings on ye' (108–9). Hymen then sang 134–5 as recitative, followed by
    another duet for Hymen and Ceres, which incorporated 136:

      Away, away, make holiday,
      Your rye-straw hats put on;
      Bring each his lass, and beat the grass,
      Let toil and care be gone.

    Nymphs and reapers then danced until Prospero started suddenly, saying 'Break off, break
    off' and 139ff.
        After 'silent', Hack's Prospero partially paraphrased 120b–2a: 'These are spirits, which by
    mine art / I have from their confines caused to enact / My present fancies / Sweet now,
    silence!'
        Hytner's Prospero lay back, remaining flat on his back for the ensuing masque, not
    needing (or bothering) to watch it (Stratford pb and CD); Ariel appeared on the SL arch,
    accompanied by a lightning flash, and remained there to present the masque (Stratford pb).
    Brook's 1990 Ariel cuddled up to Prospero, who stroked his head (CD). Bogdanov's 1992
    ' "No tongue" [became] not an injunction to silence but a prohibition on French-kissing'
    (Shuttleworth, *CiL* 3/12/92).

59sd Nineteenth-century productions staged the masque elaborately, concentrating on the vision's magic; Macready's goddesses, for instance, seemed to 'develop . . . from balmy clouds' (Forster, 'Macready's Production', p. 69). Such effects could be achieved relatively simply, as with Benson's 1891 foreground, painted on gauze so that it melted away when flooded by limelight (*BM* 25/4/1891). Kean took a very different approach, relying on complicated use of scenery, machinery and lighting. As the masque began, the gauzes, the inner cave R and the L2 wing piece worked off, as the front ground piece and third groove pieces sank. Once a large opaque cloud was off L, a panorama that had started earlier showed its view of Eleusis and the temple dedicated to Ceres. All lights went down three-quarters, apart from the back battens, which came up to show a rainbow. A child double of Iris was discovered, lit by blue limelight, floating on an iron bar in front of the panorama cloth. After a slight pause, a large cloud piece appeared, carrying Venus (another child double) and a lay figure Cupid in a dove-drawn car lit by yellow limelight; it worked in front of the Iris double, masking its removal and that of the iron bar. As the panorama moved from OP to PS, a large cloud piece moved over to OP; when it was off, Iris's cloud and rostrum were discovered behind it PS, with the real Iris standing on it (Ellis pb).

While twentieth-century productions have also paid attention to magical transformations and appearances, they have done so without Kean's elaborateness. For example, Ayrton 'changed [a smiling seascape] into a pleasant pastoral scene by lighting ingenuity' (*BM* 24/4/35), while Iden Payne had each of his 1938 goddesses rise from the ocean in a giant oyster shell. Neville's 'effects [were] restricted to a back-projected rainbow and drifting clouds' and to Juno's arrival 'in a swan-shaped chariot' (Roberts, *Tat* 20/6/62). Jones 'costumed [his other actors] in shades of ivory, gold and silver', so that 'during the Masque alone the stage burned for a moment into colour' (respectively, Bryden, *O* 21/7/68; Trewin, *ILN* 27/7/68). Some productions have concentrated their special effects on the goddesses themselves: Williams/Brook, for example, had the spirits emerge from 'ten foot high, hairy effigies' of the goddesses they portray (Alan Brien, *STel* 7/4/63); Ciulei similarly made his 'elegant . . . Gainsborough' goddesses into '10-foot giants' (respectively, Saville, *SDR* 9/81, and Hawley, *SPD* 12/6/81).

While some contemporary directors, like Daniels and Hall (1988), have treated the masque as 'a delightful mini-opera', staging it with 'glittering decorum' (Coveney, *FT*, respectively 13/8/82 and 20/5/88), Wolfe, on the other hand, turned it into a 'blissful celebration of the rites of marriage, . . . presented as a jubilant Brazilian carnival replete with campy, stilt-walking goddesses and a boogieing Prospero' who danced the samba (Brantley, *NYT* 12/7/95). Still others have treated it thematically. Miller, for example, made it an integral part of his colonialist reading in both 1970 and 1988, with the goddesses played by black singers. In 1988, dressed in a combination of African beads and straw farthingale skirts and with faces painted and half-masked, they sang baroque-style music, making a forceful point, both visibly and audibly, about the imposition of Western culture on native custom (CD). Since the 'theatrical ingenuity [of Warner's production] was principally concentrated self-reflexively upon the trickery and magic of Prospero's art', Ariel 'petulantly stage-managed a hilarious masque, set in a toy theatre with a mirror as its backdrop and Prospero as its exuberant impresario' (Stevenson, *TLS* 16/9/83). Mendes treated the masque similarly, although his production was not particularly self-reflexive: as Ariel shut the toy perspective-theatre book Prospero had given him, a life-size replica descended from the flies, its first curtain opening to reveal Iris and the second Ceres; in unison they made jerky, clockwork movements, as if they were puppets (CD).

Some directors have included the masque without embodying it; John Harrison, for example, showed 'four tall slats draped with some fluttering blue material while voices off intone[d] the lines about Ceres and dusky Dis' (*Tat* 4/75): 'Instead of the goddesses, we see . . . white billowing sails, lit . . . with alpine brightness . . . [T]he disembodying of Iris, and the bathing of the lovers in her reflected ethereal light, [gave] powerful meaning to her paean to chastity' (Lewsen, *T* 21/2/75). Many more directors, however, have solved its diffi-culties (now usually those of sustaining audience interest) by cutting it wholly or partially or by substituting something else for it. Strehler cut it: the video gives the impression that Miranda and Ferdinand, lying down in the sand-circle, watch something wonderful that the audience cannot see, whereas, in Milan, Ferdinand stood onstage while Prospero spoke the revels speech from the stalls (Warren, *TLS* 9/3/84; see note to 143–64). Donnellan mocked the masque in an extravaganza featuring eight gods and goddesses (CD), while Rylance made it 'a delicious parody of a Methodist chapel service, with the noble lords suddenly thrown into housewifely drag as the various goddesses of fruitfulness' (Rosalind Carne, *G* 24/6/91). Murray replaced it with 'a dumbshow luridly juxtaposing spiritual and sexual union' by means of 'four spirits disguised as two pairs of contemporary dancers demonstrat[ing] positions from the Kama Sutra' (respectively, Holdsworth, *TLS* 21–7/9/90; Albert Hunt, *G* 19/9/90). Hay's was 'a high-wire act', performed by 'Two chalked-up acrobats' who 'dance[d] an erotic body-sculpture' as Iris and Juno (respectively, Gore-Langton, 10/10/92; Milne, *STel* 11/10/92; St George, *FT* 5/10/92). Alexander substituted four Indian clas-sical dancers for the masque (CD), while Tipton replaced it with five Shakespeare sonnets: 78 spoken by Prospero, 23 by Miranda, 46 by Ferdinand and 43 and 8 by Ariel (programme); as they were spoken to background noises of 'cave drippings and bat squeaks', 'four spirits in white veils . . . move[d] around the darkened stage carrying geometric shapes of frosted glass that glow[ed] from within' (respectively, Canham; Shyer, 'Disenchanted', p. 28). Purcarete had the blue mid-stage curtain drawn across the SL half of the stage; standing outside it, Prospero simply announced 'Iris, Ceres, Juno' to Miranda and Ferdinand, who were sitting outside looking in. As the lovers watched the silent vision with rapt faces, at least half of the audience caught glimpses of what they saw: the skeleton that Caliban had carried in at the beginning of 2.1, the stage image itself encapsulating the 'baseless fabric' and 'insubstantial pageant' that Prospero later describes (151, 155; CD). Daniels, in a 1995 produc-tion for the American Repertory Theatre, Cambridge (not otherwise mentioned in this Com-mentary), transformed the goddesses 'into symbols of the continents Europe, the Americas and Africa', embodying Mexican philosopher José Vasconcelos's concept of 'The Cosmic or

IRIS Ceres, most bounteous lady, thy rich leas   60
      Of wheat, rye, barley, vetches, oats and peas;
      Thy turfy mountains, where live nibbling sheep,
      And flat meads thatched with stover, them to keep;
      Thy banks with pionèd, and twillèd brims
      Which spongy April at thy hest betrims   65
      To make cold nymphs chaste crowns; and thy broom-
          groves,
      Whose shadow the dismissèd bachelor loves,
      Being lass-lorn; thy pole-clipped vineyard,
      And thy sea-marge, sterile and rocky-hard,
      Where thou thyself dost air: the queen o'th'sky,   70
      Whose watery arch and messenger am I,

Fifth Race', the need 'to mix cultures and blood lines to create a new people' (Shawn René Graham, programme).

59sd–105 Cut by Garrick (1757) and Hack.

60–75 Sturgess, *Jacobean Private Theatre*, p. 93, suggests that in the original production the verse dialogue of 60–102 was spoken, 'perhaps in a kind of recitative, against the soft music' that begins to play at 58sd. Macready's, Phelps's and Daniels's Iris sang, while Burton's spoke; the latter's wore a headdress representing a basket of fruit and leaves, carried a baton, and had 'Very large wings of the gayest colours'.

    Macready, Kean and (?) Burton cut 62–3, with Kean also cutting 66b–70a. Phelps cut 66a, 67–8a; Daly 66–8; Iden Payne 68b–70a; and Daniels 69–70a. The song has had many of its words changed as well as cut: Macready adopted 'peonied and lilied' (64), Steevens's reading, and 'lass-born' (68); Kean used 'tilled' (64) and 'spungy' (65).

60–138sd Both Daly's printed text and Hoswell's rehearsal notes interpolate 124sd–33 and 106–17 after Prospero's 'revels' speech, but the rehearsal notes indicate a different arrangement: Iris and Ceres did not speak at all until after the 'revels' speech, after which they (not Juno and Ceres) 'whisper[ed] seriously' and presumably spoke 60 ff. as cut in the printed text. Juno then entered to sing 128–33, and the act ended with the Juno/Ceres song (106–17; Gurr, private correspondence). The call to the reapers and their dance with the nymphs, included in the printed text, were omitted.

    At Stratford, Hytner's goddesses were dressed in gray tunics, and their faces covered by either balaclavas or make-up; in London, they wore blue terry-cloth shifts, and their palms were painted blue. In both productions, the goddesses, who moved with stylized gestures reminiscent of modern dance, were accompanied (and sometimes mirrored) by children dressed in white and gold, who emerged from Prospero's cell and presented gifts to Miranda and Ferdinand. The gifts varied: for instance, in Stratford the Ceres child offered a casket of earth and a statue of a dolphin and in London grapes (CD).

Bids thee leave these, and with her sovereign grace,
JUNO *descends*
Here on this grass-plot, in this very place
To come and sport. Her peacocks fly amain.
Approach, rich Ceres, her to entertain.   75

Enter CERES

CERES Hail, many-coloured messenger, that ne'er
Dost disobey the wife of Jupiter;

72sd The Folio sd indicates that Juno appeared in her chariot suspended above the action.
Although many editors have assumed that the sd is misplaced, Jowett has convincingly
argued that '*descends* does not necessarily, or even usually, indicate a descent to the stage.
There was, on the contrary, what has been called "the convention of the floating deity",
whereby the deity would be expected, upon appearing from the heavens, to remain suspended in the air rather than to come down to the stage.' Both the Globe and the Blackfriars
would have allowed 'suspended free flight' for such descents ('New Created Creatures',
pp. 115–16).

75sd Ariel later says that s/he 'presented Ceres' (167), suggesting that the spirit plays this part in
Prospero's entertainment; many Ariels have doubled the roles, although some, like Brook's
(1957), simply led Ceres in.
      Phelps's staging of Ceres's entry changed greatly in the course of his production and
reflects nineteenth-century taste for spectacle. Originally, the panorama's 'dark clouding'
worked round to a bright one; Ariel then entered as Ceres, lit by a yellow light, in a car
formed by her emblems of golden corn sheaves (Phelps/Creswick pb). In 1849 the bright
sunlight clouding was accompanied by painted figures emblematic of spring who strewed
flowers in Ceres's way; however, this sd is crossed out and another added for 'Procession
of Ceres 1855': it included two satyrs with tabourines (*sic*), two swains with cymbals, two
boys with pipes, then Ceres's car drawn by a tiger; Ceres was seated in it with her
emblems of a sickle and a horn of plenty. The car was followed by two swains holding
something undecipherable and then by three pairs of youths holding a thyrsus
(Phelps/Williams pb).
      Kean's panorama moved from L to R; eight (originally twelve) attendants, dressed in
yellow and holding corn, entered L4E on a rostrum. When the OP bank piece had worked off
L, the panorama stopped and Ceres entered in a car L (Ellis pb). Even more lavishly,
McVicker's Ceres entered in a car drawn by 'glittering butterflies', and Juno 'amid filmy
clouds' in her car drawn by the 'sacred peacock'; a forest scene showed 'mermaids float[ing]
dreamily through running waters'. The masque included many dances, the most admired

Who, with thy saffron wings, upon my flowers
Diffusest honey drops, refreshing showers,
And with each end of thy blue bow dost crown   80
My bosky acres, and my unshrubbed down,
Rich scarf to my proud earth. Why hath thy queen
Summoned me hither, to this short-grazed green?

IRIS A contract of true love to celebrate,
And some donation freely to estate   85
On the blest lovers.

CERES   Tell me, heavenly bow,
If Venus or her son, as thou dost know,
Do now attend the queen? Since they did plot
The means that dusky Dis my daughter got,
Her and her blind boy's scandalled company   90
I have forsworn.

IRIS   Of her society
Be not afraid. I met her deity
Cutting the clouds towards Paphos, and her son
Dove-drawn with her. Here thought they to have done
Some wanton charm upon this man and maid,   95
Whose vows are, that no bed-right shall be paid
Till Hymen's torch be lighted – but in vain.
Mars's hot minion is returned again;
Her waspish-headed son has broke his arrows,

that of 'a throng of brightly costumed children and girls'. Juno and Ceres left their cars to 'dance in company with the sprites', after which Ariel had a dance solo (*Chicago Globe*, quoted in Nilan, ' "The Tempest" ', p. 114).

86a Kean's panorama worked off R, discovering Juno on her peacock throne C with Hymen above her, three Graces L, the Seasons R and water nymphs in water DS (Edmonds pb): 'the whole background was an airy place, filled with floating gods and goddesses. Juno drove by in her chariot drawn by peacocks whose tails glittered in the sunshine. The signs of the zodiac were displayed: the whole was a fantastic kaleidoscope . . . The entire background was in motion; landscape followed landscape, a moving panorama' (Andersen, *Pictures of Travel*, p. 284; the zodiac probably refers to the Twelve Hours that Ellis mentions, originally to be played by children and suspended on a revolving circle at the back).

86b–102 Macready, Phelps, Kean, (?) Burton, Daly, Tree and Bridges-Adams (1934) cut 86b–101a; Bridges-Adams (1930) 86b–102; Benthall and Brook (1957) 102b.

Swears he will shoot no more, but play with sparrows,   100
And be a boy right out. Highest queen of state,
Great Juno comes, I know her by her gait.
JUNO How does my bounteous sister? Go with me
          To bless this twain, that they may prosperous be,
          And honoured in their issue.   *They sing*   105

101b Benthall's Juno rose on a cloud-covered elevator, 'triumphantly throned', as 'garlands
      descended from the skies to frame her' (*NS* 7/7/51, and photos); the 'breath-taking tableau'
      incorporated 'a brilliant combination of stage and lighting effects and a medley of colour'
      (respectively, *St* 1951; *WA* 29/6/51).

102 Although the Folio gives no sd here, Ceres's preceding lines indicate that Juno's chariot
      would have descended to the stage at this point. As Jowett, 'New Created Creatures', p. 117,
      among others, explains, 'gait' does not suggest that Juno walks on stage, as the word has a
      wider meaning of 'carriage'.
          Macready interpolated 118–27 (minus 125), after which 'Juno descend[ed] slowly in a car
      drawn by peacocks'. Burton had Juno enter 'in a magnificent car driven by a Cupid [most
      inappropriately, if 87 ff. were not cut] and drawn by peacocks' with 'Flexible necks and
      working tails etc.'; Juno wore a rich radiated crown and carried a sceptre with a cuckoo on
      the top. Kean's Juno descended from her throne, while Daly's, unusually, came 'slowly forth
      from the moon'. In London, Brook's 1957 Juno descended 'from gilded clouds in a golden
      litter', which one reviewer found 'a particularly effective stroke of nineteenth-century theatri-
      cality'; another thought the 'Victorian-looking cloud attended by maidens in iridescent tinsel
      . . . tasteless and ludicrous' (respectively, Granger, *FT* 6/12/57; Geoffrey Tarran, *MA*
      23/12/57; *Sp* 13/12/57).
          Neville downplayed Juno's significance and made prominent the attendant who
      'herald[ed her arrival] . . . with the singing of Ben Jonson's "See the chariot here at hand" '
      (Trewin, *ILN* 16/6/62).
          Hall's 1974 Juno was of a piece with Iris, both appearing as 'overdressed swinging pop
      stars' (Shulman, *ES* 6/3/74): she wore an Elizabethan-style Brunel wig with a red front and
      black back, black PVC lace-up high-heeled boots, black net underskirt with padded hips, blue
      and gold taffeta skirt and bodice, cream ruff and head-dress of blue and yellow ostrich
      plumes (wig and costume lists). Her two attendants were similarly dressed and, like Juno,
      had 'glorious false breasts' 'so enormous that whilst they [were] on stage they absorb[ed] the
      attention to the exclusion of all else in fascinated horror' (respectively, staging plans 6/12/73;
      Hobson, *ST* 10/3/74). Prospero's ' "majestic vision" ' became 'a grotesque revel', greeted by
      audience laughter (Billington, *G* 6/3/74).

103–5 Jowett, 'New Created Creatures', p. 117, suggests 'Go with me' (103) invites 'Ceres to join

JUNO

Honour, riches, marriage-blessing,
Long continuance, and increasing,
Hourly joys be still upon you,
Juno sings her blessings on you.

[CERES]

Earth's increase, and foison plenty,   110
Barns and garners never empty,
Vines, with clust'ring bunches growing,
Plants, with goodly burden bowing;
Spring come to you at the farthest,
In the very end of harvest.   115
Scarcity and want shall shun you,
Ceres' blessing so is on you.

[Juno] in her throne' or chariot; they 'would then be raised to a halfway stance between the stage and the heavens for their song'.

    Cut in Daly's printed text and in Ellis's rehearsal workbook for Kean; however, Edmonds's final pb retains them (see note to 118–38sd).

105sd–17 The Folio is not precise about the song; a speech-heading indicates that Juno begins it, and the plural of 105sd that it was shared in some way. Sturgess posits that the first verse (106–9) was sung 'by Juno, the second [110–13] by Ceres, and the third [114–17] by the two in unison' (*Jacobean Private Theatre*, p. 93). Theobald's 1734 edition assigned 110–17 to Ceres, a change adopted by Macready and most directors since. However, Burton sometimes had Ceres sing alone, while Tree made the song a trio. Hack's Juno and Ceres sang together, while Daniels had Juno and Iris sing 106–9 and Ceres 110–17; while she sang 117, Juno sang 109 in harmony with her, followed by a trio that repeated 114–17. Mendes's Juno sang alone, followed by all three goddesses singing together and turning around like clockwork figures (CD). The song has gone through countless other permutations, including Phelps's use of an invisible chorus to repeat the last line.

    Kean interpolated 110–11 after 115, presumably to reflect a more 'logical' order of growing and harvest, and rather nonsensically changed 'Spring' to 'Rain' (114). Daly's printed text cut 106–17 here, interpolating it after 124sd–33 (themselves interpolated after 158a). Iden Payne cut 114–15, while Bridges-Adams (1926/30) cut the song entirely.

114–33sd Cut by Garrick (1757), who retained 116 as part of a duet between Ceres and Hymen; see note to 59.

   117 Tree gradually blacked out all the lights during the song's last notes; Juno and Ceres exited in the darkness, and naiads got into position behind the water-rows, ready to emerge at 127.

FERDINAND This is a most majestic vision, and
            Harmonious charmingly. May I be bold
            To think these spirits?
PROSPERO   Spirits, which by mine art   120
            I have from their confines called to enact
            My present fancies.
FERDINAND   Let me live here ever;
            So rare a wondered father, and a wife,
            Makes this place paradise.

Juno and Ceres whisper, and send Iris on employment

PROSPERO   Sweet now, silence.
            Juno and Ceres whisper seriously,   125
            There's something else to do. Hush, and be mute,

118–38sd Cut by Kean in Edmonds's final pb, with Ellis's rehearsal workbook showing a completely dif-
          ferent arrangement: 118–24b was followed by Juno (not Iris) singing 128–38 as recitative,
          after which nymphs and reapers entered and danced. After their exit, Juno sang 106–11 and
          Ceres 112–17. When the song finished, Prospero started suddenly and spoke 142b, making the
          spirits vanish; he then spoke 139 ff. Benthall transposed 118–27 so that they occurred during
          or at the end of the dance; Ferdinand rose to speak and was pulled back down by the 1951
          Miranda, who spoke 124b. Hack cut 118–38sd, but interpolated a version of 120b–2a after 59.
              Barton's goddesses belied Ferdinand's response at 118: 'it is impossible to understand
          what he means. Three nearly naked men, with what look like long straws in their hair, croon-
          ing in the half-dark? *Majestic*?' (Nightingale, *NS* 23/10/70). Thacker's Ferdinand moved
          himself along the floor, somewhat like Caliban, at 118–20a (CD).
      123 Whether to read 'wise' or 'wife' has been much debated. Many directors, such as Daly,
          Williams (1978), Daniels (archive video), Miller (1988) and Alexander (CD), adopted 'wise',
          while Hytner used 'wife' at Stratford and 'wise' in London.
    124sd The Folio prints this sd after 127, but Juno and Ceres must whisper and send Iris on her
          employment as Prospero describes the actions in 125–6a. Cut by Tree.
 124sd–45 Cut by Daly with 124sd–33 interpolated after 158a (printed edn); Hoswell's rehearsal notes
          indicate Ceres and Iris whispered together, as Juno had not yet entered: their opening
          speeches (60 ff.) were interpolated between 127 and 128; then Juno came on and sang
          128–33. The Juno/Ceres song (106–17) followed and then 134–8, although the latter was cut
          in rehearsal; see notes to 60–138sd and 143–64.
   124b–6a Tree cut 124b–5, Daniels 125 (but he had the described action occur at 117) and Phelps
          125–6a. Williams (1978) and Mendes gave Miranda 124b–5, with Mendes also giving her
          126a.

Or else our spell is marred.

IRIS You nymphs called naiads of the windring brooks,
    With your sedged crowns, and ever-harmless looks,
    Leave your crisp channels, and on this green land   130
    Answer your summons, Juno does command.
    Come, temperate nymphs, and help to celebrate
    A contract of true love. Be not too late.

Enter certain nymphs

127 Nineteenth-century nymphs and reapers occasioned further scenic display. Burton's 'cow-piece' was replaced by a grotto with working fountain and set waters containing four nymphs and two tritons blowing shells; the former's scarves were 'extended by the wind', an effect achieved by distending them with canes. Benson (1891) showed 'a fairy glade by moonlight. In the rear is a pool of apparently pellucid water, studded with bulrushes and water lilies. Out of this pool rise beautiful naiads, who are joined by reapers, and engage in a picturesque dance. The whole scene then disappears' (*BM* 25/4/1891).

    Brook (1957) introduced a Father Time figure in long draped robes and beard, holding an hour-glass (pb and photo).

    Mendes had the theatre's curtains open again, revealing Iris with three reapers dressed in smocks and straw hats, and holding small scythes, standing behind her; their heads were bowed so their faces could not be seen (CD).

128–38 Kean originally planned to have twelve nymphs and twelve reapers but halved the numbers. Six naiads were to enter at 131b and six reapers at 138; they were to meet the nymphs, single out partners and go in couples, six people on each side, for a dance, song and chorus. However, notes in the rehearsal workbook direct 'Cut the reapers and the nymphs out tonight', and Edmonds's final pb indicates that they were not reinstated.

    Tree transposed the lines so that 128–31 were followed by 134–5, 132–3 and 136–8. The nymphs emerged from the water when commanded and were dancing, when Cupid ran on and pointed to the reapers who had appeared on steps at the back. The frightened naiads ran back behind the water-rows, at which point Cupid indicated the reapers to Iris, who addressed them (134–5) and the nymphs, inviting them to dance together.

    Garrick (1757) cut 137–8; Bridges-Adams (1926/30) 132–3; Wright 133b, 134–8 and the reapers. Phelps gave 128–38 to Juno and cut the intervening sd (Phelps/Creswick pb). Benthall's transposition of 118–27 meant that Iris's call to the naiads followed 106–17. Barton gave 132–3a to Ceres and 134–5 to Iris; all three goddesses spoke 133b, and both Ceres and Iris 136a. Daniels gave Juno 128–31, Iris 132–3a, 136 and Ceres 134–5, 137–8; he cut 133b. The lines were sung.

133sd Burton's grotto changed to a golden wheatfield, flippers changing the set waters to sheaves of set wheat.

You sun-burned sicklemen of August weary,
Come hither from the furrow, and be merry,   135
Make holiday; your rye-straw hats put on,
And these fresh nymphs encounter every one
In country footing.

Enter certain reapers, properly habited. They join with the nymphs,
in a graceful dance, towards the end whereof Prospero starts
suddenly and speaks, after which, to a strange, hollow and
confused noise they heavily vanish

PROSPERO [*Aside*] I had forgot that foul conspiracy
Of the beast Caliban and his confederates   140

138sd Sturgess suggests that in the King's Men production 'Iris, Ceres and Juno . . . retreated upstage where Juno [sat] in the throne, the other two either side of her', while 'the four or six pairs of dancers [wove] elegant patterns over the stage' (*Jacobean Private Theatre*, p. 93); Jowett, on the other hand, argues that Juno and Ceres were more probably suspended above the stage, leaving it clear for the dancers. The spirits' heavy vanishing implies a dejected and informal exit, 'perhaps through the discovery-space curtain': 'what vanishes, in fact, is the formal construct of the masque itself' (Sturgess, *Jacobean Private Theatre*, p. 94).

Tree concocted an elaborate rationale for his dance, which was performed by children: 'Taking advantage of the chaste amiability of the Nymphs, the Reapers endeavour to embrace them, but their advances are indignantly repulsed, the maidens very rightly pointing to their ringless wedding-fingers, it being illegal (in fairy-land) to exchange kisses without a marriage certificate. Thus rebuffed, the Reapers continue their dance alone. Suddenly Cupid re-appears on the scene, and shoots a dart in the heart of each coy maiden; at once they relent, and, love conquering modesty, they sue to the Reapers. But the Reapers are now obdurate. They laugh; the maidens weep.' Cupid then shoots the Reapers with his arrows, who consequently sue to the nymphs, 'pointing to their wedding-fingers. Cupid re-appears on the scene, and an impromptu wedding is arranged, all the Reapers and Nymphs taking part in the ceremony. To the wedding song of "Honour, riches, marriage-blessing", the Nymphs assume the marriage veils which they gather from the mists of the lake, and each having received a ring and a blessing at the hands of the Rev. Master Cupid, they dance off with the Reapers in quest of everlasting happiness, thus triumphantly vindicating the ethics of the drama' (*Thoughts and Afterthoughts*, pp. 217–18). When the masque ended, Tree interpolated 148–58a, Prospero's revels speech; at its end a gong struck five times and Prospero resumed with 139ff.

Brook's 1957 dance attracted much sarcastic comment at Stratford: 'men dressed as stooks wave[d] plastic sickles and [were] surrounded by . . . vegetables' oddly 'chanting . . . what sound[ed] like a fertility rite incantation' (respectively, Kenneth Tynan, *O* 18/8/57; John Courtenay, *Tru* 23/8/57); it comprised the 'repetition . . . of four words, "barns, garners, vines, plants" ' (Trewin, *ILN* 24/8/57). Brook drastically changed this anthropological and anthropomorphic extravagance for the London transfer, staging it 'on more conventional lines' with 'reminders of the glittering scenes reproduced in the Pollock toy theatres' (Tarran, *MA* 23/12/57).

Hytner lifted the curtain behind the gauze, revealing an almost cinematic vision of grain blowing in the wind: *The Tempest* meets *Oklahoma*. Indeed, the action itself invoked the spirit of a Broadway musical, with the reapers picking flowers for the nymphs and throwing poppy petals over them (London pb and CD); at Stratford, a rainbow was projected onto the cyclorama (pb and CD). During the dance, 106–9 were repeated, and then all three goddesses sang 'Honour, riches, marriage-blessing' (106), singing it twice more as a canon, with ascending chords on 'Honour' and 'marriage' in both repetitions (London pb).

Miranda and Ferdinand sometimes join in the dance, as in Daniels's and Paige's productions; however, the moment Hall's 1974 lovers began to dance, all froze, the lights snapped on to Prospero and the spirits exited groaning. The nymphs and reapers are sometimes cut altogether, as in Miller's 1988 production. Retallack (1981) had instead 'a dance of two masked men and two masked girls', in which Ferdinand joined (Young, *FT* 2/83), while Wolfe had 'Strange little child like puppets perform a haunting ritual' (Bob Daniels, WPSC [broadcast notes, undated typescript]). Donnellan's Miranda and Ferdinand took the place of nymph and reaper, joining in a stately dance with all on stage. Ferdinand and then Miranda, however, began to hop more jazzily, eventually leading to a can-can in which confetti was thrown onto the two lovers; the words sung echoed the music: 'Da da da da / Blessing on you da da da' (CD). The masque was variously described as a 'sedate, paced dance [turning] into a barnyard romp with whoops and confetti', 'an operatic parody' that became 'a strobe-lit disco', and 'an exuberant, anarchic self-indulgence' (respectively, Hutcheon, *Tr* 9/12/88; Spencer, *DT* and McAfee, *ES*, both 28/11/88).

Directors sometimes introduce a sinister element into the masque to prompt Prospero's disruption of it. Burge, for example, had an 'obviously malign spirit, haggard' and 'reptilian . . . [fling] itself at Prospero' (respectively, Foulkes, review, p. 22; Lewsen, *T* 28/2/72). Strehler had aggressive drum beats start to overlay the stately music that had been playing, thereby upsetting Prospero (video). Hack's Prospero heard off-stage cries of 'Freedom' and 'Caliban', while Bogdanov (1992) had the 'filmy globe' in which the spirits sang 'invaded by Caliban in violent rapist mood'; he lifted Juno up, accompanied by lightning and a thunder crack (Taylor, *Ind* 30/11/92, and CD). Similarly, Mendes's middle reaper picked up his head, revealing himself as Caliban (CD), and Wolfe's masque 'dissolve[d] before the specter of would-be murderers in skeleton masks' (Brantley, *NYT* 12/7/95).

139–42a Before 139, Garrick's 1757 Prospero spoke 'Break off, break off' to the spirits. Macready's

Against my life. The minute of their plot
Is almost come. [*To the spirits*] Well done! Avoid! No more.
FERDINAND This is strange. Your father's in some passion
    That works him strongly.
MIRANDA   Never till this day   145
    Saw I him touched with anger so distempered.
PROSPERO You do look, my son, in a movèd sort,
    As if you were dismayed. Be cheerful, sir,
    Our revels now are ended; these our actors,
    As I foretold you, were all spirits, and
    Are melted into air, into thin air;   150
    And like the baseless fabric of this vision,

Prospero delivered 139–42a as an aside; Daniels's Prospero moved amongst the dancers,
speaking through the music (pb and archive video). Hall (1988) and Hytner had the spirits
freeze when Prospero spoke.

    As Purcarete's lovers watched the unseen masque, Caliban, Stephano and Trinculo
entered L and moved across the front of the stage, exiting R; at 142a, Prospero drew back the
curtain, revealing the giant skeleton surrounded by the Ariels, and sat on the floor, laughing
cynically (CD).

142b The spirits vanish, as Prospero instructs. Nineteenth-century stagings restored the pre-
masque setting: Phelps lowered the gauzes, quickly closed in the flats and raised the front
lights (Phelps/Creswick pb); Burton had the cloud cloth descend for Prospero's cave to be re-
set behind it; Kean checked the lights as the front ground rows ascended and the clouds
descended to close in all the figures of the vision, after which the back sink ascended.

    Twentieth-century productions sometimes attempt a special effect; Hytner's spirits, for
example, all stood with their arms up and then dispersed to almost cinematic effect, accompanied by a sound like that of a film winding-down in a broken projector or of a record
slowing to a stop (London pb and CD). Miller (1988), on the other hand, simply had Ariel
usher the three goddesses out: 'they scuttle[d] off as unceremoniously as if Prospero were
some Sanders of the River ordering them back to the kitchen' (pb and King, *STel* 16/10/88).

    Cut by Kemble (both versions) and Tree, and interpolated by Kean, Wright and Ayrton
before 139.

143–64 Garrick (1757) transposed 151 and 155 and cut 156b–8a. Kemble cut 143–64 here (both versions), interpolating a slightly changed 146-56a later (see notes to 5.1 and 5.1.30b); Ariel was
summoned with 'Ariel! / My industrious servant! Ariel' (1789) and with the rather curt 'What,
Ariel!' (1806). Tree cut 146-7 and interpolated 148-58a earlier (see note to 138sd); 158b
therefore followed 145. Daniels cut 159b, and Barton 160.

    Daly's printed edition reads 'Our revels are *near* ended' (italics mine), as the lines were
spoken soon after the appearance of Iris and Ceres, 'recited slowly as the accompaniment to

The cloud-capped towers, the gorgeous palaces,
The solemn temples, the great globe itself,
Yea, all which it inherit, shall dissolve,
And like this insubstantial pageant faded   155
Leave not a rack behind. We are such stuff
As dreams are made on; and our little life
Is rounded with a sleep. Sir, I am vexed.
Bear with my weakness, my old brain is troubled.
Be not disturbed with my infirmity.   160
If you be pleased, retire into my cell,
And there repose. A turn or two I'll walk
To still my beating mind.

an actual vision of gorgeous palaces and solemn temples on a "back cloth" ' (*NY Herald*, quoted in Nilan, ' "The Tempest" ', p. 116). After 158a, he interpolated 124b–133, followed by 106–17, 133sd and 134–8sd; 'the end of the spell' marked the end of Act 3. However, the reapers and final dance were cut during rehearsal, so that the act ended with Juno and Ceres's song.

Quite unlike Daly's reverie, twentieth-century Prosperos, like Gielgud for Hall (1974), often deliver the revels speech 'urgently and at speed' (Wardle, *T* 6/3/74); Williams's (1978), speaking 'in tones of rage', made it 'an urgent reminder there is pressing business to be done' (respectively, Levin, *ST* 7/5/78; Billington, *G* 15/5/78). Daniels's Prospero was bitter and very upset by the end (Cushman, *O* 15/8/82; archive video); Mendes's also made it 'a statement of baffled fury', showing a 'beautifully weary bitterness' (respectively, Billington, *G* 13/8/93; Macauley, *FT* 15/7/94). Miller's 1970 Prospero spoke 'as a man who looks into the future and sees . . . destruction . . . with a shuddering fear' (*ST* 21/6/70): ' "My old brain is troubled," [was] the key line', and Prospero 'end[ed] ill, lying full length on the ground, or kneeling in prayer' (Barber, *DT* 16/6/70; however, it is unclear if he refers to Prospero's actions here or later – see, e.g., note to 5.1.33–57). Hall's 1988 Prospero, however, 'edge[d] from the matter-of-fact to a resonant introspection' (Hiley, *L* 26/5/88), while Strehler's stood on the auditorium floor in front of the stage, literally outside the action, speaking to the audience after Miranda and Ferdinand had exited (video). His staging, which in the theatre was slightly different, seemed to be a meditation on theatrical illusion: 'Ferdinand merely [stood] silhouetted against a golden cloud formation suggestive of a baroque theatre set, while Prospero deliver[ed] "Our revels now are ended" from the front of the stalls and [made] "these our actors" refer, not to the goddesses, but to the cast of the play itself' (Warren, *TLS* 9/3/84).

158b–261 (end of scene) Cut by Daly, who had interpolated much of 165b–233 into 3.2 (see notes to 3.2).

163 Wright's Prospero, Miranda and Ferdinand exited, and the tabs closed. Then Caliban, Stephano and Trinculo entered, speaking 194–214a on the forestage; when they exited, the

FERDINAND *and* MIRANDA   We wish your peace.

                                    Exeunt [FERDINAND *and* MIRANDA]

PROSPERO Come with a thought! – I thank thee. – Ariel, come!

                        Enter ARIEL

ARIEL Thy thoughts I cleave to. What's thy pleasure?

PROSPERO   Spirit,   165

        We must prepare to meet with Caliban.

tabs opened, Prospero entered and the scene resumed with 164. Mendes's Ferdinand spoke 163b (CD).

163sd Purcarete's Ferdinand carried out the bridal-gowned Miranda as if they were newly-weds (CD).

164 Some producers, like Garrick (1757), Burton and Tree, punctuate the line or transpose its clauses so that Prospero thanks Miranda and Ferdinand; others, like Barton, have him thank Ariel. Bridges-Adams (1934), Ayrton and Burge changed 'thank' to 'think'; indeed, Benthall's 1951 Prospero spoke so 'quietly, and unemphatically . . . that when Ariel appears it really is as if thought and not mumbo-jumbo had brought him' (*BEN* 28/6/51).

165b–93sd Interpolated after 3.1.91sd in Daly's printed text. He cut 167–9, as the masque had not yet been presented, and 183–4a. After 192a, Ariel entered with the 'glistering apparel', and Prospero spoke 193b, followed by 192b–3a. After they retired to Prospero's cell and the comic trio entered, Daly interpolated 3.2.37–59a, cutting only 57a; he then returned to 4.1, interpolating 194–5 and 219–33a. Although 233a is marked as Stephano's line, as it is in Shakespeare's original, it is likely that Trinculo spoke it, as the text immediately returns to 3.2.62, where Stephano warns Trinculo to 'run into no further danger' by interrupting Caliban again; the rest of Shakespeare's 3.2 is then given, with cuts, as the end to Act 2. Hoswell's rehearsal notes, however, indicate a different order: Act 2 ended with 3.1, and this composite scene involving Caliban, Stephano and Trinculo was placed in the middle of Act 3, between the banquet and the masque scenes.

Hack cut 165b. Purcarete's Prospero laughed before answering it; no Ariel was visible on stage during 165b–85 but its form could be seen behind the blue curtain that was still partly drawn. Noticing it, Prospero approached the curtain and tried to embrace the form, but it disappeared just before 185 (CD). Paige's Prospero was 'almost hysterical' during 166–84; Ariel sat him down and knelt behind him, 'gently sooth[ing] and comfort[ing] him, [with his] arms around him', as he 'explain[ed] the whereabouts of the conspirators'. Prospero then 'leant back against him, calming visibly, to the satisfaction of both' (Carter, '*The Tempest* at Salisbury Playhouse', p. 30).

ARIEL Ay, my commander. When I presented Ceres
       I thought t' have told thee of it, but I feared
       Lest I might anger thee.
PROSPERO Say again, where didst thou leave these varlets?   170
ARIEL I told you, sir, they were red-hot with drinking,
       So full of valour that they smote the air
       For breathing in their faces, beat the ground
       For kissing of their feet; yet always bending
       Towards their project. Then I beat my tabor,   175
       At which like unbacked colts they pricked their ears,
       Advanced their eyelids, lifted up their noses
       As they smelt music. So I charmed their ears
       That calf-like they my lowing followed, through
       Toothed briars, sharp furzes, pricking gorse and thorns,   180
       Which entered their frail shins. At last I left them
       I' th' filthy mantled pool beyond your cell,
       There dancing up to th'chins, that the foul lake
       O'er-stunk their feet.
PROSPERO   This was well done, my bird!
       Thy shape invisible retain thou still.   185

167–70a Both Kemble versions cut 167b–70a, as the masque had been omitted. Kean and Bridges-
      Adams (1926/30, 1934) cut 167b–9, and Ayrton, Iden Payne and Barton 167–9; Ariel did not
      play Ceres in these productions. Macready cut 167b.
   171 Mendes's Ariel spoke 'I told you' curtly; after Prospero glared at him, he paused before
      proceeding with 'sir' (CD).
175b–82 Kemble (1789) and Kean cut 175b–81a; Kemble (1806) only 175b–8a. Word-changes some-
      times reflect staging: Hack changed 'beat my tabor' to 'clapped my hands' (175b), and
      Kemble (1806) substituted 'beside the marsh' for 'beyond your cell' (182).
   180 Retallack's Ariel was inhuman in her 'malevolent glee at leading the varlets into sharp furzes
      and pricking thorns' (Barber, *DT* 20/6[*sic*]/83).
183–4a Cut by Garrick (1757), Kemble (both versions), Macready, Phelps, (?) Burton, Daly and Tree.
      Kean cut 184a.
   184b Unlike Kemble (1806), who cut the endearment, Tree directed 'The word bird to be brought
      out strongly' (Grove's pb note).
   185 Tree interpolated 253–5a and 257a after 185. Wright cut 185b.
      Thacker's Ariel was clearly disappointed, her face making it apparent she thought
      Prospero's need for her services had come to an end (CD).

The trumpery in my house, go bring it hither
For stale to catch these thieves.

ARIEL   I go, I go.   *Exit*

PROSPERO A devil, a born devil, on whose nature
Nurture can never stick; on whom my pains
Humanely taken, all, all lost, quite lost;   190
And, as with age his body uglier grows,
So his mind cankers. I will plague them all,
Even to roaring.

186–7 Cut by Kemble (1789), who substituted this material: 'Go call the Spirits, / O'er whom I gave
thee power, quick to this place, / And let them bring the trumpery in my house, / For sake to
catch these thieves.' Then 42b–8 of the present scene were interpolated, with some minor
changes: Ariel sang 44–8 and the final, potentially poignant 'no?' was replaced by a ram-
bunctious-sounding 'ho!' After Ariel's exit, Prospero's thoughts returned to 'Oh! this Caliban!'
and Shakespeare's scene resumed with 188. The 1806 version was slightly different: 186 was
cut and 35–8 interpolated with some minor changes. Prospero's order ended with a new
version of 186 inserted before 187; 187b was cut and 42b–3 inserted in its place. Ariel then
exited, and the scene continued as in 1789.

Mendes's Ariel spoke the second 'I go' through clenched teeth, while Thacker's sounded
resigned and annoyed (CD).

188–92a Hytner's Prospero was visibly upset by Caliban's failure to respond to his nurturing; moreover, by looking at himself in disgust as he mentioned Caliban's ugly body and cankered
mind, Prospero seemed to be talking more about himself than about Caliban. His self-
revelation was given further point by Ariel's remaining in the background, listening intently
and watching Prospero with concern as the latter spoke (CD).

190 Kean cut some of Prospero's repetition, changing the first 'all' to 'are', arguably making him
sound more composed.

192a Benthall's 1952 Caliban and Stephano shushed Trinculo, who was about to sneeze; he finally
did so at 207.

192b–3 As Kermode and Orgel both note, 'line' is a variant form of 'lime' or 'linden-tree', so Shakespeare's Prospero probably refers to a stage-property tree. Subsequent productions have
usually interpreted the prop as a clothes-line (see note to 193sd), although Williams (1978)
flew in a tree bearing the frippery, Hytner's Ariel brought on a trunk and Ninagawa's used a
tree on the Noh stage.

Macready and Burton transposed 192b–3a and 193b-sd; Kean changed 'line' to 'seat'.
Phelps, Burton and Kean interpolated 253–61 while Ariel hung up the clothes
(Phelps/Williams pb; Creswick crosses the interpolation out); the first two cut 256b, while the
third changed it to 'They shall roar.' Tree, Bridges-Adams (1926/30, 1934), Hack, Williams
(1978), Daniels and Hytner cut 193b.

Enter ARIEL, *laden with glistering apparel, etc*

Come, hang them on this line.

Enter CALIBAN, STEPHANO, *and* TRINCULO, *all wet*

CALIBAN Pray you tread softly, that the blind mole may not hear a
foot fall. We now are near his cell.   195
STEPHANO Monster, your fairy, which you say is a harmless fairy,
has done little better than played the jack with us.

193sd The Folio prints both sds together after 193b, but the half-line is clearly an instruction on
Ariel's re-entry. Some stagings, like Phelps's and Burton's, had Prospero and Ariel exit;
others, like Bridges-Adams's (1926/30) and Crozier's, had them remain on-stage, unseen by
the conspirators.
　　　The frippery has been variously managed. Burton's Prospero held the end of his wand to
the R3E wing, where a stage-hand put a looped line over it; Prospero then crossed to the
opposite wing where another stage-hand fastened it. Benthall's 1951 Ariel was assisted by
two apes and two monsters, who retired back into their hole when finished. Brook (1957)
used 'some audacious slapstick when the magic garments suddenly appear[ed] across the
cave on lines, like Widow Twankey's washing-day' (*LDP* 14/8/57), while the Williams/Brook
'clothes line . . . [grew] up . . . like Jack's beanstalk' (*LP* 3/4/63), thanks to two coloured
poles that came up through the floor; Ariel appears to have had the clothes on a line that he
attached to the poles (pb). Paige's frippery 'was managed by Ariel and two other spirits . . .
wearing an academic gown each, and holding another two between them' (Carter, '*The
Tempest* at Salisbury Playhouse', p. 30), while Thacker had a rope held up by Prospero and
all the spirits, the spirits themselves representing the frippery (CD).
　　　Comic business often embellishes the trio's entrance. Tree's Caliban entered holding a
knife, followed by Stephano with a truncheon; the latter was walking heavily, prompting 194.
Brook (1990) imaginatively had the trio enter while still in the 'pool': a spirit carried a hula
hoop over their heads in which their bottle bobbed (CD and programme photo). Mendes's
Caliban dragged in the wicker basket when Ariel clapped his hands; standing up in it were
Stephano and Trinculo, their faces blackened and their clothes tattered, while Caliban had
green slime on his L shoulder (CD).
194–214a Interpolated by Wright after 163, so that 214 ff. followed 193. Much of the dialogue among
Donnellan's three conspirators took place behind the on-stage curtain (CD).
195 Kemble (both versions) had the conspirators 'at' rather than 'near' Prospero's cell. Tree's
Trinculo, carrying a mallet and nail, entered stumbling; Caliban reproved him with 'Sh!',
Stephano followed suit and Trinculo directed his own 'Sh!' off-stage.

TRINCULO Monster, I do smell all horse-piss, at which my nose is
in great indignation.

STEPHANO So is mine. Do you hear, monster? If I should take a   200
displeasure against you, look you –

TRINCULO Thou wert but a lost monster.

CALIBAN Good my lord, give me thy favour still.
Be patient, for the prize I'll bring thee to
Shall hoodwink this mischance. Therefore speak softly –   205
All's hushed as midnight yet.

TRINCULO Ay, but to lose our bottles in the pool!

STEPHANO There is not only disgrace and dishonour in that,
monster, but an infinite loss.

TRINCULO That's more to me than my wetting. Yet this is your   210
harmless fairy, monster.

STEPHANO I will fetch off my bottle, though I be o'er ears for my
labour.

CALIBAN Prithee, my king, be quiet. Seest thou here,
This is the mouth o' th' cell. No noise, and enter.   215
Do that good mischief which may make this island

---

198 Kemble (both versions), Phelps, Burton, Kean, Tree and Bridges-Adams (1926/30, 1934)
substituted 'pond' for 'piss'; Ashwell cut 'I do smell all horse-piss'.

202 Macready made Caliban a 'foul' rather than 'lost monster'. Tree's Trinculo threatened
Caliban with his mallet.

203–6 Phelps's Caliban whispered. Kemble's 1806 Caliban sang a short song, 'The owl is abroad',
after 206 (Inchbald).

207 As Tree's Trinculo tried to speak, Caliban said 'hush! hush!', and the following lines were
added:

TRINCULO Butoloosourbottlesinthepool
STEPHANO Eh?
TRINCULO Buttolooseourbottlesinthepool
STEPHANO Eh?
TRINCULO (clearing his throat) But to – loose [sic] – our – bottles – in – the – pool (Grove's pb
notes).

212–14 Some Stephanos, like Kemble's (1806) and Williams's (1978), begin to leave. Barton's tried to
rise and fell head first through the trap; Caliban and Trinculo caught him by the ankles and
dragged him up.

214–18 Phelps's Caliban again whispered.

> Thine own for ever, and I, thy Caliban,
> For aye thy foot-licker.
> STEPHANO Give me thy hand. I do begin to have bloody thoughts.
> TRINCULO O King Stephano, O peer, O worthy Stephano! Look   220
> what a wardrobe here is for thee.

218 Tree's Stephano lifted his foot, which Caliban kissed; Daniels's also kissed his foot, presumably unprompted.

Benthall's 1952 Prospero signalled to Ariel, and the spirit ran round Trinculo, making him see the garments.

219 Hall's 1988 Stephano pulled out a large knife (pb and props list), and Caliban led him towards the cell; Trinculo began to sneak away DS, where the line with its clothes was lying on the deck, but as he did so, the line was lifted and the clothes held high (pb). Hytner's Caliban put an axe into Stephano's hands and moved backward towards the cell entrance (Stratford pb).

Mendes's Ariel opened the wicker basket, which contained the frippery. Trinculo proceeded to dress himself in a blonde wig and purple gown, while Stephano donned a beard and crown; Trinculo, giving a royal wave and changing his voice, imitated the Queen, while Stephano sent up Prince Charles (CD). Trinculo, 'Decked out in stolen regal finery', reminded one critic 'irresistibly of a PG Tips chimp impersonating the Queen Mother' (Taylor, *Ind* 15/7/94).

219–49 Retallack's 'conspiratorial Stephano' spoke lines from *Macbeth*, *Richard III* and *Hamlet* 'as he don[ned] the glittering apparel' (respectively, Wardle, *T* 25/2/83; Billington, *G* 2/83).

220 Shakespeare's dialogue makes clear that, although the frippery has been visible on stage for some time, only now does Trinculo see it and alert the others.

Strehler used the discarded clothes of Alonso's court, which Ariel had put away in the traps at the end of 3.3; they included the king's ermine robe and crown. Trinculo put on the crown and opened the SR trap to pull out the rest of the king's robe, which was only partially on stage; Caliban tried to get the cloak away from him, but then Stephano took it (video). As Hirst notes, the use of the same costumes made the comic conspirators mirror-images of the political conspirators and strengthened the production's emphasis on the 'relationships between theatre and life' (*The Tempest: Text and Performance*, p. 64).

Brook's 1990 frippery scene, one of the production's highlights, began with a cloak thrown at Trinculo from off-stage; the rest of the clothes (hats and robes) were similarly thrown to him and Stephano, 'the air rain[ing] raiment in a truly marvellous sequence' (CD and Coveney, *O* 4/9/90). As the two dressed in their finery, the spirits 'form[ed] a bamboo mirror frame for Ariel to throw back a mocking reflection of the preening' pair, an action made all the funnier by the actors' different sizes: 'the large, black Ariel . . . dress[ed] up in the same ridiculous finery as the small, Balinese Trinculo . . . who, convinced he is gazing into a mirror, delightedly copie[d] all the Spirit's irreverent gestures' (respectively, Wardle, *IndS*

CALIBAN Let it alone, thou fool, it is but trash.

TRINCULO O ho, monster! We know what belongs to a frippery. O
 King Stephano!

STEPHANO Put off that gown, Trinculo! By this hand I'll have that   225
 gown.

TRINCULO Thy grace shall have it.

CALIBAN The dropsy drown this fool! What do you mean
 To dote thus on such luggage? Let't alone,
 And do the murder first. If he awake,   230
 From toe to crown he'll fill our skins with pinches,
 Make us strange stuff.

STEPHANO Be you quiet, monster! Mistress line, is not this my
 jerkin? Now is the jerkin under the line. Now, jerkin, you are
 like to lose your hair, and prove a bald jerkin.   235

4/11/90; Taylor, *Ind* 2/11/90). Stephano, in 'velvet cloak and black hat', also 'gaze[d] lovingly
at his [mistaken] mirror-image' (Billington, *G* 19/10/90).

   Thacker's Trinculo had taken off his trousers before he saw the line; when he spotted the
'frippery', represented by the spirits, he 'wore' a spirit as if it were a coat or cloak, the spirit's
stomach against his back and the spirit's arms hanging over his shoulders. Stephano
followed suit (CD).

   Just as it was needed, Purcarete's frippery descended from the flies; it consisted of what
looked like white capes, but were actually bell-shaped skirts, which during the following lines
Stephano, Trinculo and Caliban proceeded to don, one skirt on top of another, along with
wedding veils. The three were eventually identically dressed (CD).

220–7 Cut by Tree.

224 Barton's Trinculo tried to put on a gown and hand Stephano a hat.

225 Paige's Trinculo and Stephano 'each shrugged themselves into the [two] . . . empty gowns'
 held between the spirits, who then 'towed [them] about by the sleeves' (Carter, *The Tempest*
 at Salisbury Playhouse', p. 30).

227 While 227 indicates that Trinculo yields the gown to Stephano, directors have had him do so
 with varying degrees of willingness. Burton and Barton, for instance, had Stephano pull the
 gown from Trinculo at 226, while Daniels's Trinculo took the gown back from Caliban,
 putting it on Stephano.

228–32 Kemble (1789) cut 230b–2, and Benthall (1951) 229–30a. Tree cut 228b–32 and had Caliban
 speak 228a in response to Trinculo's loud laugh at 219, since the intervening lines were also
 cut. Phelps's Caliban spoke in a 'hissing whisper'.

   At 229, Hytner's Caliban grabbed the cloak from Stephano and threw it over the back of
 the trunk, only to have Trinculo put it back on Stephano.

233–9 'Mistress line . . . garment for't' is an obscure joke cut in both Kemble versions and many
 subsequent productions (e.g., Phelps's, Burton's and Benthall's 1952). Kean and Tree

TRINCULO Do, do; we steal by line and level, and't like your grace.

STEPHANO I thank thee for that jest; here's a garment for't. Wit shall
not go unrewarded while I am king of this country. 'Steal by line
and level' is an excellent pass of pate: there's another garment for't.

TRINCULO Monster, come put some lime upon your fingers, and   240
away with the rest.

CALIBAN I will have none on't. We shall lose our time,
And all be turned to barnacles, or to apes
With foreheads villainous low.

STEPHANO Monster, lay to your fingers. Help to bear this away   245
where my hogshead of wine is, or I'll turn you out of my
kingdom. Go to, carry this.

extended the cut to 242a ('none on't'); Bridges-Adams (1926/30, 1934), Ayrton, Crozier,
Wright and Daniels cut only 'Now is . . . bald jerkin' (234–5). Iden Payne cut from 'Be you
quiet' to 'Do, do' (233–6), retaining 'Mistress line, is not this my jerkin?'. Hack changed
'jerkin' to 'gown' and cut 'Now is . . . Do, do' (234–6); the pb suggests he originally rewrote
the lines, cutting the reference to 'line and level' but then reinstating it.

237 Williams's 1978 Stephano kicked the jerkin to Trinculo, who caught it and put it on, while
Daniels's took trousers from the line and gave them to Trinculo.

241–9 Kemble (1789) changed 241 to 'bear off this, and this' and cut 242–9; Bridges-Adams cut 'or
I'll . . . kingdom' (246–7). At 249, Benthall (1952) added another 'And this' for Trinculo.
Hytner interpolated four more lines of 'And this', spoken in turn by Trinculo and Stephano; at
each repetition, the speaker threw a garment to Caliban. On the penultimate one, Stephano
and Trinculo moved to the mouth of the cave, where a tapping noise started, and peered in.
    Strehler's Caliban broke his magic staff in disgusted reaction to Stephano and Trinculo's
involvement with the frippery (video).

245–261 (end of scene) Cut by Tree, who had interpolated some of the lines earlier; see note to 185.
Tree's elaborate ending to the act started with the conspirators stealthily creeping to the
entrance of Prospero's cell, saying 'hush! hush!'. On the third 'hush!', Ariel entered clashing
cymbals and dashing across stage to exit R. The cymbal clash was accompanied by a thunder
crash and black-out, during which the cloth was raised, and Roze's music for the dance of
shapes began. When the cloth was up, the blue lights came on, revealing the full cave set in
all its monstrosity and the three conspirators quaking with fear. Caliban pantomimed an
escape route through LUE, and the trio hurried that way, 'hanging on to each other's coat-
tails', with Caliban in the lead. Just as they reached their goal, 'a horrible thing . . . with a
long neck' appeared and bowed, terrifying them (Grove's pb note); thereafter they were
'met at every turn by strange shapes which . . . bow[ed] to the drunkards with a mocking and
haunting politeness' (printed sd). These gnomes, 'illuminated heads', and 'Transparent
animals' represented 'the denizens of nightmares which afflict conscience-stricken men'

TRINCULO And this.
STEPHANO Ay, and this.

A noise of hunters heard. Enter diverse spirits in shape of dogs and
hounds, hunting them about, Prospero and Ariel setting them on

(Grove's pb note; final quotation from printed sd). With Caliban in the lead, the three quickly rushed up steps and down again and exited RUE; acrobats then entered and climbed a tree, with Caliban, Stephano and Trinculo following them. The bough broke when Stephano put his foot on it, causing the three to fall and remain out of sight behind the rock row. As the yelling continued (whether from the trio or the shapes is unclear), the three re-entered and rushed DS, 'where 4 goblins drop[ped] just in front of them from bridge'; the curtain fell as they tried to 'battle with them'(Grove's pb note). The printed sd, slightly different, indicates that when the conspirators' punishment was 'complete', the 'comic Inferno dissolve[d]', revealing Prospero's cave once again, and the characters exited.

249sd Some nineteenth-century stagings were relatively modest. Accompanied by yelping, barking, hunting horns, howlings and other noises, three dogs descended from the flies and seized each of Phelps's conspirators (Phelps/Creswick pb). Macready's trio had three imps fly into their arms, while others ran on with whips, incited by Prospero and Ariel (Pattie ed. and Moore's notes in Burton pb). Burton had imps with dog's heads rush on, who tormented the trio by jumping on them, pinching them and driving them about the stage; Prospero stood at the back pointing with his wand, while Ariel laughed and enjoyed the 'sport', the act ending with this tableau. Kean, however, was more spectacular, harassing the conspirators, according to one set of Ellis's notes, with nine apes (played by 'active boys'), twelve urchin dogs (again played by boys), eight cyclopses with hammers and wings, sixteen firefiends with flashing horns (the *corps de ballet*), and five working serpents; Ariel flew above on a bat's back, setting them on.

Recent hounds have tended to be stylized. Hall (1974) had seven enter: each wore a black body-stocking, gloves, hood and pumps, as well as a dog's head, jock strap and fur fabric flanks, with tail attached; the staging plans (6/12/74) note that they were to have 'huge red tongues' and be 'larger than life'. Ariel put on a white felt hunter's hat and picked up a white hunter's horn to urge them on; the dogs then snarled slowly towards the trio. Like the grotesque shapes, these 'demon-wolves . . . with their gaping red mouths' had 'exactly the right creepiness' (Young, *FT* 6/3/74). In 1988, Ariel came with two dogs from the R corner and another spirit with three from the L; both handed Prospero the leads. The hounds were 'fierce curs', 'vicious' and 'red-eyed Maurice Sendak creatures indicative of their master's playful nastiness' (respectively, Ratcliffe, *O* 22/5/88; Shulman, *ES* 20/5/88; Coveney, *FT* 23/5/88); their huge dog- and bear-like heads had visible teeth (CD). Daniels's 'yapping skeletal dogs' were 'notably effective[ly] manipulat[ed]' by the Ariel clones wearing black cloaks (Cushman, *O* 15/8/82, and archive video); their 'glimmering eeriness' at Stratford was

PROSPERO Hey, Mountain, hey!   250
ARIEL Silver! There it goes, Silver.
PROSPERO Fury, Fury! There, Tyrant, there! Hark, hark!
　　　　　[*Caliban, Stephano, and Trinculo are driven out*]
　　　　　Go, charge my goblins that they grind their joints
　　　　　With dry convulsions, shorten up their sinews

lost in the transfer to London (King, *STel* 9/83). Other directors have found even more unusual ways to embody the dogs: Hay, for example, used 'projected, high-speed graphics' (Gore-Langton, 10/10/92), while Wolfe's trio 'fle[d] goblins in an Indonesian shadow play' (Karam, *T* 14/7/95); a photograph shows a sheet-screen with two shadows, probably Trinculo and Stephano, running SL, followed by four huge dog-like shadows on their hind legs, with front paws outstretched (*NYVV* 18/7/95).

　　　Some directors have supplanted the spirit-dogs. Benthall (1951) had his shapes (two sea-monsters, two sea hedgehogs and two barnacles) 'come alive', which suggests they had been present on stage, motionless and blending into the background. (However, the pb also notes that 'monsters [came] up from cave' at 250, not clarifying whether these were additional shapes or whether this is how they came 'alive'.) Miller (1988) had masked and 'spear-wield-ing natives' perform a tribal dance behind the fleeing trio (Edwards, *Sp* 22/10/88, and CD), while Brook's 1990 Ariel and two other spirits chased them with clap-boards. No hounds or shapes entered to harass Purcarete's trio: they simply twirled around and around, getting caught up in the strips of cloth from which the frippery had dangled (CD).

250–61 (end of scene) Garrick (1757), Kemble (1789), Macready, Burton and Kean cut 250–2; Iden Payne 250–6a, 260b–1; Bridges-Adams (1926/30, 1934) and Ayrton 250–61; Miller (1988) 253–6a. Kemble (1806) cut 257b–61, interpolating 257b–8 into 5.1, while Phelps, Burton and Kean interpolated 253–61 earlier (see note to 192b–3).

252 Only at 'hark' did Hytner have four shapes enter from the C trap (Stratford pb); they were still dressed as Prospero clones, in trousers, shirts and robes (CD). At Stratford, once the shapes entered, they and the three conspirators froze, and the tapping sound that had preceded their arrival was cut; the shapes' hounding of the conspirators did not begin until Prospero finished his speech of 252–6a. However, in London, the chase began as soon as the four shapes entered: the first shape turned Trinculo around US, whereupon the second shape punched him and the first threw him to the floor DSL. Stephano ran SL, chased by the second shape, and then crossed DSR. As the first shape pushed Trinculo DSR, the third crossed DSL to Caliban and kicked him; the fourth poked his eye and then got him in a headlock, taking him SR and punching him twice. Meanwhile the second shape punched Stephano USL and the first kneed him, while the third stamped on Trinculo's foot and pushed him US. The second shape took Trinculo off at SR, while the third and fourth took Caliban out the same way; Stephano was presumably similarly removed by the first shape. Once they were off, Prospero began his speech of 252–6a (pbs).

> With agèd cramps, and more pinch-spotted make them,   255
> Than pard, or cat-o'-mountain.
> ARIEL   Hark, they roar.
> PROSPERO Let them be hunted soundly. At this hour
> Lies at my mercy all mine enemies.
> Shortly shall all my labours end, and thou
> Shalt have the air at freedom. For a little   260
> Follow, and do me service.
>
> *Exeunt*

252sd Prospero's subsequent lines to Ariel suggest that the conspirators are no longer on stage.
  The howls of Hall's 1974 dogs and of their quarry continued when they were off-stage and
  then gave way to silence.
      Hall's 1988 Prospero let go of the dogs' leads; two of them chased Caliban, Stephano and
  Trinculo out through FOH at 255. As they exited, lower growling was heard in the auditorium.

256a Kemble (1806) had the two spirits who accompanied Prospero and Ariel go off-stage,
  whence came roars from Caliban, Stephano and Trinculo. At Stratford, Hytner's shapes
  attacked the conspirators; Caliban clearly received the worst beating of the three (CD).

257–61 Macready interpolated 3.3.83–91a after 257a and made 257b–61 the opening of 5.1. Barton
  interpolated 5.1.1–6a after 257a and 5.1.6b–7a after 261.

258 Daniels's Prospero shouted the line (archive video).

260a Some Ariels believe they are about to be liberated: Benthall's (1951) made a noise and was
  about to fly, while Daniels's began to run away (archive video).

261sd Iden Payne and Williams (1978) ran this scene straight into the next with both Prospero and
  Ariel remaining on stage. Hack interpolated 'Where the bee sucks' (5.1.88–94) after 261;
  when Ariel finished singing, the action proceeded with 5.1.
      When Daniels's Prospero and Ariel had exited, Stephano, Trinculo and Caliban entered
  separately, met C and jumped on seeing each other. The sound of growling made the trio run
  off the L proscenium; after a pause, followed by more barking, they re-entered from the
  same place, chased by three hounds. Hunted and hunters all exited through the R proscenium (Appendix E of pb).
      Hytner's Ariel picked up the trunk and exited down the cave; at Stratford Prospero exited
  with him, while in London he remained on-stage. The Stratford staging also offered a coda to
  the chase: after Prospero and Ariel had exited, Trinculo and Stephano entered, propping up
  Caliban; when they reached C, the shapes re-entered and chased them off again.

ACT 5 SCENE 1

Enter PROSPERO, *in his magic robes, and* ARIEL

PROSPERO Now does my project gather to a head.
My charms crack not, my spirits obey, and Time
Goes upright with his carriage. How's the day?
ARIEL On the sixth hour; at which time, my lord,
You said our work should cease.

5.1 The only lines retained here in any form by Dryden/Davenant and Shadwell were 95–6a,
216–20a (218b–20a given to Alonso), 224–5a (given to Prospero), 240b–1a, 268–70, 260,
289b–94 (but Caliban did not plan to 'seek for grace' (293a) and realized his mistake in wor-
shipping drunkards only when he saw that 'such as these [gallants] were in the world'),
298–302, 310b–11a, 304b–5a, 312, 314b–16a and 88–94 ('Where the bee sucks'). Interpolated
elsewhere were 1–2, 3b–5a (with 'sixth hour' changed to 'fourth'), 6b–8, 10–28. Closer to
Dryden/Davenant than to Shakespeare, Kemble (1789) similarly used little of the original
text; only 54b–7, 88–94, 179b–80, 181b–4a (divided between Dorinda and Hippolito),
200b–4a, 298–300a and 304b–14a were retained in some form. The play ended with the
masque of Neptune and Amphitrite, which incorporated 4.1.146–56a (slightly changed),
5.1.315b–16a, and a reprise of 'Where the bee sucks'. His 1806 adaptation retained more of
Shakespeare's text, as noted below. Uncharacteristically, given his handling of the rest of the
play, Phelps greatly interfered with the text in this act; see notes below for details.

Illusionistic productions, such as Tree's, set the scene at or in Prospero's cave. Restoration
elements have occasionally intruded into the twentieth century: Atkins (1933, 1934) had a
singing Neptune appear in his concluding (?) masque, an addition that 'brought perilously to
mind the Christmas theatre with its Demon Rat and fluttering juvenile fairies' (programmes;
T 13/9/33). Although his subsequent productions appear to have dispensed with such operatic additions, their influence remained in the Act 4 ballets: a 'Sea Ballet' with Amphitrite and
the Four Winds featured in 1936 (programme), while a 1938 photo shows a scene reminiscent of the masque of Amphitrite, with a trident-holding Neptune and countless nymphs
(TM). It is clear from the programmes, with their listings of principal dancers and sometimes
monstrously sized *corps de ballet*, that dance was always an important part of Atkins's Open
Air Theatre productions, in which the text was 'vigorously pared' (*T* 13/9/33).

osd This scene is unique in Shakespeare's work, in that the two characters whose exit concludes
the preceding scene immediately re-enter to begin the next. John Dover Wilson thought it
evidence of a cut, whereas W. W. Greg argued that it showed the act-division to be original; it
also suggests, as Orgel and Gurr both note, that an interval separated the two scenes (see,

PROSPERO   I did say so,   5
                When first I raised the tempest. Say, my spirit,
                How fares the king and's followers?
        ARIEL   Confined together
                In the same fashion as you gave in charge,
                Just as you left them; all prisoners, sir,
                In the line-grove which weather-fends your cell;   10
                They cannot budge till your release. The king,
                His brother, and yours, abide all three distracted,
                And the remainder mourning over them,

respectively, p. 187 n.267; '*The Tempest's* Tempest', p. 93). Many producers transpose or cut lines from the end of 4.1 or run the two scenes together in order to ease the transition: Macready, for instance, began with 4.1.257b–61, which had been omitted earlier; Iden Payne cut 4.1.260b–1, allowing Prospero and Ariel to remain on-stage; Barton integrated the opening lines of 5.1 with the final lines of 4.1.

   Lepage's actors 'graduate[d] into full makeup and costume' 'Only in Act V' (Donnelly, *MGa* 7/6/93); by the end, they were all in period costume in the middle of flags and oriflammes (Robert Lévesque, *MLD*).

 1 Gielgud, Brook's 1957 Prospero, was 'visibly agitated' at the thought of facing his enemies, prompting doubt whether 'forgiveness will after all triumph' (*T* 14/8/57).

1–7 Integrated by Barton with the closing lines of 4.1; see note to 4.1.257–61.

1–32 None of Purcarete's Ariels was present on stage: instead, the spirit manifested itself as a light, first showing under the bed on which Prospero sat (shining out from between his legs) and then as a light shining on his face (CD).

2–32sd Cut by Garrick (1756), who added 'And little further use have I for charms' as transition between the first line and 'Ye elves'.

3b–6a Cut by Kemble (1806) and Kean; Kemble interpolated 4.1.257b–8 in its place, while Kean substituted an instruction for Ariel to appear which ran straight into 7: 'Ariel! say, / How fares the king and his followers?'

 5 His fruitless reminder to Prospero made Miller's 1988 Ariel sad (CD).

 7 Miller's 1988 Ariel showed distaste for Prospero's imprisonment of the lords (CD).

9–11 Kemble (1806) cut 9b–11a and had to change slightly the lines following to accommodate the omission of characters. Macready cut 9b–10, Daly and Ashwell 9–10, Burton and Kean 10, Tree 9 and 11a, Hack 10–11a. Garrick (1757), Phelps (Williams pb), Tree and Williams (1978), following Rowe's emendation, changed 'line' to 'lime' (10). Thacker's Ariel spoke 11 angrily (CD).

13–17 Macready and Phelps cut 13–17a; Kean 14b–17a; Burton and Daly 16–17a. Thacker's Ariel seemed sorry when she reported Gonzalo's suffering (CD).

Brim full of sorrow and dismay; but chiefly
Him that you termed, sir, the good old lord Gonzalo.   15
His tears runs down his beard like winter's drops
From eaves of reeds. Your charm so strongly works 'em
That if you now beheld them, your affections
Would become tender.

PROSPERO   Dost thou think so, spirit?

ARIEL Mine would, sir, were I human.

PROSPERO   And mine shall.   20
Hast thou, which art but air, a touch, a feeling
Of their afflictions, and shall not myself,
One of their kind, that relish all as sharply
Passion as they, be kindlier moved than thou art?
Though with their high wrongs I am struck to th' quick,   25

19b Bridges-Adams's 1934 Prospero paused before his question, while Daniels's asked it in a
bitter tone, separating the words (archive video).

20 Shakespeare's text leaves ambiguous whether Prospero has always intended forgiveness or
whether Ariel influences him. For Benthall (1951), Badel spoke 20a 'with an indescribable
mixture of envy of the man's heart which *can* "become tender", and of hope that it will';
Prospero's 'sudden shamed repentance[,] and strong prayer for the power to forgive,
turn[ed] a speech which sometimes seems merely smug self-righteousness into a decisive,
victorious struggle' (Ellis, *SH* 29/6/51). Gielgud, Brook's 1957 Prospero, made palpable his
'change of heart more intensely than is common' (T. C. Worsley, *NS* 24/8/57). Strehler's Ariel
inspired Prospero to mercy, with 20a 'doubly affecting coming from one who dangle[d]
puppet-like on a flying wire' (video; Warren, *TLS* 9/3/84). The Williams/Brook Prospero, on
the other hand, had real difficulty in forgiving his enemies; Fleming disappointed several
critics in not being able to 'encompass a sudden enlargement of spirit' (Lambert, *ST* 7/4/63),
but his portrayal stemmed from the director's deliberate interpretation: 'if there is any reconciliation at the end, there is infinitely more irresolution' (Williams, programme notes).
Ninagawa's Prospero raised his wand to strike Ariel at 20a (CD), but 'force[d] himself to lose
face' (Nightingale, *T* 5/12/92). Hytner's, in contrast, played the exchange for ambiguity,
letting go of his staff and standing C: it was not clear whether Prospero had always intended
mercy or was prompted to it by Ariel (London pb and CD). For one reviewer, the exchange
proved the 'key moment' in Noble's production, with Prospero 'amazed by [Ariel's offhand]
remark, and even more astonished to find himself renouncing vengeance' (Nightingale, *Ind*
27/2/98).

21–30a Kean cut 23b–4a; Atkins (1933) 26–8a (Brown, *Observer* 17/9/33); Tree 29–30a. Mendes's
Prospero laughed as he spoke 30a (CD).

Yet, with my nobler reason, 'gainst my fury
Do I take part. The rarer action is
In virtue, than in vengeance. They being penitent,
The sole drift of my purpose doth extend
Not a frown further. Go, release them, Ariel.   30
My charms I'll break, their senses I'll restore,
And they shall be themselves.

ARIEL   I'll fetch them, sir.   *Exit*

PROSPERO Ye elves of hills, brooks, standing lakes, and groves,
And ye that on the sands with printless foot
Do chase the ebbing Neptune, and do fly him   35
When he comes back; you demi-puppets, that

30b   Kemble (1806) altered 30b to 'Follow, gentle Ariel', after which the pair exited, ending 5.1.
Kemble's 5.2. comprised, with some alteration of words and speakers and added material,
182–4a, 252–3a, 100b–1a, 102a, 179b–80, 197–204, 62, 69a, 70b–1a, 216–18a, 256–7 ('Every
man . . . fortune'), 276, 218b–20a, 260, 280–6, 275b, 287, 267b–70, 288–9a, 271–3a,
289b–95a, 223–5a, 240b–1a, 95b, 315b–16a, 88–94, 298–300a, 302b, 304–14a, 51b–2, 54b–7,
88–94 (again); it also interpolated 4.1.1–3, 5a, 7b–12, 146–56a.

30b–2a Although the changes are crossed out, the Phelps/Creswick pb shows that at one point
84b–94 ('in my cell . . . bough') were interpolated here, so that Prospero delivered the 'Ye
elves' speech dressed as the Duke of Milan. Tree cut 31–2a.

Barton's Prospero spoke 'themselves' (32a) as 'a dull, numb groan' (Nightingale, *NS*
23/10/70). Williams's 1978 Prospero also emphasized the word, 'restoring to his enemies
their freewill [*sic*] in full awareness of what they are likely to do with it' (Cushman, *O* 7/5/78).
Daniels's paused before the word and spoke it sadly and emphatically (pb, archive video and
Cushman, *O* 15/8/82).

33–57   At some point during this speech, Prospero creates a magic circle in which the charmed
courtiers will stand; nineteenth-century Prosperos tended to make it at the end (see 57sd).
Hall's 1974 Prospero used sawdust to '[weave] a circle of light around him' (Young, *FT*
6/3/74); Hytner's laid down six stones (pbs and CD). Brook's (1990) had a spirit rake a circle-
pattern in the sand; then he also created his spell with magic stones, addressing them as
spirits and placing them on the circle's periphery (CD). Ninagawa's Prospero stood in a circle
of light; Mendes's, spotlit, sprinkled sand from his fingers; Alexander's had black sand spill
from his staff (CD). Since Strehler's sand-circle set was itself a magic circle, Prospero did not
create one (video). Purcarete's Prospero simply lay prostrate on his bed; as he spoke, the
revolve moved, bringing into view two groups of music stands (CD).

Tree cut the whole speech, which his Prospero later spoke in place of the Epilogue. Garrick
(1756) cut 51b–7; Phelps 34–40a (but restored it) and 46b–8a (Williams pb); Kean 35b–9a,

By moon-shine do the green sour ringlets make,
Whereof the ewe not bites; and you, whose pastime
Is to make midnight mushrooms, that rejoice
To hear the solemn curfew; by whose aid –   40
Weak masters though ye be – I have bedimmed
The noontide sun, called forth the mutinous winds,
And 'twixt the green sea and the azured vault
Set roaring war. To the dread rattling thunder
Have I given fire, and rifted Jove's stout oak   45
With his own bolt; the strong-based promontory

48b–50a; Burton 39b–40a; Daly 36b–8a, 39b–40a, 41a, 44b–50a; Iden Payne 36b–8a. While nineteenth-century productions often omitted reference to Prospero's seemingly black magic (48b–50a), some recent ones have stressed it. Even in renouncing such power, Daniels's Prospero 'clearly relishe[d] it' (Billington, *G* 12/8/82), while Hall's 1988 Prospero reacted strongly to his past actions: he gasped, turned and put hand to head before continuing (CD).

As these two examples demonstrate, Prospero has renounced his magic in myriad ways. Benthall's 1952 Prospero spoke not 'a private meditation, but an invocation in the grand manner' (Ellis, *SH*), whereas Neville's '[addressed] the various spirits . . . severally and affectionately' (Trewin, *ILN* 16/6/62). Brook's 1957 Prospero found his magic not only a source of pride but a frightening temptation; consequently, 'the act of reconciliation [was] also an act of renunciation', and renunciation itself a 'relief', marking a 'return to the merely human state' (Worsley, *NS* 24/8/57); however, many critics also saw some 'wistfulness' in Gielgud (e.g., Trewin, *ILN* 21/12/57). Miller's 1970 Prospero '[gave] up an empire without the cover of which he will be unable to establish any real contact with his fellow-beings' (*ST* 21/6/70); as he spoke, the 'power visibly drain[ed] out of him, leaving him finally curled on the ground as a helpless foetus' (Wardle, *T* 16/6/70). Scofield, for John Harrison, was serene, 'slough[ing his powers] off as easily as last night's pajamas' (Nightingale, *NS* 8/11/74), while Gielgud, for Hall (1974), 'suddenly change[d] from a Wagnerian god into a gentle and dignified old man' (Young, *FT* 6/3/74). Mendes's Prospero 'uttered [the speech] with increasing warmth, as if looking for a new human tenderness in life after magic' (Macauley, *FT* 15/7/94).

Special effects often mark the abjuration (50–1). At 'potent art', Daniels had thunder sound, lightning flash and Prospero standing within a smoking circle (archive video). The smoke appeared to emanate from his wand as it circled the ground, sending up 'fairy rings of smoke', whereas in London, actual and '[very impressive f]lames fl[ew] up' from the floor (respectively, Chapman, *OM* 12/8/82; Cushman, *O* 9/83). Breuer had Prospero's 'book self-destruct' (Kroll, *Nw* 20/7/81), and Armfield lit up 'the globe in the flotsam pile' (Evans, *SMH* 31/5/90). Donnellan, on the other hand, simply had Prospero remove his wig and muss his make-up, since his 'rough magic' referred to theatre itself.

Have I made shake, and by the spurs plucked up
The pine and cedar; graves at my command
Have waked their sleepers, oped, and let 'em forth
By my so potent art. But this rough magic   50
I here abjure. And when I have required
Some heavenly music – which even now I do –
To work mine end upon their senses that
This airy charm is for, I'll break my staff,
Bury it certain fathoms in the earth,   55
And deeper than did ever plummet sound
I'll drown my book.

> *Solemn music. Here enters* ARIEL *before; then* ALONSO *with a*
> *frantic gesture, attended by* GONZALO; SEBASTIAN *and* ANTONIO *in*
> *like manner attended by* ADRIAN *and* FRANCISCO. *They all enter*
> *the circle which* PROSPERO *had made, and there stand charmed;*
> *which* PROSPERO *observing, speaks*

52 For Hall (1988), Prospero's 'conjuration of heavenly music . . . [became] an urgent plea from a man who has been dabbling in Satanism', Bryant giving 'a first-rate performance of a man traumatised by powers he has previously exulted in' (Billington, *G* 21/5/88).

54 Although John Harrison's Prospero was 'so lacking in bitterness that his passion . . . seem[ed] to spring from nowhere', his delivery of ' "I'll *break* my *staff*" brought me literally out of my seat. It suggest[ed] incredible pressures, even if we [were] left unsure what they [were]' (*O* 23/2/75).

57 Hall (1988) had a pause lasting at least five seconds; then as the heavenly music he had conjured reached a crescendo, Prospero broke his staff over his knee, and the shapes left. Ninagawa's Prospero referred to the script of the play which he had followed throughout the performance, so conflating the roles of Prospero and of director (CD).

57sd Macready, Phelps, Burton, Kean, Daly and Benthall had Prospero make his magic circle at the end of 57. Burton's drew 'a circle of fire' to spectacular effect: the wand was lit from under the stage, and its own top contained 'a kind of small lamp . . . from which spirits of wine can flow very gradually for circle', leaving a fiery mark on stage. Benthall's made a circle with his staff, causing nine nymphs to appear and form a 'magic O'; each carried an elaborate candelabra with twelve lighted candles, their light creating one of Benthall's most beautiful scenes (photos; *BED* 27/6/51).

Nineteenth-century productions rearranged this part of the play considerably. After making his circle, Macready's Prospero spoke a highly truncated version of the next speech as Ariel helped to dress him; the Pattie text prints only 62–4a and 82b–7, but since the courtiers had not yet entered, Prospero was presumably looking at them charmed within the

A solemn air, and the best comforter
To an unsettled fancy, cure thy brains,
Now useless, boiled within thy skull. There stand,   60
For you are spell-stopped.

cell. (Moore, in Burton's pb, notes a different Macready cut of 58–60a, 62–82a.) Prospero
then exited, leaving Ariel to sing 'Where the bee sucks', after which he and the lords entered
separately. According to Moore, Gonzalo then spoke 104–6a (before becoming transfixed?),
Prospero 95–103, 64b–8a and 106b ff. Phelps interpolated 95–6, spoken in thanks to Ariel for
leading in the king's party (a change crossed out in the Creswick pb but retained in Williams);
see also notes to 64b–103 and 94. Kean's Prospero summoned Ariel and spoke 87, 95b–6a,
97–101, 252–3a, followed by Ariel's 102–3 and exit. After Prospero's 85–6a and exit, the lords
entered and stood charmed within the circle, Gonzalo speaking 105b–6a. After an invisible
spirit sang 88–94, Prospero entered, speaking 60b–1 and 82b–3a.

The lords sometimes show physical and emotional signs of their ordeal and distress. In
1974, Hall's maddened Alonso tried to kill himself with his sword but was stopped by
Gonzalo; both Sebastian and Antonio acted 'mad' in some way. Bogdanov's 1992 lords were
not only chained but as filthy as Caliban, Stephano and Trinculo had been in the previous
scene (CD); Mendes, however, distinguished the 'men of sin' from the innocent lords: all had
lost their jackets but only the guilty were filthy. Once they had entered the magic circle, Ariel
raised his hands, causing them to cover their faces in a penitent gesture (CD).

How quickly the lords enter the circle and how still they remain is left to the director's discretion. Alexander's, for example, stood outside it until Prospero addressed them individually, whereupon each stepped inside. Ninagawa's entered as if frozen and circled round and
round the magic ring of light on the Noh stage, stopping only when named by Prospero (CD).

58–61 Garrick (1757), Phelps (Williams pb), Kean, Daly, Tree, Bridges-Adams (1926/30, 1934),
Ayrton, Iden Payne, Benthall (1952) and (?) Hack cut 58–60a; Hack's pb suggests 59b–60a
were interpolated after 'spell-stopped'. Macready and Phelps (Creswick pb) cut 58–61, the
latter interpolating 60b–1 later. See notes to 57sd and 94.

58–83a Purcarete transposed these lines with 83b–94; Prospero spoke most of them in the absence
of the lords as he continued to make himself up (see note to 88–94). Since only the Ariels
were present with him on-stage, his words became a kind of meditation on his feelings, or a
dress rehearsal for his coming encounter with his enemies; at 'flesh and blood', he hugged
the mirror, presumably anticipating reconciliation with Antonio. At 82b, the lords were
revealed behind Prospero's bed when the blue curtain was drawn back; they were now dressed
in suits and bowler hats, apart from Alonso, who continued to wear his crown (CD). Although
my notes do not indicate Purcarete's cuts, they suggest that 104 followed on from 83a.

58–103 Cut by Garrick (1756), who provided Prospero with an air, 'Let magick sounds affright no
more', after his abjuration. Then Ariel entered, followed by Alonso, Antonio and Gonzalo.

> Holy Gonzalo, honourable man,
> Mine eyes, ev'n sociable to the show of thine,
> Fall fellowly drops. The charm dissolves apace,
> And as the morning steals upon the night,   65
> Melting the darkness, so their rising senses
> Begin to chase the ignorant fumes that mantle
> Their clearer reason. O good Gonzalo –
> My true preserver, and a loyal sir
> To him thou follow'st – I will pay thy graces   70
> Home both in word and deed. Most cruelly
> Didst thou, Alonso, use me, and my daughter.
> Thy brother was a furtherer in the act –
> Th' art pinched for't now, Sebastian. Flesh and blood,

62–83a The charmed lords sometimes respond to Prospero's mention of them. Benthall had each fall to his knees when addressed by Prospero, while each of Paige's lords 'stirred and twitched, starting to come out of his trance' (Carter, '*The Tempest* at Salisbury Playhouse', p. 32). Most directors have the lords begin to show signs of returning sensibility after 64b, although many, like Crozier, emphasize the slowness of the process.

   Garrick (1757) cut 68b–71a, 76b–8a. Macready cut 64b–82a, Daly and Tree 62–82a; the former two interpolated 64b–8a after 103sd. Bridges-Adams (1926/30, 1934), (?) Ayrton and Hack cut 63–8; Iden Payne 62–8a, 77; Benthall (1952) 62–8a, 74a, 77, 78b–9a; Daniels 80b–2a. For Kean's arrangement, see note to 57sd; for Phelps's, see note to 64b–103.

64b–103 Phelps greatly rearranged the text. Williams notes that he cut 68b–103, interpolated 251b–3a and 79b–83, and then resumed with 104ff. Creswick notes an additional cut of 64b–8a and both interpolations but cancels the second. The major cut of 68b–103 is noted, although 82b–3 are retained and 83b–103 marked as if they have been restored and transposed.

74b–9a Prospero's forgiveness of Antonio is often in doubt; indeed, as noted at 62–83a, Benthall (1952) cut 78b–9a. Daniels's Prospero was furious when he addressed his brother, moving in on him as if intending harm (archive video). At 78a, Ariel went SR of Antonio (pb), so that spirit and master faced each other across the usurper (archive video). His 'sudden, silent appearance' checked Prospero's 'ungovernable fury' and led (after the pause marked in the pb) to the 'hard-wrung' forgiveness of 78b (Billington, *G* 12/8/82). Miller's 1988 Prospero 'arrested [the] gesture with which he makes to smash Antonio's face with his staff' (Taylor, *Ind* 13/10/88); Ninagawa's also stopped himself from striking Antonio (CD).

   Murray interpreted Prospero's words very differently. When the lords had entered for the first time, during the shipwreck, they each held 'in front of their faces' a mask with Prospero's features; they had them again at 57sd. Prospero 'gravely receive[d] the masks from their wearers, raise[d] them priest-like into the air, and addresse[d] them with . . . "I do forgive

You, brother mine, that entertained ambition,   75
Expelled remorse and nature, who, with Sebastian –
Whose inward pinches therefore are most strong –
Would here have killed your king; I do forgive thee,
Unnatural though thou art. Their understanding
Begins to swell, and the approaching tide   80
Will shortly fill the reasonable shore
That now lies foul and muddy. Not one of them
That yet looks on me, or would know me. Ariel,
Fetch me the hat and rapier in my cell.
I will discase me, and myself present   85
As I was sometime Milan. Quickly, spirit,
Thou shalt ere long be free.

ARIEL *sings, and helps to attire him*

thee, unnatural though thou art"' (Nightingale, *T* 15/9/90). As is clear from the staging,
Murray saw the play as focusing on Prospero's internal struggle.

82 Alexander's Prospero positioned himself DSR, striking a pose, to reveal himself to the
courtiers; then realizing that no one would recognize him, he decided to put on his ducal
robes – a Ruritanian jacket and sash – which Ariel got from a suitcase DSC (CD).

83b–7 Daly cut 83b–4; Hack, Williams (1978) and Daniels 84. Tree transposed 85–6a and 86b–7.
The lines are sometimes adapted to reflect a production's costuming; Barton, for instance,
changed 'hat' to 'robe'. Daniels's Prospero paused after calling Ariel, seemingly considering
what to do next: the donning of ducal attire was impromptu.

The passage provides opportunities to define further Prospero and Ariel's relationship.
Thacker's Ariel seemed hesitant to remove Prospero's magic cloak (CD), while Brook's 1957
Prospero broke his wand at 83b and handed it to him. Hall's 1988 Prospero embraced Ariel at
87, while Mendes's spoke the line in response to Ariel's glare (CD).

83b–106a Kean cut 83b–106a, interpolating some lines earlier (see note to 57sd). Phelps cut 83b–103
(Creswick marks them 'in' and 'transposed', while Williams interpolates 84b–94 earlier; see
notes to 30b–2a and 94); Williams resumes Folio order at 104.

87sd Ariel sometimes sings alone on stage. Garrick's (1757) did so when Prospero exited into his
cell to dress, while Macready's did so after helping to dress him. Some Prosperos forego
royal trappings: Falls's, for example, put on 'a dress shirt, vest [waistcoat], tie, and suitcoat'
(Pellowe, 'In Chicago', p. 55), while Purcarete's was given a red bathrobe, red bib with
fronds, wig with red bow tying its pigtail and shoes (CD). Burton and Tree cut the sd.

Brook's 1957 Prospero made a surprising transformation the moment he put on his ducal
robe, becoming 'suddenly gentle, smiling and approachable', 'a gay and radiant Renaissance
magnifico in the prime of life' (respectively, Rosemary Anne Sisson, *SH* 16/8/57; John

[ARIEL] Where the bee sucks, there suck I;
        In a cowslip's bell I lie;
        There I couch when owls do cry;   90
        On the bat's back I do fly
        After summer merrily.
        Merrily, merrily, shall I live now,
        Under the blossom that hangs on the bough.

Wardle, *BEN* 17/8/57). Hytner's Prospero rushed to don the accoutrements of power before the spell evaporated; in London, some comedy was added when he discovered his old sword belt no longer fit comfortably around his waist (CD).

88–94 Robert Johnson provided a setting for the song, either for a court revival or for the original production (Sturgess, *Jacobean Private Theatre*, p. 83); although it has often been used in subsequent stagings, many composers have produced new and admired settings. For example, Daniels's Ariel sounded 'almost like a counter-tenor' as he sang Stephen Oliver's 'sinuous melody accompanied by solo bassoon' (Coveney, *FT* 13/8/82). In contrast, Brook's 1957 tape-recorded *musique concrète* aroused much hostility: 'the songs are scurvily treated' by the 'plinks and plonks and grunts and groans', which provided 'a sort of eight-note recitative' (respectively, *OM* 14/8/57; *LS*; *LDP* 14/8/57). While agreeing that these were not 'passable settings for the songs', Tynan (*O* 18/8/57) found that the seeming 'combination of glockenspiel, thundersheet, Malayan nose-flute and discreetly tortured Sistine choirboy' produced an effective dreamy twangle, an opinion echoed by many other critics.

Garrick (1757), following Theobald, changed 'suck' (88) to 'lurk' and 'summer' (92) to 'sunset'. The refrain (93–4) is sometimes repeated, as in Williams's 1978 and Thacker's productions; Williams also had 90 sung twice. Purcarete had the song recited in voice-over as Prospero dressed and made up his face with white powder; because of the director's transposition, Prospero spoke 58–83a when the song finished, still applying powder as he did so (CD; see note to 58–83a).

While some producers, like Burton and Tree, cut the song, others employ it to specific effect. For example, Burge used Western pitch intervals for it, since Prospero has now renounced his magic (Foulkes, review, p. 24; programme notes). Hall (1988) had it recorded and the band amplified with reverberation so that Ariel's voice came from different places in the theatre (pb and CD).

Paige's Ariel sang under his breath, using 'a very small compass of notes' so that the effect was 'like the sound of a bee among flowers' (Carter, '*The Tempest* at Salisbury Playhouse', p. 32).

94 Macready's Prospero re-entered with the lords; 104–6a were interpolated between 94 and 95. According to the Phelps/Creswick pb, Ariel exited after the song and re-entered with the king's party, as Prospero re-entered dressed as the Duke of Milan. Then 60b–1, 95–103, 64b–8a were interpolated, the text resuming with 106b. (Such a staging contradicts an earlier

PROSPERO Why that's my dainty Ariel. I shall miss thee,   95
        But yet thou shalt have freedom. So, so, so.
        To the king's ship, invisible as thou art;
        There shalt thou find the mariners asleep
        Under the hatches. The master and the boatswain
        Being awake, enforce them to this place;   100
        And presently, I prithee.
ARIEL I drink the air before me, and return
        Or ere your pulse twice beat.   *Exit*

direction that Prospero re-enter alone after Ariel's song to speak the 'Ye elves' speech; see note to 30b–2a above.) The Phelps/Williams pb resumes Folio order with 104.
    Having been dressed in hat, coat and sword, Miller's 1988 Prospero used a mirror to check how he looked: his examination was painstaking rather than cursory (CD).

95–6 Garrick (1757) cut 96b. Daly cut 95b–6; after 95a Prospero spoke 'So, so' and interpolated 251b–3a. 95b sometimes makes Ariel fear Prospero will renege on his promise of freedom. Crozier's Ariel dropped his head slightly, raising it again at 96. Daniels's turned US, backing SL; the comment that Prospero's 'ever-repeated promises . . . that [Ariel] will have his liberty . . . seem to come from a guilty conscience' probably reflects Jacobi's delivery of 96a (Fenton, *ST* 15/8/82). Other interpretations are available: Thacker's Ariel reeled at the news that Prospero would miss her, while Mendes's Prospero touched Ariel's face and almost cooed 'so, so, so' (CD); Beale superbly 'convey[ed] that the gesture [was] both a presumption and at some level desired' (Taylor, *Ind* 13/8/93).

97–106a Macready interpolated 64b–8a after 103sd, running them straight into 106b, since 104–6a had been interpolated earlier. Burton cut 97–100 and substituted 251b–3a for 99b–100; Prospero dissolved the spell at 101. The sequence of events was presumably as follows: Ariel returned with the ducal garments as Gonzalo, uncharmed earlier than his fellows, spoke 104–6a; while Ariel helped Prospero to dress, Prospero spoke 95–6 and 251b–3a, finishing with 101. As Prospero gestured to release the rest of the courtiers from the spell, Ariel replied with 102–3 and exited. Daly cut 97–101 and interpolated 64b–8a after 103sd; Prospero then waved his wand to remove the spell from the lords. Tree cut 97–106a; Prospero spoke 95–6 to Ariel as she returned with the sword and coronet. Benthall (1952) cut 104–6a. Hack cut 97–101a, interpolating 252–3a in its place.

102–3 Daniels's Ariel put his ear to Prospero's wrist as if to judge accurately the time needed; in contrast, Hay's Ariel's was 'so relaxed [about his errands] that he scarcely justifie[d] the boast' (Milne, *STel* 11/10/92). Some of the Williams/Brook staging was 'literal almost to the point of absurdity. "I drink the air", says Ariel, opening his mouth like a fish and destroying the image of a flying spirit' (*T* 3/4/63).

103sd Not only did Benthall's Ariel exit but the nymphs broke up their circle, removing the spell from the courtiers.

GONZALO All torment, trouble, wonder, and amazement
   Inhabits here. Some heavenly power guide us   105
   Out of this fearful country!
PROSPERO   Behold, sir king,
   The wrongèd Duke of Milan, Prospero.
   For more assurance that a living prince
   Does now speak to thee, I embrace thy body,
   And to thee, and thy company, I bid   110
   A hearty welcome.
ALONSO   Whether thou beest he or no,
   Or some enchanted trifle to abuse me,
   As late I have been, I not know. Thy pulse

106b–7 The most memorable moment of Brook's 1957 production came when Gielgud, 'in his robe of turquoise', spoke 106b–7 'in a voice that . . . had the sound of an autumn night's high tide' (Trewin, *Lady* 28?/12/57); he showed 'his profound sense of release' once he had renounced his magic, greeting the lords with 'ease and gaiety' (*LSC*). In contrast, as Hytner's Prospero began to speak, none of the lords turned around to listen to him; only when he shouted the 'wronged Duke of Milan' did they do so, whereupon he softly spoke his name (CD). Breuer treated the reconciliation 'as a cocktail party awash with Mantovani-like strains of "When You Wish Upon a Star" ' (Watt, *DN* 10/7/81), while Alexander had an explosion propel the lords out of the magic circle; Prospero then entered it to deliver his speech, taking care to break it with his foot when he eventually left it (CD). Thacker's Ariel was very interested in Alonso's reaction to Prospero, while Miller's 1988 Antonio half-drew his sword when Prospero announced himself; he kept it half-drawn, sheathing it a bit at 118a and completely at 121.

109 When Hytner's Prospero embraced Alonso, the latter looked amazed (Stratford pb). Prospero's 'visible uneasiness with people' manifested itself in the 'nervous jocularity with which he greet[ed the lords]' (Billington, *G* 29/7/88). 'Facing the Neapolitan court, Wood [was] almost unendurably pathetic: they accept[ed] his kisses with the mild embarrassment they'd reserve for the harmlessly simple-minded. With his book buried, Prospero has once more become a failed elder statesman' (Renton, *Ind* 1/8/88). Purcarete's Prospero, although he spoke the words, did not embrace Alonso (CD).

110–11a Cut by Garrick (1757) and (?) Hack; Garrick (1756) simplified them to 'And bid thee welcome'.
111b–19a Tree cut 111b–19a; Ashwell 113a and 114b–19a; Kean 113b–17; Ayrton 114b–19a; Garrick (1756) 115b–16a; Daly 116–17; (?) Wright 118–20a. Kean changed 'trifle' (112) to 'devil'.

  Crozier's Alonso knelt to Prospero at 118a, followed by all the other courtiers except Antonio; Bridges-Adams's Alonso (1934) was about to kneel at 119a, but Prospero stopped him. Bogdanov's 1992 Antonio and Sebastian spent much of this scene whispering between themselves at SR (CD).

Beats as of flesh and blood; and since I saw thee,
Th' affliction of my mind amends, with which   115
I fear a madness held me. This must crave,
And if this be at all, a most strange story.
Thy dukedom I resign, and do entreat
Thou pardon me my wrongs. But how should Prospero
Be living, and be here?
PROSPERO   First, noble friend,   120
Let me embrace thine age, whose honour cannot
Be measured or confined.
GONZALO   Whether this be,
Or be not, I'll not swear.
PROSPERO   You do yet taste
Some subtleties o' th' isle, that will not let you
Believe things certain. Welcome, my friends all.   125
But you, my brace of lords, were I so minded
I here could pluck his highness' frown upon you
And justify you traitors. At this time

120a Burton, Barry and McVicker had Prospero wave his wand, releasing the courtiers from the spell (Becks's pb).

120b–5 Prospero addresses and embraces Gonzalo at 120b–1a; Purcarete's Alonso, mistakenly thinking Prospero's gesture of embrace was meant for him, was ready to reciprocate (CD). Garrick (1756) cut 120b–3a; Tree 122b–5; Phelps, Wright and Hack 125b (Phelps/Williams notes that when retained it was addressed to Adrian and Francisco).

123b–52 At about 123b, Purcarete's Ariels brought in wine and, at 125b, Prospero and the lords all drank, as if in a toast of greeting; at 134a, they drank again, as if in agreement with Prospero's demand for the return of his dukedom. Although Prospero had earlier rehearsed an embrace with his brother (see note to 58–83a), they did not do so. Although Prospero's 'movement towards forgiveness [was] affecting . . . the final scene [brought] precious little comfort. Prospero [was] still overwhelmed by his sense of sin, while his former enemies, in their smart suits and bowler hats, seem[ed] frankly bored by his long explanations, standing stiffly and sipping champagne as if at some stuffy Foreign Office reception' (Spencer, *DT* 18/9/95). The 'most telling emotion' in the production came from 'Alonso, suddenly grief-stricken on Prospero's behalf' (Kingston, *T* 12/9/95).

126–9 Cut by Garrick (both versions), Tree, and (?) Crozier; Burton and Daly cut 129. Some Prosperos speak aside to Sebastian and Antonio: Wolfe's, for instance, whispered in a way that suggested his mastery of 'Machiavellian politics' (Karam, *T* 14/7/95). Others, like Ninagawa's, speak in the hearing of all the lords (CD).

> I will tell no tales.
>
> SEBASTIAN   The devil speaks in him!
>
> PROSPERO   No.
>
> For you, most wicked sir, whom to call brother   130
> Would even infect my mouth, I do forgive
> Thy rankest fault – all of them – and require

130–4a Some Prosperos find it easier to forgive Antonio than others. Brook's 1957 Prospero paused before 130 and 131b and 'finally [forgave] his enemies . . . with a note of some asperity' (Granger, *FT* 6/12/57); Burge's showed 'profound repugnance' (Lewsen, *T* 28/2/72). Daniels's Prospero paused between 'wicked' and 'sir' (130), making his tone more civil when he resumed speaking: he paused again after 131a, presumably to regain control of himself (archive video and pb). In contrast, Hytner's Prospero put his arms around Antonio at 131a and kissed him twice on the cheek; then, weeping, he proceeded with 'I do forgive', evincing a pathetic longing for a response that Antonio was clearly unable to give (CD). (Nightingale, on the other hand, felt that 'When he plant[ed] a kiss on his brother's cheek, he nearly [threw] up, so much pain [did] the gesture cost his stomach', *P* 12/8/88.) Similarly, Brook's 1990 Prospero showed 'no great distaste for his brother': he and Antonio embraced each other (CD and Taylor, *Ind* 2/11/90).

Antonio's silence allows free interpretation of his response, both to Prospero's forgiveness and to his resumption of ducal power, and actors have run the gamut from humble gratitude to sneering villainy. When Prospero demands his dukedom, many Antonios, like those of Macready and Burton, kneel in acquiescence; Daniels's also kissed the hand Prospero held out to him, although not with any great alacrity (pb and archive video). Thacker's looked at Alonso, who nodded in agreement; Antonio then gave Prospero his ducal ring and sank down depressed on one of the chests (CD). Mendes's Antonio, however, showed no reaction, simply stepping DS FO at 135a: the way in which he remained 'ostentatiously aloof' suggested he were 'already planning a counter-coup' (CD; Nightingale, *T* 13/8/93). Alexander's Antonio grinned when Prospero forgave him, but quickly wiped the grin off his face when his brother also demanded his dukedom back (CD). Brook's 1990 Antonio, however, clearly accepted Prospero's forgiveness, kneeling to him after their embrace: 'not the usual cynical outsider . . . [Antonio] seem[ed] honestly impressed and baffled by the happy ending' (CD; Taylor, *Ind* 2/11/90). Donnellan went even further: Antonio put his hand on Prospero's heart, shrieked and embraced him, 'suddenly repentant . . . his face sunlit with pleasure at the reconciliation' (CD; Brown, *TLS* 2/12/88). In contrast, Tipton's Antonio 'literally turn[ed] his back on the scene' when Prospero forgave him and 'laugh[ed] – a cold, sneering laugh' that showed he had not changed (respectively, Shyer, 'Disenchanted', p. 64; Close, *SPPP* 15/10/91).

Garrick (1756) cut 132b–4a; Crozier 130–4a.

My dukedom of thee, which perforce I know
Thou must restore.

ALONSO   If thou beest Prospero,
Give us particulars of thy preservation,   135
How thou hast met us here, whom three hours since
Were wracked upon this shore; where I have lost –
How sharp the point of this remembrance is –
My dear son Ferdinand.

PROSPERO   I am woe for't, sir.

ALONSO Irreparable is the loss, and patience   140
Says it is past her cure.

PROSPERO   I rather think
You have not sought her help, of whose soft grace
For the like loss, I have her sovereign aid,
And rest myself content.

ALONSO   You the like loss?

PROSPERO As great to me, as late; and supportable   145
To make the dear loss have I means much weaker
Than you may call to comfort you; for I
Have lost my daughter.

ALONSO   A daughter?
O heavens, that they were living both in Naples,
The king and queen there! That they were, I wish   150
Myself were mudded in that oozy bed
Where my son lies. When did you lose your daughter?

PROSPERO In this last tempest. I perceive these lords
At this encounter do so much admire

134b–71 The section has often been severely cut. Garrick (1756) cut 134b–58a, 160b–2a, 164, 165b–70a,
with 'Alonzo, / I'll show thee a wonder' added before 170b; in 1757, he cut 145b–7a. Macready
and Kean cut 140–57a, 163–5a, with the former also cutting 170–1. Phelps cut 140–57a (later
reduced to 144b–7, 150b–2a, 153b–7a), 162b–5 and (in Creswick only) 170–1. Burton cut
140–6a, 153b–62a, 170–1; Daly 139b–62a, 170–1; Tree 139b–67a, 168–75a; Ashwell 142b,
144b–57a, 166b–7a; Bridges-Adams (1926/30, 1934) 145b–7a, 153b–65a; Ayrton 144b–7a,
150b–2a, 153b–65a; Iden Payne 145b–7a, 148b–9a, 156b–8a, 160b–5a, 166b–7a; Wright
149–52a, 153b–62a; Benthall 145b–7a, 153b–67a, with 167b interpolated after 171; Barton
145b–6a, 155b–7, 168, part of 169–70; Hack 153b–65a, 167b; and Williams (1978) 145b–7a.

153a Mendes's Prospero laughed. Purcarete's Miranda entered from SL, wearing a voluminous
skirt and carrying a chessboard; however, the lords did not notice her until the appropriate
time (CD).

That they devour their reason, and scarce think   155
Their eyes do offices of truth, their words
Are natural breath. But howsoe'er you have
Been jostled from your senses, know for certain
That I am Prospero, and that very duke
Which was thrust forth of Milan, who most strangely   160
Upon this shore, where you were wracked, was landed
To be the lord on't. No more yet of this,
For 'tis a chronicle of day by day,
Not a relation for a breakfast, nor
Befitting this first meeting. Welcome, sir;   165
This cell's my court. Here have I few attendants,
And subjects none abroad. Pray you look in.
My dukedom since you have given me again,
I will requite you with as good a thing,
At least bring forth a wonder, to content ye   170
As much as me my dukedom.

Here Prospero discovers FERDINAND *and* MIRANDA, *playing at chess*

159 Addressing Alonso, Hytner's Prospero became angry again, talking loudly and stressing 'That
     I am *Prospero*', before calming himself down (CD).

165b–6a Mendes's spirits brought on a table, screen and wicker basket, as in 1.2, thus establishing the
         cell to which he welcomes them (CD).

166a For Hall (1974) all the courtiers turned to look at Prospero's cell; at the same time the trap
      opened and the lift came up unnoticed with Miranda and Ferdinand on it. A gesture from
      Prospero cued their discovery at the appropriate point.

166b Bridges-Adams's 1934 Prospero clapped his hands and two elves entered.

171sd In the original staging, Miranda and Ferdinand were probably revealed in the discovery-
       space; eighteenth- and nineteenth-century productions opened the entrance of Prospero's
       cell to discover them. (Kean had them played by doubles to facilitate their subsequent entry.)
       Twentieth-century productions have been more inventive (and more simple): Benthall (1951)
       had the nymphs part to reveal them; Strehler had Prospero stand, holding out his robe, so
       that when he moved away, he revealed the pair; Brook (1990) had them simply walk on while
       the other characters were preoccupied (CD). Mendes had Prospero tip the screen over,
       revealing the lovers sitting on piles of books (CD). Hytner had chess pieces fly into the air and
       the courtiers scatter as Miranda and Ferdinand erupted from the cell; Ferdinand protected
       himself with the board while Miranda flung the pieces at him. Both ran around the stage,
       dodging courtiers, and ended up USC (Stratford pb and CD). Jones, however, used more
       elaborate staging: Koltai's 'lunar landscape' contained a globe that 'open[ed] with a roll-top

MIRANDA Sweet lord, you play me false.

FERDINAND   No, my dearest love,
      I would not for the world.

MIRANDA Yes, for a score of kingdoms you should wrangle,
      And I would call it fair play.

ALONSO   If this prove   175
      A vision of the island, one dear son
      Shall I twice lose.

SEBASTIAN   A most high miracle.

FERDINAND Though the seas threaten, they are merciful;
      I've cursed them without cause.
               [*kneels*]

ALONSO   Now all the blessings

---

action, revealing Miranda and Ferdinand. It's as if they'd been swallowed by a giant armadillo' (Marcus, *STel* 21/7/68).

    Modern directors have sometimes used the scene to characterize the lovers further: Donnellan's Ferdinand, for example, cheated by surreptitiously moving some pieces (CD). Some ignore the stage direction: when Simmons's lovers were 'revealed to the assembled company they [were] not exactly playing chess'; the remark's context makes clear that they were engaged in intercourse (Wardle, *T* 10/5/78). Burge had Miranda appear in 'Velasquez-style' Western clothes and shoes for the first time (Foulkes, review, p. 25).

172 The lovers are too preocupied with their game to notice the lords immediately. Daly had the vision of the pair vanish.

    Purcarete's Miranda spoke 172a although Ferdinand was nowhere to be seen; he promptly answered, however, as he came out from under her skirt, casting a different construction on her accusation of playing her 'false'. Donnellan's Miranda yelled 'Yes' (174) and scattered the chess-pieces, so that Ferdinand knelt to her in abasement; then a magic chord sounded, and the two lovers were able to see the court. Miller's 1988 Ferdinand and then Miranda tumbled out of the SL white box and 'land[ed]' in an undignified heap at the feet of Alonso'; Francisco, who in 2.1 had kept his belief that Ferdinand was alive, pointed to him while excitedly calling 'Sir, sir' to Alonso (CD; quotation from Armitstead, *HHE* 28/10/88).

    Burton, Kean and Wright cut 172–5a. Garrick (1756) inserted Ferdinand's air 'If on those endless charms you lay' between 175a and the subsequent entrance of Prospero, the courtiers and Ariel.

175b–7 Cut by Hack. Garrick (1756) and Tree cut 177b, but Brook (1990) emphasized the 'harmony. . . . Sebastian's cry "A most high miracle" . . . [was] not the usual side-of-the-mouth sceptical mutter but an exclamation of unmistrustful wonder' (Taylor, *Ind* 2/11/90).

179b–81a Cut by Tree. Ninagawa's Alonso knelt to lift up Ferdinand; they then embraced, with Alonso

Of a glad father compass thee about.   180
Arise, and say how thou cam'st here.
MIRANDA   O wonder!
How many goodly creatures are there here!
How beauteous mankind is! O brave new world
That has such people in't!
PROSPERO   'Tis new to thee.
ALONSO What is this maid with whom thou wast at play?   185
Your eld'st acquaintance cannot be three hours.

continuing to feel Ferdinand during Miranda's ensuing lines to make sure he was really alive (CD).

181b–4 The irony of Miranda's words is sometimes emphasized by having her direct them to Antonio or Sebastian; Barton, for example, had her kneel before her uncle at 183b (Trewin, *BP* 16/10/70), while Daniels's spoke while looking at him and Sebastian (archive video). However, Williams (1978) undercut the potential irony by having Miranda cross to Gonzalo, her 'wondering rapture' making her response moving (Levin, *ST* 7/5/78). Mendes, however, gave her words a very different and comical meaning: her stress on '*wonder*!' made one of the lesser lords back away in alarm, and her delivery of 183a made it appear 'as if she [were] setting off to be a coquette' (CD; Rutherford, *FT* 13/8/93). Edwards's Miranda, on the other hand, simply revealed her 'appealing, adolescent naturalness by her constant breaking into smiles of delight' (Thomson, *SundH* 20/5/90). Armfield's Miranda similarly showed a 'natural joy' that 'almost' removed the irony (Eccles, *Bul* 12/6/90).

Prospero's 184b has also been handled variously. Benthall's 1951 Prospero 'nicely [threw it] away with ironic effect', while Barton's was 'wry' and Ninagawa's amused (respectively, *LSC* 29/6/51; Barber, *DT* 17/10/70; Ratcliffe, *O* 21/8/88). John Harrison's Prospero invested the words 'with a smiling benign tenderness that warms (and breaks) the heart' (Marcus, *STel* 23/2/75). Thacker's delivered them in a humorous, knowing way, with the emphasis on 'thee' (CD). Hytner's conveyed his sense of Miranda's wonder, his delivery 'not bitterly or gently ironic but weird and wondering' (CD; Koenig, *P* 9/6/89). Daniels's Prospero emphasized ''*Tis* new – to thee' with an upward inflection on the final word (archive video), while Hall's (1988) 'spat [the words] acidly in the face of . . . Sebastian' (Coveney, *FT* 20/5/88). Wolfe's production 'particular[ly] triumph[ed]' in giving the exchange 'equally stirring due to [Miranda's] wonder and [Prospero's] melancholy' (Brantley, *NYT* 12/7/95); Miranda's dazzlement echoed Caliban's, who had been 'similarly wonderstruck seeing his first drunk' (Kissel, *DN* 12/7/95).

Garrick (1756) cut 181; Macready, Phelps, Burton and Kean 183b–4.

185b Cut by Tree, who had cut the chess game.

186–8a Kean, Tree and Barton cut 186; Burton and Daly 186–8a; Garrick (1756) the reference to severing (187).

Is she the goddess that hath severed us,
And brought us thus together?
FERDINAND   Sir, she is mortal;
But by immortal providence, she's mine.
I chose her when I could not ask my father   190
For his advice, nor thought I had one. She
Is daughter to this famous Duke of Milan,
Of whom so often I have heard renown,
But never saw before; of whom I have
Received a second life; and second father   195
This lady makes him to me.
ALONSO   I am hers.
But O, how oddly will it sound, that I
Must ask my child forgiveness!
PROSPERO   There, sir, stop.
Let us not burden our remembrances with
A heaviness that's gone.
GONZALO   I have inly wept,   200
Or should have spoke ere this. Look down, you gods,
And on this couple drop a blessèd crown;

188b–9   Williams's 1978 Gonzalo stood and 'chatted' to Miranda and embraced her; Ferdinand went
         to cross to her at 189 but, since she still was engaged with Gonzalo, he crossed to Alonso
         again. (Shakespeare signals Miranda's interest in Gonzalo at 1.2.68b–9a.)
              At 188b, Daniels's Ferdinand took Miranda's hand and led her to Alonso, joining their
         hands together. Prospero was 'touch-and-go to the very end . . . there is a fine moment
         when you see his gorge rising as Alonso places a hand on his daughter', this approach giving
         the play 'a much-needed dynamic' (Billington, *G* 14/9/83).
193–6a   Garrick (1756) cut 193–4a and 195–6a; Ferdinand sang 'Life resembles April weather' before
         196b. Barton cut 193–4a. Donnellan's Ferdinand addressed 193 to Antonio, thereby implying
         that the latter had talked admiringly about his brother since the usurpation (CD).
196b–8   Brook's 1957 Alonso kissed Miranda at 198a. Barton's knelt to her at 196b and Miranda pros-
         trated herself to him at 198a; Prospero helped her up at 198b.
   200a In a 'thrillingly transcendent moment', Noble's Prospero showed 'a man becoming suddenly
         and miraculously aware of his own freedom' (Spencer, *DT* 7/1/99).
200b–15 Garrick (1756), Macready, Phelps, Kean, Burton, Daly and Tree cut 200b–13 (Burton may
         have retained 200b–4a). Garrick (1756) followed 215a with Prospero's air to Miranda, 'With
         him thy joys shall be compleat', and cut 215b; in 1757 he cut 205–13. Brook (1957) cut
         200b–1a, 205–6a and 208b–15 (with 206b–8a interpolated before 201b at DL). Bridges-

> For it is you that have chalked forth the way
> Which brought us hither.
>
> ALONSO   I say 'amen', Gonzalo.
>
> GONZALO Was Milan thrust from Milan, that his issue   205
> Should become kings of Naples? O rejoice
> Beyond a common joy, and set it down
> With gold on lasting pillars: in one voyage
> Did Claribel her husband find at Tunis,
> And Ferdinand her brother found a wife   210
> Where he himself was lost; Prospero, his dukedom
> In a poor isle, and all of us ourselves,
> When no man was his own.
>
> ALONSO [*To Ferdinand and Miranda*] Give me your hands:
> Let grief and sorrow still embrace his heart
> That doth not wish you joy.
>
> GONZALO   Be it so, amen.   215

Enter ARIEL, *with the* MASTER *and* BOATSWAIN *amazedly*
following

> O look, sir, look, sir, here is more of us!
> I prophesied, if a gallows were on land
> This fellow could not drown. Now, blasphemy,

Adams (1926/30, 1934) and Iden Payne cut 204b–13a; (?) Miller (1988) 213b; Hack 214–15.
After 215b, Williams (1978) interpolated 'Helloa!' from the Boatswain, who was still presumably off-stage.

 Donnellan's queen, brimming with false sincerity, delivered 214–15a out to the audience as if it were one of Thatcher's speeches (CD).

215sd Strehler's Ariel led on the Master and the Boatswain, the latter unknowingly holding Ariel's hand (video). Ninagawa's two mariners entered in a trance and then awoke (CD). Many productions, however, have cut or changed the sd; see next note.

215sd–55 This section is often severely cut, with some lines interpolated elsewhere. In 1756 Garrick cut it entirely, but in 1757 he cut only 219a. Macready cut 215sd–25a, 227–40a, 242–51a; Kean 217–20a, 223, 225–53a. Phelps, Burton, Daly and Hack cut 215sd–3; the latter three had earlier interpolated 252–3a, with Hack also interpolating 240b–1 after 257. Tree cut 216–51, 253b; Ashwell 215sd–51a; Bridges-Adams (1926/30, 1934) 218b–20, 228b–45a, 247b–51a; Ayrton 218b–20, 225b–6, 243–5; Iden Payne 218b–20, 237b–40a, 243–5a, 247b–50 (except 'be cheerful'); Brook (1957) 244b–53a; Barton (who gave 220b to Alonso and 229–30a to the Master) 234, 244b–5a, 248a, 249.

That swear'st grace overboard – not an oath on shore?
Hast thou no mouth by land? What is the news? 220
BOATSWAIN The best news is, that we have safely found
    Our king and company. The next, our ship,
    Which but three glasses since we gave out split,
    Is tight and yare and bravely rigged as when
    We first put out to sea.
ARIEL [*aside to Prospero*]   Sir, all this service 225
    Have I done since I went.
PROSPERO [*aside to Ariel*]   My tricksy spirit.
ALONSO These are not natural events, they strengthen
    From strange, to stranger. Say, how came you hither?
BOATSWAIN If I did think, sir, I were well awake,
    I'd strive to tell you. We were dead of sleep, 230
    And – how we know not – all clapped under hatches,
    Where, but even now, with strange and several noises
    Of roaring, shrieking, howling, jingling chains,
    And more diversity of sounds, all horrible,
    We were awaked, straightway at liberty; 235
    Where we, in all our trim, freshly beheld
    Our royal, good, and gallant ship; our master
    Cap'ring to eye her. On a trice, so please you,
    Even in a dream, were we divided from them,
    And were brought moping hither.
ARIEL [*aside to Prospero*]   Was't well done? 240
PROSPERO [*aside to Ariel*] Bravely, my diligence. Thou shalt be free.
ALONSO This is as strange a maze as e'er men trod,
    And there is in this business more than nature
    Was ever conduct of. Some oracle
    Must rectify our knowledge.

---

221 Tipton's Boatswain entered 'speechless and amazed at having found himself so suddenly
   transported onto the island; it [was] not until Ariel place[d] a script in his hand that he [found]
   his voice and the play resume[d]. In an instant we [were] reminded both of the artifice of the
   theatre and where we began' (Shyer, 'Disenchanted', p. 31; see note to 1.1.54).

244 As Miller's 1988 Alonso wondered what 'oracle' had made these events possible, he and
   Prospero moved towards each other; Ariel followed behind Prospero who obscured him
   from Alonso (CD). The staging emblematized colonial relationships, where the unseen hard
   work of the native is disguised as 'miraculous' white achievement.

PROSPERO   Sir, my liege,   245
Do not infest your mind with beating on
The strangeness of this business. At picked leisure,
Which shall be shortly single, I'll resolve you,
Which to you shall seem probable, of every
These happened accidents. Till when, be cheerful   250
And think of each thing well. [*aside to Ariel*] Come
          hither, spirit,
Set Caliban and his companions free:
Untie the spell.
                                    [*Exit* ARIEL]
          How fares my gracious sir?
There are yet missing of your company
Some few odd lads that you remember not.   255

Enter ARIEL, *driving in* CALIBAN, STEPHANO *and* TRINCULO *in
their stolen apparel*

STEPHANO Every man shift for all the rest, and let no man take care
          for himself; for all is but fortune. Coragio, bully-monster, coragio.

251a   Daniels's Prospero, standing close to Antonio, directed 251a to him (archive video).
251b–3a Paige's Ariel did not leave the stage, instead freeing the trio 'with a gesture' (Carter, '*The
         Tempest* at Salisbury Playhouse', p. 33). Alexander's Prospero at DSL addressed the invisible
         Ariel at USR, speaking across the nobles to do so; they understandably looked puzzled, but
         Alonso then felt Ariel go past him (CD). Mendes's Ariel did not move from the ladder, but
         clapped his hands to make Caliban, Stephano and Trinculo emerge from the wicker basket at
         DSL (CD).
255   Williams's 1978 Antonio sat down 'aloof from the general rejoicing' and was 'left facing the
       audience . . . as malignant as ever' (respectively, Cushman, *O* 7/5/78; Wardle, *T* 3/5/78).
255sd   The trio can enter in varied physical and psychological states. Hall's (1974) were frightened
        and subdued, while Williams's (1978) were 'reeling ripe' (the pb quotes Alonso's description
        at 278). Purcarete's were still twirling as they had been at the end of the previous scene and
        then collapsed in a heap (CD). However, their entry allows scope for more than simple
        comedy: Daniels's Caliban, for instance, looked at the 'brave spirits' in a manner reminiscent
        of Miranda at 181b–4a (archive video). Hytner's Trinculo and Stephano wore crowns;
        because this was the only time that Trinculo did so, and because they and Prospero were the
        only ones wearing crowns, Hytner seemed to be making a point about the worth of Pros-
        pero's regained status (CD).
256–75 This section has also been greatly cut. In 1756 Garrick cut it entirely; in 1757 he cut 262b–5,
        270. Daly cut 261b–75a; Burton 262b–7a; Macready, Phelps and Kean 262b–75a; Bridges-

TRINCULO If these be true spies which I wear in my head, here's a
    goodly sight.
CALIBAN O Setebos, these be brave spirits indeed!   260
    How fine my master is! I am afraid
    He will chastise me.
SEBASTIAN   Ha, ha!
    What things are these, my lord Antonio?
    Will money buy 'em?
ANTONIO   Very like. One of them
    Is a plain fish, and no doubt marketable.   265
PROSPERO Mark but the badges of these men, my lords,
    Then say if they be true. This misshapen knave,
    His mother was a witch, and one so strong
    That could control the moon, make flows and ebbs,
    And deal in her command, without her power.   270
    These three have robbed me, and this demi-devil –
    For he's a bastard one – had plotted with them
    To take my life. Two of these fellows you
    Must know and own; this thing of darkness, I
    Acknowledge mine.

Adams (1926/30, 1934) 256–73a (with 262b retained in 1934); Iden Payne 264b–73a; Tree and Ayrton 266–75; Ashwell 267–70; Barton 267b–71; Brook (1957) 269b–70; Daniels 270. Hack interpolated 240b–1 after 257.

    The reactions of, and interactions between, Prospero, the lords and the comic trio can vary greatly. Benthall's trio tried to escape but were chased back by the barnacles or other monsters. Brook's 1957 Caliban and Stephano voluntarily knelt, but Sebastian had to push Trinculo down. Hytner's Caliban crawled to Prospero's feet and prostrated himself. Miller's 1988 Caliban knelt to Prospero, who patted his back and tousled his head like a dog (pb, CD and Wardle, *T* 12/10/88). Williams's (1978) Antonio prodded Caliban with his foot, while Hall's (1988) kicked him. Hytner's Prospero applied many of the words of 266–75 to Antonio: e.g., 'His mother was a witch', 'bastard', 'plotted with them / To take my life' (CD).

265 Alexander's Caliban gaped like a fish with his mouth, prompting Antonio's epithet (CD).

272 Donnellan's Miranda screamed when Prospero referred to Caliban as 'a bastard', sensing what was to come next (CD; see note to 274b–5a).

274b–5a Although many nineteenth-century productions cut Prospero's words (see note to 256–75), some contemporary productions make them a fulcrum of the play. Ciulei's Prospero, for instance, made it clear that he 'recognize[d] the natural human brutishness in himself, and that in that recognition he ha[d] at last become fully human' (Saville, *SDR* 9/81). Edwards had

CALIBAN   I shall be pinched to death.   275
ALONSO Is not this Stephano, my drunken butler?
SEBASTIAN He is drunk now; where had he wine?
ALONSO And Trinculo is reeling ripe. Where should they
              Find this grand liquor that hath gilded 'em?
              How cam'st thou in this pickle?   280
TRINCULO I have been in such a pickle since I saw you last, that I
              fear me will never out of my bones. I shall not fear fly-blowing.
SEBASTIAN Why how now, Stephano?
STEPHANO O touch me not! I am not Stephano, but a cramp.
PROSPERO You'd be king o' the isle, sirrah?   285
STEPHANO I should have been a sore one then.
ALONSO [*Gesturing to Caliban*] This is as strange a thing as ere I
              looked on.
PROSPERO He is as disproportioned in his manners
              As in his shape. Go, sirrah, to my cell;

Prospero and Caliban embrace (Larkin, *SA* 20/5/90); Rylance's Prospero spoke 'with soft-
ness, even love' (Kingston, *T* 10/6/91); Alexander's Prospero fondly rubbed Caliban's face,
much to the latter's delighted amazement (CD). In quite a different vein, Donnellan's Prospero acknowledged paternity of Caliban; Miranda looked sick after the admission and proceeded to assault her half-brother but then embraced him (CD). On 275b, Purcarete's
Caliban lay on his back with his hands under his head and his legs (bent at the knees) in the
air, a curiously relaxed posture given his words (CD).

276–87 Cut by Garrick (1756). Macready, Kean and Tree cut 278b–9. Daly cut 278b–9, the last sen-
              tence of 282 and 285–6; Iden Payne made the same cut at 282. Mendes's Stephano
              answered Alonso's 276 with a loud burp (CD).

   280 Wright's Alonso kicked Trinculo.

   281 Tree's Trinculo helped Stephano to get up. Daniels's Alonso had to fan Trinculo's breath away
              (archive video). Mendes's Trinculo tried to use his dummy to speak, moving his thumb
              appropriately, but then realized it was gone (CD).

   283 Stephano's 'O, touch me not' (284) indicates that a gesture should accompany Sebastian's
              line: he either touches Stephano or moves to do so. Phelps's Sebastian slapped him on the
              shoulder (Phelps/Creswick pb); Burton's clapped him there; Tree's slapped him on the back;
              Benthall's prodded him with his sword; Brook's hit him (1957); Barton's kicked him;
              Williams's prodded him (1978); Daniels's patted him on the back; Hytner's simply moved to
              touch him on the shoulder (Stratford pb).

   284 Hytner's Stephano sat up to speak; he laughed at 'cramp' (284) and at 286 (Stratford pb).

288–9 Modern directors sometimes emphasize Prospero's new relationship to Caliban. Brook's
              1957 Prospero handed Caliban his sword, perhaps implying a renewed trust. Hytner's Pros-

Take with you your companions. As you look　　290
To have my pardon, trim it handsomely.
CALIBAN Ay that I will; and I'll be wise hereafter,
And seek for grace. What a thrice-double ass
Was I to take this drunkard for a god,
And worship this dull fool!

　　　　pero knelt and looked at Caliban, his manner gentle; the laughs directed at the still prostrate
　　　　Caliban stopped (CD). Purcarete's Prospero cradled Caliban's head at 'Go, sirrah' (CD).
288–97sd Cut by Garrick (1756). Phelps cut 295b; Kean (Edmonds pb), Bridges-Adams (1926/30, 1934),
　　　　Ayrton, Iden Payne and Wright 296–7. Daly cut 289b–93a, and Tree 289c–91, 297sd; both cut
　　　　295b–7. Hack cut 296–7sd.
292–5a Caliban's repentance may be genuine, pragmatic or even unforthcoming (see preceding
　　　　note for cuts). Benthall's 1952 Caliban 'emphasis[ed] the original bond of love' between him
　　　　and Prospero and therefore 'return[ed] to allegiance with enthusiasm' (Ellis, *SH* ?/3/52); in
　　　　contrast, Mendes's Caliban 'remain[ed] an unregenerate "thing of darkness" to the bitter
　　　　end' (Spencer, *DT* 15/7/94). Williams/Brook emphasized the 'positive atmosphere of debase-
　　　　ment', making 'Caliban's grovelling humility . . . shamefully ironic' (Williams's 1963 pro-
　　　　gramme notes; he adds that 'At one point we thought of lifting all the scenery away at the end
　　　　. . . or of putting all of the characters of the finale in clown's costumes, to underline the
　　　　derisory nature of the play's "resolution" '). Similarly, although he 'has learned by his experi-
　　　　ence', Williams's 1978 Caliban made 292–3a slightly ironic: 'Caliban has learned that being
　　　　obedient he will be safe. But when anybody else should ever come to his island again he cer-
　　　　tainly won't even try to befriend them – he will kill on sight' (Suchet, 'Caliban in *The
　　　　Tempest*', p. 178). Since Murray's Caliban was 'Reviled at the close', his 'bitter submission' to
　　　　Prospero 'disrupt[ed] the comic finale far more powerfully than Antonio's failure to repent'
　　　　(Holdsworth, *TLS* 21–7/9/90). Calibans who genuinely repent have been variously sad
　　　　(Harcourt Williams, 1930), dignified (Daniels), and 'touching' (Alexander) (respectively, uc
　　　　7/10/30; archive video; Billington, *G* 15/9/94). Hytner's knelt up in front of Prospero and was
　　　　'pardoned with a compassionate pat on the shoulder' (pbs; Kemp, *Ind* 26/5/89). Ninagawa's
　　　　Trinculo polished Alonso's shoe as Caliban spoke (CD).
　295 The relationship between Caliban and his erstwhile companions can be variously portrayed.
　　　　Tree's Trinculo laughed after 295a; then Caliban, looking scornfully at Stephano, knelt at
　　　　Miranda's feet before exiting, followed by the other two. Iden Payne's Caliban kicked
　　　　Stephano and Trinculo into the cell, while Williams (1978) had Adrian and Francisco chase
　　　　the trio off-stage. Bogdanov's 1992 Caliban, however, dropped his idol, the 'dull fool' to
　　　　which he referred; thereafter Miranda touched him, and, perhaps comforted, he picked it up
　　　　again (CD). Bridges-Adams (1930) may have interpolated 'Where the bee sucks' at 295b.

PROSPERO   Go to, away.   295
ALONSO Hence, and bestow your luggage where you found it.
SEBASTIAN Or stole it rather.
                    [*Exeunt* CALIBAN, STEPHANO *and* TRINCULO]
PROSPERO Sir, I invite your highness and your train
        To my poor cell, where you shall take your rest

296 Benthall's 1951 Caliban took Trinculo to the mouth of Prospero's cave, where Trinculo fell
     down; Stephano walked there by himself but Caliban kicked him into it.

297sd The trio do not always exit together: Mendes, for instance, had Caliban exit alone through the
     DSC trap and Trinculo and Stephano via the L proscenium (CD). Strehler's Caliban exited
     alone: after throwing down a stick (Prospero's?) and a sword in disgust, he dropped through
     the trap feet first, with his arms raised above his head (video). The staging reflected 'a politi-
     cal decision' to leave Caliban with a 'choice': he 'does not want to have anything to do with
     this so-called civilized world, and crawls back into his cave, but the hole stays open, and he
     [can] . . . come up if he wishes' (Strehler, quoted in Kleber, 'Theatrical Continuities', p. 147).
     On occasion, Caliban's dismissal has been kind: Alexander's Prospero gave him Stephano's
     crown as he was about to exit; very much pleased by the gift and by Miranda's curtsey to him,
     Caliban decided to stay longer among the company, but Prospero headed him into the cell
     (CD). Ciulei had Caliban exit later; see note to Epilogue. Macready's characters (presumably
     all of them) exited through the C curtains, leaving them open and allowing the audience to
     see a bright sea, with the fleet reassembled and 'several small ships tacking and retacking'
     (Moore's notes in Burton pb).

298–309a Garrick (1756) cut 302b–4a, 308–9a; Daly 300b–5a, 308–9a; Tree and Hack 298–304;
     Ashwell, Bridges-Adams (1926/30, 1934), Ayrton, Iden Payne, Barton and Daniels 300b–4a;
     Brook (1957) 302b.
          For Barton, Ian Richardson suggested 'very delicately Prospero's reluctance to admit what
     he is about to lose' (Higgins, *T* 17/10/70). The production intended a subdued ending, with
     Prospero 'even more alone at the end of the play than he was at the beginning' (Anne
     Barton's programme note, quoted in *BgEN* 16/10/70). Miranda embraced Prospero at 305,
     and Ferdinand beckoned the lords to Prospero's cell at 307.
          His manner uneasy and his voice halting, Hytner's Prospero was visibly uncomfortable
     with people; indeed, he was awkward with them in a manner reminiscent of the Prospero
     clones who had served the banquet. Throughout this final section of the play, Ariel watched
     him very intently, perhaps warily, but his expression did not give anything away (CD).
          Paige's Prospero ushered the rest of the characters off-stage as he spoke; Miranda 'tried to
     stop for a word with Stephano and Trinculo, but was decisively recalled to Ferdinand's side'
     (Carter, '*The Tempest* at Salisbury Playhouse', p. 33). The actors playing the pair developed
     the business because they regarded their relationship 'as a first love which would probably
     not last' (p. 24).

For this one night, which, part of it, I'll waste   300
With such discourse as I not doubt shall make it
Go quick away: the story of my life,
And the particular accidents gone by
Since I came to this isle. And in the morn
I'll bring you to your ship, and so to Naples,   305
Where I have hope to see the nuptial
Of these our dear-belovèd solemnised,
And thence retire me to my Milan, where
Every third thought shall be my grave.

ALONSO   I long
To hear the story of your life; which must   310
Take the ear strangely.

PROSPERO   I'll deliver all,
And promise you calm seas, auspicious gales,
And sail so expeditious that shall catch

Gielgud, for Brook (1957), spoke 309a 'lightly', emphasizing Prospero's joy at being restored to his dukedom (John Wardle, *BEN* 17/8/57; see also notes to 87sd and 106b–7). In contrast, Daniels's Prospero directed the words to Antonio, making clear that he still regarded him a threat; indeed, at 'my Milan' (308a), Antonio had looked up sharply, and he and Prospero looked each other in the eye (archive video). Miller's 1988 Miranda looked upset and kissed Prospero when she heard of his thoughts of death, while Thacker's spirits visibly reacted to his words; however, it was unclear whether they were simply surprised or genuinely interested in his future (CD).

309b–11 Garrick (1756) cut 310b–11a and added 'In proper time' before 311b; Tree and Hack cut 309b–11.

Bogdanov's 1992 Alonso spoke 309b–10a viciously (CD). The conclusion was 'typically pessimistic', with 'Alonzo [*sic*] sneer[ing] at [Prospero] and Antonio symbolically crush[ing] him' (Arditti, *ES* 1/12/92; see following note).

311b–14a Many directors have the lords, Miranda and Ferdinand exit after 314a, so that Prospero is left alone on stage with Ariel for 314b–16a. Bridges-Adams (1926/30, 1934) also kept Antonio on-stage with Prospero and Ariel, while Hall (1988) had the other characters freeze as Prospero bid farewell to the spirit. Before leaving, Bogdanov's 1992 Antonio picked up something that looked like a weapon (CD). Purcarete had the lords all face SL and the Ariels walk on, looking oppressed, in a tightly-knit formation; the lords then fanned themselves and exited.

Phelps's Prospero broke his wand and threw it into the sea (Williams pb), while Hytner's removed his crown and sword, giving the impression that he could not get them off quickly enough for his emotional comfort; in London, he showed the physical relief of unbuckling the now-too-small sword-belt (CD). Hack cut 313b–14a.

> Your royal fleet far off. My Ariel, chick,
> That is thy charge. Then to the elements   315

314b–16a Prospero's release of Ariel has had myriad interpretations, ranging from the unproblematic to the highly charged. Brook's 1957 Ariel, for instance, knelt to Prospero, who blessed him, a treatment that seems to validate the master–servant relationship. However, as the following examples demonstrate, Prospero may be patronizing, nonchalant or wistful, and Ariel hesitant, jubilant or contemptuous; the pair may suggest a mutual or a one-sided relationship of different kinds.

Burge marked their parting with a 'long, lingering, last look from Ariel, wanting his freedom yet regretfully leaving his master, and Prospero [looking] sad at losing his spirit of youth and energy' (Foulkes, review, p. 25). Williams's 1978 Ariel sighed, backed USL and then exited USR; Prospero himself gave 'a shuddering gasp as he released him (relief? a sense of loss?)' (Warren, 'A Year of Comedies', p. 203). Brook's 1990 Ariel was upset: he 'turn[ed] hesitantly back . . . as though half-hopeful that Prospero will reinstate him' (CD; Taylor, *Ind* 2/11/90). Similarly, even though some descriptions imply Armfield's Ariel was unhappy in her enforced service (see note to 1.2.188sd), the final image of the spirit recuperated the idea of a willing female servant: 'apparently reluctant to flee [her] master', Gillian Jones seemed 'like a teenager equivocal about leaving school for the tough world outside' (Eccles, *Bul* 12/6/90).

Miller's 1988 Prospero and Ariel embraced at 314b; then Prospero smacked Ariel playfully on the cheek, broke his staff and handed it to him (CD). Donnellan's Ariel held out his hand to Prospero, who walked away without noticing it (CD), whereas Hall's 1988 Ariel was 'allowed a touching moment of human feeling when he tentatively return[ed] Prospero's embrace' (Osborne, *DT* 21/5/88).

Daniels's Prospero addressed his 'Ariel' and then paused, waiting for the spirit to appear; he then enquired 'chick?!' (archive video). When Ariel still failed to materialize, he crossed US and turned SL, moving to DSC at 'charge' (pb). At the same time he looked up, addressing the spirit and emphasizing '*then* . . . Be free'; his wish that Ariel 'fare . . . *well*' was heartfelt (archive video). Jacobi's Prospero was very effective in this passage, showing 'a palpable sense of loss' even though he knew 'that Ariel *will* perform the last task' (respectively, Billington, *G* 14/9/83; Edwards, *NS* 20/8/82).

Thacker's Ariel nodded at 'charge' (315a), but then reeled in disbelief at 'Be free' (316a). Prospero ignored her as he spoke 316b, while she looked wonderingly and tensely at him and held her hands up, her gesture probably indicating her desire that Prospero relinquish his power by breaking his staff. When he finished his half-line, they faced each other: Prospero then raised his staff in the air, echoing the posture Ariel still held, and brought it down breaking it; his action caused Ariel to collapse, either in relief or as an expression of her new freedom (CD).

Be free, and fare thou well. Please you draw near.

Exeunt omnes

At 'fare thou well', spoken by Prospero 'in tones that include[d] gratitude and affection', Mendes's Ariel quickly walked R; then he faced Prospero, giving him a long glare, before going US. When he reached a previously unseen door in the cloud cyclorama – 'a magical silhouetted door' that gave a 'sudden glimpse of a radiant white beyond this world', he turned around again to give Prospero a long look before exiting (CD; quotations from, respectively, Rutherford, *FT* 13/8/93; Morris, *TO* 20/7/94; Macauley, *FT* 15/7/94). Variously described as 'cool, 'unforgiving' and 'full of inscrutable disdain', it spoke 'volumes about the anger of the exploited' (respectively, Macauley; Billington, *G* 15/7/94; Taylor, *Ind* 15/7/94; Billington). This London staging, however, excised the most talked-about element of the Stratford production, where Ariel spat in Prospero's face – 'vicious[ly]', 'copiously', 'contemptuously' (respectively, Hoyle, *MSun* 15/8/93; Rutherford, *FT* 13/8/93; Spencer, *DT* 16/8/93).

316a   Many Prosperos, such as Benthall's (1951), snapped their staff and threw the pieces away when they released Ariel. Noble made the moment a startling one: Prospero had his staff 'jauntily slung across his shoulders as, chuckling a bit defensively, he watche[d] Ariel (whom he has just freed) loping off down the ramp [which exited through the audience]. Then, on a sudden half-beat, he snap[ped] the staff – a thrilling moment because you can see that this Prospero has had to take himself unawares to be able to perform this momentous act at all' (Taylor, *Ind* 27/2/98). Nineteenth-century Ariels, like Macready's and Burton's, often flew across the stage, singing 'Merrily, merrily shall I live now', etc.; even twentieth-century directors, like Barton, have interpolated 'Where the bee sucks' to mark the moment of Ariel's release. However, the way in which the release itself is staged can vary tremendously, with modern directors proving particularly imaginative.

Wright's Ariel moved fast from DR to exit UL, whereupon Prospero followed the invisible Ariel 'mentally through air'. Similarly, Benthall's Prospero visually 'followed Ariel's flight and made us "see" the spirit circle the auditorium and soar out of sight' (*LSC* 29/6/51). In contrast, Crozier's Ariel took actual flight only when granted his freedom, but the flying mechanism worked against the intended effect, coming across as 'a miserable bit of mechanical aid' (*EJ* 27/4/47). Donnellan's Ariel, on the other hand, tried unsuccessfully to fly away and then simply removed his turban: 'soaring back into the bosom of the winds, [Ariel] leaps . . . but can jump only six inches into the air and bumps back down with a shrug and a grin, stomping off all-actor' (respectively, CD; Hutcheon, *Tr* 9/12/88).

Most famously, Strehler marked Ariel's freedom by *releasing* her from flight: she flew down into Prospero's arms, and he unclipped her from her flying rope. She stood still at C for a while, not quite believing she was free; the staging also implied that she was now invisible, as Prospero reached out to her but appeared unable to see her. Ducking under his hand, she ran out over the ground-rows, jumped off the stage and ran down the C aisle of the auditorium and presumably out of the theatre, 'radiant with the joy of freedom' (video and

Billington, *G* 16/11/83). After she was unhooked, her rope 'audibly whined and clanged back up to the flies', drawing conscious attention to the theatrical machinery and theatrical metaphor of the production (Kleber, 'Theatrical Continuities', p. 145).

The moment of Ariel's freedom was the most commented-on aspect of Retallack's ATC production and one that reviewers found powerful. As Prospero addressed her, Ariel 'stretche[d] out her right arm in supplication and then collapse[d]', apparently dead, either into Prospero's 'arms' or 'like a shot bird at [his] feet' (respectively, Billington, *G* 2/83; Wardle, *T* 25/2/83; King, *STel* 2/83). However, Ariel had simply 'quit the body [she] was using, and Prospero watched as his darling flew invisibly, high overhead' (Barber, *DT* 20/6[*sic*]/83). Prospero then 'signal[led] a last farewell to the flying spirit', while 'Caliban carried out the abandoned corpse' (respectively, Wardle and Barber). Retallack's 1991 staging was similar (private communication).

Bogdanov's Prospero took off his magic robe and then produced a dove from his handkerchief (CD), 'a mechanical conjuring trick which only [drew] attention to the lack of genuine magic elsewhere' (Arditti, *ES* 1/12/92). The bird's release was meant to represent 'Ariel's freedom from servitude' and hence 'Prospero's freedom from the bitterness, the need for revenge, which have dogged him. His continuing to perform magic – but now a familiar, every-day magician's magic – signal[led] a kind of completion' (Neill, *Director's Notes*, p. 16).

At 'free', Purcarete's Prospero handed the Ariels wine glasses, which they raised in salute at 'well' as the blue curtain was drawn L to R in front of them, making them disappear (CD). Prospero was 'in perfect control almost to the end when, releasing Ariel, he [became] human with a sob' (Kingston, *T* 12/9/95).

Finally, a change in clothing, like Donnellan's turban, has become something of a recent motif to mark Ariel's release: Murray's Ariel made a 'breathtaking and spectacular' final exit, discarding his 'silvered parody of formal dress . . . as he [flew] to freedom' (respectively, Bill McCoid, *St* 10/1/91; Wainwright, *Ind* 15/9/90). Similarly, Tipton's Ariel 'crosse[d] the stage wearing a black motorcycle jacket and black boots. In other words, he [*sic*] has become just like everyone else' (Close, *SPPP* 15/10/91). Meckler gave the audience a 'sudden, shocking realisation that the white designer number Ariel has floated about in all evening is in fact a straitjacket' (Gardner, *G* 1/2/97).

Nineteenth-century productions often depicted Alonso's ship ready to depart; Burton, for instance, showed it tacking and re-tacking on a sunny sea. Phelps had the king's galleys work on, the sun sink and the moon rise; the galleys then came to anchor and the sink and rise worked to their former places (Creswick pb). Kean's production was even more spectacular: night descended at 316a, as clouds rose and fell discovering the spirits released by Prospero 'tak[ing] their flight from the island, into the air' (published text). The clouds closed in the spirits while a chorus sang 'Where the bee sucks'; when the clouds rose again, a ship was discovered on a calm morning sea, Ariel on its bowsprit. '[W]hen it remove[d] from its moorings, *Ariel* still remain[ed] floating in "the thin air", with all that mid-region to himself, his own' (*ILN* 18/7/1857, p. 62). Andersen explains that 'The entire stage represented a broad sea

... stirred by the wind. Prospero ... stood in the stern of the ship that came sailing down from the background to the footlights; the sails swelled, and after the final epilogue had been spoken, the ship glided down one of the side scenes [i.e., into the wings]' (*Pictures of Travel*, p. 284; see note to Epilogue 20sd).

316b   Many directors, such as Kean, Crozier, Wright, Williams (1978), Barton and Mendes, have interpolated 316b after 314a, thereby leaving Prospero and Ariel alone on stage for 314b–16a; Crozier's lords all bowed to Prospero in response. Others, such as Garrick (1756), Tree and Benthall, have cut the half-line; Garrick inserted a duet between Miranda and Ferdinand, 'Love, gentle love, now fill my breast', after 316a, ending the opera with its chorus.

Bridges-Adams used the words to mark the reconciliation of Prospero and Antonio. In 1926/30, Prospero took Antonio by the hand to lead him into the cave, presumably at 316b. In 1934, Prospero also spoke to Antonio, who (as in 1926/30) was the only courtier remaining on-stage; in reply, Antonio crossed to the cell, knelt and kissed his brother's hand before exiting into it. Hytner's Prospero addressed the words to the audience, the courtiers having exited earlier (CD).

316sd   Many nineteenth-century productions, such as Daly's and Benson's (1891), ended the play with Ariel singing 'Merrily, merrily', etc.; Daly had her appear 'in the air at the back' and showed her and the other spirits 'guiding the ship as the curtain [fell]'. Benson, like many others, also had Prospero break his magic wand and consign his magic book 'to the fathom-less ocean' (*Memoirs*, p. 298).

Some lords do not exit but remain on stage during the Epilogue. Brook's (1957), for example, grouped themselves 'in tableau' on the deck of the ship (*BM* 14/8/57; see note to Epilogue). Tipton's lords 'move[d] slowly past the wreckage of the island into the smoky void that [lay] beyond, swaying back and forth as they retreat[ed], like prisoners in formation' (Shyer, 'Disenchanted', p. 64; see note to Epilogue 20sd). The lords' exit, however, can provide an opportunity to signal Antonio's attitude: for example, during it, Mendes's Prospero faced Antonio, who walked past him and went off without any acknowledgement (CD). Hall's 1974 Antonio, on the other hand, lingered on-stage until Sebastian had gone; then he exchanged a look with Prospero and exited haughtily into the cell.

Productions often interpolate other business at the end of the play. John Ryder's 1871 pro-duction, for example, imitated Kean's handling of Ariel (see note to 316a) but also showed 'the abandonment of the island to the sole charge of Caliban, who as the curtain descend[ed lay] stretched upon the shore basking in the rays of the setting sun' (Dutton Cook, quoted in Griffiths, ' "This Island's Mine" ', p. 164). Less pointedly, Drinkwater's 'Stephano and Trinculo re-emerged with trenchers and cups and sat eating with the Boatswain and the Ship's Master, in a circle round a table. Caliban climbed from under the back of the table and sat eating an apple while Ariel gathered up Prospero's cloak and staff and threw them over the back of the rocks . . . [and] leaped off to freedom' (Cochrane, *Shakespeare and the Birmingham Reper-tory Theatre*, p. 58). Purcarete provided a poignant view of Caliban: after the Ariels disap-peared, Prospero threw the music stands about the stage, while Caliban sat on the bed, his

EPILOGUE, *spoken by* PROSPERO

Now my charms are all o'erthrown,
And what strength I have's mine own –
Which is most faint. Now 'tis true
I must be here confined by you,
Or sent to Naples, let me not,   5

back to the audience, trying to play the violin; Prospero then removed his wig and drew the curtain half-way open (CD).

Coghill's ending 'became an instant legend', with 'Much of [its] impact . . . due to the lighting [of his outdoor production] . . . [W]hen the audience came back from the interval it was just starting to get dark and, almost imperceptibly . . . artificial lighting had come on. Lights were fixed in the willows and other trees all round [Worcester College] lake, near and far, and during the final scenes they were brightened so that by the end the lake lay among delicate, beautiful trees that seemed to give off their own green light and were reflected in the black water. At the end . . . Prospero and the rest embarked on a galleon . . . and were poled away into the black distance. By this time it was completely dark, but the ship was brilliantly lit. As they went, Prospero appeared and threw his book over the stern . . . and then, as the ship receded further, Ariel suddenly darted out from behind trees . . . and ran quickly and lightly across the water, his feet raising only the tiniest splashes as they touched the surface, stopped, and – stretching out his arms – waved a passionate and heart-broken good-bye. Then he ran back to the shore and disappeared . . . Just before [the ship] disappeared, Ariel was seen again, in the distance on the far side of the lake, running steeply upwards into the air and disappearing in a brief flash of light' (Moore, 'Footing it Featly', pp. 15–16). Charles Hodgson, who played Ariel, explains that a 'bridge of duckboards . . . under the surface of the lake' allowed him to run across the water and 'a ramp' to ascend into the air: as he 'raised [his] arms, as though to command magic . . . a flare went off underneath [him] and all the lights went out in the garden' ('Rough Magic', p. 16). Both writers stress the magical effect created. (An earlier Worcester production, by the all-male Buskins, had also ended spectacularly, when a 'magnificent scarlet galley, painted with gold sea-horses', suddenly emerged from bushes and took the characters across the lake (*T* 27/7/34).)

Epilogue Garrick (1756), Kemble, Daly, Benson, Tree, Drinkwater, Ayrton and Devine/Goring cut the Epilogue; Kemble's (1789) was written by Lt. Gen. Burgoyne and spoken by Miss Farren, who had played Dorinda.

Tree believed the actor should not break the illusion by addressing the audience, and so, in place of the Epilogue, he substituted Prospero's 'Ye elves' speech (5.1.33–57 with 36b–9a and 51b–4a cut). As accompanying music ended with Prospero's final words, he broke his staff across his knee, an action greeted by thunder, lightning DSR and darkness. During the black-out, the cut cloth and back cloth were raised and the gauze lowered, so that, as the lights slowly came up again, the nymphs were heard off L singing 'Come unto these yellow sands' and the audience saw Telbin's Yellow Sands 'enveloped in a purple haze' (printed sd). Their singing was eventually drowned out by that of the boatmen homeward-bound, and soon the ship itself appeared behind row number 2 crossing from L to R, watched by Caliban, who had crept from his cave and climbed the rocks to see it depart. Ariel was heard singing 'Where the bee sucks' (5.1.88–94) and then appeared, lowered by a wire from a platform LUE to C stage, where she continued to sing. Upon reaching 'Merrily, merrily shall I live now', she flew out of sight but her voice was still heard, rising higher and higher until it was gradually transformed into that of a lark. Caliban listened to it intently before turning back 'sadly' to the departing ship, now on the horizon. The curtain fell, only to lift again, showing Caliban crouched on the rock, 'stretching out his arms towards [the ship] in mute despair. The night falls, and Caliban is left on the lonely rock. He is a King once more' (printed sd). Tree explained his intended message: 'from the conception of sorrow in solitude may spring the birth of a higher civilisation' (*Thoughts and Afterthoughts*, p. 221).

Many Prosperos, such as Burton's, Daniels's, De Berardinis's, Ninagawa's and Mendes's, break their wand before beginning the Epilogue; Wright's made the action 'a moment of mysterious awe' (*St* 15/5/47). While Macready's Prospero spoke, 'liberated sylphs were heard singing their far [away?] song of joy over the seas' (Forster, 'Macready's Production', p. 67). Kean's and Brook's (1957) spoke from the deck of the ship.

Prospero's Epilogue is unusual in that he remains in character: the words do not call attention to the actor (cf. Rosalind's in *As You Like It*). Nevertheless, some Prosperos take such an approach, particularly if the production has had a metatheatrical framework. For example, as Strehler's Prospero dropped his book and broke his magic stick in half, the set fell apart: a great sail-sheet fell from the flies, knocking over and revealing the mechanisms of the ground-rows, 'symbolising the destruction of theatrical illusion, and the renunciation of divine power'; Prospero then went down to the floor of the auditorium and stood in front of the stage, took off his white costume-robe to reveal an ordinary shirt and trousers underneath, and spoke the Epilogue 'with sadness' (video; quotations from, respectively, Billington, *G* 16/11/83, and Kleber, 'Theatrical Continuities', p. 150). Similarly, De Berardinis's Prospero delivered the Epilogue as a 'man of the theatre . . . in front of [the] now closed [red] curtain' (Manzella, *iM* 12/4/86), and Daniels's cast off 'the actor's voice and presence' (Chaillet, *T* 13/8/82); however, another view thought his delivery 'marvellously delicate and pained' (Brook, *NS* 9/83)). Hall's 1974 Prospero spoke the Epilogue DC in full stagelight in what became for one reviewer a magical moment: 'he takes off his hat to expose a 20th-century head of sparse hair, parted on the side and brushed neatly back. Instantly, Prospero changes into Sir John Gielgud. It is not the Duke of Milan that speaks the speech, it is a great actor whom we know and love, and who has just given a performance near to perfection. I hope I shall never forget how it made me feel' (Young, *FT* 6/3/74).

Prosperos who remain in character speak the Epilogue as variously as they have played the part. Wright's spoke simply, giving it 'a [most moving] human appeal' (*St* 15/5/47), while

Since I have my dukedom got
And pardoned the deceiver, dwell
In this bare island, by your spell;
But release me from my bands
With the help of your good hands.   10
Gentle breath of yours my sails
Must fill, or else my project fails,
Which was to please. Now I want
Spirits to enforce, art to enchant,
And my ending is despair,   15

Gielgud, for Brook (1957), delivered it 'wistfully, half-humorously' (*NG* 14/8/57). Hack's made it 'a kind of challenge rather than a prayer' (Bannock, *SH* 25/10/74), while Wolfe's was angry (Raphael, *CM* 18–28/7/95). Mendes's Prospero seemed 'close to tears, a lonely old man who has failed to pluck the mystery out of life and has only death to look forward to' (Spencer, *DT* 16/8/93), while Purcarete's, 'still striken by loss', was 'a whimpering wreck of a man': 'Acutely aware of the inability of his art to change anything that really matters, Prospero's final speech [became] a prayer of despair in which he seem[ed] to be pleading not so much for freedom as for the blessed relief of annihilation' (respectively, Kingston, *T* 12/9/95; Shuttleworth, *FT* 16/9/95; Spencer, *DT* 18/9/95). Ciulei's made the audience 'fully aware that the issue is freedom, the freedom of the self from the self' (Saville, *SDR* 9/81; see also note to 20). As he prepared to speak, 'the savage Caliban . . . [went] on a silent, stealthy stroll across the darkened stage', leaving the feeling that, 'sooner or later, more blood will be spilled' (Rich, *NYT* 4/7/81). Other interpretations, however, were available: it was 'a poignant image' because Caliban is 'the only character who will remain on the island amid these heaps of cultural debris about which he knows nothing' (Steele, *MT* 13/6/81). Finally, Mitchell's Prospero, in a 'tenuous but intriguing' interpretation, aimed the Epilogue 'not at the audience but at the recently freed Ariel' (Sue Gough, *Bul* 20/2/90).

2   Wolfe had 'an unexpected and altogether wonderful ending': as Prospero finished this line, 'he gesture[d] suddenly and his microphone [went] dead', reducing 'That masterful, omniscient voice . . . to human scale in an instant' (Jefferson, *NYT* 16/7/95). The gesture – waving his hand across his throat – was a deliberate signal to the sound operator (Martin A. Grove, *HR* 12/7/95).

3b–5a   Cut by Macready, Phelps, Burton, Kean and Iden Payne.

10   Purcarete's Prospero laughed (CD).

13   Barton's and Mendes's Prosperos paused after 'was' (pb and CD).

13b–14   Donnellan's Prospero was on his knees (CD).

14   Barton's Caliban entered, took Prospero's discarded wand and exited.

15   Barton's Prospero substituted 'resignation for hope, a quiet despair for faith. It is that very word, "despair", which is forced to stand out, unnaturally, from what's surely supposed to be

> Unless I be relieved by prayer
> Which pierces so, that it assaults
> Mercy itself, and frees all faults.
> As you from crimes would pardoned be,
> Let your indulgence set me free.   *Exit*   20

a conventional epilogue, politely asking the audience for indulgent applause' (Nightingale, *NS* 23/10/70). Trewin, on the other hand, thought the Epilogue was 'managed . . . perfectly' (*BP* 16/10/70).

15–18 Cut by Garrick (1757).

18 Mendes's Prospero took off his crown and held out his hands to the audience; Purcarete's laid his head on the ground (CD).

19 Changed by Garrick (1757) to 'As you would pardon'd wish to be', removing the reference to crimes.

20 Barton's Prospero extended his arms to the audience.

John Harrison's Prospero left 'the clue to his interpretation to the very end. A light [shone] from his eyes as he utter[ed] in a rapt whisper the final words "set me free". Here [was] a man who . . . [had] decided that life must take precedence over art. He [did] so not with self-pity, but with excited hope' (Marcus, *STel* 23/2/75).

Ciulei's Prospero paused before 'free', 'his mind evidently meditating upon the power, the emotion, the attachments Prospero has renounced; then, calling his faculties together, he [spoke] the word resolutely; and in that isolated and underlined "free" we [were] forcefully reminded of the play's real theme and of its desperate relevance to ourselves' (Saville, *SDR* 9/81).

20sd Nineteenth-century productions continued their spectacular staging at the end of the Epi-logue. Burton, for example, opened the curtains to discover Ariel standing on a large shell; nymphs then entered and stood in groups on each side pointing to her, while the chorus standing at the wings and the curtain took up the burden of 'Where the bee sucks' ('Merrily, merrily'). Kean's staging was grander: the ship gradually sailed off, the island receded from sight and Ariel remained alone in mid-air, watching Prospero's departure as a distant chorus of spirits sounded (printed sd in Edmonds pb); the light was contrived so that it seemed Ariel, like a 'meteor, gave the whole stage its brilliancy', causing a 'rainbow glory' to shine over the water as Prospero departed (Andersen, *Pictures of Travel*, p. 284). Twentieth-century pro-ductions were much simpler: for example, Brook (1957) had the gauzes slowly fall and then 'Darkness' (*BP* 21/8/57), while Neville's Prospero went 'off with a cheerful wave of his hat – maybe to greet some of the Old Boys' (Trewin, *ILN* 16/6/62).

Twentieth-century productions, however, often provided a coda to the play at the end of the Epilogue. Miller's 1970 Ariel, for example, 'pick[ed] up Prospero's broken staff . . . as a prelude to assuming control of the island' (Wardle, *T* 16/6/70). He used a similar staging in

1988: as Caliban waved to the departing Europeans and three islanders entered, Ariel retrieved Prospero's discarded and broken staff, pieced it together and 'held it threateningly over Caliban and his fellow-islanders' (CD; Osborne, *DT* 13/10/88); seeing Ariel's triumphant smile and gesture, Caliban's 'own grin (anticipating freedom?)' froze (Edwards, *Sp* 22/10/88). At this point, a reviewer who had wondered whether Ariel's mimickry of the mortals had been admiring or mocking realized that his 'power [was] made possible through observation and imitation' (Armitstead, *PP* 12/88)). In contrast, Wolfe had a 'final tableau of Caliban joyfully joining Ariel in freedom' (Jacobson, *NYN* 12/7/95); it is a measure of how sexual this Ariel was that another reviewer thought he was joining her 'as her consort' (Karam, *T* 14/7/95).

Quite often, the coda involves Caliban: Minor's ended the play 'draped over the twisted branches' of the set, an image 'suggesting Eve's serpent in the Garden of Eden' (Duff, *MMA* 24/6/70). Purcarete started up the revolve again, bringing Caliban into view; the lights went out while he continued to play the violin (CD). As Tipton's Prospero finished the Epilogue, 'the glowing skyline of a modern city appear[ed US] out of the darkness. The company [stood] in their flowing robes and Elizabethan costumes silently peering across the centuries into the very world that [would] inherit this play . . . Prospero join[ed] the others in the shadow of this vast, impersonal future while Caliban, the remaining inhabitant of the island, walk[ed] to the edge of the stage and stare[d] out into the auditorium. After a moment, he remove[d] his glasses, wipe[d] them and put . . . them back on, as if to get a better look at [the audience]. He regard[ed] his new kingdom and subjects – all inherited by default – with detachment as the lights fade[d]' (Shyer, 'Disenchanted', p. 64).

Finally, the end of the Epilogue provides metatheatrical productions with another opportunity to make their point: Strehler's Prospero turned to look at the stage, which was then miraculously reconstructed (video), while Walford's, in keeping with the circus setting, 'acknowledge[d] the final curtain . . . with a standing back-somersault' (he had earlier in the play 'deliver[ed] lines flat on [his] back, legs in the air, with Ariel perched on [his] feet') (Hoyle, *FT* 31/1/84). De Berardinis's Prospero 'walk[ed] backwards between the red wings of the curtain, with his arms open, bathed in light', in an image reminiscent of the 'science-fiction solitude' of Tarkovsky's *Stalker* (Zucconi, *PS* 5/4/86).

'The last sound [Hall's 1988 Prospero] emit[ted] in the play [was] a sigh of relief at having safely negotiated his return to the fold' from the realm of dangerous magic (Kemp, *Ind* 21/5/88).

Playing-time   The playing-time of twentieth-century productions generally ranged from 2 hours and 10 minutes to 2 hours and 45 minutes, including a 15-minute interval. This playing of a fuller text in such a short time gives some idea of the ponderous staging of earlier times: for example, Kemble's 1806 version, including overture, took 3 hours (Willmott), while the playing-time of Phelps's production took an average 2 hours 40 minutes (Creswick). The most pertinent example, however, comes from Kean, whose production lasted 3 hours 20 minutes; Edmonds's timing of the play includes intervals for scene-changes, since individual act timings amount to 2 hours 9 minutes. The 71 minutes devoted to scene-changes mark a considerable improvement during the play's run of 87 performances: because of the elaborate sets and machinery (which required 140 stagehands), Kean's first-night performance lasted $5\frac{1}{2}$ hours; by 7 July, an hour had been shaved off the time needed for scene-changes (see *ILN* 11/7/1857, p. 35).

APPENDIX 1: SELECTED TEXTUAL VARIATIONS

The Tempest, or The Enchanted Island (Dryden and Davenant, 1670)
Act 1 [Scene 1]

> *Enter Mustacho and Ventoso*

VENTOSO What a sea comes in?

MUSTACHO A hoaming sea! we shall have foul weather.

> *Enter Trincalo*

TRINCALO The scud comes against the wind, twill blow hard.

> *Enter Stephano*

STEPHANO Bosun!

5 TRINCALO Here, Master what cheer?

STEPHANO Ill weather! Let's off to sea.

MUSTACHO Let's have sea-room enough, and then let it blow the devil's head off.

STEPHANO Boy!

> *Enter Cabin-Boy*

BOY Yaw, yaw, here Master.

10 STEPHANO Give the pilot a dram of the bottle.

> *Exeunt Stephano and Boy*
> *Enter Mariners and pass over the stage*

TRINCALO Heigh, my hearts, cheerly, cheerly, my hearts, yare, yare.

> *Enter Alonzo, Antonio, Gonzalo*

ALONZO Good bosun have a care; where's the master? Play the men.

TRINCALO Pray keep below.

ANTONIO Where's the master, bosun?

15 TRINCALO Do you not hear him? You mar our labour: keep your cabins, you help the storm.

GONZALO Nay, good friend be patient.

TRINCALO Ay, when the sea is: hence; what care these roarers for the name of duke? To cabin; silence; trouble us not.

20 GONZALO Good friend, remember whom thou hast aboard.

TRINCALO None that I love more than myself. You are a counsellor; if you can advise these elements to silence, use your wisdom: if you cannot, make yourself ready in the cabin for the ill hour. Cheerly, good hearts! Out of our way, sirs.

> *Exeunt Trincalo and Mariners*

GONZALO I have great comfort from this fellow; methinks his complexion is perfect

25 gallows; stand fast, good Fate, to his hanging; make the rope of his destiny our cable, for our own does little advantage us: if he be not born to be hang'd we shall be drown'd.

> *Exit*
> *Enter Trincalo and Stephano*

TRINCALO Up aloft lads. Come, reef both top-sails.

STEPHANO Let's weigh, let's weigh, and off to sea.

>   *Exit Stephano*
>   *Enter two Mariners and pass over the stage*

30 TRINCALO Hands down! Man your main-capstorm.

>   *Enter Mustacho and Ventoso at the other door*

MUSTACHO Up aloft! And man your seere-capstorm.

VENTOSO My lads, my hearts of gold, get in your capstorm-bar. Hoa up, hoa up, etc.

>   *Exeunt Mustacho and Ventoso*
>   *Enter Stephano*

STEPHANO Hold on well! Hold on well! Nip well there; Quarter-Master, get's more nippers.

>   *Exit Stephano*
>   *Enter two Mariners and pass over again*

35 TRINCALO Turn out, turn out, all hands to capstorm? You dogs, is this a time to sleep? Heave together, lads.

>   *Trincalo whistles*
>   *Exeunt Mustacho and Ventoso*

MUSTACHO *within* Our viall's broke.

VENTOSO *within* 'Tis but our vial-block has given way. Come heave lads! We are fix'd again. Heave together bullies.

>   *Enter Stephano*

40 STEPHANO Cut off the hamocks! Cut off the hamocks; come my lads: come bullies, cheer up! Heave lustily. The anchor's a peek.

TRINCALO Is the anchor a peek?

STEPHANO Is a weigh! Is a weigh!

TRINCALO Up aloft my lads upon the fore-castle! Cut the anchor, cut him.

45 ALL *within* Haul catt, haul catt, etc. Haul catt, haul: haul, catt, haul. Below.

STEPHANO Aft, aft! And loose the misen!

TRINCALO Get the misen-tack aboard. Haul aft misen-sheat!

>   *Enter Mustacho*

MUSTACHO Loose the main top sail!

STEPHANO Furl him again, there's too much wind.

50 TRINCALO Loose foresail! Haul aft both sheets! Trim her right afore the wind. Aft! Aft! Lads, and hale up the misen here.

MUSTACHO A mackerel-gale, Master.

STEPHANO *within* Port hard, port! The wind grows scant, bring the tack aboard port is. Star-board, star-board, a little steady; now steady, keep her thus, no

55 nearer you cannot come.

>   *Enter Ventoso*

VENTOSO Some hands down: the guns are loose.

>   *Exit Mustacho*

TRINCALO Try the pump, try the pump!

>   *Exit Ventoso*
>   *Enter Mustacho at the other door*

MUSTACHO O Master! Six foot water in hold.

STEPHANO Clap the helm hard aboard! Flat, flat, flat in the fore-sheet there.

60 TRINCALO Over-haul your fore-boling.

STEPHANO Brace in the lar-board.

> *Exit*

TRINCALO A curse upon this howling.

> *A great cry within*

They are louder than the weather.

> *Enter Antonio and Gonzalo*

Yet again, what do you here! Shall we give o're, and drown? Ha' you a mind to
65 sink?

GONZALO A pox o' your throat, you bawling, blasphemous, uncharitable dog.

TRINCALO Work you then.

ANTONIO Hang, cur, hang, you whoreson insolent noisemaker, we are less afraid to
be drown'd than thou art.

70 TRINCALO Brace off the fore-yard.

> *Exit*

GONZALO I'll warrant him for drowning, though the ship were no stronger than a
nut-shell, and as leaky as an unstanch'd wench.

> *Enter Alonzo and Ferdinand*

FERDINAND For myself I care not, but your loss brings a thousand deaths to me.

ALONZO O name not me, I am grown old, my son; I now am tedious to the world,
75 and that, by use, is so to me: but, Ferdinand, I grieve my subjects' loss in thee:
Alas! I suffer justly for my crimes; but why thou shouldest – O Heaven!

> *A cry within*

Hark, farewell my son! a long farewell!

FERDINAND Some lucky plank, when we are lost by shipwrack, waft hither, and
submit itself beneath you.

80 Your blessing, and I die contented.

> *Embrace and exeunt*
> *Enter Trincalo, Mustacho, and Ventoso*

TRINCALO What must our mouths be cold then?

VENTOSO All's lost. To prayers, to prayers.

GONZALO The duke and prince are gone within to prayers. Let's assist them.

MUSTACHO Nay, we may e'ne pray too; our case is now alike.

85 ANTONIO We are merely cheated of our lives by drunkards.
This wide chopt rascal: would thou might'st lie drowning
The long washing of ten tides.

> *Exeunt Trincalo, Mustacho, and Ventoso*

GONZALO He'll be hang'd yet, though every drop of water swears against it; now would
I give ten thousand furlongs of sea for one acre of barren ground, long-heath,
90 broom-furs, or anything. The wills above be done, but I would fain die a dry death.

> *A confused noise within*

ANTONIO Mercy upon us! we split, we split.

GONZALO Let's all sink with the duke, and the young prince.

> *Exeunt*
> *Enter Stephano, Trincalo*

TRINCALO The ship is sinking.
> *A new cry within*

STEPHANO Run her ashore!

95 TRINCALO Luffe! luffe! or we are all lost! there's a rock upon the star-board bow.

STEPHANO She strikes, she strikes! All shift for themselves.
> *Exeunt*

The Tempest, or The Enchanted Island (Shadwell, 1674)

Shadwell made the following additions and changes to Dryden and Davenant's first scene (the Dryden/Davenant readings are shown in parentheses):

Act 1

5	(what cheer) what say you?
8	(Boy!) Boy! Boy!
11	(Heigh . . . yare.) Bring the cable to the capstorm.
15	(You mar our labour) you hinder us
29	*add* 'Make haste' *to beginning of speech*
36	*add* 'lubbord' *after* 'sleep?'
40	(off the hamocks) down the hammocks
49	(Furl him again) Let him alone
53	(The wind grows scant) The wind veers forward
55	*add* 'till the sails are loose' *to end of line*
59	(aboard) aweather
67	*add* 'and be poxt' *to end of line*
70	(Brace . . . fore-yard) Ease the fore-brace a little.
78–80sd	(Some lucky plank . . . contented. *Embrace and exeunt*) *cut*
85–90sd	(We are merely . . . dry death. *A confused noise within*) *cut*

The Tempest. An Opera. (David Garrick, 1756)

Garrick substituted this scene for Shakespeare's opening:

Act 1, Scene 1

The Stage darkened – represents a cloudy sky, a very rocky coast, and a ship on a tempestuous sea. – Ariel comes upon the stage.

AIR.

> *Arise, arise, ye subterranean winds,*
> *Arise ye deadly blighting fiends;*
> *Rise you, from whom devouring plagues have birth,*
> *You that i' th' vast and hollow womb of earth*
> *Engender earthquakes, make whole countries shake;*
> *Ye eager winds, whose rapid force can make*
> *All, but the fix'd and solid centre, shake:*
> *Come, drive yon ship to that part of the isle*
> *Where nature never yet did smile.*

Myself will fly on board, and on the beak,
In the waste, the deck, in every cabin,

I'll flame amazement. Sometimes I'll divide,
And burn in many places. On the top-mast,
The yards, and bowsprit will I flame distinctly,
Then meet and join. *Jove*'s lightnings, the precursors
Of dreadful thunder-claps, more momentary
And sight out-running, are the the [*sic*] fire and cracks
Of sulph'rous roaring; the most mighty *Neptune*
Shall seem to siege, make his bold waves tremble,
Yea, his dread trident shake.   *Exit.*
            Repeated flashes of lightning, and claps of thunder.

The Tempest; or, The Enchanted Island (J. P. Kemble, 1789)
Kemble's 1789 version of Shakespeare's Act 1, Scene 1, is printed below, with 1806 variants
given in parentheses:

Act 2, Scene 1
The Sea Shore. A Storm. A ship in the Midst of the Tempest. Ariel with Spirits assisting the
Storm. Chorus of Spirits sings:
(The Sea. A Ship in a Tempest. Ariel, firing the Ship. Spirits of the Winds dancing. Chorus by
Spirits of the Storm.)

>   Arise! ye spirits (terrors) of the storm!
>   Appal(l) the guilty eye;
>   Tear the wild waves, ye mighty winds,
>   Ye fated lightnings fly: (blasting lightnings,)
>   Dart thro' the tempest of the deep,
>   And rocks and seas confound.   *(loud thunder)*
>   Hark! how the vengeful thunders roll!
>   Amazement flames around.
>   Behold! the fate devoted bark,
> 10   Dash'd on the trembling shore:
>   Mercy: – the sinking wretches cry –
>   Mercy! – They're heard no more.

The ship sinks. Ariel and spirits disappear. (The Ship seems to founder. Ariel and all the other
Spirits disappear.)

First Dorinda/Miranda Scene (Dryden/Davenant 1670 and Shadwell 1674)

Act 1
>   *Enter Dorinda*
> DORINDA Oh sister! what have I beheld!
> MIRANDA What is it moves you so?
> DORINDA From yonder rock,
>   As I my eyes cast down upon the seas,
>   The whistling winds blew rudely on my face,
>   And the waves roar'd; at first I thought the war
>   Had been between themselves; but straight I spy'd

A huge great creature.

MIRANDA O, you mean the ship.

10 DORINDA Is't not a creature then? it seem'd alive.

MIRANDA But what of it?

DORINDA This floating ram did bear his horns above;
All ty'd with ribbands, ruffling in the wind,
Sometimes he nodded down his head awhile,
And then the waves did heave him to the moon,
He clamb'ring to the top of all the billows,
And then again he curtsy'd down so low,
I could not see him: till at last, all side long
With a great crack his belly burst in pieces.

20 MIRANDA There all had perisht
Had not my father's magic art reliev'd them.
But, sister, I have stranger news to tell you;
In this great creature there were other creatures,
And shortly we may chance to see that thing,
Which you have heard my father call, a man.

DORINDA But what is that? for yet he never told me.

MIRANDA I know no more than you: but I have heard
My father say we women were made for him.

DORINDA What, that he should eat us, sister?

30 MIRANDA No sure, you see my father is a man, and yet
He does us good. I would he were not old.

DORINDA Methinks indeed it would be finer, if we two
Had two young fathers.

MIRANDA No sister, no, if they were young, my father
Said that we must call them brothers.

DORINDA But pray how does it come that we two are not
brothers then, and have not beards like him?

MIRANDA Now I confess you pose me.

DORINDA How did he come to be our father too?

40 MIRANDA I think he found us when we both were little, and grew within the ground.

DORINDA Why could he not find more of us? Pray sister let you and I look up and
down one day, to find some little ones for us to play with.

MIRANDA Agreed; but now we must go in. This is the hour
Wherein my father's charm will work,
Which seizes all who are in open air:
Th' effect of his great art I long to see;
Which will perform as much as magic can.

50 DORINDA And I, methinks, more long to see a man.

The Tempest (directed by Keith Hack, 1974)
(The pb retains the printed sds, but does not appear to use them; the Master and
Boatswain are cut.)

Act 1, Scene 1
*The company enter and surround the stage area; Prospero, Ariel, Miranda, and Caliban are on
stage. Thunder sheet*

Prospero beats the ground with his staff.

PROSPERO:	Bestir, bestir
GONZALO:	Fall to't, or we run ourselves aground. Bestir, bestir!
PROSPERO:	Take in the topsail!
TRINCULO:	Tend to th' Master's whistle!
ALONSO:	Blow till thou burst thy wind, if room enough
ANTONIO:	Where's the Master? Play the men.
STEPHANO:	(I pray now, keep below)
ANTONIO:	Where is the Master, Boatswain?
STEPHANO:	Keep your cabins! You do assist the storm.
GONZALO:	Nay, good, be patient.
STEPHANO:	When the sea is. What cares these roarers for the name of king? To cabin! Silence!
GONZALO:	Remember whom thou hast aboard.
STEPHANO:	None that I more love than myself. You are a councillor. If you can command these elements to silence, and work the peace of the present, use your authority. If you cannot, give thanks you have lived so long, and make youself ready in your cabin for the mischance of the hour.
PROSPERO:	Down with the topmast! Yare! Lower, lower! Bring her to try with main-course.
	A cry within
STEPHANO:	A plague upon this howling! They are louder than the weather. Have you a mind to sink?
SEBASTIAN:	A pox o' your throat, you bawling, blasphemous, incharitable dog!
STEPHANO:	Work you, then.
ANTONIO:	Hang, cur, hang, you whoreson, insolent noisemaker! We are less afraid to be drowned than thou art.
ALONSO:	To prayers, to prayers! All lost!
SEBASTIAN:	I'm out of patience.
ANTONIO:	We are merely cheated of our lives by drunkards.
PROSPERO:	Lay her off to sea again! Lay her off.
GONZALO:	Now would I give a thousand furlongs of sea for an acre of barren ground. Long heath, brown furze, anything. The wills above be done, but I would fain die a dry death.
FERDINAND:	Mercy on us!
TRINCULO:	We split, we split

we split × 3 (i.e., the line was repeated three times, presumably by all the characters.
Miranda crossed to Prospero to begin 1.2.)

APPENDIX 2: LIST OF PRINCIPAL PLAYERS

Production	Prospero	Ariel	Caliban	Miranda
Alexander (1994)	Jeffery Kissoon	Rakie Ayola	Richard McCabe	Ginny Holder
Arias (1986)	Pierre Dux	Clotilde Mollet	Marilu Marini	Magali Renoire
Armfield (1990)	John Bell	Gillian Jones	Max Cullen (1995 revival: Kevin Smith)	Angie Milliken
Ashwell (1925)	A. Corney Grain	Godfrey Kenton	Philip Brandon	Diana Telby
Atkins (1933)	John Drinkwater	Leslie French	Robert Atkins	Margaretta Scott
Atkins (1934)	Drinkwater	French	Atkins	Pamela Stanley
Ayrton (1935)	Neil Porter	Margaret Field-Hyde	Roy Emerton	Gwynne Whitby
Barton (1970)	Ian Richardson	Ben Kingsley	Barry Stanton	Estelle Kohler
Baynton (1926)	B. A. Pittar	Lilian Temple	Baynton	Rosaline Courtneidge
Benson (1897)	Oscar Asche	Miss Ormerod	Benson	Constance Benson
Benson (1904)	Arthur Whitby	Ethel Dane	Benson	C. Benson
Benthall (1951)	Michael Redgrave	Alan Badel	Hugh Griffith	Hazel Penwarden
Benthall (1952)	Ralph Richardson	Margaret Leighton	Michael Hordern	Zena Walker
Bogdanov (1978)	Bill Wallis	Stephen Boxer	John Labanowski	Fiona Victory
Bogdanov (1992)	John Woodvine	Olwen Fouéré	Ravil Isyanov	Julie Saunders
Breuer (1981)	Raul Julia	eleven actors	Barry Miller	Jessica Nelson (Clove Galilee played 'young Miranda')

Production	Prospero	Ariel	Caliban	Miranda
Bridges-Adams (1919)	Charles Doran	Leah Hanman	Murray Carrington	Joyce Carey
Bridges-Adams (1926)	George Skillan	Joan Duan	Randle Ayrton	Rosaline Courtneidge
Bridges-Adams (1930)	Wilfrid Walter	Miriam Adams	George Hayes	Joyce Bland
Bridges-Adams (1934)	Neil Porter	Rachel Kempson	Baliol Holloway	Gwynne Whitby
Brook (1957)	John Gielgud	Brian Bedford	Alec Clunes	Doreen Aris
Brook (1990)	Sotigui Kouyate	Bakary Sangare	David Bennent	Shantala Malhar-Shivalingappa or Romane Bohringer
Burge (1972)	Hugh Griffith	John McEnery	Barrie Rutter	Angela Scoutar
Burton (1854)	Charles Fisher	Mrs C. B. Hill	Burton	Ms Raymond
Ciulei (1981)	Ken Ruta	François de la Giroday	Jan Triska	Frances Conroy
Coghill (1949)	David Williams	Charles Hodgson	A. W. J. (Bill) Becker	Ralda Nash
Crozier (1946)	Robert Harris	David O'Brien (child)	Julian Somers	Joy Parker
Daniels (1982)	Derek Jacobi	Mark Rylance	Bob Peck	Alice Krige
De Berardinis (1986)	De Berardinis	Francesca Mazza	Bruno Cereseto	Fernanda Hrelia
Devine/Goring (1940)	John Gielgud	Marius Goring	Jack Hawkins	Jessica Tandy (and Peggy Ashcroft)
Donnellan (1988)	Timothy Walker	Peter Darling	Duncan Duff	Cecilia Noble
Drinkwater (1915)	Felix Aylmer	E. Stuart Vinden	E. Ion Swinley	Cecily Byrne
Edwards (1990)	John Gaden	Helen Morse	Frank Gallacher	Sancia Robinson
Falls (1987)	Dennis Arndt	Don Franklin	Bruce A. Young	Anne Ryan
Gaden (1989)	Edwin Hodgeman	Daniel Witton	Steven Vidler	Ulli Birve

Production	Prospero	Ariel	Caliban	Miranda
Gellner (1951)	Clifford Evans	Terry Wale (child)	Bernard Miles	Josephine Griffin
Goddard (1988)	John Watts	Freddie Garrity	Paul Walker	
Guthrie (1934)	Charles Laughton	Elsa Lanchester	Roger Livesey	Ursula Jeans
Hack (1974)	Michael Aldridge	Robert Lloyd	Jeffery Kissoon	Debbie Bowen
Hall (1974)	John Gielgud	Michael Feast	Denis Quilley	Jenny Agutter
Hall (1988)	Michael Bryant	Steven Mackintosh	Tony Haygarth	Jennifer Hall; Shirley Henderson
Carey Harrison (1964)	Saam Dastoor	Richard Eyre	John Grillo	Jean Liddiard
John Harrison (1974)	Paul Scofield	Sam Dastor	Peter Gordon	Nicky Guadagni
Helpmann (1954)	Michael Hordern	Robert Hardy	Richard Burton	Claire Bloom
Hirsch (1982)	Len Cariou	Ian Deakin	Miles Potter	Sharry Flett
Hytner (1988)	John Wood	Duncan Bell	John Kane	Melanie Thaw
Iden Payne (1938)	Gyles Isham	Dennis Hutchinson	James Dale	Pauline Letts
Iden Payne (1941/42)	George Hayes (1941/42)	Pamela Alan (1941); Sara Jackson (1942)	Baliol Holloway (1941/42)	Olga Edwardes (1941); Barbara White (1942)
James (1989)	Peter Carmody	Elizabeth Newman, Stephen Boyle, Paul Taylor	Alan Wilson	Elizabeth Newman
Jamieson/ Quayle (1985)	Quayle	Moir Leslie	Clive Francis	Natalie Wilde
Jones (1968)	John Clements	Richard Kane	Clive Revill	Maureen O'Brian
Kean (1857)	Kean	Kate Terry (child)	Ryder	Carlotta Leclercq
Kelly (1999)	Ian McKellen	Paul Bhattacharjee	Timothy Walker	Claudie Blakely

Production	Prospero	Ariel	Caliban	Miranda
Kemble (1789)	Robert Bensley	Miss Romanzini	Mr Williames	Anna Maria Crouch
Kemble (1806)	Kemble	Miss Meadows	John Emery	Miss Brunton
Leigh (1926)	Neil Porter	Iris Roberts	Baliol Holloway	Gwynne Whitby
Lepage (1992)	Jacques-Henri Gagnon	Marie Brassard	Anne-Marie Cadieux	Macha Limonchik
Macready (1838)	Macready	Priscilla Horton	George Bennett	Helen Faucit
Meckler (1997)	Michael Cashmen	Rachel Sanders	Richard Willis	Rebecca Jackson
Mendes (1993)	Alec McCowen	Simon Russell Beale	David Troughton	Sarah Woodward
Miller (1970)	Graham Crowden	Norman Beaton	Rudolph Walker	Angela Pleasence
Miller (1988)	Max von Sydow	Cyril Nri	Rudolph Walker	Rudi Davies
Minor (1970)	Robert Pastene	Arnold Wilkerson	Charles Keating	Linda Kelsey
Mitchell (1990)	Ian Leigh Cooper	Caroline Kennison		Helen O'Leary
Murray (1990)	David Horovitch	Emil Wolk	Dan Hildebrand	Emily Raymond
Neville (1962)	Alastair Sim	Kerry Gardner	George Selway	Eileen Atkins
Ninagawa (1988)	Haruhiko Joh	Yoji Matsuda	Yutaka Matsushige (Edinburgh); Hiroki Okawa (London)	Mariko Fuji
Noble (1998)	David Calder	Scott Handy	Robert Glenister	Penny Layden
Paige (1993)	Christopher Ravenscroft	Andrew Price	Christopher McHallem	Lucy Briers
Phelps (1847)	Phelps	Julia St George	George Bennett	Miss Addison
Poel (1897 reading)	Hermann Vezin	Muriel Ashwynne	Mr Hodges	Hilda Swan
Poel (1897 performance)	Paget Bowman	Mr H. Herbert and Miss Deane	Mr Hodges	Hilda Swan

Production	Prospero	Ariel	Caliban	Miranda
Purcarete (1995)	Michael Fitzgerald	five musicians, two actors, three mannikins	Gheorghe Ilie; John Gannon (some performances)	Saira Todd
Retallack (1981)	Valerie Braddell	Christine Bishop	Jack Ellis	Susan Colverd
Retallack (1991)	Richard Durden	Diane Parish	Femi Elufowoju Jr	Juliet Aubrey
Rylance (1991)	Rylance	Julian Lyon	John Ramm	Toshie Ogura
Seale (Dryden/ Davenant) (1959)	John Phillips	Jeanette Sterke and Mary Thomas	Joss Ackland	Natasha Parry
Simmons (1978)	Chris Jordan	Sheila Burnett	Rod Beddall	Poppy Hands
Strehler (1978)	Tino Carraro	Giulia Lazzarini	Michele Placido	
Thacker (1995)	Paul Jesson	Bonnie Engstrom	Dominic Letts	Sarah-Jane Holm
Tipton (1991)	Richard S. Iglewski	Kristin Flanders	Christopher Bayes	Jennifer Campbell
Tree (1904)	William Haviland	Viola Tree	Tree	Norah Kerin
V. Tree/ Calvert (1921)	Henry Ainley	Winifred Barnes	Louis Calvert	Joyce Carey
Walford (1984)	Ricco Ross	Neil Boorman	Carl Chase	Cathy Tyson
Warner (1983)	Robert Demeger	Hilary Townley	Nicholas Jeune (1983); Edward Harbour (1984)	Julia Swift
David William (1955)	Robert Eddison	James Maxwell	Robert Atkins	June Bailey
Clifford Williams (1978)	Michael Hordern	Ian Charleson	David Suchet	Sheridan Fitzgerald
C. Williams/ Brook (1963)	Tom Fleming	Ian Holm	Roy Dotrice	Philippa Urquhart
Harcourt Williams (1930)	John Gielgud	Leslie French	Ralph Richardson	Joan Harben

Production	Prospero	Ariel	Caliban	Miranda
H. Williams (1933)	Williams	Leslie French	Malcolm Keen	Peggy Ashcroft
Wright (1947)	Robert Harris	Joy Parker	John Blatchley	Daphne Slater
Wolfe (1995)	Patrick Stewart	Aunjanue Ellis	Teagle F. Bougere	Carrie Preston

BIBLIOGRAPHY

PROMPTBOOKS AND ACTING EDITIONS

(For readers' convenience, promptbooks are cross-referenced to the standard reference work, Shattuck's *Shakespeare Promptbooks*.)

[?]. John Moore prompt copy, 7 March 1853. Folger Shakespeare Library Prompt *Tempest* 7 (Shattuck 13: Kemble–Dryden version in the Cumberland edn, 'probably' performed at the Bowery, New York).

Ashwell, Lena. Lena Ashwell Players prompt copy of *The Tempest*, 1925. Birmingham Central Library.

Ayrton, Randle. 1935 promptbook, Shakespeare Centre Library.

Barton, John. 1970 promptbook, Shakespeare Centre Library.

Becks, George (compiler). George Becks prompt copy, 1890s. Folger Prompt *Tempest* 4 (Shattuck 31: composite of nineteenth-century American productions (New York, Boston, Philadelphia, Baltimore, Chicago) and of Macready's).

Benthall, Michael. 1951 promptbook, Shakespeare Centre Library.
  1952 promptbook, Shakespeare Centre Library.

Bridges-Adams, W. 1926/1930 promptbook, Shakespeare Centre Library.
  1934 promptbook, Shakespeare Centre Library.

Brook, Peter. 1957 promptbook, Shakespeare Centre Library.

Burton, William. New York, Burton's Theatre, 11 April 1854. Folger Prompt *Tempest* 12 (Shattuck 15: John Moore's 'red ink cuts give Macready's version' and pencilled cuts Burton's).

Crozier, Eric. 1946 promptbook, Shakespeare Centre Library.

Daly, Augustin. *The Tempest* by William Shakespeare, arranged for four acts by Augustin Daly. Here printed from the promptbook, as acted at Daly's Theatre, New York, March 1897 (privately printed). Folger Prompt *Tempest* 8 (Shattuck 35: Miss Hoswell's (Iris) rehearsal copy).

[Daniel, George, ed.] *Cumberland's British Theatre, with Remarks, Biographical and Critical, by D–G*. Printed from the acting copies, as performed at the Theatres Royal, London. Vol. 7. London: John Cumberland, n.d.

Daniels, Ron. 1982 promptbook, Shakespeare Centre Library.

[Dryden, John, and William Davenant.] *The Tempest, or The Enchanted Island*. A Comedy. As it is now Acted at His Highness the Duke of York's Theatre. London: Henry Herringman at the Blew Anchor in the Lower-walk of the New Exchange, 1670.

[Dryden, John, and William Davenant.] *The Tempest, or The Enchanted Island*. 1670; rpt. in *Shakespeare Adaptations*, ed. Montague Summers. London: Jonathan Cape, 1922.

[Garrick, David.] *The Tempest*. An Opera. Taken from Shakespear [*sic*]. As it is performed at the Theatre-Royal in Drury-Lane. The Songs from Shakespear, Dryden, etc. The Music composed by Mr Smith. London: J. & R. Tonson, 1756.

[Gentleman, Francis, ed.] *The Tempest*. A Comedy, by Shakespeare. As Performed at the Theatre-Royal, Drury-Lane, Regulated from the Prompt-Book, With Permission of the Managers, by Mr Hopkins, Prompter. *Bell's Edition of Shakespeare's Plays*, vol. III, 1774. London: Printed for John Bell, near Exeter Exchange in the Strand, and C. Etherington at York, 1773. (Printed from the promptbook of Garrick's 1757 version.)

Hack, Keith. 1974 promptbook, Shakespeare Centre Library.

Hall, Peter. 1974 promptbook, Royal National Theatre.

1988 promptbook, Royal National Theatre.

Hytner, Nicholas. 1988 promptbook, Shakespeare Centre Library.

1989 promptbook, Shakespeare Centre Library.

Inchbald, Elizabeth, ed. *The Tempest; or, The Enchanted Island; A Play in Five Acts*; by William Shakespeare. Adapted to the Stage, with additions from Dryden and Davenant, by J. P. Kemble. As performed at the Theatre Royal, Covent Garden. Printed under the authority of the managers from the prompt book. London: Longman, Hurst, Rees, and Orme, [1807].

Kean, Charles. Shakespeare's Play of *The Tempest*, arranged for representation at The Princess's Theatre, with Historical and Explanatory Notes, by Charles Kean, FSA, as 1st performed on Wednesday, July 1, 1857. 3rd edn. London: John K. Chapman, n.d. Folger Prompt *Tempest* 10 (Shattuck 19: 'Final or souvenir p.b. made in 1859 by T. W. Edmonds, the prompter').

London, Princess's Theatre, 1 July 1857. Folger Prompt *Tempest* 11 (Shattuck 21: 'rehearsal workbook of George Ellis, the stage manager').

Kemble, John Philip. *The Tempest; or, The Enchanted Island*. Written by Shakspeare [*sic*]; with additions from Dryden; as compiled by J. P.

Kemble, and first acted at the Theatre Royal, Drury Lane, October 13th, 1789. London: J. Debrett, 1789.

Shakspeare's [*sic*] *Tempest; or, The Enchanted Island* [1806], a Play, adapted to the Stage, with additions from Dryden and Davenant, by J. P. Kemble; and now first published as it is acted at The Theatre Royal in Covent Garden. A New Edition. London: Longman, Hurst, Rees, & Orme, 1807. Facsimile rpt. in Shattuck, *John Philip Kemble Promptbooks*, vol. VIII. Charlottesville: Folger Shakespeare Library, 1974.

Shakspeare's [*sic*] *Tempest; or, The Enchanted Island*, a Play; adapted to the stage, with additions from Dryden and Davenant, by J. P. Kemble; and now published as it is performed at the Theatres Royal. *Select British Theatre*. London: John Miller, 1815.

[Macready, William Charles.] *The Tempest*, Part 2 of *The Dramatic Works of Shakspere* [*sic*]; after the most correct stage copies, and approved readings; with Notes, Glossary, and A Life of the Author. Embellished with finely executed portraits. London: J. Pattie, 1839. (Shattuck 14: Pattie's edition 'was printed from Macready's promptbook'.)

Miller, Jonathan. 1988 promptbook, Old Vic Theatre.

Neville, Oliver. 1962 promptbook, Theatre Museum, London.

Payne, Ben Iden. 1942 promptbook, Shakespeare Centre Library.

Phelps, Samuel. London, Sadler's Wells, 7 April 1847. Folger Prompt *Tempest* 13 (Shattuck 8: 'restored version mainly marked by Phelps, with additions by Williams, the prompter').

London, Sadler's Wells, 7 April 1847. Shakespeare Centre Library 50.31 (1709) 957 (Shattuck 10: 'excellent' transcription of Phelps's pb, with additions by William Creswick; unless otherwise noted, all production details are drawn from this pb).

[Shadwell, Thomas.] *The Tempest, or The Enchanted Island*. A Comedy. As it is now Acted at His Highness the Duke of York's Theatre. London: Henry Herringman, 1674.

The Tempest, or The Enchanted Island. 1674; rpt. (facsimile of Birmingham Shakespeare Library copy) London: Cornmarket Press, 1969.

Shattuck, Charles H. *John Philip Kemble Promptbooks*. 11 vols. Charlottesville: Folger Shakespeare Library, 1974.

Tree, Herbert Beerbohm. Shakespeare's Comedy *The Tempest* as arranged for the stage by Herbert Beerbohm Tree. With Illustrations from Original Oil Sketches by Charles A. Buchel. London: J. Miles, 1904.

London, His Majesty's, 14 September 1904. Folger Prompt *Tempest* 15 (Shattuck 39: Fred Grove's final and very full pb).

Williams, Clifford, and Peter Brook. 1963 promptbook, Shakespeare Centre Library.

Williams, Clifford. 1978 promptbook, Shakespeare Centre Library.

Wright, Norman. 1947 promptbook, Shakespeare Centre Library.

OTHER WORKS

(For newspaper and magazine reviews, please see the notes.)

Adams, J. C. 'The Staging of *The Tempest*, III.iii'. *Review of English Studies* 14, no. 56 (October 1938): 404–19.

Addenbrooke, David. *The Royal Shakespeare Company: The Peter Hall Years*. London: William Kimber, 1974.

Andersen, Hans Christian. *Pictures of Travel*. Author's edn. New York: Hurd & Houghton; Cambridge: Riverside Press, 1871.

Ashwell, Lena. *Reflections from Shakespeare*. London: Hutchinson, [1926].

Atkins, Robert. *An Unfinished Autobiography*. Ed. George Rowell. London: Society for Theatre Research, 1994.

Australia & New Zealand Theatre Record. 1989–90.

Avery, Emmett L. *The London Stage 1660–1800, Part 2: 1700–1729*. Carbondale: Southern Illinois University Press, 1965.

Babula, William. *Shakespeare in Production, 1935–1978: A Selective Catalogue*. New York and London: Garland, 1981.

Banham, Martin, ed. *The Cambridge Guide to Theatre*. Cambridge: Cambridge University Press, 1995.

Barroll, J. Leeds, and Alexander Leggatt, Richard Hosley, Alvin Kernan, eds. *The Revels History of Drama in English*, vol. III, 1576–1613. London: Methuen, 1975.

Beauman, Sally. *The Royal Shakespeare Company: A History of Ten Decades*. Oxford: Oxford University Press, 1982.

Benson, Constance. *Mainly Players*. London: Thornton Butterworth, 1926.

Benson, Frank R. *My Memoirs*. London: Ernest Benn, 1930.

Beerbohm, Max. *Around Theatres*. 1924; rpt. New York: Simon & Schuster, 1954.

Berry, Ralph. *Shakespeare in Performance*. London: Macmillan, 1993.

Blakeley, Clyde W. 'A Reconstruction of the Masque Scene from Charles Kean's *The Tempest*'. *Ohio State University Theatre Collection Bulletin* 13 (1966): 38–45.

Boaden, James. *Memoirs of the Life of John Philip Kemble Esq. including a history of the stage, from the time of Garrick to the present period*. 2 vols. London: Longman, Hurst, Rees et al., 1825.

Brown, John Russell. 'Free Shakespeare'. *Shakespeare Survey* 24 (1971): 127–35.

Shakespeare in Performance: An Introduction through Six Major Plays. New York: Harcourt Brace Jovanovich, 1976.

'Three Adaptations'. *Shakespeare Survey* 13 (1960): 137–45.

Bunn, Alfred. *The Stage: Both Before and Behind the Curtain*, vol. III. London: Richard Bentley, 1840.

Carter, Joyce. '*The Tempest* at Salisbury Playhouse: A Case Study'. Unpublished M.A. dissertation, Royal Holloway, University of London, 1994.

Child, Harold. *The Shakespearian Productions of John Philip Kemble.* London: Shakespeare Association [Oxford University Press], 1935.

Clark, William George, and John Glover, eds. *The Works of William Shakespeare*, vol. I. Cambridge and London: Macmillan, 1863.

Cochrane, Claire. *Shakespeare and the Birmingham Repertory Theatre 1913–1929.* London: Society for Theatre Research, 1993.

Cole, John William. *The Life and Theatrical Times of Charles Kean, F.S.A.* 2 vols. 2nd edn. London: Richard Bentley, 1860.

Dent, Edward J. *Foundations of English Opera: A Study of Musical Drama in England during the Seventeenth Century.* Cambridge: Cambridge University Press, 1928.

Dessen, Alan C. 'Shakespeare and the Theatrical Conventions of his Time'. In *The Cambridge Companion to Shakespeare Studies.* Ed. Stanley Wells. Cambridge: Cambridge University Press, 1986. Pp. 85–99.

Downer, Alan. *The Eminent Tragedian: William Charles Macready.* Cambridge: Harvard University Press; London: Oxford University Press, 1966.

Downes, John. *Roscius Anglicanus.* 1708; rpt., ed. Judith Milhous and Robert D. Hume. London: Society for Theatre Research, 1987.

Dymkowski, Christine. *Harley Granville Barker: A Preface to Modern Shakespeare.* Washington: Folger Shakespeare Library; London and Toronto: Associated University Presses, 1986.

Egan, Gabriel. 'Ariel's Costume in the Original Staging of *The Tempest*'. *Theatre Notebook* 51, no. 2 (1997): 62–72.

Erickson, Peter. 'A *Tempest* at the Mount'. *Shakespeare Quarterly* 32 (1981): 188–90.

Fitzgerald, Percy. *Shakespearean Representation.* London: Elliot Stock, 1908.

Forster, John. 'Macready's Production of "The Tempest"'. *Examiner* (21 October 1838). Rpt. in John Forster and George Henry Lewes,

Dramatic Essays, vol. III. Eds. William Archer and Robert W. Lowe. London: Walter Scott, 1896. Pp. 65–72.

Foulkes, Richard, ed. Extended review of Stuart Burge's 1972 *Tempest*. Birmingham: University of Birmingham Department of Extramural Studies, [1972].

Genest, John. *Some Account of the English Stage from the Restoration in 1660 to 1830*. 10 vols. Bath: H. E. Carrington, 1832.

Griffiths, Trevor R. ' "This Island's Mine": Caliban and Colonialism'. *The Yearbook of English Studies* 13 (1983): 159–80.

Gurr, Andrew. *The Shakespearean Stage, 1574–1642*. 3rd edn. Cambridge: Cambridge University Press, 1992.

Playgoing in Shakespeare's London. 2nd edn. Cambridge: Cambridge University Press, 1996.

'*The Tempest*'s Tempest at Blackfriars'. *Shakespeare Survey* 41 (1989): 91–102.

Hall, Peter. *Peter Hall's Diaries: The Story of a Dramatic Battle*. London: Hamish Hamilton, 1983.

Hazlitt, William. Review of Kemble's *Tempest*, *Examiner* (23 July 1815). Rpt. in *Dramatic Essays*, vol. II, pp. 62–6. Eds. William Archer and Robert W. Lowe. London: Walter Scott, 1895.

Hill, Errol. *Shakespeare in Sable: A History of Black Shakespearean Actors*. Amherst: University of Massachusetts Press, 1984.

Hirst, David L. *The Tempest: Text and Performance*. London: Macmillan, 1984.

Hodgson, Charles. 'Rough Magic'. *Oxford Today* 9, no. 3 (Trinity 1997): 16.

Hoffman, D. S. 'Some Shakespearian Music, 1660–1900'. *Shakespeare Survey* 18 (1965): 94–101.

Hogan, Charles Beecher. *Shakespeare in the Theatre 1701–1800*. 2 vols. Oxford: Clarendon Press, 1952–7.

Hosley, Richard. 'The Playhouses'. In *The Revels History of Drama in English*, vol. III, 1576–1613. Eds. J. Leeds Barroll et al. London: Methuen, 1975. Pp. 121–235.

Howe, Elizabeth. *The First English Actresses: Women and Drama 1660–1700*. Cambridge: Cambridge University Press, 1992.

Hunt, Leigh. *Critical Essays on the Performers of the London Theatres, including General Observations on the Practise and Genius of the Stage*. London: John Hunt, 1807.

Critical Essays. 1807; rpt. in *Dramatic Essays*, vol. I. Eds. William Archer and Robet W. Lowe. London: Walter Scott, 1894.

Jackson, Barry. 'Producing the Comedies'. *Shakespeare Survey* 8 (1955): 74–80.

Jowett, John. 'New Created Creatures: Ralph Crane and the Stage
   Directions in *The Tempest*'. *Shakespeare Survey* 36 (1983): 107–20.
Kleber, Pia. 'Theatrical Continuities on Giorgio Strehler's *The Tempest*'.
   In *Foreign Shakespeare*. Ed. Dennis Kennedy. Cambridge:
   Cambridge University Press, 1993. Pp. 140–57.
Lamming, George. *The Pleasures of Exile*. London: Michael Joseph,
   1960.
Law, Ernest. 'Shakespeare's "Tempest" as Originally Produced at Court'.
   Shakespeare Association paper No. 5 (delivered in February/March
   1918). London: Chatto and Windus, n.d.
Leacroft, Richard. *The Development of the English Playhouse: An
   Illustrated Survey of Theatre Building in England from Medieval to
   Modern Times*. 1973; revised edn. London: Methuen, 1988.
Leggatt, Alexander. 'The Companies and Actors'. In *The Revels History
   of Drama in English*, vol. III, 1576–1613. Ed. J. Leeds Barroll et al.
   London: Methuen, 1975. Pp. 97–117.
Lennep, William Van, ed. *The London Stage 1660–1800, Part 1:
   1660–1700*. Carbondale: Southern Illinois University Press, 1965.
Logan, Brian. 'On Michael Bogdanov's Tempest in Tiger Bay'. *Guardian*
   (12 July 1996), G2, pp. 6–7.
London Theatre Record. 1981–90 (from 1991, *Theatre Record*).
Mannoni, Octave. *Prospero and Caliban: The Psychology of Colonization*.
   2nd edn. Trans. Pamela Powesland. New York: Praeger, 1964.
Marker, Frederick J. 'The First Night of Charles Kean's *The Tempest* –
   From the Notebook of Hans Christian Andersen'. *Theatre Notebook*
   15 (Autumn 1970): 20–3.
Mason, Philip. *Prospero's Magic: Some Thoughts on Class and Race*.
   Oxford: Oxford University Press, 1962.
Maus, Katherine Eisaman. 'Arcadia Lost: Politics and Revision in the
   Restoration Tempest'. *Renaissance Drama* ns 13 (1982): 189–209.
McManaway, J. G. 'Songs and Masques in *The Tempest* [*c*. 1674]'. In
   *Theatre Miscellany: Six Pieces Connected with the Seventeenth-
   Century Stage* (Luttrell Society Reprints No. 140). Oxford: Basil
   Blackwell, 1953. Pp. 69–96.
Merivale, Herman Charles. *Bar, Stage and Platform: Autobiographic
   Memories*. London: Chatto & Windus, 1902.
Moore, Mary. 'Footing it Featly'. *Oxford Today* 9, no. 3 (Trinity 1997): 15–16.
Neill, Heather. *The Tempest: Director's Notes for Teachers and Students*.
   [London]: English Shakespeare Company/*Times Educational
   Supplement*, 1992.
Nilan, Mary M. ' "The Tempest" at the Turn of the Century'.
   Shakespeare Survey 25 (1972): 113–23.

Novak, Maximillian E., and George Robert Guffey, eds. *The Works of John Dryden*, vol. x. Berkeley: University of California Press, 1970.

Odell, George C. D. *Shakespeare from Betterton to Irving*. 2 vols. London: Constable, 1921.

Oxberry, W. *The New English Drama*, with Prefatory Remarks, Biographical Sketches, and Notes, Critical and Explanatory, vol. xvii. London: Simpkin & Marshall & Chapple, 1823.

Pellowe, Susan. 'In Chicago'. *Plays International* 3 (August 1987): 54–5.

Phillabaum, Corliss E. 'Panoramic Scenery at Sadler's Wells'. *Ohio State University Theatre Collection Bulletin* 6 (1959): 20–5.

Pollock, Frederick, ed. *Macready's Reminiscences, and Selections from his Diaries and Letters*. London: Macmillan, 1876.

Powell, Jocelyn. *Restoration Theatre Production*. London: Routledge & Kegan Paul, 1984.

Rees, Terence, and David Wilmore, eds. *British Theatrical Patents 1801–1900*. London: Society for Theatre Research, 1996.

Roberts, Jeanne Addison. 'The Washington Shakespeare Summer Festival, 1970'. *Shakespeare Quarterly* 21 (1970): 481–2.

Robson, William. *The Old Play-goer*. 1846; rpt. Fontwell, Sussex: Centaur Press, 1969.

Rosenfeld, Sybil. 'The Grieves Shakespearian Scene Designs'. *Shakespeare Survey* 20 (1967): 107–12.

A Short History of Scene Design in Great Britain. Oxford: Basil Blackwell, 1973.

Saenger, Michael Baird. 'The Costumes of Caliban and Ariel Qua Sea-nymph'. *Notes and Queries* ns 42 (September 1995): 334–6.

Scharf, George. *Recollections of the Scenic Effects of Covent Garden Theatre during the season 1837–9*. London: n.p., 1839.

Scott, Joan Wallach. *Gender and the Politics of History*. New York: Columbia University Press, 1988.

Shakespeare, William. *The Norton Facsimile: The First Folio of Shakespeare*. Prepared by Charlton Hinman. New York: W. W. Norton, 1968.

The Tempest. The Arden Shakespeare. Ed. Frank Kermode. 6th edn 1958; rpt. with corrections 1961 and 1962. London: Methuen, 1964.

The Tempest. The Oxford Shakespeare. Ed. Stephen Orgel. Oxford: Oxford University Press, 1987.

Shattuck, Charles H. *Shakespeare on the American Stage: From the Hallams to Edwin Booth*. Washington: Folger Shakespeare Library, 1976.

The Shakespeare Promptbooks: A Descriptive Catalogue. London and Urbana: University of Illinois Press, 1965.

Shaw, George Bernard. *Our Theatre in the Nineties*, vol III. London:
    Constable, 1932.
Shrimpton, Nick. 'Directing "The Tempest"'. *Shakespeare Survey* 29
    (1976): 63–7.
Shrimpton, Nicholas. 'Shakespeare Performances in Stratford-upon-
    Avon and London, 1981–2'. *Shakespeare Survey* 36 (1983): 149–55.
Shyer, Laurence. 'Disenchanted: A Casebook on the Making of Jennifer
    Tipton's Tempest'. *American Theatre* (January 1992): 24–31, 64–5.
Speaight, Robert. *Shakespeare on the Stage*. London: Collins, 1973.
    A Bridges-Adams Letter Book. London: Society for Theatre Research,
    1971.
    William Poel and the Elizabethan Revival. London: William
    Heinemann, 1954.
Sprague, Arthur Colby. 'Robert Atkins as a Shakespearian Director'. In
    Robert Atkins, *An Unfinished Autobiography*. Ed. George Rowell.
    London: Society for Theatre Research, 1994. Pp. 133–42.
    *Shakespeare and the Actors: The Stage Business in His Plays
    (1660–1905)*. Cambridge: Harvard University Press, 1945.
    Shakespearian Players and Performances. 1953; rpt. London: Adam and
    Charles Black, 1954.
Still, Colin. *Shakespeare's Mystery Play: A Study of 'The Tempest'*.
    London: Cecil Palmer, 1921.
Stone, George Winchester, Jr. 'Shakespeare's *Tempest* at Drury Lane
    During Garrick's Management'. *Shakespeare Quarterly* 7 (1956):
    1–7.
Sturgess, Keith. *Jacobean Private Theatre*. London: Routledge & Kegan
    Paul, 1987.
Styan, J. L. *The Shakespeare Revolution*. Cambridge: Cambridge
    University Press, 1977.
Suchet, David. 'Caliban in *The Tempest*'. *Players of Shakespeare 1*. Ed.
    Philip Brockbank. Cambridge: Cambridge University Press, 1985.
    Pp. 167–79.
Summers, Montague. *Shakespeare Adaptations*. London: Jonathan Cape,
    1922.
T., H. 'Memoir of Mr Macready'. In *The Works of William Shakespeare
    Illustrated*. London and New York: John Tallis, 1860. Pp. 3–8.
Thomas, Keith. *Religion and the Decline of Magic: Studies in Popular
    Beliefs in Sixteenth- and Seventeenth-Century England*. 1971; rpt.
    Harmondsworth: Penguin, 1978.
Thomson, Peter. *Shakespeare's Professional Career*. Cambridge:
    Cambridge University Press, 1992.

'Playhouses and Players in the Time of Shakespeare'. In *The Cambridge Companion to Shakespeare Studies*. Ed. Stanley Wells. Cambridge: Cambridge University Press, 1986. Pp. 67–83.

Toynbee, William, ed. *The Diaries of William Charles Macready, 1833–1851*. 2 vols. London: Chapman & Hall, 1912.

Tree, Herbert Beerbohm. *Thoughts and Afterthoughts*. 1913; rpt. London: Cassell, 1915.

Trewin, J. C. *Benson and the Bensonians*. London: Barrie and Rockliff, 1960.

Mr Macready: A Nineteenth-Century Tragedian and His Theatre. London: Harrap, 1955.

'Robert Atkins and the Open Air Theatre, Regents Park'. In *Robert Atkins: An Unfinished Autobiography*. Ed. George Rowell. London: Society for Theatre Research, 1994. Pp. 113–19.

Shakespeare on the English Stage 1900–1964. London: Barrie & Rockliff, 1964.

The Birmingham Repertory Theatre 1913–1963. London: Barrie & Rockliff, 1963.

Trewin, J. C., ed. *The Journal of William Charles Macready 1832–1851*. London: Longmans, 1967.

Trussler, Simon. *The Cambridge Illustrated History of British Theatre*. Cambridge: Cambridge University Press, 1994.

Vaughan, Alden T., and Virginia Mason Vaughan. *Shakespeare's Caliban: A Cultural History*. Cambridge: Cambridge University Press, 1991.

Vickers, Brian, ed. *Shakespeare: The Critical Heritage*. 6 vols. London and Boston: Routledge & Kegan Paul, 1974–81.

Walker, Roy. 'Unto Caesar: A Review of Recent Productions'. *Shakespeare Survey* 11 (1958): 128–35.

Warren, Roger. 'Shakespeare at Stratford, Ontario: The John Hirsch Years'. *Shakespeare Survey* 39 (1986): 179–90.

'A Year of Comedies: Stratford 1978'. *Shakespeare Survey* 32 (1979): 201–9.

Wearing, J. P. *The London Stage 1890–1899: A Calendar of Plays and Players*. 2 vols. Metuchen, NJ, and London: Scarecrow, 1976.

The London Stage 1900–1909: A Calendar of Plays and Players. 2 vols. Metuchen, NJ, and London: Scarecrow, 1981.

The London Stage 1910–1919: A Calendar of Plays and Players. 2 vols. Metuchen, NJ, and London: Scarecrow, 1982.

The London Stage 1920–1929: A Calendar of Plays and Players. 3 vols. Metuchen, NJ, and London: Scarecrow, 1984.

The London Stage 1930–1939: A Calendar of Plays and Players. 3 vols.
Metuchen, NJ, and London: Scarecrow, 1990.

The London Stage 1940–1949: A Calendar of Plays and Players. 2 vols.
Metuchen, NJ, and London: Scarecrow, 1991.

The London Stage 1950–1959: A Calendar of Plays and Players. 2 vols.
Metuchen, NJ, and London: Scarecrow, 1993.

Webster, Margaret. *Don't Put Your Daughter on the Stage*. New York:
Knopf, 1972.

Wells, Stanley, ed. *The Cambridge Companion to Shakespeare Studies*.
Cambridge: Cambridge University Press, 1986.

William, David. '*The Tempest* on the Stage'. In *Jacobean Theatre*. Eds.
J. R. Brown and B. Harris, 1960; rpt. New York: Capricorn, 1967.
Pp. 132–57.

Williams, John Ambrose. *Memoirs of John Philip Kemble, Esq. with an
Original Critique on his Performance*. London: J.B. Wood, 1817.

Williams, Harcourt. *Four Years at the Old Vic*. London: Putnam, 1935.

Old Vic Saga. London: Winchester, 1949.

Young, Hugo. *One of Us*. London: Macmillan, 1989.

INDEX